Statistical Methods and Reasoning for the Clinical Sciences

Evidence-Based Practice

Statistical Methods and Reasoning for the Clinical Sciences

Evidence-Based Practice

Eiki B. Satake, PhD

PLURAL
PUBLISHING
INC.

PLURAL PUBLISHING
INC.

5521 Ruffin Road
San Diego, CA 92123

e-mail: info@pluralpublishing.com
Website: http://www.pluralpublishing.com

FSC
www.fsc.org
MIX
Paper from
responsible sources
FSC® C011935

Library of Congress Cataloging-in-Publication Data

Satake, Eiki, author.
  Statistical methods and reasoning for the clinical sciences : evidence-based
practice / Eiki B. Satake.
       p. ; cm.
  Includes bibliographical references and index.
  ISBN 978-1-59756-433-5 (alk. paper)—ISBN 1-59756-433-8 (alk. paper)
  I. Title.
  [DNLM: 1. Statistics as Topic—methods—Problems and Exercises. 2. Clinical
Medicine—Problems and Exercises. 3. Evidence-Based Practice—Problems and
Exercises. WA 18.2]
  R850
  616.0072'7—dc23
                              2014009617

Contents

v

Preface

Over the past 20 years or so, we have seen the rapid rise and awareness of the importance of evidence-based practice (aka EBP) in the clinical sciences. This is a movement that has focused attention on the importance of using both empirical data analysis and clinical expertise for making better and more accurate clinical decisions, such as diagnosis, evaluation, assessment, and so on. This type of research methods clearly requires more specific types of statistical techniques that go beyond and above the traditional techniques taught at school. Unfortunately, the statistical methods that we all learned are not "evidence-based"; therefore, such traditional methods have contributed to a widespread misperception. Because of the importance of the inclusion of clinical expertise to fulfill the mission of EBP, we all need to relearn how we quantitatively combine both statistical and clinical components into a single conclusion. In other words, we need to learn "How to measure the strength of evidence both statistically and clinically." One of the most effective statistical methods to accomplish this seemingly impossible task is to use EBP statistical methods called Bayesian statistical analysis. Although Bayesian statistical methods have received an increasing amount of attention in the statistics and mathematics literatures in recent years, the use of Bayesian methods are still relatively limited in clinical decision making, especially in the fields of speech-language pathology and audiology.

Personally, I have experienced and witnessed the urgency of the use of EBP statistical methods/Bayesian methods through a series of short courses and research seminars that I have conducted at the annual American Speech-Language Hearing Association (ASHA) conventions over the past five years. There is an ever-growing number of the clinical professionals who attended my short courses, including students, practitioners, and researchers. They have become aware of the importance of evidence-based statistical methods and interested in learning more about such methods because they have finally realized that the statistical methods in current use are not useful for clinical decision making. Unfortunately, they still have to use such traditional methods for their research, mainly because there is no alternative method that they know and they can apply. Furthermore, almost all of them still believe that the effectiveness of a treatment is always contingent on the traditional statistical benchmark of p-value of 0.05. To make the matter worse, most of them do not even know the true definition of p-value or the meaning of "measuring the strength of evidence." If we want to move forward to EBP statistics, there is a serious need to teach them what EBP statistics is all about and how to use them. It must start somewhere, and we need to start sooner. This is my initial motivation of writing this book. Please do not get me wrong. A good working knowledge of traditional statistical methods is still important and fundamentals of EBP Statistical method. Knowing both types of methods certainly deepen one's statistical and clinical knowledge to a much larger extent in every aspect. So, this textbook explains and teaches what constitutes EBP statistical methods in philosophical, clinical, and mathematical perspectives.

Special features of this book include but are not limited to:

1. Provide feedback review, key terms and concepts, calculation guides, exercise questions, and several appendices to illustrate such topics as math review, clinical applications of statistical methods, calculation of p-values, calculation of statistical power, measuring disorder occurrence, sampling techniques, flowchart for traditional statistics versus Bayesian Statistical methods in hypothesis testing, single subject design, and writing a proposal for the ASHA convention nomogram.

2. Provide several clinically relevant case studies to deepen readers' knowledge and promote their learning to a larger extent.

3. Cover all necessary statistical topics for clinical professionals, such as descriptive methods, probability, and inferential methods, to improve their scientific literacy.

4. Give a greater emphasis on EBP statistical methods such as Bayesian statistical methods. It helps readers explore alternative methods that are extremely useful and powerful in clinical decision making.

5. Give clear conceptual distinction between EBP and non-EBP methods and limitations of traditional non-EBP methods, and explain why EBP is more clinically relevant and superior for clinical decision making?

6. Give step-by-step methods to show readers how to analyze data and interpret the result clinically.

7. Provide interpretations of statistical significance and clinical significance through several relevant and interesting examples in each chapter.

Introduction To Evidence-Based Statistics

Philosophical Foundation and Preliminaries for Clinical Statistics

Overview: Why Is Statistics Important for Clinical Professionals?

A growing number of clinical professionals have advocated that clinicians and researchers form collaborative relationships in collecting, evaluating, and publishing data pertaining to the efficacy of various treatment interventions. To improve communication between them, the author argues that a strong commitment will be required on the part of clinicians and researchers. As well, we must step further to clear the traditional image of clinical practitioners as "appliers" and/or "nonscientific contributors." In Figure 0–1, a traditional model of science-practice linkage (A) is compared with

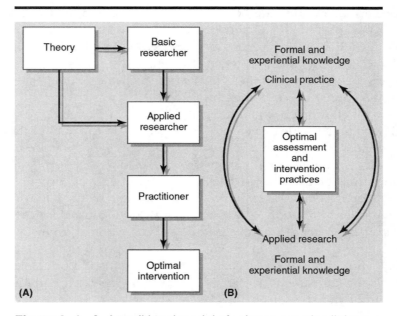

Figure 0–1. A. A traditional model of science-practice linkages; **B.** A schematic representation of the participation research process. Reprinted with permission from Thomson Delmar Learning.

another model that is more likely to foster research-practitioner partnerships (B). In the case of the traditional model, information flows in a top-down, unidirectional manner from researcher (the generator of information) to the clinician (user of information). Although the model gives a general idea to describe science-practice relationships between researchers and practitioners, several limitations were identified associated with the model (Wilcox et al, 1998.). First, practitioners may not become aware of the new research findings. Consequently, such findings fail to be implemented. Second, the research results may fail to answer questions that address practical needs such as "which treatment approach works best, under what circumstances, duration and intensity of interventions, applicability of interventions to whom)."

To further improve the model in a more practical way, Wilcox et al. proposed an alternative approach focusing on science-practitioner partnerships, shown in Figure 0–1. Their modified version is meant to depict the flow of information between researchers and practitioners as a circular, bidirectional process, thereby allowing them to "coordinate exploration of the conditions under which given procedures are appropriate as well as effective." The model is also intended to convey the notion that optimal approaches to assessment or treatment are viewed as both dynamic and evolutionary to the degree that such approaches are linked to ongoing exchanges of information among practitioners and applied researchers. Through reaching agreement so far as defining the problem to be solved, deciding an appropriate research design for doing so, and resolving problems associated with the collection, analysis, and interpretation of data. How the respon-

sibilities for these areas of cooperation are allocated also can be mutually decided.

Regardless of the clinical role that you may engage in at present or in the future or to what degree you are involved in formal research, keep in mind that you will augment your professional effectiveness by thinking and behaving like *a clinical scientist*. To perform well in any work setting, it will be necessary for you to:

- Identify problems
- Develop hypotheses about the causal relations among variables
- Formulate suitable methods of treatment
- Collect and evaluate data relevant to treatment outcomes

In other words, you, as a clinical scientist, will be using the same thinking and behaving processes that characterize the scientific method as it might be applied to a great variety of problem-solving endeavors. In so doing, you will acquire and hone the skills of a clinical scientist who is capable of doing such tasks as:

- Articulate ongoing research needs in the field of the clinical sciences that you are involved, in a manner that can be understood not only by fellow professionals but also by the laity
- Critique journal articles based on a working knowledge of appropriate research methods and statistical principles
- Apply research findings to actual problems encountered in clinical practice
- Assess and document the effectiveness of clinical practice through studies designed to

replicate research findings with different subjects and in different settings

■ Most importantly, knowing the limitations of the statistical methods in current use and explore the alternative statistical methods, that gear toward EBP, to study the subjects, analyze data, and interpret the results. The process is illustrated in Figure 0–2.

Lastly, Maxwell and Satake (2006) have outlined Twenty Science Attitudes in their book to achieve the successful partnership between researchers and practitioners. Among them, the author emphasized on the following two particular attitudes that clinicians should have in order for them to accurately evaluate and interpret clinical outcomes. They are as follows:

■ Respect for quantification and appreciation of mathematics as a language of science. (Many of nature's relationships are best revealed by patterns and mathematical relationships when reality is counted or measured, and this beauty often remains hidden without this tool.)

■ An appreciation of probability and statistics. (Correlations do not prove causal-and-effect, but some pseudoscience arises when

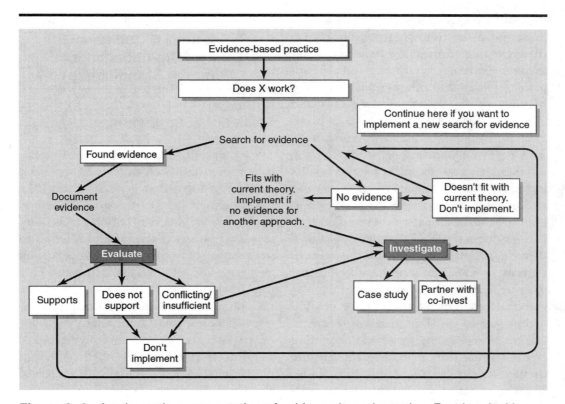

Figure 0–2. A schematic representation of evidence-based practice. Reprinted with permission from Thomson Delmar Learning.

a chance occurrence is taken as "proof." Individuals who insist on an all-or-none would and who have little experience with probability and statistics will have difficulty understanding the concept of an event occurring by chance, that is to say, they cannot distinguish between the likelihood of the treatment effect and chance errors when they make a diagnosis.)

What Kind of Statistical Reasoning Do the Clinical Professionals Need?

The statistical methods that are most desirable for the clinical professionals must fulfill the following conditions: (a) they are able to measure the strength of clinical evidence accurately for diagnosis, screening, and other clinical decision making, (b) they are able to detect and identify "Statistical Significance," "Clinical Significance," "Practical Significance," and "Personal Significance" from the data, (c) they are able to interpret the results inductively (from specific to general) and deductively (from general to specific), and (d) they must be based on the mission of EBP (evidence based practice). As I will discuss further, the statistical methods in current use are not EBP-based ones for various reasons, and consequently, the results from such methods have created erroneous conclusions that cause misinterpretations of diagnoses and screening test outcomes, that is, it has damaged the quality of clinical reasoning and integrity. For instance, the output of the standard statistical methods (aka Frequentists Methods) is neither useful nor meaning-

ful for clinical decision making because the results only indicate statistical significance (e.g., "how statistically significant is an observed difference between control group and experimental group?") but not clinical significance (e.g., "how clinically meaningful or what does the observed difference between two groups mean clinically or practically?"). Secondary, what the clinical professionals want to derive from the process is effectiveness of a given treatment/intervention or the accuracy of a diagnosis, that is to say, they need to be able to calculate the likelihood or probability of such events. Unfortunately, the frequentists methods do not calculate such probabilities. So, what kind of statistical method provides what they need?

What Are Statistical Significance, Practical Significance, Clinical Significance, and Personal Significance?

Statistical Significance

Statistical significance refers to the equality or inequality of two or more comparison groups; that is, the bottom line question here is "Do the groups differ?" In short, if an observed difference is identified, according to the standard logic and procedures of frequentists methods, such as *t*-test, ANOVA, ANCOVA, and the like, then the treatment effect is said to have resulted in a statistically significant difference. It neither mentions that the difference is how practical or clinically relevant. To address questions about the amount or the meaning of change, measures of statistical significance itself are insufficient; therefore, other measures of significance are required to properly answer the research questions. The first of such significances is called practical significance.

Practical Significance: How Much Do the Groups Differ?

Practice significance is defined as the magnitude of the observed difference between two or more comparison groups or phases (in Single Subject Design Studies). The most widely used and well-known practical significance measure is Effect Size (Cohen's *d* or omega) that can be calculated by dividing the observed differences between the means of two groups by the pooled standard deviation of the two group distributions. The reporting of effect sizes has increasingly become recommended and even required in many academic journals of the clinical sciences because of the greater emphasis on EBP in recent years.

One of the important issues on practical significance is that effect size cannot and does not fully address whether an observed difference reflects a change that any subject would describe as a good or important change in a clinical manner, not simply looking at effect size to determine the importance of the change. Therefore, we need another measure to determine how clinically meaningful or relevant such the observed difference and magnitude of the difference are. That is called clinical significance.

Clinical Significance: What Does the Observed Difference Mean Clinically?

Clinical significance refers to a certain value subjectively or objectively judged by the clinical professionals. Therefore, it implies that first the clinical professionals need to be able to interpret the results or changes derived from a screening test or diagnostic tests statistically and practically, and redefine such results clinically, that is, how do you explain the change and magnitude of the change, and what do they mean clinically? It is slightly more personal and subjective than the previous two significances.

Personal Significance: How to Measure Quality of Life? Did This Change Solve a Client's Problem?

As compared with clinical significance, *practical significance* has very little quantitative value in it, and naturally it is the most subjective significance of all. It refers to whether individual clients report feeling improvements that matter to them within the context of their own daily lives and, more importantly, whether they demonstrate functioning in ways that reflect improvements. In short, personal significance addresses the value of an observed change to a person and construct that it is labeled as the qualitative significance incorporated with the previous three significances. Please note that the personal significance may not be quantifiable, but the importance of this particular significance cannot be neglected in EBP.

What Is *Evidence-Based Practice* (EBP): Future Role of a Clinical Professional

Over the past two decades or so, we have witnessed a rapid rise of EBP in the medical and clinical sciences.

EBP has been defined in a variety of ways as it can be seen above. In general, according to an often-cited definition, Sackett et al. (1996) defines EBP as follows:

The conscientious, explicit, and judicious use of current best evidence in making decisions about the care of individual patients. *It means integrating individual clinical expertise with the best available external clinical evidence from systematic research.*

The importance of evidence-based approaches to clinical practice has been emphasized by a large number of clinical scientists and professionals in the various fields (Fey & Johnson, 1998; Apel, 1999; Wilcox, Hadley, & Bacon, 1998; Logemann, 2000; Wambaugh & Martinez, 2000; Meline & Paradiso, 2003; Peach, 1996; Dollaghan, 2004; Robey, 2004). In 2003, ASHA conducted a symposium entitled *Outcomes Research: Evidence-Based Practice* sponsored by the National Institute on Deafness and Other Communication Disorders. The goals of the symposium were to discuss recent advances in outcome research, the implications of such research for the field of communication disorders, and "levels of evidence" for evaluating outcome research (Justice & Fey, 2004). One of the most important outcomes is to develop the general process of EBP guidelines. Such guidelines contain a series of systematic steps including the following, as shown in Table 0–1.

- A comprehensive review of the professional literature
- Grading levels of evidence using preset and accepted criteria

- Developing flowcharts and decision trees to assist in evidence-supported decision making during the clinical decision making process
- Creating tables for evidence used to support the development of the guidelines (Frattali, 2004)

Additionally, Chambless and Hollon (1998) have proposed that one or more levels of questions can be asked in evaluating outcomes that pertain to the efficacy, effectiveness, or efficiency of treatment. Specifically, they are as follows:

- Has the treatment been shown to be beneficial in controlled research (*efficacy*)?
- Is treatment useful in applied clinical settings, and if so, with what patients and under what circumstances (*effectiveness*)?
- Is treatment efficient in the sense of being cost effective relative to other alternative interventions (*efficiency*)?

In a general sense, an empirically supported clinical practice is one that is able to demonstrate positive outcomes or improvements in a client's abilities that are attributable to one or more clinical interventions. Nevertheless, as Wilcox et al. (1998) observed, within the profession, there has been "persistent use of intervention techniques and programs entirely lacking in empirical support." EBP in evaluating and treating communication disorders is aimed at strengthening the field by providing such support (Dollaghan, 2004; Robey, 2004).

Last, Spring and Hitchcock (2009) is among those who have called for more

Table 0–1. Examples of Evidentiary Guidelines for Evaluating Preponderance of Evidence

Quality Designation	Criteria
	U.S. Preventive Services Task Force (1989)
Level I	Evidence from one well-conducted randomized clinical trial
Level II–1	Evidence from one well-conducted study with controls but without randomization
Level II–2	Evidence from well-designed cohort or case-control study preferably from independent researchers
Level II–3	Evidence from multiple time-series single-subject investigations or dramatic results from noncontrolled experiments
Level III	Opinions of authorities, descriptive studies, case studies, reports of expert committees
	Section 1 Task Force of the Division of Clinical Psychology of the American Psychological Association Task Force (1998)
Demonstrated Effectiveness	Two or more well-conducted group-design studies conducted by different research teams showing the treatment to be better than an alternative treatment or equivalent to an already established treatment or a large series of well-conducted single-subject studies with $n > 9$ that compare the intervention to another treatment
Probable Efficacy	Two or more well-conducted group-and/or single-subject design studies ($n < 3$) showing the treatment superior to a no-treatment, baseline, or alternative treatment condition or two well-conducted group-design studies meeting criteria for demonstrated effectiveness but both studies conducted by the same research team

Reprinted with permission from Thomson Delmar Learning.

empirical research to support the worth of the clinical profession. In her discussion of the critical need for such research, she stated the following:

The gathering of these outcome data and the necessary efficacy research cannot be left to the researchers or even the authors of these articles. Each clinician who chooses any treatment method, but especially approaches that are controversial, must assume responsibilities for regarding the intervention process as an opportunity for outcome data collection and efficacy research, including clinical trials or action based/participatory research. (p. 415)

In short, EBP is a movement that has focused on the importance of using clinical studies for empirical data based on demonstration of the treatment efficacy of clinical interventions. Until recently, a clinician and/or clinical professional are not required to have an advanced statistical knowledge and research methodologies in their fields when making a diagnosis. As the clinical decision-making process has grown to be more quantitative and complex, they are increasingly called on to make an outcome assessment of the studies and determine the accuracy of the diagnoses using the various statistical methods. Unfortunately, such methods of statistical inference in current use are not meeting the criteria of EBP, as mentioned above. Why and what's wrong with the statistical methods that we learned at school?

To understand why the standard statistical methods fail to meet EBP standard, I begin with explaining the fundamentals of the rationale behind two logical types of statistical reasoning, namely *deductive inference* and *inductive inference.*

In deductive inference, we start with a set of given hypotheses (in most cases, a null and alternative hypotheses). Next, we choose a sample from a target population to study the sample to eventually find out what we actually observed in the sample. We conclude by answering such a question as "How strongly or how well do such (conflicting) hypotheses predict the data we observed?" That is to say, we are interested in the credibility of data if that hypothesis were true. Deduction is objective in a way that the predictions about what we will observe are always true if the hypotheses are true. The difficulty of applying this reasoning to clinical decision making is that a clinician is unable to expand his or her knowledge beyond what is in the hypotheses. The standard statistical methods are all deductive-oriented. Although they are scientifically

objective, it is less useful and relevant in clinical practice.

A much more clinically useful and relevant reasoning, called inductive inference, is opposite to deductive inference (Figures 0–3 and 0–4). It goes in the reverse direction. A clinician can obtain the most likely (or tenable) hypothesis based on what was actually observed in a sample. It goes from observation to an underlying truth of the hypotheses. The basic concept behind EBP is undoubtedly inductive inference, and it allows for determining and measuring the strength of the clinical evidence directly and more accurately. The main advantages of inductive inference are (1) we can answer the question about the truth of the hypotheses, that is, "How likely is it that the treatment is effective or beneficial?," and (2) we can expand our knowledge to generate new hypotheses and learn new things.

Future Role of EBP-Oriented Clinical Professionals: What Must They Understand and Do to Become Better Investigators?

Over the past decade or so, as we discussed earlier, interest in evidence-based practice in communication disorders has steadily increased in many clinical fields —a movement that has emphasized the importance of providing empirical evidence to support various therapy interventions. To succeed in meeting the goals of EBP, clinicians must rely on more than intuition and clinical experience. In addition, they must be well-versed in the methods of research and statistics to accurately evaluate and apply evidence that seems to support a particular intervention. As Guyatt, Sackett, and Cook

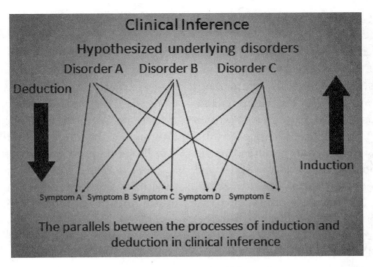

Figure 0–3. Inductive versus deductive for clinical inference. Reprinted with permission from "Toward evidence-based medical statistics. 1: The *p*-value fallacy," by S. N. Goodman, 1999, *Annals of Internal Medicine, 130*(12), p. 996.

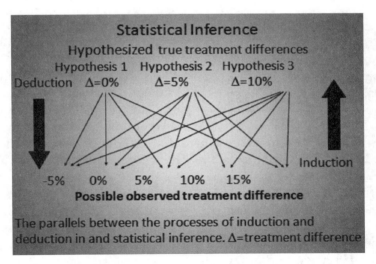

Figure 0–4. Inductive versus deductive for statistical inference. Reprinted with permission from "Toward evidence-based medical statistics. 1: The *p*-value fallacy," by S. N. Goodman, 1999, *Annals of Internal Medicine, 130*(12), p. 996.

(1993) noted, the ability to critically appraise research literature and apply such findings is an essential skill for sci- entifically based treatment. Yet, our obser- vations suggest that this concern is often neglected in graduate training programs as well as by many clinical practitioners and researchers.

One of the main reasons for this neglect is that few professionals in communication sciences and disorders seem aware of the limitations of so-called *classical* (frequentist) statistics, such as *p*-values and Null Hypothesis Significance Testing (NHST). This failure has resulted in the misuse and misinterpretation of statistical findings as reported in the literature and, in our view, has severely damaged the quality of scientific reasoning as applied to clinical problem solving. The author will address this particular issue pertaining to the fallacies of classical non-EBP statistical methods more specifically in a later section of this introduction entitled "An Alternative Method: How to Accurately Measure the Strength of the Clinical Evidence."

Moving Forward to Evidence-Based Statistics: What Really Prevents Us?

Several years ago, a colleague and I conducted a two-hour research seminar at the ASHA convention in Chicago. As always, we began with a one-item, "True or False" pop quiz. The vast majority of the participants attending the seminar were clinical professionals and graduate students in speech and language pathology and audiology. The quiz item was as follows:

True or False p-value = 0.03 means "There is a 3% chance that the null hypothesis is correct." Or, equivalently, "there is a 97% chance that the null hypothesis is incorrect."

Approximately 80% of the participants said the statement is "true." The correct answer, however, is that the statement is false.

The significance here is not that 80% of participants got the answer wrong, but rather the way the concept of *p*-value is taught, and the subsequent likelihood that it will be misinterpreted. In fact, there was a general expression of shock when, in the process of reviewing the substance of the question, that the true definition of *p*-value is much more complex than what they were led to believe.

The *p*-value is the probability of obtaining a result as an exact observed value or more extreme than the observed result derived from a sample, given that the null hypothesis (H_o) is true. However, a more challenging question is what it really suggests, and how it should be used to determine statistical significance. The *p*-value was first proposed by the English mathematical statistician R. A. Fisher in the 1920s. Initially, Fisher's intention of the use of the *p*-value was to measure the strength of evidence, and as an index to show how severely the truth of the null hypothesis (H_o) is contradicted by the actual evidence (sample data). The ground work for traditional statistics, based on inferential reasoning, was laid down early in the twentieth-century by such prominent theoreticians as Fisher, Neyman, and Pearson. In the clinical and medical sciences, generations of clinicians and researchers have been educated according to the principles of statistical inference techniques such as *p*-value and NHST. Usually, such methods do not directly address the issue of how accurate the diagnoses are. While providing the foundation for the vast majority of the clinical and experimental studies reported in the scientific literature, several clinicians and researchers have criticized the limitations and myths of p-value and NHST (Goodman, 1999a; Iversen, 1984).

Since the calculation of a p-value is based on the assumption that H_o is true, (1) it cannot be a direct measure of the probability that H_o is false (or, equivalently, that an alternate hypothesis, H_a, is true); and (2) it does not calculate the probability of the hypothesis being true or false, but rather calculates the probability of the occurrence of a sample data. The correct interpretation is that the probability of obtaining an exact result or more extreme result from the sample is 3%, given that H_o is correct.

Before discussing the reason why the p-value method does not work well in the clinical science research, we need to consider the philosophy underlying inferential statistics and how it works.

Statistical inference consists both of deductive reasoning and inductive reasoning. Deductive reasoning is exactly what p-value and Null Hypothesis Significance Testing (referred to as NHST) are all about. We begin with the assumption of the null effect (H_o is true) and predict what we will see if H_o is true. For example, we may begin by assuming that a client has no particular fluency disorder. We then evaluate and calculate the likelihood of each of the symptoms associated with the disorders as seen in the client. In short, we go from the status of the disorders (effect) to a set of the symptoms (cause). Symbolically, we can write it as **Probability (Symptom, given Disorders)**. However, the problem with this sort of reasoning is that we cannot use it to make a diagnosis based on what we actually observed. Clinically, this reasoning is not useful.

Also, this deductive method, specifically regarding p-value, uses both observed and hypothetical ("*more extreme*") data values. Very often, the inclusion of "more extreme" data values leads to a less reliable and valid conclusion. What a clinician really wants to know is the reasoning that goes in the reverse direction; from symptoms (cause) to disorders (effect), and allows her to be able to make a diagnosis based on only what is observed. Symbolically, this process can be written as **Probability (Disorders, given Symptoms)**. In other words, we need inductive reasoning that allows a clinician to make an accurate diagnosis based on what was actually observed. Inductive reasoning measures the strength of evidence more directly and is clearly "evidence-based."

However, evidence-based statistics must provide a basis for determining the credibility of a clinician's diagnosis based on the clinical observation. It must not only be clinically useful but also capable of expanding a clinician's knowledge beyond what they already know. Sadly, traditional statistical methods, such as p-value and NHST, fail to accomplish this task. The question that follows is whether there is an alternative statistical method that is suitable for evidence-based practice. Fortunately, there is such a method, namely Bayesian statistics.

In recent years, the importance of Bayesian statistical methods has been increasingly recognized and discussed in the field of clinical sciences because of its ability to state prior probabilities, representative of the initial subjective views of clinicians and then to update or revise these beliefs based on the emergence of new data to generate the posterior probability. Unlike the traditional statistics using p-value and NHST, the Bayesian approach works in a cumulative fashion, not in a terminal way. It allows for continuous revision, which allows a clinician to use the knowledge from previous research with newer findings of another research to update an estimate about a true population parameter. This cumulative treatment of data adjusts the statistical error and the amount of confounding variables (aka covariates) to increase the predictability of the final result and determine not only *statistical significance* but also *clinical significance*. In my view, a Bayesian approach is more practical and useful for clinical research because of its inductive and cumulative nature. Certainly, it is more clinically relevant and more closely synchronous to the evidence-based practice than the traditional approach. Believe it or not, all clinical professionals are natural Bayesian scientists (Figure 0–5).

Scientific Literacy and Ethical Practice: Time for a Check-Up?

Scientific literacy is necessary for promoting evidence-based practice. This book will review the components of research articles and the skills needed for their critical evaluation. Current publication guidelines for the scholastic journals, particularly in reference to reporting statistical results and the relevance of scientific literacy to ethical practice will be emphasized. Gaining the working knowledge of statistics that leads to a better understanding of data analysis and interpretation of the statistical results is absolutely essential for clinical decision making. The following are the author's recommendation for the current and future clinical professionals.

1. The clinical professionals should be able to value the importance of scientific literacy as a major ingredient of evidence/ethical practice and how academic programs can best foster such literacy.
2. The clinical professionals should be able to learn about what the author' views as several shortcomings in the current publication guidelines of the

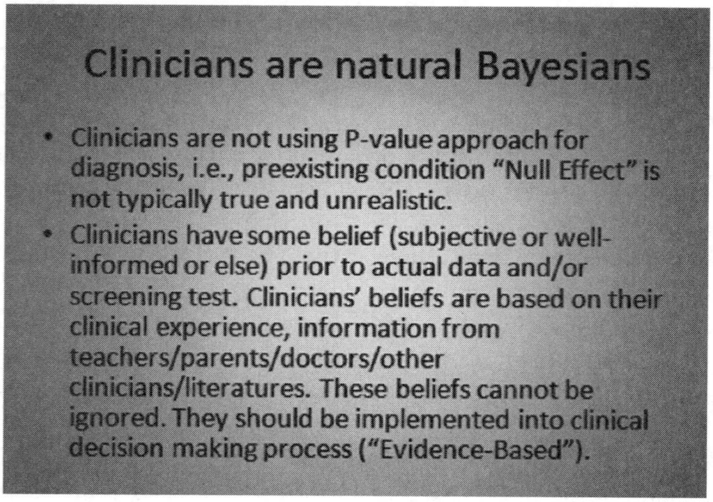

Clinicians are natural Bayesians

- Clinicians are not using P-value approach for diagnosis, i.e., preexisting condition "Null Effect" is not typically true and unrealistic.
- Clinicians have some belief (subjective or well-informed or else) prior to actual data and/or screening test. Clinicians' beliefs are based on their clinical experience, information from teachers/parents/doctors/other clinicians/literatures. These beliefs cannot be ignored. They should be implemented into clinical decision making process ("Evidence-Based").

Figure 0–5. Why are clinical practitioners Bayesians, not frequentists?

various scholastic journals including editorial policies that allow for, if not promote, null hypothesis testing (the p-value approach) in the absent of or alongside other forms of evidence such as confidence interval, effect size, replication, and alternative statistical methods.

3. The clinical professionals should be able to distinguish between "statistical significance" and "clinical significance" and become aware that the differences between these concepts are not often made clear in journal articles, and comprehend how a research article reflects a series of steps that conform with the scientific method of problem solving such as observation, hypothesis formation, hypothesis testing, verification, and evaluation.

Scientific literacy is also fundamental to the understanding of research methodology as well as the statistical assumptions and techniques used for the analysis and interpretation of data. In the absence of such understanding, it will be impossible for professionals to stay abreast of a rapidly flowing and ever-changing stream of information related to the study and treatment of speech, language, and hearing disorders. What is ultimately at stake is the credibility of the field to function as an independent discipline that presumably prides itself on contributing to a fund of knowledge leading to scientific advancements, not only in its own specialty areas but for its contributions to the arena of the health science specialties at large. In the absence of such credibility, we will practice "unethically" by failing to provide the best possible services for the people we serve.

This course will raise questions as to our "fitness" as a profession to achieve these aims. I will begin by discussing the lack of knowledge as to how many graduate programs in clinical sciences require a formal course in research methods and statistics. It appears that the Academic Council on Accreditation lauds knowledge in these areas, but makes no specific recommendations as to how competencies should be achieved beyond some ill-defined exposure to research ideas and concepts during the course of a student's graduate education. In the minds of the authors of this proposal, this falls far below the benchmark of not only the scientific aims of the profession, but also below its ethical standards of practice.

My intent in this book is to address these problems by accenting the importance of the scientific method as a thinking process that is well reflected in the various components of a scientific article about which every professional in our field needs to have knowledge whether a researcher or reader of research. These components include: (1) identifying a problem that leads to an idea for a research question or hypothesis, (2) developing a research design appropriate for the question or hypothesis, (3) collecting data and analyzing results pertinent to the questions of hypothesis, and (4) interpreting the results in a manner that refines understanding and leads to new questions/ hypotheses.

Writing up the results of a research study for publication in one's field in an intelligible manner, and the ability of readers to comprehend decisions made as to the design, methods used, and data analysis techniques comprise what the authors define as "scientific literacy." Elements of this understanding should include: why the study was done, how and to whom it was done, by what method it was done, and the results and discussion that should make clear the implications of the study.

In general, my text has the following purposes: (1) to discuss the preparation and skillful reading of research articles in view of the various sections that comprise them, (2) to make clear how each of these sections reflect the underlying thought processes of the scientific method, (3) to emphasize the importance of a clearly expressed rationale by article writers that are comprehensible to readers in all matters pertaining to the stated purpose, design, execution, and analysis of data from the study, (4) to review, critique, and make recommendations pertaining to the present publication guidelines for the various scholastic journals, (5) to discuss the potential implications of scientific literacy/or lack thereof to the future credibility of the field of the various clinical sciences, (6) to offer several recommendations as to the structure and content of our undergraduate/graduate programs so far as how best to teach scientific thinking skills, and (7) to relate all of the above to ethical practice as mandated by the journals.

An Alternative Method: How to Accurately Measure the Strength of the Clinical Evidence

The major distinction between the standard classical statistics and EBP statistics is that EBP statistics can provide such two important components of the statistical methods as (1) one is able to distinguish "*Clinical Significance*" from "*Statistical Significance*," as I will talk more about the

topic later, and (2) one is able to measure the strength of the evidence and interpret them correctly when making a diagnosis. As I noted earlier, over the past decade or so, interest in evidence-based practice has steadily increased in many clinical fields —a movement that has emphasized the importance of providing empirical evidence to support various therapy interventions. To succeed in meeting the goals of EBP, clinicians must rely on more than intuition and clinical experience. In addition, they must be well-versed in the methods of research and statistics to accurately evaluate and apply evidence that seems to support a particular intervention. As Guyatt, Sackett, and Cook (1993) noted, the ability to critically appraise research literature and apply such findings is an essential skill for scientifically based treatment. Yet, our observations suggest that this concern is often neglected in graduate training programs as well as by many clinical practitioners and researchers.

One of the main reasons for this neglect is that few professionals in the clinical sciences seem aware of the limitations of so-called classical (frequentist) statistics, such as p-values and Null Hypothesis Significance Testing. This failure has resulted in the misuse and misinterpretation of statistical findings as reported in the literature, and in our view has severely damaged the quality of scientific reasoning as applied to clinical problem solving.

One major problem in interpreting the results of classical statistics is that p-values and NHST are fundamentally two mutually exclusive and incompatible methods for accurately interpreting data. The ground work for both methods was laid down early in the twentieth century by such prominent theoreticians as Fisher, Neyman, and Pearson. Subsequently, generations of clinicians and researchers have been educated according to the principles of such statistical methods. Somehow, the philosophies underlying these two approaches were inappropriately blended and combined so that they are presently, yet mistakenly, believed to be a coherent approach to statistical inference.

Although providing the foundation for the vast majority of the clinical studies reported in the scientific literature, several clinical researchers have criticized the limitations, interpretations, and clinical relevance of classical statistical methods. One problem is that NHST requires an investigator to state two conflicting hypotheses. More specifically, the investigator predicts what should occur based on what was actually observed in the sample data while attempting to control two types of errors. The result obtained from NHST is always dichotomous, such as "Reject Null (H_o)" leads to "treatment was effective" or "Do not reject H_o" leads to "treatment was not effective." In case of Type I error, statistical conclusion validity can be threatened by concluding that there was a significant treatment effect when there was none. Statistical conclusion validity also can be threatened by a Type II error—retaining a false null hypothesis.

For purposes of interpreting p-values, an investigator wishes to determine how severely the null hypothesis was contradicted by the actual sample data. The p-value is by definition a *conditional probability*, assuming that a null hypothesis is true, of obtaining a result equal to or *more extreme* than what was actually observed in the sample data. Therefore, despite the fact that many believe that the p-value calculates the probabilities of the two hypotheses being true on the basis of actual sample data, this is actually a misinterpretation of the case. Moreover, it should be realized that the

p-value includes the calculation not only for an event that actually occurred but also includes the calculation for an event that did not occur (*more extreme*). Thus, the researcher's interpretation of the treatment effect may not be accurate because of the inclusion of events that actually never occurred.

The logic underlying the NHST and the p-value approach is called *deductive inference*. In this case, the researcher or clinician begins with a theory or hypothesis of treatment efficacy and then predicts what changes in behavior should be observed if such a theory or hypothesis was true (*effect to cause*). Because NHST and the p-value approach do not allow for more than one statistical conclusion at a time, alternative explanations for the treatment outcome cannot be entertained, thereby limiting the clinical utility of these methods.

What is needed in the clinical sciences is a reasoning process that allows researchers and clinicians to make accurate judgments about treatment efficacy by observing actual changes in client behavior. A method that allows for this determination by going in the reverse direction of deductive inference is called *inductive inference*. Based on observed behavioral outcomes following treatment, the likelihood of a theory or hypothesis being true can be evaluated (*cause to effect*). Inductive inference is a form of logic employed in the so-called *Bayesian* approach to problem solving. In contrast with classical statistics, the Bayesian method allows for the evaluation of more than one statistical conclusion at a time given the evidence. Furthermore, unlike classical statistics, this method allows for both accumulating and amalgamating clinical evidence across studies over time.

Because of the ability to incorporate prior information in generating probabilities for various outcomes based on new data as it emerges, the Bayesian method is gaining popularity in a number of disciplines. In addition, as we shall make clear, the Bayesian method allows clinicians to incorporate subjective estimates of therapy outcomes by quantitative means and to modify or update their judgment as new evidence is generated. As opposed to classical statistics, Bayesian statistics also helps to distinguish a "statistically significant result" from a "clinically significant result" by accurately measuring the strength of the evidence.

Within the context of this textbook, the history of the development of NHST and the p-value approach will be reviewed in addition to some of the more serious fallacies and misinterpretations that surround the use of these methods. An alternative to these classical statistical tests, the Bayesian method, also will be thoroughly discussed and illustrated using clinically relevant examples. More specifically, the following topics will be covered in relation to the Bayesian approach: (1) how to measure the strength of clinical evidence accurately, and (2) how to combine the results of two or more studies to generate a new research finding.

Following this text is a summary of key points of why this textbook will focus on Bayesian methods in clinical research, including the fallacies of frequentists methods.

Key Points for EBP Statistics

Frequentists Methods: Fisher's Perspectives, Neyman-Pearson's Perspectives, and the Combined Methods

1. Fisher's p-value is designed to measure the strength of evidence against the null hypothesis (H_o) and defined as "*the probability to obtain an effect exactly equal to or more extreme than the one observed presuming the null hypothesis of no effect is true.*" Symbolically, it is written as ***p [Exact Data value plus "More Extreme than Exact Data value observed in a sample | H_o is true]***. This is called Fisher's p-value (aka Imprecise p-value).

2. In general, you may state as follows: "The lower the p-value, the more unlikely the null hypothesis is, and at some point of low probability, the null hypothesis is preferably rejected. The p-value thus provides a quantitative strength of evidence against the null hypothesis stated."

3. Procedurally, Fisher's p-value is derived as follows: Let us consider the null hypothesis of no effect (H_o). Then one chooses a particular sample from a target population. He carefully studies the sample statistic and determines how severely the null hypothesis value was contradicted by the actual sample data (that is, it could serve as a measure of evidence against H_o). That is to say, the investigator computes a test statistic that measures the difference between what is observed and H_o value. This test statistic is converted into a probability, namely the p-value. Furthermore, for measuring the degree of contradiction (or discrepancies between H_o value and the actual sample data value), Fisher needed a rough numerical index guide of the strength of evidence against H_o, that is, "how small should the p-value be?" to determine the credibility of evidence against H_o. Fisher's NHST with the p-value is a practical approach whose statistical properties are derived from a hypothetical infinite population and which applies to any single experiment.

4. Fisher proposed the use of the term "significant" to be attached to the lower p-value. In his 1920 text, Statistical Methods for Research Workers, he said:

> Personally, the writer prefers to set a low standard of significance at the 5 percent point. . . . A scientific fact should be regarded as experimentally established only if a properly designed experiment rarely fails to give this level of significance.

5. This means, the operational meaning of a p-value less than 0.05 was merely that one should repeat the experiment. If subsequent studies also yielded significant p-values, one could conclude that the observed effects (or observed sample data) were unlikely to be the result of chance alone, rather due to the treatment effects.

6. Although Fisher's philosophy was centered around "inductive inference" (from "specific" to "general"), he grew disenchanted with the Bayesian subjectivism and sought to provide a more "objective" approach to inductive inference. Therefore, Fisher rejected the methods of inverse probability, that is, the probability of truth of a hypothesis (H) given the data (X), or p (H|X), in favor of the direct probability, or p (X|H). This transition was facilitated by his conviction that "It is possible to argue from consequences to causes, from observations to hypothesis" (Fisher 1925, p. 3).

7. Also, it is very important to distinguish between the "probabilities" of the observed data given H_o is true from the probability of the observed and "more extreme" data given H_o is true. It has not only caused the confu-

sion between p-value and Type I error (α) but also results in an exaggeration of the evidence against H_o by the observed data.

8. Fisher regarded p-values as constituting *inductive evidence* against H_0: the smaller the p-value, the more weight of evidence against H_0. Fisher also noted that a p-value represents an "objective" way for researchers to assess the plausibility of the null hypothesis. In other words, Fisher considered the use of probability values to be more reliable than "eyeballing" results.

9. Fisher believed that statistics could play an important part in promoting inductive inference that is drawing inferences from the particular to the general, from samples to populations. For him, the p-values assumes an epistemological role: "Inductive inference is the only process known to us by which essentially new knowledge comes into the world" (Fisher, 1925, p. 7).

10. In a sense, Fisher used some kind of casual, generic, unspecified, alternative (in replacement of the alternative rival/conflicting hypothesis against H_o) when calculating p-values, somehow implicit when identifying the test statistic and "more extreme outcomes" to compute p-values, or when talking about the "sensitivity" of an experiment. But he never explicitly defined nor used specific alternative hypothesis (H_a).

11. In a way, Fisher's p-value approach uses subjective decision for determining statistical significance, that is, he said, "If one in twenty (5%) does not seem high enough odds, we may, if we prefer it, draw the line at one in fifty (2%), or one in a hundred (1%)" (Fisher, 1925, p. 504).

12. Most investigators think and firmly believe that a p-value of 0.05, for

instance, means that the null hypothesis being true is 5%, or H_o being false is 95%. That is wishful thinking. This interpretation is logically making no sense because the p-value is calculated on the pre-existing assumption that H_o is true. Therefore, it cannot mathematically calculate the probability of truth in H_o. The only way we can calculate such the probability is by Bayes' rule. Symbolically, it is written as p [H_o is true | Exact Data observed], also termed as Posterior Probability. Recall that the calculation of a p-value is expressed as p [Exact or "more extreme" than the data observed | H_o is true] that is not equal to p [H_o is true | Exact Data observed].

13. Neyman-Pearson hypothesis tests approach has the advantages of its clear explanation. Of all the tests being carried out around the world at the 0.05 level, at most, 5% of them result in a false rejection of H_o (it is called Type I error). Its main drawback is that the performance of the procedure is always the prespecified level. Reporting the same error, say 0.05, no matter how incompatible the data seem to be with the null hypothesis is clearly worrisome in applied situations, and hence the appeal of the data-dependent p-values in research papers.

14. The chief methodological advantage of Fisher's p-value approach is that it may be taken as a quantitative measure of the "strength of evidence" against the null hypothesis. However, while p-values are very good as relative measures of evidence (inclusion of "more extreme" than the exact data values, that are unobserved and hypothetical outcomes), they are extremely difficult to interpret as absolute measures. Moreover, the various misinterpretations of p-values all result in an exaggeration of the actual evidence against the null hypothesis.

15. A common mistake by users of statistical tests is to misinterpret as the probability of the null hypothesis being true. This is not only wrong, but p-values and the Bayesian posterior probabilities of the null hypothesis can differ by several orders of magnitude, the posterior probability always being larger.

16. Researchers routinely confuse p-values with error probabilities (alpha value). This is not only wrong philosophically, but also has far-reaching practical implications. To see this, we urge those teaching statistics to simulate the frequentist performance of p-values in order to demonstrate the serious conflict between the student's intuition and reality.

17. Sophisticated statisticians may argue that p-values are just a measure of evidence in the sense that "either the null is false, or a rare event has occurred." The main flaws in this viewpoint are (1) the pre-existing assumption of p-values is "H_o is true," that is, it cannot be true and false at the same time logically, and (2) p-value is based on not only observed data but also the set of all data more extreme than the actual data. It is obvious that in this set, there can be data far more incompatible with the null than the data at hand, and hence this set provides much more "evidence" against the null (because of more rarities by inclusion of unobserved, hypothetical data) than does the actual data. This conditional fallacy, therefore, also results in an exaggeration of the

evidence against the null provided by the observed data.

18. To make it clearer when defining "the strength of evidence" against the null, one effective way is to use Bayesian measures of evidence (Minimum Bayes Factor and Posterior probabilities). On the contrary to what many believe, the Bayesian methods are easy to learn and more realistic.

19. It is disturbing that the ubiquitous p-values cannot be correctly interpreted by the majority of researchers. As a result, the p-value is viewed simultaneously in Neyman-Pearson terms as a deductive assessment of error in long-run repeated sampling situations, and in a Fisherian sense as a measure of inductive evidence in a single study. In fact, a p-value from a significance test has no place in the Neyman-Pearson hypothesis testing framework. Contrary to popular misconception, a p-value and alpha value are not the same thing, and they measure different concepts (Goodman 1999a, p. 1000).

20. The structure of the p-value and the subtlety of the fallacy that it embodied enabled the combination of the hypothesis test and p-value approaches. This combination method is characterized by setting Type I error rate (almost always 5%) and power (almost always ≥80%) before the experiment, then calculating a p-value and rejecting the null hypothesis if the p-value is less than the preset type I error rate. The combined method appears, completely deductively, to associate a probability (the p-value) with the null hypothesis within the context of a method that controls the chance of errors. The key word here is "probability," because a probability has an absoluteness that overwhelms caveats that it is not a probability of truth or that it should not be used mechanically.

21. As the philosopher Ian Hacking noted, "At no time does Fisher state why one is allowed to add the clause 'or a greater value' so as to form the region of rejection [of H_o]" (Hacking, I. [1965]. *The logic of statistical inference* [p. 82]. Cambridge, UK: Cambridge University Press.). One could argue that Fisher was implicitly acknowledging here that the p-value was an "approximate" attempt, without an alternative hypothesis, to get information like that provided by likelihood ratios. This is consistent with his vagueness about the quantitative interpretation of the p-value, his stress on its informal use, and his fury and frustration at seeing it subsumed by hypothesis testing.

22. Noting that the Gaussian standardized likelihood for $p = 0.03$ is 0.10, it would be more appropriate to say something like, "the plausibility of some relation, relative to the plausibility of no relation, is at most tenfold greater than it was before the experiment."

23. Because of its resemblance to the pretrial α error, p-value was absorbed into the hypothesis test framework. This created two illusions: that an "error rate" could be measured after an experiment, and that this post-trial "error rate" be regarded as a measure of inductive inference. One consequence is that we overestimate the evidence for associations, particularly with p-values in the range of 0.001–0.05, creating misleading impressions of their plausibility. Another result is that we

minimize the importance of judgment in inference, because its role is unclear when post-experiment evidential strength is thought to be measurable with pre-experiment "error rates." All clinical professionals, including the behavioral and social scientists, have tried to correct these problems by offering guidelines about how *p*-values should be used. But, unfortunately, still many researchers use the combined methods.

In summary, the readers of this textbook will learn:

1. About the history of NHST and the *p*-value approach and how these methods have been inappropriately combined leading to various fallacies and misinterpretations of statistical findings.
2. Why classical statistical methods currently in use are not well-designed for EBP and how NHST and *p*-values can actually hinder the development of new knowledge.
3. About several shortcomings in the current publication guidelines of ASHA's journals including editorial policies that allow for, if not promote, NHST and the *p*-value approach in the absent of or alongside other forms of evidence.
4. Why the Bayesian method is more clinically relevant to the goals of EBP than classical methods in evaluating the strength of evidence.
5. About the conceptual differences between *statistical significance* and *clinical significance* through several clinically relevant examples, and become aware that the differences between these concepts are not often

made clear in journal articles and textbooks.

Key Terms and Concepts

Evidence-based practice (EBP)

Statistical significance

Clinical significance

Practical significance

Personal significance

Deductive inference

Inductive inference

Clinical inference

Statistical inference

Frequentists methods (aka Classical/traditional statistical methods)

Bayesian methods

Bayesians

Scientific literacy

Measuring the strength of evidence

Classroom Discussions and Learning Activities

1. Define EBP.

2. What are the main differences between deductive inference and inductive inference? Clinically, which inference is more useful and meaningful? Give one clinically relevant example to support your answer.

3. Define (a) statistical significance, (b) clinical significance, (c) practical significance, and (d) personal significance.

4. Explain the difference (conceptually) between clinical inference procedure and statistical inference procedure. Which procedure is deductive or inductive? Give one clinically relevant example to support your answer.

5. Conceptually, what are the main differences between frequentists statistical methods and Bayesian statistical methods? Give one clinically relevant example to distinguish between them.

6. Why are clinicians natural Bayesians? Give several clinically relevant examples.

7. What is "scientific literacy"? Why is it important for clinical professionals? How do we develop it?

8. Philosophically, how do the clinical practitioners measure the strength of clinical evidence in a more accurate manner when they make diagnoses?

Acknowledgments

In preparing this textbook, I must say that more than words of thanks are owed to many people. For technical assistance, my many thanks go to two of my most competent research assistants at Emerson College, Ms. Kara Weasen and Ms. Kimberly Grzesik. Your contributions of this textbook are simply immeasurable. For the case studies collection and valuable suggestions for improvement, I am indebted to my former graduate students in CD 609 Research and Statistical Methods, especially very special thanks go to Ricki Feldman, Molly Riffle, Susanne Hulick, Brittany Desmarais, Christine Cleary, Jaclyn Feldman, Ali Seiderman, just to name a few. Your help is indeed statistically and clinically significant. All faculty members in my department, past or present, deserve special recognition. Words of special thanks are owed to Dr. David Maxwell and Dr. Philip Amato, longstanding teachers of research and statistical methods and distinguished scholars. I am truly grateful for your guidance and support throughout my 25 years of teaching and research career at Emerson College. I am greatly indebted to the excellent editorial, marketing, and publication professionals at Plural Publishing, especially, Ms. Angie Singh, Ms. Valerie John, Ms. Milgem Rabanera, Ms. Megan Carter, Ms. Veronica Williams, and Ms. Rachel Singer. I would also like to extend my deep appreciation to Ms. Erinn Gorey, the special program coordinator of the ASHA Short Courses. You definitely made my life easier. Additional acknowledgments must be extended to a group of several distinguished scholars at LSU-Allied Health who graciously invited me to their research symposium as the keynote speaker. From the bottom of my heart, I would like to send special thanks to Drs. Jimmy Cairo, Annette Hurley-Larmeu, Scott Rubin, and Meher Banajee. When I was delivering my keynote research presentation there, I truly felt how important and essential it is for the future clinical professionals to learn and understand evidence-based statistical methods to deepen their knowledge not only statistically but also clinically. That was the single most important moment and wake-up call for me and the audience. Thanks to LSU-Allied Health. I am ever grateful.

I would like to express a special thank you to Drs. Amir Aczel and Walter Czarnec for their incisive comments and positive suggestions that led to substantial improvements in the overall quality of this textbook. Not to mention, also thank you to my parents, my sister, and my niece for your support and love. You are always on my side, no matter what. I appreciate it more than you can possibly imagine.

Finally, I would like to dedicate this book wholeheartedly to two very special people, my wife Mary and my late father-in-law Tom, and our two very special fur babies, Hazel-Mae and Brady Boy. You are the sunshine of my life!

—Eiki Satake
February 2014

To my wife Mary,
For your continuous support and unconditional love. You always brighten
my day, no matter what kind of day I am having. I am ever grateful for that.

To my late father-in-law Tom Joyce
For your generosity, infectious enthusiasm, and
Fighting-Irish spirit, you truly inspired me.

To our precious fur babies Hazel-Mae and Brady Boy
Thanks for being there for me and making me smile every day.
No words can describe how thankful and lucky I am to have all of you in my life.

1

What Is Statistics? Descriptive and Inferential Statistics

Fundamentals of Statistics

Statistics is generally organized into two types: *descriptive* and *inferential*. The area of **descriptive statistics** consists of methods that reduce large sets of data into a manageable form that can be presented in tables or graphics and described in terms of sums, averages, relationships, differences, and so on.

The results from an experiment or survey do not arrive in an organized or structured format, ready for analysis. The data are not arranged in some magical way so that the first observed value is the highest value, the second is the next highest, and so on. Data need first to be organized so that we can see how the observed results are alike and different, and how they can be described in an objective and meaningful way. Methods of descriptive statistics help us achieve these goals for sample and population data and are the subject of the later chapters.

While useful, descriptions of data alone are rather limited, particularly in terms of developing or testing theories. More often than not, the primary goal of

a research is the ability to generalize the results from a sample to a population. For instance, suppose a clinician is interested in whether or not the nonfluent children in general exhibit a greater level of depression than fluent children. Rather than directly studying all children, we would select a representative sample of children to observe and measure and then generalize the results to the population of all children from which they were drawn. The area of **inferential statistics** provides us with the techniques and procedures for conducting sample-to-population research. These techniques and procedures are the subject of the later chapters.

Descriptive statistics consist of methods and procedures for organizing, summarizing, and describing data.

Inferential statistics include those methods and techniques for drawing inferences or making generalizations about a population on the basis of a sample from that population.

1

Population and Sample

A **population** consists of all objects, events, or individuals possessing a characteristic or characteristics of interest to a researcher. For example, "all SLP and audiologists in New York City" is a population, as is "all nonfluent children between the ages of 4 and 8" or "all autistic children of single parents." Sometimes, the size of a population under study is very large, but size alone is not the defining factor. When an entire population is measured using descriptive statistics, the process is termed a **census**. Censuses have been conducted since biblical times. But a census is very time consuming and expensive. For example, the first census conducted in the United States took nearly ten years to complete, and the 2000 census cost several billions of dollars.

> A population contains all objects, events, individuals possessing some common characteristic(s).

Rather than conducting a census, researchers usually select and study a subset or portion of a population, termed a **sample**. Ideally, the sample should be made up of a representative, cross section of the total population. Using inferential statistical methods, the researcher attempts to make predictions or generalizations about the population under study based on information observed in the sample.

> A sample is a subset or subgroup of a population.

Characteristics of populations are called **parameters**, usually symbolized

with Greek letters and occasionally with uppercase Roman letters. For example, "average age of all master degree candidates in communication disorders," or "median PPVT-R test score" would be considered parameters if used in describing a population. On the other hand, if these characteristics are used with reference to a sample of individuals from a given population, they are termed **statistics** and usually denoted both by lower- and uppercase Roman letters. For example, the Greek letter, μ (pronounced "mu"), is used to symbolize the arithmetic mean or average of a population, whereas $\overline{X}$ (pronounced "X bar") is used to denote the mean or average of a sample.

> A parameter is a quantitative characteristic of a population usually symbolized by a Greek letter. A statistic is a quantitative characteristic of a sample, usually symbolized by a Roman letter.

Types of Samples

As noted earlier, inferential statistics involves making generalizations or inferences about a population that are based on the data from a sample or subset of the population. The process of selecting a subset of a population is known as **sampling**. In selecting elements or members of a sample, one of two methods is used. Each method yields a distinct sample; one centers on probability the other does not.

Probability samples consist of elements or members that have a known chance of being selected and have been chosen on the basis of probability. This is very important because one of the crucial assumptions underlying statistical inference is that the sample has been randomly selected from a given population. The term "random" does not mean that the sample has been selected in a haphazard or seemingly unbiased manner. In statistical sampling, the term random is used to indicate that the sample has been drawn in such a way as to ensure the chance of all members of the population being selected. We examine some of the more common probability sampling techniques in Appendix G.

> Sampling is the process of selecting a subset or subgroup of objects, events, or individuals from a population.

Nonprobability samples consist of subsets of a population in which little or no attempt is made to ensure that its members are representative of the population. A group of student volunteers from a communication disorders course, a collection of individuals interviewed who visited a speech clinic, or the callers to ASHA hotline showing support for a candidate for the chief officers are examples of nonprobability samples. Although they may be subsets of defined populations, the lack of equal opportunity for all members of a given population to be selected means that the validity and reliability of such samples cannot be calculated statistically. Therefore, the ability to generalize results from observations of them to the populations from which they are selected is problematic.

> In probability samples, all of the elements or individuals have a known chance of being selected and are chosen on the basis of probability. Members of nonprobability samples are not necessarily representative of the population from which they are selected.

Variables

A **variable** is a concept or construct that consists of attributes or qualities that can differ in magnitude and variance along some dimension. Some variables that we measure are rather simple and straightforward, such as the names of religious or political affiliations; other variables, such as personality, aptitude, anxiety are more abstract and in need of more precise measures. On the other hand, a concept or construct for which the data do not vary is called a **constant**. Generally, research studies include both variables and constants. For example, in a study designed to measure math anxiety among female SLP and audiologists, gender and academic status may be constants and level of anxiety the variable.

> A variable is a concept or construct consisting of attributes or qualities that can take on different numerical values. A constant is a quantity that does not take on different values within a given context.

Continuous and Discrete Variables

The dimensions along which variables differ either are continuous or discrete. Theoretically, **continuous variables** are capable of being subdivided into an infinite number of units, although in reality this is seldom required or achieved. For example, we usually speak of one's age in terms of years and months. However, if necessary we also could measure age in units of days, hours, seconds, and fractions of seconds to infinity. The same is true when we consider the time it takes to complete a task or measures of intelligence or aptitude. Continuous variables, such as age, intelligence, aptitude, ability, and so on, represent processes, where form and substance are in flux and changing even as we try to measure them. Whatever gaps that appear to exist may be attributed to lack of adequate measuring instruments or devices rather than the absence of sub-units of measure.

A variable that can assume only designated or finite number of values between two points is termed a **discrete variable** because its measures only can be reported as fixed values. For a general example, the number of voters reported in an election or the number of members in a family represent finite points along the dimensions of the discrete variables voters and family size. Statistical treatment of discrete variables are possible but rather limited. We can, for example, report frequencies of discrete variables, as in "25 Republicans," "36 Democrats," or "41 Independents," or proportions, as in "10 percent males," "15 percent females." We also can report that the average family in a particular city has 2.43 children, although the reality is that the gap between 1 and 3 children does not contain fractional units. Nor would it be prudent to suggest that there are families out there with a .43 child. In general, nominal variables (those that categorize things by name) are discrete rather than continuous variables. We discuss the term "nominal" later in this chapter.

Most of the variables in the applied sciences are continuous in nature. Variables such as achievement, aptitude, anxiety, motivation, aggressiveness, intelligence generally are considered continuous, even though the measurement of them may be reported as discrete approximations. For example, Emily's score of 87 on a verbal aggressive scale, as measured by a clini-

cian, is considered an approximation of her verbal aggressiveness level that falls somewhere between 86.5 and 87.5. The notion of a continuum of variable measures is consistent with the modern scientific view of the world and universe where events are more probable than exact.

> Continuous variables can theoretically assume an infinite number of values between two points. Discrete variables theoretically can assume only a finite number of values between two points. Measurements of discrete variables are exact whereas those of continuous variables are approximations.

Independent and Dependent Variables

In addition to having discrete or continuous numerical values, variables are further defined according to how they are used in experimental and nonexperimental studies. For instance, variables over which an experimenter or researcher exercises control are termed as **independent variables (IV)**. In an experiment, it is the variable that is controlled or manipulated by the experimenter, who could then infer that any change in, say the behavior of subjects, and was caused by the manipulated variable. Used in this way, independent variables also are known as *predictor* or *explanatory* variables. In nonexperimental or *observational* studies, such as surveys or polls, the independent variable classifies or categorizes the objects or individuals under study. Academic status may be considered an independent variable because it classifies individuals into different categories, such as Freshman, Sophomore, Junior, or Senior. When used in this way, the variable often is referred to as a categorical variable. For another clinically relevant example, a clinician might hypothesize that recovery of linguistic ability following a stroke is related to a client's age at the time of the occurrence. This statement expresses a hypothesized relationship between the factor of age (independent variable) and recovery of linguistic ability (dependent variable) that is discussed next.

The behavior or characteristic that is said to be affected by the independent variable is termed the **dependent variable (DV)**. As the independent variable is varied, the researcher measures the changes in the dependent variable. In experiments the relationship between the two variables is one of cause and effect.

For a more complex clinical case, the clinician might wish to explore the relationship of multiple independent variables to the dependent variable within the framework of a single experiment. In this hypothetical scenario, the hypothesis might be expanded to include additional factors such as premorbid intelligence and educational achievement in the list of independent variables. Also, the clinician might wish to expand the list of dependent variables by adding such variables as the retrieval of vocational and psychological skills, and so forth to determine how strongly the dependent variable(s) will be affected by the independent variable(s). The various hypothesized relations between the independent and dependent variables are illustrated in Figure 1–1.

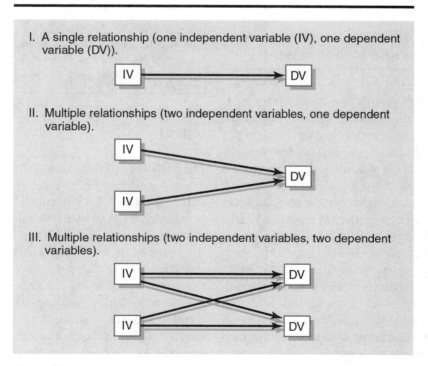

Figure 1–1. Various hypothesize relations between independent and dependent variables. Reprinted with permission from Thomson Delmar Learning.

In the field of communication disorders, an investigator thinks of and actually uses the term treatment as referring to the independent variable, whereas the outcome derived from an experiment is designated as the dependent variable. So in case that the investigator wishes to measure the outcomes associated with several different treatment options, we need to know levels of the independent (intensity of a treatment such as most intense, moderately intense, mildly intense) or levels of treatment.

> Independent variables are controlled or manipulated by the researcher and thought to influence another variable(s). Dependent variables are those variables thought to be influenced by another variable(s).

Data and Measurement

Observations made by researchers generally are recorded in numerical terms. The word observation is used here in the broadest sense. It may be an individual's response on a questionnaire or public opinion poll, or the time taken to complete a task, or a "score" on an achievement test or a response on a psychological or clinical measure. A single unit or bit of information obtained in a study, such as the response to a stimulus, or statement in a survey, is referred to as a **datum**. A record of a set of observations, such as all responses by an individual in an interview or the test scores of a group of students, is referred to as **data** or **statistical data**. Data are the basic units of information of statistical analyses.

The process of systematically assigning numerical values to direct or indirect observations according to an established or prearranged set of rules is called **measurement**. For example, if we attempted to measure what communication disorder majors consider "moderately severe fluency disorders" using a questionnaire, we would assign numerical values to each response and then compute a "score." The major concern in measurement is whether the scale or instrument meets the test of the two most important characteristics of a measuring instrument, validity and reliability.

> A single unit of information gathered in a study is referred to as a datum. A collection or record of all observations is known as data.

> Measurement involves the systematic assignment of values to observations according to an established or prearranged set of rules.

Validity

The **validity** of a measurement instrument or measurement procedures refers to the extent to which they accurately measure what they claim to measure. Suppose you develop a test protocol for measuring the severity of stuttering while reading a standard passage. You decide to calculate the number of words stuttered by two speakers and find that Speaker A stuttered significantly more than Speaker B. On the face of it, it may appear that Speaker A's problem is more severe than Speaker B's. Such a conclusion might have merit as long as you and perhaps other clinicians are content with such a narrow definition based on a single behavioral criterion, namely, frequency of stuttering during oral reading. Yet, such a restricted view of stuttering does not permit consideration of other parameters of stuttering severity. What, for example, might more frequent stuttering, exhibited by a particular speaker during an oral reading task, predict about his or her level of anxiety during social encounters or overall confidence as a communicator? Is Speaker A more avoidant of certain speaking situations than Speaker B, or vice versa? What might be the frequency of stuttering, per se, predict about educational or vocational achievement? The point of this is that simply because a test appears to accurately measure limited aspects of a phenomenon doe not make it a valid test, unless the test truly and accurately generates the outcomes that we want to measure. More generally, if the claim of a test, for instance, is that it measures one's aptitude to succeed in college, we may ask "How is aptitude defined for this test?" "How was the test developed?" "How do the test items relate to the concept or construct, aptitude?" In other words, what is it about this test that supports the claim that it makes. If the claim is supported, we say the instrument or procedure has validity.

There are three types of validity, content validity, criterion-related validity, and construct validity. An instrument is said to have content validity if its test items or procedures are representative of the concept or construct measured. The extent to which a instrument or procedure is related to some current or predictive measure is the basis of criterion-related validity. Finally, construct validity is based on how well a measurement instrument or procedure logically relates to a given concept or construct. The various methods to achieve these forms of validity are beyond the scope of this text but can be found in any research methods text.

> Validity refers to the extent to which a measurement instrument or measurement procedure accurately measures what it purports to measure.

Reliability

The **reliability** of a measurement instrument or measurement procedures refers to the extent to which they consistently measure what they claim to measure. If a personality test is administered to a random sample of individuals today and again in a month, we should expect a high to very high correlation between the two sets of scores if the test is to be considered reliable. Clinically speaking, when an investigator wished to determine the reliability of a certain test, she may consider consistency of measurement at two different times/persons/tests (from one time to another, from one client to another client, from one form of a test to another form) to see the change of the outcomes. If very little difference is observed, you may be able to conclude that the test is reliable. There are several statistical methods to actually calculate the degree of validity and reliability, that include Chronbach's alpha, Kuder and Richardson's formula 20, kappa formula (designed for observer reliability), factor analysis (determine the degree of validity of a test), just to name a few. Some of the techniques are further explained in later chapters of the book.

As a concept, validity of measurement applies to issues involving both the accuracy and reliability of a test instrument. For a measurement to be valid, it must accurately reflect the nature of the underlying variable that it is intended to represent. To be reliable, it must do so consistently with repetition over a span of time.

Relationship of Validity to Reliability

Establishing the reliability of a test is a necessary condition for establishing its validity—nothing can be true unless it is trustworthy. However, reliability alone is insufficient to establish validity. A case in point is a poorly calibrated audiometer that reliably produces invalid results in the measurement of hearing acuity. Although validity pertains to the accuracy of a test result, reliability only pertains to its replication (consistency).

The relationship between reliability and validity is illustrated and can be well described in Figure 1–2.

Using a bull's-eye target as an analogy, it can be seen that validity is based on how true one's aim is in hitting the center of the target, whereas reliability can be assessed solely on the basis of how closely the hits cluster to one another independent of their proximity to the bull's eye. In other words, validity can exist only to the degree that scores reliably cluster near the center of the target. On the other hand, reliability can exist independent of accuracy so long as the scores are not widely dispersed.

Generalizing from the bull's-eye analogy, it can be safely said that the reliability of measurement is primarily concerned with determining certain types of errors associated with the interpretation of test results.

Clinical Reliability: Kappa's Formula to Determine Observer Reliability

Observer Reliability

Professionals in clinical fields often are interested in assessing their reliability in administering diagnostic tests or treatment programs. Two types of observer reliability (also known as rater or scorer reliability) are typically of interest in any clinical study or research investigation.

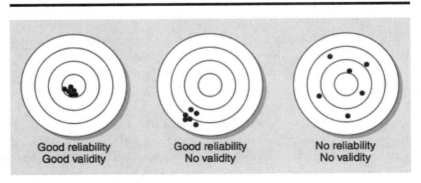

Figure 1–2. Using a bull's eye target as an analogy to describe the relationship between reliability and validity. Reprinted with permission from Thomson Delmar Learning.

The first of these, termed **intraobserver reliability**, is the degree of internal consistency of an individual observer with her or himself in administering the proscribed tests or experimental procedures and in measuring and assessing the results. Fluctuations within the observer, such as those resulting from extraneous distracters or changes in one's mental or physical state, can impair intraobserver reliability.

Although intraobserver reliability is related to the stability of judgment, another form of reliability that is of equal or greater importance to assess in most clinical studies or experiments is concerned with the accuracy of judgment. This is termed **interobserver reliability** and is often expressed as a percentage reflecting the proportion of agreements to disagreements between two or more observers. Suppose that two clinicians independently evaluate the speech of 20 randomly selected children born with a cleft palate one year after pharyngeal flap surgery. The clinicians decide to rate each child according to his or her degree of perceived nasal resonance. Assume that the ratings are assigned to one of four categories based on a numerical scale where 0 = normal resonance, 1 = mild hypernasality, 2 = moderate hypernasality, and 3 = severe hypernasality. Hypothetically, the distribution of ratings for the two clinicians could have looked something like Table 1–1.

One simple means of calculating interobserver reliability given the data in Table 1–1 is to count the frequency of agreements between the two clinicians and divide this value by the total number of observations, or:

$$\frac{Agreements}{Agreements + Disagreements} = \frac{14}{20}$$

$$= 70\% \text{ agreement}$$

A problem with this method is that when the number of observed cases decreases, the probability of observers agreeing by chance alone increases. To overcome this problem, techniques have been developed that calculate the probability for such a chance error and then subtract this probability in calculating interobserver reliability.

One relatively simple and useful method for measuring agreement between two observers in making judgments about behaviors that are assigned to one category or another is based on the so-called **kappa formula** (Cohen, 1988). The method has relevance to many clinical situations in which clinicians might wish to measure their agreement in diagnosing a particular disorder based on judgments of the presence or absence of abnormality. Such dichotomous results can be expressed as either "normal" or "abnormal" outcomes in leading to a diagnosis.

Table 1–1. Hypothetical Distribution of Two Clinicians' Ratings of Perceived Nasal Resonance for 20 Children

Case #	1	2	3	4	5	6	7	8	9	10	11	12	13	14	15	16	17	18	19	20
Rater A	1	0	1	3	2	2	1	1	3	1	1	1	0	0	1	2	1	1	0	1
Rater B	2	0	1	2	2	1	1	1	2	1	1	2	0	0	1	2	0	1	0	1

Note. 0 = normal resonance; 1 = mild hypernasality; 2 = moderate hypernasality; 3 = severe hypernasality.

Imagine that two clinicians independently evaluate 100 children suspected of stuttering and render judgments about the normality or abnormality of disfluent speech using the same diagnostic criteria. Hypothetical data based on their observations can be cast in the form of a 2 × 2 contingency table shown in Table 1–2. Based on the results shown in Table 1–1, we can proceed to illustrate the calculation of kappa (*k*), defined as the agreement beyond chance divided by the amount of agreement *possible* beyond chance, such that

$$k = \frac{o - c}{1 - c}$$

where *o* = the observed agreement, and *c* = the chance agreement. The actual steps involved in calculating kappa (*k*) are outlined below.

Calculating kappa (*k*)

Step 1: Calculate the observed agreement (*o*)

$$o = \frac{\begin{array}{c}(\text{\# of normal} \\ \text{agreements)}\end{array} + \begin{array}{c}(\text{\# of abnormality} \\ \text{agreements)}\end{array}}{\text{the grand total}}$$

$$= \frac{60 + 18}{100}$$

$$= \frac{78}{100\,(.78)} \; or \; 78\% = o$$

Step 2: Calculate the chance agreement (*c*)

a. Calculate how many observations the clinicians may agree are abnormal by chance, determined by multiplying the number each clinician found abnormal and then dividing by the grand total of 100 observations:

$$\frac{(30 \times 28)}{100} = 8.4$$

b. Calculate how many observations the two may agree are normal by chance, as determined by multiplying the number each found normal and dividing by the grand totals of 100 observations:

$$\frac{(70 \times 72)}{100} = 50.4$$

c. Add the two numbers found in the first two steps and divide by 100 to obtain the proportion of chance agreement:

$$\frac{(8.4 + 50.4)}{100} = 0.588 \; or \; 58.8\% = c$$

Step 3: Calculate kappa (*k*)

a. Given that the observed agreement (*o*) is 78%, or 0.78, the agreement beyond chance (*o* − *c*) is 0.78 − 0.588 = 0.192, representing the numerator of *k*.

b. The potential agreement beyond chance is 100% minus the chance agreement of 58.8%, or 1 − 0.588 = 0.412, the denominator of *k*. Thus, in our example,

$$k = \frac{0.192}{0.412} = 0.47 \; or \; 47\%$$

Table 1–2. Observing Agreement on Judging Disfluent Children as "Normal" or "Abnormal"

	Clinician B		
Clinician A	Abnormal	Normal	Subtotal
Abnormal	18	12	30
Normal	10	60	70
Subtotal	28	72	100

For a two-category system (or 2 by 2 categories) of the type described above, chance would dictate that the observers would agree 0.25 or 25% (1 ÷ 4 categories) of the time. Thus, based on the results of our hypothetical example in which a kappa of 47% was found, we can conclude that the extent of agreement between our two clinicians well exceeded chance expectations by approximately 22% (47%–25%).

The kappa formula represents a convenient and straightforward method for calculating the degree of reliability based on probability theory. Other more complex statistical procedures such as tests of correlation are available for determining the accuracy and stability of observations; some of these are discussed in Chapter 13. Meanwhile, remember that with respect to measurement considerations in research, the concept of reliability relates to the need for assessing errors resulting from inaccurate or unstable recording devices, including our own eyes and ears as they too may be used for such purposes.

Levels of Measurement: A General Perspective

The various types of measurement used to transform observations into statistical data generally are divided into four categories or **levels of measurement**, namely: *nominal*, *ordinal*, *interval* and *ratio*. The levels are hierarchical in nature, that is, each classifies or categorizes variables in varying degrees of precision. Each of the four levels may be viewed as a series of steps of measurement advance from measures of simple to complex variables, as shown in Figure 1–3.

Nominal Measurement

Measures that classify observations (of objects, individuals, groups, etc.) into categories by name are called **nominal measures**. It is the most general and least precise level of measurement. In nominal measurement, the categories of a variable or variables first are named

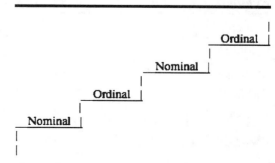

Figure 1–3. Four levels of measurement.

or labeled, such as "male" and "female" (gender); "Democrat", "Independent," and "Republican," "Libertarian," "Green Party" (political affiliation); "married," "single," divorced" (marital status); "sport utility vehicle," "sedan," "wagon," "hatchback," (car model). The frequencies or number of observations in each category are then counted and reported in tables and or graphs. Table 1–3, for example, illustrates the classification of a sample of the local speech-clinic clients (assuming that all participants agreed to share the information with a group of the investigators) according to their religious affiliation, including the number and relative frequency of observations for each affiliation. The term, relative frequency (rf) refers to the percentage of times something is observed relative to the total number of observations in a data set, as given in Formula 1–1.

Formula 1–1 $\quad rf = \dfrac{f}{n}$

Where $\quad f$ = number of times an event is observed in a data set

Table 1–3. Randomly Chosen Subjects at a Local Speech-Clinic by Religious Affiliation

Religion	Frequency	Relative Frequency
Catholic	9	0.14
Lutheran	12	0.18
Episcopal	6	0.09
Judaism	11	0.17
Baptist	8	0.12
Other	20	0.30
	Total = 66	Total = 1.00

n = total number of observed events in a data set

Ordinal Measurement

Measures that classify observations by name and puts them into categories according to degrees of differences are known as **ordinal measures**. The arrangement of categories implies that there is a prescribed ranking or logical hierarchy to the data. Values associated with variables, such as letter grades, academic and military ranks are examples of ordinal data. An ordinal measurement process consists of: (1) classifying a variable or variables into categories; (2) arranging the categories or observations into some form of rank-order; (3) assigning a numerical value to each observation or category; and (4) analyzing the data. However, the intervals between each category are not equal. For example, the hierarchy of academic ranks ranges from professor (highest) to associate professor, to assistant professor, to instructor (lowest). While there is an order to the ranks, the intervals of the scale are not equal.

What distinguishes a professor from that of an associate professor, for example, is not the same as what distinguishes an associate professor from an assistant professor, or an assistant professor from an instructor. The inequality of intervals in an ordinal scale or measures means that the mathematical manipulation of data is limited.

Interval Measurement

In interval measurement, observations are classified by name, arranged in rank-ordered categories, and the differences between the ranks are assumed to be equal. The equality in units of measure means that interval data can be treated in complex mathematical ways. However, the zero point in an interval scale does not necessarily represent the starting point of the scale or the total absence of characteristics being measured.

A Fahrenheit temperature thermometer is an example of an interval scale. The differences between degrees are the same size throughout the scale; the same 10 degree difference exists between the temperatures of 80 and 90 degrees and 50 and 60 degrees. On the other hand, a reading of zero Fahrenheit does not mean that there is a total absence of temperature. Similarly, a zero on a standardized personality or intelligence test does not mean that a person is without personality or intelligence. Finally, although arithmetic operations can be performed with interval data, the absence of a true zero point means that we can not make proportional assumptions. We can not, for instance, say that a person with a score of 80 on an anxiety scale is "twice" as anxious as someone with a score of 40.

Ratio Measurement

A **ratio** measure represents the highest or most precise level of measurement. Ratio measures have all of the properties of nominal, ordinal, and interval scales, plus an absolute zero point. Examples of common ratio measures are rulers, stopwatches, and weight scales. Someone who weighs 200 pounds is twice as heavy as one who weighs 100 pounds. A subject in an experiment who completes a task in 10 minutes is two-and-a-half times faster than one who takes 25 minutes. However,

there are few variables outside of the natural and some applied sciences that lend themselves to ratio measurement.

Level of Measurement: A Clinical Perspective

It usually refers to the nature of the numbers associated with a particular set of observations. Furthermore, the main goals of scientific research are to describe variables, the hypothesized relations among them, and the means of altering relations through systematic forms of manipulation or control. For example, a clinician might begin by describing the prevalence of certain phonological errors as observed in the speech of preschool children delayed in their expressive language development. Having classified or categorized these errors according to the type observed, the clinician might wish to understand how they vary in association with the quantity or quality of language stimulation in the home. On the basis, a parent might be instructed to interact with their children in a manner hypothesized to facilitate phonological development. The potential effect of such intervention could then be properly assessed.

Although describing, predicting, or controlling variables is the primary focus of most research, the meaning of the term *variable* is often ambiguous because of inconsistencies in usage. Perhaps this inconsistency is due in part to dictionary definitions of a "variable" as both an adjective (the tendency toward change) and as a noun (the thing that changes). For purposes of scientific research, the noun definition is the more common of the two; in it a variable "is any attribute or property in which organisms (objects, events, people) are observed to vary" (Pedhazer & Schmelkin, 1991, p. 17). Variables can be broadly classified according to: (1) their measurement properties, (2) how they are used in various types of research, and (3) the degree to which they exert an extraneous or confounding influence on the outcome of an experiment. There are three different types of variables. Classification of such variables is illustrated and summarized in Table 1–4.

Types of Data: Clinical Perspective

Before undertaking the analysis of a data set, it is important for a researcher to know the properties of the measurement scale used to represent the variables under study and the manner of their distribution. As you recall, not all data collected share the same qualities. Enumerating the

Table 1–4. Classification of Variables

Type of Variable	Characteristic(s)/Definitions	Other Terms
I. Measurement Variables		
A. Qualitative Variables	Can only be placed into certain categories	Categorical/grouping/discrete/nominal variables
(1) Dichotomous Variables	Two levels of assignment (e.g., gender)	
(2) Polyotomous Variables	More than two levels of assignment (e.g., ethnicity)	
B. Quantitative Variables	Mathematical operations can be performed, and they can be ordered/ranked according to their magnitude. Express the extent to which objects differ in degree, not in kind.	Ordinal/continuous variables
II. Research Variables		
A. Independent Variables	The antecedent factors that are manipulated, assigned, or grouped by the researcher in order to examine their affect on behavior	Cause/treatment/factor/predictor/nonmanipulated variable
B. Dependent Variables	The behaviors under study, the outcomes of a research study	Observed/criterion/outcome variables
III. Extraneous Variables	Nuisance factors unrelated to the dependent variable or independent variable that might exert unwanted influences on the outcomes of a research study	Confounding/nuisance variables

spoken opinions of jurors about "guilt" or "innocence" in a court of criminal or civil law is not the same as measuring the acoustic spectra of their various speech sounds. Data of the first type are best represented by frequency counts, whereas only the second type of data possesses properties amenable to formal mathematical operations.

Nominal and Ordinal Data

Frequency data are representative of the kind of distributions in which observations have been either: (a) placed in certain categories or (b) arranged in a meaningful order. As clinicians, we may be interested in describing various individuals or groups within our work settings according to certain qualitative categories such as children/adults, male/female, normal/impaired, improvement/no improvement, and so forth. Observations that can only be named and counted are called **nominal data**. Such data are sometimes described as dichotomous in nature because they involve "either/or" judgments about the presence or absence of a particular quality. Although such data may allow for some degree of numerical representation in terms of the frequency of the observations that fall within a given category, they have little or no quantitative meaning. For instance, we can arbitrary assign the number 1 to male clients and the number 2 to female clients as a means of designating the quality of gender. The reversal of the order of such two numbers would not make any difference in the type of gender involved. Also, quantitatively, it does not mean that one gender group is twice as much as the other gender group. To summarize the major characteristics of nominal data, it can be said:

- It classifies without arranging data in a logical order.
- Data categories are mutually exclusive and exhaustive in that a numerical value can belong to one and only one category.
- No mathematical meanings are involved in the process.

In addition to placing observations into particular categories, we often are interested in arranging them in relation to one another. Unlike the nominal scale, **ordinal measurement data** involves the ranking or logical ordering of categories. For example, should one wish to explore factors contributing toward student decisions in selecting a particular graduate program, the study might be done by devising an appropriate questionnaire. In the questionnaire, students in communication disorders at several universities were asked to rank the importance of five factors (Clinical Opportunities, Geographic Location, Faculty, Special Programs, and Small Class Size) in selecting a training program. Let's further assume that the outcomes of the study revealed that Clinical Opportunities was ranked most important followed by Geographic Location, Faculty, Special Programs, and Small Class Size, respectively. In doing so, we can rank them logically based on the importance of factors, that is, which factor influences students most in their decision making process. But ordinal level measurement does not provide information about the amount of differences. In comparing ordinal measures, we can discuss which factor ranked higher (more influential) or lower (less influential) on a particular trait, but we cannot equate differences in ranks. Therefore, the difference between the 2nd rank versus the 3rd rank is not necessarily the same degree of difference as a rank of

4th and 5th. To summarize the features of an ordinal scale:

- Data are arranged in a distinctive order.
- Data categories are mutually exclusive and exhaustive.
- Data categories are logically ranked on the basis of the amount of the characteristic possessed without mathematical meanings.

Interval and Ratio Data

An **interval scale** of measurement possesses two added features that are missing from the nominal and ordinal scale. Interval measurements are characterized by both equal intervals between data points and an arbitrary *zero point*. Whereas nominal and ordinal scales involve the measurement of **discrete variables**, those that can only be represented by integers (e.g., whole numbers 1, 2, 3, . . .), interval and ratio scales can represent continuous variables theoretically capable of taking on any value including fractional units of measurement (e.g., 1.1, 1.2, 1.3, . . .). In actual practice, continuous data are often rounded to the nearest appropriate value.

Interval scales also contain an equal amount of distance between any two comparable points of measurement along the scale. Relating this fact to many tests involving psychological measurement, we could say, for example, that the difference between 90 and 100 points of intelligence is mathematically equal to the difference between 110 and 120 points of intelligence. Although some interval scales may contain an arbitrary zero point, such a designation is actually without meaning. Thus, in the same way that it would

make no sense to conclude that the zero point on the Fahrenheit or Celsius scale means "no temperature," the idea of finding a living human without any measurable intelligence, personality, motivation, or language is equally implausible.

Nevertheless, it is often the case that both clinicians and researchers count the frequency of correct and incorrect responses without understanding whether or not the units of behavioral measurement are truly equal. For example, in the measurement of stuttering, one may not know the exact quantitative relation between one moment of stuttering and another, as these might be perceived and recorded by an observer. Yet, in many investigations, such disfluencies are often counted, averaged, and treated statistically as though they were the same. Similar dilemmas arise in the perceptual rating of other types of communication disorders where the assumption of equal intervals in the scale of measurement is tedious. Too often, the summarized ratings of a Likert-type scale (e.g., 1 = very mild, 2 = mild, 3 = moderate, 4 = severe, 5 = very severe) are treated statistically as though the intervals between these numerical values are equal when there may be no established basis for this conclusion. The principle to remember is that, so much as possible, assumptions about the applicability of any measurement scale should be consistent with the characteristics of the variables being measured. Unless equality between intervals can be determined, there is no basis for determining mathematical relations in a data set. Furthermore, regardless of the type of mathematical operation that might be permissible, good judgment must always be exercised in the interpretation of a data set. To conclude on the basis of a general test score that a person with a measured IQ of 100 is twice as intelligent as another individual having an IQ of 50 would do little to enlighten our understanding of specific differences in their cognitive abilities. In summary, the major features of an interval scale are:

- It has distinctive and logically ordered data categories.
- Data categories are mutually exclusive and exhaustive.
- Comparable differences between any two points on the scale are equal regardless of their position along the line of data points.
- An arbitrary zero point in the scale denotes neither the presence of a starting point for measurement nor the absence of the quality being measured.

A **ratio scale** not only allows numbers to be classified, ordered, and linearly specified at equal intervals, but also contains an absolute zero starting point. Measurements of length or weight are examples of physical attributes that can be interpreted using the ratio scale. Starting at zero, we can say that 4 inches is exactly twice 2 inches; the same could be said for 4 pounds as compared with 2 pounds. Thus, ratio scales permit not only the addition and subtraction of measurement units but also their division and multiplication both as whole numbers or fractions. In summary, the ratio scales has the following characteristics:

- The ability to specify amount and differences between amounts.
- The ability to arrange numerical values on a continuum.
- A true zero point exists.
- The ability to identify an absolute zero relative to a characteristic.

Feedback Review of Chapter 1

1. In statistics, the term *population* refers to
   a. the total number of people in the United States.
   b. any large group of people.
   c. all of the elements or members of a defined group.
   d. all of the above.

2. Sophomores enrolled at a college or university may be considered to constitute a
   a. sample.
   b. probability sample.
   c. population.
   d. a & c.

3. Which is the correct hierarchical order of the four common measurement scales?
   a. nominal, ordinal, interval, ratio
   b. ordinal, nominal, ratio, interval
   c. nominal, variable, ordinal, ratio
   d. nominal, ordinal, variable, interval

4. Academic letter grades are generally considered to be categories of a/an
   a. ratio variable.
   b. ordinal variable.
   c. nominal variable.
   d. continuous variable.

5. Inferential statistics are tools for
   a. describing elements of a sample.
   b. describing elements of a population.
   c. making inferences about a population.
   d. making inferences about a sample.

6. A sampling frame consists of all of the elements or members of a

a. sample.
b. defined population.
c. parameter.
d. statistic.

7. Which level of measurement has a true zero point?
   a. ratio variable.
   b. ordinal variable.
   c. nominal variable.
   d. continuous variable.

8. A statistic is to a sample as a _____ is to a population.
   a. distribution
   b. parameter.
   c. ratio
   d. frequency

9. Which of the following is an example of a constant, as opposed to a variable?
   a. number of children in a family
   b. color of eyes
   c. number of students who in a class
   d. all of the above

10. Music preferences of teenagers would most likely be measured using a/an
    a. nominal scale.
    b. ordinal scale.
    c. interval scale.
    d. ratio scale.

11. A sample of a population where all elements or members that had a known chance of being selected is known as a _____ sample.
    a. purposive
    b. strategic
    c. quota
    d. probability

12. Which type of validity is based on a statistical relationship between some current or future measure?

a. content validity
b. criterion-related
c. construct
d. logical

Fill-Ins

13. A subset of a population is called a/an _____.

14. A parameter is to a population as a/an _____ is to a sample.

15. A collection of users responding to an Internet survey is an example of a/an _____ sample.

16. In social and behavioral research, the _____ variable is controlled or manipulated by the researcher?

17. The variable affected by the manipulated or controlled variable is called the _____ variable.

18. The process of surveying all members of a population is called a _____.

19. _____ statistics consists of procedures for making generalizations about a population by studying a subset of the population.

20. Which of the following variables are continuous and which are discrete?

    math anxiety, number of items on a questionnaire, height, annual income, letter grades, personality, tennis scores, intelligence.

    Continuous   **Discrete**

21. Which type of measurement scale not only classifies and orders scores

but has equal distances along some continuum?

22. The most advanced level of measurement utilizes ratio scales, which are scales that have a true or absolute _____ point.

23. The _____ of a measurement instrument refers to the extent to which it measures what it claims to measure.

24. A _____ is a conjecture that something is so based on some theoretical or experiential evidence.

2

Organizing and Graphing Data

Overview

In this chapter, we present several ways of arranging statistical information in tabular and graphical forms. Arranging data into tables represents the first important step in the statistical analysis process since they bring a sense of order to random information. Graphs and charts come into play at the conclusion of the analysis process when the results of a study or survey are reported. They are important because they bring a sense of meaning to the consumer of statistical information.

Organizing Data

The first step in a statistical analysis is to give meaning to a set of data. Data collected by surveys, questionnaires, interviews, tests, and so on, seldom, if ever, arrive in an organized or meaningful form. For example, suppose we ask a random sample of 30 communication disorders majors to pick the most important attribute of a good clinician and obtain the results shown in Table 2–1.

Although possible, making sense of the data would be difficult. For example,

Table 2–1. Most Important Attributes of a Good Clinician Based on a Random Sample of 30 Communication Majors' Responses

precision	precision	spontaneous	precision	inventive
inventive	individualistic	precision	industrious	inventive
precision	inventive	independent	individualistic	individualistic
precision	precision	individualistic	inventive	independent
individualistic	precision	inventive	precision	independent
inventive	independent	determined	determined	industrious

we might be able to determine that "precision" is considered the most important attribute of a good clinician among our sample of communication disorder majors by simply looking at the list for a while. However, it becomes increasingly more difficult to determine which attribute ranks second or third in order of importance among those communication disorder majors.

In actual practice, the first thing we do when performing a statistical analysis is to summarize and arrange the data into a suitable format. The most common format used is tabular in nature, whether in columns generated by hand or in matrices created by spreadsheets software, such as Microsoft Excel, Minitab, or SPSS. Often, the same table used for data analysis is utilized in the written report of the analysis.

When data values, raw scores, or score intervals are arranged in an ascending or descending order, the arrangement is called a **distribution**. We examine three of the more common types: simple frequency distributions, cumulative distributions for ungrouped data, and class interval distributions for grouped data. The methods and techniques for creating these distributions are used when data sets are analyzed "by hand" using electronic calculators rather than computers and statistical software, which we illustrate from time to time throughout the text.

> An arrangement of values or scores arranged in an ascending or descending order is called a distribution.

Simple Frequency Distribution

One method of organizing data into a meaningful and efficient format is termed a **simple frequency distribution**. Because the data value are listed and treated as raw scores, rather than in groupings or intervals, simple frequency distributions also are referred to as *ungrouped data distributions* or simply as *ungrouped data*. In a simple frequency distribution, attributes, categories, or numerical values are listed in one column, and the frequency of their occurrence is listed in another. The order of arrangement may be in an ascending or descending format. Table 2–2 presents the data of our young adult survey in two simple frequency distribution formats generated on an Excel spreadsheet. One of the advantages of a computer-generated spreadsheet is that the data can be entered in a random format and later sorted into an ascending or descending format.

Looking at either table, we can easily see that "precision" is the attribute of a good clinician most frequently selected by the sample of 30 communication disorders majors in our sample. It also is easy to determine which attribute ranks second in order of importance or which is considered the least important among members of our sample. Moreover, either table is quite suited to the reporting of the results of a study.

> A simple frequency distribution is an arrangement of numerical values or variable categories in an ascending or descending order (numerically or alphabetically), with the frequency in which they are observed in the data set.

Note that in Table 2–2, we have introduced two statistical symbols, (f) representing frequency of a measure and (n) representing the total number of responses in the sample. In this text, we

Table 2–2. Frequency Attributes Considered Most Important in a Good Clinician by 30 Communication Disorders Majors

Random Order Response	f	Descending Order Response	f
Independent	4	Artistic	9
Spontaneous	1	Inventive	7
Industrious	2	Individualistic	5
Individualistic	5	Independent	4
Inventive	7	Determined	2
Determined	2	Industrious	2
Artistic	9	Spontaneous	1
	$n = 30$		$n = 30$

will use lowercase (n) to symbolize the size of a *sample* and the uppercase (N) to indicate the size of a *population*.

In short, frequency distribution tables are very efficient and effective ways of analyzing and reporting the results of a study.

Cumulative Distribution for Ungrouped Data

For analysis and reporting purposes, it often is useful to expand a simple frequency distribution to what is termed, a **cumulative distribution for ungrouped data**, as shown in Table 2–3. The data set consists of negative attitude scores of 40 clinicians toward a certain intensive speech treatment designed for a child stutterer. The first two columns, labeled X and f, contain eight distinct scores and their frequencies. The third column (cf) shows the cumulative frequency of the distribution at each distinct score level. For example, 28 scores in the distribution fall between scores 66 and 74. Note that the total of the frequency column ($n = 40$)

Table 2–3. Cumulative Distribution of Negative Attitude Scores Toward a Certain Speech Treatment

X	f	cf	%	cum%
89	1	40	2.5	100
80	4	39	10.0	97.5
77	7	35	17.5	87.5
74	13	28	32.5	70
71	7	15	17.5	37.5
69	4	8	10.0	20
67	3	4	7.5	10
66	1	1	2.5	2.5
	$n = 40$		100%	

and the value at the top of the cumulative frequency column (cf) are identical. Column four (%) contains the percentage of scores in the distribution for each distinct score. For instance, the frequency of 13 for scores 74 represents 32.5% of all the scores in the distribution. The 32.5% value, which is computed by dividing

$n = 40$ into $f = 13$, also is known as the **relative frequency** of score 74. It is derived by dividing the frequency of a score by the total number of scores in the distribution, multiplied by 100, symbolically given as $\frac{f}{n} \cdot 100 = \%$. And finally, the cumulative Percentage (*cum%*) column shows the percentages of scores in the distribution at any score level. Thus, 97.7% of all the scores in the distribution fall at and below score 80.

> The relative frequency of a score is determined by dividing the frequency of a score (f) by the total number of scores (n) of a distribution and multiplied times 100.

Data sets organized into cumulative distributions are quite useful in analyzing and describing both the results of a group as a whole and individual members. The cumulative percentage column (*cum%*), for instance, indicates the percentage of scores below a given point in the distribution. Thus, we can say that individuals with a score of 74 in Table 2–3 have a higher negative attitude toward the treatment than 37.5% of the 40 clinicians surveyed. We discuss more ways of using cumulative frequency distributions to describe individual scores.

> A cumulative distribution is an expansion of a simple frequency distribution to include the accumulation of scores at any given point (*cf*), the percentage of scores any one score represents (%), and the cumulative percentage of scores at any given point in the distribution (*cum%*).

Class Interval Distribution

Simple and cumulative distributions are quite useful and manageable with small data sets with a relatively small number of distinct scores, as seen in Table 2–3. However, when a data set is large and contains a wide range of scores, it is more convenient to arrange the values into units or classes to form a **class interval distribution**, also referred to as a *grouped data distribution* or simply as a *grouped data*. For example, suppose a clinical supervisor is interested in the incidence of "fear" toward public speaking/reporting among the first-year communication disorders majors obtains the following survey scores from a random sample of 98 students, as shown in Table 2–4. By collapsing the scores into groups or class intervals, we can substantially reduce the number of scores into a distribution and construct a table that can be analyzed efficiently.

Constructing a Class Interval Distribution Table

The first step in constructing a class interval distribution table involves determining the appropriate number of intervals. There is no fixed number of intervals that should be contained in a class interval distribution table. The rule of thumb that we suggest is to have between 8 and 15 intervals. Too few or too many intervals results in a loss of definition of the data set. In Table 2–5, the 98 test anxiety scores are organized in 11 class intervals and treated in 7 columns. We also suggest that the width of the intervals, whenever possible, be an odd rather than an even number. In that way, the interval midpoints will be whole rather than decimal values, thus making computations easier.

Table 2–4. Level of Fear Toward Public Speaking and Reporting Among Communication Disorders Majors ($n = 98$)

95	55	78	86	74	71	78	85	88	61	70
77	85	55	71	66	78	46	42	47	73	50
64	70	68	80	70	90	82	78	68	66	68
67	51	93	91	48	73	58	81	64	68	55
80	60	52	77	70	77	86	74	56	89	80
75	55	82	44	73	94	74	58	75	89	67
75	63	64	74	64	81	65	65	83	67	63
75	76	88	72	49	72	58	76	74	58	52
60	85	61	63	71	76	65	60	81	82	

Table 2–5. Class Interval Distribution of Fear Toward Public Speaking and Reporting Survey Data

ci	el	mp	f	cf	%	cum%
92–96	91.5–96.5	94	3	98	3.06	99.99*
87–91	86.5–91.5	89	6	95	6.12	96.93
82–86	81.5–86.5	84	9	89	9.18	90.81
77–81	76.5–81.5	79	13	80	13.27	81.63
72–76	71.5–76.5	74	17	67	17.35	68.36
67–71	66.5–71.5	69	14	50	14.29	51.05
62–66	61.5–66.5	64	12	36	12.24	36.72
57–61	56.5–61.5	59	9	24	9.18	24.48
52–56	51.5–56.5	54	7	15	7.14	15.30
47–51	46.5–51.5	49	5	8	5.10	8.16
42–46	41.5–46.5	44	3	3	3.06	3.06

$$n = 98$$

Source: Created by author.

Both the width and number of class intervals can be determined by dividing the range of scores (HS − LS + 1) in the distribution by 8 and 16 and selecting an odd number interval. For example, the range for the 98 scores in Table 2–4, range is 54 (95 − 42 + 1). Dividing 54 by 16 and 8 yields five possible class interval widths, 3, 4, 5, 6, and 7 (54/16 = 3.38 or 3 and 54/8 = 6.75 or 7). We selected 5 as the width of the intervals in Table 2–5, which resulted in 11 intervals. A more detailed description of the steps to follow in determining the number and width of class intervals is discussed later.

Once the width of the class intervals is determined, we can begin to construct our table, starting with the bottom interval. In Table 2–5, the bottom interval, 42–46 contains the lowest score in the distribution. After the bottom interval is established, the remaining intervals in the first or ci column are listed, each with a width of 5 score values, until last or top interval, containing the highest score in the distribution is listed, in this case 92–96.

The second column lists the exact value limits (el) of each interval, as show in Table 2–5. If we assume that the variable "homesickness" is a continuous variable, we can treat the scores on the survey as interval measures. Conceptually, score values may be thought of as numbers along a continuous rather than discrete scale. Mathematically, this means that a score represents a continuum that extends from 0.5 units below to 0.5 units above its face value. Thus, a score of, say, 67 is actually the midpoint of the interval 66.5 to 67.5 as shown in Figure 2–1.

The values 66.5 and 67.5 represent the upper limit and lower limit of raw score 67.0 of the first or bottom interval. This is the concept functioning in the exact limits of the class intervals shown in the second column of Table 2–5.

In the case of class intervals, the upper and lower limits refer to as the **exact limits** of the score interval and symbolized as (el). Thus, for the score interval 67–71 in Table 2–5, the exact lower and exact upper limits are 66.5 and 71.5, respectively, as shown in Figure 2–2, with the score value of 69 representing the midpoint of the interval.

Symbolically, the midpoint, upper limit, and lower limit of an interval are written as (m), (ul), and (ll), respectively. Some calculations require that we use the midpoint or lower limit of an interval, as we see in the next chapter.

The range of values from the exact lower to exact upper limit is referred to as the size or **width** of the interval and symbolized by the lower case of the letter

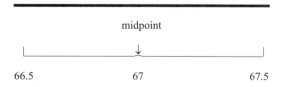

Figure 2–1. Graphical illustration of the location of the midpoint of the interval 66.5 and 67.5.

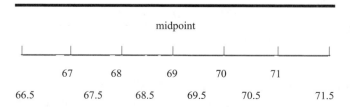

Figure 2–2. Graphical illustration of the exact limit and the location of the midpoint for the score interval 67–71.

(w). It is obtained by subtracting the exact lower limit from the exact upper limit of the interval. Thus, the size or width of the interval 67–71 is 5 (66.5–71.5); in operational terms, we can say that $ll - ul = w$. For convenience, we occasionally drop the word "exact" when referring to the term lower and upper limits of class intervals.

The **midpoint** of a class interval is the exact center of the interval and listed in the third column of a class interval distribution. It is considered to be the most representative value of an interval. This consideration is based on the theoretical assumption that the midpoint is the average of all of the values in an interval. It is obtained by one of two ways. On the one hand, we can add the lower and upper limits of the score interval and divide by 2. For example, for interval 67–71, the midpoint is 69 (67 + 71 / 2). In symbolic terms, $mp = ll + ul / 2$. The second way of obtaining the midpoint of a class interval is by adding one half of the interval width to the exact lower limit. For example, for the interval 66.5–71.5, where $w = 5$, we add 2.5 to 66.5 to obtain 69, the midpoint of the interval, as illustrated in Figure 2–3.

In symbolic terms, $mp = ll + w/2$. The same procedures are used to obtain the width and midpoint of intervals expressed in decimal terms, as in the score interval, 31.6–34.7, whose exact limits are 31.55–34.75, with an interval width of 3.2. Thus, the midpoint of the interval is 31.55 + 1.6 = 33.15. Note that when the width of an interval is an odd number, the midpoint is always a whole number.

> The exact limits (el) of a class interval (ci) consist of the upper limit (ul) and lower limit (ll). The midpoint (mp) of the interval is its exact center. And the size or width (w) is the range of values between the upper and lower limits.

In constructing class interval distributions, *tally* marks often are used to indicate the number of times a score appears within an interval, and listed as a total in the frequency (f) column, as shown in Table 2–6. The tally marks help us check the accuracy of our frequency column. They also give us a rough picture of the shape of the distribution, an important consideration in data analysis. For instance, if you rotate Table 2–6 so that the class intervals form the base of the table, you will note that the outline or shape of the tally marks is somewhat symmetrical. We say more about distribution shapes, more commonly referred to as *curves*, later in this and subsequent chapters of the text.

Earlier, we noted that simple frequency distribution tables often include

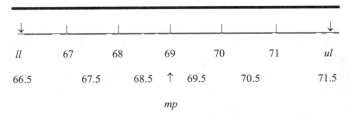

Figure 2–3. Graphical illustration of the mathematical derivations of the midpoint value for the interval 66.5–71.5.

Table 2–6. Class Intervals with Tally Marks and Frequencies of Fear Toward Public Speaking and Reporting Scores

ci	el	mp	tally	f
92–96	91.5–96.5	94	/ / /	3
87–91	86.5–91.5	89	/ / / / / /	6
82–86	81.5–86.5	84	/ / / / / / / / /	9
77–81	76.5–81.5	79	/ / / / / / / / / / / / /	13
72–76	71.5–76.5	74	/ / / / / / / / / / / / / / / / /	17
67–71	66.5–71.5	69	/ / / / / / / / / / / / / /	14
62–66	61.5–66.5	64	/ / / / / / / / / / / /	12
57–61	56.5–61.5	59	/ / / / / / / / /	9
52–56	51.5–56.5	54	/ / / / / / /	7
47–51	46.5–51.5	49	/ / / / /	5
42–46	41.5–46.5	44	/ / /	3
				$n = 98$

cumulative frequency (cf), percentage (%), and cumulative percentage ($cum\%$) columns. (See Table 2–3.) The same is true for class interval distribution, as illustrated in Table 2–5. They also function in a similar way. The values in the percentage column (%), for instance, indicate the percent of the total frequency accounted for by the frequency of any given class interval. It is computed by dividing the frequency (f) of scores in an interval by the total frequency (n) of the distribution and multiplying by 100. For example, the 12 scores in interval 62–66 represent 12.24 percent of the 98 scores in the distribution (12/98 × 100). The cumulative percentage column ($cum\%$) indicates the percentage of the total frequency of the distribution at the point of any given class interval. It may be computed either by successively adding the percentages in

the percentage (%) column or by dividing the cumulative frequency (cf) of a class interval by the total frequency of the distribution (n) and multiplying by 100. For example, for the score interval 62–66 in Table 2–5, we can arrive at the cumulative percentage value (36.72%) either by adding all of the percentages at and below the interval (3.06% + 5.10.% + 7.14% + 9.18% + 12.24%) or by adding the percentage of any given interval to the cumulative percentage of the interval below (in this case, 12.24% + 26.52%). When these columns are included in the table, class interval distributions also are referred to as *cumulative frequency* and *cumulative percentages* distributions.

Finally, one limitation of class interval distributions is the loss of some actual characteristics of a data set. For example, the distribution presented in Table 2–5 indicates that 7 students had homesickness scores in the 52–56 class interval. However, the table does not reveal which students received these scores, nor does it reveal which score occurred more than once, nor does it tell us if *anyone* even received one of the scores. As a matter of fact, a review of the actual data in Table 2–4 reveals that none of the 7 students in the 52–56 class interval received either a score of 53 or 54. On the other hand, this loss of definition does not have a serious impact on the statistical analysis of the data. In fact, the results of statistical procedures used with simple frequency and class interval distributions are identical or nearly the same as those computed with the exact scores, which we see in Chapter 3. In short, frequency distributions provide us with a convenient way of reducing large sets of data to manageable sizes without any serious disadvantage in the outcome of computations. Before moving on to more specific techniques for describing distributions and individuals scores in a distribution, we should examine some ways in which data can be organized and depicted in visual formats.

shape of the distribution?, (2) What are the measures of central tendency?, and (3) What are the measures of variation? We discuss the nature and shapes of distribution curves later in this chapter. The other two questions are discussed in Chapters 3 and 4.

There are many types of graphs or charts that can be used to display statistical data. However, the four basic graphical forms are pie charts, bar graphs, line graphs, and plot graphs. Pie charts, bar graphs, and line graphs are used primarily in reporting data, particularly in newspapers and periodicals. It would be a rare issue of *USA Today* or *Time* magazine, or the business section of most newspapers, that does not have a pie chart or bar or line graph. In statistical reporting, the particular type of graph constructed depends on the level of measurement that generated the data and whether the data represent discrete or continuous variables. For example, pie charts and bar graphs are most appropriate for nominal and ordinal measures yielding discrete data, whereas special forms of bar and line graphs are more appropriate for data representing interval or ratio measures of continuous variables.

Graphing Data

In addition to organizing data in tables, frequency distributions often are summarized and presented in the form of *graphs* or *charts*. Graphic representations are particularly useful because they can be easily understood by "consumers" of statistical data. They also provide the researcher or statistician with an image of the shape or *curve* of the distribution, which is quite useful during the exploratory phase of the data analysis. In descriptive statistics, we ask three basic questions: (1) What is the

Constructing Graphs and Charts

Generally, in graph construction, the values of the variable are presented along the horizontal or *x*-axis (formally known as the *abscissa*), and the frequency values are presented along the vertical or *y*-axis (called the *ordinate*). With the advent of computers, the task of constructing graphs using graphic and statistical software programs has been reduced to moving and clicking a mouse and/or pressing a few keys. However, computer-generated graphs vary from one program to another and may not follow the conventions noted here. We present the steps or procedures to follow in constructing graphs and charts by hand and Excel.

Graphing Nominal and Ordinal Data

Whereas tables displaying simple frequency distributions of nominal data generally are easy to understand and interpret, the impact of the data often may be enhanced by a simple graph. Two of the most widely used and most easily interpreted visual forms to depict nominal and ordinal data, such as ethnic groups, religious and political affiliations, and response modes are the pie chart and bar graph. They are effective because they provide easily understood pictures of how data are distributed among the different categories in the distribution. We briefly examine each one.

Pie Charts

A **pie chart** is basically a segmented circle whose segments represent the percentage of frequencies of the respective categories in a distribution. Table 2–7 presents a simple hypothetical frequency distribution of the ASHA-certified speech-language pathologists who favor a universal health policy by political affiliation. The first two columns show the political affiliation and frequency of those favoring a universal health policy. The third column shows the percentages corresponding to the *relative frequency* for each category. Conversion of the data into a pie chart is shown in Figure 2–4.

Constructing a pie chart is a relatively simple process consisting of the four steps outlined below.

Table 2–7. Frequency Distribution of Voters Who Favor a Universal Health Policy by Political Affiliation Among ASHA-Certified SLPs (*n* = 500)

Political Affiliation	f	%
Democrat	230	46
Republican	150	30
Independent	65	13
Libertarian	35	7
Other	20	4
	n = 500	100%

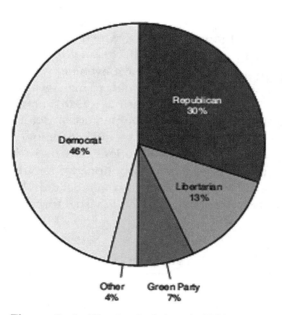

Figure 2–4. Pie chart of data in Table 2–7.

Constructing Pie Charts

Step 1: Determine the percentage of frequency for each category in the sample data set ($\frac{f}{n} \cdot 100 = \%$).

Step 2: Calculate the percentage of a circle (360°) that corresponds to the percentages found for each category. For our example, 46% of 360° is 165.5° (.46 × 360° = 165.5°); 30% of 360° = 108°; and so on.

Step 3: Use a protractor to draw a pie segment with the appropriate angle for each category.

Step 4: Create a title for the chart. Label each segment of the circle and indicate the percentage represented by each category. (It is not necessary to indicate the degrees of the angles.)

> A pie chart is a segmented circle whose segments represent the percentage of frequencies of the respective categories in a data set or frequency distribution.

Bar Graphs

Another commonly used method for graphically depicting distributions of nominal and ordinal measures is the **bar graph**. A bar graph is made up of a series of unconnected vertical or horizontal bars, whose heights correspond to the frequencies of the categories in the distribution. In a vertical bar graph, the variable categories are placed along the x-axis and the frequencies are plotted along the y-axis. The opposite is true for the horizontal bar graph, that is, the variable categories are placed along the y-axis, and the frequencies are plotted along the x-axis. Examples of vertical and horizontal bar graphs of the data in Table 2–7 are shown in Figure 2–5. Graphs in which the bars are arranged in order of frequencies, from high to low, is known as *Pareto Charts*. The three steps to follow in constructing a bar graph are outlined below.

Constructing Bar Graphs

Step 1: Using graph paper, draw and label the x- and y-axes consistent with whether it is to be a vertical or horizontal bar graph. The y-axis should be approximately three-quarters the length of the x-axis. Write a title for the graph.

Step 2: List the data values and frequencies along the x- and y-axes. For a *vertical bar graph*, list the variable categories along the x-axis and the frequencies along the y-axis. For a *horizontal bar graph*, list the variable categories along the y-axis and the frequencies along the x-axis. The units for frequencies in either type of graph should be of equal size.

Step 3: Using the frequencies as guides, draw the vertical or horizontal bars for each data value or category, arranging the bars from highest to lowest frequency either horizontally or vertically. The width of the bars should be the same for all variable categories, with spaces between each bar to indicate that there is no underlying continuum of the various categories.

Finally, although not illustrated here, a variation of the bar graph is the *picture graph*, which is frequently used to depict nominal and ordinal data in newspapers and weekly magazines. It is similar to the bar graph, except that symbols or images are used to represent frequencies rather than bars. Like the bar graph, the symbols or images may be presented in a vertical or horizontal format. The numerical value of each symbol or image is set by the person constructing the graph.

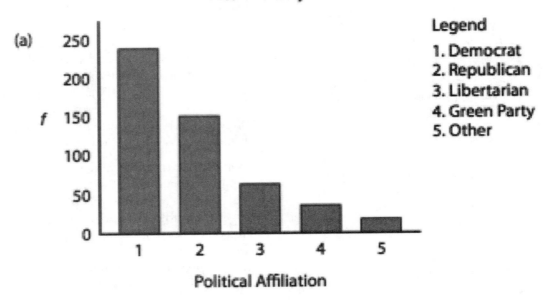

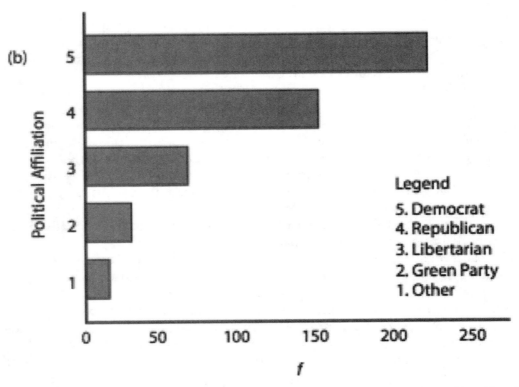

Figure 2–5. Vertical and horizontal bar graph of voters who favor a universal health policy by political affiliation among ASHA-certified SLPs; $n = 500$.

A bar graph consists of a series of unconnected vertical or horizontal bars, whose heights correspond to the frequencies of the categories in the distribution.

togram, the frequency polygon, and the cumulative frequency graph or ogive curve are used for reporting purposes. A graph often used to illustrate the relationship between variables in correlation and regression analyses is discussed in Chapters 5 and 6.

Graphing Interval and Ratio Data

When measurements are continuous along interval or ratio scales, special graphical forms are used to organize data for analysis purposes and to report the results of studies in professional journals. The most common of these are the **stem-and-leaf display**, the **histogram**, the **frequency polygon**, and the **ogive curve**, which may be plotted as a *cumulative frequency graph* or as *cumulative percentage graph*. The stem-and-leaf display and the scatter plot are particularly useful in the early stages of data analysis, whereas the his-

The Stem-and-Leaf Display

Suppose a college guidance counselor is interested in the percentage of the applicants accepted under an "early admission decision" in the communication disorders program. He selects a random sample of colleges and universities in the United States ranked among the most selective in *The Newsweek* annual "College-Admissions Survey" and obtains the results shown in Table 2–8.

As a first step in his analysis of the sample data, the guidance counselor may decide to create a stem-and-leaf display,

Table 2–8. Results of College-Admission Survey: The Percentage of the Applicants Accepted Under an Early Admission Decision in the Communication Disorders Program of a Random Sample of the Most Selective Colleges and Universities in the United States

School	Early Admissions (%)	School	Early Admissions (%)
College A	36	College G	50
College B	45	College H	55
College C	28	University F	60
College D	55	College I	27
University A	49	University G	39
University B	49	College J	53
University C	31	University H	31
University D	43	College K	43
College E	33	University I	43
College F	58	University J	44
University E	61	University K	26

as shown in Figure 2–6. A stem-and-leaf display combines the characteristics of a frequency distribution and a simple bar graph using the actual raw scores or data values in depicting the distribution. It is the graph most frequently used at the initial stages of a data analysis because it allows the researcher or statistician to quickly ascertain how the data values and their corresponding frequencies are distributed along a continuum of measures.

The format of the stem-and-leaf display is quite straightforward. It consists of a vertical line with the "tens," or "hundredths," or "thousandths" digits of the data values listed in an ascending or descending order in the **stem column**, to the left of a vertical line, and the corresponding "units" digit listed to the right in what is called the **leaf column**. For example, for data reported in hundreds, such as 53, the 5 would be placed in the stem column, and the 3 would be listed in the leaf column. Similarly, for the data values in the thousandths, as in 209, the 20 would be placed in the stem column and the 9 would be placed across from it in the leaf column.

The stem-and-leaf display also is useful because it illustrates the basic shape or curve of a distribution. The display in Figure 2–6 indicates that the distribution of the early admissions data is basically bell shaped or symmetric.

The three steps in constructing a stem-and-leaf display are outlined below.

Constructing the Stem-and-Leaf Display

Step 1: Draw a vertical line to accommodate all of the data values in the stem and leaf columns. Write a title for the plot.

Step 2: In the stem column to the left of the vertical line, list the "tens," "hundredths," or "thousandths," digits in an ascending order.

Step 3: In the leaf column to the right of the vertical line, list the corresponding "units" value of each stem value.

While useful as an initial step in the analysis process, stem-and-leaf displays seldom are used in reports of research studies. The graphs most likely to be used in technical reports and journal articles are the *histogram, frequency polygon, cumulative frequency polygon,* and the *cumulative percentage polygon.*

```
2 | 6 7 8
3 | 1 1 3 6 9
4 | 3 3 3 4 5 9 9
5 | 0 3 5 5 8
6 | 0 1
```

Figure 2–6. Stem-and-leaf display of percentage of applicants accepted under an "early admission decision" in the communication disorders program.

A stem-and-leaf display combines the characteristics of a frequency distribution and a simple bar graph, using the data values in depicting the shape of the distribution.

The Histogram

A **histogram** is basically a bar graph for interval or ratio data and the most easily interpreted of the three statistically oriented charts. It also depicts the shape of a distribution. The frequencies of scores or values, whether in ungrouped or class interval distributions, are represented by contiguous, rectangular bars along the *x*-axis and usually identified by the raw score in an ungrouped distribution or the exact upper limits of each interval in a class interval distribution. The bars are contiguous or adjacent to one another to indicate that the data values are distributed along a continuum.

A generic (nonclinical) example of a histogram is shown in Figure 2–7. The data set represents the votes for conviction on the first ballot by mock juries of varying sizes in capital offense trials. The height of each bar indicates the frequency of a score or frequency of scores in a class interval. For simple and cumulative frequency data, the bars are centered over the raw scores values along the *x*-axis, as in Figure 2–8. Also, note that the frequencies listed along the *y*-axis are calibrated in multiples of 5 rather than consecutive values from 0 to 22 in order to keep the size of the graph at a minimum.

Cumulative percentage distribution   Histogram

Jury Size	Freq.	Cum. Freq.	%	c%
16	6	89	7	100
14	10	83	11	93
12	14	73	16	82
10	22	59	25	66
8	17	37	19	41
6	12	20	13	22
4	8	8	2	9
	n = 89		100%	

Figure 2–7. Histogram of mock jury size and first ballot conviction votes.

Cumulative percentage distribution   Histogram

ci	el	mp	f	cf	%	c%
90–94	89.5–94.5	92	2	52	4	100
85–89	84.5–89.5	87	3	50	6	96
80–84	79.5–84.5	82	6	47	12	90
75–79	74.5–79.5	77	7	41	13	78
70–74	69.5–74.5	72	13	34	25	65
65–69	64.5–69.5	67	9	21	17	40
60–64	59.5–64.5	62	7	12	13	23
55–59	54.5–59.5	57	5	5	10	10
			52		100	

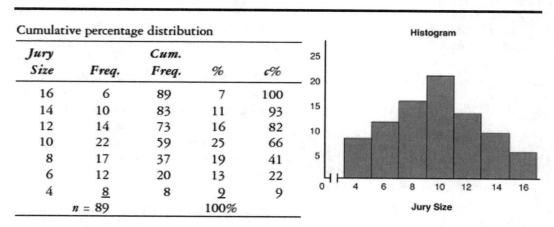

Figure 2–8. Class interval distribution and histogram for teacher competency.

An example of a histogram for class interval, cumulative frequency distribution data is shown in Figure 2–8, which presents scores on a hypothetical teacher competency test. In a class interval histogram, the boundaries of the bars are set at the exact upper limits (*ul*) of the intervals and listed along the *x*-axis. Note that the beginning of the first bar is above the lower limit (*ll*) of the first class interval in order to create a complete bar. Constructing a histogram is a relatively simple four-step process, as outlined below.

Constructing the Histogram

Step 1: Using graph paper, draw and label the *x*- and *y*-axes, with the *y*-axis three-quarters the length of the *x*-axis. Write a title for the graph.

Step 2: List the scores (simple frequency data) or the upper limits (*ul*) of the class intervals (grouped data) along the *x*-axis. For class interval data, the value of the first plot point at the left end of the *x*-axis should be the lower limit (*ll*) of the bottom interval. (See Figure 2–5.)

Step 3: List the values of the frequencies along the *y*-axis.

Step 4: Using the frequencies of the scores or class intervals as guides, draw the vertical bars for each score or class interval.

> A histogram is a bar graph in which the frequencies of scores or class intervals are represented by contiguous rectangular bars bordered by the score or upper limits of each interval along the horizontal axis.

The Frequency Polygon

A second common method used to graphically summarize data is a line graph known as a **frequency polygon**. It can be used in reporting both simple frequency and class interval distributions. Line graphs are useful in that they reflect the continuous nature of a measurement, as well as the shape or trend of the data. Like the histogram, the scores or class intervals in a frequency polygon are represented along the *x*-axis. However, instead of bars corresponding to the frequency for each score or class interval, **plot points** are placed above the scores or above the midpoints of class intervals and connected by a series of straight lines. Figure 2–9 illustrates a frequency polygon for a simple frequency distribution using the mock jury data in Figure 2–7. An example of a frequency polygon for class interval data using the teacher competency data (see Figure 2–8) above is presented in Figure 2–10.

The five steps in constructing a frequency polygon are outlined below.

Constructing the Frequency Polygon

Step 1: Draw and label the *x*- and *y*-axes. Write a title for the graph.

Step 2: List the scores (simple frequency) or the midpoints (*mp*) of the class intervals along the *x*-axis. Because the beginning and end of the frequency polygon must be anchored to the *x*-axis, place the first and last plot points on the *x*-axis one unit below and above the lowest and highest values in the distribution where the frequency is zero as shown in Figure 2–9 and Figure 2–10.

Step 3: List the values of the frequencies along the vertical or *y*-axis.

Figure 2–9. Frequency polygon for jury size data listed in Figure 2–7.

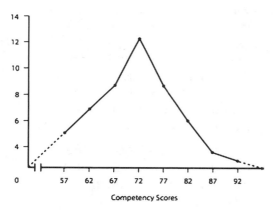

Figure 2–10. Frequency polygon for class interval distribution of teacher competency test scores listed in Figure 2–8.

Step 4: Using the scores or midpoints along the *x*-axis and their corresponding frequencies along the *y*-axis as guides, place plot points above each score or midpoint.

Step 5: Beginning at the left end of the *x*-axis, draw a straight line connecting all the dots or plot points. Use broken lines between the plot point of the first score or midpoint of the first interval and

the anchoring points at the extreme left and right sides of the *x*-axis.

One of the advantages of line graphs in general and the frequency polygon in particular is that they can be used to compare two or more distributions within the same graph. The different distributions may be differentiated by black or white or color lines, broken lines, broken lines with a dot between them. Also, when graphing more than one distribution, it is necessary to include a *legend* to identify each of the groups depicted in the graph.

> A frequency polygon is a line graph with plot points placed above the scores or class interval midpoints listed along the horizontal axis, at the intersection of their corresponding frequencies and connected by a straight line.

Cumulative Frequency and Cumulative Percentage Polygons

The **cumulative frequency polygon** and the **cumulative percentage polygon** are line graphs whose plot points represent the cumulative frequencies or cumulative percentage of scores at any given point in a distribution. They are also known as **ogive curves**. Both graphs are quite useful when we want to visually depict how many values or percentage of values fall below given scores or upper limits of class intervals.

Cumulative Frequency Polygon

Like the histogram, the raw scores or upper limits of class interval values in a cumulative frequency polygon are represented along the *x*-axis. The cumulative sum of frequencies at given points are represented by plot points placed above each score or the upper limit of each class interval because the upper limits represent the sum of the data values at any given point in the distribution. Examples of a cumulative frequency polygon for simply frequency and class interval data are shown in Figure 2–11 using the mock jury size and teacher competency test data. Constructing cumulative frequency polygons for ungrouped and class interval distributions consists of the five steps outlined below.

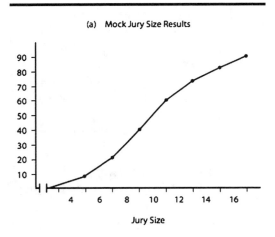

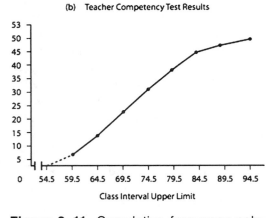

Figure 2–11. Cumulative frequency polygon for jury size and teacher competency test scores.

Constructing the Cumulative Frequency Polygon

Step 1: Draw and label the *x*- and *y*-axes. Write a title for the graph.

Step 2: List the raw scores (ungrouped data) or the *upper limits* (*ul*) of the class intervals along the *x*-axis. For class interval data, the value of the first plot point at the left end of the *x*-axis should be the *lower limit* (*ll*) of the bottom interval. (See Figure 2–11.)

Step 3: List an appropriate scale of values along the *y*-axis to represent the cumulative frequencies, such as 0, 1, 2, 3 . . . or 0, 5, 10, 15, . . . or 0, 10, 20, 30 . . . and so on, depending on the range of values in the cumulative frequency column. Do not list the actual cumulative frequency values. (See Figure 2–11.)

Step 4: Place a *plot point* above each score or upper limit of the class interval, using the frequencies along the *y*-axis as guides. Anchor the first plot point on the *x*-axis one unit value below the lowest score or the *lower limit* of the bottom interval in the distribution.

Step 5: Starting at the left end of the *x*-axis, draw a straight line connecting all the dots or plot points. Use broken lines between the plot point of the first score or midpoint of the first interval and the anchoring points at the extreme left and right sides of the *x*-axis.

Cumulative Percentage Polygon

The **cumulative percentage polygon**, also known as a **relative frequency polygon**, is identical to that of the cumulative frequency polygon, with one exception. The exception is that percentages are used in place of frequencies. An example of cumulative frequency polygons for simple frequency and class interval data, using the mock jury size and teacher competency test data are shown in Figure 2–12.

Note that the plot points represent cumulative percentages rather than frequencies.

In constructing a cumulative frequency polygon, we follow the same five-step procedure outlined above, except that in Step 3, a scale of 0 to 100 is listed along the *y*-axis to represent cumulative percentages. Figure 2–13 presents a cumulative percentage polygon for the ungrouped mock jury data. An example of a cumulative percentage polygon for the class interval data represented in Figure 2–12 is shown in Figure 2–13.

In summary, there are many types of graphs and charts available to visually represent different types of data distributions. The particular type used depends on the level of measurement and whether

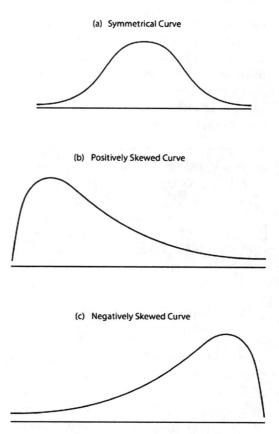

Figure 2–13. Three basic types of distribution curves.

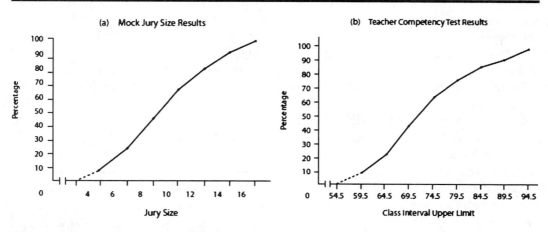

Figure 2–12. Cumulative percentage polygon of mock jury size and teacher competency test data.

the data represent a discrete or continuous variable. Generally, bar graphs and pie charts are used with nominal and ordinal measures of discrete variables, whereas histograms and frequency polygons are used with interval and ratio measures of continuous variables.

> Cumulative frequency and cumulative percentage polygons are line graphs whose plot points represent the cumulative frequencies or percentages of scores or class intervals at any given point in a distribution.

Distribution Types and Curves

Frequency distributions come in all shapes and sizes. As we noted in our discussion of graphs, the shape or curve of a distribution is determined by the spread of the data along a scale of measurement. The shape of a distribution is important because it often determines the methods and techniques that are used in statistical analyses. Although the number of possible shapes of distribution curves is unlimited, there actually are two basic forms, symmetric and nonsymmetric.

Symmetric curves, such as the one shown in Figure 2–13A, are bell-shaped, with most of the scores or data values concentrated around the center of the distribution, with progressively fewer scores toward the tails. In a perfectly shaped, symmetrical curve, each half is the mirror image of the other. If we were to draw a vertical line down the middle of the curve, the two halves would be identical in size and shape, with half of the frequencies in a distribution above the line and half of them below it. The theoretical model for this idealized distribution is known

as the *normal distribution*, and its curve referred to as the *normal curve.*

Sometimes the shape of a distribution is not normal or symmetrical. For example, if we were to measure the heights of a large, random sample of players in the National Basketball Association, most of the distribution values would most likely be at the high end of scale. Thus, the shape or curve of the distribution would not be symmetrical. Nonsymmetric curves are called **skewed curves**, and their distributions are known as **skewed distributions**. Skewed distributions and their curves are said to be "skewed to the right" or *positively skewed* or "skewed to the left" or *negatively skewed*, as in Figure 2–13B and 2–13C.

It is important to note that the skewness of a curve is represented by its "tail," where the frequencies of the data values are the fewest. For example, if the slope of the curve tails off to the right, the curve is **positively skewed** as in Figure 2–13B. In contrast, if the slope tails off to the left, the curve is **negatively skewed** as in Figure 2–13C. In other words, a distribution with most scores concentrated at the bottom or lower value end is positively skewed, whereas one with most scores at the upper or higher value end is negatively skewed. For instance, a test or task that is too easy for a particular group of individuals probably would result in a negatively skewed distribution, with most scores toward the upper range and progressively fewer scores toward the lower range of the value scale. We discuss the normal and skewed distributions in greater detail in Chapter 3.

> Distributions can take the shape of three basic forms: normal or symmetrical, positively skewed or skewed to the left, and negatively skewed or skewed to the right.

Key Terms and Concepts

Distribution

Interval lower limit

Simple frequency distributions

Class interval

Class interval distributions

Grouped data

Data set

Cumulative frequency distribution

Interval midpoint

Relative frequency distribution

Interval upper limit

Cumulative percentage distribution

Feedback Review of Chapter 2

1. A distribution that has nearly all of its scores to the extreme right of the x-axis and few at the left end is said to be
   a. bell shaped.
   b. symmetric-like.
   c. negatively skewed.
   d. positively skewed.

2. If the following scores were part of a class interval distribution, how many of them would fall in the interval with a lower limit of 9.5 and a midpoint of 11?

   10, 11, 9, 15, 12, 16, 13, 14, 13, 8, 10, 15, 11, 12, 9

   a. 5
   b. 6
   c. 7
   d. 8
   e. 9

3. The exact limits of score 75 are
   a. 75.0–75.1
   b. 75.5–75.5
   c. 75.5–75.6
   d. 74.5–75.0
   e. 74.5–75.5

4. The exact limits of score interval 35–39 are
   a. 35.0–39.0.
   b. 35.0–39.5.
   c. 35.5–39.5.
   d. 34.5–39.5.
   e. 34.5–39.6.

5. The width of the class interval, 2–6, is
   a. 3.
   b. 3.5.
   c. 4.
   d. 4.5.
   e. 5.

6. As a rule of thumb, the number of intervals that should be used in constructing a class interval distribution should be
   a. between 8 and 16.
   b. between 11 and 21.
   c. any even number.
   d. any odd number.
   e. the number equal to the width of the intervals.

7. In constructing a class interval distribution, the formula $ll + ul / 2$ is used to find
   a. exact limits of each class interval.
   b. the midpoints of class intervals.
   c. the range of scores within an interval.
   d. the frequency of scores within an interval.
   e. the percentage of scores within an interval.

Fill-Ins

8. Adding the lower and upper limits of a class interval and dividing by 2 equals the _____ of the interval.

9. In a class interval distribution, it is assumed that the average of all scores in an interval is equal to the _____ of the interval.

10. The _____ of a score is derived by dividing the frequency of a score by the total number of scores in the distribution, multiplied by 100.

For questions 11 through 16, identify the appropriate symbol.

11. class interval midpoint _____

12. interval width _____

13. population size _____

14. score _____

15. frequency _____

16. sample size _____

Calculation Guides

Determining the Number and Width of Class Intervals

Step 1

Find the *range* of scores in the distribution by subtracting the lowest score from the highest score and adding 1 (HS – LS + 1) to ensure that both extreme scores are considered within the range.

Step 2

Divide the range first by 16 and then by 8. Wherever possible, choose an interval width that is an odd number such as 3, 5, 7, 9, and so on. Using an odd number for the size or width of an interval ensures that the midpoints (*mp*) of the interval will be a whole number rather than a decimal value, thus making computations easier.

Step 3

Arrange the intervals in an ascending order in the first column of the distribution table with the lowest score values representing the bottom interval of the distribution. The bottom intervals must include the lowest score in the distribution; the top interval must contain the highest score. Examine the raw data and record the number of scores that fall into each respective interval. Note that it is not necessary to arrange the raw data in an ascending or descending order before constructing the class interval distribution.

Constructing Pie Charts

Step 1

Determine the percentage of frequency for each category in the sample data set.

Step 2

Calculate the percentage of a circle (360°) that corresponds to the percentages found for each category. For our example, 46% of 360° is 165.5° (.46 × 360° = 165.5°); 30% of 360° = 108°; and so on.

Step 3

Use a protractor to draw a pie segment with the appropriate angle for each category.

Step 4

Create a title for the chart. Label each segment of the circle and indicate the percentage represented by each category. (It is not necessary to indicate the degrees of the angles.)

Constructing Bar Graphs

Step 1

Using graph paper, draw and label the x- and y-axes consistent with whether it is to be a vertical or horizontal bar graph. The y-axis should be approximately three-quarters the length of the x-axis. Write a title for the graph.

Step 2

List the data values and frequencies along the x- and y-axes. For a *vertical bar graph*, list the variable categories along the x-axis and the frequencies along the y-axis. For a *horizontal bar graph*, list the variable categories along the y-axis and the frequencies along the x-axis. The units for frequencies in either type of graph should be of equal size.

Step 3

Using the frequencies as guides, draw the vertical or horizontal bars for each data value or category, arranging the bars from highest to lowest frequency either horizontally or vertically. The width of the bars should be the same for all variable categories, with spaces between each bar to indicate that there is no underlying continuum of the various categories.

Constructing the Stem-and-Leaf Display

Step 1

Draw a vertical line to accommodate all of the data values in the stem and leaf columns. Write a title for the plot.

Step 2

In the stem column to the left of the vertical line, list the tens, hundredths, or thousandths digits in an ascending order.

Step 3

In the leaf column to the right of the vertical line, list the corresponding "units" value of each stem value.

Constructing the Histogram

Step 1

Using graph paper, draw and label the x- and y-axes with the y-axis three-quarters the length of the x-axis. Write a title for the graph.

Step 2

List the scores (simple frequency data) or the upper limits (*ul*) of the class intervals (grouped data) along the x-axis. For class interval data, the value of the first plot point at the left end of the x-axis should be the lower limit (*ll*) of the bottom interval. (See Figure 2–8.)

Step 3

List the values of the frequencies along the *y*-axis.

Step 4

Using the frequencies of the scores or class intervals as guides, draw the vertical bars for each score or class interval.

Constructing the Frequency Polygon

Step 1

Draw and label the *x*- and *y*-axes. Write a title for the graph.

Step 2

List the scores (simple frequency) or the midpoints (*mp*) of the class intervals along the *x*-axis. Since the beginning and end of the frequency polygon must be anchored to the *x*-axis, place the first and last plot points on the *x*-axis one unit below and above the lowest and highest values in the distribution where the frequency is zero as shown in Figure 2–9 and Figure 2–10.

Step 3

List the values of the frequencies along the vertical or *y*-axis.

Step 4

Using the scores or midpoints along the *x*-axis and their corresponding frequencies along the *y*-axis as guides, place plot points above each score or midpoint.

Step 5

Beginning at the left end of the *x*-axis, draw a straight line connecting all the dots or plot points. Use broken lines between the plot point of the first score or midpoint of the first interval and the anchoring points at the extreme left and right sides of the *x*-axis.

Constructing the Cumulative Frequency Polygon

Step 1

Draw and label the *x*- and *y*-axes. Write a title for the graph.

Step 2

List the raw scores (ungrouped data) or the upper limits (*ul*) of the class intervals along the *x*-axis. For class interval data, the value of the first plot point at the left end of the *x*-axis should be the lower limit (*ll*) of the bottom interval. (See Figure 2–11.)

Step 3

List an appropriate scale of values along the *y*-axis to represent the cumulative frequencies, such as 0, 1, 2, 3 . . . or 0, 5, 10, 15 . . . or 0, 10, 20, 30 . . . , and so on, depending on the range of values in the cumulative frequency column. Do not list the use the actual cumulative frequency values. (See Figure 2–11.)

Step 4

Place a *plot point* above each score or upper limit of the class interval using the frequencies along the *y*-axis as guides. Anchor the first plot point on the *x*-axis one unit value below the lowest score or the *lower limit* of the bottom interval in the distribution.

Step 5

Starting at the left end of the *y*-axis, draw a straight line connecting all the dots or plot points. Use broken lines between the plot point of the first score or midpoint of the first interval and the anchoring points at the extreme left and right sides of the *x*-axis.

3

Descriptive Methods: Measures of Central Tendency and Variability

Overview: A General Perspective

Frequency distribution tables and graphs are very useful devices that enable us to reduce and give meaning to a mass of data and indicate whether a distribution is symmetric-like or skewed to one side or the other. They provide us a picture of a distribution as a whole. However, often we wish to describe data in more specific terms. To do so, we apply statistical methods that yield a single *data value* that tells us something about a characteristic of the entire distribution or the value itself.[1] For example, when someone says that the "average age of Internet user is such and such," we learn something specific about the population of all Internet users. In this case, the average age is a single data value that summarizes and represents a distribution in a particular way. We also can use this average to describe the position of individual scores or values, as in "above average" or "below average." In other cases, we may want to understand how individuals within a group differ from one another on some measure.

At the outset of the data analysis process, there are several summary measures of interest. These include measures that describe similarity and differences among scores or values in a distribution. These measures are commonly known as *measures of central tendency* and *measures of variability* (or *s*). They focus on characteristics that describe the distribution as a whole. Several of the measures also are useful in describing individual scores within a distribution, both in terms of position and relationship to other scores. In this chapter, we introduce concepts and computational techniques related to measures of central tendency and measures of variability as descriptors of distributions. In Chapter 4, we consider descriptors of individual scores.

---

[1]For the sake of convenience, we use the terms "score" and "value" interchangeably.

Measures of Central Tendency

In the last chapter, we noted that in normal distributions or those that approximate them, most of the data values tend to cluster around the center of a distribution. Thus the data value that best represents or characterizes the distribution will probably lie in that middle area. This value is called a **measure of central tendency**. There are three of these summary measures: the *mode*, the *median*, and the *mean*, more commonly known as the *average*. Actually, each of these measures is a type of "average" that tells us something about the characteristic of an entire distribution. A knowledge and understanding of them is considered fundamental to many aspects of everyday life. The National Council of Teachers of Mathematics, for example, considers the ability "to determine mean, median, and mode for given numerical data" one of the 48 mathematical competencies and skills "essential for enlightened citizens."

Consider the following scenario. Suppose a clinician is interested in how her young clients' favorite (children aged 4 to 8) television programs, such as *Sesame Street*, *Barney*, and *Bob the Builder*, affect the development of prosocial behavior in children. An investigator develops an instrument designed to detect the extent to which these types of programs influenced the development of prosocial skills. She then administers it to a random sample of 30 adolescents who reported viewing such programs on a regular basis as a child. The results of her survey, which we shall refer to as the "prosocial skills survey," are summarized in a simple frequency distribution shown in Table 3–1. The higher the score, the greater the perception by an adolescent of influence on

Table 3–1. Simple Frequency Distribution of Prosocial Skills Survey Scores; $n = 30$

X*	f	X	f	X	f	X	f	X	f
48	1	41	2	37	1	33	2	29	3
46	1	40	1	36	2	32	1	27	1
45	1	39	1	35	1	31	2	26	1
42	1	38	2	34	1	30	3	25	2

*Where X represents a data value and f represents frequency.

the development of prosocial behavior. As we begin the process of analyzing the results of the survey, our interest may be on any number of outcomes. However, for our purposes here, we first focus on the three measures of central tendency in general and how they related to the survey data in particular. We also consider how these measures are determined for ungrouped and grouped data.

> *Measures of central tendency*, known as the *mode*, the *median*, and the *mean*, are summary data values that best represents or characterizes a distribution. They tend to lie in the middle of the distribution.

Mode

The score or value with the highest frequency in a distribution is termed the **mode**, denoted by the symbol, *mo*. It is the simplest and easiest measure of central tendency to detect. In a distribution of ungrouped data, it is the value that occurs most often or with the greatest frequency; in a graph, it is the highest peak; in a pie chart, it is the largest segment. For example, in the following set of scores: 20, 19, 18, 17, 17, 17, 16, 15, the mode is 17, since it is the score that occurs most often.[2] Some distributions have no mode; others have two or more. When two values or scores share the same highest frequency, the distribution is known as a **bimodal distribution**. Table 3–1 reveals that two scores, 29 and 30, have the highest frequency of 3. Thus, we can say that our prosocial survey data distribution is bimodal. When there are more than two modes, the distribution is called a muti- or *polymodal distribution*.

For data organized into a class interval distribution, the *midpoint (mp)* of the interval with the highest frequency represented is considered the mode of the distribution. The interval is called the *modal interval*, of which they can be more than one, as in the case of bimodal or multimodal distributions. In Table 3–2, the data from our prosocial skills survey is arranged in a class interval distribution. Since the interval 30–32 has the highest frequency of scores, namely 6, the modal interval of the distribution and its midpoint, 31, is considered the mode of the sample.

> The *mode* is the score or value in an ungrouped data distribution that occurs with the highest frequency. In a class interval distribution, the midpoint of the interval with the highest frequency functions as the mode and the interval is called the modal interval.

Table 3–2. Class Interval Distribution of Prosocial Skills Survey Scores; $n = 30$

ci	el	mp	f	cf	fmp
48–50	47.5–50.5	49	1	30	49
45–47	44.5–47.5	46	2	29	92
42–44	41.5–44.5	43	1	27	43
39–41	38.5–41.5	40	4	26	160
36–38	35.5–38.5	37	5	22	185
33–35	32.5–35.5	34	4	17	136
30–32	29.5–32.5	31	6	13	186
27–29	26.5–29.5	28	5	7	140
24–26	23.5–26.5	25	2	2	50
			$n = 30$		1041

---

[2]For purposes of convenience, small samples of data are used to illustrate computational techniques and procedures throughout the text, as well as in Review Problems at the end of each chapter.

Median

A second measure of central tendency that is useful in describing a distribution is called the median. The **median**, symbolized as (*mdn*), is the *point* in a distribution above and below which half of the measures lie; that is to say, 50% of the scores or values fall above the median and 50% fall below it. Also, because the median is a point or location in a distribution, it does not necessarily have to be an actual score, which often is the case when the size of the distribution (*n*) is an even number.

Suppose we decide to conduct a follow-up study of the top half of adolescents in our prosocial skills survey. We can easily identify these students by first locating the median of the distribution. For example, since the sample size (*n*) is 30, the median is at the point in the distribution above and below which lie 15 scores. Referring to the frequency column in Table 3–1, we count up 15 scores, which bring us to score 33. However, if we assume that score 33 represents the median of the distribution, we would be wrong because only 14 scores fall above it.

To locate the exact point in the distribution that represents the median when the size of a sample is an *even* number, we proceed as follows. We first arrange the scores in a simple frequency distribution in an ascending or descending order. Next, we divide the size of the sample by two ($n/2$) and count up (or down) to the $n/2$ value in the distribution. The median is the average of the value *at* the $n/2$ point *and* the value above (or below) it. Applying the procedure to the data in Table 3–1, we count up 15 scores (30/2) to score 33. The average of 33 and the score just above it, 34, is 33.5 (77/2). Therefore, the median is at the 33.5 point in the distribution. The four-step procedure followed here is discussed later.

For distributions where the number of scores is an *odd* number, we follow a different four-step procedure. For example, for the data set 80, 76, 71, 64, 60, 58, 52, the median is 64; half of the scores are above 64, and half fall below. Locating the median can be defined by the equation $\frac{n+1}{2}$; in this case $\frac{7+1}{2} = 4$, the fourth value up from the bottom (or down from the top) is 64.

The process followed to locate the exact point in the distribution that represents the median when the size of a sample is an odd number can be summarized in the following four-step procedure. First, we arrange the scores in an ascending or descending order. Next, we add 1 to the number of scores and divide the total by 2, and count up or down to the $\frac{n+1}{2}$ point in the distribution. The value at that point is the midpoint or median of the distribution. In the case of the seven numbers listed at the beginning of the paragraph, we add 1 to 7 scores and divide the total of 8 by 2 (that is equal to 4), and count up or down to the 4th point in the distribution.

For future reference, these four steps are outlined at a later section of the chapter.

> The *median* is the point in a distribution above and below that falls 50% of the scores or values. In a class interval distribution, the interval containing the median is known as the median interval.

Locating the Median in Class Interval Distributions

For class interval distributions, the median is located using Formula 3–1. Do not be put off by the symbols in the formula. All of them were introduced in Chapter 2. Once you recall what they represent, substituting the appropriate values and evaluating the equation becomes quite simple. The legend below the formula will help you do so.

Formula 3–1

$$Mdn = ll + \left(\frac{n(50) - cf}{f}\right)(w)$$

Where

ll = the exact lower limit of the interval containing the median value or score

n = the number of scores in the distribution

cf = cumulative frequency of scores below the interval containing the median

f = frequency of scores in the interval containing the median

w = the size or width of the class intervals

Consider the prosocial skills, class interval distribution in Table 3–2. To find the median using Formula 3–1, we proceed as follows. We first multiply the total number of scores (*n*) by .50. For the data in Table 3–2, the middle score is 15, [30 (.50)], which falls within the class interval 33–35, known as the *median interval*. We then identify the exact lower limit (*ll*) of the median interval, which in this case is 32.5. Applying Formula 3–1, we find the median to be $Mdn = 32.5 + \left(\frac{15 - 13}{4}\right)(3) =$ 32.5 + 1.5 = 34, the three steps outlined below. Thus, the midpoint or median of the prosocial skills, class interval distribution is 34. Put another way, 50% of the scores fall *above* the 34 point in the dis-

tribution, and 50% fall *below* it. The three steps to follow in locating the median for class interval data are listed in a later section of the chapter.

Mean

The mean is the "arithmetic average" of the values in a distribution. It is the measure of central tendency most frequently used in statistical analyses. Symbolically, the mean is denoted by, $\overline{X}$, (pronounced "X-bar") for sample data and by the Greek symbol, μ, (pronounced "mu") for population data. In general, we present formulas for sample data within the text and, where appropriate, indicate the population formulas in footnotes, keeping in mind that the results of sample data represent only an estimate of the population parameter.

Calculating the mean for different types of distributions is pretty straightforward. For ungrouped values, such as 9, 6, 8, 8, 4, 4, 10, 3, 3, 3, the mean is obtained by adding all of the values and dividing the sum by the number of values. In this case, the mean is 5.8

$$\text{Mean} = \frac{9 + 6 + 8 + 8 + 4 + 4 + 10 + 3 + 3 + 3}{10} =$$

$$\frac{58}{10} = 5.8$$

Operationally, the mean for ungrouped data is expressed in Formula 3–2.

Formula 3–2[3]

$$\overline{X} = \frac{\Sigma X}{n} \quad \text{i.e.,} \quad \frac{X_1 + X_2 + X_3 + \dots X_n}{n}$$

---

[3]For population data, Formula 3–2 is expressed as $\mu = \frac{\Sigma X}{N}$.

In statistics, the Greek letter, Σ (*sigma*), means "summation" or "total of." Thus, in Formula 3–2, the combined symbols, ΣX, tell us to add all the values in the distribution. It does not matter whether the values are arranged in a ranked (high to low or vice versa) or random order; the result will be the same.

When data are arranged in a simple frequency distribution, as in Table 3–1, the mean is obtained by: (1) multiplying each value (X) by its frequency (f), and (2) dividing the sum by the number of values (n) in the distribution, as given in Formula 3–3.

Formula 3–3[4]

$$\overline{X} = \frac{\Sigma fx}{n} \quad \text{i.e.,}$$

$$\frac{fX_1 + fX_2 + fX_3 + \ldots fX_n}{n}$$

The calculation process is facilitated by adding a column labeled (fX) in the simple frequency table, as shown in Table 3–3, with the 10 values used above.

Applying Formula 3–3 to the data, we find that the mean of the distribution to be 5.8 (58/10). Note that Formula 3–2 and Formula 3–3 yield identical means; that is to say, the mean will be the same whether the data are arranged in a frequency distribution or as a set of individual scores in rank or random order. Consider the prosocial skills data in Table 3–1. What is the mean? Construct the appropriate table and apply Formula 3–3.

Table 3–3. Frequency Distribution for Computing the Mean—Ungrouped Data

X	f	fX
10	1	10
9	1	9
8	2	16
6	1	6
4	2	8
3	3	9
	$n = 10$	$\Sigma fx = 58$

Finding the Mean in Class Interval Distributions

When data are arranged in a class interval distribution, the mean is calculated using the midpoints (mp) of the intervals as representatives scores, as is the case when finding the mode. The convention is based on the theoretical assumption that the midpoint of an interval is the average of all the values within it. This outcome becomes increasing evident as the number of values in an interval increases and are normally distributed.

The procedure for computing the mean for class interval distributions is expressed in Formula 3–4.

Formula 3–4[5]

$$\overline{X} = \frac{\Sigma f(mp)}{n} \quad \text{i.e.,}$$

$$\frac{f(mp_1) + f(mp_2) + f(mp_3) + \ldots f(mp_n)}{n}$$

---

[4]For population data, Formula 3–3 is expressed as $\mu = \dfrac{\Sigma fx}{N}$.

[5]For population data, Formula 3–4 is expressed as $\mu = \dfrac{\Sigma fmp}{N}$.

Operationally the midpoint (*mp*) of each interval is multiplied by its frequency (*f*) and the total (Σfmp) divided by *n*. In calculating the mean for class interval data, we add an *fmp* column to the distribution table, as shown in Table 3–2. Applying Formula 3–4, we find the mean to be $\frac{1041}{30} = 34.7$.

Note that the mean of 34.7 is slightly different than the mean of 34.53 computed using the simple frequency distribution in Table 3–1. The difference is from the grouping of the raw data into intervals. Recall that when data are arranged in class interval distributions, some of the exactness of its values may be lost and some error introduced in the results. However, the differences tend to be modest, especially with large data sets and off-set by the convenience of being able to treat the data in a more manageable way. In the case of the prosocial skills survey data, the difference between the two means becomes meaningless when both values, 34.53 and 34.7, are rounded to 35.

> The *mean* is the arithmetic average of scores or values in a distribution. For ungrouped data, it is the sum of all values divided by the number of values in a distribution.

Applying Measures of Central Tendency

When a distribution is perfectly symmetrical, the values of the mode, median, and mean are identical, as shown in Figure 3–1A. Of course, perfectly symmetrical distributions are not commonly observed in statistical analyses. Therefore, the appropriateness of a measure must be considered when interpreting results. Two other common types of so-called skewed distributions can often be seen in the scientific literatures, namely positively skewed curve (shown in Figure 3–1B, and negatively skewed curve (shown in Figure 3–1C).

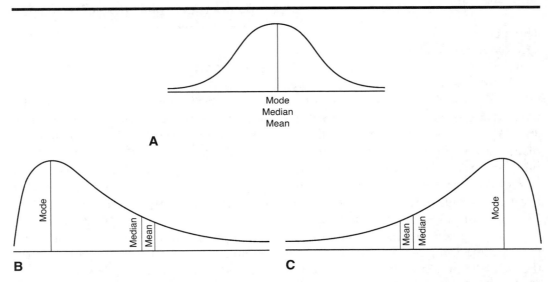

Figure 3–1. A. Symmetrical ("Normal") curve. **B.** Positively skewed curve. **C.** Negatively skewed curve.

The Mode

The mode is an appropriate measure of central tendency when the data are nominal. For example, if work preference is the variable for a sample of communication disorders majors, the workplace they desire to be with the highest frequency of the students may be the only appropriate measure. We cannot compute the average of say, 6 medical centers, 9 schools, and 14 private practices, and arrive at a meaningful statistic. The principal advantage of the mode is the ease with which it can be detected, whether the data are nominal, ordinal, interval, or ratio. However, it is the least statistically informative of the three measures of central tendency, since it does little beyond identifying the value or score with the highest frequency. The median and mean, in contrast with the mode, can be applied to the data of all four levels of measurement, that is, nominal, ordinal, interval, or ratio.

The Median

The median is the most appropriate measure of central tendency when a distribution is markedly skewed. For instance, in skewed distributions, most of the scores are concentrated at one end or the other of the distribution, such as in Figure 3–1B and Figure 3–1C. In positively skewed distributions, the mode and most of the other scores are closer to the extreme left side of the curve, and the mean is drawn toward the right tail of the distribution; in negatively skewed distributions, the order is reversed; that is, the mode is to the extreme right side of the curve, and the mean is pulled to the left tail of the distribution. In both cases, the median falls between the other two measures of central tendency.

The median also is less affected by **outliers**, which are extreme values that fall well beyond the general pattern of the data. Consider what happens to the variable, "average income," if Madonna, Warren Buffet, Oprah, or Alex Rodriguez walks into a room full of 20 first-year speech-pathology and audiology graduate students and teachers? In this instance, their respective income makes them outliers. Including the income of any one of them to the mix obviously would distort considerably mean or average income of those in the room. On the other hand, their incomes, individually or combined, will not change the value of the median; it would remain the income value above and below that falls to 50% of the people in the room. Note that the mode of a distribution also is unaffected by outliers, and therefore may be reported along with the median.

> *Outliers* are values that fall well beyond the general pattern of the data.

The Mean

When distributions are normally distributed, the most appropriate and versatile measure of central tendency for interval and ratio is the mean. Because it is derived from *all* of the values in a distribution, it may be thought of as a fulcrum point that *balances* the data in actual terms. Consider the bar graph of self-esteem scores of communication disorders majors campaigning for graduate student government offices at a large university shown in Figure 3–2.

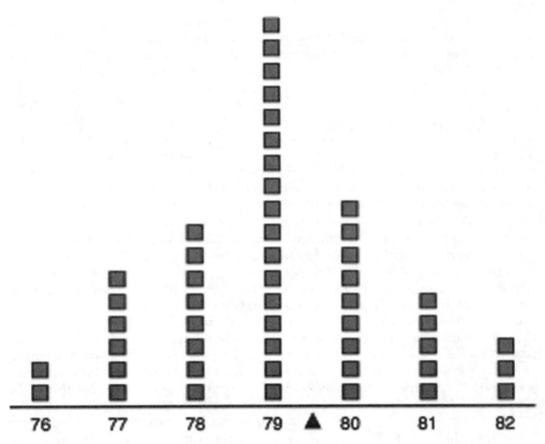

Figure 3–2. Bar graph of self-esteem frequency distribution.

If we think of the data as equal units along a plank, we can graphically illustrate how the mean represents the fulcrum or balancing point of a distribution. It is this property that makes the mean such a unique measure, and useful in more advanced statistical calculations. Specifically, the property demonstrates that the difference between the sum of the deviations of scores *above* and *below* the mean will always equal zero. For example, if we subtract the mean of 79.04 from each score in Figure 3–1 and add them up, we end up with a total of zero. If any value other than 79.04 is subtracted from each score, the sum of the deviations will be greater than zero in absolute terms.

Finally, the properties of the mean not only demonstrate its power in describing distributions but also its versatility as a descriptive measure of individual scores within distributions. For example, at a very basic level, the difference between the mean and a given value in a distribution, known as a **deviation score**, reveals both the direction and magnitude of individual scores. A deviation score of 3 or –5 indicates that a score is 3 units above or 5 units below the average score in the distribution. We discuss several measures for describing and comparing individual scores in a distribution in Chapter 5.

Measures of Variability

Focusing solely on measures of central tendency within an analysis of data could be problematic, since distributions can have identical measures of central tendency and yet be very different. Consider the distributions of three groups on the same measure shown in Table 3–4. Although the means and medians of all three groups are identical, there are considerable differences in how the values in each distribution vary. For example, suppose 21 test scores (derived from a certain clinical screening test and used to determine the effectiveness of three different

treatments at a later stage) were obtained and measured by a clinical investigator at a university speech clinic. The difference in values between the highest and lowest scores Group A is 60 (70–10), while the differences for Group B and Group C are 50 (70–20) and 30 (55–25), respectively.

Just as scores have a tendency to cluster around the center of a normal distribution, so is there a tendency for scores to vary both from one another and from the mean. This tendency for scores to differ along a continuum is referred to as **variability**. The concept of variability is central to statistics, particularly inferential statistics. If there is no variability in a distribution, then all of the scores are identical, and there is no need for statistical analysis.

There are several methods of measuring variability. The three most common are the *range*, *variance*, and the *standard deviation*. Each describes how values or scores are dispersed. Of the three, the variance and standard deviation of a distribution are the most important measures because of their role in inferential statistics. We consider each of these measures.

Table 3–4. Three Simple Distributions

Group A X	Group B X	Group C X
70	70	55
60	50	50
50	45	45
40	40	40
30	30	35
20	25	30
10	20	25
$\overline{X} = 40$	$\overline{X} = 40$	$\overline{X} = 40$
$mdn = 40$	$mdn = 40$	$mdn = 40$

Range

The **range** of a distribution, symbolized as Rg, is the most basic measure of variability. It indicates the distance between the lowest and highest values in a distribution. To find the range, we simply subtract the lowest score from the highest score and add 1, as defined in Formula 3–5[6].

Formula 3–5

$$Rg = HS - LS + 1$$

---

[6]The range often is computed without the addition of 1. However, we use it to ensure that the highest and lowest scores are included in the calculation.

Thus by definition, the ranges of the three distributions in Table 3–5 are 61 (70 − 10 + 1), 51 (70 − 20 + 1), and 31 (55 − 25 + 1), respectively.

When there are few scores in a data set or when scores are somewhat evenly dispersed throughout a distribution, the range can be a quick, useful measure of variability, much the same as the mode is a quick measure of central tendency for symmetrical distributions. However, when distributions contain outliers or extreme scores, the range can be a poor descriptor of variability. For example, consider a simple distribution of values of a certain clinical screening test, that is, 90, 88, 85, 80, 77, 73, 71, 70, and 15. By definition, the range is 76 (90 − 15 + 1). However, if the outlier, 15, is omitted, the range is only 21 (90 − 70 + 1). In other words, a measure of variability that excludes outliers is a more useful measure of differences among values in a distribution.

Table 3–5. Ounces of M&Ms Candy Consumed by Young Adults Under Stress

Student	Ounces Consumed
A	14
B	13
C	12
D	12
E	9
F	8
G	7
H	5
$n = 8$	80

$mo = 12$ (frequency is 2); $mdn = 10.5$ ((12 + 9)/2); $\bar{X} = 10$ (80/8).

> The *range* reflects the numerical spread or distance between the highest and lowest values in a distribution. Operationally, it is defined as the highest score in a distribution minus the lowest score, plus one, that is, $Rg = HS - LS + 1$.

Variance

Consider the following. A simple experiment is conducted by a food nutritional scientist and a clinician to determine the amount of "comfort food" consumed by a sample of eight young communication disorders majors, who report eating chocolate candy as one means of combating stress during the semester (due to their hectic schedule such as courses, clinical practicum, etc.). Various conditions of stress served as the independent variable, and the number of ounces of M&Ms candy consumed served as the dependent variable. The results are shown in Table 3–5. For convenience, I will refer to the experiment and its results as the "M&Ms study" and "M&Ms data."

An analysis of the data indicates that the three measures of central tendency or "averages" are relatively close to one another: $mo = 12$, $mdn = 10.5$ ((12 + 9)/2), and $\bar{X} = 10$ (80/8). Looking at Table 3–5, we find that there is a 10-ounce difference between Participant A, who consumed 14 ounces of M&Ms and Participant H who consumed 5 ounces ($Rg = 14 - 5 + 1$). While of some use, this information is rather limited, since the range reveals only the difference between the highest and lowest scores. Of greater statistical interest is how the participants differ in the number of ounces of candy consumed.

Finding the variance of each distribution would give us that answer.

Variance is an index of the average distance from the mean of all values in an interval or ratio distribution, expressed in squared units. It is one of the most versatile and extensively used measures of variability in experimental work and research studies. Symbolically, variance is denoted by s^2 (pronounced "s squared") for sample data and by the Greek symbol, σ^2 (pronounced "sigma squared"), for population data.

There are several methods for calculating variance depending on whether the size of a sample is small and the values ungrouped or large, with a wide range of values, grouped in intervals. For small, ungrouped data sets, the two techniques are known as the *deviation score method* and the *raw score method*. Both methods express variance in squared units of measurement, that is, the deviation and original raw scores are squared. The two methods are algebraically equivalent and yield identical results. Therefore, the method selected for application depends on the preference of the user. For larger data sets, the raw score method is recommended.

> *Variance* is an index of variability that reflects the average distance of scores from the mean in an interval/ratio distribution, expressed in squared units.

Deviation Score Method

The process of finding variance with small, ungrouped data using the deviation score method is pretty straight forward. Each score in (X) a distribution is subtracted from the mean $(X - \overline{X})$ and squared $(X - \overline{X})^2$ to form a distribution of squared deviation scores, as shown in Table 3–6.

Squaring each of the deviation scores resolves the issue of the sum of the signed deviation score values equaling zero. The sum of the squared deviation scores is then divided by the size of the sample, less than one, as expressed in Formula 3–6.

Formula 3–6[7]

$$s^2 = \frac{\Sigma(X - \overline{X})^2}{n - 1}$$

Applying Formula 3–6 to the data in Table 3–6, we find that the average dif-

Table 3–6. Variance Table for M&Ms Study Data: Deviation Score Method

	X	**(X – X̄)**	**(X – X̄)²**
	14	4	16
	13	3	9
	12	2	4
	12	2	4
	9	–1	1
	8	–2	4
	7	–3	9
	5	–5	25
Total Sum	80	0	72

Given $\overline{X} = 10$

---

[7]For population data, Formula 3–6 is expressed as $\sigma^2 = \frac{\Sigma(X - \mu)^2}{N}$.

ference in M&Ms candy consumed by the "Type A" students, under various conditions of stress, is approximately 10.29.

$$s^2 = \frac{\Sigma(X - \bar{X})^2}{n - 1} = \frac{72}{7} = 10.286 \approx 10.29$$

Keep in mind that the "average" in this case is in squared units. The four-step process used in calculating variance using the deviation method for ungrouped data are outlined later.

Degrees of Freedom. As noted above, the denominator in Formula 3–6 for sample data is expressed as $n - 1$. This algebraic term is known as **degrees of freedom**, denoted by the symbol, df. It is used to minimize one of the limitations of samples. Briefly, sample statistics, such as the mean ($\bar{X}$) and variance (s^2) are used as estimates of the population parameters, μ and σ^2. Without adjustment, sample data tend to underestimate population parameters, particularly for samples where n less than 30. By subtracting the sample size by 1, it has been shown to minimize the degree of skewness in sample data, thereby improving its estimating power. Statistics derived using degrees of freedom often are referred to as *unbiased estimates* of population parameters. We discuss degrees of freedom and unbiased estimates in greater detail later in the text.

Raw Score Method

Of the two methods for calculating variance for ungrouped data, the raw score method is the easier to calculate. The table used consists of two columns. The first column (X) lists each of the scores in the distribution; the second columns lists the sum of each score, squared (X^2). The computational definition for sample data is expressed in Formula 3–7.

Formula 3–7[8]

$$s^2 = \frac{\Sigma X^2 - [\frac{(\Sigma X)^2}{n}]}{n - 1} \quad \text{or}$$

$$s^2 = \frac{872 - \left[\frac{(80)^2}{8}\right]}{7} = 10.29$$

While the formula may appear daunting, the computational process is rather simple. First we arrange the data in table form with two headings: X and X^2 and list all of the raw scores in the first (X) column, as shown in Table 3–7. We then square each score and list the products in the X^2 column. Finally, we find the sum of each column and apply Formula 3–7.

$$s^2 = \frac{872 - \left[\frac{(80)^2}{8}\right]}{7} = 10.29$$

---

[8]Formula 3–7 also may be expressed as $s^2 = \frac{n\Sigma X^2 - (\Sigma X)^2}{n(n - 1)}$.

The population formula is given as $\sigma^2 = \frac{\Sigma X^2 - [\frac{(\Sigma X)^2}{n}]}{N}$

or equivalently as $\frac{N \times \Sigma X^2 - [(\Sigma X)^2]}{N^2}$.

Table 3–7. Variance Table for M&Ms Study Data: Raw Score Method

X	X²
14	196
13	169
12	144
12	144
9	81
8	64
7	49
5	25
Total Sum 80	872

Note that the variance value of 10.29 is identical to that found using the deviation score method, which is what we would expect given that Formula 3–6 and Formula 3–7 are algebraic equivalents. The three steps for calculating variance using the raw score method are outlined in Appendix G.

Although versatile and useful, as we see in future chapters, a limitation of variance as a measure of variability is that it is expressed in *squared units* of measurement. This can be a source of confusion when viewing variance literally as an "average" variation of scores within a distribution, rather than an index of variability in squared units. For example, consider the distribution of scores for the M&Ms study in Table 3–6. The computed variance says that on average, the scores differ by 10.29 points. Yet, even a cursory review of the data indicates that no score

differs from another by that wide of a margin. Therefore, in many instances, a more appropriate measure of variability is the *standard deviation*.

Standard Deviation

The **standard deviation**, like variance, it is an index of variability that reflects the average difference of all the scores or values in a distribution in relation to the mean. However, unlike variance, the index is expressed in the *actual* rather than in squared units of measurement. The standard deviation actually builds upon variance by extracting the square root of variance, thereby returning the overall data to the original units of measure. In short, the standard deviation is the square root of variance.

Symbolically, the standard deviation is written as, s, for sample data, and by the Greek letter sigma, σ, for population data. The same procedures and algebraic expressions for calculating the variance for ungrouped data are used to find the standard deviation, except that the variance formulas are enclosed within the radical (square root) sign. The formulas for each method are illustrated below.

Deviation Score Method

The operational definition for the standard deviation using the deviation score method is summarized in Formula 3–8.

Formula 3–8[9]

$$s = \sqrt{\frac{\Sigma(X - \bar{X})^2}{n - 1}}$$

---

[9]For population data, Formula 3–8 is expressed as $\sigma = \sqrt{\dfrac{\Sigma(X - \bar{X})^2}{N}}$

To obtain the standard deviation for ungrouped data, we follow the same steps outlined above for finding variance via the deviation score method and extract the square root as a final step. Thus, for data in the M&Ms study (see Table 3–6), the standard deviation is 3.56, as given in

$$s = \sqrt{\frac{\Sigma(X - \bar{X})^2}{n - 1}} = \sqrt{\frac{72}{7}} = 3.207 \approx 3.21$$

Raw Score Method

The operation for calculating the standard deviation using the raw score method is summarized in Formula 3–9.

Formula 3–9[10]

$$s = \sqrt{\frac{\Sigma X^2 - \left[\frac{(\Sigma X)^2}{n}\right]}{n - 1}} \quad \text{or}$$

$$s = \sqrt{\frac{n \cdot \Sigma X^2 - [(\Sigma X)^2]}{n \cdot (n - 1)}}$$

The process involves the same steps as those outlined above for finding variance via the raw score method, with a final step in which the square root of variance is extracted. Because Formula 3–9 is the algebraic equivalent of Formula 3–8, the standard deviation for the M&Ms study using the raw score method (see Table 3–6) also is 3.21, as given in

$$s^2 = \sqrt{\frac{\Sigma X^2 - \left[\frac{(\Sigma X)^2}{n}\right]}{n - 1}} = \sqrt{\frac{872 - \left[\frac{(80)^2}{8}\right]}{7}}$$

$$= \sqrt{10.286} = 3.207 \approx 3.21$$

As noted above, reporting the variability of scores in terms of the original units of measure is a more meaningful way of describing how values in a distribution, on average, differ from one another. In the case of the data of the M&Ms experiment shown in Table 3–6, the standard deviation is intuitively more comprehensible than variance. Meaning it makes more sense to describe the results of the study by saying that, on average, the research participants differed in the amount of M&Ms candy consumed by 3.21 ounces (standard deviation) than saying they differed by 10.29 ounces (variance).

> The *standard deviation* is an index of variability that reflects the average distance of scores from the mean in an interval/ratio distribution, expressed in the original units of measurement.

Functionality of the Standard Deviation

The importance and function of the standard deviation, when considering the mean of a distribution, cannot be overstated. For most statistical analyses, it is generally considered the standard measure for describing the extent to which

---

[10]For population data, Formula 3–9 is expressed as $\sigma = \sqrt{\dfrac{\Sigma X^2 - \left[\frac{(\Sigma X)^2}{N}\right]}{N}}$ or $\sigma = \sqrt{\dfrac{N \cdot \Sigma X^2 - \left[\frac{(\Sigma X)^2}{N}\right]}{N^2}}$

scores in a distribution deviate from the mean. It also is quite useful in comparing distributions. For example, consider the following scenario in which the mean is the only statistic reported.

It has been a real tough term and a group of well-deserved communication disorders majors is really looking forward to the upcoming "Spring Break." A local travel agency advertises two packages at the same price. One package takes you to one of two warm-weather resorts. Resort A has an average temperature of 80; Resort B's average is 85. The other package takes you to one of two ski resorts, each with slopes with great packed bases. Resort X has an average weekly snow fall of 12 inches; Resort Y's average is 19 inches.

Question: If you wanted a warm weather vacation, which of the resorts would you choose, A or B?

Question: If you wanted to ski or snowboard over the "Break," which of the resorts would you choose, X or Y?

Given your choice, suppose that in addition to the mean, the standard deviations related to the temperatures and weekly snow falls are reported by the travel agency, as shown in Figure 3–3. Now which resort would you chose? All things being equal, given the values of the standard deviations, the temperature and snowfall conditions Resort A and Resort X, respectively, are far more stable and predictable than those of Resort B and Resort Y. In short, when the mean is coupled with the standard deviation of a distribution, we can make a more informed decision. You will see more of the advantages of using these two measures when we discuss standard scores in the next chapter.

Resort	Average Temperature	Standard Deviation
A	80	2
B	85	10

Resort	Average Snowfall	Standard Deviation
X	12	1.5
Y	16	10

Figure 3–3. Mean and standard deviation of temperature levels and snowfall amounts at four vacation resorts.

Descriptive Statistical Methods for Behavioral and Clinical Research

The following three measures may not be often seen in the standard textbooks, but they are extremely useful and practical for clinical investigators for evaluation and analysis of the clinical outcomes.

Chebysheff's Theorem

According to Chebysheff's theorem, for any set of data, at least $100 \cdot [(1 - (1/k)^2]$ % of the data values are lying within k standard deviations of the mean, given that $k > 1$. Although many frequency distributions have different patterns of variation, it is true of all sets of data values that at least $100 \cdot [1 - (1 - (1/2)^2]\% = 75\%$ are lying within two standard deviations and at least $100 \cdot [1 - (1 - (1/3)^2]\% = 88.89\%$ are lying within three standard deviations from the mean. The importance of the theorem is that it helps guide clinicians to where the major portions of the clinical data values are located and how much variation there is in a set of data. A small standard deviation indicates that the data values are clustered near the mean. A large standard deviation indicates that the data values are widely dispersed about the mean.

Coefficient of Variation

To determine whether a set of data values has much variation (the degree of spread-out) or whether a number of measurements are precise, the ratio of the mean to the standard deviation is calculated. This value, called the coefficient of variation (CV), is calculated by the following:

$$CV = 100 \cdot (S/\overline{X}) \%$$

For example, the coefficient of variation of the set $\overline{X} = 10$ and $S = 0.3$ is $100 \cdot (0.3/10) = 3\%$. This data set has very little variation. On the other hand, for the set $\overline{X} = 10$ and $S = 3$, the coefficient of variation is determined to be $100 \cdot (3/10) = 30\%$, suggesting that this latter data set is relatively varied.

Pearsonian Measure of Skewness

Previously, several different shapes of frequency distribution curves were shown in Figure 3–1 A–C. In a normal distribution, the mean, median, and mode are all equal. In a positively skewed distribution, the mean is the largest of the three measures of central tendency. This distribution occurs when the extreme items are large in value compared with the vast majority of other data values. A distribution called a negatively skewed distribution contains some data values that are significantly smaller than the vast majority of all data values, that is, the mean is the smallest of the three measures of central tendency; the mode is the point of largest frequency because it is unaffected by extreme data values (outliers), and the median, less affected by extreme data values, is located between the mode and mean. Karl Pearson, a notable statistician in the mid 19th century to early 20th century, found that the median is generally located about two-thirds of the distance from the mode to the mean in moderately skewed frequency distributions. Mathematically, such a measure, called the Pearsonian measure of skewness (denoted by S_K), is calculated as follows:

$$S_K = \left[3 \cdot \frac{(Mean - Median)}{S} \right]$$

where S represents the standard deviation.

If $S_K > 0$, then the distribution is positively skewed, whereas it is negatively skewed if $S_K < 0$. When $S_K = 0$, the distribution is normal. Generally S_K is used to: (1) describe the shape of a frequency distribution, (2) select the most representative measure of central tendency, and (3) measure the lack of normality in a given frequency distribution. Suppose that the value of $S_K = 0.88$ is derived when we measure the degree of skewness of the distribution of the hypothetical data values on PPVT-R (Peabody Picture Vocabulary Test-Revised) among young fluent children. We may conclude that the distribution of the sample forms positively skewed curve.

Key Terms and Concepts

Mode

Bimodal distribution

Median

Mean

Outlier

Deviation score

Variability

Range

Variance

Degrees of freedom

Feedback Review of Chapter 3

1. The measure of central tendency most appropriate for nominal data is the
   a. mode.
   b. mean.
   c. median.
   d. all of the above.

2. The median is the point in the distribution
   a. least affected by extreme scores.
   b. above and below which fall fifty percent of the values.
   c. where the sum of the distances of all of scores is zero.
   d. where the sum of the squared distances of all scores is zero.
   e. a & b

3. In a negatively skewed distribution, mean is located to the
   a. right of the mode.
   b. left of the mode.
   c. right of the median.
   d. left of the median.
   e. b & d.

4. In a truly symmetrical distribution, which of the following measures of central tendency are equal?
   a. mode and median
   b. mode and mean
   c. median and mean
   d. mode, mean, and median

5. When the number of scores in a distribution is odd, the median
   a. is the $n + 1/2$ score from the top or bottom of an ordered distribution.
   b. is the $n/2$ value from the top or bottom of an ordered distribution.

c. is the midpoint between the $n + 1/2$ score and $n/2$ value.
d. all of the above.
e. none of the above.

6. If each raw score in a distribution was doubled, which of the following would remain unchanged?
a. mode.
b. median.
c. mean.
d. a & b.
e. a & c.

7. Which of the following is not a measure of variability?
a. range
b. median
c. variance
d. standard deviation
e. a & d.

8. The range of a distribution is generally defined as the distance between the
a. first and third quartiles.
b. mean and the standard deviation.
c. mean and variance.
d. variance and the standard deviation.
e. lowest and highest scores.

9. The _____ of a distribution is defined as the average of the sum of the squared deviations of the scores from the mean divided by $n - 1$.
a. mean.
b. median.
c. deviation score.
d. variance.
e. standard deviation.

10. The results of a measure to determine advertising and public relations aptitude among a sample of 50 college students yield a mean of 10 and a standard deviation of 4. What is the variance of the sample?
a. 16
b. 40
c. 5.0
d. 4.6
e. 12

11. In which measure of variability is the square root extracted from the sum of squared deviations from the mean divided by one?
a. range.
b. median.
c. variance
d. standard deviation.
e. a & d

12. Which measure of variability is expressed in the original units of measurement?
a. range
b. variance
c. median
d. mean
e. standard deviation

Fill-Ins

13. In distributions with a few extreme scores in one direction, the preferred measure of central tendency is the _____.

14. The score that has the highest frequency in a distribution is called the _____.

15. A deviation score is computed by subtracting a raw score from the _____.

16. Given the following set of scores: 22 67 69 73 74 74 76 77. The score 32 is called a/an _____.

17. In a class interval distribution, it is assumed that the average of all scores in an interval are equal to the _____ of the interval.

18. The square of the standard deviation is the _____ of a distribution.

For questions 19 through 28, identify the appropriate symbol.

19. "sum of" _____

20. raw score _____

21. population size _____

22. sample mean _____

23. median _____

24. population mean _____

25. sample variance _____

26. population standard deviation _____

27. degrees of freedom _____

28. sample standard deviation _____

Calculation Guides

Locating the Median for Ungrouped Data: *n* = Even Number

Step 1: Arrange the scores in a simple frequency distribution in an ascending or descending order.

Step 2: Divide the size of the sample by two, or n/2.

Step 3: Count up (or down) to the n/2 value in the distribution. The median is the average of the value at the n/2 point and the value above (or below) it.

Locating the Median for Ungrouped Data: *n* = Odd Number

Step 1: Arrange the scores in an ascending or descending order.

Step 2: Add 1 to the number of scores and divide the total by 2 $(n + 1/2)$.

Step 3: Count up or down to the $n + 1/2$ point in the distribution. The value at that point is the midpoint or median of the distribution.

Locating the Median for Class Interval Data

Step 1: Multiply the total number of scores (n) by 0.50. In the frequency (f) or cumulative frequency (cf) column, count up to the interval in which the n (0.50) score falls. This interval is known as the median interval.

Step 2: Identify the exact lower limit of the median interval (el).

Step 3: Substitute the appropriate values for each symbol and calculate the median using Formula 3–1.

Calculating Variance: Deviation Score Method

Step 1: Arrange the data in table form with three column headings: X, $(X - \overline{X})$, and $(X - \overline{X})^2$.

Step 2: Subtract each score from the distribution mean $(X - \overline{X})$; that is, find the deviation score for each value.

Step 3: Square each deviation score. (See column 3 in Table 3–5.)

Step 4: Sum the deviation scores and plug in Formula 3–6.

Calculating Variance: Raw Score Method

Step 1: Arrange the data in table form with two headings: X and X^2.

Step 2: Square each raw score (X) and list in the X^2 column.

Step 3: Find the sum of each column and apply Formula 3–7.

4

Foundation of Standard Normal Distribution: Describing Individual Scores

Overview

So far we have considered procedures for organizing and graphing data and for calculating measures of central tendency and variability. Taken together they represent four common methods for describing distributions. In this section, we are discussing procedures and methods for describing individual scores or values in a distribution. Although researchers are concerned with the characteristics of, say, a distribution of test scores, the people who take a test are more concerned with their performance on it. It matters little whether the test is one of academic achievement, intelligence, personality, strength, blood pressure, stress, and so on. The bottom line invariably is, "How did I do?"

Most of us have an intuitive understanding that raw scores tell us little about our performance on a given task unless they are framed within a particular context. We know that a score of 85 on an achievement test is meaningless without some point of reference, such as the number of items on a test or the position of a score in relation to other scores in the distribution. Earlier we noted that deviation scores can be used to describe individual scores, since they indicate both the magnitude and direction of a score in relationship to the mean of a distribution. However, deviation scores are somewhat limited because they do not express a score's position in relation to other scores in a distribution. *Percentiles*, *percentile ranks*, and *standard scores*, on the other hand, are more informative because they describe the relational position of an individual score or data value in a distribution.

Percentiles

A distribution of scores arranged in an ascending or descending order, which we shall refer to as a *rank-order distribution*, may be thought of as falling along a continuum of 100 equal units.[1] Each unit represents a percentile. Most, if not all, of us are familiar with percentiles or percentile ranks because many standardized tests use them to indicate a score's relative standing. For example, a score that is said to be at the 90th percentile is equal to or higher than 90% of the scores in a distribution. The significance of a value at the 90th percentile is visually represented in the bell-shaped, normal curve shown in Figure 4–1. Note that a value is not needed to indicate the percentile. Thus, a **percentile** may be defined as a *point* in a distribution at or below which fall a given percentage of scores. The concept is easy to understand and test results reported in percentile terms are easy to interpret, which is one of the reasons why percentiles are used widely.

We use the uppercase P_x, with a subscript to indicate a given percentile, such as P_{90}. In any distribution, the *median* and P_{50} are identical because all are points at or below which fall 50% of the values. Percentiles for simple, rank-ordered distributions are operationally defined in Formula 4–1.

Formula 4–1

$$Percentile_x =$$

$$\frac{n\ of\ scores\ less\ than\ or\ equal\ to\ X}{total\ n\ of\ scores} \cdot 100$$

Locating Percentiles for Ungrouped Data

Consider the 30 clinical screening test scores for voice articulation listed in Table 4–1. Suppose we are interested in knowing the score or point in the distri-

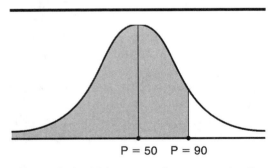

Figure 4–1. 90th percentile area under the normal curve.

Table 4–1. Simple Rank Order Distribution of Clinical Screening Test Scores for Voice Articulation; $n = 30$

X*		
48	37	30
46	36	30
45	36	30
42	35	29
41	34	29
41	33	29
40	33	28
39	32	27
38	31	26
38	31	25

*Raw score symbol.

[1]When we rank scores or attributes, we arrange them according to some criterion, such as highest to lowest, most effective to least effective, very best to poorest, and so on. A *simple rank-ordered distribution* lists all scores without regard to the frequency with which they occur. A *simple rank-ordered frequency distribution* includes observed frequencies.

bution that represents the 60th percentile (P_{60}). Because the data in Table 4–1 already are arranged in a simple rank order, we proceed as follows. First, we multiply $0.60 \times 30 = 18$. Second, counting up 18 values from the bottom of the distribution we come to score 36.[2] Thus, $P_{60} = 36$, that is, the raw score 36 represents the 60th percentile, or the point in the distribution at or below which fall 60% of the scores. If the scores in Table 4–1 were arranged from the lowest to highest score, we would count *down* 18 scores to the percentile of interest. The three steps summarizing the process for calculating percentiles when scores are arranged in a simple rank-ordered distribution are listed in the Calculation Guides section at the end of the chapter.

> A *percentile* is a point in a distribution at or below which a given percentage of values fall.

Percentiles for Grouped Data

The procedure for finding percentiles when data sets are organized into class interval distributions is slightly more involved than with simple rank order distributions. Consider the 30 clinical screening test scores for voice articulation in Table 4–1 arranged in the class interval distribution shown in Table 4–2. To find the score or point in the distribution that represents the 60th percentile (P_{60}), we follow a six-step process using Formula 4–2.[3]

Table 4–2. Cumulative Frequency of Clinical Screening Test Scores for Voice Articulation; $n = 30$

c.i.	e.l.	mp	f	cf
46–48	45.5–48.5	47	2	30
43–45	42.5–45.5	44	1	28
40–42	39.5–42.5	41	4	27
37–39	36.5–39.5	38	4	23
34–36	33.5–36.5	35	4	19
31–33	30.5–33.5	32	5	15
28–30	27.5–30.5	29	7	10
25–27	24.5–27.5	26	3	3

Formula 4–2

$$P_n = ll + \left(\frac{np - cf}{f} \right)(w)$$

Where

ll = the lower limit of the interval containing the percentile of interest

n = total number of scores in the distribution

p = the decimal value of the percentile of interest

cf = cumulative frequency of scores below the interval containing the percentile of interest

f = frequency of scores in the interval containing the percentile of interest

w = the width of the class intervals

---

[2]The location of the percentile of interest [P_x] may be operationally defined as $L = n(.P) .P$, where, L = the location of the P_x; n = number of scores in the distribution; and $(.P)$ = the decimal value of the percentile of interest.

[3]Formula 4–2 is nearly identical to Formula 4–1 used to compute the median, which would be expected, since the median and 50th percentile are one and the same. The only difference is that in Formula 4–1, np is expressed by the constant, $n (.50)$.

As in the case of rank-order distributions, we begin by multiplying the decimal value of the percentile of interest, in this case P_{60}, by the total number of scores in the distribution (n); that is, $0.60 \times 0.30 = 18$. We then substitute 18 for np in Formula 4–2. Next, we refer either to the frequency (f) or cumulative frequency (cf) column and count up 18 scores from the bottom interval (25–27) to the *percentile interval*, 34–36.[4] Again, referring to Formula 4–1, we substitute 33.5 for ll, 4 for f, 15 for cf, and 3 for the width of the class intervals, w. Finally, we complete the arithmetic operations.

$$P_{60} = 33.5 + \left(\frac{18 - 15}{4}\right)(3)$$

$$= 33.5 + \left(\frac{3}{4}\right)3$$

$$= 35.75$$

Thus, 35.75 is the value representing P_{60}, which matches what we found using the simple rank-order method.

Keep in mind that because a percentile is a *point* in a distribution, it may be either a score or a value that falls between two scores. For example, the 73rd percentile is represented by the value 38.68 $\left[P_{73} = 36.5 + \left(\frac{21.9 - 19}{4}\right)(3) = 38.675\right]$ rather than an actual score in the distribution (see Table 6–1). However, for purposes of convenience and ease of interpretation, we would round the value to 39. The six steps to follow in calculating percentiles for class interval data are outlined in the Calculation Guides section at the end of the chapter.

Percentile Ranks

Percentile ranks are probably the most widely used measures of relative standing of scores in a distribution. This is particularly true in the case of commercially published standardized tests, including the Peabody Picture Vocabulary Test (PPVT), Wechsler Intelligence Scale for Children-Third Edition (WISC-III), Scholastic Aptitude Test (SAT), College Entrance Examination Board (CEEB) test, the Graduate Record Exam (GRE), and many others. The popularity of percentile ranks stems from the ease with which they can be interpreted and understood both by professionals and laypersons. While percentiles refer to *points* in a distribution, percentile ranks, also known as *percentile scores*, refer to actual scores. A **percentile rank** is a value that corresponds to a particular score in a distribution, indicating the percentage of scores less than or equal to it. We use the upper letters, PR_x, with a subscript to symbolize a given percentile rank. Percentiles for simple, rank-ordered distributions are operationally defined in Formula 4–3.

Formula 4–3

$$PR_n = \frac{n \text{ of scores at and below } X}{n \text{ of scores in distribution}} \cdot 100$$

Where X = score of interest

Percentile Ranks for Ungrouped Data

The computational process for finding percentile ranks for ungrouped data fol-

---

[4]Looking at the cumulative frequency column (cf) in Table 6–2, we find that there are 15 scores up to interval 31–33. However, because there are 18 scores at or below the 60th percentile, we must use the next interval (34–36) as the percentile interval.

lows three steps, which we illustrate using the data in Table 4–1 above. For example, to find the percentile rank for raw score 41 (PR_{41}), we first count the number of scores *at and below* 41, of which there are 26. Next we would divide that number by the size of the distribution (n) and multiply the result by 100, that is, $\frac{26}{30} \cdot 100$ = 86.666 ~ 87. In other words, approximately 87% of the scores in the distribution fall at and below the raw score of 41. Put another way, the raw score 41 is at the 87th percentile, which is what we would find if we were to apply Formula 4–1 to the data. The three steps in the computational process for ungrouped data are outlined in the Calculation Guides section at the end of the chapter.

> A *percentile rank* is a score converted to the percentile at or below which a given percentage of values in a distribution fall.

Percentile Ranks for Grouped Data

When the data are organized into a class interval distribution, percentile ranks are derived by a five-step process using Formula 4–4.

Formula 4–4

$$PR_n = \left\{ \frac{cf + \left(\frac{X - ll}{w}\right)f}{n} \right\} \cdot 100$$

Where

cf = cumulative frequency of scores below the score of interest

X = the score of interest

ll = the lower limit of the interval containing the score of interest

w = the width of the class intervals

f = frequency of scores in the interval containing the score of interest

n = total number of scores in the distribution

For example, consider once again the class interval distribution of the 30 clinical screening test scores for articulation introduced in Table 4–2. To determine the percentile rank of raw score 29 (PR_{29}), we first identify the *percentile interval*, that is the interval in which the percentile of interest falls. In this case, score 29 falls within the interval 28–30. Referring to Formula 4–4, we substitute 27.5 for ll, 7 for f, and 3, the cumulative frequency (cf) of scores *below* the percentile rank interval. We also substitute 3 for the width (w) of the class intervals and 30 for the size (n) of the distribution. Finally, we do the arithmetic and find that the percentile rank of raw score 29 is 21.666.

$$\left[PR_{29} = \left\{ \frac{3 + \left(\frac{29 - 27.5}{3}\right)7}{30} \right\} \cdot 100 = 21.666 \right]$$

In short, approximately 22% of the test anxiety scores fall at and below the raw score of 29. An outline of the steps to follow in calculating percentile ranks for class interval data listed is in the Calculation Guides section at the end of the chapter.

Limitations of Percentiles and Percentile Ranks

Although percentiles and percentile ranks are useful in describing the relative position of scores in a distribution, they are limited by their ordinal nature, particularly in making comparisons across different distributions. As mentioned earlier, the intervals or distances from point to point in ordinal scales are not equal. Because most of the values in a symmetrical or bell-shaped distribution are centered near the mean of the group, the absence of equal intervals results in distortions among percentile and percentile ranks, which are clustered around the center of the scale, as shown in Figure 4–2. As a result, differences in raw scores at the center of distributions tend to be exaggerated in terms of percentiles or percentile ranks, whereas differences between scores at the tails of the distribution tend to be underestimated.

Consider the raw scores and percentile ranks for the simple frequency distribution of scores in Table 4–3. The distance from the raw scores 15 to 17 and from 13 to 15 is only 3 points. Yet an individual with a raw score of 15 is considered to be at the 33rd percentile, whereas someone with a raw score of 17 is at the 86th percentile, a difference of 53 percentile ranks. On the other hand, an individual with a raw score of 13 is at the 2nd percentile, whereas someone with a raw score of 15 is at the 33rd percentile, a difference of only 31 percentile ranks. In other words, although the raw score

differences between the two sets of scores are the same, the percentile rank differences are significantly different.

The ordinal nature of the percentile scale also means that percentiles and percentile ranks cannot be manipulated mathematically. Neither can they be added nor multiplied nor averaged nor combined in complex calculations. We cannot, for example, average the percentile ranks of a subject on three or four different tests or measures. Nor can we compare the percentile ranks of different students on different measures. In short, percentiles and percentile ranks are limited to describing the points or values in a single distribution. However, in cases where the data

Table 4–3. Simple Frequency Distribution with Percentile Ranks; $n = 57$

X	f	PR
19	3	99
18	5	95
17	11	86
16	19	67
15	11	33
14	5	14
13	3	2

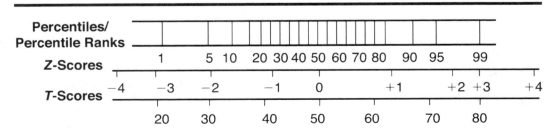

Figure 4–2. Scale showing a symmetrical or bell-shaped distribution.

set is normal or symmetrical, scores can be converted into distributions that overcome the limitations of percentiles and percentile ranks. These converted scores are known as *standard scores* and *transformed standard scores*.

Standard Scores

When a distribution is symmetrical, its values can be transformed into a distribution of scores based on equal interval units, as depicted in Figure 4–2. These scores, which are based on the mean and standard deviation of the original distribution, are known as **standard scores**. They express the relative position of individual scores in terms of the number of standard deviation units they deviate from the mean.

The conceptual operation of a standard score is expressed in Formula 4–5.

Formula 4–5

$$Standard\ Score = \frac{Raw\ Score - Mean}{Standard\ Deviation}$$

$$= Standard\ deviation\ units$$

We consider two standard scores, the z-score and the T-score.

z-Scores

The **z-score** is the most common standard score used in statistics. It indicates the number of standard deviations a given score is above or below the mean. To convert a raw score to a z-score, we simply subtract it from the mean of the distribution and divide the quotient by the standard deviation, as expressed in Formula 4–6.

Formula 4–6.[5]

$$z = \frac{X - \mu}{\sigma}$$

Where

X = raw score of interest

μ = mean of the distribution

σ = standard deviation of the distribution

z-scores have a standardized mean of zero (0) and standard deviations in units of 1. Even though raw scores are changed to new values, the properties of the distribution remain the same. The steps to calculate z-scores are outlined in the Calculation Guides section at the end of the chapter.

Because the z-scores are standardized, they can be compared with scores within a distribution, across different measures, and across different distributions. For example, suppose a student obtains a score of 65 on a psychology test in which the distribution is 55 and the standard deviation 5. The z-score for the raw score would equal 2.

$$\left[z = \frac{65 - 55}{5} = 2 \right]$$

Suppose another student obtains a score of 48 on the same test. In this case, the z-score would be -1.4 $\left[\frac{48 - 55}{5} \right]$.

In terms of describing and comparing these individual scores, what do these two

---

[5]For sample data, Formula 4–6 is expressed as $z = \frac{X - \bar{X}}{s}$.

z-scores tell us about the performance of the two students?

Interpreting z-Scores

There is an empirical rule for symmetrical or normal distributions that states that approximately 68% of all scores or values are within 1 standard deviation of the mean; that approximately 95% are within 2 standard deviations of the mean; and that approximately 99.7% are within 3 standard deviations.[6] Thus, the z-score of 2 tells us that the student with a raw score of 65 performed 2 standard deviation units *above* the mean or better than approximately 95% of those taking the test. Similarly, the student with the raw score of 48 performed 1.4 standard deviation units *below* the mean. Later on in the text, when we discuss the areas under the normal curve, we know that a z-score falling 1.4 units below the mean is better than only 8% of all the other scores in a distribution. In short, positive z-scores indicate that raw scores are above the mean; negative z-scores indicate that they are below the mean. We discuss how percentage points corresponding to z-scores are derived in Chapter 7.

The functionality of z-scores extends beyond single distributions. Unlike percentiles and percentile ranks, z-scores can be used to compare values across different distributions, even those from two or more different populations. This is because z-scores reflect the relative position of a value in a distribution. For example, suppose Maria's score on a clinical screening test measure for voice articulation is 58 and James's score is 54 on the test. Because Maria's score is obviously higher than James's score by 4 points, we could conclude that she is more articulate vocally than James. However, since the variable gender may well be an influential factor in voice articulation among young children, we may want to determine if Maria is more articulate than James in *relative* terms; that is, in relation to other females and males. By standardizing the parameters of both populations (females and males) in the form of z-scores, we can make such a comparison.

Suppose, for illustration purposes, the mean and standard deviation for test scores among women is 54 and 2.1, respectively, and that the mean and standard deviation for males is 48 and 1.9. We can now derive the standardized scores for Maria and James, as follows, using Formula 4–6.

$$\text{Maria} \quad z = \frac{X - \mu}{\sigma} = \frac{58 - 54}{2.1} = 1.9$$

$$\text{James} \quad z = \frac{X - \mu}{\sigma} = \frac{54 - 48}{1.9} = 3.16$$

Although Maria's score of 1.9 standard deviations above the mean is high compared with other females, James's z-score of 3.16 in comparison with other males is considerably higher. Therefore, in relative terms, we can conclude that James's is more articulate vocally than Maria.[7]

Because transformed distributions share a common mean of zero and standard deviations in units of 1, z-scores can be manipulated mathematically and compared, regardless of the size, mean, and standard deviation values of the original

---

[6]These concepts are discussed in greater detail in Chapter 7.

[7]In cases where population means and standard deviations are unknown, the means and standard deviations of samples can be used to create *z-distributions*. (See formula in Footnote 4.)

distributions. Although the transformation of scores to a z-distribution alters the mean and standard deviations, it does not change the shape of the original distribution of raw scores, nor does it change the location or relative positions of the raw scores. Also, the means and standard deviations of z-distributions will always be 0 and 1 regardless of the values of the mean and standard deviation of the raw score distribution.

> A *z-score* is a standardized value that represents the number of standard deviations a given score is above or below the mean.

Transformed Standard Scores

One limitation of z-scores is that they are expressed in decimals and, sometimes, negative numbers, as seen in Table 4–4. These properties make them unattractive,

if not confusing, when reporting results of tests to nonstatisticians. Imagine a teacher reporting to a parent that her daughter received a z-score of 1.00 on a screening test. Imagine the response of a high school senior upon learning that his z-score on the test is 2.00. Neither score appears attractive, even though their relative positions are higher than approximately 84 and 95% of other scores in a distribution. To avoid problems associated with decimals and negative values, z-scores often are converted into *transformed standard scores*.

A **transformed standard score** is a converted z-score derived from a transformed distribution. One such distribution, known as the **T distribution**, has a mean of 50 and standard deviation units of 1. Its values are known as **T-scores** and symbolized as T. To convert a z-score of 1.5 to a T-score, we multiply it by the standard deviation, 10, and add 50. The result is a transformed score of 65. In other words, a z-score of 1.5 is equal to a T-score of 65. The operational definition of a T-score for sample and population data is expressed in Formula 4–7.

Table 4–4. Cumulative Frequency Distribution of Hypothetical Sample Data

c.i.	e.l.	mp	f	cf
48–50	47.5–50.5	49	1	30
45–47	44.5–47.5	46	2	29
42–44	41.5–44.5	43	1	27
39–41	38.5–41.5	40	4	26
36–38	35.5–38.5	37	5	22
33–35	32.5–35.5	34	4	17
30–32	29.5–32.5	31	6	13
27–29	26.5–29.5	28	5	7
24–26	23.5–26.5	25	2	2

Formula 4–7

$$T = (s)\,(z) + \overline{X} \text{ (sample)}$$
$$T = (\sigma)\,(z) + \mu \text{ (population)}$$

Where

s or σ = the standard deviation of the T distribution

z = the z-score of the original raw score

$\overline{X}$ or μ = the mean of the T distribution

Remember the z-scores of 1.90 and 3.16 for Maria and James, which were based on their raw scores of 58 and 54, respectively. Applying Formula 4–7, their respective T-scores would be 69 [(10)(1.90) + 50] and 82 [(10)(3.16) + 50] rounded.

Raw scores can be converted directly to T-scores using Formula 4–8, which combine the operations given in Formula 4–6 and Formula 4–7.

Formula 4–8

$$T = 10\left(\frac{X - \overline{X}}{s}\right) + 50 \text{ (sample)}$$

$$T = 10\left(\frac{X - \mu}{\sigma}\right) + 50 \text{ (population)}$$

Many standardized tests, such as the Stanford-Binet Intelligence Test, the SAT (Scholastic Achievement Test), GRE (Graduate Record Exam), and LSAT (Law Scholastic Aptitude Test), report results in terms of transformed standard scores rather than raw score or z-scores. For example, the distribution of SAT scores is based on a mean of 500, with standard deviation units of 100.

Any distribution of raw scores can be converted into a transformed standard distribution without the loss of any of its basic properties, including its shape, its measures of central tendency, and its measures of variability. Both a raw score and its corresponding z- and T-scores lie at the same point in a distribution. The only difference is in the values used to express them.

Finally, the same basic operation expressed in Formula 4–7 can be used to convert a transformed standard score to its original raw score, as shown in Formula 4–9. In other words, given the mean and standard deviation of a transformed distribution and a particularly z-score, we can determine the original raw score (RS).

Formula 4–9

$$RS = (s)(z) + \overline{X}$$

where

s = standard deviation of the transformed distribution

z = standard score

$\overline{X}$ = mean of the transformed distribution

Suppose we want to know the original raw score value of the z-score 1.2, given a transformed score distribution with a mean of 62 and a standard deviation of 5. Applying Formula 4–9, we find that the original raw score is 68 [(5) (1.2) + 62].

A *transformed standard score* (*TS*) is a converted z-score derived from a transformed distribution with a prescribed mean and standard deviation.

Basic concepts associated with the correlation of two variables is one of the most common techniques for measuring this relationship. In Chapter 6, we present the basic concepts associated with regression and a common method for making predictions about correlated variables.

Correlation refers to the statistical relationship between two or more variables.

Key Terms and Concepts

Percentile

Percentile rank

z-distribution

Standard Scores

z-score

Transformed standard score distribution

T distribution

T-score

Feedback Review

1. Which type of score is the following statement describing? "At the center of a normal distribution, the use of _____ scores tend to exaggerate small, nearly nonexistent differences, while in the tails of the distribution, they tend to underestimate actual differences."
   a. raw
   b. standard
   c. percentile
   d. transformed
   e. normalized

2. Transformed scores, such as T-scores, differ from z-scores in that they
   a. are smaller in values.
   b. are more accurate mathematically.
   c. are based in part on the mean.
   d. do not involve negative values.
   e. a & c

3. Percentiles and percentile ranks are considered to be at the _____ level of measurement.
   a. nominal
   b. ordinal
   c. interval
   d. ratio
   e. c & d

4. If 67% of scores are below the raw score of 44, the percentile rank of 44 is
   a. 33
   b. 44
   c. 56
   d. 67
   e. none of the above

5. Carol's SAT-Verbal score has a percentile rank of 82, which means that
   a. her raw score was above average.
   b. her raw score was below average.
   c. 82% of her answers were correct.
   d. her score was equal to or greater than 82% of other test takers.
   e. a & d

6. Which of the following is an example of a transformed score?
   a. a SAT-Verbal score
   b. a SAT-Math score
   c. an IQ score on the Stanford Binet Intelligence Test
   d. a GRE score
   e. all of the above

7. If 35% of scores are above the raw score of 72, the percentile rank of 72 is
   a. 35
   b. 45
   c. 65
   d. 72
   e. none of the above

8. Given a mean of 50 and a standard deviation of 5, the z-score of raw score 40 is
   a. −1
   b. −2
   c. 0
   d. 1
   e. 2

Fill-Ins

9. A/an _____ is a point in a distribution at or below which falls a given percentage of scores.

10. The values of the mean and standard deviation of the z-distribution are _____ and _____ respectively.

11. One of the limitations of percentiles and percentile ranks is that at the center of a normal distribution, they tend to _____ small and nonexistent differences between raw scores, and at the tails of the distribution they tend to _____ differences.

For questions 12 and 13, identify the appropriate symbol.

12. percentile _____

13. percentile rank _____

Review Problems (Computation Questions)

1. Consider the following sample of raw scores ($n = 15$) arranged from highest to lowest.

   28 26 25 24 24 24 20 20
   18 18 17 16 15 14 12

   Find the following:

   a. 40th percentile (P_{40})
   b. 75th percentile (P_{75})
   c. percentile rank for raw score 17 (PR_{17})
   d. percentile rank for raw score 24 (PR_{24})

2. Given that the mean and standard deviation of the data set in Problem 1 are 20.67 and 4.86, respectively, find the z-score for the following raw scores.

   a. 18   b. 24

3. Given a transformed score distribution with a mean of 100, and standard deviation units of 20, find the TS-score of raw score (a) 17 and (b) 25.

4. Given that a standardized test designed to measure reflective thinking has a mean of 78 and a standard deviation of 6:
   a. what would be the z-score of a student who achieved a raw score of 84?
   b. what would be the z-score of a student who achieved a raw score of 63?

5. Given a standardized test designed to measure spatial relations in autistic children that uses a transformed standard score with a mean of 60 and standard deviation units of 10:
   a. what would be the TS-score of a student who achieved a z-score of −1.3?
   b. what would be the TS-score of a student who achieved a z-score of 2.1?

6. Consider a sample of data with a mean of 5.6 and a standard deviation of 2.1:
   a. what score would have a z-score equal to 3.3?
   b. what score would have a z-score equal to 0.36?

7. A test designed to waive communication disorders students from the required introductory research and statistics course has a mean of 72.75 and standard deviation units of 5.5. If a standard z-score of 1.5 is required to have the course requirement waived, what raw score must a student achieve?

8. Consider the cumulative frequency distribution of sample data, $n = 30$, in Table 4–4.
   a. Find the following percentiles:
      (a1) 20th   (a2) 45th   (a3) 65th
   b. Find the percentile rank for raw score: (b1) 32   (b2) 38   (b3) 45

Calculation Guides

Calculating Percentiles for Simple Rank-Ordered Data

Step 1: Arrange scores in a rank-order from highest to lowest score.

Step 2: Multiply the decimal value of the percentile of interest by the total number of scores in the distribution and round to the nearest whole number. The result is the number of scores at or below the percentile of interest.

Step 3: Count up that number of scores from the bottom of the distribution. This is the location of P_x, that is, the score or value that represents the percentile of interest.

Calculating Percentiles for Class Interval Data

Step 1: Multiply the decimal value of the percentile (p) of interest by the total number of scores in the distribution (n). Do not round if the product is a decimal value. Substitute this value for np in Formula 4–2.

Step 2: Count up that number of np scores from the bottom interval using the frequency (f) or (cf) column. The interval containing the percentile of interest is called the *percentile interval*.

Step 3: Enter into the equation of Formula 4–2 the values of the lower limit (ll), and frequency of scores (f) within the *percentile interval*.

Step 4: Enter the cumulative frequency (cf) of scores *below* the *percentile interval*.

Step 5: Enter the size or width of the class intervals (w).

Step 6: Complete the arithmetic operations in Formula 4–2.

$$P_n = ll + \left(\frac{np - cf}{f}\right)(w)$$

Calculating Percentile Ranks for Simple Frequency Data

Step 1: Count the number of scores at and below the score of interest (X).

Step 2: Divide the number of scores at and below the score of interest (X) by the total number of scores in the distribution (n).

Step 3: Multiply the product by 100. The result is the percentile rank, which indicates the percentage of scores at and below it.

Calculating Percentile Ranks for Class-Interval Data

Step 1: Locate the interval that contains the score of interest (X). This interval is referred to as the *percentile rank interval*.

Step 2: Enter into the equation the values of the lower limit (ll), and frequency of scores (f) in the *percentile rank interval*.

Step 3: Enter the cumulative frequency (cf) of scores *below* the *percentile rank interval*.

Step 4: Enter the size or width of the class intervals (w) and the total number of scores in the distribution (n).

Step 5: Complete the arithmetic operations in Formula 4–4.

Calculating *z*-scores

Step 1: Compute the mean and standard deviation of the distribution.

Step 2: Subtract the mean from the raw score of interest.

Step 3: Divide the difference between the raw score and mean by the standard deviation.

Chapters 5 and 6

Measuring the Strength of Association and Making Predictions: Correlation and Regression

5

Part 1.
Measuring Relationships:
Correlation

General Overview

To this point, we have been mainly concerned with a single variable or *univariate* characteristics of a sample. However, it often is the case that the purpose of a research investigation is to determine whether a statistical relationship exists between two or more variables (*bivariate* or *multivariate*) and/or whether it is possible to predict one or more variables based on other variables. For example, a clinical researcher may want to know if viewing cartoons with aggressive and violent content is related to aggressive behavior in children with a particular disorder, or whether negative political ads are related to voter apathy, or if a person's locus of control is related to his or her attitude toward academic performance. Variables related to one another in a systematic way are said to be *corelated* or *correlated*.

Often, the discovery of a relationship between variables can lead to the ability to predict one from the other. For example, if the relationship between state-trait anxiety inventory score (STAI) and Profile of Mood

State score (POMS) among autistic children is strong, we may be able to predict a child's POMS score from the child's STAI score. Because prediction is one of the major goals of the clinical and behavioral sciences, the discovery of such a relationship becomes a very important outcome of research.

The relationship between two variables is usually determined by a statistical measure known as **correlation**. The technique commonly used to predict one or more variables based on other variables is known as **regression**. In this chapter, we present the **scattergram**, also known as a *scatter diagram* or *scatterplot*. A scattergram is essentially a line graph that indicates the direction and magnitude of the relationship between two variables. In a scatterplot, the values of one of variable, in this case *drug dosage*, are listed along the vertical axis (y), with the lowest value at the bottom, and the values of the other variable, *reaction time*, listed along the horizontal (x) axis, with the lowest value placed at that the extreme left. Each pair of values is represented by a **plot point**, in this case a dot. For example, Subject C received a drug dosage of 3 and had a reaction time score of 4.0. To plot these two scores, we locate the value 3 along the drug dosage axis (*y*) and the value 4.0 on the reaction time axis (*x*). At the intersection where an imaginary horizontal and a vertical line meet (here represented by dashes), we place a plot point, as shown in Figure 5–1. This one dot represents the two measures of Student C.

> A *scattergram* is a line graph that indicates the direction and magnitude of the relationship between two variables by plotting pairs of scores along the vertical and horizontal axes for each individual. Each pair is represented by a dot, known as a *plot point*.

When the relationship between two variables (*X* and *Y*) is such that an increase in one is accompanied by an increase in

the other or vice versa, we say that they have a straight line or **linear relationship**. The direction of the linearity indicates the type of relationship between the two variables. If an *increase* in a score on one variable, *X*, is accompanied by an *increase* in a paired score on the other variable, *Y*, the variables are said to have a **positive correlation**. Height and weight, fear and motivation, SAT scores and grade-point average, and stress and blood pressure are examples of variables that tend to be positively related. On the other hand, if an *increase* in the values of *X* is accompanied by a *decrease* in the values of *Y*, the variables are said to exhibit a **negative correlation**. Car speed and fuel consumption, exercise and weight, and anxiety and performance are examples of variables that usually reflect negative correlations.

When a scattergram shows that for every *increase* in the score value of one

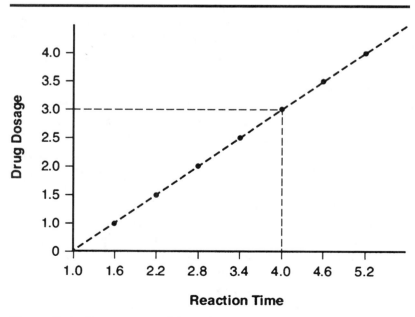

Figure 5–1. Scattergram of drug dosage and reaction time variables.

variable is accompanied by a corresponding *increase* in the score value of the other variable, the relationship between the two variables is said to have a *perfect positive correlation*. In the scattergram in Figure 5–1, the changes in drug dosage values are exactly proportional to the changes in reaction time values. Thus, we say that there is a perfect positive correlation between drug dosage and reaction time. A scattergram depicting a *perfect negative correlation*, in this case between the variables *math anxiety* and *math achievement*, is represented in Figure 5–2. Here the math anxiety scores are inversely related in a proportional way to the math achievement scores, where an *increase* in a math anxiety score is accompanied by a commensurate *decrease* in a math achievement score. In scattergrams of perfect correlations, the plot points are aligned exactly in a straight line that runs through all of the dots.

> A *linear relationship* between two variables exists when a distinct change in one is associated with a similar change in the other. When the change in the variables is in the same direction, the relationship is said to be *positive*; when the change in the variables is in opposite directions, the relationship is said to be *negative*.

Correlation Coefficients

In reality, there are few variables that are perfectly related, mostly what we observe are variables with relationships that range somewhere between zero and 1. The plot points in scattergrams for such variables reflect trends in direction rather than exact straight lines. While useful as a visual representation of the direction of the relationship between two variables, a scattergram is limited in its ability to express the magnitude of relationships that are neither perfectly positive nor perfectly negative. To express the magnitude of the relationship between two variables statistically, we need a numerical index that represents the degree to which a correlation exists. The statistic that expresses the degree to which two sets of data are related is known as a **correlation coefficient**.

A range of correlation coefficients along a continuum starts from negative one (–1), to zero, to positive one (+1). The sign of the coefficient indicates direction of the relationship between two variables; the numeric value expresses the magnitude of the relationship. A coefficient of –1 or +1 indicates a perfect relationship while one of –.15 or +.15 suggests a weak

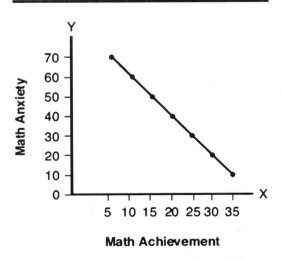

Figure 5–2. Scattergram of perfect negative relationship between math anxiety and math achievement.

relationship. When there is no relationship between two variables, the coefficient is equal to zero (0).

Hypothetical scattergrams of five types
of correlations are shown in Figure 5–3.

> The numerical expression summariz-
> ing the size and direction of a statistical
> relationship is known as a *correlation
> coefficient*.

There are cases when two variables
may be related in what is known as a
curvilinear relationship. In such cases,
both variables begin changing in the same
direction but end up changing in opposite
directions. Consider the two variables, fear

and motivation, mentioned above as having a positive relationship. In general, as
the level of fear increases, the motivation
for change also increases. However, if the
level of fear continues to increase beyond
a certain point, there is a tendency for
the motivation to decrease or cease, as
in cases where individuals suppress the
root of the fear or are "paralyzed" by it.
Thus, what starts out as a positive relationship between two variables ends up as a
negative relationship, as depicted in the
inverted U-shaped curve in Figure 5–3(d).
On the other hand, consider the variables'
age and car value. At the outset, the variables are negatively related, that is to say,
as a car ages its value decreases. However, at some point in time an old, deval-

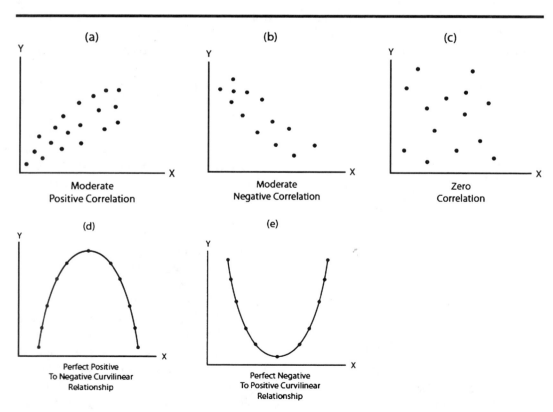

Figure 5–3. Hypothetical scattergrams depicting various types of correlations.

ued car becomes a "classic" or antique, and its value appreciates as it ages. Thus, what starts out as a negative relationship ends up as a positive one, as shown in the U-shaped curve in Figure 5–3(e). In this text, we are concerned only with methods of computing correlations for straight-line, linear relationships.

> When the positive association between two variables becomes negative or vice versa, the variables are said to have a *curvilinear relationship*, characterized by a U-shape or an inverted U-shape (∩) curve.

Two of the more common methods for deriving correlation coefficients are the *Pearson product-moment correlation method* and the *Spearman rank-order method*.

Pearson Product-Moment Method

The Pearson product-moment correlation coefficient, denoted by the symbol r, is probably the most frequently used coefficient to express the relationship between two variables. There are three assumptions or conditions that must be satisfied when applying the Pearson product-moment method.

> 1. The data must consist of paired X and Y values for each member of a sample.
> 2. The variables must be continuous and come from normally distributed populations.
> 3. The relationship between the variables must be linear.

If the conditions for assumption 2 and 3 cannot be satisfied, the Pearson r is an inappropriate measure and other techniques must be used.

Scenario

Suppose the behavioral science researchers and clinical investigators of speech-language pathology are interested in determining if the variables *voice attraction* and *self-disclosure* are correlated. That is to say, is what we disclose about ourselves related to how vocally attracted we are to someone? We administer and score two survey instruments and obtain the following voice attraction (X) and self-disclosure (Y) scores for eight young adults, illustrated in Figure 5–4. While the scattergram in Figure 5–4 indicates a strong positive relationship between the two variables, we need to calculate a coefficient to objectively describe the magnitude of the correlation.

Calculating the Pearson Coefficient r

The most common method of deriving r is given in Formula 5–1.

Formula 5–1

$$r = \frac{n(\Sigma XY) - (\Sigma X)(\Sigma Y)}{\sqrt{[n(\Sigma X^2) - (\Sigma X)^2][n(\Sigma Y^2) - (\Sigma Y)^2]}}$$

We shall refer to this technique as the *raw score method*. Although seemingly complex and daunting, the computational procedure is relatively simple and similar to the raw score methods used in calculating variance and the standard deviation. To compute r, we need six values: n (sample size), ΣX and ΣY (the sums

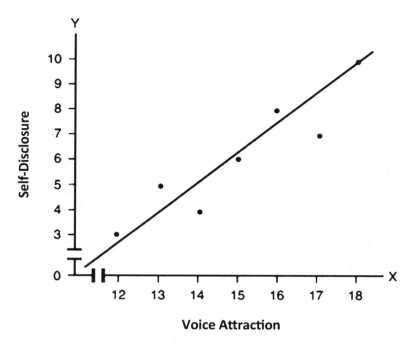

Figure 5–4. Distribution and scattergram of voice attraction and self-disclosure variables.

of the two frequency distributions), ΣXY (the sum of the products of the paired-scores for each individual), and squared ΣX^2, ΣY^2 (the sums of each paired score, squared). To obtain these values, construct a table with the data of the two measures extended in five columns, as also shown in Table 5–1, which is an expansion of the Voice Attraction/Self-Disclosure scores of the eight teenagers in Figure 5–4.

In constructing the raw score method table, we list the paired X, Y scores for each individual in Columns 1 and 2. Next, we multiply the X score times the Y score of each participant and place the product in Column 3. We then square each X and Y score in Columns 1 and 2 and put the products in Column 4 and 5. Finally, the totals of each column are computed. (A summary of these four steps is listed in the Calculation Guides section at the end of the chapter.) For our illustration, these values are as follows: $n = 8$, $\Sigma X = 124$, $\Sigma Y = 52$, $\Sigma XY = 845$, $\Sigma X^2 = 1964$, $\Sigma Y^2 = 380$. Referring to Formula 5–1, we compute the Pearson coefficient r as follows:

$$r = \frac{8(845) - (124)(52)}{\sqrt{[8(1964) - (124)^2][8(380) - (52)^2]}}$$

$$= \frac{6760 - 6448}{\sqrt{[15712 - 15376][3040 - 2704]}}$$

$$= 0.929 \sim 0.93$$

Given the magnitude of the coefficient 0.93, we may conclude that the positive linear relationship between voice attraction and self-disclosure is quite high.

Table 5–1. Pearson Product-Moment Correlation Coefficient Table—Voice Attraction (X) and Self-Disclosure (Y)

(1) Subject	(2) X	(3) Y	(4) XY	(5) X^2	(6) Y^2
A	18	10	180	324	100
B	13	5	65	169	25
C	15	6	90	225	36
D	17	7	119	289	49
E	19	9	171	361	81
F	16	8	128	256	64
G	14	4	56	196	16
H	12	3	36	144	9
Total Sum	124	52	845	1964	380

Interpreting Correlation Coefficients

The interpretation of correlation coefficients is somewhat subjective and relative to a number of factors, including the variables being correlated and the nature and properties of coefficients. For example, although an assumption of the Pearson coefficient is that the variables are continuous, the scale of coefficients from −1 to +1 is ordinal, not interval or ratio. Therefore, in interpreting a Pearson r, it is inappropriate to say that a correlation coefficient of 0.90 is twice as strong as one of 0.45. Nor is it appropriate to say that a coefficient of $r = 0.60$ indicates that there is a 60% agreement between the values of the two variables. A correlation coefficient is simply a numerical index of the magnitude of the relationship between the frequency distributions of two variables, with a sign indicating the direction of the relationship.

Finally, if the relationship between the variables is not linear, the Pearson product-moment correlation coefficient tends to underestimate the value of the actual relationship between the two variables. Therefore, we need to be cautious in how we express the significance of a correlation coefficient and the types of conclusions or inferences we draw from them.

The qualitative terms we use to express correlation coefficients range from "very high" to "very low." Although somewhat arbitrary, the scale shown in Table 5–2 can serve as a guide in interpreting the size of a correlation coefficient, given the cautionary notes above. Perhaps the greatest caution should be focused on avoiding an assumption that coefficients indicate a causal relationship between two variables. Although there are cases where a causal relationship exists, the coefficient of the correlation itself is not proof of it. Besides the clinical standpoint, consider a 1998 Purdue University study that found

Table 5–2. Spearman Rank-Order Correlation Table: Locus of Control and Self-Handicapping Survey Results

Coefficient Range (r is the absolute value positive number)	Interpretation
$0.9 < r < 1$	Very high correlation
$0.7 < r \leq 0.9$	High correlation
$0.5 < r \leq 0.7$	Moderate correlation
$0.3 < r \leq 0.5$	Low correlation
Below or at $r = 0.3$	No to very low correlation

that obesity is associated with religious participation.[1] Accordingly, Southern Baptists, on average, have the highest body-mass index, with Catholics in the center, and Jews and other non-Christians at the low end. Does religious participation cause obesity in Southern Baptists? Is the body-mass index lowest in some people because they participate in non-Christian religions? Anything is possible, but logic tells us that it is improbable. It is more likely to reason that other factors, such as cultural and socioeconomic variables, are influencing the relationship between obesity and religious participation. In short, whether causality between two variables can be inferred directly or indirectly depends on information other than that of the correlation coefficient. Therefore, it is important that we not overstate the significance of correlation coefficients.

Coefficient of Determination

There is another important reason why researchers and statisticians are cautious in the conclusions they draw from correlational data. It has to do with the variances of the distributions of the two variables. Variables with large variances tend to have higher correlation coefficients than those that are more homogeneous. However, at another level, a measure related to the variances of two distributions can tell us much more than simple correlation coefficients. The measure, known as the **coefficient of determination** and denoted by the symbol r^2, is obtained by squaring the correlation coefficient.

Statisticians and researchers prefer to use the coefficient of determination for two reasons: (1) it is a more conservative measure of the degree to which two variables are related; and (2) it tells us something about the effect of one variable on another. For example, according to Table 5–2, a coefficient of $r = 0.71$ is considered a moderate to high correlation. However, squaring the coefficient $r = 0.71$ yields a coefficient of determination, $r^2 = .5041$ or 50.41%. What this coefficient of determination tells us is that 50.41% of the variance of Y is accounted for or explained

[1]K. Clark & K. F. Ferraro. (2005, August 12). "Does Religion Increase the Prevalence and Incidence of Obesity and Severe Obesity in Adulthood?" Paper presented at the annual meeting of the American Sociological Association, Philadelphia, PA.

by X or vice versa. The remaining 49.59% is not accounted for and may be because of other factors, including sampling error and/or chance. Similarly, the case of a low to moderate coefficient of $r = 0.50$, with an $r^2 = 0.25$ coefficient of determination, indicates that only 25% of the variance of Y is accounted for or explained by X or vice versa. The remaining 75% is not accounted for and may be because of other factors, including random fluctuations due to chance. (See Figure 5–5B.) The significance of this reduction in relationship strength can be better understood by considering the second reason why r^2 is a more meaningful measure than r.

Unlike r, the coefficient of determination is a proportion or percentage. Specifically, r^2 may be defined as the proportion or percentage of the variance of the X variable that is associated with the variance of the Y variable. The higher the coefficient of determination, the more we know about the effect of one variable on another.

The concept of the coefficient of determination can be illustrated by using circles to represent the variance of each variable, as in Figure 5–5. The extent to which the circles overlap reflects the proportion of variable Y that can be associated with variable X. When the r and r^2

coefficients equal zero, the variances of the two variables have nothing in common and the circles are apart, as in Figure 5–5A. When the coefficients are high, as in the case of the Voice Attraction and Self Disclosure variables illustrated above, where $r = 0.929$ and $r^2 = 0.863$, there is much overlap, as shown in Figure 5–5C. In this case, we can say that approximately 86% of the variance in self-disclosure (Y) can be explained or accounted for by the positive linear relationship between voice attraction and self-disclosure or vice versa. The remaining 14% of variation in self-disclosure values cannot be explained by the voice attraction variable.

Other factors, including the random fluctuation of values from sampling error, may account for the variation in the self-disclosure distribution. Nevertheless, we can conclude that the predictability of one variable from the other is quite strong. In Chapter 6, we illustrate how correlations with high coefficients form the basis for predicting individual Y scores based on what we know about X, and vice versa.

> The *coefficient of determination* represents the percentage of variance shared by two correlated variables.

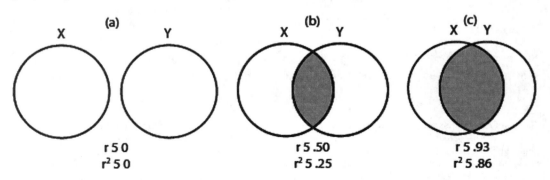

Figure 5–5. Variance of variables X and Y.

The Spearman Rank-Order Correlation Method

The Pearson product-moment correlation method is quite useful in describing linear relationships between two continuous variables when the data are expressed along a numerical scale. However, there are many instances where differences are expressed in the form of ranks or where the relationship between two variables is *nonlinear* and cannot be described by the Pearson coefficient. In such cases, the ***Spearman rank-order correlation method*** can be used as an alternative to the Pearson rank-order method to determine relationships between variables.

The **Spearman rank-order correlation coefficient**, denoted by the symbol, r_s, is a measure of the relationship between two variables whose paired data are expressed in the form of ranks for each individual on each variable. It is particularly useful when the sample size is less than 30, and scores or ratings have been ranked in some order of merit. It also can be applied to numerical data by converting numerical values to ranks. The values of r_s range from −1 to 1 inclusive. In computing the coefficient r_s between the two sets of ranks, the Spearman technique takes into account the relative position of each value or score.

Scenario

Suppose a sample of 10 communication disorders majors is surveyed to determine the relationship between the variables locus-of-control and self-handicapping behavior,[22] with the results shown in Table 5–3. The scores for each student on the two measures are listed in the first two columns. The higher the locus-of-control score, the stronger the perception that others have more control over one's life and behavior. The higher the self-handicapping scores are, the greater the reliance on self-handicapping strategies becomes.

Computing the Spearman Correlation Coefficient

The Spearman rank-order correlation coefficient, r_s, is calculated using Formula 5–2.

Formula 5–2

$$r_s = 1 - \frac{6\Sigma d^2}{n(n^2 - 1)}$$

Where

6 = a constant

Σd^2 = sum of the squared differences between each paired ranks

n = size of the sample

Algebraically, the formula is equivalent to the formula used to derive the Pearson product-moment coefficient, r, except that ranks are used instead of raw scores. When there are no ties in the rankings, the correlation coefficients of the Spearman and Pearson formulas are the same.

---

[2]Locus of control refers to the perception a person has regarding forces affecting his or her behavior. Individuals with *internal* locus of control perceive that they have more direct control over their lives and behavior. Those with an *external* locus of control perceive that others have more control over their lives and behavior than they do. Self-handicapping behavior refers to face saving strategies that may be consciously or subconsciously adopted when a person anticipates failure in order to maintain self-esteem and/or the illusion of competence—as in, "I would have aced the exam if my dog didn't eat most of my notes."

Table 5–3. Spearman Rank-Order Correlation Table: Locus of Control and Self-Handicapping Survey Results

Student SS	Locus . . . X	Self-Hand. Y	R_X	R_Y	d	d^2
A	19	16	6	8	−2	4
B	15	14	8.5	9	−0.5	0.25
C	21	50	4	1.5	2.5	6.25
D	23	42	3	5	−2	4
E	20	43	5	4	1	1
F	15	24	8.5	7	1.5	2.25
G	28	50	1	1.5	−0.5	0.25
H	25	45	2	3	−1	1
I	12	13	10	10	0	0
J	18	35	7	6	1	1
Total Sum					0	20

The sum of the squared differences between each paired ranks, Σd^2, is derived from a table, such as Table 5–3. In the case of the 10 communication disorders students surveyed to determine the relationship between locus-of-control and self-handicapping behavior, the table is constructed following four steps. First, the name (or symbol) and paired scores for each research participant are listed in the first three columns, labeled SS, X, and Y. Second, in the fourth and fifth columns, labeled R_X and R_Y, enter the ranks of the scores in columns 2 and 3, assigning 1 to the highest score, 2 to the next highest score, and so on. In cases of tied scores (15 for X; 50 for Y in Table 5–3), assign to them the average of the next two ranks. For example, the two 15s would occupy the ranks of 8 and 9 if they were not tied scores. Thus, each is assigned the rank of 8.5 [(8 + 9/2)]. The two 50s would be ranked 1.5 [(1 + 2/2)]. (A review of pro-

cedures for ranking scores is included at the end of the chapter in the Calculation Guides section.) In the third step, enter the differences between the paired ranks, R_X and R_Y, in the sixth column, labeled d. Finally, in the seventh column, d^3, enter and sum the squared differences between the paired ranks to obtain $\Sigma d^2 = 20$. A summary of the steps followed in constructing a Spearman Rank-Order table is included in the Calculation Guides section at the end of the chapter.

To apply Formula 5–2 to our illustration, substitute 20 for Σd^2 and 10 for n. In this case, the Spearman correlation coefficient is 0.879 or approximately 0.88.

$$r_s = 1 - \frac{6(20)}{10(10^2 - 1)}$$

$$= 1 - \frac{120}{990}$$

$$= 0.879 \sim 0.88$$

Thus, we may conclude that there is a high, positive relationship between self-handicapping and the perception of who among us is more directly involved in the control of our lives and behavior.

Comparing Pearson and Spearman Coefficients

One of the advantages of the Spearman rank-order method is the ease with which we can compute the coefficient, r_s. This is particularly true whenever the size of a sample (n) is small. As noted earlier, when there are no ties in the scores in the two distributions, the calculation of the Spearman r_s is equal to the Pearson r coefficient. When the number of ties in the distributions is small, the difference between r_s and r tends to be minimal. For example, if we calculate the Pearson coefficient treating the ranks in Table 5–3 as scores, taken as deviations from an assumed mean of zero, the Pearson coefficient r is 0.878, virtually the same coefficient as that of the Spearman $r_s = 0.879$. The slight difference is because of the loss of information when we use ranks instead of the original data.

While the Spearman coefficient r_s takes into account the relative position of each value or score in the two distributions, it does not allow for the differences between adjacent scores. For example, the scores of 85, 80, and 78 in a distribution would be ranked 1, 2, and 3 without regard to the difference of 5 points between scores 85 and 80 and the difference of 2 points between the scores of 80 and 78. Thus, some information and the accuracy of the measure are lost when scores are converted to ranks. Nevertheless, the Spearman rank-order technique provides a quick and convenient method for estimating the relationship between two variables, and under certain conditions it provides as adequate a measure of relationships as that obtained by the more laborious and time-consuming Pearson product-moment method.

Key Terms and Concepts

Correlation

Regression

Linear relationship

Positive correlation

Negative correlation

Curvilinear relationship

Scatterplot

Ranking

Correlation coefficient

Pearson product-moment coefficient

Coefficient of determination

Spearman rank-order correlation

Spearman correlation coefficient r_s

Feedback Review of Chapter 5

1. A scatterplot in which one variable decreases as another variable increases is an example of
   a. a positive correlation.
   b. a negative correlation.
   c. a curvilinear relationship.
   d. no correlation.
   e. c or d

2. Knowing that there is a correlation of 0.72 between the number of cigarettes smoked and the incidence of cancer, you can validly conclude that
   a. cigarette smoking causes cancer.
   b. there is a high probability that cigarette smoking causes cancer.
   c. a third variable, related to cigarette smoking, causes cancer.
   d. 72% of people who are heavy smokers will get cancer.
   e. none of the above

3. Which correlation coefficient indicates the strongest relationship between the two variables?
   a. 0.05
   b. −0.03
   c. 0.77
   d. −0.77
   e. c and d

4. Which of the following must be satisfied before the Pearson product-moment correlation coefficient can be computed?
   a. The variables must be measured using interval or ratio data.
   b. The size of the sample must be more than 30.
   c. The relationship between the two variables must be positive.
   d. The relationship between the two variables must be curvilinear.
   e. The relationship between the two variables must be negative.

5. If the correlation coefficient is −0.80, the coefficient of determination is
   a. −0.40
   b. 0.40
   c. 0.64
   d. −0.64
   e. a and d

6. Two variables that are likely to have a negative correlation coefficient are
   a. height and weight.
   b. aptitude and achievement.
   c. income and education.
   d. test anxiety and test performance.
   e. none of the above.

7. When the plot points in a scatterplot are essentially in a straight line, the Pearson correlation coefficient is
   a. positive.
   b. negative.
   c. near +1.
   d. near −1.
   e. c or d.

8. Which would explain the greatest proportion (percentage) of total variance in Y that is accounted for by the variance of variable X?
   a. A correlation of zero (0)
   b. A correlation of 0.61
   c. A coefficient of determination of .61
   d. A coefficient of determination of .72
   e. b and c

9. A psychological study finds that the more a clinical practitioner attempts to be "friendly and outgoing," the more "trustworthy" they are considered by their peers and clients—but only up to a certain point. Beyond that point, the more they try, the less trustworthy they are perceived to be. This relationship between amount of effort put into being "friendly and outgoing," and perceived trustworthiness represents a
   a. positive linear correlation.
   b. negative linear correlation.
   c. curvilinear correlation.
   d. all of the above.
   e. none of the above.

10. If the correlation between a statistics aptitude test and grades in a statistics course is $r = 0.84$, we may assume that the test has _____.
    a. a curvilinear relationship.
    b. predictive reliability.
    c. predictive regression.
    d. a and b
    e. a and c

11. The sizes of correlation coefficients range from
    a. −0 to +1.
    b. −1 to 0.
    c. −1 to +1.
    d. −0.00 to 1.00.
    e. +0.00 to 1.00.

Fill-In the Blanks

12. A study finds that the correlation between verbal aggressiveness and personality type is $r = 0.70$. What percentage of the variance in personality type can be explained by the correlation?

    _____

13. If the linear correlation between two variables is perfect, $r =$ _____ or

    _____.

For questions 14 and 15 identify the appropriate symbol.

14. Pearson product-moment correlation coefficient _____

15. Coefficient of determination _____

Review Problems
(Computation Questions)

1. The following data represent two frequency distributions for ten graduate students in communication disorders program in an attitude study. The X data are scores on an attitude-toward-research-oriented education measure; the Y data are scores on an attitude-toward-clinical-oriented education scale. The results of the study are shown in Table 5–4.
    a. Draw a scatterplot of the data
    b. Compute the Pearson product-moment correlation coefficient
    c. Compute the coefficient of determination

2. The following data represent two distributions for 12 subjects in a study focusing on the relationship between hand-eye coordination (X) and spatial relation skills (Y) of 12 randomly selected clients who recently visited the College's speech clinic. The results of the study are shown in Table 5–5.
    a. Draw a scattergram of the data
    b. Compute the Pearson product-moment correlation coefficient
    c. What percent of spatial relation skills can be explained by hand-eye coordination?

3. A researcher wants to know if there is any relationship between the number of hours individuals work as volunteers for a candidate for the ASHA (American Speech-Language Hearing Association) national office (X) and their knowledge of the key issues of the campaign (Y). The following data were obtained for a random sample of 17 volunteers a month before the election. The results of the study are shown in Table 5–6.
    a. Draw a scatterplot of the data
    b. Compute the Pearson product-moment correlation coefficient
    c. Compute the coefficient of determination.

Table 5–4. Frequency Distributions of a Hypothetical Attitude Study Concerning the Relationship Between Attitude-Toward-Education Measure (X) and Attitude-Toward-Wealth Scale (Y)

Ss*	X	Y
1	18	22
2	13	14
3	9	18
4	18	16
5	17	25
6	12	19
7	12	20
8	16	24
9	17	26
10	11	18

* = Subjects.

Table 5–5. The Results of a Hypothetical Study Concerning Relationships Between Hand-Eye Coordination (X) and Spatial Relation Skills (Y)

Ss*	A	B	C	D	E	F	G	H	I	J	K	L
X	9	8	8	7	6	6	5	4	4	3	2	1
Y	8	9	4	5	7	3	2	6	4	2	4	1

* = Subjects.

Table 5–6. The Results of a Hypothetical Study Concerning the Relationship between the Number of Working Hours at National Office (X) and Their Knowledge of the Key Issues (Y)

X	5	5	11	8	13	7	10	9	11	7	9	12	11	11	11	12	2
Y	33	39	41	50	59	38	45	56	45	22	52	54	63	44	41	54	6

4. The following two frequency distributions are for ten subjects in a behavioral study. The data are ordinal (i.e., they are from ordinal scales of measurement). The X values are ratings on a scale measuring aggressiveness; the Y values are ratings on a popularity scale. The results of the study are shown in Table 5–7.

   a. Draw a scattergram of the data (use graph paper).
   b. Compute the Spearman rho (ρ) correlation coefficient.

Table 5–7. The Results of a Hypothetical Behavioral Study Concerning the Relationship Between Ratings on a Scale Measuring Aggressiveness (X) and Ratings on a Popularity Scale (Y)

Ss	X	Y
1	20	5
2	5	1
3	5	2
4	40	7
5	30	8
6	35	9
7	5	3
8	5	2
9	15	5
10	40	8

Calculation Guides

Constructing the Table for r: Raw Score Method

Step 1: List the subjects in Column 1 and their paired X, Y scores in Columns 2 and 3.

Step 2: Multiply the X score times the Y score of each participant, and place the product in Column 4.

Step 3: Square each X and Y score in Columns 1 and 2, and put the products in Columns 5 and 6.

Step 4: Total columns 2 through 6.

Review: Ranking Ungrouped Distributions

To determine the ranks of values in a simple distribution, construct a table, such as the one shown in Table 5–8.

Step 1: Label the first column "Order," and list the order of scores from 1 to n, ignoring tied scores.

Step 2: In the second column, X, list the actual scores in the distribution.

Step 3: In the third column, labeled "Rank," enter the rank of each score using the value listed in the Order column, except in the cases of tied scores. The ranks for tied scores are derived by averaging their "order" values. In the case of the two scores of 24, the average of their order values, 3 and 4, is 3.5 (7/2). In the case of three scores of 17, their respective rank is 8, derived by adding their order values and dividing the sum by 3 (7 + 8 + 9 = 24/3).

Table 5–8. Determining the Ranks of the Hypothetical Data Values in an Ungrouped Distribution

Order	X	Rank
1	30	1
2	28	2
3	24	3.5
4	24	3.5
5	21	5
6	20	6
7	17	8
8	17	8
9	17	8
10	16	10
–	–	–
–	–	–
n	n_x	n_R

Constructing the Spearman Rank-Order Table for Σd^2

Step 1: List the name (or symbol) and paired scores for each individual in the first three columns. Label the columns SS, X, and Y.

Step 2: Label columns four and five, R_X and R_Y, and enter the ranks for each of the X and Y scores from high to low, assigning 1 to the highest score, 2 to the next highest score, and so on. In cases of tied scores, assign to them the average of the next two (three, four, etc.) ranks. For example,

if the fourth and fifth values in a column are tied scores, assign to them the average of the two ranks they would occupy if not tied, in this case $4 + 5 = 9/2 = 4.5$. Thus, each of the tied scores would be ranked 4.5.

Step 3: List the differences between the paired ranks in the sixth column (d).

Step 4: Enter and sum the squared differences between the paired ranks in the last column to obtain Σd^2.

$$r = \frac{10(374.5) - (55)(55)}{\sqrt{[10(384.5) - (55)^2][10(384.5) - (55)^2]}}$$

$$= \frac{720}{\sqrt{672400}}$$

$$= 0.878 \sim 0.88$$

6

Part 2.
Making Predictions:
Regression

We have seen that measures of correlation are indicators of the relationship between two variables and that the degree of the relationship is expressed by a correlation coefficient. The higher the coefficient becomes, the stronger the relationship gets. We also have seen how the coefficient of determination (r^2) is a useful basis for describing a functional relationship between two variables. Recall that in a functional relationship, a change in one variable is accompanied by a concomitant change in the other.

When a functional relationship is strong, meaning a high correlation coefficient, the ability to predict the outcome of values for one variable based on what is known about the other variable becomes increasing more accurate. The higher the coefficient becomes, the greater the accuracy of prediction becomes. If the correlation between two variables is perfect (±1.00), we can predict with absolute accuracy. However, few variables are perfectly correlated. Nevertheless, when the coefficient between two variables is high, we can make reasonably good predictions of an individual's performance on one

measure based on what we know of his or her performance on a correlated measure. The process that examines the relationship between two or more variables in order to predict outcomes from one another is known as **regression analysis**.

The importance of regression analysis is its usefulness in applications where estimates of outcomes are desired. Once a functional relationship between specific variables has been established, instruments or methodologies can be developed and applied over a wide range of topics and disciplines. Generally speaking, aptitudes tests, such as the Scholastic Aptitude Test (SAT), Graduate Record Exam (GRE), and Law Scholastic Aptitude Test (LSAT), are examples of how regression analysis has been applied in education. Since a high positive correlation between scholastic aptitude and academic performance has been established, these tests are used to help institutions admit students who are likely to succeed in their programs. However, because the correlations are not perfect, there is no guarantee that students with high scholastic aptitude will perform as expected. Some students with high academic aptitude may have poor test taking skills or suffer from test anxiety. Others with high aptitude may simply goof off or lack the discipline and rigor of academic studies.

As noted earlier, in this text we are focusing on variables that have a linear relationship, such as scholastic aptitude and academic performance; social status and religious or racial tolerance; political affiliation and attitudes on abortion or the role of government, and so on. The statistical technique for analyzing variables that are linearly related is known as *linear regression*.

> *Regression analysis* refers to the process that examines the relationship between two or more variables in order to predict an outcome from one another.

Linear Regression

Linear regression refers to the process of predicting scores of variables that are linearly related. In Chapter 5, we illustrated the concept of linear correlation graphically with a scattergram, where the plot points tend to fall along a straight line. In a scattergram, the regression line is the straight line that best fits through the plot points. Recall that when two variables are linearly related, the dots in a scattergram are disbursed elliptically around some imaginary straight line. The closer the fit of the plot marks to the regression line, the higher the absolute value of the correlation coefficient (r) and the more accurate the prediction of Y from X. In practice, we do not try to draw the best-fitting line to show the functional relationship

between the variables; rather, we use the equation for a straight line.

The process of prediction involves two steps. In the first step, we determine the regression line, using the mathematical equation of a straight line. In the second step we use the mathematical equation to predict scores. In this chapter, we examine two basic approaches that will be predicting Y scores from X scores, and that of predicting X scores from Y scores.

> The process of predicting scores of variables that are linearly related is known as *linear regression*.

The Regression of *Y* on *X*

In predicting Y scores from X scores, we say that Y is a function of X and use the *slope-intercept form* of the equations for a straight line. The form of the equation that we use is expressed in Formula 6–1.

Formula 6–1

$$\hat{Y} = a + bX$$

Where

$\hat{Y}$ = predicted score (read "Y hat")

$a = Y -$ intercept

b = slope of the line

To illustrate the slope-intercept form, consider the graph of a regression line of Y on X shown in Figure 6–1. (The actual scatter of plot points around the regression line is omitted for illustration purposes.) The slope of the Y on X line (b) indicates the amount of increase on the Y variable that accompanies a unit of increase on the X variable, sometimes

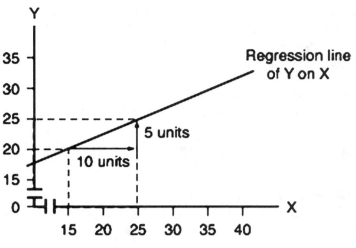

Figure 6–1. Regression line of Y on X.

referred to as the *rate of change*. In Figure 6–1, the slope of the line indicates that for every 10 units of change on the X variable, there are 5 units of change on the Y variable. In other words, the ratio of vertical change (on the Y variable) to the horizontal change (on the X variable) is b = 5 unit/10 units, as depicted by the broken lines. Therefore, the coefficient of the slope for the data in this illustration is 1/2 or 0.5. Note that a positive b indicates the amount of increase in Y that corresponds to an increase in X; a negative b indicates the amount of *increase* in Y that corresponds to a *decrease* in X.

The Y-intercept, a, represents the value of Y when X = 0, that is the value of Y when the regression line crosses or intercepts the y-axis. In Figure 6–1, the regression line crosses or intercepts the y-axis at the midpoint of the Y values 15 and 20. Therefore, for this illustration, the intercept, a, is 17.5 and the straight line equation, using Formula 6–1, is given as $\hat{Y}$ = 17.5 + 0.5(X).

To predict a particular Y value ($\hat{Y}$) for a given value X value, we would simply multiply the X value of interest by 0.5 and add 17.5. For example, if an individual received an X score of 8, we would predict that his or hers will be $\hat{Y}$ = 17.5 + 0.5(8) = 21.5 *or* ~22. In regression analysis, the slope of the line is referred to as *regression coefficient*, and the Y-intercept is known as the *regression constant*. The formulas used to derive their values are discussed below.

Step One: Determining the Regression Line

The line that best describes the functional relationship between the two variables, such that a change in the value of one variable, X, is accompanied by a concomitant (successive) change in the value of another variable, Y, is called the **regression line**. It is drawn in such a way that the sum of squares of the vertical distances of plot points from the line in a scattergram is at a minimum. It is referred to as the "best fitting" line because it yields the smallest possible sum of squares. The most common statistical technique used to determine the "best fitting" line is known as the **method of least squares.** In order to draw a regression line in such a precise way, we need to locate two points through which it can be drawn. We determine these two points by using the equation for a straight line given in Formula 6–1, $\hat{Y} = a + bX$, and illustrated in Figure 6–1. In regression analysis, we refer to the slope-intercept form equation as the *regression equation*.

Scenario. Suppose we find two variables, hours-at-speech clinic per week (X) and self-esteem (Y), to be highly correlated with a coefficient $r = 0.793$, as shown in Table 6–1 and graphically depicted in Figure 6–2. Since the correlation is high, we can expect the

$$\bar{X} = 5.417 \qquad \bar{Y} = 4.792 \qquad n = 24$$

$$s_x = 2.469 \qquad s_y = 2.45$$

$$r = \frac{24(733) - 130(115)}{\sqrt{[24(844) - (130)^2][24(689) - (115)^2]}}$$

*Using Formula 5–1

estimates of a self-esteem based on hours at a speech clinic to be reasonably accurate.

For $X = 1$, we find
$\hat{Y} = 0.529 + 0.787(1) = 1.316$

For $X = 9$, we find
$\hat{Y} = 0.529 + 0.787(9) = 7.612$

that will be accompanied by a concomitant change in self-esteem (Y), and reflect in the regression equation.

The slope (b) and Y-intercept (a) of the regression equation, $\hat{Y} = a + bX$, as noted above, are called the **regression coefficient** and **regression constant**, and calculated using Formula 6–2 and Formula 6–3.

Table 6–1. Summarized Data on Hours-in-Speech Clinic (X) and Self-Esteem (Y)

X	Y	XY	X²	X²
2	4	8	4	16
4	4	16	16	16
1	1	1	1	1
6	3	18	36	9
6	5	30	36	25
5	6	30	25	36
9	9	81	81	81
8	8	64	64	64
9	8	72	81	64
2	1	2	4	1
2	3	6	4	9
6	7	42	36	49
7	5	35	49	25
3	2	6	9	4
3	2	6	9	4
7	5	35	49	25
7	7	49	49	49
4	4	16	16	16
4	6	24	16	36
8	4	32	64	16
8	9	72	64	81
5	2	10	25	4
5	3	15	25	9
9	7	63	81	49
130	115	733	844	689

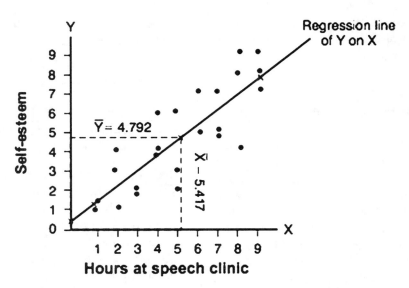

Figure 6–2. Hours at speech clinic and degree of self-esteem part 1.

Formula 6–2[1]

$$b = \frac{[n\Sigma XY] - [\Sigma X][\Sigma Y]}{[\Sigma X^2] - (\Sigma X)^2}$$

Formula 6–3[2]

$$a = \overline{Y} - bX$$

Where

$\hat{Y}$ = mean of Y variable values

$\overline{X}$ = mean of Y variable values

The numerator in Formula 6–2 represents the sum of squares of the X variable.

For the data shown in Table 6–1, we calculate the regression coefficient, b, and the regression constant, a, as follows:[3]

$$b = \frac{24(733) - (130)(115)}{24(844) - (130)^2}$$
(regression coefficient)

$$= \frac{2642}{3356} = 0.787$$

$$a = 4.792 - .787(5.417)$$
(regression constant)

$$= 0.529$$

---

[1]An alternative formula for the regression coefficient for Y on X is given as $b = (r)\frac{S_y}{S_x}$, where r is the correlation coefficient between variables X and Y; is the standard deviation of Y values and is the standard deviation of X values.

[2]An alternative formula for the regression constant is given as $a_{XY} = \frac{\Sigma X - b_{XY}\Sigma Y}{n}$

[3]Alternatively $b = (r)\frac{S_y}{S_x} = (0.793)\frac{2.45}{2.469} = 0.787 / a_{XY} = \frac{\Sigma X - b_{XY}\Sigma Y}{n} = \frac{115 - 0.787(130)}{24} = 0.529$

Thus, the regression equation for the variables hours-at-speech clinic (X) and self-esteem (Y) is given as $\hat{Y} = 0.529 + 0.787(X)$.

The Regression Line of *Y* on *X*

It is possible to predict Y values using the regression line in a scattergram by locating the point above a given X value and reading the corresponding Y value on the vertical axis. In Figure 6–1, we illustrated the concept of how b and a are determined by examining the placement and slope of the regression line in a scattergram. In practice, however, we would proceed to draw the regression line for Y on X in reverse fashion using one of two methods. Each method consists of a set of procedures for identifying the two points in a scattergram through which the regression line will pass. We illustrate both methods using the data in Table 6–1 and the scattergram in Figure 6–2.

Method 1. The two points through which the regression line will pass are derived as follows. Locate the intersection of two predicted Y and corresponding X values using the regression equation, $\hat{Y} = a + bX$, and place plot points, such as a small x, at each point. Next, draw a line through the two plot points. For example, suppose we want to predict the self-esteem score for an individual who spent one hour per week at the speech clinic and for someone who spent nine hours per week at the speech clinic. Applying the regression equation for this illustration, we find the two plot points as follows:

  i. For $X = 1$, we find $\hat{Y} = 0.529 + 0.787(1) = 1.316 \approx 1.3$

  ii. For $X = 9$, we find $\hat{Y} = 0.529 + 0.787(9) = 7.612 \approx 7.6$

To draw the regression line of Y on X in Figure 6–2, we simply place a small x at $X = 1$, $\hat{Y} = 1.3$, and a small x at $X = 9$, $\hat{Y} = 7.6$ and draw a line between the two points as shown in Figure 6–2.

Method 2. The second method is based on the fact that the regression line always passes through the point where the means of the X and Y distributions intersect, which serves as the location for one plot point. The other is located at the Y intercept, that is, the point on the vertical axis where $X = 0$. For our illustration, we place a small x at the intersection of $\overline{X} = 5.417$ and $\overline{Y} = 4.792$ (see dash marks in Figure 6–2) and another at the Y intercept, $a = 0.529$. Next, we draw the regression line through the two points as shown in Figure 6–2.

However, as mentioned earlier, we generally do not construct scattergrams and draw regressions lines to predict Y scores. Instead, we simply develop a regression equation using Formulas 6–2 and 6–3, and use the equation to determine $\hat{Y}$ for any X value. In the second step of the process of calculating the regression of Y on X, we apply the equation, substituting X values of interest to predict their corresponding Y value.

Step Two: Predicting Y from X

The second step in a regression analysis is using the derived values of the regression coefficient (b) and regression constant (a) in the regression equation given in Formula 6–1 and solve for the predicted score, $\hat{Y}$. For the data in our illustration, the regression equation we computed for predicting self-esteem scores based on hours-at-speech-clinic scores $\hat{Y} = 0.529 + 0.787(X)$. Thus, if an individual's hours-at-speech-clinic score is 3, we would predict that his or her self-esteem score will be 2.9 or approximately 3[$\hat{Y} = 0.529 + 0.787(3) = 2.89$]. Likewise, we would predict that the self-esteem score of an individual's hours-at-speech-clinic score of 5 will be approximately 4.5[$\hat{Y} = 0.529 + 0.787(35) = 4.464$]. The sample distributions of the original hours-at-speech-clinic (X) and self-esteem (Y) and the predicted self-esteem scores ($\hat{Y}$) are shown in Table 6–2. Note that the predicted self-esteem scores vary somewhat from the original Y scores in the second column. The difference between an actual score and a score predicted using the regression equation is referred to as **prediction error**. The higher the correlation between two variables becomes, the lower the difference between an actual score and the predicted score derived by the regression equation becomes. In cases where variables are perfectly correlated with coefficients equal to ±1.00, prediction errors equal zero. However, since few variables are perfectly related with coefficients equal to ±1.00, some prediction error is likely to be present in the regression analysis.

> *Prediction error* refers to the difference between an actual score and a score predicted using the regression equation.

Table 6–2. Sample Distribution of Original Hours-at-Speech Clinic (X) and Self-Esteem Scores (Y) and Predicted Self-Esteem Values ($\hat{Y}$)

X	Y	$\hat{Y}$
1	1	1.316
2	3	2.103
2	4	2.103
3	2	2.89
4	6	3.677
5	2	4.464
5	6	4.464
6	3	5.251
6	7	5.251
7	5	6.038
7	7	6.038
8	4	6.825
8	9	6.825
9	8	7.612
9	9	7.612

The Regression of *X* on *Y*

When two variables of interest are interchangeable in terms of independent and dependent functions, it is possible to develop two regression equations, one defining the regression line of Y on X and the other of X on Y. For example, if we find that hours-at-speech clinic (X) and self-esteem (Y) variables are highly correlated and interchangeable, we could develop a regression equation to predict the regression of Y on X, as illustrated above or regression equation to predict the regression of X on Y, as we illustrate in this section.

Scenario. We know from the illustration above that the variables self-esteem and hours-at-speech clinic per week are highly correlated. Suppose we establish that they also are interchangeable. That being the case, we would now be able to develop a regression equation and regression line to predict the number of hours per week an individual will spend at a speech clinic (X) based on his or her self-esteem score (Y).

In this section, we examine the two-step process for developing such a regression equation and their regression lines to predict X values from Y values. We continue to use the data in Table 6–1.

Step One: Determining the Regression Line

The regression line of X on Y differs from the line depicting the regression of Y on X whenever the correlation between two variables is less than perfect. When $r = -1.00$ or $r = 1.00$, the two regression lines are identical, and prediction is 100% (perfectlY) accurate.

The formulas used in calculating the regression of X on Y are identical to those used in predicting Y values corresponding to X values, except for the reversal of symbols. The regression equation of X on Y is given in Formula 6–4 (written form) and Formula 6–5 (symbolic form). They are as follows:

Formula 6–4

Predictive Value of X = X intercept + The product of (the slope of XY) and (a given value of Y)

Formula 6–5

$$\hat{X} = a_{xy} + b_{xy}Y$$

Here the predicted value of X is denoted by the symbol (read "X hat"). The calculation for determining the regression coefficient b_{xy} (rather than b as in Formula 6–3) is expressed in Formula 6–6.

Formula 6–6

$$b_{xy} = \frac{[n\Sigma XY] - [\Sigma X][\Sigma Y]}{[n\Sigma Y^2] - (\Sigma Y)^2}$$

Here the numerator is the same as in Formula 6–2. However, the denominator represents the sum of squares of the Y variable. Finally, Formula 6–7

Formula 6–7

$$a_{xy} = \bar{X} - b_{xy}\bar{Y}$$

expresses the calculation for the Y intercept, which is the value of X at the point where the regression line crosses the y-axis, that is, when $Y = 0$.

To illustrate the computation of the regression equation for X on Y, suppose we want to predict an individual's hours-at-speech-clinic score (X) on the basis of his or her self-esteem score (Y), using the distributions shown in Table 6–1.

Applying Formulas 6–6 and 6–7, we find the regression coefficient b_{xy} and the regression constant a_{xy} to be as follows:

$$b_{xy} = \frac{24(733) - 130(115)}{24(689) - (115)^2} = \frac{2642}{3311} = 0.80$$

(regression coefficient)

$$a_{xy} = 5.417 - 0.80(4.792) = 1.583$$

(regression constant)

Thus, the regression equation for predicting hours-at-speech clinic scores (X) based on what we know about self-esteem scores, as given in Formula 6–5, is as follows:

$$\hat{X} = 1.583 + 0.80(Y)$$

We now can use this regression equation to predict hours-at-speech-clinic scores (X) that correspond to self-esteem scores. For example, if an individual's self-esteem score is 1, we would predict that he or she will have his or her hours-at-speech clinic score be approximately 2 [$\hat{X}$ = 1.583 + 0.80(1) = 2.283]. Likewise, we would predict that the hours-at-speech-clinic-center score of an individual with a self-esteem score of 8 will be approximately 8 [$\hat{X}$ = 1.583 + 0.80(8) = 7.983]. As mentioned earlier, although these predicted values are not precisely those in the Y distribution shown in Table 6–1, they are reasonable close estimates of those values and are most likely values of the dependent variable. The sample distributions of original hours-at-speech-clinic

Table 6–3. Sample Distribution of Original Hours-at-Speech Clinic (X) and Self-Esteem Scores (Y) and Predicted Hours-at-Speech Clinic Values ($\hat{X}$)

X	Y	$\hat{X}$
1	1	2.383
2	3	3.983
2	4	4.783
3	2	3.183
4	6	6.383
5	2	3.183
5	6	6.383
6	3	3.983
6	7	7.183
7	5	5.583
7	7	6.038
8	4	4.783
8	9	8.783
9	8	7.983
9	9	8.783

scores (X) and self-esteem scores (Y) and the predicted hours-at-speech-clinic scores ($\hat{X}$) are shown in Table 6–3.

The scattergram shown in Figure 6–3 depicts the two regression lines for the two distributions derived from the Y on X and X on Y regression equations.[4] When the correlation between two variables is less than perfect, the two regression lines in a scattergram cross each other at the point where the means of the two distributions ($\overline{X}$, $\overline{Y}$) coincide. Note that the two regression lines cross at the point where the means of the two distributions, $\overline{X}$ = 5.417 and $\overline{Y}$ = 4.792, coincide.

To draw the regression line of X on Y using the predicted X values above, we place a small x at Y = 1, $\hat{X}$ = 2.383, and a small x at Y = 8, $\hat{X}$ = 7.983, and draw a line between the two points as shown in Figure 6–3.

Interpreting Predicted Values

We have seen that the predicted values of Y on X and X on Y in the illustrations above often do not equal the actual values from which they were derived by the regression equation. For example, in the first illustration above, the predicted self-esteem ($\hat{Y}$) score of an individual with 2 hours-at-speech-clinic hours is 2.103. However, a review of the X and Y distributions in Table 6–2 shows 2 hours-at-speech-clinic-center cases corresponding with self-esteem scores of 3 and 4. The discrepancy, as we mentioned, is referred to as *prediction error*, which occurs whenever correlations between the two variables are less than perfect. Therefore, in the absence of a perfect correlation between two variables, it is more prudent to interpret the predicted scores as the

---

[4]Recall the regression equation for Y on X is $\hat{Y}$ = a + bX = $\hat{Y}$ = 0.529 + 0.787(X).

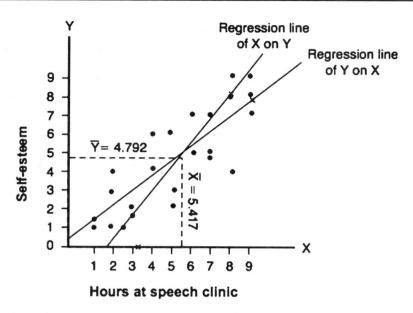

Figure 6–3. Hours at speech clinic and degree of self-esteem part 2.

expected average or mean value of a Y or X score, rather than a precise score.

Increasing the Accuracy of Predictions

Although we may not be able to predict a precise Y or X value or X or Y, it is possible to establish a range or interval within which a Y or X value falls, and thereby increase the accuracy of the prediction. As with all estimations, to determine the interval within which the "true" predicted value falls, we need to derive a standard error of estimate of a Y or X measure predicted from an X or Y score in the regression equation. However, in order to use this estimate in predicting, three assumptions or conditions must be satisfied. The first assumption is that relationship between the two variables must be linear. The second assumption is that the distributions of X and Y are normal,

or approximately normal. Finally, the third assumption is that the standard deviations of the two distributions are equal. This condition is known as **homoscedasticity**. If these three conditions are met, we can obtain the appropriate standard error of estimate and compute the interval within which a predicted X or Y score will fall. Let us examine both of these approaches to prediction.

> The condition known as *homoscedasticity* refers to the assumption that the standard deviations of two correlated variables are equal.

The Standard Error of Estimate in Predicting $\hat{Y}$

The standard error of estimate in regression analysis is a measure of the amount of error in prediction. It is a kind of standard deviation, reflecting the variability of observed scores around the regression line. As we have seen, when the correlation between X and Y is perfect, all of the data points are perfectly aligned on the regression line, and the standard error of estimate is equal to zero. Therefore, the larger the standard error of estimate becomes, the greater the scatter or dispersion of scores around the regression line becomes.

When Y scores are predicted from X scores, the standard error of estimate is denoted by the symbol, (read "$s\,y$ dot x"), and calculated as given in Formula 6–8.

Formula 6–8

$$s_{y \cdot x} = s_y \sqrt{1 - r^2}$$

Where

s_y = the standard deviation of the Y distribution

r^2 = the coefficient of determination

Consider again, the data in Table 6–1 and our interest in predicting an individual's self-esteem (Y) score based on an hours-at-speech-clinic value (X). As indicated in Table 6–1, given the coefficient of determination $r^2 = 0.629$ ($r = 0.793$) and the standard deviation of the Y distribution $s_y = 2.45$, the standard estimate of Y using Formula 6–8 is calculated as follows:

$$s_{y \cdot x} = 2.45 \sqrt{1 - 0.629}$$

$$= 2.45(0.609)$$

$$= 1.492$$

For the data in our scenario, the interval that contains the best estimate for predicting a self-esteem score (Y) is a given hours-at-speech-clinic value, plus or minus ($\pm$) 1.492, as denoted in Formula 6–9.

Formula 6–9

$$\hat{Y} = X_x \pm s_{y \cdot x}$$

Where

$\hat{Y}$ = predicted Y value

X_x = an X value

$s_{y \cdot x}$ = the standard error of estimate for Y on X

For example, the best estimate of the self-esteem score for an individual who spends 4 hours per week at a speech-clinic center, applying Formula 6–9, falls between the lower and upper limits of the following interval.

$$\hat{Y} = 4 \pm 1.492$$

$$= (2.508, 5.492)$$

Note that the standard error of estimate for Y on X (or X on Y) is a form of maximum error in estimating the interval containing the true predicted value. Therefore, we can say that the best estimate of a self-esteem score for someone who spends 4 hours per week at a speech-clinic-center is 4 ± 1.492 points. Finally, recall that the predicted self-esteem score ($\hat{Y}$) for someone who spends 4 hours per week at a speech clinic, using the regression equation in Formula 6–1, for values 4 was 3.667, as shown in Table 6–2 [$\hat{Y} = 0.529 + 0.787(4) = 3.677$].

The Standard Error of Estimate in Predicting

The formula for computing the standard estimate error of estimate to determine the interval that contains the true predicted values for X scores is shown in Formula 6–10.

Formula 6–10

$$s_{x \cdot y} = s_x \sqrt{1 - r^2}$$

Where

s_x = the standard deviation of the X distribution

r^2 = the coefficient of determination

The equation is identical in function to that expressed in Formula 6–8, except for the subscripts to denote that predicted X values are the values of interest. Applying Formula 6–10 to the data in our illustration, the standard error of estimate for X on Y, where the standard deviation for hours-at-speech-clinic is s_x = 2.469 and the coefficient of determination is r^2 = 0.629, is calculated as follows:

$$s_{x \cdot y} = 2.469 \sqrt{1 - 0.629}$$

$$= 2.469(0.609)$$

$$= 1.504$$

The equation for predicting hours-at-speech-clinic-center (X) values from self-esteem scores (Y) is identical in function to that of Formula 6– 9 except for symbols as given in Formula 6–11

Formula 6–11

$$\hat{X} = Y_x \pm s_{x \cdot y}$$

Where

$\hat{X}$ = predicted X value

$\hat{Y}_x$ = a Y value

$s_{x \cdot y}$ = the standard error of estimate for X on Y

For the data in our scenario, the interval that contains the best estimate for predicting an hours-at-speech clinic (X) value is a given self-esteem score, plus or minus ($\pm$) 1.504. In this case, the equation for the interval containing the best estimate of hours-at-speech clinic values, based on the self-esteem score, is given as $\hat{X} = Y_x \pm$ 1.504. For example, the best estimate of the number of hours an individual will spend at a speech clinic center, based on his or her self-esteem score of 5, using Formula 6–11, falls within the interval, 3.496 – 5.704 [$\hat{X}$ = 5 $\pm$ 1.504 = (3.496, 6.504)]. Similarly, the best estimate of the hours-at-speech-clinic value for someone with a self-esteem score of 6 is 6 $\pm$ 1.504 or between 4.496 and 7.504 hours per week. Finally, recall that the predicted hours-at speech clinic value ($\hat{X}$) for someone with self-esteem scores of 5 and 6, using the regression equation in Formula 6–1, were 5.583, [$\hat{X}$ = 1.583 $\pm$ 0.80(5) = 5.583] and 6.383 [$\hat{X}$ = 1.583 $\pm$ 0.806 = 6.383] respectively, as shown in Table 6–3.

Multiple Regression

When a regression analysis is extended to include two or more predictor variables, the technique is referred to as **multiple regression**. It is reasoned that two or more predictor variables, if correlated with the criterion variable, increase the accuracy of prediction. From a research perspective, a multiple regression analysis may be used in several ways. For example, a researcher may be interested in predicting some outcome based on what is known about two or more variables. Consider the admissions department at a graduate school interested in determining which applicants will succeed in the communication disorders program, where success is defined as maintaining an acceptable grade point average and graduating within a fixed time period. Or the researcher whose interest is more theoretical or basic, such as a psychologist who wants to identify trait characteristics, such as intelligence, self-concept, extroversion, that may be predictors of risk tolerance levels.

Basic Principles and Underlying Logic

The principles and basic logic of multiple regression analysis are the same as those for simple linear regression, where a criterion (dependent) variable (Y or X) is predicted from a correlated predictor (independent) variable (X or Y). In multiple regression analysis, the criterion or dependent variable is predicted from two or more predictor or independent variables, such as X_1, X_2 . . . X_k. In fact, the multiple regression equation is quite similar to that used in a simple regression analysis. For example, the multiple regression equation using two independent variables, X_1 and X_2, to predict Y is basically an extension of the formula used in the case of single predictor variable and given in Formula 6–1.

Formula 6–12

$$\hat{Y} = b_1X_1 + b_2X_2 + a$$

Where

a = regression constant

b_1 and b_2 = partial regression coefficients

X_1 and X_2 = values of two predictor variables

Most of the statistical techniques of multiple regression are beyond the scope of this text. However, we can develop a general understanding of their concepts and functions by examining the formulas and procedures used in developing a multiple regression equation for predicting values of a criterion variable (Y), using two predictor variables (X_1 and X_2). The following scenario may not be directly related to the field of communication disorders (a clinically relevant example of a multiple linear regression model will be presented at a later section), although, it is a good example that illustrates the application of the method to the general behavioral and clinical sciences among young children that all clinical investigators may want to know.

Scenario

Consider the problem of youth violence, which at times appears to be pervasive throughout the United States, particularly among high school students. For example, a nationwide survey conducted by the researchers at the Centers for Disease Control and Prevention in 1998, found that more than 36% of the 10,000 high school students surveyed, reported having been "in at least one fight in the past 12 months," where fighting was defined as two or more individuals hitting, punching, kicking, slapping, or pushing each other.[5] The problem is intensified because early aggressive and/or violent behavior are two of the strongest predictors of adult violence.

---

[5]Grunbaum, J. A. et. al. (2003). *Youth Risk Behavior Surveillance—United States*. Division of Adolescent and School Health, National Center for Chronic Disease Prevention and Health Promotion, CDC, USA.

According to the theory of reasoned action, the best determinants of behavior are: (1) a person's attitude toward performing or not performing the behavior and (2) the perception he or she has of how "relevant others" (peers, parents, school officials, etc.) view the behavior.[6] This latter factor is referred to as "subjective norms." Now suppose a researcher is interested in the predisposition to fight among high school girls who have expressed an interest in joining a street gang. Specifically, the researcher wants to determine the extent to which attitudes toward fighting and subjective norms predict a willingness to fight among girls in this population. In this hypothetical study, attitude-toward-fighting and subjective-norms are the independent (predictor) variables and willingness-to-fight is the dependent (criterion) variable.

The researcher administers three survey instruments to a random sample of 12 high school girls who have expressed an interest in joining a street gang and obtains the data shown in Table 6–4.

In the multiple regression equation for this illustration, the two predictor variables, attitude-toward-fighting and subjective-norms will be denoted by the symbols X_1 and X_2, respectively. The criterion variable, willingness-to-fight, is represented by the symbol Y.

Developing the Multiple Regression Equation

The process of developing the multiple regression equation expressed in Formula 6–12 involves two steps. First, the values b_1 and b_2, referred to as *partial regres-*

Table 6–4. Attitude-Toward-Fighting (X_1), "Subjective Norms" (X_2), and Willingness-to-Fight (Y) Survey Data

X_1	X_2	Y
6	12	52
10	22	49
12	20	53
13	12	50
15	7	48
17	28	60
19	21	63
19	23	59
20	18	70
22	27	64
25	22	67
27	18	69
Σ 205	230	704
$\overline{X}$ 17.083	19.167	58.667
s 6.19	6.24	8.05

sion coefficients and the regression constant, a., are calculated. Next, the multiple regression equation is used to predict a criterion value, $\hat{Y}$. The formulas used to calculate b_1, b_2, and a are given as in Formulas 6–13, 6–14, and 6–15.

Formula 6–13

$$b_1 = \left[\frac{r_{X_1 Y} - (r_{X_2 Y})(r_{X_1 X_2})}{1 - r_{X_1 X_2}} \right] \left(\frac{s_y}{s_{x_1}} \right)$$

---

[6]See, for example, I. Ajzen & M. Fishbein. (1980). *Understanding Attitudes and Predicting Social Behavior.* Englewood Cliffs, NJ: Prentice Hall.

Where

$r_{X_1 X_Y}$ = the correlation between the first predictor variable and the criterion variable

$r_{X_2 X_Y}$ = the correlation between the second predictor variable and the criterion variable

$r_{X_1 X_2}$ = the correlation between the first and second predictor variables

s_y = the standard deviation of the criterion variable (Y)

s_{X_1} = the standard deviation of the first predictor variable (X)

Formula 6–14

$$b_2 = \left[\frac{r_{X_2 Y} - (r_{X_2 X_Y})(r_{X_2 X_2})}{1 - r_{X_2 X_2}}\right]\left(\frac{s_Y}{s_{X_2}}\right)$$

Where

s_{X_2} = standard deviation of the second predictor variable

Formula 6–15

$$a = \overline{Y} - [(b_1)(\overline{X}_1) + (b_2)(\overline{X}_2)]$$

Where

$\overline{Y}$ = mean of the criterion variable

$\overline{X}_1$ = mean of the first predictor variable

$\overline{X}_2$ = mean of the second predictor variable

Note that calculations in these three formulas utilize the means and standard deviations of the two predictor variables X_1 and X_2 and the criterion variable Y, and the correlation coefficients for each pair of variables $(r_{X_1 X_2}; r_{X_1 X_Y};$ and $r_{X_2 X_Y})$. In the multiple regression equation with two predictors, b_1 is the expected change in Y when X_1 changes one unit, whereas X_2 remains constant. Similarly, b_2 is the expected change in Y when X_2 changes one unit and X_1 remains constant.

For the data in our illustration, the means and standard deviations for the three variables as shown in Table 6–2 are as follows:

attitude-toward-fighting (X_1)
$$\overline{X}_1 = 17.083 \qquad s_1 = 6.19$$

subjective-norms (X_2)
$$\overline{X}_3 = 19.167 \qquad s_1 = 6.24$$

willingness-to-fight (Y)
$$\overline{Y} = 58.667 \qquad s_1 = 8.05$$

The correlations between the distributions are as follows:

attitude-toward-fighting
and subjective-norms $r_{X_1 X_2} = .391$

attitude-toward-fighting and
willingness-to-fight $r_{X_1 X_Y} = .85$

subjective-norms and
willingness-to-fight $r_{X_2 X_Y} = .487$

For these data, the correlation between the two predictor variables, attitude-toward-fighting and subjective-norms is very low $(r_{X_1 X_2} = .391)$. The correlation between the variables subjective-norms and willingness-to-fight $(r_{X_2 X_Y} = .487)$ is low to moderate. And, the correlation between attitude-toward-fighting and willingness-to-fight $(r_{X_1 X_Y} = .85)$ is high and significantly greater than the correlation coefficients of the other two correlations. In an ideal situation, the most accurate prediction of $\hat{Y}$ scores would occur when the correlation between the two independent variables is low and the correlations between each predictor and the criterion variable is high.[7] This is not the case of the data in our illustration. Therefore, in our illustration the attitude-toward-fighting scores (X_1), when entered into the regression equation, will have a greater effect in predicting willingness-to-fight scores $(\hat{Y})$ than will the scores of the subjective-norms variable (X_2).

Applying Formulas 6–13, 6–14, and 6–15 to the data in this scenario, we find the partial regression coefficients to be

$$b_1 = \left[\frac{.85 - (.487)(.391)}{1 - .391}\right] \cdot \left(\frac{8.05}{6.19}\right)$$

$$= 1.01$$

$$b_2 = \left[\frac{.487 - (.85)(.391)}{1 - .391}\right] \cdot \left(\frac{8.05}{6.24}\right)$$

$$= 0.236$$

Here the partial regression coefficient associated with the first predictor variable, b_1, is greater than the coefficient of the second predictor, b_2. This is expected since the correlation between attitude-toward-fighting and willingness-to-fight is higher than the correlation between subjective-norms and willingness-to-fight.

Applying Formula 6–15, we find the regression constant to be,

$$= 36.9$$

and the multiple regression equation, applying Formula 6–12, is given as

$$\hat{Y} = 36.9 + 1.01X_1 + 0.236X_2$$

With this equation, we can calculate the predicted Y scores (willingness-to-fight) for any given values of attitude-toward-fighting (X_1) and subjective-norms scores (X_2). For example, for a high school female, with an attitude-toward-fighting score of 12 and a subjective-norms score of 20, we would predict a willingness-to-fight score of 53.74, that is,

$$\hat{Y} = 36.9 + 1.01(12) + 0.236(20)$$

$$= 53.74$$

Again, it is important to keep in mind that predicted values are estimates rather than absolutes. And in the case of our illustration, with a sample size of only 12, the estimates are to be considered illustrative but very tentative.

Clinical Applications of Measures of Association

In general, correlation and regression help the clinical investigators to identify, examine, measure, and predict the trend or tendency between the variables of interest. Specifically, correlation examines the strength of association between two or more variables, none of which is considered the variable one tries to predict from the others. On the other hand, regression analysis examines the ability of one or more influential factors (independent variables) to predict the clinical outcomes of interest (dependent variables). So, the key issue here is how well the dependent

---

[7]Of course, if the predictor variables are perfectly correlated ($r = 1.00$), using one of them in a simple regression equation provides as much accuracy in prediction as using both of them in a multiple regression equation.

measure is affected and predicted by a set of selected independent measures. In a clinical setting, a regression model can be used to construct clinical prediction rules that help to guide clinical decisions, whereas correlation analysis can be used to measure the strength of association between the variables (independent and dependent measures), that is to say, how strongly or closely two or more target variables are related to one another without prediction of the variable. Therefore, in this section, I discuss the fundamentals of clinical applications of such two techniques. I refer to the first technique—measuring the magnitude of the association between different variables or phenomena —as "correlation method," and the second technique—making a prediction or causal inference—as "regression method."

Clinical Applications of Correlation Method

As I noted earlier, "correlation method" is the statistical technique that measures the strength of the relation between the variables of interest. But what does it really mean in a clinical setting? The easiest way to interpret the test result is to consider the following hypothetical, yet realistic, two clinically relevant examples.

Example 1

Let us now illustrate an application of correlation methods in the analysis of an example involving the association between hearing vocabulary and IQ scores. For this purpose, imagine that we have randomly chosen a group of nine

subjects for whom scores on the Peabody Picture Vocabulary Test-Revisited (PPVT-R, denoted by X) and the Stanford-Binet Intelligence Scale (SBIS, denoted by Y) were obtained. Using the formula and steps, as discussed in the chapter of Correlation, the following hypothetical data set can be derived and summarized in Table 6–5.

As noted earlier, a correlation in this range is indicative of a moderate relationship between two variables. Also, as previously discussed in the earlier session of the chapter, the coefficient of determination R^2 is calculated as 0.4356 (43.56%). Therefore, based on the previous example pertaining to the PPVT-R and SBIS, the proportion of variance in Y (SBIS) predictable from X (PPVT-R) is 43.56%. The common variance shared by X and Y variables is slightly below 50%.

As mentioned earlier, the range of the correlation is −1 and +1, so what is the case that the value of r gets closer to +1 or −1 in a clinical setting? The following hypothetical example illustrates such a case.

Example 2

Suppose a clinician wants to investigate the relationship between severity of stuttering and the test scores on a diagnostic screening test for determining the degree of speech fluencies among young children. Historically, several clinical researchers have attempted to develop useful diagnostic criteria for differentiating the nonfluencies of children who are incipient stutterers from normal fluent children. Based on an amalgam of the data, Adams (1984) noted common profile characteristics which included the following

Table 6–5. Calculation of the Pearson Product-Moment Correlation Coefficient (r) Based on Hypothetical Data for PPVT-R Test Scores (X) and SBIS Test Scores (Y)

X	Y	X²	Y²	X·Y
115	105	13225	11025	12075
105	90	11025	8100	9450
110	94	12100	8836	10340
95	120	9025	14400	11400
89	104	7921	10816	9256
126	135	15876	18225	17010
77	70	5929	4900	5390
100	80	10000	6400	8000
90	70	8100	4900	6300
$\Sigma X = 907$	$\Sigma Y = 868$	$\Sigma X^2 = 93201$	$\Sigma X^2 = 87602$	$\Sigma X \cdot Y = 89221$

Result $r = 0.66$ (moderate strength of association)
$R^2 = (0.66)^2 = 0.4356$ or 43.56%

signs and symptoms: (1) part-word repetitions and prolongations make up in excess of 7% of all words spoken, (2) the part-word repetitions are marked by at least 3 unit repetitions (e.g., "bee-bee-bee-beet" versus "bee-bee-beet"), (3) the part-word repetitions are also perceived as containing the schwa in place of the vowel normally found in the syllable that is being repeated (e.g., "buh-buh-buh-beet" versus "bee-bee-beet"), (4) the prolongations last longer than one second, and (5) difficulty in starting or stopping airflow and/or sustaining airflow is heard in association with the part-word repetitions and prolongation.

According to Adams (1984), if a client exhibits none or only one of these signs, a differential evaluation of Normal disfluency is usually made. However, if the client should exhibit two or three of the five signs, a more ambiguous or borderline clinical picture would emerge; therefore, (s)he is usually diagnosed as Moderately Severe. Finally, for the client showing four or all five of the listed symptoms, a diagnosis of incipient stuttering would be made along with recommendations for therapy intervention, that is to say, the client is diagnosed as Severe.

The purpose of this example is not to argue for or against the validity of these behavioral criteria or any others that might be emphasized in the diagnostic process. Rather, I have chosen to use these particular indicators for purposes of illustrating an example application of the methods of association (especially the case that r gets closer to the extreme points +1 or −1) for measuring the strength of relation between a clinician's diagnostic decision (severitY) and the number of symptoms observed. Suppose we let X designate the number of symptoms that the clinician observed, and Y designates the degree of severity (say, 1 = Normal, 2 = Moderately Severe, and 3 = Severe). It is obvious to see that the correlation coefficient r between X and Y is very strongly positive (close enough to be a +1). On the other hand, if the severity is reversed such as 1 = Severe, 2 = Moderately Severe, and 3 = Normal, the correlation coefficient r will get closer to a −1.

Very often when we use the statistical software, we will see a p-value provided with a correlation coefficient. Although more details about p-value and hypothesis tests are discussed in later chapters, the author gives an overview of p-value associated with correlation.

Normally we state two conflicting hypotheses about r in a target population. Symbolically, we write them as follows:

H_o (the null hypothesis): $r = 0$ (No relation exists between X and Y)

H_a (alternative hypothesis): $r \neq 0$ (A significant relation between X and Y exists)

As a rule of thumb, the smaller the p-value, the less likely it is that chance explains the apparent association between the two variables. Within the context of hypothesis tests method, we will reject H_o in favor of H_a.

The p-value derived from the correlation analysis is contingent upon not only the strength of association (the value of r itself), but also the sample size (n). If n becomes larger, the threshold for rejecting H_o gets smaller. For instance, with $n = 50$, if the observed r-value is less than 0.2732; we reject H_o in favor of H_a. But with $n = 100$, if the observed r-value is less than 0.1946, we will reject H_o in favor of H_a.

As discussed in the Introduction, the Bayesian approach (EBP Statistical Methods) gives much more informative results than the traditional p-value and hypothesis tests approaches. The Bayesian version of a p-value (called the Minimum Bayes Factor) is presented and illustrated through clinically relevant examples in later chapters. Using the Minimum Bayes Factor, we can measure the strength of association between the variables more accurately (that leads to a more credible and reliable diagnosis). After all, under the EBP, a clinician needs to know how to evaluate the amount of clinical evidence against her clinical belief based on what she observed, and interpret the results correctly.

Clinical Applications of Regression Method

As noted earlier, when the main goal of the clinical investigation is to measure or quantify the relationship between variables of interest, the correlation method is the most useful tool for this purpose. However, given that the correlation observed between two data sets is reasonably high, next a clinician might want to estimate individual scores on one of two correlated variables from scores obtained on the other. Such an estimate is made possible by the use of the various regression techniques (simple, multiple, or logistic), as discussed in the previous chapter. As a clinical practitioner/researcher, we are often interested in predictions: we may wish to know which client(s) will have a particular fluency disorder and which will not, and which client(s) will fare well after the completion of the intense speech therapy sessions and which will fare poorly. In a clinical setting, regression analysis is one of the most powerful tools in addressing these kind of important issues.

Let us now illustrate the use of a simple linear regression model in predicting an individual's SBIS score from a test score obtained on the PPVT-R, as we previously discussed. For this purpose, we calculate the slope and y-intercept of the regression line, and it is given by $\hat{Y} = 0.97 \cdot X - 1.32$. We further assume that one client of interest scored an 103 on the PPVT-R. Given these knowledge, how can we use this information to estimate the SBIS score obtained by the same individual? As we did before, we replace X in the equation above by the PPVT-R score of 103. This yields the predicted SBIS score (approximately 99). Given this hypothetical result, we can conclude that hearing vocabulary, as assessed by the PPVT-R, was a good predictor of intelligence as measured by SBIS.

There are many types of regression techniques in addition to simple linear regression that have application to a variety of clinical and research problems. Suppose a clinician wants to estimate a score on the SBIS from more than one predictor (PPVT-R and several other factors that might influence intelligence). In this case, the clinician necessitates the use of more comprehensive regression techniques. As noted earlier, one of these methods, called multiple regression, permits the simultaneous estimation of a criterion variable from several predictor variables. Thus, instead of using only the scores obtained on the PPVT-R to predict IQ scores, we might have incorporated such other semantic language measures as found on the Clinical Evaluation of Language Fundamentals (CELF-R) and the Woodcock-Johnson Psycho-Educational Battery (WJ-R) among many others. For the illustration purpose, a clinician has decided to use PPVT-R and WJ-R to predict SBIS score. Since there

are two predictors, we call it a two-way multiple regression line. Furthermore, the clinician might want to determine the interaction effect of PPVT-R and WJ-R, in addition to such two main effects as PPVT-R (denoted by X_1) and WJ-R (denoted by X_2). The interaction effect of the two is symbolically denoted by X_{1x2}. The equation of the multiple linear regression line is expressed as follows:

$$\hat{Y} = b_0 \text{ (y-intercept)} + b_1 \cdot X_1$$
$$\text{(PPVT-R effect)} + b_2 \cdot X_2 \text{ (WJ-R effect)}$$
$$+ b_{1x2} \cdot X_{1x2} \text{ (Interaction effect)}$$

We further assume that such p-values are derived. The results are summarized in Table 6–6 shown below.

The hypothetical results shown above reveal that a highly strong interaction effect, moderately strong main effect 1, and weak main effect 2 were observed. The coefficient of determination $R^2 = 0.62$ indicates that 62% of the variability in the SBIS scores can be accounted for by knowing three predictors. But what if R^2 is much weaker (smaller), say, for instance, 0.005? This would mean that only 0.5% of the total variability in the SBIS is predicted (or explained) by the three predictors. This is the case that the clinician

Table 6–6. Calculation Tables for the Multiple Linear Regression Study: Predicting SBIS Scores from PPVT-R and WJ-R Scores

Effect(s)	p-value
Main Effect 1 (PPVT-R)	0.03
Main Effect 2 (WJ-R)	0.15
Interaction Effect (1 × 2)	0.01
	$R^2 = 0.62$

may want to apply an appropriate type of nonlinear (curvilinear) regression method to increase the accuracy of prediction, that is, increase the amount of R^2 to a larger extent.

This example gives us two important key points about regression analysis. First, we always have to check if all given data points would form the linearity of relationships and the shapes of distributions. This can be checked by a Linear Fit Test as seen in several statistical software like MINITAB, SAS, SPSS, and so on, to determine whether or not the linear regression model is appropriate. Second, the clinician must know that choosing an appropriate regression model has a definitive positive impact on the accuracy of the findings. An inappropriate analysis may hinder a true relationship that might actually exist in the data. For instance, there are a number of multivariate techniques that can be used to predict a binary dependent measure from a set of independent measures. Among these, multiple regression techniques have numerous applications in answering a variety of clinical and research questions, such as: What factors in a client's history best predict a certain communication disorder? What clinical and laboratory data best identify clients with such disorders? What therapy procedures are most likely to predict favorable clinical outcomes? On the other hand, such techniques have major limitations when the dependent variable has dichotomous values, for instance, an event either occurs or does not occur. In this situation, the assumptions required for performing multiple regression analysis, such as normality and/or homogeneity of the variances, will be violated.

In most cases, both correlation and regression assume that the existence of a linear relationship between variables of interest. When the data fail to meet this requirement, the clinical investigator has three alternatives. They are as follows.

Linear Transformation of the Data

In some cases, a linear relationship can be created by an appropriate transformation of the data. For example, in Communication Sciences and Disorders, the treatment-response relationship among young children is less likely to form a linear relationship, because of covariates (the secondary unwanted variables, other than the treatment effect, that may affect a dependent measure; that is, anxiety, stress, and the like), while the corresponding logarithm of treatment-response relationship may be linear. The logarithm with base 10 or e, or square/cube roots, is most commonly used on transformation functions to maintain linearity.

Nonlinear Regression Analysis

Although it is mathematically possible to use more complex regression methods without maintaining linearity, such as identify the relationships between the variables by means of trigonometric functions, and so on. But these methods are considerably more complex and time consuming; every effort should be made to identify a suitable linear transformation of the original data.

Reduce/Add/Replace Predictors

In some cases, an investigator may want to convert or modify the nonlinear regression model to linear regression model by dropping, adding, or replacing predictors till it forms linearity. Several difficulties are as follows: (a) in case that the original data values are dichotomous, we need

Table 6–7. Test Results for Hypothetical Linear Regression Study: Investigating a Relationship Between the Intensity of a New Speech Therapy Treatment for Stuttering (X) and a Number of Correct Responses on a Post-Test (Y)

Intensity Level (X)	# of Correct Responses (Y)
1	4
2	7
3	8
4	14
5	15

Note. (1) Intensity level was divided into five categories such as 1 = weak, 2 = moderately weak, 3 = moderate, 4 = moderately strong, 5 = strong. (2) Observed t-value concerning the test of a slope = 7.034 (two-sided test H_o: $\beta_1 = 0$ (X and Y are not linearly related) versus H_a: $\beta_1 \neq 0$ (X and Y are linearly related)), $n = 5$, d.f. = 3, b_1 (the slope of the regression line) = 2.9, b_0 (the y-intercept of the regression line) = 0.9, Fisher's p-value (two-sided test) = 0.0059, and $R^2 = 0.943$.

to use logistic regression model, as we discussed previously. This method is only useful when we estimate the probability of occurrence of an event, so it is rather limited, (b) it may lose the original intention of the study, that is, we may not be able to answer the original research questions in an accurate manner, and (c) it is a time consuming task to identify a set of new suitable predictors and unsuitable predictors to build a linear regression model.

A Clinically Relevant Example of Linear Regression Model: A Bayesian Perspective

Suppose a clinical investigator wishes to investigate a relationship between the intensity of a new speech therapy treatment for stuttering (X) and the number of correct responses on a post-test (Y). The hypothetical data and results are illustrated in Table 6–7 shown below:

Next, we find MBF (Minimum Bayes Factor) and Posterior probabilities of H_o and H_a. The results are showin in Table 6–8.

Key Terms and Concepts

Regression analysis

Principle of regression

Linear regression

Regression line

Method of least squares

Regression of Y on X

Regression coefficient

Slope

Regression constant

Intercept

Regression equation

Regression of X on Y

Prediction error

Homoscedasticity

Multiple regression

Partial regression coefficients

Table 6–8. Minimum Bayes Factor (MBF) and Posterior Probabilities of H_o and H_a Based on the Hypothetical Study Illustrated in Table 6–7

Prior for H_o	Prior for H_a	MBF*	Posterior for H_o	Posterior for H_a
0.1	0.9	0.00905	0.0010	0.9990
0.2	0.8	0.00905	0.0023	0.9977
0.3	0.7	0.00905	0.0039	0.9961
0.4	0.6	0.00905	0.0060	0.9940
0.5	0.5	0.00905	0.0090	0.9910
0.6	0.4	0.00905	0.0134	0.9986
0.7	0.3	0.00905	0.0207	0.9793
0.8	0.2	0.00905	0.0349	0.9651
0.9	0.1	0.00905	0.0753	0.9247
0.8533**	0.1467	0.00905	0.05**	

*Sources for Calculation of MBF: Perception and Cognitive Lab, Department of Psychological Sciences, University of Missouri, http://www.pcl.missouri.edu/bayesfactor

**MBF of 0.00905 indicates that the amount of evidence against H_o, in a Bayesian perspective, is only *Moderately Strong*, whereas frequentists Fisher's *p*-value 0.0059 suggests that the result was *Statistically Highly Significant*. Therefore, MBF shows that the *p*-value obtained from the study overstates the evidence against H_o and, consequently, the result exaggerates the degree of statistical significance. It also shows how low initial confidence in H_o (Prior for H_o) must be the result in 5% confidence after observing data (that is 95% confidence in a non-null effect), or equivalently, the posterior probability of H_o is less than 0.05). With the conventional Fisher's *p*-value of 0.05 thresholds, the prior probability of H_o must be at most 0.8533 (85.33%) to allow an investigator to conclude with 95% confidence that H_o is false. This means even when you start out stating $P(H_o) = 0.8533$, believing that the null effect is most likely than the non-null effect before seeing data, the actual sample data have led the investigator to believe that the true treatment effect will be more than a 95% chance, that is, the actual evidence is strong enough to move 85.33% skepticism about the effectiveness of the treatment to less than a 5% skepticism about it. This calculation is not meant to interpret "95%" in the Bayesian approach, but rather to show the readers what will happen when similar benchmarks are used in the two approaches.

Feedback Review of Chapter 6

1. In the regression equation $\hat{Y} = a + bX$, b is called the
   a. regression constant.
   b. regression coefficient.
   c. regression line.
   d. regression estimate.
   e. *Y*-intercept.

2. In the regression equation, $\hat{Y} = a + bX$, a is called the
   a. regression constant.
   b. regression coefficient.
   c. regression line.
   d. regression estimate.
   e. slope.

3. At the *Y*-intercept of the regression line of *Y* on *X*, the value of *X* equals

a. 1.0
b. −1.0
c. 0
d. 0.5
e. X^2

4. Galton referred to the tendency for tall fathers to have shorter sons, and short fathers to have taller sons as the principle of
   a. regression.
   b. linearity.
   c. bivariate correlation.
   d. homoscedasticity.
   e. all of the above.

5. The statistical technique that determines the line that best fits the data is known as the
   a. correlation analysis.
   b. linear regression.
   c. regression analysis.
   d. regression principle.
   e. method of least squares.

6. In multiple regression analysis, b_1 and b_2 are referred to as
   a. slope and Y intercept of a straight line.
   b. Y intercept and slope of a straight line.
   c. mean and standard deviation of the X variable.
   d. mean and standard deviation of the Y variable.
   e. a & c

7. In multiple regression analysis, b_1 and b_2, are referred to as
   a. independent variables.
   b. dependent variables.
   c. partial regression constants.
   d. partial regression coefficients.
   e. criterion variables.

8. The standard error of estimate
   a. is a measure of the amount of error in prediction.
   b. is a kind of standard deviation.
   c. denoted by the symbol $s_{y \cdot x}$
   d. denoted by the symbol $s_{x \cdot y}$
   e. all of the above

9. In regression analysis, the condition where the standard deviation of the Y distribution is equal to the standard deviation of the distribution of X scores is known as
   a. bivariate linearity.
   b. residual variance.
   c. homogeneity of variance.
   d. homoscedascity.
   e. all of the above.

10. In an ideal multiple regression situation, the most accurate prediction of $\hat{Y}$ scores would occur when the correlations between the predictor variables
    a. are high but each is highly correlated with the criterion variable.
    b. are low but each is highly correlated with the criterion variable.
    c. and the criterion variable are high.
    d. and the criterion variable are low.
    e. none of the above

Fill-Ins

1. The predicted score in regression is denoted by the symbol _____.

2. The line that best describes the linear relationship between two variables is called the _____ line.

3. When the independent and dependent variables are perfectly correlated, the standard error of estimate is equal to _____.

4. The difference between an actual score and the score predicted by the regression equation is known as _____.

5. A best-fit, regression line is one in which the sum of the squared distances from the data points to the line is at a _____.

6. In regression analysis, the X variable is known as the _____ variable, and the Y variable is known as the _____ variable.

7. In cases where we want to predict Y scores from X, the technique is known as the regression of _____.

Review Problems

1. A researcher notices that communication disorders students who work out regularly at the college's fitness center appear to have higher levels of self-esteem as a clinician than those who use the center occasionally. He observes a random sample of students over a 6-week period and records the average number of hours each spends in the center on a weekly basis. He also obtains the self-esteem score of each student. The results are shown in Table 6–9.
   a. Construct a scatterplot of the distributions of the two variables.
   b. Determine the regression equation for Y on X, that is, self-esteem score (Y) based on the average number of hours spent in the fitness center on a weekly basis (X).

Table 6–9. The Results of a Hypothetical Study Concerning the Average Number of Hours Each Clinician Spends in the College's Fitness Center (X) and Their Self-Esteem Scores (Y)

Hours (X)	Self-Esteem (Y)	Hours (X)	Self-Esteem (Y)
13	9	9	7
12	10	9	7
12	10	8	6
11	9	8	7
11	10	8	6
11	9	7	8
11	8	7	6
10	5	7	5
10	8	5	5
10	9	5	4

c. In the scatterplot, draw the regression line of Y on X.

d. Using the regression equation for Y on X, predict the self-esteem score of a student who spends an average of 10 hours per week in the fitness center. Predict the self-esteem score of the student who spends 5 hours per week on average.

e. Determine the regression equation for X on Y, that is, the average number of hours spent in the fitness center per week (X) based on self-esteem (Y) score.

f. Using the regression equation for X on Y, predict the average number of hours per week a student with a self-esteem score of 12 spends in the fitness center. Also, for a student with a self-esteem score of 6.

g. In the scatterplot, draw the regression line of on Y on X.

2. Using the data in Question 1:

a. Determine the standard error of estimate for predicting Y scores from X. (Review procedures for finding standard deviations in Chapter 3.)

b. What is the best estimate for the self-esteem score of a student who spends an average of 12 hours per week in the fitness center?

c. Determine the standard error of estimate for predicting X scores from Y.

d. For the student with a self-esteem score of 8, what is the best estimate of the average number of hours he or she will spend in the fitness center per week?

3. A research team of educators and communication disorders researchers is interested in the relationship between delays in language development (X) and the onset of stuttering behavior among children who stutter (Y). The team gathers data on a sample of 10 children and obtains the following results:

$\Sigma X = 106$ $\Sigma Y = 121$ $\Sigma XY = 1557$
$\Sigma X^2 = 1484$ $\Sigma Y^2 = 1739$

Missing data: $\overline{X}$ s_x $\overline{Y}$ s_y r

a. Determine the regression equation for predicting the onset of stuttering behavior among children with delays in language development.

b. Using the regression equation predict the onset of stuttering score for a child with a delay-in-language-development score of 3. Also, for a child with a delay-in-language-development score of 7.

c. Determine the standard error of estimate for predicting Y scores from X.

d. Determine the standard error of estimate for predicting X scores from Y.

4. A college admissions director wants to predict the ratings of his Applicant Review Committee (ARC) using the ratings of an applicant's high school homeroom teacher (HST) and guidance counselor (GC) as predictors. He collects the data (Table 6–10) from a random sample of recently accepted applicants to the college.

a. Determine the regression equation for predicting the rating scores of the Applicant Review Committee (ARC).

Table 6–10. The Results of a Hypothetical Predictive Study Concerning the Ratings of Applicant Review Committee (ARC) Using Two Predictors as the Ratings of an Applicant's High School Homeroom Teacher (HST) and Guidance Counselor (GC)

GC	HST	ARC	GC	HST	ARC
X_1	X_2	Y	X_1	X_2	Y
4	8	5	14	18	15
5	9	7	13	17	13
8	8	9	14	7	15
8	7	10	15	13	14
9	12	11	15	12	13
10	14	12	16	11	17
11	8	12	17	12	16
11	13	14	18	14	18

b. Predict the ARC score of an applicant who had a guidance counselor (GC) rating of 9 and a high school teacher (HST) rating of 12.

c. Predict the ARC score of an applicant who had a guidance counselor (GC) rating of 15 and a high school teacher (HST) rating of 13.

5. A clinical/behavioral researcher is interested in predicting relational satisfaction (Y) for young adults who have been in a close (dating) relationship for more than 6 months, using measures of "openness" (X_1) and "positivity" (X_2) as predictor variables. She surveys a random sample of 30 young adults from the target population and obtains the following results on the three measures.

Openness (X_1)
$$\overline{X}_1 = 31.517 \quad s_1 = 5.223$$
Positivity (X_2)
$$\overline{X}_2 = 8.321 \quad s_2 = 2.130$$
Relational satisfaction (Y)
$$\overline{Y} = 16.53 \quad s_y = 3.414$$

The correlations between the distributions are as follows:

Openness and positivity
$$r_{X_1X_2} = .382$$
Openness and relational satisfaction $\quad r_{X_1X_Y} = .85$

Positivity and relational satisfaction $\quad r_{X_2X_Y} = .625$

a. Determine the regression equation for predicting relational satisfaction.

b. What is the predicted relational satisfaction score for someone who has an openness score of 52 and a positivity score of 16?

c. What is the predicted relational

satisfaction score for someone who has an openness score of 26 and a positivity score of 7?

7

The Standard Normal Distribution

Overview

Earlier we noted that researchers use inferential statistics to make generalizations about populations based on the observed results of samples. For instance, public opinion pollsters interested in voter preferences for presidential candidates do not survey every potential voter in the country. A clinical investigator interested in determining the prevalence rate of a particular fluency disorder does not investigate every subject who has the disorders. Rather, they survey a relatively small proportion of them and generalize the results to the population as a whole. How is this accomplished? How does a Gallop Poll manage to predict the outcome of presidential elections from samples as small as three thousand potential voters when the population of voters can exceed two hundred million?[1] From a statistical stand-point, the answer to such questions, in part, rests in the use of what are termed *sampling distributions*.

Briefly, **sampling distributions** are theoretical distributions that serve as the bases for generalizations about populations based on samples, supported by inferential statistics. Sampling distributions are derived from theorems with precise mathematical formulas and consist of an infinite number of values and distinct properties that define their makeup. These properties allow them to be used as probabilities distributions in comparing sample data from different distributions. We say more about sampling distributions throughout the remainder of the text. In this chapter, we focus on one of the more widely used theoretical distributions in inferential statistics, namely the *standard normal distribution*. However, by way of introduction, we first discuss theoretical distributions in general.

---

[1]Since 1948, for example, national polling organizations have accurately predicted the winner of presidential elections, usually within the margin of error of their polls.

The Nature of Theoretical Distributions

For any given set of data, the shape of the curve of a distribution may be symmetric or bell shaped; in others, it may be skewed. Distributions that are somewhat symmetric tend to become increasingly more symmetrical as more values are added to the sample. This characteristic is illustrated by the histograms of hypothetical distributions of caffeine levels of students during final exam week as shown in Figure 7–1. Note that as the size of the sample increases and the size or width of the intervals decrease, the shape of the distributions becomes "smoother" and less jagged.[2] Such a distribution may be said to have an infinite number of values (keeping in mind that the actual meaning of the word infinite is "without end").

> *Theoretical distributions* consist of an infinite number of values and a distinct set of properties that define their shape and characteristics. A *sampling distribution* is a theoretical distribution that serves as the basis for generalizations about populations based on samples.

The Normal Distribution

The theoretical distribution described above is known as the **normal distri-**

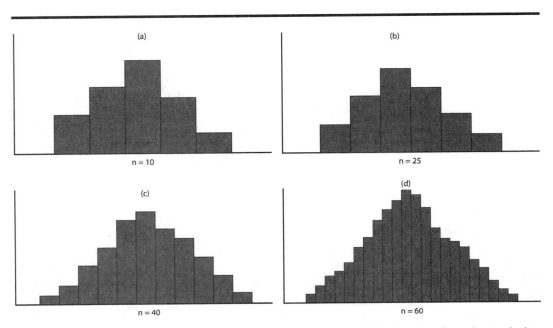

Figure 7–1. Histograms of hypothetical distributions of caffeine levels of students during final exam week.

[2]However, at some point, adding values and decreasing interval widths has little or no effect on the shape of the distribution.

bution. It is an idealized mathematical construct of what would be true or what we might expect if an infinite number of scores or values were obtained. In such a case, the result would be a perfectly symmetrical curve that is bell-shaped, such that its midpoint is at the highest point of the curve, with an identical value corresponding to the mode, mean, and median of the distribution, as depicted in Figure 7–2.[3] In reality, the normal distribution is not a single distribution but a family of distributions, each defined by an equation based on two parameters, the *population mean* (μ) and *standard deviation* (σ). The graph that depicts a normal distribution is called the **normal curve**, as depicted in Figure 7–1C.

> The *normal distribution* is a theoretical model of a distribution in which the values form a bell-shaped curve, its midpoint is at the highest point, corresponding to the mode, mean, and median of the distribution. The graph that depicts it is called the ***normal curve***.

Properties of the Normal Curve

While normal distributions and their respective curves may vary, depending on their respective means and standard deviation, they all share the same distinct properties that are inherent in Figure 7–2.

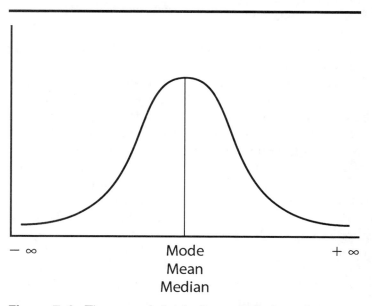

Figure 7–2. The normal distribution or bell-shaped curve.

---

[3]It was first derived in 1733 by the French mathematician Abraham DeMoivre and a hundred years later by Pierre Laplace in France and Carl Fredrich Gauss in Germany, independent of each other and unaware of DeMoivre's work. At the time of his discovery, DeMoivre was interested in probabilities associated with binomial variables, such as the outcomes of tossed coins. He observed that as the size of the sample increases (say from 5 to 10 coins), the histogram of the frequency distribution becomes increasingly more symmetric or bell-shaped, as illustrated in Figure 7–1.

1. The distribution is *unimodal.* In a normal distribution, the most frequently observed score or value (*X*) falls exactly at the midpoint and mean of the distribution. As the distance between the population mean (μ) and scores increases, the frequency with which a score occurs decreases, thus defining the bell shape of the distribution curve.

2. The normal distribution is symmetric about the mean, such that if the distribution were folded in half, the right and left sides would fall exactly on top of one another. In other words, the frequencies and proportion of the scores *above* the mean are identical to those *below* the mean.

3. The unimodal and symmetric properties of the distribution account for the mode, median, and mean having the same value.

4. The normal distribution is continuous, reflecting an infinite number of values, and for every value of *X*, there is a value of *Y*.

5. Finally, the distribution is said to be **asymptotic** to the horizontal axis, that is, as the tails of the distribution extend farther from the mean, they get closer and closer to *x*-axis but never touch it. This is because, in theory, the normal distribution actually extends from negative infinity ($-\infty$) to positive infinity ($+\infty$).

Many variables in the social, natural, and applied sciences are continuous and normally distributed, with symmetrical curves. These include: physical characteristics such as height, weight, and blood pressure levels; standardized tests scores in academic areas; and performance ratings in business and economics areas. The distributions of these variables, although not always perfectly bell-shaped, have the same properties as the theoretical normal distribution. Thus, when sample data approximate a symmetric distribution, they can be analyzed and described in a variety of ways based on the properties of the theoretical normal distribution and its applied model, the *standard normal distribution*.

> *Asymptotic* is the characteristic of the normal curve in which the tails of the distribution get closer to the horizontal axis (*x*-axis), but never touch it as they extend away from the mean to infinity.

The Standard Normal Distribution

Since most variables that are normally distributed have different means and standard deviations, comparing them or the individual data values within them becomes problematic. However, we can overcome this problem by converting different normal distributions to a common or standardized distribution. One such distribution is the **standard normal distribution**, also known as the *z-distribution*. It is a distribution of standard scores, specifically *z*-scores, with a population mean (μ) equal to zero and standard deviation (σ) units equal to one (1).[4] Recall that the raw scores of a normally distributed variable can be standardized into a distribution of *z*-scores using Formula 4–6, $\left| z = \frac{X - \bar{X}}{s} \right|$, introduced in Chapter 4. Because they are

---

[4]It can be demonstrated that if a given variable is normally distributed with parameters μ and σ, then $z = \frac{X - \bar{X}}{s}$ is normally distributed with parameters of 0 and 1.

standardized, z-scores across different distributions can be compared. Moreover, we can use them to determine proportions, percentiles, and percentile ranks. However, before we discuss these applications, we need to understand a little more about the structure of the standard normal distribution.

> The *standard normal distribution*, also referred to as the *z*-distribution, is a theoretical distribution with a mean of zero and standard deviation of one and the properties of the normal distribution.

Areas Under the Standard Normal Curve

The standard normal curve is divided into eight major areas representing four standard deviation units above and below its midpoint ($z = 0$). Because the area beyond the third standard deviation is so small, illustrations of the distribution show only three units on either side of the midpoint, as depicted in Figure 7–3.[5] Note that approximately 50% of the area under the curve falls above and below the z-score of zero ($z = 0$). The total area on either side of the mean actually equals 0.5, reflecting the infinite, asymptotic nature of the normal distribution. However, since there is a mathematical proof that demonstrates that the variance (and standard deviation) of z-scores always equal 1, statisticians often express the total area under the standard normal curve as being equal to 1.

Looking at Figure 7–3, we can easily determine the area under the curve between the mean and a given standard deviation. For example, 0.3413 of the area under the curve falls between $z = 0$ and $z = +1$. Put another way, we can say that

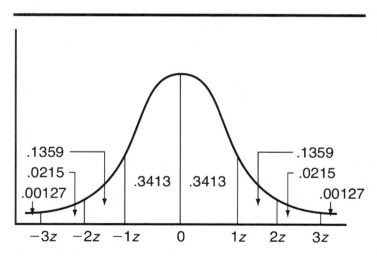

Figure 7–3. Areas under the standard normal curve.

---

[5]As mentioned earlier, transforming a raw score distribution into a standard score distribution does not change the shape of the distribution, just the mean and standard deviation or total area under the curve. Also, since the focus of interest in applied statistics is on the area under the standard normal distribution, graphs of the distribution generally omit values along the y-axis.

34.13% of the z-scores in the standard normal distribution fall between $z = 0$ and $z = +1$. Similarly, 0.3413 or 34.13% of the area under the curve falls between $z = 0$ and $z = -1$. Thus, 0.6826 of the area under the curve falls between one standard deviation above and below the mean, symbolically expressed as $z = \pm 1 = 0.6826$. In similar fashion, 0.9554% of the area falls within two standard deviations of the mean; 0.9974% falls within three standard deviations; and 0.9998% of the area falls within four standard deviations. These combined areas, as illustrated in Figure 7–3, form the basis of what is called the **empirical rule**, which states that for any symmetrical distribution, approximately 68% of all observations will fall within one standard deviation of the mean; 95% will fall within two standard deviations of the mean; and that 99.7% will fall within three standard deviations of the mean.[6] Thus, for a normal distribution, nearly all of the values will fall within 3 standard deviations ($\pm 1z$, $2z$, $3z$) of the mean.

To find the areas between the mean ($z = 0$) and any given standard deviation ($\pm 1z$, $2z$, $3z$, $4z$), we turn to Tables K–1, K–2, and K–3 found in Appendix K. A portion of the table is shown in Figure 7–4. The values of z are listed in Column A, and the area between the mean ($z = 0.00$) and a given z-score is listed in Column B; the area beyond a given z-score is listed in Column C. Tables K–1, K–2, and K–3 contain only the positive values of z-scores

A	B	C	A	B	C	A	B	C
	Area	Area		Area	Area		Area	Area
	Between	Beyond		Between	Beyond		Between	Beyond
z	$\overline{X}$ and z	z	z	$\overline{X}$ and z	z	z	$\overline{X}$ and z	z
0.00	.0000	.5000	0.40	.1554	.3446	0.80	.2881	.2119
...	...	...	...	...	...	...	...	...
0.20	.0793	.4207	0.60	.2257	.2743	1.00	.3413	.1587
...	...	...	...	...	...	...	...	...
1.20	.3849	.1151	1.60	.4452	.0548	2.00	.4772	.0228
...	...	...	...	...	...	...	...	...
2.55	.4946	.0054	2.95	.4984	.0016	4.00	.49997	.00003
...	...	...	...	...	...	...	...	...
2.60	.4953	.0047	3.00	.4987	.0013			

Figure 7–4. Areas between mean ($z - 0$) and any given standard deviation.

[6]A well-known theorem, known as *Chebyshev's rule*, states that for any set of population or sample data, the percentage of values within k standard deviations of the mean is *at least* $100 \left(1 - \frac{1}{k^2}\right)$%; that is, $1 - \frac{1}{16} = 94\%$. Using the Chebyshev rule, we find that at least 94% of the values in the distribution will fall within 4 standard deviations of the mean. The attractiveness of the Chebyshev rule is that it is applicable to any set of data, whether normal or skewed.

from 0.00 to 4.00. Because the standard normal curve is symmetrical, negative z-scores represent the same areas as positive z-scores, except that they fall below the mean ($z = 0$). For example, the area between $z = 0.00$ and $z = -1.00$ (0.3413), is identical to the area between $z = 0.00$ and $z = +1.00$ (0.3413). Finally, since the normal distribution represents continuous variables and contains an infinite number of values, Tables K–1, K–2, and K–3 are asymptotic, as indicated by the areas for $z = 4.00$ in Figure 7–2.

When a sample of data approximates the normal distribution, we can use the standard normal distribution and its curve to describe scores or values in a variety of ways, including proportions, percentiles, and percentile ranks, without the limitations inherent in their scales, which are ordinal with unequal intervals. As we noted in Chapter 4, ordinal scales tend to exaggerate differences between percentiles and percentile ranks at the center of the distribution and underestimate differences away from the center of the distribution. In the following sections, we introduce procedures for determining proportions, percentiles, and percentile ranks using the equal-interval scale of the standard normal distribution.

Determining Proportions

In cases where distributions are normally distributed, describing proportions of distribution in terms of the standard normal distribution has the distinct advantage of equal intervals. To illustrate, let us consider the following hypothetical situation that is relevant to communication and behavioral sciences.

Scenario

A researcher surveys a random sample of 2,200 first-year graduate students in a communication disorders program nationwide, administering a self-report measure related to a variable dealing with some of the rituals exhibited at the early stages of a friendship between members of the opposite sex. (We refer to this variable simply as "interpersonal-ritual.") Let us assume that the mean of the sample distribution is 65 ($\overline{X}$) and the standard deviations (s) are in units of 5. The distribution of these statistics and their corresponding z-values are listed along the baseline of the normal curve shown in Figure 7–5. With these two sample statistics, we can determine both

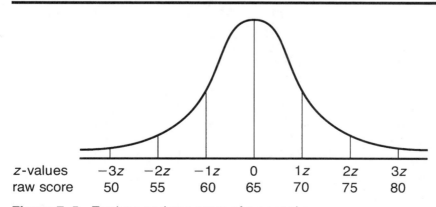

z-values	−3z	−2z	−1z	0	1z	2z	3z
raw score	50	55	60	65	70	75	80

Figure 7–5. *Z*-values and raw score of a normal curve.

the proportion and the number of cases or scores in the sample. Looking at Figure 7–5, we can readily see that approximately two thirds of the first-year graduate students in the program scores fall between scores 60 and 70, or within one standard deviation above and below the mean of 65. In raw score terms, we can say that 0.6826 or approximately 68% of the freshmen in the sample have scores between 60 and 70. In z-score terms, we say that 0.6826 scores fall between $z = -1.00$ (0.3413) and $z = +1.00$ (0.3413). To find the actual number of students with scores between two points, we multiply the proportion of cases by the size of the sample, in this case 0.6826 × 2,200, or 1,502 students.

The graph depicted in Figure 7–5 is useful when the raw score of interest falls exactly at a point corresponding to a z-score of ± 1 z, ± 2 z, or ± 3 z. But what about z-scores that fall between these whole units? To determine the proportion and/or number of raw scores that fall between whole standard units, we refer to the z-distribution in Tables K–1, K–2, and K–3. The process involves four steps, which we illustrate with reference to the data in our hypothetical scenario.

Suppose we are interested in both the proportion *and* the number of students with interpersonal-rituals scores in the 62 to 72 range. The first thing we would do is to convert the raw scores into z-scores using Formula 4–6, $\left[z = \frac{X - \bar{X}}{s} \right]$, as shown in the first step.

Step 1: We convert each of the two raw scores to z-scores.

$$z_{62} = \frac{62 - 65}{5} = -0.60$$

$$z_{72} = \frac{72 - 65}{5} = 1.4$$

In the second step, we sketch a bell-shaped curve and mark off and shade the area(s) related to the z-value(s) (Figure 7–6). The sketch is not necessary, but it will help you visualize the area(s) of interest under the curve corresponding to the z-value(s) of interest. For the data in our scenario, the areas of the curve related to $z = -0.60$ and $z = 1.4$ are marked off and shaded as illustrated below.

Step 2: See Figure 7–6.

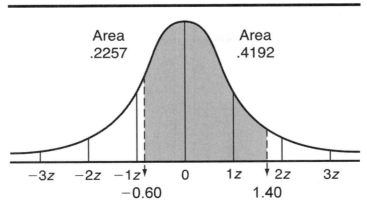

Figure 7–6. Sketch of bell-shaped curve with shaded area for $z = -0.60$ to $z = 1.40$.

In Step 3, we refer to Table L–1 in Appendix L to find the area(s) between $z = 0.00$ and the z-score(s) of interest. If there are two z-scores and they are on opposite sides of the mean, we add the two area values to find the total proportion. We shall refer to this operation as the "**Addition Rule**." If the z-scores are on the same side of the mean, we subtract the two area values and refer to the operation as the "**Subtraction Rule**." For the z-scores of 0.60 and 1.4 in our scenario, we refer to Columns A and B in Table L–1 to locate and add the two areas of interest, because they are on opposite sides of the mean, as shown below.

Step 3:

Area between $z = 0.00$ and $z = -0.60$	$= 0.2257$
Area between $z = 0.00$ and $z = 1.4$	$= \underline{0.4192}$
Addition Rule	0.6449

Thus, 0.6449 or approximately 64% of the students had raw scores between 62 and 72.

In the final step, to determine the *number* of cases that fall within a given z-score range, we multiply the value of the total area by the number of cases in the distribution, as illustrated below.

Step 4:

$0.6449 * 2200 = 1418.78 \approx 1419$

So in this scenario, approximately 1,419 students had interpersonal-ritual scores between 62 and 72.

A summary of these four steps, used in calculating proportions and frequency of cases under the standard normal curve, is included in the Calculation Guides section at the end of the chapter.

> The *Addition Rule* states that when two z-scores are on opposite sides of the mean, add the two area values to find the total proportion. The *Subtraction Rule* states that when two z-scores are on the same side of the mean, subtract the two area values to find the total proportion.

Scenario

The director of human resources at a large medical center wants to know the proportion and frequency of SLP and audiologists who achieved work performance scores (as measured by their supervisors) between 1 and 2 standard deviations above the mean. She obtains a random sample of 150 SLP and audiologists with a mean of $\overline{X} = 71$ and a standard deviation of $s = 4$. The two raw score values of interest in this case are 76 and 80, as shown in Figure 7–7.

Using the four-step process outlined above, the director would proceed as follows:

Step 1: Conversion of raw scores to z-scores.

$$z_{76} = \frac{75 - 71}{4} = 1.00$$

$$z_{80} = \frac{79 - 71}{4} = 2.00$$

Step 2: Sketch of bell-shaped curve with shaded areas for $z = 1.00$ to $z = 2.00$ (see Figure 7–7).

Step 3: Refer to Columns A and B in Tables K–1, K–2, and K–3.

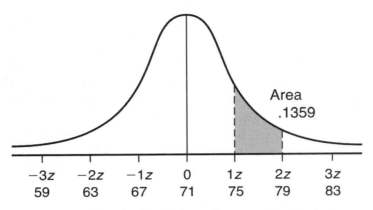

Figure 7–7. Sketch of bell-shaped curve with shaded area for $z = 1.00$ to $z = 2.00$.

Area between
$z = 0.00$ and $z = 1.00$ $= 0.3413$

Area between
$z = 0.00$ and $z = 2.00$ $= \underline{0.4772}$

Subtraction Rule* 0.1359**

*The two z-scores are on opposite sides of the mean.

**No minus sign before total area. Areas cannot be negative.

Step 4: Number of students with raw scores between one and two standard deviations above the mean.

$0.1359 * 150 = 20.385 \approx 20.4$

In this case, the director of human resources can conclude that approximately 14%, or 20.4 SLP and audiologists, achieved work performance scores between one and two standard deviations above the mean.

In addition to the proportion of values *between* two points in a distribution, we may want to know the proportion of values *above* or *below* a particular point in

the z-distribution. If the value is above the mean, we proceed as follows. Suppose we want to know the proportion and number of the first-year graduate students in the communication disorders program with interpersonal ritual scores *greater* than 75. First we convert the raw score of 75 to a z-score, as given in $z_{73} = \frac{73-65}{5} = 1.60$. We then draw a bell-shaped curve with the area of interest shaded (Figure 7–8).

In the second step, we refer to Column C, "Area Beyond" in Tables K–1, K–2, and K–3. In this case, the Area Beyond $z = 1.60$ is 0.0548. Finally, to determine the number of students with scores greater than 73, we multiply the proportion of area by the size of the sample, in this case, $0.0548 * 2200 = 120.56$. Therefore, we can conclude that approximately 5%, or 121, of the 2,200 students have interpersonal ritual scores above 73. The same procedure would be followed if the raw score of interest is *below* the mean of the distribution, except that a minus sign (−) would be placed before the value of z. A summary of these four steps, used to calculate proportions and frequency

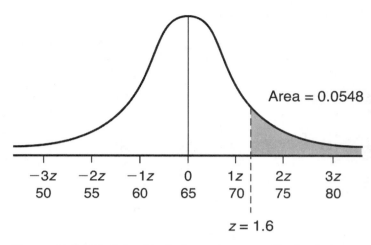

Figure 7–8. Sketch of bell-shaped curve with shaded area for proportion of values above $z = 1.60$, percentile rank of 75.

of cases that are either *greater* than or *less* than a given raw score above or below the mean, is included in the Calculation Guides section at the end of the chapter.

Determining Percentiles

The process to determine percentiles using the standard normal or z-distribution is relatively simple. Percentiles above 50 are expressed as positive z-values; whereas those below 50 are expressed negative z-values. As we presented in Chapter 4, the author continues to use the symbol P_x to represent percentiles of a given value.

Whereas it is possible to use Tables K–1, K–2, and K–3 to determine z-values that correspond to percentiles of interest, the format of Table L–1 in Appendix L is considerably easier to apply. A portion of the table is shown in Figure 7–9. The table consists of two columns. Column A lists all

of the percentiles from 50 to 99 as decimal values. Column B lists the corresponding z-value of each percentile.

Determining a particular percentile for a distribution of values using the standard normal curve is a three-step process. First, the percentile is expressed as a decimal value. Second, the decimal value and its corresponding z–score are located in Columns A and B in Table L–1. The z-score represents the point in the distribution of the percentile of interest. Third, a bell-shaped curve is sketched with the area below the z-value shaded. A summary of these steps is included in the Calculation Guides section at the end of the chapter.

To illustrate, let us suppose we want to determine the 75th percentile (P_{75}) of the interpersonal-rituals-in-friendship distribution. Applying the three-step process outlined above, we proceed as follows:

Step 1: We express the 75th percentile or P_{75} as 0.75.

A Percentile	B z-score	A Percentile	B z-score	A Percentile	B z-score
.500	.0000	.675	.4538	.850	1.0364
.505	.0125	.680	.4677	.855	1.0581
...	...	...	...	...	...
.545	.1130	.720	.5828	.895	1.2536
.550	.1257	.725	.5978	.900	1.2816
...	...	...	...	...	...
.605	.2663	.780	.7722	.955	1.6954
.610	.2793	.785	.7892	.960	1.7507
...	...	...	...	...	...
.665	.4261	.840	.9945	.999	3.0902
.670	.4399	.845	1.0152	.9995	3.2905

Figure 7–9. Z-values that correspond to percentiles of interest.

Step 2: Referring to Columns A and B in Tables K–1, K–2, and K–3, we find that the corresponding z-value for .75 is 0.6745, which consists of the area 0.1745 above the mean and the area 0.5 below the mean.

Step 3: We then draw a bell-shaped curve, mark and shade the area below the z-value 0.6745, which represents the area at and below the 75th percentile (Figure 7–10).

Thus, the z-score 0.6745 represents the point in the distribution of the interpersonal-ritual variable at and below which fall 75% of the scores. Put another way, 75% of the students had z-scores of 0.6745 or less on the interpersonal-rituals-in-friendship survey.

> To determine *percentiles*, use Tables K–1, K–2, and K–3 and Table L–1 to locate the z-score that corresponds to the proportion of the area to its left under the normal curve.

To derive the raw score that marks the 75th percentile of the interpersonal-ritual distribution (the score that corresponds to $z = 0.6745$), we apply the transformation Formula 4–9 [$RS = (s)(z) = \overline{X}$] introduced in Chapter 4. In this case, we substitute 5 for the standard deviation (s), 0.6745 for z, and 65 for the mean ($\overline{X}$), as in $(5)(.6745) + 65 = 68.373$. Thus, in terms of the original raw score distribution, we would say that the approximate score of 68 represents the 75th percentile or the point at and below which fall 75% of the scores in the distribution.

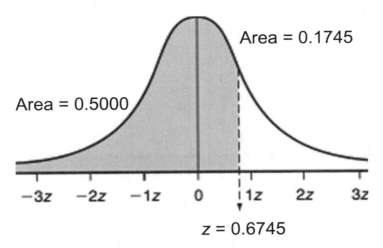

Figure 7–10 Sketch of bell-shaped curve with shaded area for proportion of values below $z = 0.6745$, the 75th percentile.

On the other hand, suppose we are interested in determining a percentile below 50. Since Table L–1 lists only percentiles of 50 and above, we follow a modification of the three-step procedure illustrated above, using the complement of the percentile of interest $(1 - P_x)$ and expressing z as a negative value. (A summary of the three-step process is in the Calculation Guides section at the end of the chapter.)

To illustrate, suppose we want to determine the 37th percentile (P_{37}) of the distribution of interpersonal-rituals-in-friendship scores. In this case, we proceed as follows:

Step 1: We express the 37th percentile or P_{37} as 0.37. Its complement is 0.63 $(1 - 0.37)$.

Step 2: Referring to Columns A and B in Tables K–1, K–2, and K–3, we locate the corresponding z-score for 0.63 and express it as a negative value, in this case, $P_{37} = -0.3319$, to be more exact by using the software packages.

Step 3: We then draw a bell-shaped curve, mark and shade the area below the z-value -0.3319, which represents the area at and below the 37th percentile (Figure 7–11).

Thus, a z-score of -0.3319 represents the point in the distribution of the interpersonal-rituals-in-friendship variable at and below which fall 37% of the scores. Applying Formula 4–9 $[RS = (s)(z) = \overline{X}$ or $(5)(-.3319) + 65]$ we find that the raw score value 63.341 or 63 represents the 37th percentile, or the point at and below which fall 37% of the scores in the distribution.

> To determine *percentiles* below 50, use the complement of the percentile of interest to locate the z-score in Table L–1 that corresponds to the proportion of the area to its left under the normal curve.

Determining Percentile Ranks

In addition to proportions and percentiles, we can use the standard normal or

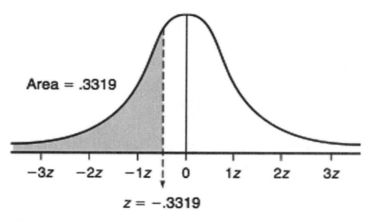

Figure 7–11. Sketch of bell-shaped curve with shaded area for proportion of values below $z = -0.3319$, the 37th percentile.

z-distribution to find the *percentile rank* (*PR*) of any given score in a distribution. Recall that in Chapter 4 we described a percentile rank as the percentage of scores that fall at and below a given score. As in the case of percentiles, percentile ranks are determined using a three-step process. First, the raw score of interest is converted to a z-score using Formula 4–6, $Z = \frac{X-\bar{X}}{s}$. Second, draw a bell-shaped curve and shade the area related to the z-value of interest. Finally, refer to Tables K–1, K–2, and K–3 in Appendix K. If the z-score is positive, find the proportion of the total area *below* it, that is, add the 0.5 area below the mean to the area from z = 0.00 to $z = n$, referring to Columns A and B. If the z-score is negative, find the area *beyond* it using Columns A and C. These three steps are summarized in the Calculation Guides section at the end of the chapter.

Seems complicated? Let's illustrate how it works.

Suppose we want to determine the percentile rank of score 71 (PR_{71}) in the distribution of interpersonal-rituals scores,

where $\bar{X} = 65$ and $s = 5$. Applying the three steps above, we would proceed as follows:

Step 1: First we convert the raw score 71 to the z-score of 1.20; as in

$$z = \frac{71 - 65}{5} = 1.20$$

Step 2: We then draw a bell-shaped curve, mark and shade the area below $z = 1.20$ (Figure 7–12).

Step 3: Referring to Tables K–1, K–2, and K–3, we find that 0.3849 of the area under the curve is between $z = 0.00$ and $z = 1.20$. Since the z-score is positive, we apply the *Addition Rule* and add 0.3849 to the 0.4999 area *below* the mean, as in

Area between $z = 0.00$ and $z = 1.20$	= 0.3849
Area below $z = 0.00$	= + 0.5
Apply the Addition Rule	0.8849

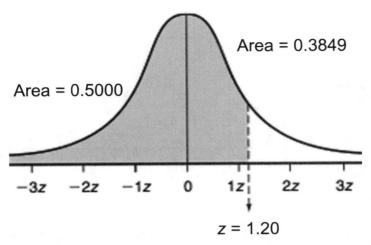

Figure 7–12. Sketch of bell-shaped curve with shaded area for proportion of values below $z = 1.20$.

Thus, the percentile rank of score 71 (PR_{71}) is 0.8849. Put another way, approximately 88.49% of the interpersonal-rituals-in-friendship distribution scores fall at and below a score of 71. The number of students with scores at or below score 71 is 1947 (0.8849 × 2200).

Similarly, if we want to find the percentile rank of a raw score that falls below the mean, a score of 57, for example, we use the same basic three-step procedure, except that in Step 3 we refer to Columns A and C.

Step 1: First we convert the raw score 57 to a z-score, as in

$$z = \frac{57 - 65}{5} = -1.6$$

Step 2: We then draw a bell-shaped curve, mark and shade the area below $z = -1.60$ (Figure 7–13).

Step 3: Referring to Tables K–1, K–2, and K–3, Columns A and C, we find that 0.0548 of the

area under the curve falls below (beyond) $z = -1.60$, that is,

Area below $z = -1.60 = 0.0548$

Thus, the percentile rank of score 57 (PR_{57}) is 0.0548, which means that approximately 5.48% or 121 students (0.0548 × 2200) had scores on the interpersonal-rituals-in-friendship measure among the first-year communication disorders majors at and below the raw score 57.

Finally, it is important to note that while a standardized normal distribution can be used to describe any normally distributed variable, converting or standardizing nonnormal or skewed distributions does not make them "normal." Nor does it change the shape or curve of the original data. The curve of z-scores of a nonnormal distribution will still be skewed to the left or to the right. The original distribution of raw scores must either be normal or approximately normal to apply the standard normal distribution to determine proportions, percentiles, and percentile ranks.

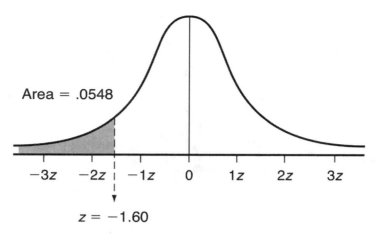

Area = .0548

z = −1.60

Figure 7–13. Sketch of bell-shaped curve with shaded area for proportion of values below z = −1.60.

Key Terms and Concepts

Sampling distributions

Theoretical distributions

Normal distribution

z-distribution

Normal curve

Asymptotic

Standard normal distribution

Empirical rule

Addition rule

Subtraction rule

Proportions

Percentiles

Percentile ranks

Feedback Review of Chapter 7

1. One of the properties of the normal distribution finds that as the tails of the distribution extend away from the mean, they come closer and closer to the x-axis but never touch it. Thus, the normal distribution is said to be
   a. symmetric.
   b. bell shaped.
   c. asymptotic.
   d. theoretical.
   e. a & d.

2. The normal distribution that has a population mean equal to zero and standard deviation units equal to 1 is known as the
   a. basic normal distribution.
   b. standard normal distribution.
   c. z-distribution.
   d. theoretical distribution.
   e. b & c

3. Approximately _____ of all the scores or cases under the standard normal curve would fall between −3.00 z and +3.00 z.
   a. 68%
   b. 75%

c. 80.5%

d. 99.7%

e. 100%

4. A score subtracted from the mean of a distribution and divided by the standard deviation is called a/an
   a. percentile rank.
   b. *z*-score.
   c. *T*-score.
   d. statistic.
   e. percentile score.

5. Which of the following is a property of the normal distribution?
   a. The distribution is unimodal.
   b. It is symmetric about the mean.
   c. The values under the curve are continuous.
   d. All of the above.
   e. a and c.

6. In a normal distribution, which measures have the same value?
   a. mean deviation, variance, and standard deviation
   b. range, variance, and standard deviation
   c. mode, mean, median
   d. mode, variance, and standard deviation
   e. variance and standard deviation

7. In the normal curve, approximately 68% of all the scores or cases would fall within
   a. −1.00 *z* and +1.00 *z*
   b. +1.00 *z* and 1.50 *z*
   c. +1.00 *z* and 2.00 *z*
   d. −2.00 *z* and +2.00 *z*
   e. −1.00 *z* and −2.00 *z*

8. The normal distribution can be used to determine
   a. proportions.

b. percentiles.

c. percentile ranks.

d. all of the above.

e. b & c.

9. The _____ of a raw score indicates the percentage of scores in a distribution that fall at and below it.
   a. *z*-score
   b. percentile rank
   c. standard deviation
   d. proportion
   e. median

10. Converting a distribution of raw scores into a distribution of *z*-scores changes the
    a. total area under the curve.
    b. shape of the distribution.
    c. mean (μ) and standard deviation (σ) of the distribution.
    d. numerical values of the scores (*X*).
    e. c & d

11. Which standard deviation in the standard normal distribution corresponds to the 84th percentile?
    a. 0
    b. 1
    c. 2
    d. 3
    e. −2

Fill-Ins

12. When finding areas between *z*-scores in the standard normal distribution, you _____ the areas if the *z*-scores are on the same side of the mean.

13. The _____ rule states that approximately 99.7% of all observations will fall within three standard deviations of the mean.

14. Theoretically, as the number of values in a distribution increases, the shape of the distribution becomes increasingly more _____.

15. In a standard normal distribution, if 0.0668 of the area under the curve falls below a z-score of −1.5, what proportion of area falls above a z-score of 1.5? _____

16. A raw score value that represents the point in a distribution that falls at or below a given proportion of values is called a _____.

17. The standard normal distribution is also known as the _____ distribution.

18. The actual number of cases of a given proportion of scores in a standard normal distribution can be obtained by multiplying the proportion by the _____ of the sample.

Review Problems

Directions: For the problems listed below, consider the total area under the standard normal distribution curve to equal 1.00, that is, 0.5 to the left of the mean ($\mu = 0$) and 0.5 to the right of the mean.

1. Given a standard normal distribution of z-scores determine the following areas. (Sketching a picture of a normal curve may be helpful.)
   a. The area between $z = 0$ and $z = 1.5$ is _____
   b. The area between $z = 1.8$ and $z = −1.6$ is _____
   c. The area between $z = 1.3$ and $z = 1.8$ is _____

d. The area beyond $z = 1.2$ is _____

e. The area beyond $z = −2.51$ is _____

2. Consider a random sample of 1,000 women whose scores on a verbal ability measure are normally distributed with a mean of 67 inches and a standard deviation of 2 inches.
   a. What percent of women would have scores below 69 inches?
   b. What percent of women would have scores greater than 71 inches?
   c. How many women would have scores between 62 and 64?

3. Consider a normally distributed collection of scores with a mean of 50 and a standard deviation of 10.
   a. What raw score would be at the 87th percentile?
   b. What raw score would be at the 35th percentile?

4. Consider a normally distributed set of scores with a mean of 30 and a standard deviation of 5.
   a. What is the percentile rank of score 40?
   b. What is the percentile rank of score 26?

5. The entire freshman class of 500 students completed a standardized test of critical thinking skills. Assume the scores are normally distributed with a sample mean $\overline{X} = 72$ and a standard deviation $s = 10$, and determine the following. (Remember to draw a curve and use the appropriate tables.)
   a. What percentage of scores will fall between the scores of 50 and 85?

b. What percentage of scores will fall between the scores of 81 and 93?

c. What number of students achieved a score greater than 88?

d. What number of students scored less than 60?

e. What is the 75 percentile, and what raw score is at that point in the distribution?

f. What is the 30th percentile, and what raw score is at that point in the distribution?

g. What is the percentile rank of score 65?

6. Jennifer scored 92 on the New Wave Musical Aptitude Test, which has a mean of 83 and a standard deviation of 7. Brittney scored a 57 on the Hip Hop Test of Agility, which has a mean of 51 and a standard deviation of 4. Compare their scores. Who had a better score on their respective test? How did their scores compare with others who took the same tests?

Calculation Guides

Calculating Proportions and Frequencies Under the Standard Normal Curve

Step 1: Convert the raw score(s) to a z-score(s) using Formula 4–6

$$\left[z = \frac{X - \bar{X}}{s} \right]$$

Step 2: Sketch a bell-shaped curve. Mark off and shade the area(s) related to the z-value(s). The sketch is not necessary, but it will help you visualize the area(s) of interest under the curve corresponding to the z-value(s) of interest.

Step 3: Referring to Tables K–1, K–2, and K–3, find the area(s) between z = 0.00 and the z-score(s) of interest. If there are two z-scores and they are on opposite sides of the mean, add the two area values to find the total proportion (**Addition Rule**). If the z-scores are on the same side of the mean, subtract the two area values (**Subtraction Rule**).

Step 4: To determine the *number* of cases that fall within the given z-score range, multiply the total area value by the n of the distribution.

Finding Proportions and Frequency of Cases Greater than X

Step 1: Convert raw score to z-score.

Step 2: Sketch bell-shaped curve with area of interest shaded.

Step 3: Refer to Column C, "Area Beyond," in Tables K–1, K–2, and K–3.

Step 4: Multiply the proportion value by the number of cases in the sample to find the actual number of cases below the raw score.

Finding the Proportion and Frequency of Cases Less than X

Step 1: Express the percentile of interest as a decimal value.

Step 2: Refer to Columns A and B in Tables K–1, K–2, and L–1 to locate the corresponding z-value.

Step 3: Draw a bell-shaped curve and shade the area below the z-value that represents the area at and below the percentile of interest.

Determining Percentiles (P_x) from 50 to 99 Using Table L–1

Step 1: Express the percentile of interest (P_x) as a decimal value.

Step 2: Refer to Columns A and B in Table L–1 to locate its corresponding z-value.

Step 3: Draw a bell-shaped curve, mark and shade the area below the z-value that represents the area at and below the percentile of interest.

Determining Percentiles (P_x) Below 50 using Table L–1

Step 1: Express the percentile of interest (P_x) as a decimal value and determine its complement by subtracting its value from one ($1 - P_x$).

Step 2: Refer to Columns A and B in Table L–1 to locate the z-score of the complement percentile and express it as a negative z.

Step 3: Draw a bell-shaped curve, mark and shade the area below the negative z-value that represents the area at and below the percentile of interest.

Determining Percentile Ranks Using the Standard Normal Curve

Step 1: Convert the raw score to a z-score using Formula 4–6:

$$\left[z = \frac{X - \bar{X}}{s} \right]$$

Step 2: Draw a bell-shaped curve. Mark off and shade the area related to the z value of interest.

Step 3: Refer to Tables K–1, K–2, and K–3. If the z-score is positive, find the proportion of the total area *below* it, that is, add the area 0.4999 area below the mean to the area from $z = 0.00$ to $z = n$, referring to Columns A and B. If the z-score is negative, find the area *beyond* it using Columns A and C.

8

Probability

General Overview

The concept of probability is tied to prediction and central to the rational underlying inferential statistics. In scientific research, one of the most important considerations is whether the observed results occurred because of some intervention or treatment or whether they simply occurred within reasonable levels of chance. Did the responses of college students in an experiment about drug and alcohol abuse messages occur because of the controlled presentation of the message or were the responses caused by some other factor or factors? Would the students have responded the same way without any special treatment of the message? Are abused children more likely to become abusers of children as adults? Do children's programs such as *Sesame Street* and family situation comedies such as *The Brady Bunch* or *The Cosby Show* foster significant prosocial behavior in children and young adults? What is the relationship between rap music lyrics and teen violence? Each of these questions reflects a degree of uncertainty, and each requires that probability be taken into consideration in constructing answers to them.

In inferential statistics, there are no absolutes, only probabilities and interpretations of them. The question is not whether individuals in an experimental group respond to messages in a particular way or whether the outcomes of a home environment or television viewing or music listening results in a particular behavior, but rather whether the response or behavior exceeds some fixed or subjectively defined probable level. Finding the answer to such questions is central to the process of statistical inference.

Whenever we engage in experimental or observational research, of primary concern is whether observed events occur because of chance or random fluctuations in measurement, or because of some experimental intervention, or because of some attribute, trait or attitude in the participants of the study. If we conclude that the probability of some behavior or event is high, beyond our chance expectancies, we would have greater confidence in our ability to predict such behavior and perhaps even control it. As we shall see throughout the remaining chapters, the significance of observed results is governed by the probability criterion we set for them. Therefore, it is important that we have a solid grasp of the concept of probability and how it relates to inferential statistics.

Some Basic Terms and Concepts

In mathematics and statistics, the topic of probability usually is introduced within the context of games of chance, which are quite useful in illustrating fundamental concepts and principles. This tradition stems from the fact that the origins of probability and statistics are inextricably tied to games of chance. We follow this tradition using small data sets to explain and demonstrate basic principles and functions, keeping in mind that in research, data sets are generally much larger.

Illustrations of probability usually are presented in the context of a trial or **experiment**, that is, a procedure or process that yields specific, observable outcomes. The outcome of an experiment, such as heads in a coin flip, is known as an **event**. Events also may be simple or complex. The total number of possible events or outcomes for a given experiment is known as the **sample space**. In the flip of a single coin, for example, the sample space consists of a head and a tail. In the toss of a single die, the sample space consists of the six possible outcomes, 1, 2, 3, 4, 5, and 6. The author denotes the uppercase letter P to represent probability of a particular event of an investigator's interest and uppercase letters, such as A, B, C, and so on, to represent the events themselves of the investigator's interest.

Probabilities are expressed as positive integers that range from 0 to 1; each extreme representing absolute certainty. The probability that New Year's Day in the United States will fall on January 1 or that an unbiased penny will land on either heads or tails is 1. The probability that pennies will rain from heaven is 0 (except perhaps in a song or a movie or a Harry Potter novel). Probabilities of 0 and 1 are rare. Most probability values fall somewhere between the two extremes. Another characteristic of probability is that the sum of all possible outcomes in an experiment always equals 1, as in a coin flip where 0.5 (heads) + 0.5 (tails) = 1.00. We also can say that the probability of an event is the fractional proportion of the total number of outcomes, as in the probability of randomly drawing an ace of spades from a deck of cards is 1/52 or 0.02.

Randomness

In discussions of probability, we often see phrases, such as "a true coin," "a balanced die," "a shuffled deck of cards," and "a well shaken box," as conditions of an experiment. The purpose of these conditions is to ensure that the outcomes of an experiment are random and not predictable at any given time. By random, we mean that every possible outcome has an equal chance of occurring at any given time.

The concept of randomness is fundamental to inferential statistics. Indeed, it is the basis upon which all statistical decisions are made. It also is central to an understanding of probability distributions and how they function in inferential statistics. For example, when we speak of a **random sample**, implicit in the term is the notion that every person or object in the population from which the sample is drawn has an *equal* chance

> In probability illustrations, an *experiment* refers to a process or procedure that yields specific, observable outcome(s). The outcome of an experiment is known as an *event*. The total number of possible events or outcomes for a given experiment is known as the *sample space*.

of being selected. If this condition is not met, we can never know whether our results reflect the population from which the sample was drawn or a bias in the selection process. Sometimes the identification of all members in a population is not practical or even possible. In such cases, researchers will utilize techniques to minimize bias in various aspects of a study. For example, in experimental studies, researchers often utilize a method of treatment known as a *double-blind procedure*, where neither the experimenter nor the participant knows who is receiving treatment or being manipulated. A discussion of the more common sampling methods is included in Appendix G.

Random sample: One in which every person or object in the population from which the sample is drawn has an *equal* chance of being selected.

Probability generally is classified into three types, *classical* or *theoretical probability*, *empirical probability*, and *subjective probability*. Although we examine all three types, the two of particular interest in this chapter are the classical and empirical models. While both models differ with respect to the basis for determining a probability, they share a common underlying principle, which is the relative frequency of an occurrence. That is to say, over the course of many experiments or trials, the probability of an outcome is related to how frequently it can occur.

Classical Probability Model

The **classical or theoretical probability model**, also known as the *equally likely model*, focuses on experiments in which the total number of outcomes in a sam-

ple space is known and equally likely to occur, as in games of chance. For example, we know that in the flip of an unbiased coin (an experiment), there are two possible events in the sample space, a head or a tail, and that the probability (P) of either outcome is 1/2 or 50%. Similarly, if we were to write the names of 10 individuals on equal size slips of paper and shake them together in a hat, so that each has an equal chance of being selected, the sample space would consists of 10 events and the probability of obtaining any given name is 1/10 or 10%. Thus, in the classical probability model, the probability of an event is a fraction of all possible outcomes in the sample space. We shall refer to this definition as the **equally likely probability rule**, which can be generalized in the form of a ratio, as shown in Formula 8–1.

Formula 8–1

$$\text{Probability } (A) = \frac{\text{number of ways } A \text{ can occur}}{\text{total number of distinct outcomes}}$$

The *classical or theoretical probability model* is used to describe experiments in which the total number of outcomes in a sample space is known and each outcome is equally likely to occur. This also is known as the *equally likely model*.

The *equally likely probability rule* states that the probability of an event is the fraction of all possible outcomes in a sample space.

It is important to remember that when we say there is a 50% chance that a head or a tail will occur in the flip of a coin or that there is a 10% chance of drawing any given name out of a hat containing ten names, we are not assuming that these outcomes will actually occur; rather, we are assuming that they are the probabilities associated with long-term outcomes. Theoretically, we know that the probability of drawing an ace from a well-shuffled deck of cards is 4/52. On a short-term basis, the observed occurrences of events may not equal the theoretical probability. However, as the experiment is conducted repeatedly over a very long period of time, the probabilities will increasingly approach and eventually equal the theoretical probability. This is the underlying principle for all probabilities, whether they are theoretically or empirically derived. Perhaps a more precise definition of probability is that *it is a measure of the proportion of times that an outcome would occur if an experiment were repeated an infinite number of times.* We get a clearer understanding of this definition by examining how classical probabilities are determined.

> *Probability* may be specifically defined as a measure of the proportion of times an outcome would occur if an experiment were repeated an infinite number of times.

Determining Classical Probabilities

As we said earlier, when all of the possible outcomes of an experiment are known, and each is equally likely to occur, we can determine the probability of each outcome. For example, if we toss a balanced, six-sided die, the probability of getting any of the six values is 1/6, since each value is likely to occur on any given roll.

So, if we are interested in the probability of obtaining a 5 on a single toss of the die, the *equally likely probability rule* is given as $P(A) = \frac{1}{6}$ *or* 0.167.

The equally likely rule of an event expressed in Formula 8–1 can be operationalized in a simply three-step process. First, identify the number of outcomes of interest (numerator). Next, determine the total number of distinct outcomes in the sample space when an experiment is performed. Finally, divide the number of outcomes of interest by the total number of distinct outcomes. The quotient is the probability of equally likely events. These three steps are summarized in the Calculation Guides section at the end of the chapter.

Table 8–1 presents a distribution of probabilities for each possible outcome in the toss of a die. Note that the sum of the probabilities equals 1.002. This is due to rounding error. A distribution of probabilities for all equally likely outcomes is known as a *probability distribution*. (We say more about probability distributions in the next chapter.) Finally, note that in

Table 8–1. Outcomes and Probabilities of a Balanced, Six-Sided Die

Face Value	Probability	Rounded Probability
1	0.16666 …	0.167
2	0.16666 …	0.167
3	0.16666 …	0.167
4	0.16666 …	0.167
5	0.16666 …	0.167
6	0.16666 …	0.167
		1.002*

*Due to rounding.

addition to fractions, we express probabilities as proportions between 0 and 1 (as in, "The probability of getting a head is 0.50.") or as a percent between 0% and 100% (as in, "There is a 50% probability of getting a head.").

The equally likely rule of an event being a fraction of all possible known outcomes in the sample space holds even in cases where the occurrences and probabilities of events are *not* equal. What is central to the rule is that all of the possible outcomes are *known*. For example, in the roll of a pair of six-sided dice, there are 11 possible face value outcomes; that is to say, the total face value of the two die can be a number between 2 and 12, inclusive, as shown in Table 8–2. However, as we can see each of the 11 outcomes is

not equally likely to occur. Whereas a 2 or 12 can occur only one way, a 3 can occur two ways, a 9 four ways, and so on. In all, there are 36 possible combinations of dice surfaces for the 11 different possible outcomes, and the probabilities for these outcomes reflect the relative frequencies of these combinations. For example, since a 2 only can occur one way, its probability is 1/36 or 0.028, meaning it is likely to occur less than 3% of the time. In contrast, since a seven can occur 6 times, its probability is 6/36 or 0.167, meaning it is likely to occur approximately 17% of the time.

There are many day-to-day occurrences in which the classical probability model can be used. For example, we might be interested in the probability of randomly selecting a couple with three children, two of whom are boys. If we assume that having a boy or having a girl are equally likely events, and that the birth of one does not affect the birth of the other, then the total number of possible outcomes is 8, that is, there are 8 equally likely events in the sample space, as seen in Figure 8–1. Of the eight equally likely,

Table 8–2. Frequency and Probability of Face Value Totals for a Pair of Dice

Event (Face value of dice)	Ways of Occurring	Probability
2	1	0.028
3	2	0.056
4	3	0.083
5	4	0.111
6	5	0.139
7	6	0.167
8	5	0.139
9	4	0.111
10	3	0.083
11	2	0.056
12	1	0.028
Total	**36**	**1.010***

*Due to rounding.

Event	*(Birth order)*		
1	boy	boy	boy
2	boy	boy	girl
3	boy	girl	boy
4	boy	girl	girl
5	girl	boy	boy
6	girl	boy	girl
7	girl	girl	boy
8	girl	girl	girl

Figure 8–1. Probability of randomly selecting a couple with three children, two of whom are boys.

three events consist of two boys and one girl. Therefore, the probability is 3/8 or 0.375 that a couple could have three children, two of whom are boys. Applying the equally likely rule, where A equals exactly 2 boys in 3 births, we can express the probability of such an event as $P(A) = \frac{3}{8} = 0.375$.

There is an easier way of determining probabilities for combinations of elements, which we discuss later in this chapter.

Empirical Probability Model

In the classical probability model, probabilities are based on outcomes that are theoretically known and, in the long run, equally likely to occur. The sample space is a constant, such as two sides to a coin, six sides to a die, and 52 cards to a deck, and all probable outcomes are equally likely to occur. In contrast, the **empirical probability model** consists of events where the total number of outcomes is unknown but specified and not equally likely to occur, except over a long period of trials. Probabilities are based on observations with reference to the specified sample space (total number of all distinct outcomes). For example, suppose a randomly sample of 154 likely voters in a communication disorders graduate student government election contains 87 SLP majors. If a potential voter is selected at random, what is the probability (P) that the voter is a SLP (A)? Once the sample space has been specified, in this case 154, the probability of A (selecting a SLP), is the fraction of all possible outcomes in the sample space, as was the case in the classical probability model, specifically $P(A) = \frac{87}{154} = 0.565$, or approximately 57%.

> The *empirical probability model* consists of events not equally likely to occur and where the total number of outcomes is unknown but specified and not equally likely to occur, except over long periods of trials.

The empirical probability model is based on the concept of relative frequency and is often referred to as the *relative frequency probability model*. The relative frequency is the proportion of times each event can occur relative to the total number of possible outcomes. When all of the possible outcomes of an event can be specified, we can determine both the relative frequency and probability of each outcome. We shall refer to this definition as the **relative frequency probability rule**, which can be generalized in the form of a ratio, as given in Formula 8–2.

Formula 8–2

$$\text{Probability } (A) = \frac{\text{number of times } A \text{ observed}}{\begin{array}{c}\text{total number of outcomes} \\ \text{in the sample space}\end{array}}$$

The primary difference between Formula 8–1 and Formula 8–2 is in how the total number of events is expressed in the denominator. The term "sample space" is used in Formula 8–2 to indicate that the total number of possible outcomes is unknown and that we are using specified possible outcomes. Determining probabilities using the relative frequency probability rule follows a simple three-step process that is identical in procedures to those used for the equally likely rule. The only difference is in the use of the term "sample space" in the denominator for the ratio. To illustrate both the concept of the relative frequency model and its probability rule, consider the following scenario.

> The *relative frequency probability rule* states that when the total number of outcomes can be specified, the probability of each outcome can be determined.

Scenario

The School Dean of Communication Sciences and Disorders at a small private college is interested in the reasons why students withdraw from the college before the end their first year of the program. Survey data compiled by his office over a two-year period indicates that: (A) 16 students withdrew for academic reasons; (B) 11 left for financial reasons; (C) 4 left because they did not feel challenged by the curriculum in their major; and (D) 9 dropped out or transferred for other reasons. If one of these students is randomly selected for a follow-up interview by the dean, what is the probability that the reason given for dropping out was B (financial)? Since the events (reasons for leaving school) are neither equally likely to occur nor known, the relative frequency probability rule is the appropriate means of determining the probability of event B.

> The *relative frequency **probability rule*** refers to the proportion of times an event can occur, relative to the specified total number of possible outcomes.

Applying the relative frequency probability rule follows the same three-step procedure used for the *equally likely probability rule*, an explanation of which is included in the Calculation Guides section at the end of the chapter. In the case of our illustration, we would proceed as follows:

Step 1: We first identify the number of times B (leaving school for financial reasons) occurred, which is 11.

Step 2: We then determine the total number of students leaving for reasons A, B, C, and D, specifically, $16 + 11 + 7 + 6 = 40$.

Step 3: Finally, we apply the relative frequency probability rule and find that $P(B) = \frac{11}{40} = 0.275$.

In short, the probability of randomly selecting a student who withdrew from the college for financial reasons is slightly less than 30%. Table 8–3 presents a breakdown of the frequency and relative frequency for each possible reason for leaving the college. You may have gathered by this point that the terms "relative frequency" and "probability" are synonymous. Looking

Table 8–3. Reported Reasons for Leaving College

Reason	Frequency	Relative Frequency
A. Academic	16	0.40
B. Financial	11	0.275
C. No challenge	4	0.10
D. Other	9	0.225
Total	**40**	**1.00**

back at Table 8–2, we can see that the probabilities for tossing a pair of dice are relative frequency probabilities. This is why we say that the true distinction between theoretical and empirical probabilities is in the denominator of their respective rules, that is, in the theoretical probability model the total number of possible outcomes is known or readily derived, whereas in the empirical model the total number of possible outcomes is specified from observations.

Probability Laws and Computational Rules

In addition to the *equally likely* and *relative frequency* probability rules, there are several laws and rules of interest when considering questions of probability. Of particular relevance and interest to concepts and procedures related to inferential statistics is the *law of large numbers* and the rules for *single* and *compound events*. The compound events of interest follow either an *addition* or *multiplication rule* in determining probabilities.

Law of Large Numbers

We noted earlier that probabilities associated with flipping coins or tossing dice actually are based on the theoretical number of outcomes that can be expected over a long period of time. We know that it is quite possible to flip an unbiased coin six times and get heads each time; we also know that we can flip the coin another six times and get another six heads. However, if we repeat this experiment over a very long period of time, the outcomes will eventually even out to 50% heads and 50% tails. That is to say, the probability of getting heads or tails is relative to an

infinite number of flips. The same is true for tosses of dice or drawing names out of a hat. This notion of actual probabilities being tied to long time or infinite trials is, as we noted earlier, the underlying principle of the theoretical and empirical models of probability. Both models reflect a mathematical theorem commonly known as the **law of large numbers**, which states that as an experiment is repeated over and over, the probability of an event tends to approach the actual probability. In other words, probabilities of single experiments are relative to or approximations of the actual probability of long-term, repeated experiments.

> The *law of large numbers* states that as an experiment is repeated over and over, the probability of an event tends to approach the actual probability.

Determining Probabilities for Single Events: The General Rule

For single events, the *equally likely* or *relative frequency* rules for theoretical and empirical probabilities events are applied in the computational process depending on whether the total number of possible outcomes is known. Recall that the ratios expressed in Formulas 8–1 and 8–2 are identical, with the only difference being the reference point of the denominator. Regardless of whether we are interested in computing the probability of a coin flip, the toss of dice, the drawing of a name from a hat, or randomly selecting a student with a particular reason for dropping out of school, the ratio of the number of ways the outcome can occur to the total number of possible outcomes at a given time is the same.

Complementary Rule

The probability that an event *does not* occur is the complement that it does occur, or 1 minus the probability of a given event. This proposition is known as the **complementary rule**, and is symbolized as $P(\overline{A})$, read as "the probability of not A." It is operationally defined in Formula 8–3.

Formula 8–3

$$P(\overline{A}) = 1 - P(\overline{A})$$

Note that the probability of an event and its complement always equals 1, except in cases where error is introduced due to rounding. For example, in the toss of a six-sided die, the probability of not obtaining a 5 (for which $P = \frac{1}{6}$ *or* .167) using Formula 8–2 is given as P (not 5) = 1 − 0.167 = 0.835 (slight error due to rounding). Similarly, the probability of there being at least 1 boy family in a family of 3 children, using the complementary rule, is given as P (at least 1 boy) = 1 − P (no boy).

> The *complementary rule*, symbolized as $P(\overline{A})$, refers to the probability that an event *does not* occur.

Addition Rule: Mutually Exclusive Compound Events

A **compound event** consists of two or more single events. For example, drawing the ace of spades **or** the queen of hearts from a deck of cards is considered a compound event. The same would be true if we were interested in the probability of tossing a pair of dice and obtaining a 2 **or** 7 **or** 11, **or** 12. Each of these events is distinct and singular, with nothing in common, meaning only one of them can occur at a given time. When two or more events contain no outcomes in common, they are said to be **mutually exclusive** or **disjointed events**. *For mutually exclusive, compound events, the probability of any given event is the sum total of the probabilities of the separate events.* This is known as the **addition rule for mutually exclusive compound events**, expressed in Formula 8–4.

Formula 8–4

$$P(A \text{ or } B) = P(A) + P(B)$$

Implicit in the addition rule for mutually exclusive compound events is the proposition that there can be more than two mutually exclusive events. Therefore, Formula 8–4 also may be stated as: $P(A \text{ or } B \text{ or } \ldots k) = P(A) + P(B) + \ldots P(k)$, where the symbol k represents the final event of interest. The key to determining whether to use the addition rule, as you may have gathered, is the word "or," whether stated or implied. For instance, if the problem is to "find the probability of obtaining a number greater than 4" when tossing a die, it means obtaining a 5 **or** a 6 (mutually exclusive outcomes). Thus, we would add the separate probabilities: $\frac{1}{6} + \frac{1}{6}$.

> A *compound event* consists of two or more single events. When compound events have no outcomes in common, they are known as *mutually exclusive* or *disjointed events*. The *addition rule for mutually exclusive compound events* is the probability of mutually exclusive events occurring, and it is the sum total of the probabilities of the separate events.

Applying Formula 8–4 to the case of drawing either the ace of spades or the queen of hearts, we find the following:

$$P(A \text{ or } B) = \frac{1}{52} + \frac{1}{52}$$

$$= 0.019 + 0.019 = 0.038$$

Where

A = the probability of drawing the ace of spades

B = the probability of drawing the queen of hearts

In the case of the probability of obtaining either a 2, 7, 11, or 12 in the toss of a pair of dice, the application of the addition rule in Formula 8–4 yields the following:

$$P(A \text{ or } B \text{ or } C \text{ or } D) = \frac{1}{36} + \frac{6}{36} + \frac{2}{36} + \frac{1}{36}$$

$$= 0.028 + 0.167 + 0.056 + 0.028$$

$$= 0.279$$

Where

A = the probability of obtaining a 2

B = the probability of obtaining a 7

C = the probability of obtaining a 11

D = the probability of obtaining a 12

Finally, in cases where the total number of categories and possible outcomes are known, the events may be both mutually exclusive and exhaustive. For example, in the roll of a six-sided die, the six possible outcomes are both mutually exclusive and exhaustive, meaning that on any given toss there are only six possible outcomes (exhaustive), only one of which can occur at any given time. Note that if events are both mutually exclusive and exhaustive, the sum of the probabilities for all events is equal to 1 (see Table 8–1.)

The concept of mutually exclusive and exhaustive events extends to categories and observations in research studies. For example, if participants in a study are classified by gender, the class of males and the class of females are mutually exclusive, since it is impossible for anyone to be placed in both of the two categories. Moreover, if within the system of classification every observation must be in at least one of the given classes, then those classes are said to be exhaustive. Thus, the classes of males and females are said to be both mutually exclusive and exhaustive. We can illustrate these concepts by considering the following hypothetical scenario. Suppose a survey of 120 subjects with a particular disorder is conducted to determine the incidence of smoking, with the results by gender shown in Table 8–4.

Table 8–4. Smoking Survey Results by Gender

Event	Description	Frequency	Probability
A	Male smoker	20	.167
B	Female smoker	16	.133
C	Male nonsmoker	38	.317
D	Female nonsmoker	46	.383
Total		**120**	**1.000**

What is the probability of randomly selecting a male or a female smoker? Since any given observation can only be classified in one way, we can say that the possible compound events (A or B), (A or C), and (B or C) identified in Table 8–4 are mutually exclusive and exhaustive. Thus, the probability of randomly selecting a male or female student who is a smoker is given as:

$$P(A \text{ or } B) = \frac{20}{120} + \frac{16}{120} = 0.167 + 0.13$$

$$= 0.297 \approx 0.3 \text{ (or 3\%)}$$

Where

A = the probability of selecting a male smoker

B = the probability of selecting a female smoker

Addition Rule: Nonmutually Exclusive Compound Events

When compound events share a common or overlapping element, they are said to be **nonmutually exclusive**. The event is still a case of either/or, but with a distinction that accounts for the element common to both possibilities. For instance, the elements in drawing the ace of spades **or** a spade are nonmutually exclusive since both events share a common element— the suit of spades. Similarly, drawing a seven or a red card represent two events that have common elements—the seven of hearts and the seven of diamonds. *When two events (or more) have a common element and are not mutually exclusive, the probability of obtaining A or B is equal to the sum of the probability of A and the probability of B, minus the probability of A and B, that is, the probability of the common element.* This, then, is the **addition rule for nonmutually exclusive compound events,** symbolically defined in Formula 8–5. Let us examine the logic behind this expression.

Formula 8–5

$$P(A \text{ or } B) = P(A) + P(B) - P(A \text{ and } B)$$

Where $P(A \text{ and } B)$ is the probability of the element common to both events

Note that if A and B are mutually exclusive, then $P(A \text{ and } B) = 0$ and vice versa.

Example 1. Suppose the results of the smoking survey discussed earlier were reported by category in the format shown in Table 8–5. If a subject is selected at random, what is the probability that she is a female or a nonsmoker? Since the two events share a common element, namely the class of female, the events are not mutually exclusive. If we were to simply

Table 8–5. Smoking Survey Results by Category

Event	Description	Male	Female	Total
A	Smoker	20	16	36
B	Nonsmoker	38	46	84
Total		**58**	**62**	**120**

compute the probability of selecting a female ($\frac{62}{120} = 0.517$) and add it to the probability of selecting a nonsmoker ($\frac{84}{120} = .7$), we would end up with a probability value of 1.217, which is impossible since a probability cannot exceed the value of 1. What happened? The answer is "double counting," that is to say, since the element of female is common to each event, its probable outcome is counted twice. However, the problem, as we have seen, can be resolved by applying the addition rule for nonmutually exclusive compound events. Using Formula 8–5, the probability of randomly selecting a female or a nonsmoker is computed as follows:

$$P(A \text{ or } B) = (Female) + P(Smoker) - P(Female \text{ and } Smoker)$$

$$= \frac{62}{120} + \frac{84}{120} - \frac{46}{120}$$

$$= 0.517 + 0.7 - 0.383$$

$$= 0.834 \text{ or } 83\%$$

Example 2. Suppose ten equal-sized cubes numbered 1 to 10 are contained in a well-shaken container. What is the probability of randomly selecting cube number 6 or a cube with an even number? Applying Formula 8–5, we find the following:

$$P(6 \text{ or an even number}) = P(6) + P(even \text{ number}) - P(6 \text{ and even number})$$

$$= \frac{1}{10} + \frac{5}{10} - \frac{1}{10}$$

$$= 0.10 + 0.5 - 0.10$$

$$= 0.50$$

Note that since both the number 6 and the even numbers share a common element (both are even numbers), the probability

of that common element must be subtracted from the sum of the two separate probabilities.

The *addition rule for nonmutually exclusive compound events* states that when two or more events have a common element and are not mutually exclusive, the probability of obtaining A or B is equal to the sum of the probabilities of A and B, minus the probability of the common element in A and B.

Example 3. Applying Formula 8–5 to the case of drawing either the ace of spades or a spade from a well-shuffled deck of cards, we find the following:

$$P(A \text{ or } B) = P\left(\frac{1}{52}\right) + P\left(\frac{13}{52}\right) - P\left(\frac{1}{52}\right)$$

$$= 0.019 + 0.25 - 0.019$$

$$= 0.025 \text{ or } 25\%$$

Where

A = the probability of drawing the ace of spades

B = the probability of drawing a spade

Example 4. Applying Formula 8–5 to the case of drawing either a seven or a red card, from a deck of well-shuffled cards, we find the following:

$$P(A \text{ or } B) = P\left(\frac{4}{52}\right) + P\left(\frac{26}{52}\right) - P\left(\frac{2}{52}\right)$$

$$= 0.077 + 50 - 0.038$$

$$= 0.253 \text{ or } 54\%$$

Where

A = the probability of drawing a 7

B = the probability of drawing a red card

Determining Probabilities for Successive Events

Compound events in which one event follows another or where both events occur simultaneously are known as **successive** or **joint events**. In each case, the terms are distinguished by the word "and," and the probability of both events occurring is the product of their separate probabilities. For example, the events of drawing an ace *and* then a king from a deck of cards are considered successive events. Similarly, tossing two coins and obtaining a head on one *and* a head on the other or any combination of the two possible outcomes, is considered an example of joint events.

When considering probabilities for events that can occur in succession or concurrently, the major consideration is the independence of the events. Two events are said to be statistically **independent** if the outcome of one event has no effect on the probable outcome of the other. On the other hand, two events are considered to be **dependent** or **nonindependent** if the probable outcome of one event affects the outcome of the other. The importance of the concept of independence extends to sampling methods utilized in research. If the method of selecting research participants is conducted in such a way that the selection of participants for one group is not affected by the selection of any other, the groups are said to be independent. The computation of probabilities of independent and nonindependent events follows simple rules of multiplication.

Successive or *joint events* are compound events in which one event follows another, or where both events occur simultaneously. If the outcome of one event has no effect on the probable outcome of the other, the events are said to be statistically *independent*; if it does have an effect, the two events are said to be *dependent* or *nonindependent*.

The Multiplication Rule for Independent Events

If two events, A and B, are statistically independent, the probability of Event A will have no affect on the outcome of Event B. From a computational point of view, the size of the sample space remains the same. The concept holds both for successive and joint compound events. For example, if we draw an ace from a shuffled deck of cards, replace it, and reshuffle the deck, the probability of obtaining an ace on the second draw is still 4/52. We could repeat the experiment indefinitely and the probability of obtaining an ace will still be 4/52. This concept of independence also is known as **sampling with replacement**, since the replacement of the selected item ensures that the total number of possible distinct outcomes in the sample space remains the same. Similarly, if we toss two fair dice at the same time, the probability of obtaining a sum of seven is 6/36 (or 1/6) on any given toss, regardless of the number of times we repeat the experiment.

For successive or joint events, the probability that two or more outcomes will occur is the product of the probabilities of the separate events. This is known as the **multiplication rule for independent successive or joint events,** given in Formula 8–6.

Formula 8–6

$$P(A \text{ and } B) = P(A) \cdot P(B)$$

If we apply Formula 8–6 to our two examples above, the probability of drawing an ace, replacing it in the deck, and then drawing a king is computed as follows:

$$P(A \text{ and } B) = \frac{4}{52} \cdot \frac{4}{52} = 0.077 \cdot 0.077 = 0.006$$

Where

A = drawing a ace

B = drawing a king

Similarly, the probability of tossing two coins at the same time and obtaining, say a head on one coin and a head on the other is computed as follows:

$$P(A \text{ and } B) = \frac{1}{2} \cdot \frac{1}{2}$$

$$= 0.5 \cdot 0.5 = 0.25 \text{ or } 25\%$$

Where

A = obtaining a head on one coin

B = obtaining a head on the other

> The *multiplication rule for independent successive* or *joint events*, also known as *sampling with replacement*, refers to the probability that the outcome of two or more joint or successive events is the product of the probabilities of the separate events.

The two examples above reflect classical probabilities. We can extend the concept of independence to cases of relative frequencies. Consider the results of a hypothetical nationwide study in which 900 randomly selected undergraduate students who major in communication disorders were asked if they would consider using an online statistical program for their research projects in replacement of SPSS or MINITAB software packages provided by the college. A demographic breakdown of the 380 students who responded positively is shown in Table 8–6. If one of these students is selected at random, what is the probability that he is male and a junior? Since the joint events,

Table 8–6. Breakdown of "Yes" Responses to the Question: "Would You Consider Using an Online Dating Service?" by Gender and Class

Class	Male	Female	Total
Freshman	32	24	56
Sophomore	44	33	77
Junior	57	59	116
Senior	82	49	131
Total	**215**	**165**	**380**

being male (*A*) *and* being a junior (*B*) are dependent, we apply Formula 8–6, with the following result:

$$P(A \text{ and } B) = P \text{ (male and junior)}$$

$$= \frac{215}{380} \cdot \frac{57}{215} = 0.560 \cdot 0.265$$

$$= 0.15 \text{ or } 15\%$$

In short, the probability of selecting a male student in his junior year from among the 380 students who said they would consider using an online statistical program is approximately 15%.

Ignoring or failing to understand the concept of independent events often leads to what is known as the **gambler's fallacy**, where one assumes that the probability of an outcome increases because it does not occur over some expected number of trials or period of time. Consider the case where someone comes to believe that the more a coin comes up heads, the greater the probability that on the next flip the coin will come up tails, or the longer we go without a date, the better our chances that we will get one. This is not so. The fallacious phrase often heard in these cases is, "*The law of averages says* . . . [fill in the blank]."

While the probability of getting ten heads in ten successive tosses of a coin, as we shall see later in this chapter, is quite low, each coin flip represents an independent event and the probability of obtaining a head or a tail on any given flip is always 1/2 or 0.5. So if you find yourself in a situation where someone claims that he/she can get a head on ten successive flips, it would be a safer bet to presume that the coin is unfair or biased rather than to assume some "law of average." As for the chances related to droughts in dating, we have no rationale or advice.

> The *gambler's fallacy* refers to instances where one assumes that the probability of an outcome increases because it has not occurred over an expected period of time.

The Multiplication Rule for Nonindependent Events

If the probability of a given event is dependent on the occurrence or nonoccurrence of another event, the events are said to be **dependent** or **nonindependent**. For example, consider an experiment where 20 numbered cubes are contained in a box. Given that each cube is identical in size and weight and that the box is well shaken, the probability of selecting cube number 9 is 1/20 or 0.05. The probability of selecting cube number 16 (or any other numbered cube for that matter) is still 1/20 or 0.05, *provided* that cube number 9 was returned to the box. In such cases, each event is considered independent of the other. However, if the first cube (number 9) is *not* returned to the box, the probability of selecting the second cube (number 16) is no longer 1/20 but 1/19, or approximately 0.053, because only 19 cubes remain in the box. This concept of nonindependence of events also is known as **sampling without replacement**.

Another perspective of nonindependent events is to say that the probability of one is conditioned by the probability of the other. For this reason, nonindependent probability also is known as **conditional probability**. It is symbolically denoted as $P(B|A)$, read as "the probability of *B* given *A*" or "the probability of *B* given that *A* has already occurred." The operational definition generally used to define the conditional probability is given in Formula 8–7.

Formula 8–7

$$P(B|A) = \frac{P(A \text{ and } B)}{P(A)}$$

This formula is known as the **multiplication rule for nondependent successive or joint events**.

A less daunting and algebraically equivalent definition, which we use in our illustrations, is expressed in Formula 8–8.

Formula 8–8

$$P(A \text{ and } B) = P(A) \cdot P(B|A)$$

Example 1. Consider 20 cubes numbered 1 to 20. The probability of randomly selecting cube 9 and cube 16 in succession, without replacing the first cube before selecting the second, applying Formula 8–8, is computed as follows:

$$P(9 \text{ and } 16) = P(9) \cdot P(16|9)$$

$$= \left(\frac{1}{20}\right) \cdot \left(\frac{1}{19}\right)$$

$$= (1/20) \cdot (1/19)$$

$$= 0.05 \cdot 0.053$$

$$= 0.003$$

The *multiplication rule for nondependent successive or joint events*, also known as *sampling without replacement* and *conditional probability*, refers to the probability of a *dependent* or *nonindependent event* where the occurrence or nonoccurrence of one (or more) event is dependent or conditioned by another event.

Example 2. An experiment is conducted where three cards are drawn from a shuffled deck of cards as follows. First, a diamond is drawn and put aside. Next, a heart is drawn and put aside. Question. What is the probability of drawing a club from the same deck on the third draw? Applying an extension of Formula 8–8, we find the following:

$$P(A \text{ and } B \text{ and } C) =$$
$$P(A) \cdot P(B|A) \cdot P(C|B|A)$$

$$= \frac{13}{52} \cdot \frac{13}{51} \cdot \frac{13}{50}$$

$$= 13/52 \cdot 13/51 \cdot 13/50$$

$$= 0.25 \cdot 0.255 \cdot 0.26$$

$$= 0.017$$

Where

A = probability of drawing a diamond

B = probability drawing a heart, given event A

C = probability drawing a club, given event B

Example 3. Remember the survey of the undergraduate students in communication disorders who said they would consider using an online statistical program? (See Table 8–6.) Suppose a researcher decides to interview two freshmen and two seniors from among those surveyed. He writes the names of all 380 students on same-sized slips of paper, places them in a box, and gives the box a good shake so that each name has an equal chance of being selected. He then draws four slips from the box, putting each one aside and shaking the box again before drawing another slip. Whew! Question. What is the probability that he will randomly select two freshmen and two seniors (the order of outcome is not important)? In this case, the calculation of the probability is similar to the illustration above of drawing a diamond, a heart, and a club from a deck of cards. Suppose the outcome of the first selection is a senior (*A*), the second a freshman (*B*), the third another freshman (*C*), and the last selection a senior (*D*). Expanding Formula 8–8, we find as follows:

$$P(A \text{ and } B \text{ and } C \text{ and } D) = P(A) \cdot P(B|A)$$
$$\cdot P(C|B|A) \cdot P(D|C|B|A))$$

$$= \frac{131}{380} \cdot \frac{56}{379} \cdot \frac{55}{378} \cdot \frac{130}{377}$$

$$= 0.3 \cdot 45 \cdot 0.148 \cdot 0.146 \cdot 0.345$$

$$= 0.003$$

Where

A = probability of selecting a senior

B = probability of selecting a freshman given that the prior selection was a senior

C = probability of selecting a freshman given that the prior selection was a freshman

D = probability of selecting a senior given that the prior selection was a freshman

Note that in this case, both the numerator and the denominator for the selection of the second freshman and the second senior are reduced by 1 because of sampling without replacement.

Bayes's Rule

Conditional probabilities are important in decision-making situations in many of the sciences. However, Formula 8–8 is only applicable when the total outcomes in a sample space or the population mean(s) are known. In many practical situations, population parameters are not known. A researcher may know that an event has occurred but not know the probability of such an outcome prior to research. In such cases, an extension of the conditional probability concept in Formula 8–8, known as **Bayes's Rule**, is applied. The rule states that the conditional probability of a particular event is based on all events that precede it. The rule, which is named after Thomas Bayes, an 18th-century English minister who first described the theorem, is expressed in Formula 8–9.

Formula 8–9

$$P(B|A) = \frac{P(B) \cdot P(A|B)}{P(B) \cdot P(A|B) + P(\bar{B}) \cdot P(A|\bar{B})}$$

Suppose, for example, event *A* represents the first stage of an experiment and *B* is the second stage. Applying Formula 8–9 allows us to calculate *B* based on *A*. A more detailed discussion of Bayes's Rule, including methods of calculating conditional probabilities and illustrations, is included in Appendix D and Appendix E.

Subjective Probability

Most of us have a general or intuitive sense of the concept of probability. This is not surprising, considering that the concept is basic and ever present in our informal reasoning and decision-making processes. Much of what we do is predicated on some level of probability we assign to an anticipated action. The concept is evident in our everyday speech, as when we say, "He'll probably not agree with me on the diagnosis of the severity of stuttering," or, " I think there is a good chance that my client will be cured," or, "What's the likelihood that the ASHA will have the convention outside of the U.S.A?" These expressions of probabilities are referred to as *subjective probabilities*.

While our interactions with concepts related to probability are mostly intuitive and subjective, *subjective probability* is a relative term. In theory and application, it can range from being based on little more than generalized clinicians' professional experiences and guesses to a proposition rooted in well-structured and intellectually sound methods of observation. For a more general nonclinical example, weather predictions by the National Weather Bureau are not based on the ramblings of someone at the bureau who reports what she has seen looking out a window. They actually are based on long-term data of previous days with similar attributes and characteristics, a process somewhat analogous to the relative frequency probability model.

At the high end of the subjective probability scale is a very sophisticated statistical method known as Bayesian statistics, based on the theorem introduced above and discussed in greater detail in Appendix D and Appendix E.

Probability and Underlying Distributions

Distributions of equally likely outcomes are known as **probability distributions**, and they have three important properties. The first property is that the outcomes occur by chance and are free of any bias. The second property is that they include all of the possible outcomes of an experiment and the sum of the probabilities equals 1. For this reason, probability dis-

tributions also are referred to **underlying distributions**. In a toss of two coins, for example, there are four possible outcomes: two heads, a head and a tail, a tail and a head, and two tails, as shown in Table 8–7 and also in Table 8–2.

The third property of probability distributions is that they are normally distributed. The larger the number of outcomes, the more symmetrical the distribution curve, as illustrated in the histograms of the outcomes for two coins and a toss of two dice, shown in Figure 8–2.

> A *probability* or *underlying distribution* is random and free of bias, symmetrical, and includes all the possible outcomes of an event.

The *z*-Distribution as a Probability Distribution

Because the standard normal or *z*-distribution introduced in the Chapter 7 has all of the properties of an underlying distribution, it can be used to determine probabilities of outcomes of variables that are normally distributed. The sum of the area under its curve theoretically equals 1, even though the asymptotic property of normal curves means that the fractional total

Table 8–7. Probability Distribution for Two Coins

Event	*Frequency*	*Probability*
Two Heads	1	1/4 = 0.25
One Head and One Tail	2	2/4 = 0.5
Two Tails	1	1/4 = 0.25
Total	**4**	**1**

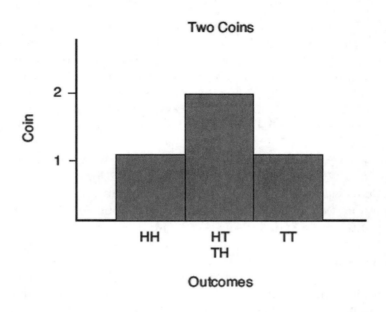

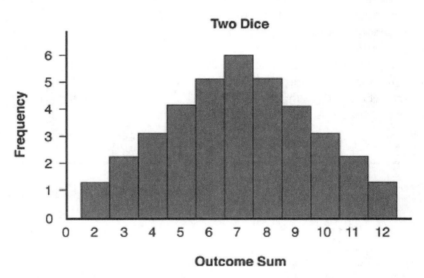

Figure 8–2. Histogram of the outcomes for two coins and a toss of two dice.

equals 0.9999 . . . ∞, as seen in Tables K–1, K–2, and K–3 in Appendix K. For purposes of convenience, in some illustrations, we consider the area equal to 1.

In Chapter 7 we illustrated how the standard normal z-distribution can be used to determine proportions, percentiles, and percentile ranks. Here we discuss how it can be used to determine probabilities of outcomes, specifically in terms of the areas under the curve in which they fall. The procedures used to determine probability outcomes are the same as those followed for determining proportions, percentiles, and percentile ranks, which as you may recall are summarized in the Calculation Guides section at the end of Chapter 7. We apply these procedures in the illustrations that follow. You should refer to them when working through the Review Problems at the end of this chapter.

Consider the results of a hypothetical test anxiety survey administered to a random sample of 220 undergraduate and graduate students who participated in the ASHA convention over the past 5 years with a mean of 65 and a standard deviation of 5, as shown in Figure 8–3, with corresponding z-values and areas under the normal curve.

To determine the probability of a given score location within the distribution, we follow the same procedures used to determine proportions in Chapter 7. In this case, as mentioned above, the areas under the curve represent probabilities rather than proportions. Thus, the probability of a score falling one standard deviation above the mean is approximately 34%, since the area between $z = 0.00$ and $z = 1.00$ is 0.3413. The same would be true for a score falling one standard deviation below the mean. This would be the case for a score falling between 65 and 70 (or between 60 and 65).

To determine probabilities for scores that fall between the standard units in Figure 8–3, we use the same procedures for finding proportions, using Tables K–1, K–2, and K–3. For example, to find the probability of randomly selecting a score between 58 and 73, we first calculate the z-score of the two raw scores as illustrated in Step 1 below. Next, referring to Tables K–1, K–2, and K–3, we locate the areas in Column B that correspond to each z-score and total them, as shown in Step 2.

Step 1: $z = \dfrac{58 - 65}{5} = -1.40$

$z = \dfrac{73 - 65}{5} = +1.60$

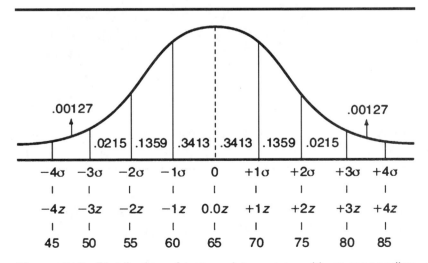

Figure 8–3. Distribution of test anxiety scores with corresponding standard deviations, z-scores, and areas under the standard normal curve.

Step 2: Area between
$z = 0.00$ and $z = -1.40$ = 0.4192

Area between $z = 0.00$
and $z = +1.60$ = 0.4452

Apply Addition Rule 0.8644

Thus, the probability of selecting a score between 58 and 73 is 0.8644, or approximately 86%. Recall that when the two scores (raw and z) are on opposite sides of the mean, the Addition Rule is used to compute the areas under the curve. The Subtraction Rule is applied when the score values fall on the same side of the mean. (It may be useful for you to refer to Tables K–1, K–2, and K–3, and work through the steps in the illustrations that follow.)

To determine the probabilities of scores falling above or below given points in the distribution, we refer to Column C in Tables K–1, K–2, and K–3. For example, to determine the probability of selecting a raw score *greater* than one standard deviation above the mean, we first calculate the z-score of the raw score. Next, referring to Column C, we locate the area *beyond* the z-score. The following example illustrates this procedure for the raw score of 78.

Step 1: $z = \dfrac{78 - 65}{5} = 2.60$

Step 2: Area *beyond* $z = 2.60$
= 0.0047 (Column C)

Thus, the probability of selecting a raw score *greater* than 78 is less that one half of 1%, or less than 5 times in a thousand. The same procedure is used to calculate the probability of selecting a score *less* than a score *below* the mean, as illustrated for the raw score 59.

Step 1: $z = \dfrac{59 - 65}{5} = -1.20$

Step 2: Area *beyond* $z = -1.20$ =
0.1151 (Column C)

Therefore, the probability of randomly selecting a raw score less than 59 is 0.1151, or approximately 12%.

To calculate the probability of selecting a score *greater* than a score that is below the mean, we follow the procedure shown below for the raw score 62. Note that after calculating the z-score, its area is added to the total area below the mean as shown below and illustrated in Figure 8–4.

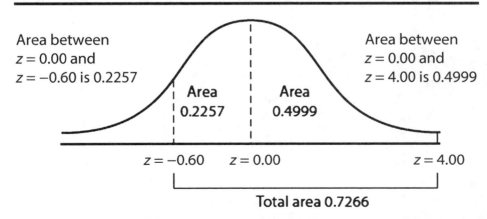

Area between $z = 0.00$ and $z = -0.60$ is 0.2257

Area 0.2257

Area 0.4999

Area between $z = 0.00$ and $z = 4.00$ is 0.4999

$z = -0.60$ $z = 0.00$ $z = 4.00$

Total area 0.7266

Figure 8–4. Probability of selecting a score greater than a score below the mean.

Step 1: $z = \dfrac{62 - 65}{5} = -0.60$

Step 2: Area between
$z = 0.00$ and $z = -0.60$ = 0.2257

Area between $z = 0.00$
and $z = +4.00$ = 0.4999

Apply Addition Rule 0.7256

Therefore, there is a 0.7256 or 72.56% chance of randomly selecting a score below 62.

The same procedure is used to determine the probability of selecting a raw score *less* than a given score *above* the mean, as shown below and illustrated in Figure 8–5 for the raw score 72.

Step 1: $z = \dfrac{72 - 65}{5} = 1.40$

Step 2: Area between
$z = 0.00$ and $z = 1.40$ = 0.4192

Area between $z = 0.00$
and $z = -4.00$ = 0.4999

Apply Addition Rule 0.9191

Thus, the probability of selecting a score less than 72 is 0.9191, or 91.91%.

Clinical Applications of Probability: Fundamentals of Test Construction Theory

Accuracy of a Diagnostic Test

Despite the many applications of diagnostic test findings, the primary objective of any such test is to detect a particular disorder or disease when present. A good diagnostic test normally identifies people who have the particular disorder or disease of interest and excludes people who do not. To accurately measure the outcomes of a new test or a screening test, results obtained from it are generally compared with some other established test(s) viewed as the **gold standard** in yielding valid results. Even though such tests may not prove to be 100% accurate, they serve as the standard against which the merit of a new test can be judged. A logical question to ask is, "If a test judged as the gold standard is doing a good job in accurately diagnosing a particular disorder or disease, why not use it in all cases?" The answer is that the gold standard for diagnosis can be time-consuming, expensive, and

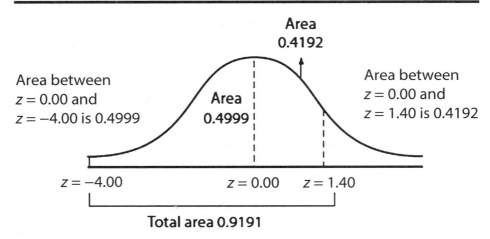

Figure 8–5. Probability of selecting a score less than a given score above the mean.

more difficult to perform. For this reason, a screening test is often used as an option during initial testing to decide who among people should be given a more definitive evaluation and who should not. Thus, an audiologist might give an audiometric screening test to decide when a more complete audiometric evaluation might be warranted. There are several major probabilities that constitute a screening test for determining the accuracy of the results. They are namely as follows:

Prevalence of a Disorder (denoted by D)

P (D+) = Probability that the disorder (or disease) is present, whereas P (D−) = Probability that the disorder is absent.

Test Results (denoted by T)

P (T+) = Probability that the test is positive, whereas P (T−) = Probability that the test is negative.

True Positive

P (D+ and T+) = Probability that the disorder is present and the test result is positive. People with the disorder are correctly identified as test positive.

False Positive

P (D− and T+) = Probability that the disorder is absent but the test result shows positive. People without the disorder are falsely labeled as test positive.

True Negative

P (D− and T−) = Probability that the disorder is absent and the test result is negative. People without the disorder are correctly identified as test negative.

False Negative

P (D+ and T−) = Probability that the disorder is positive but the test result is negative. People with the disorder are falsely identified as test negative.

Sensitivity of a Test

It is defined as the probability that the test result is positive (T+) given that the disorder actually exists (D+). Symbolically, it is written as:

$$P(T+|D+) = \frac{[P(T+ \text{ and } D+)]}{P(D+)}$$

$$= (True\ Positive) \div (Prevalence\ Rate)$$

If a test has high sensitivity, it will have a *low false negative rate*, that is, the probability that a subject who tests out as negative but who is actually positive, denoted by P (T−|D+). In such a case, the test result will seldom indicate that the disorder is not present when in fact it is present.

Specificity of a Test

It is defined as the probability that the test result is negative (T−) given that the disorder actually does not exist (D−). Symbolically, this is written as follows:

$$P(T-|D-) = \frac{[P(T- \text{ and } D-)]}{P(D-)}$$

$$= (True\ Negative) \div (1 - Prevalence\ Rate)$$

A test that has high specificity is one that has a low false positive rate, denoted by P (T+|D−), meaning that it will seldom predict the presence of a disorder that does not exist.

Although test sensitivity and specificity are important preliminary steps in constructing a diagnostic screening test, these indices alone have limited application to actual diagnosis and clinical decision making. More specifically, although these values may be used to estimate the accuracy of a particular diagnostic test, it is the **predictive values of a test** that actually have practical/clinical values in detecting a disorder or disease. In the case of measures of sensitivity and specificity, in contrast with predictive values, the disorder or disease status is already known. However, as noted previously, what a clinician really wants to obtain is whether or not a disorder or disease actually exists based on the test result of a diagnostic screening test. Only the predictive values allow for forecasting actual clinical outcomes (EBP) based on test results. There are two major components of predictive values of a diagnostic screening test, namely *predictive value positive* (PV+), and *predictive value negative* (PV−).

Predictive Value Positive (PV+)

It refers to the probability that a disorder or disease exists when the test result is positive (T+). Symbolically, this is expressed as follows:

$$P(D+\,|\,T+) = \frac{[P(D+ \text{ and } T+)]}{P(T+)}$$

$$= (True\ Positive) \div (Test\ Positive)$$

Predictive Value Negative (PV−)

It refers to the probability that a disorder or disease does not exist when the test result is negative. Symbolically, this is written as follows:

$$P(D-\,|\,T-) = \frac{[P(D- \text{ and } T-)]}{P(T-)}$$

$$= (True\ Negative) \div (Test\ Negative)$$

All probabilities defined above are summarized in Table 8–8 shown below.

In communication disorders, clinical practitioners often look at the results of clinical trials they are investigating and interested in the association (or relationship) between a treatment and an outcome. In some cases, they may find a strong association or, in another case, there may be no significant association. When clinical investigators try to show the degree of association between two events (control versus experimental, treatment A versus Treatment B, etc.), they need to know how to measure the strength of association based on what they observed. Next, I examine: (1) the procedures of several different measures of association that can be frequently seen and used in the clinical science research, and (2) interpretation of the results. The first of these measures is called relative risk.

Table 8–8. Probability Estimates of Test Results

Test Results	Disorders		
	D+	D−	Row Total
T+	P (D+ and T+)	P (D− and T+)	P (T+)
T−	P (D+ and T−)	P (D− and T−)	P (T−)
Column Total	P (D+)	P (D−)	P (S) = 1

For illustration purpose, the following measures of association are defined and expressed based on Table 8–9 and Table 8–10.

Relative Risk (RR)

In a clinical setting, RR is usually calculated when a clinician wants to know the risk ratio of Experimental group (T+) to that of Control group (T–). In other words, it compares the risk of developing the disorder or disease when exposed (D+) or not exposed (D–) to the risk factor to that in the presence or absence of the intervention. Therefore, we define the following probabilities for several events shown in Table 8–10. They are as follows:

P (T+) = Experimental intervention = A + B

P (T–) = Control intervention = C + D

P (D+) = Unfavorable clinical outcomes (Exposed to a risk factor) = A + C

P (D–) = Favorable clinical outcomes (Not exposed to a risk factor) = B + D

Symbolically, RR can be expressed as

$$RR = \frac{[P(D+|T+)]}{[P(D+|T-)]}$$

Based on our hypothetical scenario in Table 8–10, the RR can be calculated as follows:

$$RR = \left[\frac{\frac{A}{(A+B)}}{\frac{C}{(C+D)}}\right] = \left[\frac{\frac{10}{(10+30)}}{\frac{16}{(16+24)}}\right] = 0.625$$

That is, the risk of having an unfavorable outcome after experimental therapy is

Table 8–9. Clinical Outcomes of Intervention

Intervention (Treatment)	Clinical Outcomes	
	Unfavorable (Undesirable)	Favorable (Desirable)
Experimental	A	B
Control	C	D

Table 8–10. Relative Risk of Clinical Outcomes

Intervention	Clinical Outcomes		Row Total
	Unfavorable (Exposed to a risk factor)	Favorable (Not exposed to a risk factor)	
Experimental	10	30	40
Control	16	24	40
Column Total	26	54	80

about 62.5% as great as the risk of having an unfavorable outcome after control therapy.

Absolute Risk Reduction (ARR)

It is the difference in the risk of an event between the two groups (therapies). It also defines the excess risk of a disorder or disease that can be ascribed to exposure to the risk factor of interest, over and above that experienced by subjects who are not exposed. It provides an estimate of the number of cases of the disorder or disease that might be prevented if the exposure to the risk factor were eliminated and is meaningful and useful for determining the magnitude of the test results to a larger population. It is calculated by:

$$ARR = \left[\frac{C}{(C + D)}\right] - \left[\frac{A}{(A + B)}\right]$$
$$= P(D+|T-) - P(D+|T+)$$

Based on our hypothetical experiment, ARR is calculated as:

$$\left[\frac{16}{(16 + 24)}\right] - \left[\frac{10}{(10 + 30)}\right] = 0.4 - 0.25 = 0.15$$

It tells us the proportion of clients who are spared the unfavorable outcomes as a result of having received the experimental therapy rather than the control therapy, that is, in our case, 15%.

Relative Risk Reduction (RRR)

It tells us the percentage of the baseline risk (the risk of an event in the control therapy group) removed as a result of therapy. It also refers to the difference in the prevalence (or incidence) of a disorder or disease between subjects who are exposed to the risk factor and those who are not exposed. The calculation of RRR is as follows:

$$RRR = \frac{(ARR)}{\left[\frac{C}{(C + D)}\right]} = 1 - RR$$
$$= \frac{[P(D+|T+) - P(D+|T-)]}{P(D+|T+)}$$

In our example, RRR = 1 − 0.625 = 0.375.

Odds Ratio (OR)

It is the risk ratio (obtaining unfavorable outcomes) of an event in the experimental group to those in the control group. It tells us the ratio of the ratio of "unfavorable outcomes" to "favorable outcomes" under the two therapies. It also compares the odds that a disorder or disease will occur among subjects who have a particular characteristic or who have been exposed to a risk factor to the odds that a disorder will occur in subjects who lack the characteristic or who have not been exposed to the risk factor. In the conditional probability term,

$$OR = \frac{\left[\frac{P(D+|T+)}{P(D-|T+)}\right]}{\left[\frac{P(D+|T-)}{P(D-|T-)}\right]}$$

In short, we can directly calculate OR to estimate the odds of an event occurring. It is derived as follows:

$$OR = \left[\frac{\frac{A}{C}}{\frac{B}{D}}\right] = \frac{\left[\frac{P(D+|T+)}{P(D-|T+)}\right]}{\left[\frac{P(D+|T-)}{P(D-|T-)}\right]}$$

In our example, OR is calculated as:

$$\frac{\left[\frac{10}{16}\right]}{\left[\frac{30}{24}\right]} = 0.5$$

Overall (combining two types of therapies), the occurrence of unfavorable outcomes is 0.5 times as likely as the occurrence of favorable outcomes.

The OR and the RR give limited information in reporting the results of prospective trials because they do not reflect changes in the baseline risk. Generally, the OR and the RR do not address the magnitude of the absolute risk, that is to say, it cannot properly measure practical significance of the result. For instance, an RR of 50% may mean that the experimental therapy reduces the risk of an unfavorable outcome from 2% to 1% or 70% to 35%. The clinical implications of these two cases are quite different, especially when you evaluate the amount of severe side effect associated with a therapy. In the first case (2% to 1%), a clinician may not institute the therapy because the amount of the reduction of side effects is not so large quantitatively (1%), whereas the clinician may be willing to accept the second case because the therapy reduces the probability of an unfavorable outcome by 35%. The RRR is also very similar to the characteristic of RR, that is, it does not reflect the change in the underlying risk in the control therapy group.

Number Needed to Treat (NNT)

This is the latest measure of treatment efficacy. Let us return to our hypothetical case study. We obtained that the risk of having an unfavorable outcome in the experimental therapy group is 25% and in the control therapy group 40%. Therefore, say, treating 1,000 clients with experimental therapy rather than control therapy will improve their clinical outcomes of 150 clients, as shown by the ARR. If treating 1,000 clients prevents 150 unfavorable outcomes, how many subjects do we need to treat to prevent one event? The answer

is $1,000 \div 15 =$ approximately 67. This figure is defined as NNT. Simply, NNT can be calculated as the reciprocal of **ARR (or NNT = 1/ARR)**. In our example, the NNT is calculated by $\frac{1}{0.15} = 6.7$.

In general, the NNT changes inversely in relation to the baseline risk. If the risk of an unfavorable outcome doubles, we need to treat only half as many clients to prevent the same number of unfavorable events. If the risk decreases by a factor of 3, we need to treat three times as many clients to accomplish the same goal.

Key Terms and Concepts

Experiment

Event

Sample

Sample space

Classical probability

Addition rule

Equally likely probability rule

Empirical probability

Randomness

Relative frequency probability rule

Law of large numbers

Complementary rule

Compound events

Mutually exclusive events

Nonmutually exclusive events

Independent events

Nonindependent events

Sampling with/without replacement

Multiplication rule

Conditional probability

Subjective probability

Statistical inference

Feedback Review of Chapter 8

1. In the process of determining probabilities, the observed outcome of the process is referred as a/an
   a. experiment.
   b. probability model.
   c. event.
   d. likelihood.
   e. all of the above.

2. According to the classical model of probability, if the outcome of 100 fair coin tosses is a head every time, the probability of it coming up heads on the next toss (i.e., 101st toss) is:
   a. 1/4.
   b. 1/2.
   c. 3/4.
   d. 1/101.
   e. cannot be determined.

3. The set of all possible outcomes in an experiment is known as
   a. an event.
   b. a compound event.
   c. a successive event.
   d. a probability.
   e. the sample space.

4. The probability law P(A or B) = P(A) + P(B) – P(A and B)
   a. applies only if events A and B are statistically independent.
   b. applies only if events A and B are statistically dependent.
   c. applies only if events A and B are mutually exclusive.
   d. applies only if events A and B are nonmutually exclusive.
   e. applies only if events A and B are conditional.

5. The expression, P(A or B) refers to
   a. the probability that either A or B will occur.
   b. the probability that both A and B will occur.
   c. independent events.
   d. the first multiplication rule.

6. If P(B|A), the events are said to be
   a. statistically independent.
   b. mutually exclusive.
   c. nonmutually exclusive.
   d. none of the above

7. When flipping a coin, heads and tails are mutually exclusive events because
   a. if the coin comes up heads, it cannot also come up tails.
   b. if the coin comes up heads on one toss, it has no influence on whether the coin comes up heads or tails on the next toss.
   c. the samples are dependent or conditional.
   d. sampling is with replacement.
   e. sampling is without replacement.

8. In an experiment where a single die is tossed, which expression refers to the probability of observing a 5 or a number greater than 4?
   a. P(A and B) = P(A) P(B)
   b. P(A and B) = P(A) P(B|A)
   c. P(A or B) = P(A) + P(B) – P(A and B)
   d. P(A or B) = P(A) + P(B)

9. Which of the following represents a formal approach to subjective probability?
   a. Classical statistics
   b. Theoretical statistics
   c. Empirical statistics
   d. Bayesian statistics
   e. a & c

10. The probability rule P(A and B) = P(A) · P(B) applies when two events are
    a. mutually exclusive.
    b. nonmutually exclusive.
    c. independent.
    d. dependent.
    e. b & d

11. A container contains 5 red balls, 3 green balls, and 7 yellow balls. If 3 balls are randomly selected, what is the probability of selecting a ball of each color, without replacement?

    a. $\left(\frac{1}{5}\right) + \left(\frac{1}{3}\right) + \left(\frac{1}{7}\right)$

    b. $\left(\frac{5}{15}\right) + \left(\frac{3}{15}\right) + \left(\frac{7}{15}\right)$

    c. $\left(\frac{1}{5}\right)\left(\frac{1}{3}\right)\left(\frac{1}{7}\right)$

    d. $\left(\frac{5}{15}\right)\left(\frac{3}{14}\right)\left(\frac{7}{13}\right)$

12. Which of the following is a property of probabilities?
    a. The sum total of all probabilities in a sample space equals 1.
    b. Probabilities range from 0 to 1.
    c. The probability of an absolute event is always equal to 1.
    d. a & c
    e. all of the above.

Fill-Ins

13. The outcome of an experiment is called a/an _____.

14 A _____ is the collection of all possible outcomes that can occur in an experiment.

15. When events are dependent, the probability is known as _____ probability.

16. Which mathematical law or theorem states that as an experiment is repeated over and over, the probability of an event tends to approach its actual probability? _____

17. The probability that an event *does not* occur is 1 minus the probability of the event occurring, and is known as the _____ rule.

For questions 18 through 20 write the appropriate symbol.

18. _____ the probability of success

19. _____ the probability of not success

20. _____ the probability of not A

Review Problems

1. Given a jar with 100 cubes (numbered 1 to 100), what is the probability of randomly selecting a cube
   a. with a number 27 on it?
   b. with a number less than 20 or greater than 75?
   c. with the number 9 or less than 13?

2. There are 10 blue and 8 red hats in a box, mixed thoroughly.
   a. What is the probability of randomly selecting a blue hat and then selecting a red hat and then selecting a blue hat? Assume the events (selecting a hat) are

statistically independent events (i.e., with replacement).

b. What is the probability of selecting a blue hat and then selecting a second blue hat? Assume the events (selecting a hat) are dependent events (not statistically independent or without replacement).

3. Given a normal deck of 52 cards, what is the probability of selecting a queen or a diamond?

4. Given a normal deck of 52 cards, what is the probability of selecting a face card and an ace?

5. In the toss of a single die, what is the probability of getting an odd number or a number less than 4?

6. In a toss of a pair of dice, what is the probability of getting a
   a. 3?
   b. 7?
   c. 2 or 12?

7. Consider a random sample of 18 students consisting of 7 communication disorders majors—5 of whom are females and 2 of whom are males, and 11 psychology majors, and 8 of whom are females and 3 of whom are males. (Instead of trying to formulate an answer directly from the wording of the problem, it is better to first summarize the data in the form of a table as outlined as instructed in part "a" below.)

a. Construct a table with top headings of: "Major, Females, Males, and Total," and under the heading of "Major" list psychology on the first row and communication disorders on the second row. Fill in the table.

b. What is the probability that a student selected at random is a male or communication disorders major?

c. What is the probability that a student selected at random is a female psychology major?

d. What is the probability of randomly selecting a student who is neither a psychology major nor a communication disorders major?

8. A study concluded that 12% of American adults are considered "high communication apprehensives (HCA)," that is, they report experiencing much stress when called upon to deliver a public speech. What is the probability of randomly selecting three American adults who are high communication apprehensives?

9. Eight (8) students in the Communication Disorders Program—Roxy, Nicole, Carol, Maria, Michael, Howard, James, and Siggy—are candidates for a campus committee. If the committee is to be made up of 6 members, how many different committees of 6 members are possible from the group of 8 students?

Calculation Guides

Determining Equally Likely Probabilities

$$\text{Probability } (A) = \frac{\text{number of ways } A \text{ can occur}}{\text{total number of distinct outcomes}}$$

Step 1: Identify the number of outcomes of interest (numerator).

Step 2: Determine the total number of distinct outcomes in the sample space when an experiment is performed.

Step 3: Divide the number of outcomes of interest by the total number of distinct outcomes. The quotient of the division is the probability of equally likely events.

9

Hypothesis Testing: One Sample Case for the Mean

Overview: Frequentists' Approach

This chapter is the first of several that focus on that body of statistical methods known as *inferential statistics*, where sample data are used to make generalizations or inferences about populations. The chapter, more specifically, explains the statistical concepts of hypothesis testing, including Fisher's *p*-value, Neyman-Pearson's hypothesis tests, and the Minimum Bayes Factor approaches. The data obtained from samples are subjected to one of two types of statistical tests, parametric and nonparametric. Parametric tests are so-called because they are based on population parameters and involve procedures for evaluating hypotheses or developing estimates of parameters. Underlying these procedures are certain assumptions that must be satisfied before they can be applied, such as the requirement that samples are independent and randomly selected. We discuss these and other assumptions when introducing specific parametric tests. Nonparametric tests

also are used for testing hypotheses and estimating population parameters. However, they are applied when assumptions about the nature and shape of population distributions are unknown or not required. In this chapter, we introduce two of the most commonly applied parametric tests within the context of hypothesis testing.

Consider the following research scenario. A speech pathologist is interested in investigating the effectiveness of a new treatment for stutters, particularly at the early stages. The findings of her sample study suggest that the stutters will show elevated levels of depression levels. Can she conclude that stutters in general have a mean depression level of more than the mean of the norm? Or compared with the mean of nonstutters, is there any significant difference in means between two groups? How do we test this speech-language pathologist's test claim? However, in the absence of empirical evidence of a population, the belief is more conjecture than fact. If an investigator chooses to obtain empirical evidence and conducts an experiment or survey to test the claim, he or she will undertake a process known as *hypothesis testing* (aka, Neyman-Pearson Hypothesis Tests). So, let us start how this approach operates to generalize the characteristic(s) of interest in a target population based on a sample.

Hypothesis testing is a decision-making process in which a research claim is subjected to a series of steps to determine its tenability, that is, its ability to be defended and sustained. The claim is framed as an assertion of no difference known as a *null hypothesis*, as in, "There is no difference in the mean depression levels between stutters and nonstutters." An *alternative hypothesis*, the one of interest to the investigator, may state, "The mean depression level among stutters is more than that of nonstutters," "The mean depression level among stutters is different from that of nonstutters," and so on. Samples of subjects are randomly selected and the obtained data are analyzed for generalization.

On the basis of the observed results, the researcher either will draw conclusions regarding the null hypothesis or inferences about the population from which the samples were drawn. If the difference between what is observed and what could be expected is within the realm of chance or sampling error, the null hypothesis is retained and considered tenable. On the other hand, if the difference between the observed and expected exceeds a level of probability chosen by the researcher, the null hypothesis is considered to be false and rejected, and attention is drawn to the alternative hypothesis.

The importance of hypothesis *testing* in inferential statistics cannot be overstated. In fact, much of the remainder of this text deals with various statistical techniques and procedures for testing hypotheses under various conditions. In this chapter we introduce the general terms, concepts, and procedures used in hypothesis testing in general and single sample cases for the mean in particular. Since we will mainly be concerned with test hypotheses concerning sample means, we need to first consider one of the probability distributions used in the process, namely, *sampling distributions of the mean*.

> *Hypothesis testing* is a decision-making process in which a claim is subjected to a series of steps in order to determine its tenability.

Sampling Distributions of the Mean

In the previous chapter, we noted that sampling distributions are theoretical distributions that include the probability values of all possible outcomes. In testing the significance of sample means, the probability values are taken from **sampling distributions of the mean**. The sampling distribution used depends on the size or some other characteristic of a sample. In this chapter, we are concerned with sampling distributions used both with large and small samples. We focus first on the distribution used with large samples, those with more than 30 subjects. Later in the chapter, we will consider the sampling distribution for samples less than or equal to 30 subjects.

Although sampling distributions are derived from mathematical theorems, it may be useful, at this point, to describe the empirical basis of the sampling distribution of the mean for large samples. Suppose we were to randomly select 50 first-year graduate students majoring in communication disorders from a large

Midwestern college and record the mean GRE score for the sample. Suppose we repeat the procedure an infinite number of times, using sampling-with-replacement. Eventually, we will end up with a frequency distribution of sample means, with all of the parameters of central tendency and variability discussed in Chapter 3. There would be a mode, median, and mean, as well as a range, variability, and standard deviation of this distribution of sample means. And if we graphed the values in the distribution, the result would be a perfectly normal, bell-shaped curve. Since our distribution would contain all possible sample means, it could be used as a probability distribution. This, then, is the concept of the sampling distribution of the mean.

In reality, we do not construct sampling distributions. Instead, we utilize those derived from mathematical constructs and governed by theorems that describe three major characteristics or properties, *shape*, *central tendency*, and *variability*.

The theorem that describes the shape or curve of the sampling distribution of the mean for large samples is known as the **central limit theorem**. It states that as the number of equal-sized samples drawn from normally distributed population approaches infinity, the distribution of their means approaches the normal distribution. The significance of this characteristic is that the standard normal z-distribution introduced in Chapter 7 and its probability values listed in Tables K–1, K–2, and K–3 can be used with samples greater than 30 (>30).

> *Sampling distributions of the mean* are underlying probability distributions of all possible outcomes for hypothesis testing of means.

> The *central limit theorem* states that as the number of equal-sized, samples drawn from normally distributed population approaches infinity, the distribution of their means approaches the normal distribution.

The theorem that describes the central tendency property of the sampling distribution of the mean states that the sampling distribution mean is equal to the mean of the population. This is denoted symbolically as μ_x, where μ_x represents the mean of all distinctly possible sample means with size n. The research implication of this characteristic is that the mean of a random sample with a normal distribution is equal to the mean of the population from which it is drawn. In fact, sample statistics that can be characterized as having this property are known as **unbiased estimators** of population of their parameters. It does not matter if they are measures of central tendency or measures of variability.

The variability theorem that defines the third property of the sampling distribution of the mean, states that the standard deviation of the distribution is the **standard error of the mean**. It is operationally defined in Formula 9–1.

Formula 9–1

$$\sigma_{\bar{X}} = \frac{\sigma}{\sqrt{n}}$$

Where

σ = standard deviation of the population

n = size of the sample

Since the standard deviations of populations are seldom known, estimates of the standard error of the mean are derived using the standard deviation of the sample, as given in Formula 9–2.

Formula 9–2

$$s_{\bar{X}} = \frac{s}{\sqrt{n}}$$

Where

s = standard deviation of the sample

n = size of the sample

In summary, the three properties of the sampling distribution of the mean are defined as follows. For equal-sized samples drawn from a normally distributed population, the sampling distribution: (1) is normally distributed with a bell-shaped curve; (2) has a mean equal to the population mean, $\mu_x = \mu$; and (3) the standard deviation, called the standard error of the mean, is equal to $\sigma_{\bar{X}} = \frac{\sigma}{\sqrt{n}}$ for the population data and $s_{\bar{X}} = \frac{s}{\sqrt{n}}$ for sample data.

The function of these three properties of the sampling distribution of the mean for large samples will become clearer as we test hypotheses for large samples. However, at this point, we need to become familiar with some general terms and concepts associated with hypothesis testing and the model used in the process.

> A statistic is an *unbiased estimator* if the mean of the sampling distribution of the statistic is equal to the parameter being estimated.

> The standard deviation of the sampling distribution is known as the *standard error of the mean* and is defined as $\sigma_{\bar{X}} = \frac{\sigma}{\sqrt{n}}$ for population data and $s_{\bar{X}} = \frac{s}{\sqrt{n}}$ for sample data.

Research Questions, Claims, and Hypotheses

Asking questions often represents the first phase of a research process. The questions may ask whether a particular phenomenon exists under certain conditions or if certain variables are related. For example, an educational psychologist may ask, "What happens in the brain when children or young adults experience anxiety while working on a difficult math problem?" A sociologist may ask, "Do children from same sex households differ significantly from children from opposite sex households in attitudes toward marriage and the family?" A communication researcher may want to know: "Is argumentativeness negatively related to marital satisfaction?" A speech-language pathologist and an audiologist may want to ask, "Will EBP improve the quality of patient care in audiology and speech-language-pathology?" These types of questions are called **research questions** because they identify problems in need of study or resolution.

Sometimes a researcher may believe that there is a particular relationship between two variables or that one variable has a particular effect upon another. For instance, a clinical child psychologist may believe that language delay in children is related to a particular neurological dysfunction. A sociologist may feel that the same two particular variables are present in discrimination against youth and the elderly or that one factor is more prevalent for youth than the elderly. A political scientist may believe that negative advertisements have a significantly negative influence on voter attitudes The claims underlying these beliefs often are based on theory or the results of previous research, and, as such, they are referred to as **research claims** because they assert a specific relationship between variables or an influence of one variable upon another.

Research questions and claims are useful in identifying and framing problems into hypotheses to be tested. A **hypothesis** may be described as a conjecture, that is, a statement of fact about a condition or relationship presumed to be true. However, by definition a conjecture is a statement based on inconclusive or incomplete evidence; the word "conjecture" is synonymous with words such as "speculate" and "guess." That is why a "hypothesis" is sometimes referred to as an "educated guess," that is, a guess based on valid but inconclusive prior information. In short, hypotheses are to be tested before being accepted. Hypotheses state research questions or claims in a succinct, specific, and straightforward manner. They also state them in simple, declarative sentences. For example, a clinical research question might ask: "Is there a positive correlation between the severity of language delay and low self-esteem?" A hypothesis, on the other hand, might claim: "There is (is not) a positive correlation between verbal aggression and self-esteem." Specifically, in empirical research hypotheses are claims made about one or more population parameters that serve as the focal point of the research design. They reflect the broad question or questions of the research topic and guide the search for evidence in support of the researcher's propositions.

A *hypothesis* is a conjecture or statement of fact about a condition or relationship assumed to be true.

The Hypothesis Testing Model

Fisher/Neyman-Pearson/ Combined Methods

The framework of the model that we will use in testing hypotheses consists of four steps: (1) stating a null hypothesis to be tested and an alternative hypothesis to consider if the tested hypothesis is rejected; (2) setting the criterion for rejecting the hypothesis to be tested; (3) computing a test statistic to compare with the criterion; and (4) making a decision regarding the outcome of the process. The formal structure of the model is labeled as follows:

Step 1. State the two conflicting hypotheses, namely H_o and H_a (or H_1).

Step 2. Set the criterion for rejecting the null hypothesis (H_o).

Step 3. Compute the test statistic.

Step 4. Apply the decision rule.

Each of these steps requires consideration of the terms, concepts, and procedures introduced in this chapter and illustrated using the results of hypothetical research studies with large and small samples.

The model outlined above represents the *traditional method* of testing hypotheses. A more recent method, known as the Fisher's ***p*-value method**, has emerged since the introduction of computers and statistical calculators. It is similar to the traditional model, except with reference to how the criterion for rejecting the null hypothesis is stated. We use the tradition model in this text. However, we note some of these differences in our discussion of the traditional model, with a more detailed discussion of how to use the p-value method in Appendix I. We include these references and the detailed discussion in Appendix I because many computer statistical software packages report probability values for both traditional and p-value hypothesis tests.

Hypothesis Testing with Large Samples

Research Study 1

Scenario. A behavioral scientist interested in young female SLP's who develop romantic relationships via Internet chat rooms wants to know if their level of introversion is significantly different than the population mean or norm of 44 (μ), with a standard deviation of 6. For the sake of brevity, we shall refer to the these young female SLPs as "online romantics." The researcher randomly selects a sample of 36 (n =36) young female SLPs who recently developed romantic online relationships and finds an average introversion score of 47 ($\overline{X}$). The four steps in the hypothesis test that she would follow are described in some detail in the sections that follow. The actual test is outlined in Figure 9–1.

At this point, you are not expected to understand where the elements and for-

---

Step 1: State the hypotheses.

$$H_o: \mu = 44 \qquad H_1 \text{ (or } H_a): \mu \neq 44$$

Step 2: Set the criterion for rejecting the null hypothesis.

$$\alpha = .05 \quad \text{Two-Tailed Test} \quad z_{cv} = \pm 1.96$$

Step 3: Compute the test statistic.

$$n = 36 \qquad \sigma = 6 \qquad \overline{X} = 47$$

$$z = \frac{47 - 44}{1} \qquad\qquad \sigma_{\overline{x}} = \frac{\sigma}{\sqrt{n}}$$

$$= \frac{3}{1} \qquad\qquad\qquad = \frac{6}{\sqrt{36}}$$

$$= 3 \qquad\qquad\qquad\quad = 1$$

Step 4: Apply the decision rule.

Decision Statement: **Since** $z = 3 \qquad > z_{cv} = \pm 1.96$

H_o **is rejected;** p <.05

Figure 9–1. Four steps in hypothesis testing with large samples.

mulas come from or how they are derived. That is the purpose of later portions of this chapter. Let us now examine what all this means, step by step.

Step 1: State the Hypotheses

In the scenario outlined above, the question of interest to the researcher is whether the 3-point difference between the population introversion mean of 44 (μ) and the sample mean of 47 ($\overline{X}$) is great enough to reject a null hypothesis of no difference between the two. Or could the difference be due to sampling error or chance?

The first step within the hypothesis testing model involves framing the *null hypothesis* and an *alternative hypothesis*. As noted above, the **null hypothesis** is the research claim that is tested. It asserts that there is no difference or no relationship between a sample statistic and the hypothesized population parameter, or between two or more samples. It is symbolized as H_o: (read as "H naught" or "H oh") and always contains the equal (=) sign. For our scenario, the null hypothesis would be stated as: H_o: $\mu = 44$, which claims that from a significance point of view, there is no difference between the population introversion mean of 44 and introversion mean of 47 for the sample.

> The *null hypothesis*, symbolized as H_o:, is a research claim of no difference or relationship between a sample statistic and a population parameter, or between two or more samples. It always contains the equal sign.

While the null hypothesis is the hypothesis to be tested, it is the *alternative hypothesis* that is of interest to the researcher. For that reason, it also is known as the *research hypothesis*, since it stems from the research question or claim. The alternative hypothesis, symbolized by **H_1: (or H_a)**, asserts that there *is* a difference or relationship between a sample statistic and the hypothesized population parameter, or that there *is* a difference or relationship between two or more parameters or samples. In contrast with the null, the alternative hypothesis is stated using one of three terms: ≠ (not equal to), > (greater than), or < (less than). When the null hypothesis is rejected, support for the credibility of the research hypothesis increases. This is not to say that rejecting the null hypothesis proves that the alternative hypothesis is true. After all, it was the null and not the alternative hypothesis that was tested.

Since the researcher in our scenario simply wants to find out if the means of the sample and population are significantly different, the alternative hypothesis is stated as H_1: $\mu \neq 44$. If, on the other hand, the researcher believed that the introversion level of the population was significantly higher or lower than the mean of online romantics, the alternative hypothesis would be either stated as H_1 (H_a): $\mu < 44$ or as $\mu > 44$. These latter two hypotheses are known as **directional hypotheses,** in contrast with H_1: $\mu \neq 44$, which is known as a **nondirectional hypothesis**. Note that the null and the alternative hypotheses are mutually exclusive and exhaustive, that is, either the population value *is* equal to x or it *is not* equal to x. Both hypotheses cannot be true at the same time.

> The *alternative* or *research hypothesis*, symbolized by **H_1 or H_a**, asserts that a difference or relationship exists between a sample statistic and the hypothesized population parameter.

In our scenario, the null hypotheses H_o claims that the population mean (μ) from which the sample was drawn is 44; the alternative or research hypothesis H_1 (or H_a) asserts that it is not equal to 44. Thus, the hypotheses in the first step are stated as follows:

Step 1: H_o: $\mu = 4$ H_1: $\mu \neq 44$

We suggest that you copy this and subsequent steps on a sheet of paper that you can refer to as we proceed through the hypothesis testing of the hypothetical illustration.

Step 2: Set the Criterion for Rejecting H_o

Recall that in order for the researcher to consider the implication of the alternative hypothesis, the null hypothesis must first be rejected. If it is not, then the claim of the null hypothesis is true. This is the underlying rationale for setting a criterion for rejecting H_o. In setting the criterion for rejecting the null hypothesis, there are several concepts and considerations: a *level of significance*, the *direction of significance test*, *critical values*, the *region of rejection*, and the role of *error* within the process. We consider each of these factors in general and in relation to our hypothetical scenario.

Level of Significance

The criterion for rejecting the null hypothesis is stated as a probability value. If the observed difference in means between a sample and a population or between two or more samples is unlikely in terms of the probability criterion, the null hypothesis is rejected. If the null hypothesis is

not rejected, it is assumed that the difference in the means is not significant and probably due to chance, sampling error, or some other factor.

The criterion for rejecting the null hypothesis is known as the **level of significance**, denoted by the lower case Greek letter, **α** (read "Alpha"). It is the probability value below which the null hypothesis is rejected. While there are several levels of significance that a researcher may choose, the two most common are 0.05 and 0.01. (Less common but often used alpha levels include 0.10, 0.005, and 0.001.) The smaller the level of significance, the more likely the difference between the observed and hypothesized values is true and not due to chance, sampling error, or some other factor. This is because at 0.05, the researcher is noting that the observed difference would occur only 5% of the time; at the 0.01 level, a significant difference would be one that occurs only 1 time in a 100. Since these are relatively infrequent possibilities, the difference is considered significant, and the null hypothesis would be rejected. For these reasons, hypothesis tests are also referred to as *tests of significance*.

> *Level of significance*, symbolized as **α**, refers to the probability level below which the null hypothesis is rejected.

Direction of Significance

In setting the criterion for rejecting the null hypothesis, the researcher indicates the direction of the expected or predicted difference between the observed and hypothesized values. This is done with specific reference to the alternative hypothesis and tails of the sampling distribution curve. If the alternative hypothesis claims that the population mean is greater than (>) or less than (<) the hypothesized value stated in the null hypothesis, the test is referred to as a **one-tailed test** of significance, also known as a **directional test**. Alternative hypotheses that predict no significant difference (≠) between the observed and hypothesized values are known as **two-tailed** or **nondirectional tests**.

Critical Values

The probability values associated with levels of significance are referred to as the **critical values** of the hypothesis test. They are known as such because they are the values against which the test statistic, computed in Step 3, is compared. Briefly, if the absolute value of the computed test statistic is greater than the absolute value of the critical value, the null hypothesis is rejected; if it is less, the null hypothesis is retained. So far we have considered two of the three factors related to critical values, the *level of significance* chosen by the researcher and the *direction of the test* specified in the alternative hypothesis. The third factor is concerned with the *sampling distribution of the statistic*.

The Sampling Distribution of the Statistic

The critical value that corresponds to the level of significance in a hypothesis test is derived from a sampling distribution of the statistic, namely the mean. For samples equal to or greater than 30, the sampling distribution of the mean is the standard normal or z-distribution. Therefore, the critical values for hypothesis tests are represented by z-values in Tables K–1, K–2, and K–3, which we will denote symbolically as z_{cv}. For example, the critical value for a 0.05 two-tailed test of significance is a z-score of ±1.96, which cuts off 5% of the area of the normal distribution curve, specifically 0.025 on either side, as shown in Figure 9–2. This can be verified by looking at the "Area Beyond" column in Tables K–1, K–2, and K–3 for $z = 1.96$.

For a one-tailed test, the z-score for the critical value $\alpha = 0.05$ as found in Tables K–1, K–2, and K–3 or Table L–1 is 1.65. The exact z-score that cuts off 5% of the area on either side of the curve is 1.645. Since only a limited number of significance levels are used in hypothesis testing, it is not necessary that we go to Tables K–1, K–2, and K–3 for each test.

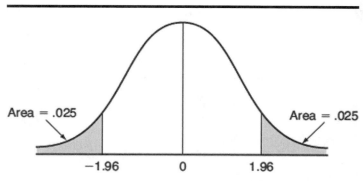

Figure 9–2. Critical values for a 0.05 two-tailed test of significance.

Instead, we can refer to Table 9–1 to find the appropriate critical value. Recall that the values in Table 9–1 are those of the right side of the *z*-distribution, which are identical to the negative values for the left side of the distribution.

> The direction of a test of significance is dictated by the alternative or research hypothesis. A **one-tailed test**, also known as a **directional test**, is one that predicts a significant difference between the hypothesized and observed values that will occur at one of the two extremes of the sampling distribution curve (> or <). A **two-tailed** or **nondirectional test** predicts that the difference will not be significant (≠).

Region of Rejection

Critical values mark the proportion of areas under the sampling distribution curve for rejecting the null hypothesis. These areas are known as **regions of rejection**. Figure 9–3 shows the regions of rejection for one-tailed and two-tailed tests. If the *z*-value (or a *t*-value to be discussed soon) of the test statistic computed in Step 3 falls in the area beyond the critical value, the null hypothesis is rejected.

For purposes of illustration, let us suppose the researcher in our scenario sets her level of significance at $\alpha = 0.05$. Since her alternative hypothesis is non-directional, (H_1: $\mu \neq 44$), indicating a two-tailed test, the critical value is expressed as $z_{cv} = \pm 1.96$. Step 2 of the hypothesis test for the scenario is stated as follows:

Table 9–1. Critical Values and Levels of Significance Under the Standard Normal *z* Curve

Alpha α Level Two-Tailed Test	Alpha α Level One-Tailed Test	Tables K–1, K–2, and K–3 Critical Values
0.20	0.10	1.282
0.10	0.05	1.645
0.05	0.025	1.960
0.02	0.01	2.326
0.01	0.005	2.576
0.001	0.0005	3.291

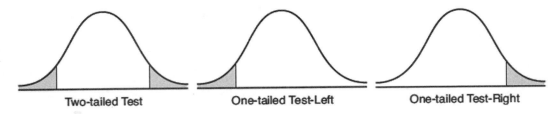

Two-tailed Test   One-tailed Test-Left   One-tailed Test-Right

Figure 9–3. Regions of rejection for one-tailed and two-tailed tests of significance.

Step 2: $\alpha = 0.05$ 2-Tailed Test
$z_{cv} = \pm 1.96$

It is suggested that we draw a sketch of the sampling distribution curve with shaded cut-offs for the rejection region, as in Figure 9–2. This helps us visualize both the directionality of the test and the area(s) for rejecting the null hypothesis. Shading the region of rejection helps to remind us that if a test statistic (in this case z) falls within the shaded area of the curve, the null hypothesis is to be rejected. We follow this practice in our illustrations.

The *region of rejection* sets off the proportion of areas under the sampling distribution curve beyond which a null hypothesis is rejected.

Errors in Testing Hypotheses

Although we prefer to avoid them, the possibility of error is present in virtually every research process. Here we are concerned with errors associated with hypothesis testing, particularly as they relate to establishing the criterion for rejecting the null hypothesis (H_o). In fact, the decision we make is subject to one of two types of error, commonly referred to as *Type I* and *Type II* error.

Type I Error. If a true null hypothesis is rejected, the committed error is referred to as a Type I error. It also is known as **alpha error** (α) because it is the probability of committing the error. There are two ways of looking at a level of significance. On the one hand, it represents the criterion for rejecting the null hypothesis. On the other hand, it represents the probability or degree to which we are willing to be wrong. When the researcher in our hypo-

thetical scenario chooses 0.05 as her level of significance, she is establishing both a criterion for rejecting the null hypothesis and a tolerance level for committing Type I error. In this case, she is willing to be wrong 5% of the time in rejecting a null hypothesis when it is true.

Type II Error. The probability of retaining a false null hypothesis is known as Type II error. It is denoted by the Greek letter beta (β) and is often referred to as **beta error**. If the hypothesized population mean (μ) of 44 in the null hypothesis in our scenario is false and the hypothesis test fails to reject it, the result is a Type II error.

In tests of hypotheses, there are two possibilities regarding the null hypothesis, H_o; either it is true, or it is false. Based on the results of the test of significance, H_o is either rejected or not rejected. In terms of decision-making, these results reflect the four possible outcomes illustrated in Figure 9–4. If the null hypothesis is true and rejected, Type I error occurs. If H_o is true and not rejected, the decision is correct. Similarly, if the null hypothesis is false and not rejected, Type II error occurs. If H_o is false and is rejected, the decision is correct.

Avoiding making the wrong decision is not an easy task. The relationship between Type I and Type II error is such that reducing one type of error increases the probability of committing the other. For example, while a smaller level of significance, such as $\alpha = 0.01$ or 0.05, lessens the chances of rejecting a *true* null hypothesis or Type I error, it increases the likelihood of failing to reject a *false* null hypothesis or Type II error. The converse also is true, that is, increasing the level of significance, say to $\alpha = 0.10$ or greater, lessens the probability of committing Type II error while increasing the

Circumstance

Decision	The null hypothesis H_o is true	The null hypothesis H_o is false
Reject H_o	Type I error α	Correct decision $1 - \beta$
Do not reject H_o	Correct decision $1 - \alpha$	Type II error β

Figure 9–4. Possible outcomes regarding the null hypothesis.

chance of committing a Type I error. This is not to suggest that a level of significance can be selected for Type II error. Beta (β) error probabilities are difficult to compute and are not set in advance as in the case of Type I or alpha (α) errors. Although, in a typical clinical practice scenario, investigators attempt to control Type I (almost always 0.05) and Type II errors (almost always ≤ 0.2) by setting values for and *n*, so that a value of β can be determined and minimized by what is called the *power of a test*.

The Power of a Test. The power of a statistical test is the probability of rejecting a false null hypothesis, denoted as $1 - \beta$. It is the counterpart of Type II error (β), which is the probability of failing to reject a false null hypothesis. The higher the power of a test, the greater the chance of detecting a true difference between the parameters stated in the null and alternative hypotheses. Although the specific methods of calculating the power of a test are beyond the scope of this text, it is important for us to have a general understanding of the concepts underlying the procedures. Again, in a typical research situation on communication disorders, it is desirable for a test to have at least 80% of the power (90% Power is most desirable in the medical sciences).

Briefly, the power of a test is computed by using a level of significance (α) and a population parameter that is an alternative to the hypothesized value that is assumed to be true in the null hypothesis, as in H_o: $\mu = 44$: H_1: $\mu = 46$. The values for the power of a test, like all probabilities, range from zero to one and are expressed as a decimal or percentage. If the probability of Type II error for a particular test is $\beta = 0.05$, then the power of that test $(1 - \beta)$ would be 0.95 or 95%. In this case, the test is highly capable of rejecting a false null hypothesis.

There are several ways to increase the power of a test. One way is to increase the size of a sample. For instance, suppose we set a 0.05 α level to compute the power of the test to reject the null hypothesis that the average age of ASHA short-courses presenters is 44 years old, with an alternative hypothesis that the average age is 46, as in H_o: $\mu = 44$, H_1: $\mu = 46$. If our sample consists of 15 subjects, the power of the test will be low, but if we increase it to 50, the power will be much higher. Recall that a larger sample size causes a reduction in the standard error of the mean, which, in turn, reduces β.

We also can increase the power of the test by increasing the significance level. For example, we may choose to use $\alpha = 0.05$ instead of $\alpha = 0.01$. As noted at the outset of this discussion, as the level of significance increases, beta or Type II error (β) decreases; therefore, $1 - \beta$ will increase the power of the test. In general, a 0.05 level of significance and a power of at least 80% often are set by many clinical investigators and highly suggested by many statisticians, particularly those in the social, behavioral, and clinical/health sciences, to determine whether a hypothesis test will be effective in minimizing Type II error.

The Consequence of Error

The tolerance for one type of error or the other is generally dictated by the resulting consequence. Consider a scenario where an over-the-counter test to detect the HIV virus (or some other deadly disease, such as anthrax, that terrorists may try to use as a weapon of mass destruction) is being developed and tested by a pharmaceutical company. Assume that the test is significantly more expensive than the traditional procedure conducted in laboratories. However, the promise of the test is that it can be self-administered with results as accurate as those determined under laboratory conditions. In a hypothesis test for this case, the null might assert that there is no significant difference in the effectiveness of the new test and current laboratory pro-

cedures. The alternative hypothesis might state that the new test is more effective. Thus, there are four outcomes related to possible decisions regarding the null hypothesis: two are correct and two are in error. What are the consequences of the two possible wrong decisions? Which error is worse, Type I or Type II?

If the null hypothesis is true but rejected (Type I error), the pharmaceutical company would needlessly spend a great deal of money in developing and marketing a test that is no more effective than its current method of detection. Consumers who purchase the test would spend a lot of money for something that is no more effective than the laboratory method of detection. On the other hand, suppose the null hypothesis is false and *not* rejected (Type II error). In this case, the consequence of the decision is that the pharmaceutical company would cease developing and marketing a test that would be more efficient and effective in detecting a deadly disease than current methods. In this case, the consequence of Type II error is worse than that of Type I error.

It is obvious from this illustration that some errors are more costly than others. However, the level of significance chosen for a hypothesis test can help avoid the consequences of Type I and Type II errors. Here are some guidelines for setting alpha.

1. If the consequence of Type I error is more costly than Type II error, set the level of significance very low, say $\alpha = 0.05$ or less.
2. If the consequence of Type II error is more costly than Type I error, set the level of significance higher, say $\alpha = 0.10$ or greater.
3. If the consequence of both types of error is unacceptable, set the level of

significance very low and increase the size of the sample. This reduces the chances of making a Type II error. Keep in mind, however, that large samples are costly in terms of time and cost.

> *Type I* or *alpha error* is the probability of rejecting a null hypothesis when it is, in fact, true. *Type II error* is the probability of retaining a null hypothesis when it is, in fact, false.

Step 3: Computing the Test Statistic

In the first two steps of hypothesis testing, we are concerned with: (1) stating the null (H_o) and alternative (H_1) hypotheses; and (2) setting the criterion for rejecting the null hypothesis. In the third step, we focus on analyzing the data gathered in the study. Specifically, we compute a standard score, such as a z-score, to compare with the critical value. The computed value from the sample data is known as the **test statistic**. The formulas used to calculate test statistics vary in terms of number and size of samples. To this point, our focus has been on single, large-sized samples, those greater than 30. Later in this chapter, we consider samples with less than or equal to 30 members.

The test statistic formula for single sample data with more than 30 members is expressed in Formula 9–3.

Formula 9–3

$$z = \frac{\overline{X} - \mu}{\sigma_{\overline{X}}}$$

Where

$\overline{X}$ = sample mean

μ = hypothesized mean of the population

$\sigma_{\overline{X}}$ = standard error of the mean when $n > 30 = \frac{\sigma}{\sqrt{n}}$ (Formula 9–1)

It is similar to Formula 4–6, introduced in Chapter 4, except that in this case the sample and population means are listed in the numerator and the standard error of the mean is expressed in the denominator. The hypothesis test is also referred to as a **z-test**.

In our scenario, the sample mean is 47 and the hypothesized population mean is 44, with a standard deviation of 6. Since the population standard deviation is known, the standard error of the mean is computed using Formula 9–1. Therefore, the test statistic is computed as follows:

Step 3: $n = 36 \quad \sigma = 6 \quad \overline{X} = 47$

$$z = \frac{47 - 44}{1} \qquad \sigma_{\overline{X}} = \frac{\sigma}{\sqrt{n}}$$

$$= 3 \qquad\qquad = 1$$

Step 4: Apply the Decision Rule

The final step in hypothesis testing consists of two statements: the *decision statement* and the *probability statement*. The **decision statement** reflects the outcome of the **decision rule**, which is defined as follows:

> If the *test statistic* is greater than the *critical value*, the *null hypothesis* is rejected. If the value of the *test statistic* is less than the critical value, the *null hypothesis* is not rejected.

From a graphic point of view, the decision rule may be stated as follows:

> If the value of the observed *test statistic* falls within the shaded area of the normal curve, the *null hypothesis* is

rejected. If the value of the *test statistic* falls outside the shaded area, the *null hypothesis* is not rejected.

The two possible decision statements (based on the combined method that the author is opposed to but frequently seen in many research articles) are expressed symbolically as follows:

Since z is $> z_{cv}$, H_o is rejected. $p < \alpha$

or

Since z is $< z_{cv}$, H_o is not rejected. $p > \alpha$

The value of p indicates the probability of obtaining the actual or more extreme data value, given that the null hypothesis is true.

For our scenario, since the test statistic $z = 3$ is greater than $z_{cv} = 1.96$, the null hypothesis is rejected and the decision statement is written as follows:

Step 4: Decision Statement:
Since $z = 3 > z_{cv} = \pm 1.96$

H_o is rejected; $p < .05$

Note that when the test statistic is a negative value, the decision statement is expressed in terms of an absolute value. For example, if the observed z-value in this illustration was -3, the decision statement would read, "Since $z = -3$ is greater than $z_{cv} = -1.96$ in absolute value, H_o is rejected; $p < 0.05$." Or "Since $z = |-3| > z_{cv} = |-1.96|$, H_o is rejected; $p < 0.05$."

> The *decision statement* reflects the outcome of the *decision rule*, which states that the null hypothesis is rejected when the test statistic is less than the critical value.

Research Study 2

Scenario. In order to investigate the cultural myth of "Six degrees of Separation," a social scientist is interested in testing the validity of the popular notion of only six degrees of separation, which states that if a person is one step away from each person he or she knows and two steps away from each person who is known by one of the people he or she knows, then everyone is on average six steps away from every other person on Earth. The scientist believes that the number of chains needed to reach a target person is greater than 6 and decides to conduct a study to assess his claim. He selects a random sample of 49 students from a local college and finds that it takes an average of 6.96, with a standard deviation of 2.3, chains to reach a targeted individual.

The salient data in this study are as follows. The presumed population mean $\mu = 6$; the sample mean $= 6.84$; the standard deviation of the sample $s = 0.84$; and the sample size $n = 49$. Is the 0.84 difference between the population and sample means sufficient to reject the null hypothesis? The scientist wishes to be conservative and selects an alpha of 0.01 as a level of significance. Since n is greater than 30, the test of significance will be a z-test. The standard error of the mean will be computed using the standard deviation of the sample (Formula 9–2) because the population standard deviation is unknown. The test will be directional because of the scientist's belief. The four steps followed in the hypothesis test are outlined below.

Step 1: State the hypotheses
H_o: $\mu = 6$ H_1: $\mu > 6$

Step 2: Find the critical value(s) for rejecting H_o

$\alpha = 0.01$ 1-Tailed Test $z_{cv} = 2.576$

Step 3: Compute the test statistic

$$n = 49 \quad s = 2.3 \quad X = 6.84$$

$$z = \frac{6.84 - 6}{0.329} \qquad s_{\bar{X}} = \frac{s}{\sqrt{n}}$$

$$= 2.553 \qquad\qquad = 0.329$$

Step 4: Apply the decision rule

Decision statement: **Since z = 2.553 is less that z_{cv} = 2.576**

H_o is not rejected; $p > 0.01$

Since the null hypothesis is not rejected, the scientist may conclude that the null hypothesis is true, that only 6 chains are needed to reach a target individual. Another way of stating a conclusion is to say that there is not sufficient evidence to support the research or alternative hypothesis.

Hypothesis Testing with Small Samples

When the size of a sample becomes less than 30 (in many cases, less than or equal to 30 if one wishes to be more conservative) and the population standard deviation is unknown, the standard normal distribution is an inappropriate sampling distribution of the mean. In such cases, the distribution of the sample cannot be assumed to be equal, as is the case when $n \leq 30$, and Tables K–1, K–2, and K–3 cannot be used as the probability distribution. Instead, a different theoretical distribution, known as the Student's t distribution or simply as the t distribution, is used as the sampling distribution of the mean, and Formula 9–2 is used to compute the standard error of the mean.

The (Student's) t Distribution

In many ways, the theoretical t distribution is quite similar to standard normal z distribution. It is symmetrical, with a bell-shaped curve that is asymptotic and at the midpoint of the curve the mode, median, and mean are equal to 0. It also is a relative frequency or probability distribution. The t distribution differs from the normal distribution in that its curve, although bell-shaped, is flatter and the variance is greater than 1. The distribution was first described in the early twentieth century by William S. Gosset, who wrote about his findings under the pseudonym "Student." For this reason, the distribution also is known as "Student's t distribution."

At the time of his discovery, Gosset was working for the Guinness Brewery in Dublin, Ireland, in quality control. He noticed that sampling distributions for small samples were considerably different than the normal distribution, and as the size of samples changed, so did the sampling distribution. Rather than a single t distribution, he noted that there actually is a family of t distributions. While z distributions are distinguished by two population parameters (μ and σ), each t distribution is associated with a unique number of *degrees of freedom*, (*df*), one for every sample size.

Degrees of Freedom

Degrees of freedom is a mathematical construct that is beyond the scope of this text. However, the general concept, which we touched upon in Chapter 3, is relatively easy to understand. At one conceptual level, **degrees of freedom** refers to the number of values in a sample that are free to vary (take on any value) in the calculation of a sample statistic. For example, suppose a sample of five scores ranging from 0 to 50 are randomly drawn from a population. If the first four scores are given as 11, 10, 8, and 7, can you determine the fifth score? Perhaps, but not likely. But suppose you are told that the sum of the five scores in the sample is 40 or that the mean is 8. Given these points of reference, determining the value of the fifth score becomes rather simple, since the value can only be 4. In this case, we can say that four scores in the sample are free to vary until a reference point is established, at which time the one remaining score becomes restricted to a single value. Thus, for this example, we would say that there are four degrees of freedom.

> *Degrees of freedom* refers to the number of values in a sample that are free to vary (take on any value) in the calculation of a sample statistic.

As previously mentioned in Chapter 3, subtracting the sample size by 1 minimizes the degree of skewness in sample data, thereby improving the estimating power of variance. (See Formula 3–7.) If the variance of a sample is computed with n as the denominator, it would result in an underestimation of the statistic and therefore would not be an *unbiased estimator*. For one-sample cases, degrees of freedom are defined as $n - 1$. As we shall see in future chapters, different sample statistics are based on different numbers of degrees of freedom.

The shape or curve of a given t distribution is affected by the number of degrees of freedom. The fewer the degrees of freedom, the flatter the shape of a t distribution. Figure 9–5 shows the shapes of three different t distributions with varying degrees of freedom.

As the sample size increases, the t distribution approaches the normal distribution so that at the point of infinity they converge and $t = z$.

Critical Values of the t Distribution

The critical values for t-tests, denoted by the symbol t_{cv}, are found in Table M–1 in Appendix M. The table consists of critical values for degrees of freedom, from 1 to infinity. Selected values and levels of

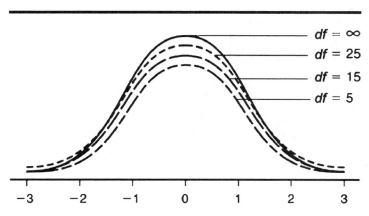

Figure 9–5. t distributions with varying degrees of freedom.

significance for one- and two-tailed tests of significance from Table M–1 are shown in Table 9–2.

The top two rows of the table list six levels of confidence for one- and two-tailed tests. The first column lists the degrees of freedom, with each *df* forming a row of critical values. Only positive values are listed, since positive and negative t_{cv} values are identical, except for sign.

To find the critical value for a single sample, two-tailed, nondirectional hypothesis test where $n = 10$ and $\alpha = 0.05$, we proceed as follows, using Table M–1. First we subtract $n - 1$ $(10 - 1 = 9)$ for degrees of freedom. Next, we locate the critical value by going to the intersection of row 9 (Column 1) and $\alpha = 0.05$ for a two-tailed test (Column 4). In this case, $t_{cv} = 2.262$ (see Table 9–2). These four steps are listed at the end of the chapter in the Calculation Guides section.

The following hypothetical research study illustrates the procedure for testing hypotheses for one sample case for the mean, when the size of the sample is less than 30, using the *t* distribution as the sampling distribution of the mean.

Research Study 3

The Scenario. An undergraduate student in the communication disorders program wants to know if the tuition and fees cost at public four-year colleges in New England is significantly higher than the national average of $6,185 reported by the College Board for 2007–2008. She believes that it is the case. Using a cluster sampling method, she surveys 25 public colleges in New England and finds that the average tuition cost is $6,571, with a standard deviation of $642. The underlying research question is whether the difference of $386 between the national mean (μ) and the sample mean ($\overline{X}$) is significantly higher than the claim of the College Board, or if the difference is the result of random sampling error. Let's assume that the researcher chooses a 0.01 level of

Table 9–2. Levels of Significance for Two-Tailed Tests

	Levels of Significance for Two-Tailed Tests					
	0.10	0.05	0.025	0.01	0.005	0.0005
	Level of Significance for Two-Tailed Tests					
df	0.20	0.10	0.05	0.02	0.01	0.001
1	3.078	6.314	12.706	31.821	63.657	636.619
9	1.383	1.833	2.262	2.821	3.250	4.781
16	1.337	1.746	2.120	2.583	2.921	4.015
28	1.313	1.701	2.052	2.473	2.771	3.690
60	1.296	1.671	2.000	2.390	2.660	3.460
∞	1.282	1.645	1.960	2.326	2.576	3.291

significance and proceed through the four steps in hypothesis testing to see what she will conclude.

Step 1: State the Hypotheses

For this example, the null and alternative hypotheses are stated as follows:

$$H_o: \mu = \$6,185 \quad H_1: \mu > \$6,185$$

The greater than sign is used in the alternative hypothesis because the researcher believes that the tuition cost at public colleges in New England is higher than the $6,185 reported by the College Board.

Step 2: Set the Criterion for Rejecting the Null Hypothesis

As we noted earlier, the three considerations in setting the criterion level for rejecting H_o are: (1) the appropriate sampling distribution; (2) the level of significance; and (3) the direction of the test. Since the sample n is less than or equal to 30, the t distribution will be the sampling distribution of the mean. Let's assume that the researcher is concerned about making a Type I error and chooses a conserva-

tive 0.01 level of significance. From the statement of the alternative hypothesis, we know that the test of significance will be one-tailed with the region of rejection located at the extreme right side of the sampling distribution curve.

Recall that when a t distribution is used in hypothesis testing, a fourth factor is considered, specifically sample size and corresponding degrees of freedom, which for single samples is $df = n - 1$. Thus, for this example, $\alpha = 0.01$ and $df = 25 - 1 = 24$. Referring to Column 5 in Table M–1, we find that the critical value for a one-tailed test at the 0.01 level of significance is $t_{cv} = 2.492$. For this research scenario, the criterion for rejecting H_o is stated as follows:

> **Step 2:** $\alpha = 0.01$ 1-Tailed Test
> $df = 24$ $t_{cv} = 2.492$

The critical value and region of rejection are illustrated in Figure 9–6.

Step 3: Compute the Test Statistic

For samples with less than or equal to 30 members, the test statistic (t) is derived using Formula 9–4.

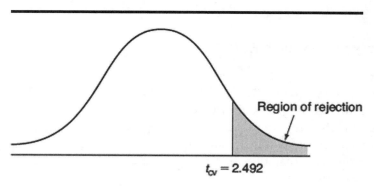

Figure 9–6. Critical value and region of rejection for a one-tailed t-test.

Formula 9–4

$$t = \frac{\bar{X} - \mu}{s_{\bar{X}}}$$

Where

$\bar{X}$ = sample mean

μ = hypothesized population mean

$s_{\bar{X}}$ = standard error of the mean (Formula 9–2)

Operationally, the calculation for the *t*-test is identical in that of the *z*-test in Formula 9–3. In our scenario, the relevant data are as follows: (1) the hypothesized population mean (μ) is \$6,185; (2) the sample mean ($\bar{X}$) is \$6,571, and the sample standard deviation is \$642; (3) the sample size (*n*) is 25 with *df* = 24 degrees of freedom; and (4) the level of significance is $\alpha = 0.01$. For this research scenario, the criterion for rejecting H$_o$ is stated as follows:

Step 3: $n = 25 \quad s = 642 \quad \bar{X} = 6571$

$$t = \frac{6571 - 6185}{128.4} \qquad s_{\bar{X}} = \frac{s}{\sqrt{n}}$$

$$= \frac{386}{128.4} \qquad\qquad = \frac{642}{\sqrt{25}}$$

$$= 3.006 \qquad\qquad\quad = 128.4$$

Thus, the test statistic is given as $t = 3.006$

Step 4: Apply the Decision Rule

Since the test statistic, $t = 3.006$, is greater than the critical value, $t_a = 2.492$, the null hypothesis is rejected. The probability is less than 1% that the hypothesized null of \$6,185 is true. The researcher in this scenario may conclude that the average 2007–2008 tuition and fee costs for public colleges in New England is significantly higher than the national average as reported by the College Board. The deci-

sion statement for this step is included in the summary of the four hypothesis test steps in Figure 9–7.

Which Test the Reasoning Process

An outline of the reasoning process that may be useful in determining which test is appropriate in conducting hypothesis tests for the mean is shown below.

Line of Reasoning

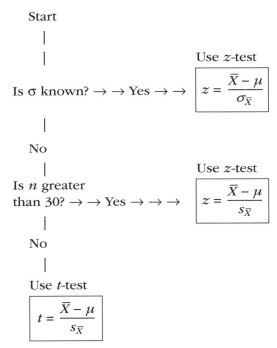

"Statistical" Versus "Practical/Clinical" Significance

An additional note related to hypothesis testing concerns the significance of "significance" in rejecting the null hypothesis.

Step 1: State the Hypotheses

$H_o: \mu = \$6,185$ H_1 (or H_a): $\mu > \$6,185$

Step 2: Set the Criterion for Rejecting H_o

$\alpha = .01$ 1-Tailed Test $df = n - 1 = 24$ $t_{cv} = 2.492$

Step 3: Compute the Test Statistic

$n = 25$ $s = 642$ $\bar{X} = 6571$

$$t = \frac{6571 - 6185}{128.4} \qquad s_{\bar{x}} = \frac{s}{\sqrt{n}}$$

$$= \frac{386}{128.4} \qquad\qquad = \frac{642}{\sqrt{25}}$$

$$= 3.006 \qquad\qquad\quad = 128.4$$

Step 4: Apply the Decision Rule

Decision Statement: Since $t = 3.006 > t_{cv} = 2.492$

H_o is rejected; $p < .01$.

Figure 9–7. Four steps in hypothesis testing.

The underlying assumption when rejecting H_o is that the observed difference between the test statistic and the hypothesized parameter is not because of chance or sampling error and is therefore statistically significant. However, the difference may have little or no practical significance.

Statistical significance is a concept set by theory. If the value of a test statistic is greater than the critical value, the null hypothesis is rejected. Theoretically,

the magnitude of a z or t statistic is not a factor in deciding whether to reject H_o. It does not matter whether the result of a two-tailed hypothesis test, with a $\alpha = 0.05$ level of significance is $z = 1.97$ or $z = 3.97$. Since both statistics exceed the critical value of ± 1.96, both are considered statistically significant outcomes.

Practical/Clinical significance, on the other hand, is set by the subjectivity of the researcher and others involved in the practical application of research findings. For example, the outcome of a marketing study may impact one of two options. Failing to reject H_o supports Option A, which is to continue marketing the current product. Rejecting H_o supports Option B, which is to produce and market a "new and improved" version of a product.

The researcher and decision makers in this case may consider a test statistic of $z = 1.97$ to be of no practical use since it barely manages to exceed the critical value of ± 1.96, particularly since the cost of producing and marketing the "new and improved" version of the product could run into millions of dollars. So while the outcome of the hypothesis test may be statistically significant, the practicality of the outcome may be insignificant.

Frequentists' Methods Cannot Control "Error Rates" in the Long Run: Why Are Their Methods Incorrect?

The major goal in traditional frequentists statistical methods, especially Neyman-Pearson's Hypothesis Tests, is to use decision procedures with known controlled long-term error rates (α and β) for rejecting and retaining the null hypothesis H_o. As the readers are quite aware by now, you can be in error by rejecting H_o when it is actually true (type 1 error rate α) or failing to reject H_o (retaining H_o) when it is actually false (type 2 error rate β). To draw a reliable and credible conclusion, that is to say, accurately measure the strength of evidence against or for H_o, both of the error rates must be controlled to minimize potential damages to the conclusion you desire to derive about a true treatment

effect. So, first, let me start out explaining how frequentists normally control type 1 error rate, type 2 error rate, and finally how the limitations and incorrect procedures are remedied by Bayesian methods.

Controlling Type 1 Error Rate

In the classroom instructions, students are in general taught about controlling type 1 error rate as follows: Type error rate must be set small enough (usually its threshold is set at 0.05) to determine whether or not an observed value (Z, t, Chi-square, F, and so on) derived from an actual sample will fall under the critical region of α. Using a combined method (although the method is incorrect, as noted earlier), the result is said to be *statistically significant if $p < 0.05$ (or "reject H_o")*, or otherwise, the result is said to be *statistically nonsignificant (or "failing to reject H_o")*. It is this sentiment that has led to some of the frequent criticism of the traditional methods (e.g., Fisher's p-value, Neyman-Pearson's Hypothesis Tests, Combined Method, and so on). To some extent, these criticism reflect the clinical practice of only trying to control α and not employing the rest of the Neyman-Pearson's logic. As far as an investigator conducts an experiment that involves two or less populations, such as paired t-test, unpaired z-test, or unpaired t-test, it will not be a complicated task to control and maintain the original type 1 error rate throughout. But when more than two significant pairwise tests (e.g., (M)ANOVA post hoc pairwise test) are conducted, the question will arise as to the long-term error rates of the group (or "family") of tests as a whole. The family-wise error rate is the probability of falsely rejecting *at least one null hypothesis*. Usually, Bonferonni is a generic and most widely used method when we conduct a multiple number of significant family-wise pairwise tests. For instance, suppose your family consists of K-tests and wishes to set the original α at 0.05. If this is the case, we need to make some adjustment to maintain $\alpha = 0.05$ throughout the whole process. This can be accomplished by setting $\alpha = (0.05)/K$ (or more mathematically, the precise formula is $\alpha = 1 - (1 - 0.05)^{1/K}$) as the significance level for each individual pairwise post hoc test. For example, if you were conducting three t-tests ($K = 3$), you could reject any individual null hypothesis only if its $p < [(0.05)/3] = 0.17$. With such a decision procedure, you would reject one or more of three null hypotheses no more than 5% of the time in the long run. Bonferonni method controls the family-wise error rate to be no more than 5%, but it does so more severely than needed. So, suppose that your p-values from post hoc test were given as 0.022, 0.003, 0.15, and 0.023 ($K = 4$, in this hypothetical case example), you would first order them from lowest p-value to highest p-value. Namely, it is shown in Table 9–3.

Next we construct a threshold value for each p-value: p (1)'s threshold is $[\frac{(0.05)}{(K)}]$, p (2)'s threshold is $[\frac{(0.05)}{(K-1)}]$, p (3)'s is $[\frac{(0.05)}{(K-2)}]$, and so forth till the value in the denominator becomes 1. It is illustrated in Table 9–3.

Next, we start at the bottom of the table and check if the last value there is less than its threshold. It is not in our case, since p (4) = 0.15 exceeds its threshold of 0.05, so that this test is nonsignificant. Move up to the next level and check the value. Here we have p (3) = 0.023 is less than the threshold value of 0.025, so it is significant and all p-values above it in the table are automatically significant too whether they exceed their threshold or not. For example, in our case, p (2) is significant even though it is higher than its threshold value of 0.017. Under Bonferonni's rule, p (2) would not have been significant if the other tests below it had not been. This decision rule is guaranteed to control family-wise error rate at 0.05 as a whole if you were to use Bonferonni

Table 9–3. True Type 1 Error Rate When Conducting Three t-Tests Concurrently: Bonferonni Pairwise t-Test Method for Adjustment

p-Values from Pairwise Comparison	Threshold for Bonferonni Test
p (1) = 0.03	$\left(\frac{0.05}{4} = 0.0125\right)$
p (2) = 0.022	$\left(\frac{0.05}{3} = 0.017\right)$
p (3) = 0.023	$\left(\frac{0.05}{2} = 0.025\right)$
p (4) = 0.15	$\left(\frac{0.05}{1} = 0.5\right)$

instead of the usual ANOVA methods for detecting statistical significance. But you can see the major flaw of the process. The method clearly overstates the amount of evidence against or for H_o; therefore, whatever the conclusion we derive from this method, it is more likely that we exaggerate the degree of statistical significance.

Controlling Type 2 Error Rate: How Do We Calculate and Interpret Power of a Test

As noted earlier, the most common conceptual error in the practical use of inferential statistical methods is that many investigators ignore the sensitivity of a test. Sensitivity can be determined by power of a test (basic calculation of power is illustrated in Appendix C and Confidence Intervals). For calculations, most statistical software packages (e.g., SPSS, SAS, BMDP, MINITAB, and the like) will report them.

Power calculation involves determining the minimally interesting effect size (as measured by Cohen's d). Based on Cohen's rule, the following guideline is normally used: $d = 0.2$ (small effect), $d = 0.5$ (medium effect), and $d = 0.8$ (large effect) for the between-subject case. If you were to use Cohen's d to determine effect size and its impact on effectiveness of a treatment in a simpler yet practical manner, you could follow such a procedure: Set up power (almost always 80% to 90%) to detect a medium effect size, and follow the Cohen's guideline for whatever experiment you run. However, power is something you decide on before running an experiment in order to determine subject number. Many statistical software packages offer automatic power calculations along with significance tests results. These power calculations have very little practical meaning and are indeed worthless. They calculate a power to detect the effect size actually measured, and this is a straightforward function of the p-value. You will obtain very little information from such automatic power calculations. Power should be calculated for the effect size you are interested in detecting. Under the frequentists methods, the best way to determine the sensitivity of the experiment after collecting data is with confidence intervals. They tell you the set of values you reject as possible population means and the set you still hold under consideration. Furthermore, confidence intervals naturally allow you to assess if the effects allowed by the data are larger than some minimal interesting amount.

Using the Minimum Bayes Factor to Control Long-Term Error Rates

The hypothesis with the largest amount of evidence for it has the maximum (mathematical) likelihood against H_o, which means that it predicts the observed data best among all possible distinct alternative values. If a clinical investigator observes a 15% difference on the cure rates for stuttering between two different speech therapy treatments, the alternative (testing) hypothesis with the maximum likelihood would be that the true population means difference would be 15%. In other words, whatever effect size we are measuring, the best-supported hypothesis is always that the unknown true populations mean effect is equal to the observed effect. This fact makes the calculation of power with effect size (aka meta-analysis) straightforward and more clinically relevant and practical under the Bayesian methods. The Bayesian methods are conceptually different than frequentists methods as discussed earlier. The Bayesian methods can allow us to combine the evidence provided by each experiment for each hypothesis and directly test H_o and H_a (the best-supported hypothesis) for measuring the strength of evidence to calculate truth of H_o and H_a). With frequentists methods, an investigator must take a weighted average of the observed effects derived from all possible distinct samples and pool their standard errors. Then we recalculate a new *p*-value based on the average effect and pooled standard error. But, in reality, this new *p*-value and standard error have little relation to the *p*-values for the individual effects, and taking a weighted average of all observed effects obscures the fact that all experiments actually provide the identical evidence for the same hypothesis. So, while the frequentists claim that they are combining evidence from similar studies, they do not have a standard measure of evidence that is directly combined. Furthermore, in securing the assumptions of normality and homogeneity of several variances, the investigator must check all necessary conditions required for meta-analysis. As we discussed previously, the use of MBF definitely has an edge when we measure the strength of evidence against because of the Bayesian statistics' cumulative nature. Although the calculation of MBF is more complex than those of frequentists methods, the readers can visit the following website for computation: http://www.pcl.missouri.edu/bayesfactor.

Additionally, in Bayesian methods, the critical prior intervals (CPS) is often used in replacement of confidence intervals. The CPR gears more toward the clinical decision making process than confidence intervals. It is more useful and suitable especially when we have substantial amount of external evidence prior to an experiment and wish to implement it into clinical diagnoses and a decision-making process in general. For those who are mathematically inclined, the author highly recommends that they should read the article, entitled "Why should clinicians care about Bayesian methods?" (Matthews, R. A. J. [2001]. *Journal of Statistical Planning and Inference, 94,* 43–58).

Clinically Important Difference: Effect Size (Cohen's *d*)

The *clinically important or relevant difference (effect size)* refers to the difference between two population parameters (μ, σ^2, etc.) that is meaningful from a clinical standpoint of view. Two parameters that differ by less than the clinically important difference are assumed to have equivalent treatment efficacy. In many occasions, a clinician wants to calculate the size of the difference between two population parameters based on what was observed in a sample, we often use a method called *Cohen's d (denoted by Δ)*, that is, it refers to the difference between two population means divided by the pooled standard deviation of the two distributions. In a symbolic form, it can be expressed as follows:

$$\Delta = \frac{|(\textit{Mean of Group 1}) - (\textit{Mean of Group 2})|}{(\textit{the pooled standard deviation denoted by } SD_{POOLED})}$$

Where the pooled *t*-test assumes homogeneity, that is, equal variances. If the paired *t*-test is conducted, we will replace the pooled standard deviation by the standard deviation of the sample (or population) of differences, denoted by $SD_{DIFFERENCE}$.

For instance, $\Delta = 1.5$ can be interpreted as showing that the mean post-treatment score is 1.5 pretreatment standard deviations away from the mean pretreatment score. So, how do we know if an observed difference between two phases (or groups) shows clinically important? Cohen (1988) gives such index values as: if $\Delta = 0.2$ (small clinical effect), $\Delta = 0.5$ (moderate clinical effect), and $\Delta = 0.2$ (large clinical effect) to measure the size of the difference from a clinical perspective. It is also called measures of clinical practice significance level. Although the reporting of effect size has increasingly become popular and highly recommended in many journals of the communication sciences and disorders lately, it should not be overinterpreted. The main reason is that the effect size is still sensitive to the sample size (n). So, it is more common that the authors report both confidence intervals and effect size together to answer their research questions of interest. Furthermore, a measure of effect size does not address whether an observed difference (the value of Δ) reflect a change that any clinician would describe as a good change or a clinically important change. It simply measures the magnitude of the difference without clinical interpretations. That is the reason why the measure of effect size itself is not considered to be the one and only solution when we evaluate the strength of clinical evidence that is one of the major goals to achieve EBP in the communication sciences and disorders (Satake & Maxwell, 2011). But, this limitation and/or shortcoming can be over-come by adding another construct called *clinical significance*. The bottom line question here is, "What does the difference between two group populations parameters mean clinically?" In the language of EBP, it refers to a clinical value placed upon a result by a subject (e.g., investigator, practitioner, client, or other parties) who attempts to interpret, ascribe meaning to, or make her clinical judgment about the test results. As noted earlier, practical significance is defined as the magnitude of an observed change without clinical implications, whereas clinical significance refers to the clinical meaning and interpretations of the observed change(s) between two groups or phases. One of the most widely used statistical methods to measure the strength of clinical significance pertaining to an observed change between two groups and/or phases is called *Reliable Change Index*. It is given as:

RC = [(post-test score − pretest score)] / $SE_{DIFFERENCE}$

Where $\mathbf{SE_{DIFFERENCE}}$ represents the standard error of the difference between two different phases (groups). It is calculated as:

$$SE_{DIFFERENCE} = (SD_{PRETEST}) \cdot (2)^{\frac{1}{2}} \cdot (1 - r)^{\frac{1}{2}}$$

Where *r* is the reliability of the measurement of a test.

For instance, when a clinician conducts a two-sided 95% confidence interval test to measure an observed change, she can conclude that the observed change is clinically significant if RC > 1.96 (1.96 to approximate a 95% confidence interval). Computation of RC can be easily done by such statistical software packages as SPSS, MINITAB, and the like.

Most recently, Satake and Maxwell (2011) have provided a more clinically relevant and rather elegant statistical model called a Bayesian model in measuring statistical significance, practical significance, clinical significance, and personal significance of the test results. Although Bayesian methods have not quite caught on in clinical decision making in the field of communication sciences and disorders, there are several main advantages over the traditional frequentists statistical methods such as Cohen's d and RC. I shall discuss this particular matter at a later chapter.

A Clinically Relevant Example of Testing Hypothesis for a Single Population: A Bayesian Perspective

Suppose that a clinical investigator is interested in examining the intelligence of school-age children born with clefts of the palate and testing the claim that their intelligence is different from the norm of 100 on a score of WISA-III (the Wechsler Intelligence Scale for Children). To do so, the investigator randomly selected a hypothetical group of 36 subjects from the target population of children with this particular type of clefts who are being followed by a certain group of craniofacial clinics. Further assume that the clinical investigator administered WISC-III to her sample with the following test results: Sample Mean = 95, $\sigma = 15$, $\mu = 100$, and SE (standard error of the mean) = $(95 - 100)/SQR (36) = -2$, Fisher's p-value (two-sided) = 0.0456, and MBF = 0.1353. Furthermore, we will test the following null (H_o) and alternative (H_a) hypotheses concerning the clinical investigator's test claim.

H_o: The mean intelligence of the group of interest is no different from 100.

H_a: The mean difference of the group of interest is different from 100.

Next, we find MBF (Minimum Bayes Factor) and posterior probabilities of H_o and H_a. The results are summarized in Table 9–4.

Table 9–4. Minimum Bayes Factor and Posterior Probabilities of H_o and H_a: The Results from the Hypothetical Case Study

Prior for H_o	Prior for H_a	MBF*	Posterior for H_o	Posterior for H_a
0.1	0.9	0.1353	0.0148	0.9852
0.2	0.8	0.1353	0.0327	0.9673
0.3	0.7	0.1353	0.0548	0.9452
0.4	0.6	0.1353	0.0827	0.9173
0.5	0.5	0.1353	0.1192	0.8808
0.6	0.4	0.1353	0.1687	0.8313
0.7	0.3	0.1353	0.2399	0.7601
0.8	0.2	0.1353	0.3512	0.6488
0.9	0.1	0.1353	0.5491	0.4509
0.28**	0.72	0.1353	0.05**	

*Sources for Calculation of MBF: Perception and Cognitive Lab, Department of Psychological Sciences, University of Missouri, http://www.pcl.missouri.edu/bayesfactor

**MBF of 0.1353 indicates that the amount of evidence against H_o, in a Bayesian perspective, is only *Moderately Weak*, whereas frequentists Fisher's p-value 0.0456 suggests that the result was *Statistically Significant*. Therefore, MBF shows that the p-value obtained from the study overstates the evidence against H_o and, consequently, the result exaggerates the degree of statistical significance. It also shows how low initial confidence in H_o (Prior for H_o) must be to result in 5% confidence after observing data (that is 95% confidence in a non-null effect), or equivalently (the posterior probability of H_o is less than 0.05). With the conventional Fisher's p-value of 0.05 thresholds, the prior probability of H_o must be at most 0.28 (28%) to allow an investigator to conclude with 95% confidence that H_o is false. This means even when you start out stating $p(H_o) = 0.28$, believing that the null effect is less likely than the non-null effect before seeing data; the actual sample data have led the investigator to believe that the true treatment effect will be more than a 95% chance, that is, the actual evidence is strong enough to move 28% skepticism about the effectiveness of the treatment to less than a 5% skepticism about it. This calculation is not meant to interpret "95%" in the Bayesian approach but rather to show the readers what will happen when similar benchmarks are used in the two approaches.

Key Terms and Concepts

Test of significance

Null hypothesis

Alternative hypothesis

Degrees of freedom

Research hypothesis

One- and two-tailed tests

Test statistic

z-test

t-test

Decision rule

Decision statement

Feedback Review of Chapter 9

1. When the sample size is greater than 30, the sampling distribution when testing a hypothesis for one sample case for the mean is the
   a. z distribution with degrees of freedom.
   b. t distribution with degrees of freedom.
   c. t distribution.
   d. z distribution.
   e. binomial distribution.

2. The complement of the level of significance is
   a. a point estimate.
   b. an interval estimate.
   c. alpha.
   d. the standard error.
   e. a level of confidence.

3. When the alternative hypothesis is directional, the test is called a
   a. one sample test of the mean.
   b. two-tailed test.
   c. one-tailed test.
   d. test of the research hypothesis.
   e. significance test.

4. The critical values of a test statistic are those values in the sampling distribution that are:
   a. inside the region of rejection.
   b. outside the region of rejection.
   c. beyond the region of rejection.
   d. at the beginning of the region of rejection.
   e. none of the above.

5. The t distribution is the appropriate sampling distribution when
   a. σ is known.
   b. σ is unknown.

   c. when $n \geq 30$.
   d. when $n \leq 30$.
   e. b & c.

6. The statistic computed to compare with the critical value(s) in hypothesis testing is know as a/an
   a. point estimate.
   b. test statistic.
   c. sample statistic.
   d. alpha level.
   e. random statistic.

7. When testing a hypothesis, the sample mean is compared with the
   a. sample mean that would occur if the null hypothesis were true.
   b. sample mean that would occur if the null hypothesis were false.
   c. population mean that would occur if the null hypothesis were true.
   d. population mean that would occur if the null hypothesis were false.
   e. b & d

8. If the test statistic is equal to 1.75 and the critical value for a one-tailed test is equal to 1.65, the decision rule is symbolically stated as
   a. since $z > z_{cv}$, reject H_o, $p < \alpha$.
   b. since $z < z_{cv}$, reject H_o, $p < \alpha$.
   c. since $z < z_{cv}$, do not reject H_o, $p < \alpha$.
   d. since $z > z_{cv}$, reject H_o, $p < \alpha$.
   e. since $z \neq z_{cv}$, do not reject H_o, $p > \alpha$.

9. Which of the following steps is out of sequence?
   a. State the hypotheses.
   b. Compute the test statistic.
   c. Find the critical value(s) for rejecting H_o.

d. Apply the decision rule.

e. All are in the correct order.

10. When the population standard deviation is unknown and the sample size is less or equal to than 30, the standard error of the sample mean is symbolized as

   a. z_{cv}.

   b. z_α.

   c. $z_{\alpha/2}$.

   d. $s_{\bar{\sigma}} = \dfrac{\sigma}{\sqrt{n}}$.

   e. $s_{\bar{X}} = \dfrac{s}{\sqrt{n}}$.

11. Which of the following hypothesis statements is an acceptable null hypothesis?

   a. $H_o: \mu > 100$

   b. $H_o: \mu < 100$

   c. $H_o: \mu = 100$

   d. $H_1: \mu = 100$

   e. All are acceptable null hypotheses.

12. Efforts to minimize Type I error result in a/an

   a. increase in statistical power.

   b. decrease in statistical power.

   c. effect size.

   d. increase in Type II error.

   e. decrease in Type II error.

Fill-Ins

13. In a nondirectional test of a hypothesis, the region of rejection of the sampling distribution is located in _____.

14. What is the decision of the researcher if the test statistic falls in the region of rejection at the extreme right side of the sampling distribution curve? _____

15. Given the alternative hypothesis, H_1: $u > 106$, where is the region of rejection located? _____

16. If the null hypothesis is rejected, how can a researcher locate a possible true value for the population parameter of interest? _____

17. In a one-tailed t-test of significance with a sample size of 27, the degrees of freedom is equal to _____.

18. What is the symbol for degrees of freedom? _____

19. A researcher believes that the average age of rock stars in 2003 is 18. In a hypothesis test, how will the null and alternative hypotheses be stated? _____

20. In one sample case for the mean where the size of the sample is less than or equal to 30 and the population standard deviation is unknown, what is the appropriate sampling distribution of the mean? _____

21. If the null hypothesis is not rejected at the 0.05 level of significance, what can be said about rejecting or failing to reject at the 0.01 level of significance (i.e., would you reject or fail to reject H_o:)? _____

22. If the null hypothesis is rejected at the 0.01 level of significance, what can be said about rejecting or failing to reject at the 0.05 level of significance (i.e., would you reject or fail to reject H_o:)? _____

23. If the null hypothesis is rejected at the 0.05 level of significance, what can be said about rejecting or failing to reject at the 0.01 level of significance (i.e., would you reject or fail to reject H_o:)?

_____

Review Problems

1. For each of the following levels of significance, indicate the critical value using the normal curve as the underlying distribution.

Level of significance	Critical Value One-tailed	Two-tailed
0.05		
0.10		
0.01		
0.02	± 2.055	
0.025		± 2.24

2. Using the t-distribution as the underlying distribution, state the critical values for each of the following.

Level of significance	Degrees of freedom	Critical Value One-tailed	Two-tailed
0.05	20		
0.05	200		
0.01	27		
0.01	270		
0.10	10		

3. The following sets of hypotheses are related to variables where the population means and standard deviations are known. For each set, draw a distribution curve and illustrate the critical values and their placement along the horizontal axis. (For example, for a nondirectional, two-tailed test at the 0.05 level of significance, the curve would show a line at the boundaries of the regions of rejection and the critical values −1.96 and +1.96 would be shown below the boundary marks.)

a. H_o: = 65
   H_a: ≠ 65
   $\alpha = 0.10$

b. H_o: = 3,700
   H_a: > 3700
   $\alpha = 0.01$

c. H_o: = 243
   H_a: ≠ 243
   $\alpha = 0.02$

d. H_o: = 5.75
   H_a: < 5.75
   $\alpha = 0.05$

4. The following sets of hypotheses are related to variables where the population means and standard deviations are unknown. For each set, draw a distribution curve and illustrate the critical values and their placement along the horizontal axis.

a. H_o: = 65
   H_a: ≠ 65
   $\alpha = 0.10$
   $n = 30$

b. H_o: = 3,700
   H_a: > 3,700
   $\alpha = 0.01$
   $n = 50$

c. H_o: = 243
   H_a: ≠ 243
   $\alpha = 0.02$
   $n = 25$

d. H_o: = 5.75
   H_a: < 5.75
   $\alpha = 0.05$
   $n = 20$

5. A director of the National ASHA office believes that a specific population of conservative voters for a candidate for the professional development committee has a mean age of 47 years. She selects and surveys a random sample of 150 people from the population and finds that the mean age is 49.4, with a standard deviation of 13 years. At the alpha = 0.05 level of significance:
   a. What is the sampling distribution of the mean?

b. What is the critical value that will be used to reject the null hypothesis?

c. What is the standard error of the mean equal to?

6. Using the data above and the four steps followed in testing hypotheses for one sample case for the mean, test the appropriate null hypothesis. (Label each step; show all data and information contained in each step.)

7. Using the same data above, and the four steps followed in testing hypotheses for one sample case for the mean, test the appropriate null hypothesis against the alternative hypothesis claim that the mean age of the population is greater than 47 years. Set alpha at 0.01. (Label each step; show all data and information contained in each step.)

8. A communication researcher hypothesizes that the average collegiate debater has an argumentative level of 13.5 (that's high). She randomly selects 25 debaters and finds the following results: $\Sigma X = 312$; $\Sigma X^2 = 4,182$. At the 0.05 level of significance, what does she conclude?

Note: All of the data needed to test the hypothesis are included in the problem—none are missing. Pause and think about what values are missing and how you can find them.

9. A national study reports that the average score of students who cram the night before a test is 70 (out of a possible 100), with a standard deviation of 3.3. The dean of students decides to see if the claim is true. He randomly selects a sample of 40 students who reported that they crammed for their last exam and finds that their average score was 68. At the 0.05 level of significance, what can the dean conclude? Follow the four steps in testing the null hypothesis. Label each step. Show all data and information contained in each step.

Calculation Guide

Finding Critical Values Using Table M–1 in Appendix M

Step 1: Calculate the degrees of freedom for the sample.

Step 2: Referring to Table M–1 in Appendix A, locate the row within the first column (*df*) listing the degrees of freedom corresponding critical values.

Step 3: Locate the "level of significance" column of a two-tailed test for the level of confidence of interest.

Step 4: The value at the intersection of the located row and column is the critical value *t* for the confidence interval.

10

Hypothesis Testing: Two Sample Cases for the Mean

Overview

In scientific research, there often are cases where hypothesis testing involves two samples. For example, a clinical psychologist may want to determine if children in an experimental group perform significantly better on a measure of self-esteem than their counterparts in a non-experimental group. A political scientist may want to know if negative television advertisements are more effective than neutral ads. A sociologist may be interested in whether inner-city teenagers are more prone to violence than suburban teens. Each of these cases, at a basic level, involves two samples. Each may be the basis for a research study whose results are compared in a hypothesis test to determine if the populations from which the samples were drawn are significantly different on some parameter.

The population means (μ_1 and μ_2) are most often the focus of comparison of two groups, although any population characteristic can be compared using sample statistics. The question addressed by the hypothesis test is whether the population means are equal (H_o: $\mu_1 = \mu_2$ or, equivalently, H_o: $\mu_1 - \mu_2 = 0$), which would be the claim of the null hypothesis. Since sample data are used to determine the answer, the question is whether the samples reflect the mean of a single population or different populations. The research hypothesis would assert that the population means are not equal ($\neq$) or that one is greater than ($>$) or less than ($<$) the other. The hypotheses in the first step of the process are stated as follows:

$$H_o: \mu_1 = \mu_2 \qquad H_1 \ (or\ H_a): \mu_1 \neq \mu_2$$

$$(or\ \mu_1 > \mu_2,\ or\ \mu_1 < \mu_2)$$

Where

μ_1 = mean of population from which sample 1 is drawn

μ_2 = mean of population from which sample 2 is drawn

Note that the population means need not be known or hypothesized in order to determine whether a significant difference exists between them. Whatever difference exists between the population means can be determined by testing the difference between the means of the two samples drawn from each population. This is the underlying rationale of inferential statistics, namely, that sample statistics are used to infer population parameters.

The test statistics, including the standard error of the differences between the means, are based on variances rather than standard deviations. When the variances of the populations (σ_1^2, σ_2^2) are unknown, the variances of the samples (s_1^2, s_2^2) are used as best estimates. We will say more about the standard error of the differences between the means as we proceed through the chapter. For the sake of brevity, we will sometimes refer to the term simply as "the standard error."

There are other considerations that must be addressed in deciding which test statistic and standard error are to be used. These considerations relate to several assumptions, which we will discuss at various points in the chapter. Three assumptions that are of considerable importance are the assumptions of independent samples, normality, and homogeneity of variance.

Assumption of Independent Samples

Two samples are assumed to be independent if their members have been randomly assigned, and the scores of one sample are neither related to nor influenced by the scores of the other sample. One way to achieve this is by first selecting a random sample of individuals from a population and then randomly assigning one half to an experimental group and the other half to a control group. Another method, often used in observational studies, involves randomly selecting individuals from two distinct populations. The purpose of these sampling techniques is to ensure that differences that may exist among the sample members are randomly distributed into the two groups. In that way, significant differences in sample means may be attributed to some treatment or variable of interest rather than to chance or error. On the other hand, if the scores for the two samples are obtained from the same individuals or from individuals who have been paired or matched with respect to a particular variable or characteristic, the two groups are said to be dependent samples, and their means are said to be dependent sample means. For this reason, dependent samples also are known as paired or matched samples.

> Two samples are said to be independent if their members have been randomly assigned and the scores of one sample are neither related to nor influenced by the scores of the other sample.

> Two samples are said to be dependent if their members have been paired or matched with respect to a particular variable of interest.

Assumption of Normality

In Chapter 7, we noted that many variables in the social and natural sciences are continuous and normally distributed, with symmetrical curves. The distributions of these variables, while not always perfectly bell-shaped, have the same properties as the theoretical normal distribution. For this reason, when sample data approximate a normal distribution, they can be analyzed and described using the standard normal z distribution. It also is the underlying reason why the assumption of normality must be satisfied in order to use the standard normal distribution as a sampling distribution and z-tests of significance.

In Chapter 9, we learned that when the population standard deviation, σ, is known or when the sample size is greater than 30, the standard normal z distribution and the z-test can be used for one sample case for the mean. Otherwise, the less powerful, but nevertheless useful, t-test must be applied. For two sample cases, the requirement is that both populations must satisfy the assumption of normality. As in one samples case, the assumption is satisfied when the population standard deviations, and , are known or when the size of the two samples are greater than 30 (>30).

If the assumption of normality is violated, a t-test of significance can be conducted based on whether the homogeneity of the variances of the two populations from which the samples are drawn can or cannot be assumed.

Assumption of Homogeneity of Variance

When the populations from which the samples are drawn are normally distributed and their variances known, or when the samples are greater than 30 (both n_1 and n_2 >30), the standard normal or z distribution is the sampling distribution of the means. In such cases, a modified version of the z-test is used to compare the sample means. When the size of independent samples is less than or equal to 30, a modified t-test is used for the significance test of the mean. In such cases, the assumption of homogeneity of variance must be addressed before the test of significance can be conducted. The concern of the assumption is whether the variance of population 1 (σ_1^2) is equal to the variance of population 2 (σ_2^2). The concern is one of importance because the condition of homogeneity of variance dictates how the standard error of the differences between the means is computed. We discuss the procedures for determining which standard error to use later in this chapter.

> The assumption of homogeneity of variance is concerned with whether the variance of population 1 (σ_1^2) is equal to the variance of population 2 (σ_2^2).

> The pooled estimate of population variance (σ^2) refers to the outcome of computing the standard error of the differences between the means using the variances of the two samples.

Comparing Large Independent Samples

It was noted earlier that when the variances of normally distributed populations from which two samples are drawn are known, the standard normal or z distribution is the sampling distribution for testing hypotheses for two sample cases for the mean. The same is true when the sample sizes are greater than thirty (>30), even if the population variances, σ_1^2 and σ_2^2, are unknown, which often is the case. In such instances, the variances of the respective samples, s_1^2 and s_2^2, are used as the best estimates of the population variances and a modified version of the z-test is used as the test of significance. The major difference in the z-test is reflected in the standard error of the differences between the means, denoted by the symbol $s_{\bar{x}_1 - \bar{x}_2}$, and defined in Formula 10–1. In Formula 10–2, which we use in this text, the computation equation of the standard error is incorporated with that of the test statistic.

Formula 10–1

$$\sqrt{\frac{s_1^2}{n_1} + \frac{s_2^2}{n_2}}$$

Where

s_1^2 and s_2^2 = sample variances

n_1, n_2 = sample sizes

Formula 10–2

$$z = \frac{(\bar{X}_1 - \bar{X}_2) - (\mu_1 - \mu_2)}{\sqrt{\frac{s_1^2}{n_1} + \frac{s_2^2}{n_2}}}$$

Where

$\bar{X}_1 - \bar{X}_2$ = difference in sample means

$\mu_1 - \mu_2$ = difference in population means or hypothesized mean difference (in most cases the difference is zero)

$\sqrt{\frac{s_1^2}{n_1} + \frac{s_2^2}{n_2}}$ = standard error of the differences between the means

The three assumptions and conditions for testing hypotheses for two sample cases for the mean are: (1) the populations of the samples are normally distributed; (2) the samples are randomly drawn and independent; and (3) the population variances are known or the sample sizes are greater than 30.

The procedure for testing hypotheses with independent samples >30 is illustrated using the results of a hypothetical research study and the four-step model introduced in the previous chapter.

Step 1. State the hypotheses.

Step 2. Set the criterion for rejecting the H_o.

Step 3. Compute the test statistic.

Step 4. Apply the decision rule.

Scenario 1

A clinical scientist believes that the attitudes of younger SLPs (less than or equal to 10 years of clinical experience as a certified SLP) toward a certain intensive and aggressive speech treatment are less negative than those of older SLPs (more than 10 years of clinical experience as a certified SLP). He decides to test his belief and conducts a survey using a random sample from each population. The results are summarized in Table 10–1. The lower the survey score, the lower the level of negative attitude. Given the sampling method, the two samples are assumed to be independent of each other. Since the samples are greater than 30, the standard normal distribution can be used as

Table 10–1. Results of Survey on Attitudes Toward a Certain Intensive and Aggressive Speech Therapy by Younger and Older SLPs

$\bar{X}_1 = 59$	$\bar{X}_2 = 61$
$s_1^2 = 12$	$s_2^2 = 14$
$n_1 = 32*$	$n_2 = 31*$

*It is not necessary that both samples be equal.

the sampling distribution of differences between the means, with a *z-test* as the test of significance. At $\alpha = 0.05$ level of significance, what will the hypothesis test for these data conclude? (Again, we suggest that you work through the steps with us on a sheet of paper.)

Step 1: State the Hypotheses

Since the clinical scientist believes that the average negative attitude score for young SLPs will be less than the average score of older SLPs, the hypotheses are stated as follows:

$$H_o: \mu_1 = \mu_2 \quad H_o: \mu_1 < \mu_2$$

Where

μ_1 = mean negative attitude score for young SLPs

μ_2 = mean negative attitude score for older SLPs

The less than symbol is included in the alternative hypothesis (H_1) because the implied claim of the null hypothesis is that the population mean, μ_1, of young SLPs is equal to or greater than the popula-

tion mean, μ_2, of older SLPs. Therefore, if H_o is rejected, the researcher is directed toward the claim of the alternative or research hypothesis, H_1, which asserts that the average negative attitude score for younger SLPs is less than the average negative attitude score for older SLPs.

Step 2: Set the Criterion for Rejecting H_o

The alternative hypothesis, H_1, specifies that the test for significance will be one-tailed with the region of rejection located at the lower or extreme left end of the distribution curve as shown in Figure 10–1.

At $\alpha = 0.05$, the critical value, z_{cv}, for rejecting the null hypothesis is −1.645. (See Table 9–1.) Thus, Step 2 of the hypothesis test is stated as follows:

Step 2: $\alpha = 0.05$ 1-Tailed Test
$z_{cv} = -1.645$

Step 3: Compute the Test Statistic

Since the population variances in this study are unknown, the test statistic z is derived using Formula 10–2.

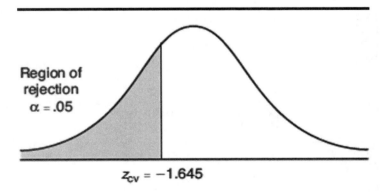

Region of
rejection
$\alpha = .05$

$z_{cv} = -1.645$

Figure 10–1. Critical value and region of rejection for a one-tailed hypothesis test.

$$z = \frac{(59 - 61) - (0)}{\sqrt{\frac{12}{32} + \frac{14}{31}}}$$

$$= \frac{(-2)}{\sqrt{0.375 + 0.452}}$$

$$= -2.20$$

When values are not specified for population means, $\mu_1 - \mu_2$ will always equal zero.

Step 4: Apply the Decision Rule

Since the test statistic, $z = -2.20$, is greater in absolute value than the critical value, $z = -1.645$, as shown in Figure 10–2, the null hypothesis (H_o) is rejected. The belief and claim of the clinical scientist is confirmed at the 5% level of significance. A summary of the four steps followed in the hypothesis test is outlined in Table 10–2.

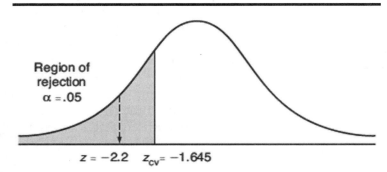

Figure 10–2. Critical value and test significance for Scenario 1 test of significance.

Table 10–2. A Summary of the Basic Four Step for Scenario 1

Step 1: State the hypotheses
H_o: $\mu_1 = \mu_2$ H_1: $\mu_1 < \mu_2$
Step 2: Set the criterion for rejecting H_o
$\alpha = 0.05$ 1-Tailed Test $z_{cv} = -1.645$
Step 3: Compute the test statistic
$n_1 = 32$ $n_2 = 31$ $\overline{X}_1 = 59$ $\overline{X}_2 = 61$
$z = \dfrac{(59 - 61) - (0)}{\sqrt{\frac{12}{32} + \frac{14}{31}}} = \dfrac{-2}{\sqrt{0.375 + 0.452}} = -2.20$
Step 4: Apply the decision rule
Since $z = \lvert -2.20 \rvert > = \lvert -1.645 \rvert$
Decision Statement:
H_o is rejected at the 5% level of significance. $p < 0.05$

Before continuing with procedures for testing hypotheses for the mean with independent samples, we need to consider further the assumption of homogeneity of variance, which asks whether the population variances are equal. The question is answered using a procedure designed to test the difference between two variances, known as the F-test. The implications of the test results will become clear when we discuss comparing small, independent samples.

Comparing Variances: The *F*-Test

As we noted earlier, any population parameter may be used to determine whether significant differences exist between two or more populations. Sometimes, researchers may be interested in comparing two groups, such as men and women, fluency children and disfluency children, liberals and conservatives, or introverts and extroverts, using two variances or standard deviations rather than the mean. In such cases, the test of comparison is known as the *F*-test. Our primary interest in this text is in role the *F*-test plays in hypothesis tests of the mean for two or more

small, independent samples. However, to best understand its role in the process, we need to know something about its sampling distribution and the test itself.

The sampling distribution for the F-test comes from the F distribution. The theoretical basis for the distribution is the same as for other sampling distributions, meaning that if we repeatedly select two random samples from a normally distributed population and compute the ratio of each pair, $\frac{s_1^2}{s_2^2}$, the distribution of ratios, called *F*-ratios, would form an *F* distribution. Actually, there is a family of *F* distributions, each of which is positively skewed and based on the degrees of freedom for each sample. Because of the skewness of the distribution, the values of *F* are always positive or zero, ranging from zero to +1, since variances cannot be negative, as shown in Figure 10–3. The mean of *F* is approximately equal to 1. The four distinguishing characteristics of the *F* distribution are summarized below.

Properties of the *F* Distribution:

1. The distribution is positively skewed.
2. Values of the distribution cannot be negative.
3. The mean of the distribution is approximately equal to 1.

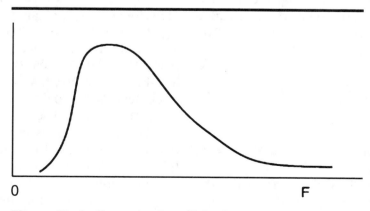

Figure 10–3. Example of an *F* distribution curve.

4. The distribution is a family of distributions based on the degrees of freedom for each distribution.

The *F*-Test

The *F*-test uses the samples variances, s_1^2 and s_2^2, to compare the variances of the populations from which they are drawn. The test is based on two assumptions. The first is that the two populations are normally distributed. The second is that the two populations are independent of each other. Since the variance of one sample is not likely to equal the variance of another, the test of the null hypothesis is concerned with the magnitude of the difference between the sample variances. The *F*-test may be viewed as a hypothesis test that follows the same four-step process we have been using in hypothesis tests for means. This is the approach we will take to describe and illustrate the concepts and procedures related to the test.

Step 1: State The Hypotheses

If two populations have equal variances ($\sigma_1^2 = \sigma_1^2$), then the ratio of $\frac{\sigma_1^2}{\sigma_1^2}$ equals 1. This is the expected value of *F* in the test for homogeneity of variance. The null hypothesis claims that the population variances are equal; the alternative hypothesis is that they are not equal. The hypotheses are stated as follows:

$$H_o: \frac{\sigma_1^2}{\sigma_1^2} = 1 \qquad H_I: \frac{\sigma_1^2}{\sigma_1^2} \neq 1$$

This is essentially the same as: $H_o: \sigma_1^2 = \sigma_1^2$ versus $H_o: \sigma_1^2 \neq \sigma_1^2$.

Theoretically, if the variances of the two populations are equal: (1) the *F*-ratio of the samples will tend to be close to 1; (2) the null hypothesis will not be rejected; and (3) the assumption of homogeneity of variance is confirmed. On the other hand, if the populations have significantly different variances, then the *F*-ratio will be greater than 1, the claim of the null hypothesis will be rejected, and homogeneity of variance cannot be assumed. We consider the implications of both conditions when we discuss hypothesis tests comparing two or more small, independent samples. For now, we simply continue to outline the procedures for the *F*-test.

Step 2: Set the Criterion for Rejecting H_o

The *F*-test, as a prerequisite of independent *t*, is always a nondirectional, two-tailed test of significance, since our concern is whether *F* exceeds a critical value, denoted by F_{cv}. The critical values for the *F* distribution are listed in three tables in Appendix N: Tables N–1, N–2, and N–3. The tables correspond to three levels of significance, $\alpha = 0.05$, $\alpha = 0.0.25$, and $\alpha = 0.01$ for right side values of the *F* distribution curve. Since the *F*-test used for homogeneity of variance is always two-tailed, the right side values of the distribution at the $\alpha/2$ level of significance are used when comparing two sample variances. Thus, for an *F*-test with an $\alpha = 0.10$ level of significance, the 0.05 ($\alpha/2$) critical values are found Table N–1. For an *F*-test with an $\alpha = 0.05$, the 0.025 (.05/2) critical values in Table N–2 are used. And for a test with alpha level set at 0.02, Table N–3, with $\alpha = 0.01$ F_{cv} values, is used.

The critical values in the *F* distribution tables are based on the degrees of freedom associated with the numerator and denominator of the *F*-ratio. The degrees of freedom for the numerator, symbolized as df_{n1}, is defined as $n_1 - 1$ and shown as column headings along the top of the tables. The degrees of freedom for the denominator, symbolized as df_{n2}, is defined as $n_2 - 1$ and shown as rows of the tables. In conducting F-tests for homogeneity of variance, it is suggested that the larger of the sample variances always be designated as the numerator in determining the critical value, F_{cv}. This greatly simplifies computations and ensure that the F-ratio will always be a value greater than 1.00.

For illustration purposes, consider the following data:

Sample A	Sample B
$s_1^2 = 31.7$	$s_2^2 = 29.3$
$n_1 = 16$	$n_2 = 12$

To determine the critical value (F_{cv}) for these data, we follow a simple three-step process. First, we designate the variance of Sample A ($s_1^2 = 31.7$) as the numerator and that of Sample B ($s_2^2 = 29.3$) as the denominator. Next, we define the degrees of freedom. In this case, the numerator, df_{n1} is given as $16 - 1$ or 15, and the degrees of freedom for the denominator, df_{n2}, is given as $12 - 1$ or 11. Finally, assuming an $\alpha = 0.05$ level of significance, we refer to Table N–2, column 16 and row 11, to find the 0.025 ($\alpha/2$) critical value, in this case, $F_{cv} = 3.33$. See the partially reproduced Table N–2 in Figure 10–4.

Thus, in a hypothesis test for homogeneity of variance for the data in this illustration, the criterion step would be stated as follows:

Step 2: Set the criterion for rejecting H_o

$$\alpha = 0.025 \quad df_{n1} = 16 - 1 = 15$$

$$df_{n2} = 12 - 1 = 11 \quad F_{cv} = 3.33$$

In cases where Tables N–1, N–2, and N–3 do not list degrees of freedom for samples of interest, use the critical values

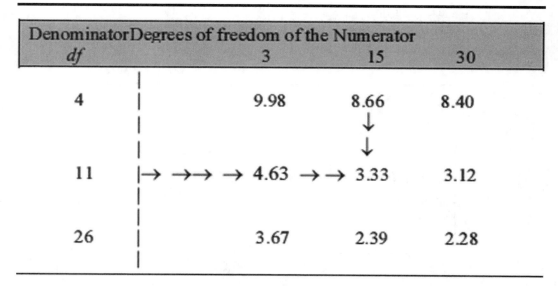

Denominator df	Degrees of freedom of the Numerator		
	3	15	30
4	9.98	8.66	8.40
11	4.63	3.33	3.12
26	3.67	2.39	2.28

Figure 10–4. Degrees of freedom for the numerator.

of the degrees of freedom that fall below those of the two samples, that is, choose the next smaller degrees of freedom. For example, for samples of 22, 23, or 24, use the critical values listed for 20 degrees of freedom.

Step 3: Compute the Test Statistic

The equation for computing the test statistic, F, is given in Formula 10–3.

Formula 10–3

$$F = \frac{s_1^2}{s_2^2}$$

Where

s_1^2 = the larger of the sample variances

s_2^2 = the smaller of the sample variances

For the data in the illustration above, the F-ratio or test statistics is given as

$$F = \frac{31.7}{29.3} = 1.082$$

Step 4: Apply the Decision Rule

Since the observed $F = 1.082$ is less than the upper $F_{cv} = 3.33$, the null hypothesis (H_o) is not rejected. (See Figure 10–5.) Therefore, we can conclude that homogeneity of variances can be assumed.

We now discuss how homogeneity of variance impacts the testing of hypotheses for small, independent samples.

Comparing Small Independent Samples

We mentioned earlier that when population variances are unknown, or sample sizes are less than or equal to 30, the t distribution is the appropriate sampling distribution for conducting tests of significance for the mean. The test is a modified version of the t-test for one sample cases. The major differences are reflected in how degrees of freedom and the estimate of the standard error of the differences between means are calculated. Actually, there are two approaches in conducting t-tests for small samples. One approach

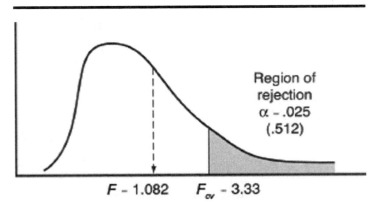

Figure 10–5. Critical value (F_{cv}).

is used when the assumption of homogeneity of variance is confirmed ($\sigma_1^2 = \sigma_2^2$); the other is used when homogeneity of variance cannot be assumed ($\sigma_1^2 \neq \sigma_2^2$). Each approach uses different formulas to calculate df and $s_{\bar{x}_1 - \bar{x}_2}$ in the process of conducting the t-test.

When testing small samples, two hypothesis tests are conducted, an F-test to determine if homogeneity of variance can be assumed and a t-test to determine the significance of differences in means. In the sections that follow, we illustrate how the t-tests are conducted based on the outcome of the F-test, specifically when the outcome indicates that homogeneity of variance cannot be assumed.

The t-Test: Homogeneity of Variance Assumed

In cases where homogeneity of variance can be assumed, the standard error in the t-test is computed using a combined variance of the two samples. The single variance is known as the **pooled estimate of the variance** and denoted by the symbol s^2. We refer to this type of t-test as a **pooled t-test**. When homogeneity of variance cannot be assumed, the standard error of the difference between the two means, as well as degrees of freedom, are derived using correction formulas. We refer to this type of t-test as a **nonpooled t-test**.

Scenario 2

A national survey by a media advocacy group reports that the prosocial skills of the average teenager may have been learned or reinforced from viewing prosocial children's television programs such as Sesame Street, Thomas and His Friends, and Bob the Builder, to name a few.

A developmental psychologist agrees with the report but believes that viewing prosocial children's television programs had a greater impact on teenage boys than teenage girls. He conducts a pilot study to test his belief. He selects a random sample of 19 teenagers, 9 boys and 10 girls, who reported watching children's television programs regularly as young children. Each of the participants is asked to complete a questionnaire consisting of items related to learning prosocial skills as a child. The results are summarized in Table 10–3.

Table 10–3. Summary Data from Prosocial Skills Study

Group 1 (Teenage Boys)	Group 2 (Teenage Girls)
57	85
42	57
48	78
59	61
66	81
55	70
52	75
79	55
46	72
	77
$n_1 = 9$	$n_2 = 10$
$\Sigma X_1 = 505$	$\Sigma X_2 = 71.1$
$X_1 = 56$	$X_2 = 71.1$
$\Sigma X_1^2 = 29{,}240$	$\Sigma X_2^2 = 51{,}503$
$s_1^2 = 127$	$s_2^2 = 105.656$
$s_1 = 11.269$	$s^2 = 10.279$

From an analysis point of view, the question is whether the 15.1 point sample mean difference between teenage boys ($\overline{X}_1 = 56$) and teenage girls ($\overline{X}_2 = 71.1$) can be attributed to random sampling fluctuation or some other treatment. In other words, is the difference statistically significant, suggesting that boys, in general, are less affected by prosocial children's television programs than girls, in terms of learning prosocial skills?

As mentioned above, when the sample sizes are less than or equal to 30, two hypothesis tests must be conducted as part of the analysis of the research data prior to conducting a hypothesis test to determine the significance of the difference between the sample means.

Let us assume the psychologist wants to be conservative and chooses an alpha level of 0.01 for the t-test of significance of means. However, before conducting the test of the sample means, the psychologist must first conduct a hypothesis test to determine whether homogeneity of variance can be assumed. For the F-test, he chooses a significance level of 0.10.

Of course, we know from the heading of this section that homogeneity of variance will be assumed and that a pooled t-test will be used to compare the sample means, but the developmental psychologist does not know what we know. So for illustration purposes, we will conduct both the F-test and the pooled t-test from the perspective of the psychologist. Meaning that we will pretend we don't know the outcome in advance.

The *F*-test for Homogeneity of Variance

The relevant data in Table 10–3 for the hypothesis test to determine homogeneity of variance are as follows:

Group 1 (boys):
$$n_1 = 9 \quad \overline{X}_1 = 56 \quad s_1^2 = 127$$

Group 2 (girls):
$$n_2 = 10 \quad \overline{X}_2 = 71.1 \quad s_2^2 = 105.656$$

Because of the sampling procedures followed by the researcher, we will assume that the two samples are independent.

Step 1: State the Hypotheses

For the test for homogeneity of variance, the null and alternative hypotheses are stated as follows:

$$H_o: \sigma_1^2 = \sigma_2^2 \quad H_1: \sigma_1^2 \neq \sigma_2^2$$

or, equivalently,

$$H_o: \frac{\sigma_1^2}{\sigma_1^2} = 1 \quad H_o: \frac{\sigma_1^2}{\sigma_2^2} \neq 1$$

Step 2: Set the Criterion for Rejecting H₀

Since the F-test is always two-tailed and the alpha level chosen in this case is 0.10, the $0.05(\frac{10}{2})$ value is used in Table N–1. Also, since the variance of the sample with boys (Group 1) is larger than that for girls (Group 2), the degrees of freedom are set as: $df_{n1} = 9 - 1$ or 8 (numerator) and $df_{n2} = 10 - 1$ or 9 (denominator). Referring to column 8, row 9 in Table N–1 we find the critical value to be 3.23. Therefore, Step 2 is stated as follows:

$$\alpha = 0.05 \quad df_{n1} = 9 - 1 = 8$$
$$df_{n2} = 10 - 1 = 9 \quad F_{cv} = 3.23$$

Step 3: Compute the Test Statistic

Apply Formula 10–4.

$$F = \frac{s_1^2}{s_2^2} = \frac{127}{105.656} = 1.202$$

Step 4: Apply Decision Rule

Since $F = 1.202$, which is less than the critical value $F_{cv} = 3.23$, the null hypothesis is *not* rejected. Therefore, the population variances from which the samples were drawn are considered equal, and homogeneity of variance can be assumed.

The Pooled *t*-test for Small Sample Means

Since homogeneity can be assumed, the developmental psychologist is able to conduct a pooled *t*-test to determine if boys are less affected than girls by prosocial television programs for children. The pooled *t*-test is conducted using the combined variances and degrees of freedom of the two samples. The combined variance, denoted by the symbol s^2, is known as a *pooled estimate of the variance*, or simply as *pooled variance*. It is used in computing the estimated standard error of the difference between the sample means, $s_{\bar{x}_1 - \bar{x}_2}$. Before examining the methodology for the pooled *t*-test, let's consider two methods of calculating pooled variance.

Pooled Variance

The two ways for estimating the population variance, s^2, using the combined variances of the samples are known as the raw score method and the variance method. The raw score method, shown in Formula 10–5, combines or pools the sums of squares and degrees of freedom of the two samples.

Formula 10–5

$$s^2 = \frac{[\sum X_1^2 - (\sum X_1)^2/n_1] + [\sum X_2^2 - (\sum X_2)^2/n_2]}{n_1 + n_2 - 2}$$

It is an expansion of the raw score method (Formula 3–7) for estimating the population variance for a single sample, introduced in Chapter 3.

> Pooled estimate of the variance, also referred to as pooled variance, s^2, is the combined variances of the two samples used in computing the estimated standard error of the difference between the sample means, $s_{\bar{x}_1 - \bar{x}_2}$.

The variance method, expressed in Formula 10–6, combines the variance estimates of the two samples.

Formula 10–6

$$s^2 = \frac{(n_1 - 1)s_1^2 + (n_2 - 1)s_2^2}{n_1 + n_2 - 2}$$

(Variance Method)

Both methods are algebraic equivalents and yield identical estimates of the population variance. Table 10–3 contains all of the data needed to compute pooled variance using either method.

The Hypothesis *t*-Test Using Pooled Variance

Step 1: State the Hypotheses

Since the research interest of the developmental psychologist is that boys are affected less by viewing prosocial children's television programs than teenage girls, the hypotheses are stated as follows:

$$H_o: \mu_1 = \mu_2 \quad H_1: \mu_1 < \mu_2$$

Step 2: Set the Criterion for Rejecting H_o

Recall that the psychologist chose $\alpha = 0.01$ as the level of significance for this one-tailed, directional test. The degrees of freedom (df) for a pooled t-test is derived by subtracting 2 from the sum of the n's of the two samples as shown in Formula 10–7.

Formula 10–7

$$df = n_1 + n_2 - 2$$

In this case, $df = 9 + 10 - 2 = 17$. Referring to Table M–1 in Appendix M, we find that for 17 degrees of freedom, given an $\alpha = 0.01$ level of significance, the critical value (t_{cv}) for a one-tailed test is −2.567. Thus, Step 2 is stated as follows:

$$\alpha = 0.01 \quad \text{1-Tailed Test}$$
$$df = 9 + 10 - 2 = 17 \quad t_{cv} = -2.567$$

Step 3: Compute the Test Statistic

The test statistic (t) for independent samples when homogeneity of variance is derived from Formula 10–8; it involves three separate calculations: (1) the pooled estimate of the variance, (2) standard error, and (3) a modified t-test.

Formula 10–8

$$t = \frac{(\bar{X}_1 - \bar{X}_2) - (\mu_1 - \mu_2)}{\sqrt{s^2 \left(\frac{1}{n_1} + \frac{1}{n_2}\right)}}$$

Where

$\bar{X}_1 - \bar{X}_2$ = difference between two sample means

$\mu_1 - \mu_2$ = zero, unless specified in the hypotheses

$\sqrt{s^2 \left(\frac{1}{n_1} + \frac{1}{n_2}\right)}$ = estimated standard error of the difference between the means, $s_{\bar{x}_1 - \bar{x}_2}$, where s^2 represents the pooled estimate of the population variance

(1) The pooled estimate of the population variance using Formula 10–6.

$$s^2 = \frac{(9-1) \cdot 127 + (10-1) \cdot 105.656}{9 + 10 - 2}$$

$$= \frac{(1016 + 950.9)}{17} = 115.7$$

(2) The estimated standard error.

$$s_{\bar{x}_1 - \bar{x}_2} = \sqrt{s^2 \left(\frac{1}{n_1} + \frac{1}{n_2}\right)}$$

$$= \sqrt{115.7 \left(\frac{1}{9} + \frac{1}{10}\right)} = \sqrt{24.413} = 4.941$$

(3) The t-test statistic using Formula 10–8.

$$= \frac{(56 - 71.1) - (0)}{4.91} = -3.075$$

Recall that when populations means are not specified, $\mu_1 - \mu_2$ equals zero.

Step 4: Apply the Decision Rule

Since the observed t-ratio −3.075 is greater than the critical value $t_{cv} = -2.567$ in absolute value, the null hypothesis is rejected and the alternative or research hypothesis is supported (Figure 10–6). At the 0.01 level of significance, the psychologist may conclude that boys appear to be less affected than girls by the prosocial nature of children television programs.

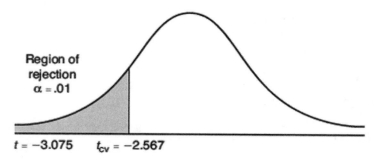

Figure 10–6. Critical value (t_{cv}) and test significance (t) for Scenario 2 test of significance.

The *t*-Test: Homogeneity of Variance Not Assumed

In this section we consider a hypothetical situation where the null hypothesis of an *F*-test is rejected, and homogeneity cannot be assumed. In the subsequent, nonpooled *t*-test, two alternative formulas are introduced to determine degrees of freedom and the standard error of the difference between the means.

Scenario 3

A communication sciences and disorders researcher wants to know if there is a significant difference between college-age male and female compulsive communicators, known as "talkaholics." Is one group more talkative on average than the other? The dependent variable is the average length of time (in seconds) before pauses in a conversation. Under controlled laboratory conditions, the results of observed samples from each population in conversation are as follows:

Males: $n_1 = 25$ $\overline{X}_1 = 32.8$
$s_1^2 = 90.9$

Females: $n_2 = 31$ $\overline{X}_2 = 33.0$
$s_2^2 = 41.7$

Since the population variances are unknown, and one of the samples is less than or equal to 30, the researcher must first conduct an *F*-test, which, as we shall see, indicates that homogeneity of variance cannot be assumed. For this illustration, we will assume that the researcher chooses $\alpha = 0.05$ for the *F*-test and $\alpha = 0.05$ for the *t*-test of significance.

The *F*-Test for Homogeneity of Variance. For this test, males are designated as Group 1 because they have the larger sample variance and females as Group 2. The variable, average length-of-time before pauses, is assumed to be normally distributed. At $\alpha = 0.10$, what will a test of homogeneity of variance conclude? The four-step procedure for hypothesis testing is applied.

Step 1: State the hypotheses.

$$H_a: \sigma_1^2 = \sigma_2^2 \quad H_1: \sigma_1^2 \neq \sigma_2^2$$

Step 2: Set the criterion for rejecting H_o. Since the variance for males is the larger of the two samples ($s_1^2 = 90.9$ versus $s_2^2 = 41.7$ for females), the degrees of freedom of the numerator is 24 ($n_1 - 1$), leaving 30 ($n_2 - 1$) as the denominator.

Referring to column 24, row 30, in Table N–1 the 0.05 critical value for this *F*-test is 1.89, and Step 2 is stated as follows:

$$\alpha = 0.025 \quad df_{n1} = n_1 - 1 = 24$$
$$df_{n2} = n_2 - 1 = 30 \quad F_{cv} = 1.89$$

Step 3: Compute the test statistic.

$$F = \frac{s_1^2}{s_2^2} = \frac{90.9}{41.7} = 2.180$$

Step 4: Apply decision rule. Since the observed *F*-ratio, 2.18, is greater than the critical value, $F_{cv} = 1.89$, the null hypothesis is rejected (Figure 10–7). Thus, the communication sciences and disorders researcher can conclude that the population variances are not equal (H_1: $\sigma_1^2 \neq \sigma_2^2$) and that homogeneity of variance cannot be assumed. In such cases, a nonpooled *t* must be used in testing the significance of differences among the sample means.

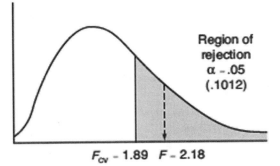

Figure 10–7. Critical value (F_{cv}) and test statistic (*F*) for Scenario 3 test of homogeneity of variance.

when homogeneity of variance cannot be assumed. In this text, we use the methods suggested by Welch (1938) for calculating degrees of freedom and the method suggested by Cochran and Cox (1957) for estimating the standard error of the difference between the means.

The Nonpooled *t*-Test for Small Sample Means

When sample sizes are less than or equal to 30 and the variances of the populations are unknown, violation of the assumption of homogeneity of variance increases the probability of a Type II error (failing to reject a false null hypothesis) in a *t*-test. To diminish the likelihood of Type II error, corrective procedures for determining degrees of freedom and the estimate of the standard error of the differences between the means must be applied.

Corrective Methods for Computing df and $s_{\bar{x}_1 - \bar{x}_2}$ When $\sigma_1^2 \neq \sigma_2^2$

There are several algebraically equivalent methods for determining degrees of freedom and estimating the standard error

Welch Method for Calculating Degrees of Freedom

While Formula 10–9 may appear daunting, it requires only the variances and sizes of the two samples to calculate the degrees of freedom needed for finding the critical value for the *t*-test.

Formula 10–9

$$df = \frac{\left(s_{\bar{X}_1}^2 + s_{\bar{X}_2}^2\right)^2}{\left(s_{\bar{X}_1}^2\right)^2 / (n_1 + 1) + \left(s_{\bar{X}_1}^2\right)^2 / (n_2 + 1)} - 2$$

Cochran and Cox Method for Calculating the Standard Error

Formula 10–10, like the Welch method, requires only the variances and sizes of the two samples to compute the estimate of the standard error of the difference between the means.

Formula 10–10

$$s_{\bar{x}_1 - \bar{x}_2} = \sqrt{\frac{s_1^2}{n_1} + \frac{s_2^2}{n_2}}$$

The Nonpooled t-Test

The t-test when homogeneity of variance cannot be assumed is expressed in Formula 10–11.

Formula 10–11

$$t = \frac{(\bar{X}_1 - \bar{X}_2) - (\mu_1 - \mu_2)}{s_{\bar{x}_1 - \bar{x}_2}}$$

The Nonpooled Variance Hypothesis t-Test

Step 1: State the Hypotheses. Since the researcher makes no claim regarding the direction of difference, the alternative hypothesis is nondirectional.

$$H_o: \mu_1 = \mu_2 \quad H_1: \mu_1 \neq \mu_2$$

Step 2: Set the Criterion for Rejecting H_o. The chosen level of significance is 0.05. The degrees of freedom is calculated using Formula 10–9.

$$df = \frac{(90.9 + 41.7)^2}{(90.9)^2/(25 + 1) + (41.7)^2/(31 + 1)} - 2$$

$$= \frac{17582.76}{317.8 + 54.34} - 2 = 45.248 \text{ or } 45$$

Referring to Column 1 and Row 40 in Table M–1, the critical value for a two-tailed test at $\alpha = 0.05$ with 49 df is 2.021. (Recall that when a table does not contain particular critical values, the suggestion

is to use the one in the row below the computed df.) Step 2 is stated as follows:

$$\alpha = 0.05 \quad \text{Two-Tailed Test}$$
$$df = 45^* \quad t = \pm 2.021^*$$

*Since there are no probability values for $df = 45$ in Table M–1, the critical value for $df = 40$ is used.

Step 3: Compute the Test Statistic. Two calculations are conducted. First is the standard error using the Cochran and Cox method (Formula 10–10); second is the t-test using Formula 10–11.

(1) Cochran and Cox standard error.

$$s_{\bar{x}_1 - \bar{x}_2} = \sqrt{\frac{90.9}{25} + \frac{41.7}{31}} = \sqrt{3.636 + 1.345}$$

$$= \sqrt{4.981} = 2.232$$

(2) $\quad t = \dfrac{(\bar{X}_1 - \bar{X}_2) - (\mu_1 - \mu_2)}{s_{\bar{x}_1 - \bar{x}_2}}$

$$= \frac{(32.8 - 33) - (0)}{2.232} = -0.09$$

Step 4: Apply the Decision Rule. Since the observed $t = -0.09$, does not exceed the critical value of $t_{cv} = 2.021$ in absolute value; the null hypothesis is rejected (Figure 10–8). Thus, the communication researcher may conclude that there is no significant difference among male and female talkaholics on the criterion variable, average length of speech before pauses.

Testing Hypotheses for Dependent Sample Means

We noted earlier that two samples are considered to be dependent when the scores or values of individuals in one group

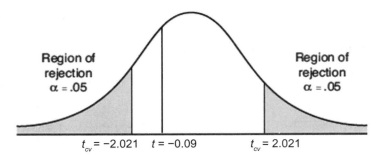

Figure 10–8. Critical value (t_{cv}) and test statistic (t) for Scenario 3 test of significance.

are related to those in another group. Dependent samples also are referred to as paired or matched samples. Samples are considered paired when the two scores for each member represent pretest-posttest or before-after treatment measures. For example, elementary and secondary school students often are given one form of a standardized achievement test in the fall ("pretest") and an alternative version in the spring ("post-test") to determine gains in academic achievement during the school year. This results in a pair of scores for each student; the two sets of scores are then compared to determine if the academic curriculum or program had a significant effect on their test scores.

Samples are considered matched when the pair of scores is for sample members who share a particular characteristic(s), which often is the case in experimental studies. For example, a researcher randomly selects a group of 20 young adults who believe that major events in their lives are "other directed" and not fully in their control. The variable is known as "locus-of-control." The subjects are then randomly assigned to one of two groups in a fashion that ensures the equivalency of the two groups. This may be accomplished by taking the two individuals with

the highest scores and randomly assigning one to the "experimental group" and the other to the "control group." The procedure would continue for the individuals with the third and fourth highest scores and be repeated until the process is complete. In this way, the two groups may be considered equivalent in the shared characteristic or variable, locus-of-control. Thus, any observed post treatment differences between the two samples are assumed to be due to the effects of treatment received or not received.

> Dependent samples are considered paired when the two samples represent the scores of each individual, as in pretest-post-test scores. Matched samples consist of individuals who share a particular characteristic(s).

The data for dependent samples are evaluated using the t-test for dependent samples. The test is essentially the same as the one used for independent groups, except that the sampling distribution of differences is for paired or matched data. The test statistic t is derived using the same three-stage process whether population parameters are known or not known.

The calculations are essentially the same, except for symbols. However, we continue to use sample statistics as estimates of the population parameters. The process involves the computation of: (1) an estimate of the population's standard deviation; (2) an estimate of the population variance; and (3) the test statistic itself. Since the equivalency of the two groups is assured, the distributions of pretest scores and post-test scores are assumed to be homogeneous; that is to say, it is not necessary in this case to conduct an *F*-test.

Estimating σ_d for Dependent Samples

There are several algebraically equivalent methods for calculating an estimate of the population's standard deviation of the differences between paired or matched scores. The method we present here, denoted by the symbol s_d, is identical to Formula 3–8 introduced in Chapter 3 for calculating the standard deviation for single samples. Only the symbols are different, as in Formula 10–12.

Formula 10–12

$$s_d = \sqrt{\frac{n \sum d^2 - [(\sum d)^2/n]}{n-1}}$$

Where

d = difference between pretest and post-test = $X_1 - X_2$

$\sum d^2$ = sum of the squared difference for each pair of scores

$\sum d$ = sum of the difference for each pair of scores

n = number of paired scores

This estimate of the standard deviation of differences is used to compute an estimate of the standard error of differences, denoted by symbol $s_{\bar{d}}$.

Estimating $\sigma_{\bar{d}}$ for Dependent Samples

An estimate of the population standard error of the difference between the paired or matched scores is determined by dividing the standard deviation estimate, s_d, by the square root of n as given in Formula 10–13.

Formula 10–13

$$s_{\bar{d}} = \frac{s_d}{\sqrt{n}}$$

Computing the Test Statistic

The test statistic, t, is computed using Formula 10–14, which includes the estimates of the standard deviation and standard error of the difference between the dependent samples.

Formula 10–14

$$t = \frac{\bar{d} - \Delta}{s_{\bar{d}}}$$

Where

$\bar{d}$ = mean of the difference between each pair of scores, that is ($\bar{d} = \bar{X}_1 - \bar{X}_2$ or, equivalently, $\bar{d} = \sum d/n$)

Δ = hypothesized difference between the two populations or zero

$s_{\bar{d}}$ = estimate of the standard error

Degrees of Freedom

Finally, in testing the significance of differences between dependent samples, degrees of freedom are defined as $df = n - 1$, where n represents the number of paired or matched scores, rather than the total number of scores.

Scenario 4

An audiologist decides to conduct an experiment to see if a new type of hearing aid is more effective than the type used with a more traditional audiological hearing device, which we refer to as "earbuds." Recent research suggest that earbuds can effect a severe damage to their ears (nearly loss of hearing) in young people similar to that found in aging adults. The researcher selects a random sample of 20 young adults who use earbuds on a regular basis. Using the matched-pair procedure described

above, he assigns half to an experimental group, X_1, that will wear the new hearing devices. The other half is assigned to a control group, X_2, that continues to use earbuds. At the end of the 9 months, both groups are given hearing tests.

The results of the hearing test are summarized in Table 10–4. Note that the arrangement of the data in the table generates all of the data needed to perform the calculations in Formulas 10–11, 10–12, and 10–13. A review of the data in Table 10–4 shows a 2.4 difference between the mean score of the experimental group and the control group. The lower the score, the less hearing loss detected.

From an analysis point of view is the 2.4 difference between the means of the two samples $(\overline{X}_1 - \overline{X}_2)$ statistically significant? Or is the difference indicative of random sampling error or some chance factor? The hypothesis test to answer this question is as follows:

Table 10–4. New Headphone Experiment Data

Pair	(X_1)	(X_2)	d	d^2
1	24	26	−2	4
2	24	24	0	0
3	20	23	−3	9
4	20	22	−2	4
5	13	19	−6	36
6	20	18	2	4
7	15	16	−1	1
8	11	15	−4	16
9	8	13	−5	25
10	9	12	−3	9
$n = 10$	$\Sigma X_1 = 164$	$\Sigma X_2 = 188$	$\Sigma X_1 = -24$	$\Sigma d^2 = 108$
	$X_1 = 16.4$	$X_2 = 18.8$		

Step 1: State the Hypotheses. The hypotheses for the matched pairs are stated as

$$H_o: \Delta = 0 \qquad H_1: \Delta \neq 0$$

or, equivalently,

$$H_o: \Delta = \mu_1 - \mu_2 = 0 \quad H_1: \Delta = \mu_1 - \mu_2 \neq 0$$

The symbol delta, Δ, is used to denote the difference between populations.

Step 2: Set the Criterion for Rejecting H_o. The critical values are found in Table M–1. The criterion for this nondirectional test is stated as follows:

$$\alpha = 0.05 \qquad \text{Two-Tailed Test}$$

$$df = n = 10 - 1 = 9^* \qquad t_{cv} = 2.262$$

*Recall that for dependent samples, n is represented by the number of samples.

Step 3: Compute the Test Statistic. The three-stage process for the test statistic for the data in Table 10–4 is as follows:

Stage 1: Estimate of population standard deviation of the difference

between the means, s_d. (Formula 10–11)

$$s_d = \sqrt{\frac{108 - [(-24)^2/10]}{9}} = \sqrt{5.6} = 2.366$$

Stage 2: Estimate the standard error of the mean difference, $s_{\bar{d}}$. (Formula 10–12)

$$s_{\bar{d}} = \frac{2.366}{\sqrt{10}} = 0.748$$

Stage 3: Calculate the statistic t. (Formula 10–13)

$$t = \frac{-2.4 - 0}{0.748} = -3.21$$

Step 4: Apply the Decision Rule. Since $t = -3.419$ is greater than $t_{cv} = -2.262$ in absolute value, the null hypothesis is rejected at $\alpha = 0.05$ level of significance (Figure 10–9). The results suggest that at the 0.05 level of significance, the severe hearing damages to their ears among young adults using the new type of hearing devices (experimental group) is significantly less than the young adults using earbuds.

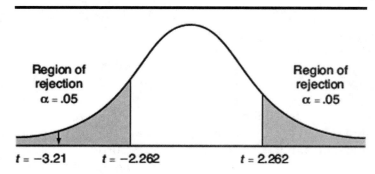

Figure 10–9. Critical value (t_{cv}) and test statistic (t) for Scenario 4 test of significance.

Which Test?
A Reasoning Process

An outline of the reasoning process that may be useful in determining which approach is appropriate in conducting hypothesis tests for two sample cases for the mean is shown in Figure 10–10.

Key Terms and Concepts

Independent sample

Dependent sample

Standard error

F-ratio

Homogeneity of variance

F-test

F distribution

Pooled variance

Pooled t-test

Nonpooled t-test

Paired samples

Matched samples

Feedback Review of Chapter 10

1. Homogeneity of variance is an assumption that
   a. two samples are dependent.
   b. two sample variances are equal.
   c. two population variances are equal.
   d. the samples are independent.
   e. b and c

2. The t distribution is used in hypothesis testing for two sample cases for the mean when
   a. $\sigma_1^2 = \sigma_2^2$.
   b. $\sigma_1^2 \neq \sigma_2^2$.
   c. σ^2 is known.
   d. σ^2 is not known.
   e. a & b

3. In hypothesis testing for two sample cases for independent sample means, $p > 0.05$ means that
   a. the sample means are not significantly different.
   b. there is statistical significance for a one-tailed test.
   c. the population means are not significantly different.
   d. 5% of the time the results will be statistically significant.
   e. none of the above.

4. The means of two groups are compared using a t-test. There are 10 subjects in each group. The degrees of freedom are
   a. 19 if the groups are independent and the pooled estimate of variance is used.
   b. 18 if the groups are independent and the pooled estimate of variance is used.
   c. 9 if the groups are dependent.
   d. 8 if the groups are dependent.
   e. b & c

5. Hypothesis testing for two dependent samples does not include
   a. a decision to use a one-tailed or a two-tailed test.
   b. a sampling distribution of the statistic.
   c. degrees of freedom.
   d. use of the population variances.
   e. a confidence interval.

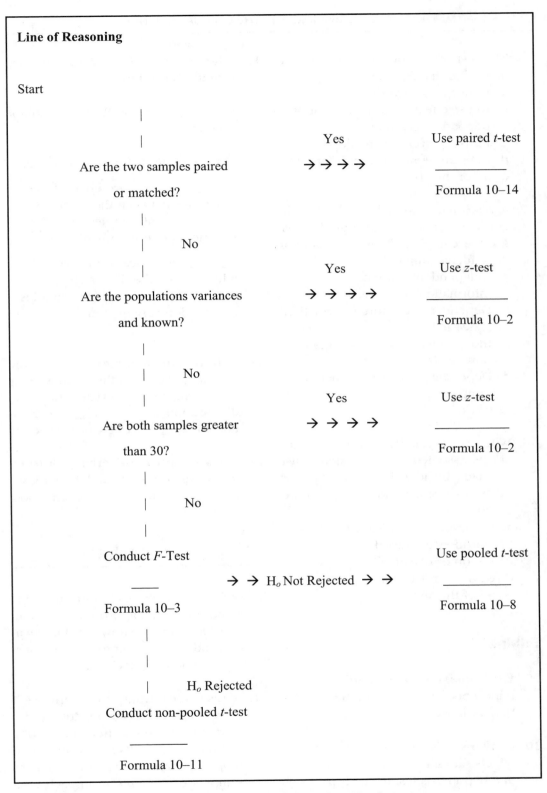

Line of Reasoning

Start

|

| Yes   Use paired *t*-test

Are the two samples paired   → → → →   _____

or matched?   Formula 10–14

|

| No

| Yes   Use *z*-test

Are the populations variances   → → → →   _____

and known?   Formula 10–2

|

| No

| Yes   Use *z*-test

Are both samples greater   → → → →   _____

than 30?   Formula 10–2

|

| No

|

Conduct *F*-Test   Use pooled *t*-test

_____   → → H$_o$ Not Rejected → →   _____

Formula 10–3   Formula 10–8

|

|

| H$_o$ Rejected

Conduct non-pooled *t*-test

_____

Formula 10–11

Figure 10–10. Flowchart of a reasoning process for hypothesis test.

6. The test of homogeneity of variance is used to decide whether
   a. to use pooled variance.
   b. to use a test for independent or dependent samples.
   c. to use degrees of freedom.
   d. the sample means are different.
   e. all of the above.

7. A researcher has data on 20 fourth-grade boys and 15 fourth-grade girls. Are these likely to be independent or dependent samples?
   a. Independent but more information is needed.
   b. Dependent but more information is needed.
   c. Independent because of unequal sample size.
   d. Dependent because of unequal sample size.
   e. b & d

8. When homogeneity of variance cannot be assumed, an adjustment must be made in how the standard error of the difference and _____ is/are determined.
   a. the level of significance
   b. confidence interval
   c. region of rejection
   d. degrees of freedom
   e. all of the above

Fill-Ins

9. List (name) the two methods to determine a pooled estimate of the population variance. _____

10. In two-sample cases for the mean, which sampling distribution is used in a hypothesis test to see if $\sigma_1^2 = \sigma_2^2$?

   _____

11. When $\sigma_1^2 \neq \sigma_2^2$, the Cochran and Cox formula is used to _____.

12. When $\sigma_1^2 \neq \sigma_2^2$, the Welch formula is used to _____.

13. List the symbols for the following:

   _____ the standard error of the difference between the means of two dependent samples (population variances are not known)

   _____ the critical value symbol when testing the difference between two independent samples (population variances are not known)

14. In testing the null hypothesis for the two-sample case for the mean when is unknown, the appropriate underlying distribution is the _____ distribution with _____ degrees of freedom.

15. The appropriate underlying distribution when testing the null hypothesis, $H_o: \sigma_1^2 = \sigma_2^2$, is the _____ distribution.

Review Problems

Directions. Organize your answers; label and follow the appropriate steps in hypothesis testing as shown in the Calculations Guide. Remember to carry answers 3 places beyond the decimal.

1. A researcher wants to determine if there is any difference in attitudes toward all-college requirements among communication disorders and sociology majors. She randomly selects samples of students from each area and observes the results in Table 10–5.

Table 10-5. The Results of a Hypothetical Study Concerning Attitudes Toward All-College Requirements among Communication Disorders Majors and Sociology Majors

Communication Disorders Majors	Sociology Majors
$n_1 = 41$	$n_2 = 41$
$\bar{X}_1 = 84.5$	$\bar{X}_2 = 81.4$
$s_1^2 = 6.4$	$s_2^2 = 3.5$

Table 10-6. A Summary of the Results of Comparison Study Between Two Different Methods in Determining the Effectiveness of Reducing Statistics Anxiety Among Communication Disorders Majors

Method 1	Method 2
$n_1 = 8$	$n_2 = 9$
$\Sigma X_1 = 551$	$\Sigma X_2 = 445$
$\Sigma X_1^2 = 39009$	$\Sigma X_2^2 = 22865$
$\bar{X}_1 = 68.88$	$\bar{X}_2 = 49.44$

a. At the 0.20 level of significance, what will she conclude about the homogeneity of variance of the two groups? (Show breakdown of all work, including her probability statement.)

b. If she were to conduct a test of significance between the population means (H_o: $\mu_1 = \mu_2$ H_1: $\mu_1 \neq \mu_2$), her degrees of freedom would be

_____.

c. Her standard error of the differences between the means would be _____.

2. Table 10-6 shows the results of two methods of reducing statistics anxiety among communication disorders majors: Method 1 (systematic desensitization); and Method 2 (cognitive restructuring). The samples were randomly selected and are independent. Also, you can assume homogeneity of variance.

a. In a two-tailed test of significance with $\alpha = 0.05$, the degrees of freedom would be _____, and the critical value would be

_____.

b. The standard error of the differences between the means would be _____.

c. Assuming that the null hypothesis for a two-tailed test at the 0.05 level of significance was rejected, what would be the confidence interval? (Come back to this problem after working through Chapter 12.)

3. An educational researcher wants to determine if there is any difference in the effectiveness of a new type of computer-assisted program with language-delayed children. Five (5) language-delayed children are randomly selected and tested for achievement levels before and after exposure to the computer-assisted program. The results are shown in Table 10-7.

At the 0.10 level of significance, what will the researcher conclude regarding the effectiveness of the new type of computer-assisted program with language-delayed children?

4. A psychologist experiments with two types of reinforcers and gets the following results.

Table 10–7. A Summary of Pre- and Post-Results of a Hypothetical Study Concerning the Effectiveness of a New Type of Computer-Assisted Program with Language-Delayed Children

Subject	Before	After
1	78	73
2	63	60
3	66	72
4	89	85
5	49	51

Type A: $n_1 = 17$ $s_1^2 = 225$
Type B: $n_2 = 10$ $s_2^2 = 100$

Before conducting a full analysis of the data, she wants to determine if the variances of the two populations from which the samples are drawn are equal ($\sigma_1^2 = \sigma_2^2$). At the alpha = 0.05 level, what does she conclude and where does she go from there if she continues with her analysis of all of the data?

5. An educational researcher develops two methods of evaluating small group class interaction. A random sample of 13 scores computed by judges using Method A has a variance of 0.80, and a random sample of 10 scores computed by judges using Method B has a variance of 0.64. At the alpha = 0.01 level, what does he conclude about the variances of the two groups and where does he go from there if he continues with his analysis of all of the data?

6. An educational psychologist believes that there is a difference between boys and girls in their preference for television programming. Specifically, she claims that girls watch more educationally oriented shows than boys. She conducts a survey and finds the results in Table 10–8 of viewing hours of educationally oriented programs over a six-month period.

Assume that $\sigma_1^2 = \sigma_2^2$, (homogeneity of variance) and test the appropriate hypothesis using alpha = 0.05. You may also assume that the variable, viewing preference, is normally distributed and that the samples are independent.

7. A communication researcher develops two methods of improving persuasive messages. Method 1 uses videotaped instructions and an illustrated text; Method 2 uses audiotaped instructions and a self-paced text. The two methods are employed with independent samples of students with the results in Table 10–9.

Assume the variable, method of persuasive messages, is normally distributed. Conduct the following two tests. Part I: at $\alpha = 0.05$, test for homogeneity of variance. Part II: at $\alpha = 0.05$, conduct a test of the means.

8. A behavioral scientist is interested in the effect of stress on hand-eye coordination in filling out hand ballots by first time voters during an election for statewide and national elections. He believes that more errors are likely under stressful conditions than under neutral conditions. (Sounds like common sense, but he wants to know if common sense reasoning holds up under empirical conditions.) The researcher randomly selects 16 individuals who plan to vote for the first

Table 10–8. A Summary of the Results of Gender Difference Concerning Their Preference for Television Programming

Girls	Boys
$n_1 = 13$	$n_2 = 12$
—	—
$\bar{X}_1 = 26.9$	$\bar{X}_2 = 21.3$
$\Sigma X_1 = 350$	$\Sigma X_2 = 256$
$\Sigma X_1^2 = 9876$	$\Sigma X_2^2 = 6003$

Table 10–9. A Summary of the Results of a Comparison Study Involving Two Different Methods of Improving Persuasive Messages

Method 1	Method 2
$n_1 = 25$	$n_2 = 31$
$\bar{X}_1 = 32.8$	$\bar{X}_2 = 33.0$
$s_1^2 = 90.9$	$s_2^2 = 41.7$
$s_1 = 9.53$	$s_2 = 6.46$

time in an upcoming national election and then randomly assigns them to one of two matched groups, "Neutral" and "Stressful." Both groups are tested under their respective conditions with the results in Table 10–10.

Assume that you are analyzing the data for matched pairs. (1) Complete the table. (2) At the 0.05 level, test the null hypothesis of no difference against the claim that there is higher hand-eye coordination under neutral conditions than under stressful conditions.

9. A psychologist believes that a new method of desensitization for test anxiety is more effective than a traditional method. She randomly selects 20 children with similar backgrounds and skills, and randomly assigns them to one of two groups. In short, the groups are considered paired or matched. Group$_1$ is treated with the traditional method, and Group$_2$ is treated with the new or experimental

Table 10–10. A Partial Summary of the Results of Comparison of Two Different Conditions Concerning the Effect of Stress on Hand-Eye Coordination in Filling Out Hand Ballots by First-Time Voters

Ss	Neutral	Stressful	d	d²
A	16	13		
B	19	15		
C	14	14		
D	20	16		
E	18	15		
F	11	13		
G	15	15		
H	17	14		

Table 10–11. A Summary of the Results of Comparison of Two Different Methods Concerning the Effect of Reducing Test Anxiety

Pair:	1	2	3	4	5	6	7	8	9	10
Group$_1$ (traditional method):	18	19	17	22	15	16	18	19	13	20
Group$_2$ (new method):	16	19	16	18	17	15	14	12	10	17

method. The achievement scores of each group are shown in Table 10–11.

Assume that you are analyzing the data for matched pairs. (1) Complete the table. (2) At the 0.05 level, test the null hypothesis of no difference against the claim that there is a difference between the two methods.

Calculation Guide

Determining Critical Values (F_{cv}) for F-tests for Homogeneity of Variance

Step 1: Designate the variance of the larger sample as the numerator and the variance of the smaller sample as the denominator.

Step 2: Define the degrees of freedom for the numerator, df_{n1}, and the denominator, df_{n2}, as follows: $df_{n1} = n_1 - 1$ and $df_{n2} = n_2 - 1$.

Step 3: Refer to the value at the column/row intersection of the appropriate table in Appendix N.

11

Making Inferences About Population Proportions

Overview

To this point, we have been mainly concerned with population and sample means and the inferences that can be drawn from hypothesis tests that focus on differences among one and two sample cases. In this chapter, we examine parameters and statistics of proportions.

The variety of studies in which proportions are the focus of interest is virtually endless. However, the most common are those designed to measure public opinion. Few of us have not been asked to respond to a questionnaire or survey. At many colleges and universities, students complete a teacher/course evaluation or feedback survey at the end of every term. As consumers, we constantly are asked how we feel about a particular product or service. As television viewers, radio listeners, and Internet users, we often are asked to respond to questions about some political issue or candidate(s), or about some social or religious issue. In short, it would seem that everyone wants to know how we feel about something, or someone, or some place.

In proportion studies, the critical issues relate to the size of a percentage or the comparison of two or more percentages. For example, is the percentage of cases benefiting from an experimental treatment for some psychological or physiological disorder, such as schizophrenia or AIDS, statistically significant? Is the percentage of cases that will benefit from the new treatment greater than the percentage of cases benefiting from the current method of treatment? Is the percentage of voters who favor social services for illegal immigrants greater than the percentage of voters against such services.

In the following sections, the general concepts and computational methods used in testing hypotheses about population proportions are presented. Again we encourage you to work through the problems in the illustrations in addition to the review problems at the end of the chapter.

General Terms and Concepts

A **proportion** represents some part of a whole. For example, numerous research studies indicate that as many as 10% of college students have a severe, almost phobic fear of speaking in public. The

10% proportion parameter also may be expressed as a fraction or decimal, as in $\frac{10}{100}$ or 0.10. In the statement, "4 out of 5 dentists recommend X Toothpaste," each dentist is a proportion of the whole, or 4/5, or 0.80, or 80% of the population. A proportion also can be expressed as a probability, as in the statement: The probability of randomly selecting a dentist who recommends "X Toothpaste" is 0.80 or 80%.

Data used in proportion studies are generally obtained through surveys conducted by telephone, through the Internet, by mail, or in-person. In some cases, physical instruments such as television monitoring devices used by media rating companies, such as Neilson, are used to gather proportion data. A **population proportion**, denoted by the symbol p, is generally defined as the percentage of a population that possesses some characteristic or attribute of interest. For example, if the attribute of interest is body piercing jewelry, and the population is college students in Massachusetts, then the population proportion of interest is the percentage of college students in Massachusetts that wear body piercing jewelry. The proportion of the population not having the characteristic of interest is symbolized by the letter q, or $1 - p$.

> A proportion is a part of a whole and may be expressed as a fraction, decimal, or percentage.

Usually, the population of interest is too large to be surveyed or observed in its entirety. Imagine the time and money it would take for a public opinion organization, such as the Gallup Poll, to ask each of the more than 200 million voters in the United States who they plan to vote for in a presidential election. Instead, random samples are selected as surveyed. A **sample proportion**, denoted by the symbol $\hat{p}$ (read "p hat"), is defined as the percentage of the sample possessing the character of interest. It is obtained using Formula 11–1.

Formula 11–1

$$\hat{p} = \frac{f}{n}$$

Where

f = frequency of cases in the sample having the characteristic of interest

n = number of cases in the sample (sample size)

The proportion of the sample not having the characteristic of interest is symbolized by the letter $\hat{q}$, which is equal to $(1 - \hat{p})$. In the case of the 4 out of 5 dentists mentioned above, the sample proportion possessing the characteristic of research interest would be given as $\hat{p} = \frac{4}{5} = 0.80$. The proportion of the sample not having the characteristic of interest would be given as $\hat{q} = 1 - 0.80 = 0.20$.

> A population proportion (p) refers to the percentage of a population that has a characteristic or attribute of interest. A sample proportion ($\hat{p}$) refers to the percentage of a population that has a characteristic or attribute of interest. The proportion not having the characteristic of interest is designated by q and $\hat{q}$.

In the sections that follow, we examine methods for testing hypotheses for single and two sample cases. However, at this point, we need to consider some important assumptions and conditions that must be verified in testing hypotheses about proportions.

Assumptions and Conditions

The probability or sampling distribution for dichotomous variables is the binomial distribution, provided that two assumptions are met. The first assumption is that there are only two possible outcomes. This is because proportion testing is essentially a test of a dichotomous variable or discrete variable with only two mutually exclusive and exhaustive categories. For instance, *male* and *female* are two categories of the variable *gender*. Sometimes, a researcher may find it convenient to treat a continuous variable as if it were dichotomous by dividing a population into two distinct groups, as in *voters age 40 and below* and *voters above age 40*. Each of these conditions satisfies the first assumption.

The second assumption is that the outcomes are independently sampled. This can be accomplished by using a random sampling technique in selecting members of a sample. In that way, the researcher can assume that the responses are independent since the sample is representative of the population. Without the assurance of a representative sample, there would be no way of knowing if the obtained data are normally distributed.

A classic example of what can go wrong when unrepresentative samples are used in proportion studies occurred during the 1936 presidential election. One of the country's most popular news magazines, the *Literary Digest,* conducted a straw-poll sending 10 million ballots to people listed in telephone directories and on lists of automobile owners. More than 2 million ballots were returned, giving the Republican candidate, Alf Landon, a stunning 57 to 43% margin over the incumbent president, Franklin Delano Roosevelt. When the election was held a few weeks later, Roosevelt won by a landslide with 63% of the vote. What happened? The first issue is the fact that only 22% of those polled by the *Digest* returned their ballots. More important though is the sample was distinctly unrepresentative of the voter population, given the fact that in 1936 telephones and automobiles could be afforded only by the affluent, who were decidedly Republican.

In proportions testing, the two assumptions that must be met are: (1) that there are only two possible outcomes; and (2) that the outcomes are independently sampled.

The Standard Normal Distribution

Although the binomial distribution represents the underlying sampling distribution of discrete variables, it often is more convenient to use the standard normal z distribution in proportion testing. This is certainly true for us, since we already have some understanding of the z distribution and z-tests of significance. However, certain conditions related to the size of samples and their proportions must be present in order to do so. When the products of np and nq are equal to or greater than 5, the standard normal distribution is an adequate approximation of the binomial distribution, and therefore can be used as the sampling distribution of proportion parameter. If the condition is not met, an alternative method for testing hypotheses about proportions, one that is beyond the scope of this text, must be used.

> When $np \geq 5$ and $nq \geq 5$, the standard normal or z distribution can be used as the sampling distribution in proportion testing.

Proportion Testing: One Sample Cases

There are many instances when a researcher is interested in determining whether the observed proportion of a sample having a characteristic of interest is the same or significantly different than one reported for a population or that of a previous study. Consider the following. In 2002, an article in a widely read Sunday newspaper reported that 25% of Americans would abandon all their friends for $10 million. If the survey was valid, we could say that the proportion of the population (p) possessing this characteristic of interest is 0.25 and the proportion not having this characteristic of interest (q) is 0.75.

Scenario

Suppose we randomly select a sample of 50 adults and find that 6, (6/50) or 12%, respond positively to the question: "Would you abandon all of your friends for $10 million?" In this case, the sample proportion is $\hat{p} = 0.12$. The research question in this case asks whether the difference between the proportion reported by the newspaper and that of our sample could have occurred simply by chance or whether the difference is statistically significant. Put another way, are the people in our sample similar in their attitude about abandoning

all friends for $10 million to the adults in the newspaper report?

The process followed in testing a hypothesis about the proportion for a single population is similar to that used in testing hypotheses for single cases for the mean shown in Chapter 9. Therefore, we apply the same four-step model.

The Hypothesis Test

Pretest Considerations

Before conducting the hypothesis test, we must first verify that the two assumptions related to proportion testing in general and the conditions necessary for use of the standard normal distribution in particular have been satisfied. For our illustration, we can assume that the sampling method and phrasing of the survey question are adequate to satisfy the assumptions of independence and distribution of only two possible outcomes, "yes" and "no." The condition $np \geq 5$ and $nq \geq 5$ required to use the standard normal z distribution also has been satisfied where $np = 50(0.25) = 12.5$ and $nq = 50(0.75) = 37.5$.

The population and sample data for this illustration are summarized below.

Population:
N = unknown $p = 0.25$ $q = 0.75$

Sample:
$n = 50$ $\hat{p} = 0.12$ $\hat{q} = 0.88$

The Test

Step 1: State the Hypotheses

Since our interest in this study is simply to determine if a significant difference exists between the results reported in the newspaper article and our sample, the test of significance will be two-tailed and the hypotheses stated as follows:

$$H_o: p = 0.25 \qquad H_1: p \neq 0.25$$

Step 2: Set the Criterion for Rejecting H_o

For this test, assume we choose a 0.05 level of significance with a critical value of $z_{cv} = \pm 1.96$ (Table 9–1), since our sample size is large enough to use the standard normal distribution. Thus, our criterion for rejecting the null hypothesis is set as shown below.

$$\alpha = 0.05 \qquad \text{Two-Tailed Test}$$
$$z_{cv} = \pm 1.96$$

Again we remind you that it will be helpful to draw a normal curve with the boundaries set off at the region of rejection.

Step 3: Compute the Test Statistic

The standard error, $s_{\hat{p}}$, which is incorporated in the test statistic, z_p, is derived using Formulas 11–2 and 11–3.

Formula 11–2

$$s_{\hat{p}} = \sqrt{pq/n}$$

Where

pq = product of the hypothesized population proportions having *and* not having the characteristic of interest

n = size of sample

Formula 11–3

$$z_p = \frac{\hat{p} - p}{\sqrt{pq/n}}$$

Where

$\hat{p}$ = hypothesized proportion of the sample having the characteristic of interest

p = hypothesized proportion of population having the characteristic of interest

$\sqrt{pq/n}$ = the standard error of the proportion, $s_{\hat{p}}$.

For our illustration, the test statistic is computed as follows:

$$z_p = \frac{0.12 - 0.25}{\sqrt{(0.25)(0.75)/50}}$$

$$= -\frac{0.13}{0.061}$$

$$= -2.13$$

Step 4: Apply the Decision Rule

Since the test statistic, $z_p = -2.13$, is greater in absolute value than the critical value, $z_{cv} = -1.96$, the null hypothesis is rejected, $p < 0.05$ (Figure 11–1). Therefore, we can conclude that there is no statistical basis for assuming that the young adults in our sample are from the same population of adults who said they would abandon all of their friends for $10 million. A summary of the hypothesis test is shown in Table 11–1.

Proportion Testing for Two Independent Samples

There are many instances when a researcher is interested in whether two populations are significantly different with regard to some characteristic of interest. In this section, we consider instances when the two populations from which the samples

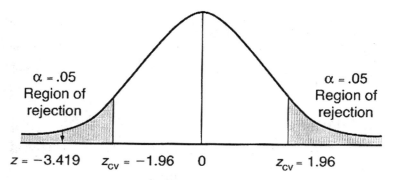

Figure 11–1. Location of z-score in relation to critical value z_{cv} and region of rejection; $\alpha = 0.5$.

Table 11–1. Summary of Hypothesis Test

Preanalysis:

Preanalysis:

$n = 50$ $p = 0.25$ $q = 0.75$ $\hat{p} = \dfrac{6}{50} = 0.12$

$np = (50)(0.25) = 12.5$ $nq = (50)(0.75) = 37.5$

Step 1: State the hypothesis

$H_o: p = 0.25$ $H_1: p \neq 0.25$

Step 2: Set the criterion for rejecting H_o

$\alpha = 0.05$ Two-Tailed Test $z_{cv} = \pm 1.96$

Step 3: Compute the test statistic

$$z_p = \frac{0.12 - 0.25}{\sqrt{\dfrac{(0.25)(0.75)}{50}}} = \frac{-0.13}{0.061} = -2.13$$

Step 4: Apply the decision rule

Decision Statement:

Since $z_{cv} = |{-2.13}| > z_p = |{-1.96}|$, H_o is rejected: $p < 0.05$

are drawn are considered independent. As noted in the last chapter, two samples are considered *independent* when the selection and data of one sample does not affect the selection and data of another.

When testing hypotheses about two population proportions using independent samples, the theoretical sampling distribution represents the differences between $\hat{p}_1$ and $\hat{p}_2$ for all possible samples of a given size. The standard deviation of this sampling distribution of the difference between proportions is known as the **estimated standard error of the difference between the proportions**, and is denoted by the symbol $s_{\hat{p}_1 - \hat{p}_2}$.

It is a pooled estimate of the sample proportion, as defined in Formula 11–4, consisting of the proportion that possesses the characteristic of interest, denoted as $\hat{p}_d$, and the proportion that does not, denoted as $\hat{q}_d$.

Formula 11–4

$$s_{\hat{p}_1 - \hat{p}_2} = \sqrt{\hat{p}_d \hat{q}_d \left(\frac{1}{n_1} + \frac{1}{n_2} \right)}$$

Where

$\hat{p}_d = \frac{f_1 + f_2}{n_1 + n_2}$ where f = frequency of the characteristic of interest

$\hat{q}_d = 1 - \hat{p}_d$

The *standard error of the difference between the proportions*, $s_{\hat{p}_1 - \hat{p}_2}$, is a pooled sample proportion, where $\hat{p}_d$ symbolizes the proportion that possess the characteristic of interest and $\hat{q}_d$ represents the sample proportion that does not possess the characteristic of interest.

The test statistic, shown in Formula 11–5, is similar to that used for comparing population means.

Formula 11–5

$$z_p = \frac{(\hat{p}_1 - \hat{p}_2) - (p_1 - p_2)}{s_{\hat{p}_1 - \hat{p}_2}}$$

or, equivalently,

$$z_p = \frac{(\hat{p}_1 - \hat{p}_2) - (p_1 - p_2)}{\sqrt{\hat{p}_d \hat{q}_d \left(\frac{1}{n_1} + \frac{1}{n_2} \right)}}$$

Where

$\hat{p}_1 - \hat{p}_2$ = difference in sample proportions

$p_1 - p_2$ = null hypothesis, zero (0) value, indicating "no difference"

$\sqrt{\hat{p}_d \hat{q}_d (\frac{1}{n_1} + \frac{1}{n_2})}$ = standard error of the difference between the proportions, $s_{\hat{p}_1 - \hat{p}_2}$.

Scenario

For many high school seniors, the college admissions process can be a slow and nerve-wracking experience. It therefore should come as no surprise to learn that the number of applications for early admission has risen dramatically in recent years. Schools see it as a way of attracting high academic achievers. Students see it as a way of locking in their school of choice and reducing anxiety. The percentage of students who apply and are accepted for early admission varies widely from school to school and year to year. While the practice may be attractive to students and admissions officers, the question considered here is whether early admission students fare better academically than students who are admitted through the regular admissions process.

Let's assume a researcher wants to determine if a significant difference in academic performance exists between early and regular admission students at public colleges and universities in the northeast. She selects a random sample of 5% of the students from the two populations of college applicants (early admission and regular admission) and obtains the following results. Of the 2,084 early admissions students, 517 made the dean's list in the first semester of their freshman year, whereas 1,373 of the 6,166 regular admissions students achieved the same honor. What will she conclude from her results?

The sample proportions of early admissions students ($\hat{p}_1$) and regular admissions students ($\hat{p}_2$) are calculated using Formula 11–1, using different subscripts for each sample.

$$\hat{p}_1 = \frac{517}{2084} = 0.248$$

$$\hat{p}_2 = \frac{1373}{6166} = 0.223$$

The proportions that do not have the characteristic of interest are designated as $\hat{q}_1$ and $\hat{q}_2$, which in this case are 0.752 ($1 - 0.248$) and 0.777 ($1 - 0.223$), respectively. The purpose of the hypothesis test illustrated here is to determine if the 0.025 percentage point difference between the two samples is statistically significant or due to chance or sampling error?

Pretest Considerations

In this scenario, the two categories of measure, "dean's list," and "not dean's list," and the sampling method used satisfy the assumptions of two outcomes and independence. For two sample cases, the sample size requirement, given as $n_1\hat{p}_1$ and $n_1\hat{q}_1 \geq 5$ and $n_2\hat{p}_2$ and $n_2\hat{q}_2 \geq 5$, is determined using the sample proportions. Since the requirement is met, the hypothesis test can be conducted using the standard normal z distribution as the sampling distribution.

$n_1\hat{p}_1 = (2084)\,(0.248) = 517$ and
$n_1\hat{q}_1 = (2084)\,(0.752) = 1567$

$n_2\hat{p}_2 = (6166)\,(0.223) = 1375$ and
$n_2\hat{q}_2 = (6166)\,(0.777) = 4791$

The Test

Step 1: State the Hypotheses. For this scenario, the population proportions are given as follows:

p_1 = all early admissions students who make the dean's list.

p_2 = all regular admissions students who make the dean's list.

Since the research interest is not one of directionality, the hypotheses are stated as follows:

$$H_o:\ p_1 = p_2 \qquad H_1:\ p_1 \neq p_2$$

or, equivalently,

$$H_o:\ p_1 - p_2 = 0 \qquad H_1:\ p_1 - p_2 \neq 0$$

Step 2: Set the Criterion for Rejecting H_o. Let's assume that the researcher chooses an alpha level of 0.10. Since the sample size is adequate, the critical value for the two-tailed significance test (see Table 9–1) is $z_{cv} = 1.645$. Thus, the second step of the hypothesis test is set as follows:

$$\alpha = 0.10 \qquad \text{Two-Tailed Test}$$
$$z_{cv} = \pm 1.645$$

Step 3: Compute the Test Statistic. The test statistic z_p is derived using Formula 11–5.

$$z_p = \frac{(0.248 - 0.223) - (0)}{\sqrt{(0.229)(0.771)\left[\frac{1}{2084} + \frac{1}{6166}\right]}}$$

$$= \frac{0.025}{\sqrt{0.177[(0.00048)+(0.00016)]}}$$

$$= \frac{0.025}{0.011} = 2.272$$

*Note that we continue to use the rounding rule of carrying solutions to two non-zero digits after the decimal. A breakdown of the standard error, $s_{\hat{p}_1 - \hat{p}_2}$, is shown below.

$$\hat{p}_d = \frac{517 + 1373}{2084 + 6166} = 0.229$$

$$\hat{q}_d = 1 - 0.229 = 0.771$$

$$s_{\hat{p}_1 - \hat{p}_2} = \sqrt{(0.229)(0.771)\left[\frac{1}{2084} + \frac{1}{6166}\right]}$$

$$= \sqrt{(0.177)(0.00064)}$$

$$= 0.011$$

Step 4: Apply the Decision Rule. Since the test statistic, $z_p = 2.272$ is greater than the critical value, $z_{cv} = 1.645$, the null hypothesis is rejected (Figure 11–2).

It would appear from this example that the academic performance of the early admissions student was statistically better than regular admissions students during the first semester of their freshman year. However, it is important for us to keep in mind that the results are valid only to the extent that the samples selected are representative of their respective populations, and that the results of this study only apply to performance in the first term.

A summary of symbols and notations used in testing two-population proportions hypotheses is presented in Table 11–2.

Clinical Applications of Paired *t*-Test and Unpaired *t*-Test: A Bayesian Perspective

Paired *t*-Test

Let us now illustrate the use of the paired *t*-test as it might be applied to a clinical problem in the area of fluency disorders. There is evidence that the adrenergic blocking agent propranolol is useful in controlling certain neuromotor disorders such as essential tremor and tardive dyskinesia. Hypothetically, assume that we

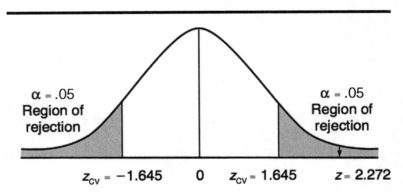

Figure 11–2. Location of *z* score in relation to critical value z_α, and region of rejection at $\alpha = 0.10$.

Table 11–2. Symbols and Notations for Two-Population Proportions Testing

p_1 = proportion of population one having the characteristic of interest
q_1 = proportion of population one not having the characteristic of interest ($q_1 = 1 - p_1$)
p_2 = proportion of a second population having the characteristic of interest
q_2 = population proportion not having the characteristic of interest ($q_2 = 1 - p_2$)
$\hat{p}_1$ = symbol for proportion of sample n_1 from population p_1 with the characteristic of interest $\hat{p}_1 = \frac{f_1}{n_1}$
$\hat{p}_2$ = symbol for proportion of sample n_2 from population p_2 with the characteristic of interest $\hat{p}_2 = \frac{f_2}{n_2}$ Where f = frequency of cases having characteristics of interest and n = number of cases in the sample
The standard error of the difference between two proportions is given as $$s_{\hat{p}_1 - \hat{p}_2} = \sqrt{\hat{p}_d \hat{q}_d \left(\frac{1}{n_1} + \frac{1}{n_2} \right)}$$ Where $\hat{p}_d$ is the pooled sample proportion and $\hat{q}_d = 1 - \hat{p}_d$. See Formula 11–4.
The test statistic is given as $$z_p = \frac{(\hat{p}_1 - \hat{p}_2) - (p_1 - p_2)}{s_{\hat{p}_1 - \hat{p}_2}}$$ or   See Formula 11–5 $$z_p = \frac{(\hat{p}_1 - \hat{p}_2) - (p_1 - p_2)}{\sqrt{\hat{p}_d \hat{q}_d \left(\frac{1}{n_1} + \frac{1}{n_2} \right)}}$$
$$z_p = \frac{0.12 - 0.25}{\sqrt{\dfrac{(0.25)(0.75)}{50}}} = \frac{-0.13}{0.061} = -2.13$$

want to investigate the potential effect of minimal therapeutic dose of this drug against a placebo on self-rating of stuttering severity using a Likert-type scale in which 1 = least severe to 5 = most severe. For purposes of this hypothetical study, a crossover design is chosen for use in which half of ten subjects initially will be treated with propranolol and the other half treated with placebo for a two-week period, at the end of which they will provide self-ratings of stuttering severity. A six-week "wash-out" period will separate the two treatments before crossing over to the alternate form. At the end of the second two-week treatment period, self ratings of stuttering severity will be made again. All pairs for the study were matched by the investigator. We illustrate the results by Fisher's *p*-value and the Minimum

Bayes Factor (MBF). The null and alternative hypotheses are stated as follows:

H_o: No significant mean difference between two groups exists.

H_a: A significant mean difference between two groups exists.

The results are illustrated in Table 11–3.

Next, we will find MBF (see and read special chapter first for details) and posterior probabilities of H_o and H_a. The results are as follows, shown in Table 11–4.

Unpaired *t*-Test

Suppose a clinical investigator is interested in evaluating the effectiveness of "therapy approach 1" as compared with "therapy

Table 11–3. Paired *t*-Test for the Self-Rating of Stuttering Under Two Treatments

Subject	Propranolol	Placebo
1	4	5
2	0	1
3	0	0
4	2	4
5	1	4
6	3	5
7	3	3
8	1	3
9	2	2
10	1	4

Note: Observed *t*-value = –3.78 (Propranolol – Placebo), $n = 10$, d.f. = 9, and *p*-value (two-sided test) = 0.00435

Table 11–4. Minimum Bayes Factor and Posterior Probabilities of H_o and H_a

Prior for H_o	Prior for H_a	MBF*	Posterior for H_o	Posterior for H_a
0.1	0.9	0.0561	0.0063	0.9937
0.2	0.8	0.0561	0.0142	0.9858
0.3	0.7	0.0561	0.0246	0.9754
0.4	0.6	0.0561	0.0388	0.9612
0.5	0.5	0.0561	0.0592	0.9408
0.6	0.4	0.0561	0.0912	0.9088
0.7	0.3	0.0561	0.1480	0.8520
0.8	0.2	0.0561	0.2748	0.7252
0.9	0.1	0.0561	0.7598	0.2402
0.484**	0.516	0.0561	0.05**	

*Sources for Calculation of MBF: Perception and Cognitive Lab, Department of Psychological Sciences, University of Missouri: http://www.pcl.missouri.edu/bayesfactor

**It shows how low initial confidence in H_o (Prior for H_o) must be to result in 5% confidence after observing data (that is 95% confidence in a non-null effect). With the conventional Fisher's *p*-value of 0.05 threshold, the prior probability of H_o must be at most 0.484 (48.4%) to allow an investigator to conclude with 95% confidence that H_o is false. This calculation is not meant to interpret "95%" in the Bayesian approach but rather to show the readers what will happen when similar benchmarks are used in the two approaches.

approach 2." Assume further that, from a common pool of available subjects, 14 subjects are randomly assigned to group 1 and 11 subjects to group 2. She wishes to know whether the performance of group 1 will differ from that of group 2.

The hypothetical data for two samples are summarized as follows:

Sample 1: Mean = 100, SD = 12, $n = 14$

Sample 2: Mean = 88, SD = 15, $n = 11$

The two distributions were found to be homogeneous (Bartlett's F-test: $p \geq 0.05$). Observed t-value = 2.23. P-value (two-sided) = 0.0358, d.f. = 23, MBF* = 0.365.

Let us calculate the posterior probabilities for H_o and H_a to accurately determine the strength of evidence against H_o and H_a. The results are summarized in Table 11–5.

Again, MBF shows that the traditional Fisher's p-value clearly overstates the amount of evidence against H_o (or exaggerates the degree of statistical significance); therefore, the true strength of evidence against the null effect is not nearly as strong and credible as the p-value suggests.

As noted earlier in the section of Bayes factor, the exchange rate table between MBF and Fisher's p-value (under the standard normal distribution) is summarized in Table 11–6.

Table 11–5. Summary of Unpaired t-Test Example Using MBF to Calculate Posterior Probabilities of Truth in H_o and H_a: A Bayesian Approach

Prior for H_o	Prior for H_a	MBF*	Posterior for H_o	Posterior for H_a
0.1	0.9	0.3650	0.0390	0.9610
0.2	0.8	0.3650	0.0836	0.9164
0.3	0.7	0.3650	0.1353	0.8647
0.4	0.6	0.3650	0.1957	0.8043
0.5	0.5	0.3650	0.2674	0.7326
0.6	0.4	0.3650	0.3538	0.6462
0.7	0.3	0.3650	0.4599	0.5401
0.8	0.2	0.3650	0.5935	0.4065
0.9	0.1	0.3650	0.7666	0.2334
0.126**	0.874	0.3650	0.05**	

*Sources for Calculation of MBF: Perception and Cognitive Lab, Department of Psychological Sciences, University of Missouri: http://www.pcl.missouri.edu/bayesfactor

**It shows how low initial confidence in H_o (Prior for H_o) must be to result in 5% confidence after observing data (that is 95% confidence in a non-null effect). With the conventional Fisher's p-value of 0.05 threshold, the prior probability of H_o must be at most 0.126 (12.6%) to allow an investigator to conclude with 95% confidence that H_o is false. This calculation is not meant to interpret "95%" in the Bayesian approach, but rather to show the readers what will happen when similar bench marks are used in the two approaches.

Table 11–6. A Table for Exchange Rate for Measuring the Strength of Evidence Against H_o Between Fisher's p-Value and MBF

Fisher's p-Value (Two-sided)	MBF	Strength of Evidence
0.10	0.26	Weak
0.05	0.15	Weak to moderate
0.03	0.095	Moderate
0.01	0.036	Moderate to strong
0.001	0.005	Strong to very strong

Key Terms and Concepts

Proportion

Population proportion

Sample proportion

Point estimate

Dichotomous variable

Population parameter

Sample statistic

Margin of error

Maximum error

Standard error of the proportion

Pooled sample proportion

Standard error of the difference between two proportions

Feedback Review of Chapter 11

1. The sampling distribution in two sample proportions testing (when $n_1 p_1$ and $n_2 p_2$ are equal to or greater than 5) is the
   a. normal distribution.
   b. p distribution.
   c. binomial distribution.
   d. t distribution.
   e. F distribution.

2. A proportion may be expressed as a
   a. fraction.
   b. decimal.
   c. percentage.
   d. probability.
   e. all of the above.

3. A poll conducted during the first war in Iraq found that 53% of men and 44% of women supported the conflict. The research question is: "Is there a significant difference between men and women in support of the war?" This is an example of a test of the
   a. difference in means using independent samples.
   b. difference in means using the dependent samples.
   c. difference in proportions using independent samples.
   d. difference in proportions using the t distribution.
   e. a and d

4. In a confidence interval, the differ-ence between $p_1 - p_2$ is known as
   a. the sample proportion.
   b. the sample statistic.
   c. an interval estimate p.
   d. a point estimate.
   e. b and d

5. The critical value in constructing a confidence interval for two indepen-dent populations is
   a. denoted by the symbol E.
   b. that of a two-tailed z-test.
   c. that of a one-tailed z-test.
   d. a and c
   e. none of the above

6. The expression $\hat{p} = \frac{f}{n}$ is used to calcu-late the
   a. standard error of the proportion.
   b. population proportion.
   c. sample proportion.
   d. population proportion with the characteristic of interest.
   e. population proportion without the characteristic of interest.

7. Which of the following is a property of the sampling distribution of the proportion?
   a. The distribution is normal when $np \geq 5$ and $nq \geq 5$.
   b. The shape of the distribution is skewed to the right.
   c. The shape of the distribution is skewed to the left.
   d. all of the above
   e. none of the above

8 One of the components of a confi-dence interval for a single population proportion is
   a. the point estimate.
   b. the critical values.
   c. the standard error of the proportion.
   d. all of the above
   e. none of the above

9. The expression $n = pq\left[\frac{z_{\alpha/2}}{E}\right]^2$ is used to calculate
   a. population size.
   b. sample size.
   c. the critical values of a confidence interval.
   d. the standard error of the proportion.
   e. none of the above

10. In the expression above, the symbol E is known as
   a. error.
   b. maximum error.
   c. margin of error.
   d. the standard error of the proportion.
   e. b and c

For questions 11 through 13, refer to the following sets of hypotheses:

   a. $H_o: p_1 = p_2$ $H_1: p_1 < p_2$
   b. $H_o: p_1 - p_2 = 0$ $H_1: p_1 - p_2 > 0$
   c. $H_o: p_1 - p_2 = 0$ $H_1: p_1 - p_2 \neq 0$
   d. $H_o: p_1 - p_2 = 0$ $H_1: p_1 - p_2 = 0$
   e. $H_o: p_1 - p_2 = 0$ $H_1: p_1 - p_2 < 0$

11. Which pair of hypotheses would be used to test the claim that "the pro-portion of men who smoke is signifi-cantly more than that of females?"

12. Which pair would be used to test the claim of no difference between the two populations of smokers?

13. Which pair does not have a valid alter-native hypothesis?

Fill-Ins

14. The standard deviation of the sam-pling distribution is known as the _____.

15. In general, the underlying sampling distribution for sample proportions is the _____ distribution.

16. What is the expression in calculating the proportion of the population that does not possess the characteristic of interest? _____

17. State the null and alternative hypotheses that would be used to the claim, "the proportion of females who report they can't get out of bed in the morning is less than the proportion of males who claim they can't get out of bed in the morning." _____

For questions 18 through 22, write the appropriate symbol.

18. _____ sample proportion

19. _____ population proportion not possessing the characteristic of interest

20. _____ standard error of the proportion

21. _____ test statistic for large sample proportion testing

22. _____ pooled sample proportion

Review Problems

Applications to the clinical, behavioral and social sciences

1. The campaign manager for a U.S. Senate candidate believes that her candidate's views on a gun control issue are supported by more than 65% of the state's voters. A survey of 300 random voters is conducted, and the results reveal that 204 voters agree with the candidate's views. At the 0.01 level of significance, what will be the conclusion of this study? Use the four-step hypothesis test model.

2. A researcher believes that teenage girls with low self-esteem are significantly more vulnerable to gossip than teen girls with high self-esteem. His research hypothesis states that $H_1: p_1 - p_2 > 0$ (where p_1 represents the population of girls with low self-esteem). Given the following data: 93 of the 150 girls with low self-esteem are found to be affected by gossip, while 87 of the 200 girls with high self-esteem are found to be affected by gossip. At the 0.10 level of significance, what will the researcher conclude? (Do not round off values after the decimal in the zp-test.)

3. A earlier study of jury decision making suggested that more than 90% of capital crime decisions were based on first ballot votes by a jury. A sociologist reviews a random sample of decisions over a five-year period and finds that 186 out of 200 jury decisions were based on the first ballot. Using a 0.05 level of significance, should the claim of the earlier study be revised?

4. A researcher claims that Internet ads for computer software have a greater impact on college students than non-college students. He selects two random samples of people who recently bought software. Of the 75 college students who bought software, 25 were motivated to purchase a software product by an Internet ad. Of the 80 noncollege students, 20 were motivated to buy because of an Internet ad. At the 0.05 level of significance, what will the researcher conclude?

12

Estimating Population Parameters

General Overview

A researcher is interested in how males perceive the height of females as an attribute of physical attractiveness. Specifically, she wants to determine if males exhibit a significant preference for females who are shorter than themselves. She randomly selects a random sample of 35 college age males, administers an instrument that measures perceptions of attractiveness, and calculates the mean of the sample. From a statistical inference standpoint, she can address her interest in one of two ways. She can determine the probability of her observed mean in terms of some claim or hypothesis, or she can determine how closely the mean of her sample is to the population mean. The first method, as we have seen, is known as *hypothesis testing*; the second is known as *statistical estimation*.

In this chapter, we examine the concepts and procedures used in statistical estimation, which seeks to determine population parameters from the results of samples. While hypothesis testing is used more frequently in social and behavioral science research, estimation has great

functionality and, in some cases, can serve as a complement to hypothesis testing. This is particularly the case when the null hypothesis has been rejected. An underlying assumption of the alternative hypothesis is that there are an infinite number of population parameters greater than or less than the specified hypothesized value in the null hypothesis. Therefore, even when the null hypothesis is rejected, there is still the problem of knowing which of the infinite number of population means is the true one. That is why statistical estimation may be used in concert with hypothesis testing.

Point and Interval Estimates

The process involved in using sample statistics to estimate their corresponding population parameters is known as **statistical estimation**, or simply *estimation*. For example, the sample mean ($\overline{X}$) derived from the physical attraction scores of the 35 males may be considered an estimate of the population mean (μ) of all college-age males. In this case, the sample mean is referred to as a *point estimate*. A **point**

estimate is a sample statistic, such as $\overline{X}$, s^2, or s, that is used to estimate a population's parameters, such as μ, or σ. In inferential statistics, a point estimate of the population parameter, such as the mean, often is referred to as the **sample statistic**. In the absence of any other information, a point estimate, derived from a random sample, is considered the best estimate of the population parameter, and the mean of the sample is the best estimator of central tendency for populations. However, in reality, a single-sample statistic cannot adequately represent a population parameter.

As we know from our understanding of sampling distributions, the mean of an infinite number of sample means is equal to the population mean. However, we also know that the mean of individual samples will vary widely and that estimates based on sample statistics, such as the mean, are subject to *sampling error*. For this reason, it is difficult to have much confidence in the mean of a single sample.

> *Statistical estimation* is the process of using sample statistics to estimate their corresponding population parameters.

There is a way, however, in which we can use a point estimate to derive an estimate of the population parameter of interest and be significantly confident that our estimate is accurate. The method is referred to as *interval estimation*. An **interval estimate** is a range of values within which we can be quite confident the true population parameter lies. For instance, in which statement would you place more confidence? "The temperature tomorrow will be 82," or, "The temperature tomorrow will be between 79 and 85." In the first instance, the statement is too exact, especially where weather forecasting is concerned. The statement leaves no room for even the slightest difference in the forecast. The second statement is more flexible. The prediction may still be wrong, but the interval provides us with a margin of error and, therefore, a basis for more confidence in the claim. For this reason, interval estimates are more commonly referred to as *confidence intervals*.

> A *point estimate* is a sample statistic, such as the mean or standard deviation, that is used to estimate a population's parameters, such as μ, or σ. Point estimates are often referred to as *sample statistics*.

> An *interval estimate* is the range of values within which we can be quite confident the true population parameter lies.

Confidence Intervals

Interval estimates are referred to as **confidence intervals** because they indicate the degree to which we feel sure of the location of a population parameter. The degree to which we are confident that a given interval may contain the population parameter is known as **level of confidence**. It is expressed as a percentage, as in, "I am 95% confident that the population mean is between 60.5 and 70.9." As in so many other areas of statistics, we have an intuitive understanding of confidence intervals. Statements that begin with, "I'm (some percentage value) sure that . . . , or,

"I am practically certain that it is between such and such," reflect our feel for the concept. However, in statistical estimation, our estimates are derived objectively and in quantitative terms.

We can think of a confidence interval as a continuum having a lower and an upper limit, with a point estimate at the center of the range, as shown in Figure 12–1.

We also can think of a confidence interval in terms of the *empirical rule* in Chapter 7, and our discussion of using the normal distribution as the *sampling distribution of the mean* in Chapter 9. Recall that the percentages of area between 1, 2, 3, and 4 standard deviations under the standard normal curve described by the empirical rule are identical to the percentages for the standard deviations of the sampling distribution of the mean, known as the *standard error of the mean*. Therefore, if we are considering an infinite number of a sample means as estimates of the true value of the population mean, we could say that 95.54% of the means will fall within two standard errors above and below the point estimate. Similarly, for an infinite number of sample means, 99.74% would fall within three standard errors above and below the point estimate. There is a little bit more to this, which we shall see shortly, but it serves as a generalized conception of how confidence intervals are derived and perhaps provides some insight into the properties of confidence intervals.

> Interval estimates are referred to as *confidence intervals* because they indicate the degree to which one is sure of the location of a population parameter. The degree to which the confidence is expressed, in percentage terms, is known as a *level of confidence*.

Properties of Confidence Intervals

A confidence interval, symbolized as *CI*, is derived from three factors: (1) the *point estimate* of the population parameter, which was discussed above; (2) the *critical values* associated with some percentage of confidence; and (3) the *standard error* of the sampling distribution. The generalized operation for computing a confidence interval is given as: $CI_{\_\%}$ = point estimate of the population parameter ± (critical value; standard error of the sampling distribution), as shown in Formula 12–1.

Formula 12–1

$$CI_{\_\%} = pe \pm (cv_{\alpha/2})(se)$$

Where

$_{\_\%}$ = percentage of confidence

pe = the point estimate of the population parameter

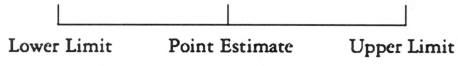

Lower Limit   Point Estimate   Upper Limit

Figure 12–1. Confidence interval continuum.

$cv_{\alpha/2}$ = the critical value for the confidence interval (two-tailed)

se = the standard error of the sampling distribution

Note that the value of the point estimate of the population parameter will be that of the sample statistic of interest. For example, for confidence intervals estimating the mean of the population (μ), the point estimate will be represented by the value of the sample mean ($\overline{X}$). Thus, if the mean of a sample is 76.4 and we are using it to estimate the mean of the population from which the sample was drawn, we refer to 76.4 as the point estimate (sample statistic) of the confidence interval.

Critical Values

In hypothesis testing, critical values represent the boundaries of the region of rejection for rejecting the null hypothesis. In statistical estimation, the *critical values* of confidence intervals correspond to the lower and upper limits of the continuum shown in Figure 12–1. They serve as boundary markers for a given percentage of area under the sampling distribution related to the expressed level of confidence. Each boundary is expressed as a standard score, such as the z scores of the standard normal distribution, which we will use as a point of reference in this discussion. For example, if one is expressing 95% confidence that the true population mean lies between the lower and upper boundaries of a particular continuum, the critical values will be represented by z scores. However, the standard score representing the critical value in Formula 12–1 actually represents one-half the area of the confidence interval, since, as we have seen, the tables of z, t, and F contain only the positive values to the right of the distribution mean. Recall, for example, that Tables K–1, K–2, and K–3 in Appendix K list only z scores from $z = 0.00$ to $z = 4.00$, and since the z distribution is symmetric, the z scores and corresponding areas between $z = 0.00$ to $z = -4.00$ are identical to those for $z = 0.00$ to $z = 4.00$.

The three most common confidence levels for estimating population parameters are 90%, 95%, and 99%, which correspond to the 0.10, 0.05, and 0.01 alpha levels of significance. The critical values for each of these intervals are shown in Table 12–1.

For example, in cases where the standard normal or z distribution is used in constructing a 90% confidence interval, the critical value $z_{cv} = 1.645$ is used

Table 12–1. Three Commonly Used Critical Values of Confidence Intervals Using the Standard Normal z Distribution

Level of Confidence	Alpha for Two-Tailed Test and for One-Tailed test	Critical z-value (Two- and One-Tailed tests, respectively)
90%	0.10	1.645, 1.28
95%	0.05	1.96, 1.645
99%	0.01	2.58, 2.33

because 0.9000 of the area under the normal curves is between $z = -1.645$ and $z = +1.645$, as depicted in Figure 12–2. This can be confirmed by referring to Table L–1 in Appendix L, noting that the 1.645 value represents the mean of the critical values $z = \pm1.64$, which accounts for 0.8990 of the area under the normal curve, and $z = \pm1.65$, which accounts for 0.9010 of the area. Therefore, we use the mean of 1.64 and 1.65, $z = 1.645$, to construct a 90% confidence interval, that is, $CV_{0.05} = CV_{\frac{10}{2}} = 1.645$.

Following the same procedure, we find that the critical z-values ±1.96 and ±2.58 cut off 95% and 99% of the areas under the standard normal curve as shown in Figures 12–2B and 12–2C. Keep in mind that the level of confidence can be set as almost any level, that is, we can express confidence as 75%, 80%, 85%, and so on.

(Table 9–1 includes the critical values for confidence intervals of 80%, 98%, and 99%.)

The Standard Error

The third property of confidence intervals is the *standard error* of the sampling distribution, symbolized as (*se*) in Formula 12–1. In Chapter 9, the *standard error of the mean* was defined as a numerical index of the variability among the samples in the sampling distribution, and symbolized as ($\sigma_{\bar{x}}$) when the standard deviation of the population is known, and as ($s_{\bar{x}}$) when the population standard deviation is unknown. We continue to use these symbols in constructing confidence intervals. The definitions for standard errors of other sample statistics, such as for the mean or proportions of samples, are nearly identical except for the subscripts

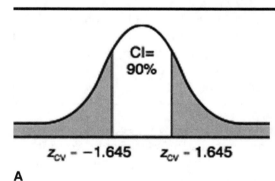

A

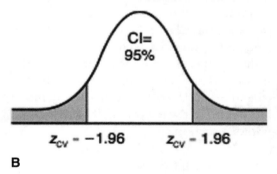

B

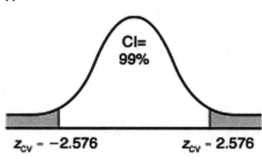

C

Figure 12–2. A. Critical z-value for the 90% confidence interval. **B.** Critical z-value for the 95% confidence interval. **C.** Critical z-value for the 99% confidence interval.

in the formula expressions. Also, recall that the calculation for the standard error of the mean is $\sigma_{\bar{x}} = \frac{\sigma}{\sqrt{n}}$ when the population standard deviation is known, and $s_{\bar{x}} = \frac{s}{\sqrt{n}}$ when is unknown. In this chapter, we continue to use the standard error of the mean since it is appropriate in constructing confidence intervals to estimate population means.

Constructing Confidence Intervals

Constructing a confidence interval to estimate a population parameter follows a relatively simple four-step process. For the generalized confidence interval expressed Formula 12–1 above, proceed as follows. First, set a level of confidence, such as 90%, 95%, or 99%, for the interval. Next, multiply the critical value (cv) of the interval by the standard error of the sampling distribution (se). Label the product of (cv)(se) "E," which is known as *maximum error*. Next, subtract E from the point estimate (pe) to obtain the lower limit of the interval. Finally, add E to the point estimate to obtain the upper limit of the interval. These four steps are included at the end of the chapter in the Calculation Guides section.

The generalized confidence interval expressing these four steps is shown in Formula 12–2.

Formula 12–2

$$CI_{\_\%} = pe \pm E$$

Where

$_\% $ = percentage of confidence for the interval

pe = the point estimate of the population parameter

E = maximum error (product of the critical value (cv) times the standard error of the sampling distribution (se))

The term E (*maximum error*) is commonly referred to in news reports of surveys or public opinion polls as the *margin of error*, which we discuss later in greater detail. Briefly, **maximum error** (E) is half the width of the confidence interval. It expresses the number of standard errors on either side of the point estimate or the most a confidence level can be off on either side of the point estimate. If the point estimate of an interval is 50 and maximum error is 3, we say that the true population parameter lies between 47 and 53, or that 50 is the true population parameter, give or take 3 points. We say more about this concept later in the chapter.

> *Maximum error*, also referred to as *margin of error* and denoted by the symbol E, is the product of the critical value times the standard error and equals half the width of the confidence interval.

In the following sections, we examine methods for constructing confidence intervals when the point estimate or sample statistic is the mean for both large and small samples and for when the sample statistic is a proportion. In some cases, we refer back to illustrations used in Chapters 9, 10, and 11.

Constructing CI: σ_1, σ_2 Known and/or $n > 30$

Recall that when the standard deviation (σ) of a population is known or when the size of the sample is larger than 30 (>30), the normal z distribution is used to establish confidence intervals for the mean. The *critical values*, as noted earlier, represent the number of standard errors on either side of point estimate, and are denoted symbolically as z_{cv}. The z-value also is known as the *interval coefficient*; it corresponds to a decision maker's level of confidence that the interval contains the true population parameter.

Single-Sample Cases

The formula to compute the confidence interval for single sample cases when is known or when the sample size is 30 are algebraically defined in Formulas 12–3 and Formula 12–4.

Formula 12–3

$$CI_{\_\%} = \bar{X} \pm (z_{cv})(\sigma_{\bar{X}})$$

Formula 12–4

$$CI_{\_\%} = \bar{X} \pm (z_{cv})(s_{\bar{X}})$$

Where

$_\%$ = percentage of confidence

$\bar{X}$ = sample mean (point estimate)

z_{cv} = z-value of half the confidence interval (critical value)

$\sigma_{\bar{X}}$ = standard error of the mean

$s_{\bar{X}}$ = standard error of the mean

Scenario. A sociologist is interested in estimating the average IQ of people who audition for "reality" type television shows. He randomly samples 100 contestant hopefuls and finds that the average IQ is 102. The sociologist knows that the point estimate of 102 may or may not be representative of all the people who try out for these shows. He decides to establish an interval in which he can be 90% confident lies the true average IQ of the population of contestant hopefuls.

Assuming that the sociologist uses a standardized IQ test that has a mean of 100 (μ) and a standard deviation of 15 (σ), the 90% confidence interval, using Formula 12–3, is derived as follows:

$$CI_{90\%} = 102 \pm (1.645)(15/\sqrt{100})$$

$$= 102 \pm 2.468$$

$$= (99.532, 104.468)$$

There are two ways in which the sociologist can express his results. He can say that he is 90% confident that the interval 99.532 to 104.468 contains the average IQ of people who try out for reality type television shows. Or he can say that he is 90% confident that the average IQ of contestants for reality type shows is 102, plus or minus 2.468 IQ points. This statement reflects both the point estimate and the maximum error (E) or margin of error for the confidence interval.

Two-Sample Cases

The confidence interval for two-sample cases when σ_1^2 and σ_2^2 are known or where the size of both samples, n_1, n_2, is larger than 30 (both n_1 and n_2 >30) are operationally defined in Formula 12–5 and Formula 12–6.

Formula 12–5

$$CI_{\_\%} = (\bar{X}_1 - \bar{X}_2) \pm (z_{cv})(\sigma_{\bar{X}_2 - \bar{X}_2})$$

Formula 12–6

$$CI_{\_\%} = (\bar{X}_1 - \bar{X}_2) \pm (z_{cv})(s_{\bar{X}_2 - \bar{X}_2})$$

Where

$\_\%$ = percentage of confidence

$(\overline{X}_1 - \overline{X}_2)$ = difference between two sample means

z_{cv} = z-value corresponding to the level of confidence for a two-tailed test

$\sigma_{\overline{X}_2 - \overline{X}_2}$ = standard error of the difference between two means $\sqrt{\dfrac{\sigma_1^2}{n_1} + \dfrac{\sigma_2^2}{n_2}}$ (Read Chapter 10 for details)

$s_{\overline{X}_2 - \overline{X}_2}$ = estimated standard error of the difference between two means $\sqrt{\dfrac{s_1^2}{n_1} + \dfrac{s_2^2}{n_2}}$ (Formula 10–1)

As noted above, the estimation of where the true population parameter lies may be determined either by constructing a confidence interval from sample data or a fifth step in hypothesis, when the null hypothesis is rejected, as illustrated in the following example.

Scenario. A behavioral science researcher interested in height and the perception of physical attractiveness decides to test if there is a significant difference between male and female perceptions. She selects and surveys a random sample of 35 college age males and 35 college-age females and obtains the results shown in Table 12–2.

A one-tailed hypothesis test at the $\alpha = 0.01$ level is conducted to determine if the 3-point difference between the means of males and females is statistically significant. The test ends in the rejection of the null hypothesis, concluding no significant difference between the two sample means (z_{cv} = 2.326 versus z = 3.788, with a standard error $s_{\overline{X}_2 - \overline{X}_2}$ = 0.792). This leaves the researcher asking the question: "If the 3-point difference between the samples is not significant, what is the interval in which the true difference lies?" The answer to the question can be obtained by constructing a confidence interval.

In constructing a confidence interval following the rejection of a null hypothesis, there are two things to keep in mind. The first is that the complement of the alpha level chosen for the hypothesis test is the confidence level for the interval. In the example illustrated here, the alpha level was 0.01. Therefore, the confidence level for the interval will be 99%. The second thing to keep in mind is that the critical value used in the equation must always be that of a two-tailed test, since an interval has both a lower and upper limit. Therefore, in our illustration, the two-tailed test, $\alpha = 0.01$, and the critical value z_{cv} = 2.576 will be used rather than the z_{cv} = 2.326 of the one-tailed test. The remaining relevant statistics for constructing the 99% confidence interval using For-

Table 12–2. Results of Survey on Perception of Physical Attractiveness Based on Height

Males	Females
Sample Mean = 72	Sample Mean = 69
Sample Variance = s_2 = 11	Sample Variance = s_2 = 10
Sample Size = n = 35	Sample Size = n = 35

mula 12–6 are: $\overline{X}_1 = 72$, $\overline{X}_2 = 69$, and $s_{\overline{X}_2 - \overline{X}_2} = 0.792$. They are computed as follows:

$$CI_{99\%} = (72 - 69) \pm (2.576)(0.792)$$

$$= 3 \pm 2.040$$

$$= (0.96, 5.040)$$

Our researcher may state with 99% confidence that the true difference between the population means of college-age males and females on the perception of height and physical attractiveness falls between a low of 0.96 to a high of 5.040.

There are two other notes of interest regarding confidence intervals. The first is that the hypothesized value of the null, 0, is not included within the interval because it was rejected. Therefore, we can think of the range of values in a confidence interval as a range of true null hypothesis. The second note of interest is that there is a tendency to look upon the percentage of confidence as a probability. It is not. We say more on this topic in the section on interpreting confidence intervals later in the chapter.

Constructing CI: σ_1, σ_2 Unknown and $n \leq 30$

As we have seen with single and two sample cases for the mean, when the standard deviations of the populations from which the samples are drawn are unknown and when the size of the sample is less than or equal to 30 (≤ 30), the standard normal distribution is inappropriate as a sampling distribution. In such cases, the t distribution is used as the sampling distribution both in hypothesis testing and in estimation. This section illustrates constructing confidence intervals for one- and two-sample cases for the mean.

Critical Values Using the t Distribution

When we conduct a z-test, the level of significance values 0.20, 0.10, 0.05, 0.02, 0.01, and 0.001 for a two-tailed test in Table L–1 in Appendix L correspond to the 80%, 90%, 95%, 98%, 99%, and 99.9% confidence levels for confidence intervals. As noted earlier, levels of confidence are the complements of levels of significance. When we conduct a t-test, the procedure introduced in Chapter 9 to find the critical value, denoted by t_{cv} (we must use Appendix M for the derivation), in hypothesis testing are used in constructing confidence intervals.

Single-Sample Cases

The formula for single sample cases when σ is unknown and where the size of the sample is less than or equal to 30 (≤ 30) is identical to Formula 12–4, except that the critical value t_{cv} is substituted for z_{cv}, as given in Formula 12–7.

Formula 12–7

$$CI_{\_\%} = \overline{X}(t_{cv})(s_{\overline{X}})$$

Where

$\_\% =$ percentage of confidence

$\overline{X} =$ sample mean (point estimate)

$t_{cv} = t$-value of half the confidence interval (critical value)

$s_{\overline{X}} =$ standard error of the mean
$s_{\overline{X}} = \frac{s}{\sqrt{n}}$

Scenario. A communication researcher is interested in estimating the "willingness to communicate" level of individuals who visit a particular online chat room more than once a week. The researcher surveys a random sample of 20 individuals from the population of such users and finds that the average willingness-to-communicate score is 61.7, with a standard deviation of 5. In constructing her confidence interval, the researcher wants to be 95% confident that the interval contains the true population average of all visitors to the online chat room of interest.

In constructing the confidence interval, she: (1) finds the degrees of freedom to be 19 ($20 - 1 = 19$ df); (2) finds the critical value for the 95% confidence level to be $t_{cv} = 2.093$ (the value at the intersection of the row for 19 df and the 0.05 column for a two-tailed test in Table M–1, Appendix M); and (3) constructs the confidence interval using Formula 12–7, as follows:

$$CI_{95\%} = 61.7 \pm (2.0932)(5/\sqrt{20})$$

$$= 61.7 \pm 2.34$$

$$= (59.36, 64.04)$$

Thus, the researcher can be 95% confident that the interval 56.36 to 64.04 contains the true willingness-to-communicate population mean for online users who visit the chat room of interest more than once a week.

Two-Sample Cases

The confidence interval for two-sample cases when σ_1^2 and σ_2^2 are unknown and where the size of at least one of two samples, n_1, n_2, is less than or equal to 30 (both n_1 and $n_2 \leq 30$ or either n_1 or $n_2 \leq 30$) is operationally defined in Formula 12–8, which, except for the symbol of the critical value, t_{cv}, is the same as Formula 12–6.

Formula 12–8

$$CI_{\_\%} = (\overline{X}_1 - \overline{X}_2) \pm (t_{cv})(s_{\overline{X}_2 - \overline{X}_1})$$

Where

$\_\%$ = percentage of confidence

$(\overline{X}_1 - \overline{X}_2)$ = difference between two sample means

t_{cv} = z-value corresponding to the level of confidence for a two-tailed test

$s_{\overline{X}_2 - \overline{X}_2}$ = estimated standard error of the difference between two means
$\sqrt{\dfrac{s_1^2}{n_1} + \dfrac{s_2^2}{n_2}}$ (Formula 10–1)

Recall the illustration in Chapter 10 in which a developmental psychologist conducted a pilot study to determine if teenage boys who, as young children, regularly viewed prosocial children's television programs were less affected in the development of prosocial skills than teenage girls who viewed such programs as young children. The null hypothesis was rejected, which led to support for the alternative hypothesis that boys were less affected. However, the test revealed nothing about the true difference between the population means, which could lead the psychologist to construct a confidence interval. If so, the relevant data from the hypothesis test are as follows:

$n_1 = 9$ $n_2 = 10$ $\overline{X}_1 = 56$ $\overline{X}_2 = 71.1$

$s_{\overline{X}_2 - \overline{X}_2} = 4.941$ $\alpha = 0.01$

One-Tailed Test $df = 9 + 10 - 2 = 17$

$t_{cv} = -2.898$

For the 99% confidence interval, which is always a two-tailed test, the critical value t_{cv} will be 2.898 and Formula 12–8 will be applied.

$$CI_{99\%} = (56 - 71.1) \pm (2.898)(4.941)$$

$$= -15.1 \pm 14.319$$

$$= (-29.419, -0.781)$$

The developmental psychologist can be 99% confident that the true average difference among teenage girls and boys in learning prosocial skills is between −29.419 and −0.781.

Constructing CI: Proportions

The procedures for constructing confidence intervals for one and two sample cases for proportions are similar to those employed for the mean. In each case, the size of samples dictates which sampling distribution and test statistic is used. In the case of proportions, we have seen that when samples sizes are ≥5, the standard normal z distribution may be used as the sampling distribution. When the condition is met, the process of constructing confidence intervals is identical to that used above for cases of the mean, either as a standalone method or as a fifth step following the rejection of the null hypothesis. In the following two examples, which were illustrated in the last chapter, we use both approaches for estimating the interval in which a true population parameter lies.

Single-Sample Cases

The confidence interval for single-sample cases for proportions, when the sample size is equal to or greater than 5, is defined in Formula 12–9.

Formula 12–9

$$CI_{\_\%} = \hat{p} \pm \left(z_{\alpha/2}\right)\left(s_{\hat{p}}\right)$$

Where

$\_\%$ = percentage of confidence

$\hat{p}$ = point estimate or sample statistic of proportion having the characteristic of interest

$z_{\alpha/2}$ = the critical value of a two-tailed, z-test

$s_{\hat{p}}$ = the estimated standard error of the proportion $s_p = \frac{s}{\sqrt{n}}$

In the last chapter, we illustrated a scenario in which 50 adults were asked if they would abandon all of their friends for $10 million. The sample proportion $\hat{p}$ = 0.12 was observed to be large enough for the null hypothesis to be rejected. Also, recall that the test of significance was two-tailed, $\alpha = 0.05$, with a critical value, $z_{cv} = \pm 1.96$. Since H_o was rejected, we could decide to determine the interval in which the true percentage of the population would abandon all of their friends for $10 million.

In constructing the confidence interval in this case, the point estimate is 0.12, the standard error is $s_{\hat{p}} = 0.061$, the confidence level is 95%, and the interval is calculated as follows:

$$CI_{95\%} = 0.12 \pm (1.96)(0.061)$$

$$= 0.12 \pm 0.012 \ (E)$$

$$= (0.108, 0.132)$$

Thus, we would be able to conclude that the true percentage of adults who would abandon all of their friends for $10 million falls somewhere between approximately 10 and 13%, with an approximate margin of error of 1%. The conclusion is much more meaningful than simply saying "the null hypothesis is not tenable, and there is support for the alternative hypothesis."

Two-Sample Cases

In two-sample cases, when the condition, and n_1 and $n_2 \geq 5$, is satisfied, the standard normal distribution may be used as the sampling distribution, and the process for constructing a confidence interval for proportions is defined in Formula 12–10.

Formula 12–10

$$CI\_\% = (\hat{p}_1 - \hat{p}_2) \pm (z_{cv})\left(s_{\hat{p}_1 - \hat{p}_2}\right)$$

Where

$\_\%$ = percentage of confidence

$(\hat{p}_1 - \hat{p}_2)$ = point estimate or difference between two sample proportions (sample statistic)

z_{cv} = z-value corresponding to the level of confidence for a two-tailed test ($z_{\alpha/2}$)

$s_{\hat{p}_1 - \hat{p}_2}$ = estimated standard error of the difference between two proportions, $\sqrt{\hat{p}_d \hat{q}_d \left(\frac{1}{n_1} + \frac{1}{n_2}\right)}$. (Formula 11–5)

Let us assume that the researcher in the last chapter who was interested in comparing the academic achievement of early and regular admission college students decides to derive an estimate of parameter differences rather than conducting a hypothesis test. Recall that of the 2,084 early admissions students surveyed, 517 or 0.248 made the dean's list in the first term of their freshman year, while 1,373 of the 6,166 or 0.223 of regular admissions students achieved the same honor. In constructing the confidence interval, she uses a confidence level of 90, the two-tailed test critical value $z_{cv} = 1.645$, and the computed standard error of differences $s_{\hat{p}_1 - \hat{p}_2} = 0.011$, as calculated in

Chapter 11. Referring to Formula 12–10, the interval is constructed as follows:

$$CI_{90\%} = (0.248 - 0.223) \pm (1.645)(0.011)$$

$$= 0.025 \pm 0.018 \ (E)$$

$$= (0.007, 0.043)$$

Therefore, the researcher would be able to state with 90% confidence that the true difference between the population proportions of early and regular admissions students making the dean's list in the first semester of their freshman year is between approximately 1 and 4%, or, equivalently, (0.007, 0.043). She also may say that the difference is approximately 3%, plus or minus approximately 2% (maximum error).

Interpreting Confidence Intervals

It is important to keep in mind when interpreting confidence intervals that a confidence level is not a probability statement. The sociologist in the scenario about contestants in reality type television shows cannot say, "There is a 90% probability that the interval 98.53 to 104.48 contains the average IQ of people who try out for the show." Nor can the researcher investigating willingness-to-communicate say there is a 0.95 probability that the interval 59.36 to 63.34 contains the average level of online users who visit the chat room of interest more than once a week. Probability statements can only be made *before* a confidence interval is constructed and only in a general rather than a specific sense.

When interpreting confidence intervals, we should keep in mind that what a confidence interval tells us is similar to what we know about sampling in general.

Meaning, if we took an indefinite number of samples and calculated the confidence interval for each sample, we would end up with a distribution of intervals with varying lower and upper limits because of sampling error. Moreover, a significant number of these intervals will contain the true population parameter, such as μ, and a few will not. For example, when the population standard deviation σ is known or when $n \geq 30$, we know that 90% of the intervals between $z = -1.65$ and $z = +1.65$ will contain the true population mean, μ, and that $z = -1.96$ and $z = +1.96$ represent the lower and upper limits of 95% of all possible intervals. Put another way, we can say that there is a 90% or 95% probability that μ will be contained in intervals between $z = +1.65$ and $z = -1.96$, respectively, over an infinite number of samples. However, in reality we only construct one confidence interval from which we draw our conclusion regarding the location of the true population parameter. Therefore, we only can make probability statements about confidence intervals in general, before they are computed, and once a confidence interval has been established, we can only express a level of confidence that the computed interval contains the true population mean. This, then, is one factor to consider in interpreting confidence intervals. Another factor to consider is associated with the concept of *maximum error (E)*.

Maximum Error

In the generalized operation for computing a confidence interval, we noted that the product of the critical value (*cv*) and the standard error (*se*) is known as the **maximum error of estimate**, which we refer to simply as **maximum error** or by

its symbol *E*. The operation for calculating *E* is expressed in Formula 12–11.

Formula 12–11

$$E = (cv)(se)$$

Where

cv = critical value for z or t

se = standard error $\sigma_{\bar{X}} = \frac{\sigma}{\sqrt{n}}$ or $s_{\bar{X}} = \frac{s}{\sqrt{n}}$

In a confidence interval, *E* falls on both sides of the point estimate. We also can think of maximum error as the maximum amount of error that is tolerable in a statistical estimate and analogous to the common expression, "give or take," as in, "I'll be there at five, give or take a few minutes."

The maximum error of estimate, as mentioned earlier, is commonly known as the **margin of error**, a term most of us are familiar with from reports of public opinion polls. The results of polls in the popular media are not reported in terms of confidence interval but rather in terms of a point estimate and a maximum error of estimate. For example, a *Washington Post-ABC News* poll of teenagers, one week after the shooting of students at Columbine High School in Littleton, Colorado, reported that 40% of those surveyed believed their school had the potential for such an incident. The report noted, "The margin of error for the survey results is plus or minus 4.5 percentage points." With reference to the generalized confidence interval expressed in Formula 12–1, the 40% represents the point estimate (*pe*) and 4.5 is the maximum error (*E*). In short, the true percentage of all teenagers holding such an opinion was somewhere between 35.5% and 44.5%. Finally, the maximum error of a confidence interval also is a factor to be taken into account when considering the accuracy or precision of a statistical estimation.

Statistical Precision

Statistical precision is a matter of importance and concern for the researcher who decides to use a confidence interval to determine the location of the true population parameter of interest. In inferential statistics, the distance or width between the lower and upper limits of the confidence interval represents the **statistical precision** of the estimation. In general, the smaller the interval width, the greater the precision of the estimate.

There are two ways to increase the statistical precision of a point estimate. One way is to decrease the confidence level. For example, in our illustration of the sociologist interested in estimating the average IQ of possible contestants for reality type television shows, the interval width was calculated as 7.74 (98.13, 105.87) for the 99% confidence interval, repeated below.

$$CI_{99\%} = 102 \pm (2.58)(15/\sqrt{100})$$

$$= 102 \pm 3.87$$

$$= (98.13, 105.87)$$

By reducing the confidence level from 99% to 90%, the interval width is reduced from 7.74 to 4.95 (99.525 − 104.475), as shown below.

$$CI_{90\%} = 102 \pm (1.65)(15/\sqrt{100})$$

$$= 102 \pm 2.475$$

$$= (99.525, 104.475)$$

However, decreasing the width of a confidence interval lessens the possibility that the interval will contain the true population parameter. Reducing the confidence level from 99% to 90%, for example, means that of all the possible intervals for our sample, only 90% will contain the true population parameter.

A second way of increasing the statistical precision of a confidence interval is by increasing the size of the sample. This is because sample size affects the standard error, which, in turn, affects the maximum error of an estimate. For example, by increasing the sample size from 100 to 200 in the 99% confidence interval illustrated above, the width of the interval is reduced from 7.74 (105.87 − 98.13) to 5.474 (104.737 − 98.263), as shown below.

$$CI_{99\%} = 102 \pm (2.58)(15/\sqrt{200})$$

$$= 102 \pm 2.737$$

$$= (99.263, 104.737)$$

However, the size of a sample often carries a cost both in time and money. In general, the larger the sample size, the greater the expenditure of time and money, and in the real world of research, time and money are very important considerations. Thus, the issue of proper sample size is important in statistical estimation.

Determining Sample Size

The size of a sample is an important consideration in statistical estimation. We know, in general, that the larger the sample size, the smaller the width or maximum error of a confidence interval and the more precise the statistical estimate. However, as mentioned above, the larger the sample, the more time, effort, and expense is required in conducting a study. The dilemma is this: too small a sample may invite significant error in our findings; too large a sample may be unnecessary and costly.

So how do you determine the minimum sample size for constructing a confidence interval to estimate a population parameter? The answer depends on three factors: (1) a level of confidence (α); (2) the standard deviation (σ or s); and (3) the maximum error (E) tolerable. These three factors are incorporated in Formula 12–12, which represents a generalized procedure for calculated sample size.

Formula 12–12

$$n = \left[\frac{cv \cdot se}{E}\right]^2$$

Where

cv = the z- or t-value of half the confidence interval (critical value)

se = standard error of a known population, the results of a pilot study, or previous research findings

E = maximum error

Determining Sample Size When σ Is Known

When the standard deviation of the population σ is known, the minimum required sample size for a given confidence interval is computed using Formula 12–13.

Formula 12–13

$$n = \left[\frac{z_{cv} \cdot \sigma}{E}\right]^2$$

Where

z_{cv} = critical value of the confidence interval

σ = standard deviation of the population

E = maximum error

Scenario

A behavioral science researcher is interested in estimating the average effect of action video games on hand-eye coordination among preteens. Suppose the goal of the researcher is to be 95% confident that his interval estimate is accurate within 6 units of the point estimate. How large a sample does the researcher need? For purposes of illustration, let us assume that previous studies have determined that the population standard deviation (σ) for preteen hand-eye coordination is 12.55. Thus, the three factors that will be used to determine the minimum sample size are: (1) a critical value, z_{cv} = 1.96, which corresponds to the 95% level of confidence when the standard deviation of the population is known; (2) the value of the population standard deviation, σ = 12.55; and (3) the maximum error of interest, in this case 6 points on either side of the point estimate or sample mean.

Referring to Formula 12–13, the minimum sample size is computed as follows:

$$n = \left[\frac{(1.96)(12.55)}{6}\right]^2$$

$$= \left[\frac{24.598}{6}\right]^2$$

$$= 16.81 \approx 17$$

Note that when determining sample size, all fractional (decimal) values should be *rounded up* to the next larger integer. Therefore, a minimum sample size of $n = 17$ is needed to estimate the 95% confidence interval that contains the true average level of hand-eye coordination among preteens, with a maximum error (margin of error) of 6 points. Suppose the researcher wants to increase the precision of his estimate by reducing the maximum error tolerable on either side of the point estimate from 6 points to 3 points. What effect would this reduction of maximum error have on the sample size needed for the estimate? Using Formula 12–13, the required sample size is computed as follows:

$$n = \left[\frac{(1.96)(12.55)}{3} \right]^2$$

$$= \left[\frac{24.598}{3} \right]^2$$

$$= 67.224 \approx 68$$

In this case, the minimum size of the sample required to estimate the 95% confidence interval increases from 17 to 68. Of course, as noted above, although the increase in sample size decreases the maximum error of the confidence interval, it significantly increases the time, money, and effort that will be expended in the study. Therefore, researchers need to keep in mind the cost of a research study and the need for statistical precision in estimating population parameters.

Determining Sample Size When σ Is Unknown

When the population standard deviation is unknown, the standard deviation of a sample from a pilot or from previous research may be used as an estimate of σ in computing a sample size. The calculation for such cases is given in Formula 12–14.

Formula 12–14

$$n = \left[\frac{z_{\alpha/2} \cdot s}{E} \right]^2$$

Where

$z_{\alpha/2}$ = z-value of half the confidence interval (critical value)

s = standard deviation of a sample from a pilot study

E = maximum error

Scenario

A director of a juvenile delinquent facility wants to estimate the average level of verbal aggression among first-time offenders and wants to be 99% confident that his estimate is accurate to within 7 points. The results of earlier studies reported in research journals indicate that the standard deviation of verbal aggression among juvenile delinquents is 15. In this case, since the population standard deviation is unknown, the standard deviation of a sample from a previous study, such as one reported in a research journal or in a pilot study, may be used as an estimate.

The three factors used to determine the minimum sample size in this case are: (1) the critical value of 2.576, which corresponds to the 99% level of confidence; (2) the estimated standard deviation from the pilot study, 15; and (3) the maximum error of 7 points on either side of the point estimate (sample mean). Applying Formula 12–14, the minimum sample size needed to conduct the study is calculated as follows:

$$n = \left[\frac{(2.576)(15)}{7}\right]^2$$

$$= \left[\frac{38.64}{7}\right]^2$$

$$= 30.47 \approx 31$$

Thus, to estimate the average level of verbal aggression among juvenile delinquents, with a 7 point margin of error, the director of the juvenile delinquent facility would need a minimum sample of 31 participants to construct the 99% confidence interval.

Key Terms and Concepts

Statistical estimation

Point estimate

Interval estimate

Confidence interval

Level of confidence

Level of significance

Sample statistic

Critical values

Standard error

z distribution

t distribution

Degrees of freedom

Maximum error

Margin of error

Interval coefficient

Statistical precision

Sample size

Feedback Review of Chapter 12

1. In statistical estimation, a point estimate is
   a. an interval along a number continuum.
   b. one-half the width of a confidence interval.
   c. a population parameter.
   d. a sample statistic.
   e. none of the above.

2. Which of the following symbols represents a possible point estimate?
   a. μ
   b. σ
   c. $\overline{X}$
   d. s
   e. c & d

3. In estimating a population parameter with a confidence interval, the maximum error of estimate, E, is
   a. a range of the possible true parameters.
   b. one-half the width of the interval.
   c. equal to the entire width of the interval.
   d. the complement of the level of confidence.
   e. a & c.

4. Which of the following represents a way of increasing the precision of a statistical estimate?
   a. use the point estimate of the parameter.
   b. increase sample size.
   c. decrease the level of confidence.
   d. a & b.
   e. b & c.

5. If you were to construct 95% confidence intervals from a distribution of

300 sample means randomly selected from a population, how many of the 300 interval estimates would you expect to contain the true population mean (μ)?

a. 15
b. 95
c. 285
d. 295
e. 300

6. Which of the following is a factor in determining sample size?
   a. maximum error (E).
   b. the z-value of half the confidence interval ($z_{\alpha/2}$).
   c. the standard deviation of the population.
   d. all of the above.
   e. none of the above.

7. The complement of the level of confidence is
   a. level of significance.
   b. standard error of the mean.
   c. the critical value of the interval.
   d. a point estimate.
   e. alpha.

8. In a confidence interval, $\overline{X}$ refers to the
   a. maximum error of the estimate.
   b. width of the interval.
   c. critical values of the interval.
   d. point estimate.
   e. the product of the critical value and the standard error.

9. Increasing the size of a sample
   a. increases the width of the confidence interval.
   b. decreases the width of the confidence interval.
   c. increases the maximum error of the interval estimate.

   d. reduces the maximum error of the interval estimate.
   e. b & d.

10. Increasing the maximum error in the process of determining the minimum sample size for a confident interval
    a. increases the width of the confidence interval.
    b. decreases the width of the confidence interval.
    c. increases the required size of the sample.
    d. reduces the required size of the sample.
    e. increases the statistical precision of the estimate.

11. Which of the following statements concerning the 95% confidence interval is true?
    a. It contains the true population parameter 95% of the time.
    b. It contains the true population parameter 0.95% of the time.
    c. It probably contains the true population parameter 95% of the time.
    d. It probably contains the sample mean 95% of the time.
    e. None of the above.

12. Large sample sizes are reflected in
    a. increased statistical precision.
    b. decreases in the width of a confidence interval.
    c. increases in the size of the maximum error of estimate.
    d. all of the above.

13. Which of the following levels of confidence produces a narrower interval?
    a. 90%
    b. 93%
    c. 95%

d. 97%

e. 99%

14. When the population standard deviation is unknown, the critical values for a confidence interval is/are
   a. determined using the t distribution.
   b. symbolized as $t_{\alpha/2}$.
   c. symbolized as $z_{\alpha/2}$.
   d. a & b.
   e. a & c.

Fill-Ins

15. What term is synonymous with the term "maximum error"? _____

16. When the population standard deviation (σ) is known, degrees of freedom are defined as n _____.

17. If the point estimate of a confidence interval is 31 and the tolerable maximum error is 4,
   a. what are the limits of the interval? _____
   b. what is the width of the interval?

   _____

18. In estimating the population parameter μ, what is the sample statistic?

   _____

19. In estimating the population parameter μ, when the population standard deviation σ is unknown, how many degrees of freedom would there be for a sample of 28? _____

20. The critical values of a confidence interval are based on the level of significance of a _____-tailed test.

21. Given the following in constructing the 90% confidence interval to detect the population mean: $n = 12$, $\overline{X} = 8$, and $s_x = 2.6$,
   a. what is the point estimate of the interval? _____
   b. how many degrees of freedom are there in determining the critical value? _____

22. In estimating the population mean from a population in which is unknown, the confidence interval is *symbolized* $CI = \overline{X} \pm (\ \ )(\ \ )$

For questions 23 through 26, indicate the appropriate symbol.

23. _____ maximum error

24. _____ value of half the confidence interval (critical value) when is known

25. _____ degrees of freedom

26. _____ sample size

Review Problems

1. Using the normal or z distribution as the underlying distribution, indicate the critical value and confidence level for each level of significance listed in the first column of Table 12–3.

2. Using the t distribution as the underlying distribution, indicate the critical values and confidence level for each of the following in Table 12–4.

3. The director of a teacher education program wants to estimate the grade point average (4.0 GPA) of students

Table 12–3. Corresponding Critical Values and Confidence Intervals at 0.05, 0.10, and 0.01 Significance Level Under the z Distribution

Significance Level	Critical Value	Confidence Level
0.05	±1.96	95%
0.10		
0.01		

Table 12–4. Corresponding Critical Values and Confidence Intervals Under the t-Distribution When Significance Level at 0.01, 0.05, and 0.10, and Degrees of Freedom (df) Are Given

Significance Level	df	Critical Value	Confidence Level
0.01	25	2.787	99%
0.05	30		
0.10	225		

who enter the program at the beginning of their junior year. A random sample of 27 students yields a mean of 2.75, with a standard deviation of 0.81.

a. What is the 90% confidence interval for estimating the true mean of the population of students entering the program at the beginning of their junior year?

b. What is the 98% confidence interval for estimating the true mean of the population of students entering the program at the beginning of their junior year?

4. A random sample of 60 students majoring in communication disorders in New England colleges is selected to estimate the average or mean age of all students in such programs. The results of the data analysis show that the average age of the sample students is 20.3 years. The variance of the population found in a previous large-scale study is 16. (Hint: Read problem very carefully.)

a. What is a point estimate for the population mean?

b. Estimate the 95% confidence interval.

c. Estimate the 99% confidence interval.

5. A psychologist asks his research assistant to give him a "good" estimate of the average time readers who are single and in their mid-thirties spend reading the personal advertisements section of the Sunday edition of the

New York Times. The researcher surveys a random sample of 29 readers and finds that the group spends an average of 13 minutes reading the ads, with a standard deviation of 5 minutes.

a. What is the interval estimate that the researcher can report to the psychologist with 95% confidence?

b. What is the 99% confidence interval estimate?

6. A national child advocacy group is interested in estimating the average number of commercials aired during Saturday morning cartoon programs in 2001. The standard deviation of a study done by the same group in 2000 had a population standard deviation of 5. Assume that the group wants to be 90% confident that the estimated interval in which the true population average falls is accurate within 3 points.

a. How large a sample does the group need to conduct this study?

b. How large a sample is required for the group to be 99% confident?

7. The chief academic officer (CAO) at a large university wants to estimate the average teacher/course evaluation rating of untenured instructors. A pilot study using a random sample of 20 instructors had a standard deviation of $s = 3.4$ points. If the CAO wants to be 99% confident that a sample mean ($\overline{X}$) does not differ from the true population mean (μ) by more that a half point (0.5), how large a sample should he use?

8. What sample size would you need to estimate with 90% confidence the average level of communication competency of the communication disorders students and be accurate to within 2 points on either side of the point estimate? A pilot study using a sample of 15 students yielded a sample standard deviation of 9.

Calculation Guides

Constructing Confidence Intervals

Step 1: Set the level of confidence for the interval, e.g., 90%, 95%, or 99%.

Step 2: Multiply the critical value (*cv*) of the interval by the sampling distribution (*se*). Symbolize the product of *cv* × *se* as *E* for "*maximum error.*"

Step 3: Subtract *E* from the point estimate (*pe*) to obtain the lower limit of the interval.

Step 4: Add *E* to the point estimate (*pe*) to obtain the upper limit of the interval.

13

Analysis of Variance: One-Way

Overview

Tests of significance for the mean are not restricted to one- and two-sample cases. Very often, researchers are interested in more than the difference between two population means obtained from an experiment or observational study. Suppose a clinical psychology researcher is interested in comparing the effectiveness of three methods of reducing test anxiety among high school students: behavior modification, cognitive restructuring, and systematic desensitization. If she randomly assigns students to three experimental or treatment groups, she can measure their anxiety levels at the end of the treatment period and obtain a mean score for each of the three samples for comparison purposes. On the other hand, a speech-language pathologist may want to investigate the effectiveness of several different types of the therapies in reducing stuttering to determine which therapy is most effective. Or a sociologist or political scientist may be interested in the attitudes of Democrats, Republicans, and Independents toward some public policy, such as the use of military tribunals in prosecuting terrorists. In such a study, individuals would be randomly sampled from each politically affiliated group and given an attitude measure. Differences in the mean attitude of individuals in the three groups could then be compared.

The one-way analysis of variance technique is actually concerned with two basic questions. First, does a significant difference or differences exist anywhere among the means of the groups being compared? And second, if so, where does the difference exist? If the answer to the first question is "no," the data analysis ends, and we conclude that there is no basis for rejecting the null hypothesis. If the answer is "yes," that is, if the null hypothesis is rejected, we move on to the second question and ask, "Where does the significant difference (or differences) exist?" In the case of the test anxiety study, if a significant difference is detected and the null hypothesis rejected, the secondary question is pursued, namely, "Which treatment method or methods has the greater effect?"

In this chapter, we examine a statistical technique that permits the comparison of more than two group means. The technique is known as **analysis of variance**, usually abbreviated as **ANOVA**. It is so-called because the procedure involves the comparison of two kinds of variations. Specifically, we are examining a specific type of ANOVA that tests hypotheses involving one independent variable, known as **one-way analysis of variance**. It is referred to as "one-way" because it tests hypotheses involving one independent variable that has three or more categories or levels.

Assumptions and the *F* Distribution

The application of a one-way analysis of variance technique for independent samples depends on the same three assumptions, namely: (1) that the populations from which the samples are drawn must be normally distributed; (2) that the samples be independent of one another; and (3) that the variances of the populations must be equal. The first two assumptions, as noted in Chapter 10, can be satisfied by randomly selecting samples greater than thirty (>30). The assumption of equal variances requires the variability of the scores within the groups to have approximately the same spread. A ratio of 2 or less of the highest to the lowest sample standard deviations has been suggested as a guide for testing this assumption. We follow this guideline.

The *F* Distribution

In an ANOVA procedure, the sampling distribution of interest is the *F* distribution, and the significance of the differences between the between-groups and within-groups variances is determined by an *F*-test. Conceptually, the *F*-test used in ANOVA is an extension of the *F*-test for homogeneity of variance for two sample cases for the mean, introduced in Chapter 10. The test was conducted using the sample variances to determine if the population variances were equal (homogeneous). In ANOVA, the between-groups and within-groups estimates are used to test the equality of the populations from which the sample groups are drawn. In both cases, the *F* distribution is the sampling distribution from which the critical values for *F*-tests are derived.

In a one-way ANOVA, the *F*-ratio is computed using the between-groups estimate as the numerator and the within-groups estimate as the denominator. Mathematically, if the null hypothesis in an ANOVA test is true, the ratio of the estimates of population variance $[s_b^2/s_w^2]$ is approximately 1.00. If the null hypothesis is *not* true, the ratio of s_b^2 to s_w^2 is expected to be significantly greater than 1.00.

Computing a One-Way ANOVA

The basic function of the one-way ANOVA technique is to compare two estimates of population variance. The first is the variability of scores within the sample groups, referred to as the **within-groups variance estimate**, denoted by the symbol s_{within}^2 or s_w^2. It is obtained by computing a sum of squares for each of the samples separately and then combining them into a single estimate of population variance. Since all members of a given sample receive the same treatment, it is assumed that the variability of scores within the groups is due to sampling error or some other random chance factor. The second estimate is the variability of means among the sample groups, referred to as the **between-groups variance estimate**, denoted by the symbol $s^2_{between}$ or s^2_b. It is obtained by computing the mean for each sample and then calculating a variance estimate using these means and the sizes of the samples. Since each group receives a different treatment, it is assumed that the variability among the group means is due to sampling error and possible treatment effects.

If the difference between the two estimates, s^2_w and s^2_b, is less than the chosen level of significance, we conclude that the samples are probably from populations with identical means and that the variability of means among the samples is due solely to chance or sampling error. In the case of the test anxiety study mentioned earlier, we would conclude that there is no difference in the effectiveness of the three methods of reducing test anxiety. If, on the other hand, the variance estimate based on variability between the sample means is significantly larger than the variance estimate of variability of scores within the samples, the null hypothesis is rejected. In this case, we say that the samples do not come from populations with identical means and conclude that the between-group variance estimate is too large to have occurred by chance or sampling error, and must have occurred because of a significant difference in the effectiveness of the three anxiety reduction methods.

The *within-groups variance estimate*, s^2_w, represents the difference of scores within sample groups. The *between-groups variance estimate*, s^2_b, reflects the difference between the means of the sample groups.

The computations needed to perform an analysis of variance can be quite tedious and complex. This is particularly true when many samples are involved and, in such cases, it is best left to the speed and utility of statistical software such as Excel, Minitab, and SPSS. However, for cases where there are relatively few small samples and only one or two independent variables, hand calculations of ANOVA are not difficult to understand and are quite manageable. The illustration presented here is an example of such a case, and our purpose is twofold. First, it allows us to present the procedures executed in computing a one-way ANOVA. Second, the process can help us gain further insight into some of its basic concepts and functions.

Scenario. Consider the following hypothetical research scenario. Clinical psychologists are interested in determining the relative effectiveness of the three anxiety reduction methods mentioned earlier, namely, behavior modification, cognitive restructuring, and systematic desensitization, as they relate to teenagers identified as having high levels of test anxiety. We select 35 of these teenagers and randomly assign them to three experimental or treatment groups: behavior modification [*bm*], cognitive restructuring [*cr*], and systematic desensitization [*sd*]. After six weeks of treatment, the test anxiety levels of the research participants are again measured, with the results shown in Table 13–1. We refer to the data in this table as we proceed through the various data analysis procedures that follow.

In computing a one-way ANOVA, the between-group and within-group variance estimates, s^2_w and s^2_b, are used to calculate the test statistic F. However, several preliminary procedures must be completed before the F-test can be computed. The procedures represent a two-part process. In Part I, Preliminary Data Analysis, the between-group and within-group variance estimates are organized and calculated in

Table 13–1. Test Anxiety Survey, Post-Treatment Results

| Treatment Groups | | | | | | Grand Total |
| bm | | cr | | sd | | (t) |
ΣX_{bm}	ΣX^2_{bm}	ΣX_{cr}	ΣX^2_{cr}	ΣX_{sd}	ΣX^2_{sd}	
52	2704	48	2304	42	1764	
49	2401	48	2304	40	1600	
49	2401	42	1764	40	1600	
46	2116	41	1681	39	1521	
46	2116	41	1681	38	1444	
44	1936	39	1521	37	1369	
44	1936	39	1521	36	1296	
44	1936	39	1521	30	900	
42	1764	39	1521	30	900	
42	1764	38	1444	28	784	
42	1764	38	1444			
40	1600	35	1225			
		33	1089			
$\Sigma X_{bm} = 540$		$\Sigma X_{cr} = 520$		$\Sigma X_{sd} = 360$		$\Sigma X_t = 1420$
$\overline{X}_{bm} = 45$		$\overline{X}_{cr} = 40$		$\overline{X}_{sd} = 36$		$\overline{X}_{bm} = 40.57$
$\Sigma X^2_{bm} = 24438$		$\Sigma X^2_{cr} = 21020$		$\Sigma X^2_{sd} = 13178$		$\Sigma X^2_t = 58636$
$n_{bm} = 12$		$n_{cr} = 13$		$n_{sd} = 10$		$n_t = 35$

a four-step process. In Part II, an *F*-test of significance is conducted in a four-step sequence.

Part I: Preliminary Data Analysis

The four steps involved in computing the between-group and within-group variance estimates listed below represent a sequential process, wherein the procedures followed in one step yield the necessary values for executing the procedures in the next step.

Step 1: Organize and summarize the raw data.

Step 2: Calculate the sum of squares (denoted by *SS*) for the total group, between-group, and within-group.

Step 3: Calculate the degrees of freedom (denoted by *df*) for the total group, between-group, and within-group.

Step 4: Calculate the mean square (estimated variance, denoted by

MS) for the between-group and within-group.

We illustrate each step in detail using the data in Table 13–1.

Step 1: Organize and Summarize Raw Data

The summarized data in Table 13–1 represents the first step of the preliminary data analysis. In this step, the sample size, mean, sum of scores, and sum of squared scores for the three treatment groups (behavior modification *bm*, cognitive restructuring *cr*, systematic desensitization *sd*) individually and combined are computed. Sample statistics for the group as a whole (symbolized by subscript *t*) are computed because the null hypothesis assumes that the data for each of the three samples comes from populations having identical means.

An examination of the data in Table 13–1 shows that the means for the three groups ($\overline{X}_{bm} = 45$, $\overline{X}_{cr} = 40$, $\overline{X}_{sd} = 36$) differ from one another as well as from the combined or *grand mean* of the three groups, 40.57. However, the critical question, as always, is not whether the sample means differ but whether the differences are great enough to be attributed to the treatment received by the participants in the different groups rather than random sampling error. We address this question in Part II when we conduct the *F*-test of significance using the values derived in the steps below.

Step 2: Calculate the Sum of Squares

The calculations of the between-group, within-group, and total group sum of squares provide us with estimates of the between-groups and within-groups variances. The between-groups variance estimate (s_b^2) and within-groups variance estimate (s_w^2) are derived from the deviations of the research participant scores from their group means and from the deviations of group means to the mean of all groups combined (total group). The concept can be illustrated by looking at a single score in a distribution. In Table 13–1, the highlighted bold score 52 in the behavior modification group (*bm*) deviates from the total mean ($\overline{X}_t = 40.57$) by 11.43 points. This deviation value is partitioned into the within-group and between-group categories. Specifically, 7 of the 11.43 points represent the amount of deviation from its within-group mean (52–45), and 4.43 is the amount that the *bm* group mean deviates from total group mean (45–40.57). In other words, the deviation of a participant's score from the total mean is equal to its deviation from its group mean plus the deviation of its group mean from the total group mean.

The estimates of the between-groups and within-groups variances (s_b^2 and s_w^2) are termed **mean squares** and symbolized as MS_b (*mean square between-groups*) and MS_w (*mean square within-groups*). Recall that in Chapter 3, the variance of a sample, as given in Formulas 3–6 and 3–7 (deviation and whole score methods), is determined by dividing the sum of squares (*SS*) for score values by the degrees of freedom (*df*), as given in $MS = \frac{SS}{df}$. Therefore, in order to determine MS_b and MS_w, we must first compute the sum of squares for the between-group and within-group, as well as for the total group.

> Between-groups and within-groups variance estimates, (s_b^2) and (s_w^2), also are known as *mean square between-groups* (MS_b) and *mean square within-groups* (MS_w).

There are two methods for computing the sum of squares. The first method is a two-step procedure that provides us with some insight into the calculation process. The second method is a four-step procedure with a much easier computational process but without the insight. Both methods are algebraically equivalent and yield the same results. We examine each technique, but in subsequent illustrations, we use the second method.

Calculating Sum of Squares: Method One. The first technique for computing the sum of squares in a one-way ANOVA consisting of two steps in which we first calculate the sum of squares for the total group and each of the subgroups (Step 1); and then calculate the sum of squares for the between- and within-groups (Step 2). We examine each step in general and with reference to our test anxiety study example in particular.

Step 1: Calculate SS_t, SS_1, $SS_2 \ldots SS_k$. The sum of squares for the total group (SS) and each of the subgroups or samples (SS_1, $SS_2 \ldots SS_k$) is determined by using the generic equation shown in Formula 13–1.

Formula 13–1

$$SS_J = \Sigma X_J^2 - \frac{(\Sigma X_J)^2}{n}$$

Where

$J = 1, 2, \ldots k$ (In our example, $J = bm$, cr, and sd)

pe = the point estimate of the population parameter

$cv_{\alpha/2}$ = the critical value for the confidence interval (two-tailed)

For the test anxiety data in Table 13–1, the total sum of squares for the total group

and the three treatment groups are computed as follows:

Sum of squares for total group:

$$SS_t = 58636 - \frac{(1420)^2}{35} = 1024.57$$

Sum of squares for each subgroup:

$$SS_{bm} = 24438 - \frac{(540)^2}{12} = 138$$

$$SS_{cr} = 21020 - \frac{(520)^2}{13} = 220$$

$$SS_{sd} = 13178 - \frac{(360)^2}{10} = 218$$

Step 2: Calculate SS_b and SS_w. To estimate the between-group and within-group variances (MS_b and MS_w,), the sum of squares for the total group is partitioned into the between-groups (SS_b) and within-groups (SS_w) categories using the sum of squares of the subgroups, as defined in Formulas 13–2 and 13–3.

Formula 13–2

$$SS_b = SS_t - SS_w$$

Sum of squares between-groups

Formula 13–3

$$SS_w = SS_1 + SS_2 + \ldots SS_k$$

Sum of squares within-groups

Applying Formula 13–2 to the test anxiety data, the between-groups sum of squares is:

$$SS_b = 1024.57 - 576 = 448.57$$

For the within-groups, using Formula 13–3, the sum of squares is:

$$SS_w = 138 + 220 + 218 = 576$$

In short, the combined sum of scores for the between- and within-groups are equal to the sum of scores for the total groups, that is, $SS_t = SS_b + SS_w$.

Before continuing our illustration, let us consider another underlying concept of the one-way analysis of variance, namely the effect of the means of the subgroups and the total group on the mean squares. As indicated in Formula 13–3, the within-groups sum of squares (SS_w) is determined by adding the sum of squares of the subgroups, and its mean square (MS_w) will not be affected by the means of the groups, regardless of their values. In our test anxiety illustration, the SS_w will be 576 regardless of the values of the subgroup means. On the other hand, the between-groups sum of squares [SS_b] and its subsequent mean square (MS_b) are affected by the differences between the subgroup means and the total group mean. This can be illustrated using Formula 13–4, which is an alternative equation to Formula 13–3 for calculating SS_b.

Formula 13–4

$$SS_b = n_1(\overline{X}_1 - \overline{X}_t)^2 + n_2(\overline{X}_2 - \overline{X}_t)^2 \ldots$$
$$n_k(\overline{X}_k - \overline{X}_t)^2$$

For our illustration,

$$SS_b = 12(45 - 40.57)^2 + 13(40 - 40.57)^2$$
$$+ 10(36 - 40.57)^2 = 448.57$$

Calculating Sum of Squares: Method Two. This is the easier of the two methods to compute the sum of squares needed for the variance estimates for the between- and within-groups. The procedure followed is defined by Formulas 13–5 through 13–8.

Formula 13–5

$$C = \frac{(\Sigma X_t)^2}{n_t} \quad \text{Correction term}$$

Formula 13–6

$$SS_t = \Sigma X_t^2 - C \quad \text{Total sum of squares}$$

Formula 13–7

$$SS_b = \frac{(\Sigma X_1)^2}{n_1} + \frac{(\Sigma X_2)^2}{n_2} + \ldots \frac{(\Sigma X_k)^2}{n_k} - C$$
$$\text{Between-groups } SS$$

Formula 13–8

$$SS_w = SS_t - SS_b \quad \text{Within-groups } SS$$

The four formulas actually represent a four-step sequence. In Formula 13–5, a correction term is calculated. The correction term is then used in the second and third steps to compute the sum of squares for the total group (SS_t) and the between-group (SS_b). Finally, using Formula 13–8, the within-group sum of squares (SS_w), which is the difference between SS_t and SS_b, is calculated.

Applying these four equations to the test anxiety data in Table 13–1, we obtain the following results:

Step 1: $C = \frac{(1420)^2}{35} = 57611.43$
(Formula 13–5)

Step 2: $SS_t = 58636 - 57611.428 = 1024.57$ (Formula 13–6)

Step 3: $SS_b = \frac{(540_{bm})^2}{12_{bm}} + \frac{(520_{cr})^2}{13_{cr}} + \frac{(360_{sd})^2}{10_{sd}} - 57611.43 = 448.57$ (Formula 13–7)

Step 4: $SS_w = 1024.57 - 448.57 = 576$
(Formula 13–8)

Note that the results of this sequence are identical to those found using Method One.

Step 3: Calculating Degrees of Freedom

The calculations of degrees of freedom for the total group (df_t), the between-groups (df_b), and the within-groups (df_w) are given in Formulas 13–9 through 13–11.

Formula 13–9

$$df_t = N - 1 \quad \text{(total group)}$$

Formula 13–10

$$df_b = \text{total number of groups, } n - 1$$
$$\text{(between-groups)}$$

Formula 13–11

$$df_w = df_t - df_b \quad \text{(within-groups)}$$

Applied to the data in our test anxiety illustration, we obtain the following degrees of freedom: $df_t = 35 - 1 = 34$, $df_b = 3 - 1 = 2$, and df_w $34 - 2 = 32$.

Step 4: Calculating Mean Squares

The equations for calculating the mean squares or variance estimates for the between- and within-groups (MS_b, Ms_w) are given in Formulas 13–12 and 13–13.

Formula 13–12

$$MS_b = \frac{SS_b}{df_b}$$

Formula 13–13

$$MS_w = \frac{SS_w}{df_w}$$

Applying these formulas to the test anxiety data in Table 13–1, we obtain the following:

$$MS_b = \frac{448.57}{2} = 224.29$$

$$MS_w = \frac{576}{32} = 18$$

If the null hypothesis in a one-way ANOVA is true, we would expect the variance estimates of the between- and within-groups to be the same value, which is not the case for the data in our illustration. For the test anxiety data, the mean square of the between-groups, $MS_b = 224.29$, is obviously greater than that of the within-groups, $MS_w = 18$. To determine whether the difference is great enough to reject the null hypothesis, the F-test is applied. A summary of the results of the preliminary data analysis for the test anxiety illustration is shown in Box 13–1.

Part Two: Conducting the F-Test

The second stage in a one-way ANOVA consists of an F-test of significance using the data derived from the preliminary analysis of data in Part I. In illustrating the procedures for the test, we continue to use the test anxiety reduction data in Table 13–1 and the results of the preliminary data analysis.

Step 1: State the Hypotheses

For the test anxiety reduction data, the hypotheses are stated as:

H_o: $\mu_{bm} = \mu_{cr} = \mu_{sd}$

H_1: *At least one mean is different from the others.*

Here the null hypothesis claims that the scores for the 3 treatment groups are from populations with identical means. The alternative hypothesis states that the means are different for some of the populations.

Box 13–1. A Summary of the Results of the Preliminary Data Analysis for the Test Anxiety

Step 1: See Table 13.1

Step 2: Sum of Squares

METHOD ONE

Formula 13.1: Total group and each sample group (Step 1)

$$SS_t = 58636 - \frac{(1420)^2}{35} = 1024.57 \quad SS_{bm} = 24438 - \frac{(540)^2}{12} = 138$$

$$SS_{cr} = 21020 - \frac{(520)^2}{13} = 220 \qquad SS_{sd} = 13178 - \frac{(360)^2}{10} = 218$$

Formula 13.2: Between-group (Ss_b) (Step 2)

$$SS_b = 1024.57 - 576 = 448.57$$

Formula 13.3: Between-group [Ss_w] (Step 2)

$$SS_w = 138 + 220 + 218 = 576$$

METHOD TWO

Formula 13.5: Correction term (Step 1)

$$C = \frac{(1420)^2}{35} = 57611.43$$

Formula 13.6: Total sum of squares (Step 2)

$$SS_t = 58636 - 57611.428 = 1024.57$$

Formula 13.7: Between-groups sum of squares (Step 3)

$$SS_b = \frac{(540_{bm})^2}{12_{bm}} + \frac{(520_{cr})^2}{13_{cr}} + \frac{(360_{sd})^2}{10_{sd}} - 57611.43 = 448.57$$

Formula 13.8: Within-groups sum of squares (Step 4)

$$SS_w = 1024.57 - 448.57 = 576$$

Step 3: Degrees of Freedom

    Total group $df_t = 35 - 1 = 3$ Formula 13.9

    Between-groups $df_b = 3 - 1 = 2$ Formula 13.10

    Within-groups $df_w = 34 - 2 = 32$ Formula 13.11

Step 4: Calculate the mean squares (variance estimates).

    Between-group $MS_b = \dfrac{448.57}{2} = 224.29$ Formula 13.12

    Within-group $MS_w = \dfrac{576}{32} = 18$ Formula 13.13

Step 2: Set the Criterion for Rejecting H_o

As noted earlier, ANOVA tests are two-tailed, nondirectional tests, since the alternative hypothesis ("H_1: *At least one mean is different from the others*") does not specify the direction of the differences among the sample means. As in the *F*-test for homogeneity of variance, the estimate of the larger variance, in this case the mean squares of the between-groups (MS_b), is the numerator and the mean squares of the within-groups (MS_w) is the denominator. Similarly, the degrees of freedom of the between-groups (df_b) and within-groups (df_w) are used to derive the critical value (F_{cv}). However, since F $\left[F = \frac{MS_b}{MS_w} \right]$ is a ratio of two nonnegative values, the region of rejection is only in the right tail of the *F* distribution of critical values, as listed in Table N–1 (Appendix N).

For the *F*-test, we have selected a 0.05 level of significance. Referring to Table N–1 ($\alpha = 0.05$) at the intersection of 2 *df* and 30 *df* (which are closest to *df* = 2 and *df* = 32), we find the F_{cv} for our test to be 3.32.

Step 3: Compute the Test Statistic F

The *F*-test for one-way ANOVA is given in Formula 13–14.

Formula 13–14

$$F = \frac{MS_b}{MS_w}$$

Where

MS_b = mean square between groups

MS_w = mean square within groups

For the data in our test anxiety illustration, we find the following:

$$F = \frac{224.29}{18} = 12.46$$

Step 4: Apply the Decision Rule

The format for reporting the results of a one-way ANOVA, using the data in our test anxiety illustration, is shown in Table 13–2. Note that a right-tailed test is always performed.

Recall that the decision rule states that if the value of the test statistic exceeds the critical value of the level of significance, the null hypothesis is rejected. In a one-way ANOVA, the decision maker may then conclude that at least one of the population means differs from the others. On the other hand, if the *F*-ratio in an ANOVA does not exceed the critical value of the level of significance, the null hypothesis cannot be rejected and the decision maker must conclude that there is no difference

Table 13–2. ANOVA Results

Source of variation	Sum of squares	Degrees of freedom	Mean square	F
Between-groups	$SS_b = 448.57$	$df_b = 2$	$MS_b = 224.29$	12.46 $p < 0.05$
Within-groups	$SS_w = 576$	$df_w = 32$	$MS_w = 18$	
Total	$SS_t = 1024.57$	$df_t = 34$		

among the population means from which the samples are selected.

In our illustration, since $F = 12.46$ is greater than $F_{cv} = 3.32$, we reject the null hypothesis (H_o: $\mu_{bm} = \mu_{cr} = \mu_{sd}$). Thus, we can conclude that at least one of the population means of the treatment groups (μ_{bm}, μ_{cr}, μ_{sd}) differs from the other two. A summary of the F-test for the test anxiety reduction scenario is shown in Box 13–2.

When the null hypothesis in an ANOVA procedure is rejected, further tests must be conducted to determine which population means are not equal. These tests are known as *multiple comparison tests* (also called *post hoc ANOVA tests*), two of which are illustrated below.

Multiple Comparison Tests

In one sense, an ANOVA may be thought of as an exploratory statistical procedure, the purpose of which is to determine if there is any significant difference among the data representing experimental treatment or categorical groups. If the analysis yields an F-ratio less than 1.00, the null hypothesis cannot be rejected because the variability of the sample mean was less

Box 13–2. A Summary of the F-Test for the Test Anxiety Reduction Scenario

<u>Step 1:</u> State the Hypotheses

$H_0 : \mu_{bm} = \mu_{cr} = \mu_{sd}$

H_1 : At least one mean is different from the others.

<u>Step 2:</u> Find the Critical Value for Rejecting H_0:

$\alpha = 05$ $F_{cv} = 3.32$ (numerator; denominator)

(**df**$_{between}$ = 2 for the numerator: **df**$_{within}$ = 32 for the denominator)

<u>Step 3:</u> Compute the Test Statistic

$$F = \frac{224.29}{18} = 12.46$$

<u>Step 4:</u> Apply the Decision Rule (Use a right-tailed test.)

Construct summary table.

Since $F = 12.46$ is greater than $F_{cv} = 3.32$, H_0 is rejected; $p < .05$.

than what would be expected by chance or sampling error. On the other hand, when the F-ratio is greater than the critical value, F_{cv}, the claim of the null hypothesis is untenable, and we must conclude that there is a significant difference between the means of the samples. Since an ANOVA does not reveal which groups or samples are significantly different from the others, a test of comparisons must be conducted to determine which population mean or means differs significantly from the others.

While it may be possible to conduct multiple t-tests for all possible pairs of means, the approach is inappropriate for several reasons. Perhaps the most important reason is the increased threat of rejecting a true null hypothesis, which is, committing Type I error. For example, at a 0.05 level of significance, we would expect to reject a true null hypothesis 5 times out of 100 just by chance or sampling error. However, when multiple t-tests are conducted, the pairs of means are no longer independent, and each t-test increases the rate of rejecting a true null hypothesis, sometimes referred to as *experiment-wise error rate*.

In making pairwise comparisons among treatment groups, **experiment-wise error rate** is the probability of concluding at least two treatments to be different when, in fact, there are no differences among the groups. Consider the test anxiety study above, if we computed t-tests comparing the three treatments using $\alpha = 0.05$ for each test, the probability of making at least one Type I error would no longer be 0.05 but approximately 0.14. If the number of treatment groups or pairwise comparisons is large enough, it is almost a certainty that we would find at least one statistical difference just by chance rather than the result of some treatment or true difference between the paired groups.

> *Experiment-wise error rate* refers to the probability rate of increase in Type I error (rejecting a true null hypothesis) when pairs of means are no longer independent, as in the case of multiple t-tests.

There are a number of statistical tests that can be used to make multiple comparisons between sample means without any increase in the pre-established Type I error. They also allow us to rank treatments or groups in terms of effectiveness or magnitude of difference. The tests are called **multiple comparison tests**. Since these tests are performed after an analysis of variance reveals an overall level of significance among the sample means, they often are referred to as **post hoc tests**. We consider two of the more commonly used tests, the *Tukey Multiple Comparison Test* and the *Scheffe's Test*. Both tests assume: (1) that the samples under consideration are independent (randomly selected); (2) that the populations from which the samples are drawn are normal; and (3) that the variances of the populations are equal. If you recall, these are the assumptions required to conduct a one-way ANOVA.

> Tests used to detect pairwise significant differences among group means following an ANOVA where the null hypothesis is rejected are known as *multiple comparison* or *post hoc tests*.

The Tukey Test

The **Tukey Multiple Comparison Test** may be used to make pairwise comparisons of all means when the size (n) of the treatment or sample groups are equal. In conducting the test, all possible combinations of means are compared two at a time. For example, if there are three treatment groups or subgroups, three pairwise comparisons are conducted, as shown below:

$$\overline{X}_1 \text{ vs. } \overline{X}_2 \quad \overline{X}_1 \text{ vs. } \overline{X}_3 \quad \overline{X}_2 \text{ vs. } \overline{X}_3$$

The null hypothesis for the pairwise comparisons asserts that each pair of population means is equal, that is $H_o: \mu_i = \mu_k$.

The Tukey test, sometimes referred to as the Q-test, is quite similar to the t-test except that the sampling distribution, Q, is used to determine if the difference between the paired means are statistically significant. The Q distribution, like the z and t distributions, is actually a family of distributions defined by the number of samples and the degrees of freedom (df) for the within-groups mean square (MS_w). The test statistic, denoted by the symbol Q, is derived using Formula 13–15.

Formula 13–15

$$Q = \frac{\overline{X}_i - \overline{X}_j}{\sqrt{MS_w/n}}$$

Where

$\overline{X}_i - \overline{X}_j =$ difference between all possible samples

$MS_w =$ mean squares of the within-group

$n =$ size of each sample

The critical values, Q_{cv}, for Q-tests at the 0.05 and 0.01 levels of significance for various numbers of samples based on degrees of freedom are listed in Table O–1 (Appendix O). The symbol r denotes the number of means being compared, and df represents the number of degrees of freedom associated with mean squares of the within-group (Ms_w). For example, consider a three sample multiple comparison test with 3 groups of 10 subjects, and a 0.05 level of significance ($\alpha = 0.05$). In such a case, the number of means to be compared is 3 ($r = 3$), the within-group (Ms_w) degrees of freedom is 27 ($df_w = 27$), and critical value is $Q_{cv} = 3.53$. (From Table O–1). In a Q-test of significance, any Q-ratio equal to or greater than $Q_{cv} = 3.96$ indicates a statistically significant difference between the means of the paired sample tested.

Scenario. The "catharsis hypothesis" asserts that acting aggressive or even viewing aggressive behavior is an effective way of reducing anger and aggressive feeling. Suppose a communication science researcher is interested in the relative effectiveness of print, video, and audio media in presenting procatharsis messages. She randomly assigns 40 college students to one of four groups, three experimental (print, video, audio) and one control. The participants in the experimental groups are presented the same basic message supporting the notion that aggressive activities, such as hitting a punching bag, are healthy ways of dealing with anger and aggressive feelings. We refer to these messages as "procatharsis aggressive messages." Participants in the control group are presented with a neutral message. Following the message presentation, all participants completed a survey in which they were asked to rate various ways of venting anger, including hitting inanimate objects. The higher the total rating score, the greater the willingness of participants to engage in procatharsis aggressive behavior. The survey results are summarized in Table 13–3. The summary of the preliminary data analysis are

Table 13–3. Results of "Procatharsis Message" Survey

Treatment Groups				
Print (p)	Video (v)	Audio (a)	Control (ctrl)	Total (t)
9	8	5	3	
8	9	6	6	
6	9	7	4	
10	10	3	5	
9	7	8	3	
7	9	7	6	
4	10	9	4	
10	10	8	4	
5	8	3	2	
7	10	4	3	
$n_p = 10$	$n_v = 10$	$n_a = 10$	$n_{ctrl} = 10$	$n_t = 40$
$\Sigma X_p = 75$	$\Sigma X_v = 90$	$\Sigma X_a = 60$	$\Sigma X_{ctrl} = 40$	$\Sigma X_t = 265$
$\Sigma X^2_p = 601$	$\Sigma X^2_v = 820$	$\Sigma X^2_a = 402$	$\Sigma X^2_{ctrl} = 176$	$\Sigma X^2_t = 1999$
$\Sigma \overline{X}_p = 7.5$	$\Sigma \overline{X}_v = 9$	$\Sigma \overline{X}_a = 6$	$\Sigma \overline{X}_{ctrl} = 4$	$\Sigma \overline{X}_t = 6.63$

shown in Figure 13–1. And the results of the one-way ANOVA, using an alpha level of .05 with a critical value $F_{cv} = 3.32$ (df_b = 3 numerator; df_w = 6 denominator), are presented in Table 13–4.

Since the F-ratio, 15.42, in Table 13–4 exceeded the critical value, 3.32, in the F-test, the null hypothesis of no difference between the sample means is rejected. The researcher may conclude that at least one of the sample means differs significantly from the other three and that a multiple comparison test is in order. Since the size of the samples is equal, the Tukey Test may be applied to compare the four treatments (print, video, audio, control).

The *Tukey Multiple Comparison Test* may be used for pairwise comparisons of group means when the size of the samples is equal.

Applying the Tukey Test for Multiple Comparisons

The process followed in conducting the Tukey Test is a simple two-step sequence. First, find the critical value, Q_{cv}, for evaluating the magnitude of the test statistic, Q. Second, conduct a Q-test for all possible pairs of samples to determine which

Step 1: See Table 13.3

Step 2: Sum of Squares: Method Two

$$C = \frac{(265)^2}{40} = 1755.63 \quad \text{(correction term)} \qquad \text{Formula 13.5}$$

$$SS_t = 1999 - 1755.63 = 243.37 \qquad \text{Formula 13.6}$$

$$SS_b = \frac{(75)^2}{10} + \frac{(90)^2}{10} + \frac{(60)^2}{10} + \frac{(40)^2}{10} - 1755.63 = 136.88$$

$$\text{Formula 13.7}$$

$$SS_w = 243.37 - 136.87 = 106.5 \qquad \text{Formula 13.8}$$

Step 3: Calculate the Degrees of Freedom

Total group	$df_t = 40 - 1 = 39$	Formula 13.9
Between-groups	$df_b = 4 - 1 = 3$	Formula 13.10
Within-groups	$df_w = 39 - 3 = 36$	Formula 13.11

Step 4: Calculate the mean squares (variance estimates)

$$\text{Between-group} \quad MS_b = \frac{4136.87}{2} = 45.62 \qquad \text{Formula 13.12}$$

$$\text{Within-group} \quad MS_w = \frac{106.5}{36} = 2.96 \qquad \text{Formula 13.13}$$

Step 5: Calculate F Ratio

$$\text{Observed } F = \frac{MS_b}{MS_w} = 15.42 \left(\frac{45.63}{2.96} = 15.42 \right)$$

Figure 13–1. Summary of preliminary data analysis for procatharsis data.

Table 13–4. ANOVA Results of "Procatharsis Message" Survey

Source of variation	Sum of squares	Degrees of freedom	Mean square	$F = \dfrac{MS_b}{MS_w} = \dfrac{45.63}{2.96}$
Between-groups	$SS_b = 136.88$	$df_b = 3$	$MS_b = 45.63$	15.42 $p < 0.05$
Within-groups	$SS_w = 106.5$	$df_w = 36$	$MS_w = 2.958$	
Total	$SS_t = 243.38$	$df_t = 39$		

sample mean(s) is significantly greater than the others.

Step 1: Find the Critical Value Q_{cv} for Procatharsis Study.

Where $df_w = 36$ (within-group degrees of freedom), $r = 4$ (sample groups), and $\alpha = 0.05$ (level of significance), the critical value, Q_{cv}, is 3.85. (The within-groups degrees of freedom, $df_\omega = 30$, is used because there is no 36 df_w in Table O–1.) Therefore, a Q-ratio of at least 3.85 is needed to reject the null hypothesis.

Step 2: Conduct a Q-Test for All Sample Pairs.

Calculating the Q-ratio for each of the pairwise comparisons also is a two-step process. First, the means of the samples in order from high to low, as shown in Table 13–5, are ranked. Second, a Q-test

Table 13–5. "Procatharsis Message" Survey Means

Treatment Group	Mean
Video message	9
Print message	7.5
Audio message	6
Control message	4

with each pair of samples is conducted using Formula 13–15 to determine the significance of the differences between the means. For example, a Q-ratio for the video versus print groups is derived as follows:

$$Q = \frac{\bar{X}_i - \bar{X}_j}{\sqrt{MS_w/n}} = \frac{9 - 7.5}{\sqrt{2.958/10}} = \frac{1.5}{0.544} = 2.76$$

The summary of the six pairwise comparisons, in order of the magnitude of the means, is presented in Table 13–6, with asterisks beside Q-ratios significantly greater than the critical value, $Q_{cv} = 3.85$. The results indicate that significant differences in message effectiveness exist between several of the media. While there is no significant difference in the effectiveness between video and print media, the video medium was significantly more effective in presenting aggressive procatharsis messages than audio and the control method. In addition, although the difference between the means of the print and control groups was significant, there was no significant difference in effectiveness between the print and audio. Finally, no significant difference in message effectiveness was detected between the audio and control groups.

Table 13–6. Pairwise Comparisons of "Procatharsis Message" Media

Paired Samples	Sample Means	Difference	Q-Ratio
Video versus Print	9–7.5	1.5	2.76
Video versus Audio	9–6	3	5.52*
Video versus Control	9–4	5	9.19*
Print versus Audio	7–6	1	1.84
Print versus Control	7–4	3	5.52*
Audio versus Control	6–4	2	3.68

*Significant at the 0.05 level.

The Scheffe's Test

The **Scheffe's Multiple Comparison Test** can be used to make pairwise comparisons of all means when the size of the treatment or subgroups of the sample are unequal. As in the case of the Tukey test, all possible combinations of means are compared two at a time. The claim of the null hypothesis for each pairwise comparison is that the means of the populations from which the samples are drawn are equal ($H_o: \mu_i = \mu_k$). The sampling distribution for the test statistic is the F distribution. The test statistic for each pairwise comparison is calculated using Formula 13–16.

Formula 13–16

$$F = \frac{(\bar{X}_i - \bar{X}_k)^2}{MS_w(1/n_i + 1/n_k)}$$

Where

$(\bar{X}_i - \bar{X}_k)$ = difference between all possible samples

MS_w = mean squares of the within-groups

The critical value, symbolized as F' (read "F prime"), is not taken directly from Tables N–1, N–2, and N–3. Rather, it is obtained by multiplying the critical value used in the ANOVA by the number of subgroups minus 1, as given in Formula 13–17.

Formula 13–17

$$F' = (k - 1)(F_{cv})$$

Where

k = number of treatment or subgroups

F_{cv} = critical value of the ANOVA (Tables N–1, N–2, and N–3)

df for numerator = $k - 1$ and df for denominator = $N - k$ where N = number of all participants.

We illustrate the procedures followed in the Scheffe's test using the data obtained for the three test anxiety reduction methods ANOVA, behavior modification, cognitive restructuring, and systematic desensitization (see Tables 13–1 and 13–2).

To evaluate the significance of each pairwise F-ratio, we first compute the critical value F' using Formula 13–17. Recall that the level of significance used in the ANOVA for the illustration was set at α = 0.05, and that the F_{cv} obtained from Table N–1 was 3.32 (the table value closest to our 2 and 32 degrees of freedom). Applying Formula 13–17, we obtain the following:

$$F' = (k - 1)(F_{cv}) = 2(3.32) = 6.64$$

Thus, any F-ratio greater than 6.64 is considered statistically significant. F-ratios obtained with Formula 13–16 that exceed the critical value, F', are considered statistically significant.

A summary of the Scheffe's test results for the data in test anxiety reduction methods are in Figure 13–2. The results of the F-tests indicate that there are significant differences in the three treatment methods to reduce test anxiety among teenagers identified as having high anxiety levels. Specifically, the behavior modification method (bm), with a group mean of $\bar{X}$ = 45 and an F-ratio of 24.55, appears to be the most effective of the three anxiety reduction methods. The results also show that the cognitive restructuring method (cr), with a group mean of $\bar{X}$ = 40 and an F-ratio of 8.67, while not as effective as behavior modification (bm), appears significantly more effective than systematic desensitization (sd), with a group mean of $\bar{X}$ = 36

Step 1: State the Hypotheses

$$H_0: \mu_{bm} = \mu_{cr} = \mu_{sd}$$

H_1: *At least one mean is different from the others.*

Step 2: Find the Critical Value for Rejecting H_0:

$$\alpha = 05 \qquad F_{cv} = 3.32, \text{ and } F' = 6.64$$

$(df_b = 2 \text{ numerator}; \; df_w = 32 \text{ denominator})$

Step 3: Compute the Test Statistic

$$F = \frac{224.29}{18} = 12.46$$

Step 4: Apply the Decision Rule (Use a right-tailed test.)

Construct summary table.

Since $F = 12.46$ is greater than $F_{cv} = 3.32$, H_0 is rejected; $p < .05$.

Observed F value of 12.46 is greater than $F' = 6.64$

Figure 13–2. Summary of Scheffe's test results for data in the test anxiety reduction method.

and an *F*-ratio of 5.02. Thus, one can conclude that in this study, both behavior modification and cognitive restructuring are significantly more effective in reducing test anxiety among teenagers than systematic desensitization, and of the two, behavior modification is the more effective treatment method.

The *Scheffe's Test* is useful in making pairwise comparisons of group means when the size of the samples is unequal.

Clinical Perspectives, Applications, and Logic: Multivariate ANOVA, (M)ANCOVA, Nonparametric Methods, Meta-Analysis, and Several Clinically Useful Post Hoc Tests

In this section of the chapter, we mainly discussed one-way ANOVA to detect a difference among three or more population means along with the test of homogeneity (Bartlett's *F*-test or Levene's *F*-test). In a clinical setting, it is often necessary for a clinician to answer questions that go beyond the one-way ANOVA questions, that is to say, the clinician might want to compare the treatment effectiveness of intervention approaches or the performance of several groups on a particular dependent variables. It is also possible to study combined treatment effects that might result from the interactions of treatment (A × B, A × C, B × C, etc.).

First let us go back to the logic behind analysis of variance in general. One may ask, "Why not perform a single t-test for each pairwise statistical comparison of mean scores that might need to be made?" For instance, suppose we wish to determine the effectiveness of three treatments, namely A, B, and C. Why not conduct three independent t-tests to detect differences among three, that is, A versus B, A versus C, and B versus C. A major problem relating to the use of multiple numbers of t-tests is the probability of one or more of them reaching significance merely by chance. Because multiple t-tests typically are not independent of one another, the probability of a type 1 error (α) becomes greater with the number of t-tests performed. In my example, assuming that three t-tests are performed where $\alpha = 0.05$, the actual probability of obtaining a significant result by chance from any of the three tests is not exactly equal to 0.05. Rather, the true probability is given by:

$$p \text{ (type 1 error)} = 1 - (1 - \alpha)^n$$

Where n represents the number of the t-tests conducted. Thus, the true probability of a type 1 error is:

$$1 - (1 - 0.05)^3 = 0.14, \text{ not } 0.05.$$

Then, if you were to still use multiple t-tests for detecting a difference instead

of performing ANOVA to obtain the final α value of 0.05, you must set the original α value at:

$$0.05 = 1 - (1 - \alpha)^3,$$

after a great deal of algebra, you will obtain 0.017. In other words, you need to set α at 0.017 to maintain a 5% level of significance. Algebraically, conducting a multiple number of t-tests in order to make this "dry gulch" determination is a needless waste of time.

In this chapter, we briefly discussed the conceptual basis of systematic variance (between variances) versus error variance (within variances) in accounting for the results of an experiment. The main goal of ANOVA is to compute the ratio of systematic variance (the amount of variations owing to a treatment effect) to the degree of error variance that may involve both sampling errors and measurement errors. So, the observed F-ratio is symbolically expressed as:

$$F = (V_{\text{between}}) / (V_{\text{within}})$$

where the denominator in the equation shown above is error variance, and the numerator is systematic variance.

In reality, the degree of systematic variance in any experiment is the consequence of not only treatment effects, but also some chance fluctuations as well. Therefore, the total variability in data sets can also be expressed as:

Total variability of effects = variability owing to main treatment + variability within groups (error variance) for one-way ANOVA

In case, as we briefly discussed previously, if you wish to investigate two different treatments, then two-way ANOVA will be used. The conceptual basis for computing the two-way ANOVA is illustrated below:

Total variability of effects = variability owing to main effect 1 + variability owing to main effect 2 + variability owing to interaction effect (1 × 2) + variability within groups (error variance) for two-way ANOVA

ANOVA provides a convenient method of calculating whether the variability between group means is greater than the variability within group means. This can be accomplished by dividing up sources of variance into two major components: (1) the variation of the score of each subject from the mean of their groups and (2) the variation between each group mean and grand mean for the sample. If there are large differences between the group means, the variation between them and the grand mean will be large compared with the amount of variation within each group. If this is found to be true on the basis of an F-test, then H_o is rejected under the frequentists method. On the other hand, if the group means are similar in size, their variation from the grand mean should not differ substantially from the variation among the subjects within each group beyond chance expectation. Under the rule of Neyman-Pearson hypothesis tests, H_o is retained to conclude that the difference of interest was not detected.

If the data values were analyzed based on the multiple factor designs (two or more independent factors or independent variables with the various levels), we normally use the method called **MANOVA** (Multi-Variables Analysis of Variance). The simplest form of MANOVA is two-way ANOVA with two different factors.

The interpretation of the test results derived from MANOVA is complex and much harder to explain the findings. First, we illustrate a clinically relevant hypothetical two-way ANOVA example. Suppose a clinical investigator wishes to determine whether or not her clients can successfully improve their speech (based on a test score at the end of session, that is, we further assume that this particular experiment is the randomized post-test only design) by the following two independent variables of interest, namely (1) Main Effect 1 (Factor 1)—the effectiveness of two treatments (experimental versus conventional) and (2) Main Effect 2 (Factor 2)—the intensity of speech therapy sessions (twice a week versus four times a week). The clinical investigator's hypotheses are written as follows:

For Main Effect 1:

H_o: No difference exists between two levels of treatment

H_a: A difference exists between two levels of treatment

For Main Effect 2:

H_o: No difference exists between two levels of intensity

H_a: A difference exists between two levels of intensity

For Interaction Effect 1 × 2:

H_o: No interaction effect exists

H_a: An interaction effect exists

Note that any differences associated with the independent variables are termed as *Main Effects*, and the differences associated with the combination of two independent variables are termed as *Interaction*

Effects. A hypothetical test result of the study is illustrated in Table 13–7.

A Hypothetical Two-Way ANOVA Results

Under the frequentists *p*-value method, the results were found to be statistically significant for Main Effect 1 (Type of treatment: Experimental treatment is more effective as shown in a line graph—and Interaction Effect (Treatment by Intensity) but not statistically significant for Main Effect 2 (Intensity) (Figure 13–3).

Note that a statistically significant interaction means that the outcome for one of the main effects (factors) detected a difference depending on the level of other main effect (factor). In our hypothetical clinical example, the outcome for type of treatment was different depending on the level of intensity. In our hypothetical clinical example, the outcome for type of treatment was different depend-

ing on the level of intensity. Whenever we detect a significant interaction effect, it is a common practice that we examine this source first before we get to main effects for evaluation. The first step is, although it is primitive, to use a line graph (or plot the data points on an *XY* plane) to identify the place where the significant interaction occurs. In our example, the mean score for the experimental treatment group was higher than that of the conventional treatment group (that is to say, when the session becomes more intense and more frequent, the difference between two treatment group means becomes larger), while there is no significant difference in mean scores between two treatment groups when the session is held less frequently. We can also use post hoc ANOVA pairwise comparison tests, as discussed earlier, such as Tukey's simultaneous 95% confidence interval, Scheffe's test, and the other popular methods like Fisher's 95% confidence interval. The purpose of using such tests is to find out which individual

Table 13–7. A Hypothetical Two-Way ANOVA Results

Sources	p-Values	95% Confidence Interval for Pairwise Comparison
Main Effect 1 (Type of Treatment)	0.04 (significant)	(0.5 1.1) (significant)
Main Effect 2 (Intensity)	0.07 (not significant)	(−0.05, 0.3) (not significant)
Interaction Effect (1 × 2)	0.025 (significant)	All significant except the case that intensity is low, that is, no significant mean difference between two levels of treatment when the intensity level is twice a week.
Error		

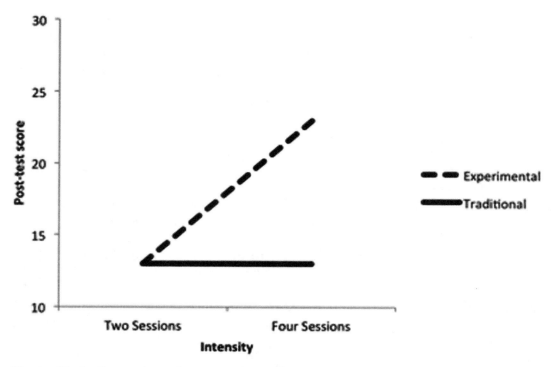

Figure 13–3. Comparison of post-test scores between experimental and traditional therapy groups based on two different levels of intensity (two sessions versus four sessions).

group pairwise comparisons show statistically significant results. As the number of individual groups increase, such post-hoc ANOVA tests become more useful and practical than the visual methods such as Factor Plots or Line Graph, especially when we detect an interaction effects. So, what must a clinician do and interpret the results when she observed a significant interaction effect? Using our hypothetical example, the clinician can conclude that the most effective way to improve the clients' mean scores (or conditions) is to: (1) provide an experimental treatment while maintaining intense treatment, and (2) investigate if there are any unwanted secondary factors that might have affected the clients' test scores, other than two main effects? Such a variable (if it exists)

is called covariate. If a clinical investigator wishes to determine true effects (without covariate effect), another type of ANOVA method called **Analysis of Covariance (ANCOVA or MANCOVA** if there are two or more main effects) is more desirable for that purpose.

In general, especially when an investigator wishes to detect a true treatment effect, she first needs to identify the existence of such the influence or unwanted variables in an experiment and remove them from an experiment. This process can be best dealt with through statistical control methods. One such method is the *Analysis of Covariance* or *Multi-Variable Analysis of Covariance*, as noted earlier. These methods are designed to remove the influence of extraneous variables when they can be identified. This is accomplished by treating secondary variables that are predicted to have such an influence as covariates to be measured and then, through the use of combined correlation methods and ANOVA procedures, removing their sources of variation. In essence, ANCOVA or MANCOVA is a mathematical correction procedure for controlling covariates statistically.

A study conducted by Erler and Garstecki (2002), who examined the degree of stigma that women in three different age groups attached to hearing loss and hearing aid use provides an example of how ANCOVA or MANCOVA can be employed to control for a potentially confounding covariate. The three groups of women were asked to complete statements designed to assess their perceptions related to hearing loss and hearing aid use. Although all participants in the study were determined to have hearing within normal limits based on age-related norms, the ANCOVA or MANCOVA was used to control for the effect of hearing variations across the three groups (the unwanted covariate). This was done so that a true age-related difference in the perceptions of the three groups of women could be detected, if present, uncomplicated by the covariate of their own hearing ability. Theoretically, the manner in which this was accomplished by such multivariate statistical methods as ANOVA and MANOVA procedures, as previously mentioned in this chapter. The results of the study indicated that younger women perceive greater stigma related to hearing loss than older women, among other findings.

For another illustration of ANCOVA (or MANCOVA), suppose a clinical investigator wishes to measure the maintenance of clinical gains in response to some treatment for three groups of sub-

jects following the termination of therapy. Group A will be evaluated 6 months after therapy, Group B after 12 months, and Group C after 18 months. There are several within-group and between-group variables besides the independent variable that might potentially influence the outcome of such a study. For example, an investigator may wish to control for the degree of improvement that occurred during the course of therapy. It is possible that subjects who made more progress in therapy will be the same individuals who best maintain clinical gains through time. Although this is an interesting question in its own right, it is not the purpose of the study, which seeks only to determine the degree of maintenance across different spans of time. Thus, we might wish to control for within- and between-group differences for the degree of progress that occurred during therapy by factoring these gain scores into the analysis of the dependent variable. The intelligence, the level of anxiety, and the motivation of subjects are examples of other control variables that might need to be seriously considered to obtain a true clinical gains or treatment effect due to only therapy.

ANCOVA or MANCOVA methods uses pretest–post-test designs to make sure that the suspected covariate will greatly influence the dependent outcome, that is, the existence of such covariate may potentially prevent us from detecting a true treatment effect or true clinical gains (due to only therapy). Generally, the correlation between covariate (pretest) and post-test scores is above 0.60; it will be more powerful (a greater ability to detect a true treatment effect) for us to use (M) ANCOVA than (M)ANOVA.

In the (M)ANCOVA, the total variability among scores on the dependent variable can be partitioned into several sources of variability. For instance, the MANCOVA (two main treatment effects with the interaction) can be expressed as follows:

Total variability of effects = variability owing to main effect 1 + variability owing to main effect 2 + variability owing to interaction effect (1 × 2) + variability owing to covariates + variability within groups (error variance) for two-way ANCOVA

Now, an investigator has identified the existence of covariate and removed it from the original equation shown above. The equation for Adjusted Two-Way ANCOVA is now given as follows:

Total variability of effects = [(variability owing to main effect 1 – variability owing to covariates)] + [(variability owing to main effect 2 – variability owing to covariates)] + [(variability owing to interaction effect (1 × 2) – variability owing to covariates)] + [(variability within groups (error variance) – variability owing to covariates)] for two-way ANCOVA

Because the mathematical calculation of (M)ANCOVA is highly complex, I urge the readers to use the statistical software packages such as MINITAB, SPSS, SAS, and the like.

(M)ANOVA and (M)ANCOVE Table: Logic Behind (M) ANOVA and (M)ANCOVA

Table 13–8 illustrates the general model for all multivariate ANOVA and ANCOVA statistical methods. The main theme for the

model building is to determine whether or not there is a significant treatment difference between two or more groups with respect to main treatment effect and interaction treatment effect. Each model includes *Sources, Variances, Observed Values*, and *Research Questions*.

A Clinically Relevant Example: Two-Way ANCOVA

Suppose a clinical investigator wishes to determine the effectiveness of a newly developed innovative treatment, which is designed to increase one's PPVT-R score. Two treatments (Experimental and Conventional) were given to a group of 40 young children who were diagnosed as "Moderately Severe Fluency Disorders." The clinical investigator decided to use pretest–post-test design to test several research hypotheses concerning comparison in the children's mean gain scores between experimental group (20 subjects) and conventional group (20 subjects). She further divided all participants into four different levels based on their Grade level (3rd grade, 4th grade, 5th grade, and 6th grade) to conduct two-way ANCOVA. The investigator designated pretest scores as covariate for data analysis. The results are illustrated in Table 13–9.

The calculation of MBF and the interpretations of it in the multifactorial designs is mathematically very complex and goes beyond the main scope of this textbook; therefore, the readers should use *Bayes Factor Calculator* at http://www.pcl.missouri.edu/bayesfactor.

As can be seen, MBF shows that the traditional Fisher's *p*-value overstates the amount of evidence against H_0 (exaggerate statistical significance). That is to say, the weight of clinical evidence we observed

Table 13–8. The General Calculation Tables for the Most Widely Used Univariate and Multivariate Analyses of Variance

One-Way ANOVA General Model

Sources	Variances	Observed F-Ratio	Research Question
Treatment I	V_I	$F = V_I / V_E$	Observed changes due to Treatment I effect?
Error	V_E		

Two-way ANOVA general model (aka MANOVA general model)

Sources	Variances	Observed F-Ratio	Research Question(s)
Treatment I	V_I	$F_1 = V_I / V_E$	Observed changes are due to Treatment I effect
Treatment II	V_{II}	$F_1 = V_{II} / V_E$	Due to Treatment II effect
Treatment I*II	V_{I*II}	$F_1 = V_{I*II} / V_E$	Due to Interaction I*II effect
Error	V_E		

One-way ANCOVA general model.

Sources	Variances	Adjusted Variances	Observed F-Ratio	Research Question(s)
Treatment I	V_I	$V_I - V_{cov} = V_{adj.I}$	$F = V_{adj.I} / V_{adj.E}$	Observed changes are due to True Treatment I effect
Covariate	V_{cov}			
Error	V_E	$V_E - V_{cov} = V_{adj.E}$		

Two-way ANCOVA general model (aka MANCOVA model).

Sources	Variances	Observed F-Ratio	Observed F-Ratio	Research Question(s)
Treatment I	V_I	$V_I - V_{cov} = V_{adj.I}$	$F_I = V_{adj.I} / V_{adj.E}$	Observed changes are due to Treatment I effect
Treatment II	V_{II}	$V_{II} - V_{cov} = V_{adj.II}$	$F_{II} = V_{adj.II} / V_{adj.E}$	Due to Treatment II effect
Treatment I*II	V_{I*II}	$V_{I*II} - V_{cov} = V_{adj.I*II}$	$F = V_{adj.I*II} / V_{adj.E}$	Due to Interaction I*II effect
Covariate	V_{cov}			
Error	V_E			

Table 13–9. A Hypothetical Example of Determining Effectiveness of a Newly Developed Innovative Treatment on Increment of PPVT-R Score Among Young Disfluency Children

Grade Level	Conventional		Experimental	
	Pretest	Post-test	Pretest	Post-test
3rd grade	90	98	80	102
	93	103	100	106
	104	107	105	107
	108	100	110	111
	125	125	119	119
4th grade	95	95	95	102
	100	108	99	102
	104	108	104	107
	106	104	110	116
	110	116	120	120
5th grade	75	106	85	112
	88	106	90	110
	90	95	100	115
	105	115	110	119
	120	124	115	125
6th grade	80	97	79	96
	95	102	100	120
	100	110	105	117
	110	98	106	110
	120	122	110	116

Notes: (1) $R^2 > 60\%$ (The total variability in post-test scores Y that can be accounted for by knowing group and grade level exceeds 60%), (2) The distributions of post-test scores are homogeneous to both group and grade level, since Bartlett's F-test shows $p \geq 0.05$, (3) Pearson correlation (r) between covariate (pretest scores) and the dependent variable of interest (post-test scores) is equal to 0.698 (p-value = 0.000), therefore, the ANCOVA model is more appropriate than the ANOVA model.

here is not nearly as strong and credible as the magnitude of Fisher's p-value indicates. This MBF method is the correct way to measure the strength of evidence, that is, what EBP statistics is all about, as can be seen in Table 13–10.

Table 13–10. A Summary of the Results of Hypothetical PPVT-R Example: Classical Fisher's *p*-Value Versus Minimum Bayes Factor (MBF) in Measuring the Strength of Clinical Evidence

Sources	p-Values	Statistical Significance (under Frequentists Methods)	Interpretations	MBF* (The Strength of Clinical Evidence)
Main Effect 1 (Group)	0.026	Significant	A true group effect exists	Moderate
Main Effect 2 (Group Level)	0.006	Highly significant	A true grade level effect exists	Moderately strong
Interaction Effect (Group X Grade Level; 1 × 2)	0.779	Not significant	No interaction effect exists	Very weak
Covariate (Pretest)	0.000	Highly significant	Covariate effect is very strong	Strong
Error (Within)				

*Minimum Bayes Factor calculates the credibility of exact clinical evidence, given that the null hypothesis (no treatment effect exists) is true.

Frequentists Nonparametric Alternatives to Parametric Statistics: Theory with Several Clinically Relevant Examples

Nonparametric Alternatives to Parametric Statistics

Thus far, our discussion of statistical inference has focused on the use of parametric tests of significance, which generally include the following assumptions:

1. *Normality.* The population distribution is normal.
2. *Homogeneity of variances.* When two populations are being compared, especially in the case of independent observations, their distribution values should have relatively equal variances.
3. *Randomness.* Subjects should be chosen randomly.
4. *Interval/ratio data.* The data should be quantifiable on a numerical scale when common arithmetic is appropriate.

When these assumptions cannot be met, then the use of such parametric statistics as the mean, standard deviation, and *t*-test may be inappropriate and may lead to invalid conclusions. Three **nonparametric statistics** that do not make these assumptions are discussed next.

Chi-Square Test (χ^2)

A test that is useful in evaluating hypotheses about the relationship between nominal variables having two or more independent categories is the χ^2 statistic or chi- (pronounced "kai") square. The inventor of this test, Karl Pearson, also developed a well-known method for computing correlation coefficients as discussed in Chapter 11. Throughout his career, this acknowledged founder of modern statistics was interested in studying the relations among variables. One of the most modern thinkers of his time, Pearson rejected the search for causality in favor of studying the association or *contingency* of phenomenon. Pearson's fervent interest in the topic of association also extended into the social realm, to such matters as the relations between the sexes. In 1885, he founded a "Men and Women's Club" in England to promote the discussion of such relations, where he met his future wife (Peters, 1987). Apparently, their interests were indeed contingent—that is, a "good fit!"

In essence, the chi-square test provides a means of determining the *independence* between two or more nominal variables by calculating the discrepancy between the *observed frequencies* (actual counts) for a set of categories and the *expected frequencies* for the same categories (probability estimates). Suppose we wish to determine whether graduate students preparing for clinical careers in either speech-language pathology *or* audiology have different preferences for the type of setting in which they might choose to work, say, a medical versus nonmedical setting. Imagine further that our two-sample case is based on the job preferences expressed by 50 students who wish to be certified as speech-language pathologists and an equal number who desire certification in audiology. Let us now illustrate the steps involved in testing to see whether the variables of interest are independent or in some way associated. Before we begin, it is important for us to

understand some of the important characteristics about a chi-square distribution. So, we first introduce the properties of a chi-square distribution.

A chi-square distribution has the following properties:

1. There are an infinite number of chi-square distributions. Each one has a number (or index number) with it called its *degrees of freedom*. We use the degrees of freedom to specify which chi-square distribution we are using.
2. The shape of a chi-square distribution curve is not symmetric but is skewed to the right (positively skewed). It begins at 0 and extends indefinitely in a positive direction. The total area under the curve is 1.

With that background, to perform a chi-square test do the following.

Step 1. Form the hypothesis in statistical terms.

H_o: The proportion of subjects from each sample selecting a particular preference category will be independent (unrelated).

H_1: The proportion of subjects from each sample selecting a particular preference category will *not* be independent (somehow related).

Step 2. Select an appropriate statistical test. The chi-square test is appropriate for our problem because two samples of subjects are being compared on a nominal variable that has two categories.

Step 3. Choose the significance level. We will set the significance level (alpha) at

0.05 for a one-tailed test. A one-tailed test is employed for interpreting the statistical significance of chi-square value because the result is used to evaluate whether the discrepancy between the observed and expected frequencies is *greater* than can be accounted for by chance.

Step 4. Organize the data in a 2 × 2 contingency table and calculate the test statistic.

The data are organized into a contingency table, like that shown in Table 13–11 in order to compare the frequency of responses in each cell that actually occurred (observed frequency) with the number of responses estimated to occur (expected frequency). The latter proportion can be calculated with the following formula:

$$E = \frac{Row\ total\ \times\ Column\ total}{Grand\ total}$$

For example, the expected frequency of speech-language pathology students preferring to work in a medical setting is the computational result of 50 (first row sum) times 49 (first column sum) divided by 100 (grand sum), which is equal to 24.5. The same computation is performed for the remaining cells to yield an expected frequency for each category.

Once the observed values have been entered into a 2 × 2 contingency table, we can perform the chi-square test in accordance with one of the following formulas, depending on the number of degrees of freedom.

a. $\chi^2 = \Sigma^k_{i=1} = \frac{(O_i - E_i)^2}{E_i}$

for degrees of freedom greater than 1, where O = the observed frequency (actual counts), and E = the expected frequency (probability estimates)

b. $\chi^2 = \dfrac{N(ad - bc)}{(a + b)(c + d)(a + c)(b + d)}$

Where

N = the total number of subjects

a = the observed frequency of the first row and first column

b = the observed frequency of the first row and second column

c = the observed frequency of the second row and first column

d = the observed frequency of the second row and second column

Table 13–11. Hypothetical Survey of Work Preference Among Speech-Language Pathology Students and Audiology Students

	Work Preference			
	Medical	*Nonmedical*	*Row Sum*	*N = 100*
Sp-Lang. Path.	18	32	50	
Audiology	31	19	50	
Column Sum	49	51	100	

Source: From *Research and Statistical Methods in Communication Sciences and Disorders* (p. 338), by D. L. Maxwell and E. Satake, 2006, Clifton Park, NY: Thomson Delmar Learning.

For degrees of freedom equal to 1, the second formula, called **Yates's correction for continuity**, should be used instead of the first formula. Generally, Yates's formula deals with the inconsistency between the theoretical chi-square distribution and the actual sampling distribution having 1 degree of freedom. Based on our example, it can be seen that Yates's correction must be used because $df = (r - 1)(c - 1) = (2 - 1)(2 - 1) = 1$ where r represents the total number of rows and c represents the total number of columns. Next, enter the appropriate values into the formula to calculate the χ^2 value.

$$\chi^2 \text{ (observed)} =$$

$$\frac{100(18 \cdot 19 - 32 \cdot 31)^2}{(18 + 32)(31 + 19)(18 + 31)(32 + 19)}$$

$$= 6.76$$

Step 5. Draw conclusions on the basis of critical value(s). For a 2 × 2 contingency table, like the one in our example, there are two rows and two columns, so the degrees of freedom $(df) = (2 - 1) \cdot (2 - 1) = 1$. Chi-square table has been constructed that allow the statistical significance of x^2 to be assessed directly (See Table P–1 in Appendix P). By referring to such a table, as that found in Table P–1 in Appendix P, we note that with $df = 1$, the critical value that must be exceeded to achieve a 0.05 level of significance is 3.841 for a one-tailed test. Because the calculated (observed) value of χ^2 obtained from our sample exceeds the critical value of 3.841, we would reject the null hypothesis of independence. Given the fictitious results of our example, we are able to conclude that there is a significant relationship between emphasis in graduate training and preferences for future employment. More specifically, it appears that there is a difference in job setting preferences between students of speech-language pathology and audiology. Whereas the majority of the former group in our sample preferred a nonmedical as opposed to medical work setting, the opposite was true for the latter group.

Because of its wide range of applications, the chi-square test is useful for many problems involving the comparison of proportions. The example we used involved only two groups and two categories of variables. However, the number of rows and columns can be extended for the study of relationships among multiple groups and variables depending on the nature of the research question.

The chi-square test is often referred to as a "goodness-of-fit" test when the question pertains to whether distributions of scores fall into certain categories according to an investigator's expectation. Other uses include testing to see whether an obtained distribution drawn by random sampling reflects a normally distributed population. A nonsignificant chi-square would indicate that the shape of the obtained distribution fits the shape of the normal curve. On the other hand, a significant chi-square would be interpreted as a lack of fit between the obtained and normal distribution.

Unfortunately, the chi-square test is often applied inappropriately to statistical problems for which it is not intended. Remember that it is most suited for categorical data in which each case falling within a category or cell is independent of every other case. This is necessary to determine the true relationship between column and row variables—whether they are indeed independent of one another. In the case of our example, had we inadvertently mixed among our categories graduate students pursing certification in *both* speech-language pathology and audiology, such a linkage would have violated the assumption of independence. In the use of the chi-square, the best policy is to have only one frequency count per subject and to have the subjects as unrelated to one another as possible.

Nonparametric Rank-Order Methods

There are two highly useful alternative methods to the *t*-test that were developed by Wilcoxon and are said to be "distribution free" for two reasons. First, like the chi-square, they are free of assumptions about the shape of the underlying population distribution. Second, they both entail *transforming* scores to ranks. Such tests are well suited for ordinal scales of measurement when the scores in a distribution can be logically arranged from most to least frequent, but the intervals between the data points are either unknown or skewed.

The **Wilcoxon matched-pairs signed ranks test** is a commonly used nonparametric analog of the paired *t*-test that utilizes information about both the *magnitude* and *direction* of differences for pairs of scores. Within the behavioral sciences, it is the most commonly used nonparametric test of the significance of difference between dependent samples. This test is appropriate for studies involving repeated measures, as in pretest-post-test designs in which the same subjects serve as their own control, or in cases that use matched pairs of subjects. The ranking procedures used by the Wilcoxon test allow for: (1) determining which member of a pair of scores is larger or smaller than the other, as denoted by the sign of the difference (+ or −, respectively), and (2) the ranking of such size differences. The null hypothesis under this test is that the median difference among pairs of ranked scores is zero.

Let us illustrate the steps in hypothesis testing using the Wilcoxon test in conjunction with some hypothetical data that might be generated in a study of the relationship between grammatical complexity and phonological production. More specifically, suppose we wish to determine whether preschool children with impairments in both grammar and phonology will make more speech sound errors when imitating grammatically complex sentences than when imitating relatively simple sentences that are comparable in length. The results were shown and summarized in Table 13–12.

We can proceed as follows:

Step 1 Form the hypothesis in statistical terms.

H_o: There is no difference in the occurrence of phonologic errors when subjects imitate complex and simple sentences of the same length.

H_1: Phonologic errors will occur more often in the production of complex sentences than in that of simple sentences of the same length.

Step 2. Select an appropriate statistical test.

As an alternative to the paired *t*-test, the Wilcoxon test has been selected because it also is an appropriate test for the analysis of dependent or correlated samples. With respect to its overall *power* (probability for rejecting a false null hypothesis), the Wilcoxon test closely approximates the efficiency of the parametric *t* for large *n*'s. For small *n*'s, the power efficiency of the Wilcoxon test is approximately 95% of its counterpart (Siegel, 1956). For data that are not normally

Table 13–12. Hypothetical Study of Speech Sound Errors for Preschool Children During Imitation of Complex and Simple Sentences

Subject	Complex	Simple	d	Rank	Less Frequent Rank
1	17	18	−1	−1.5	1.5
2	14	11	3	4.5	
3	16	13	3	4.5	
4	11	11	0	0	
5	13	7	6	9	
6	31	29	2	3	
7	12	7	5	6.5	
8	29	21	8	9	
9	17	12	5	6.5	
10	9	10	−1	−1.5	

Source: From *Research and Statistical Methods in Communication Sciences and Disorders* (p. 341), by D. L. Maxwell and E. Satake, 2006, Clifton Park, NY: Thomson Delmar Learning.

distributed, the Wilcoxon test is more powerful than the *t*-test. The likelihood of scenes increases as *n* becomes small, as in the case of our sample.

Step 3. Choose the significance level. The significance level (a) is set at 0.05 in a one-tailed test. We have chosen a one-tailed test in view of some preexisting evidence that phonological errors occur more often in the production of complex sentences than simple sentence (Menyuk & Looney, 1972; Panagos & Prelock, 1982).

Step 4. Organize the paired-scores into a table and calculate the test statistic. The difference score is positive if the first number of a pair is larger than the second or, conversely, carries a negative sign if the second number is larger than the first. The

sign of a number has no real mathematical significance in the Wilcoxon test, but serves to mark the direction of difference between the pairs of scores. The next step is to rank the difference scores according to their relative magnitude, assigning an average rank score to each tie irrespective of whether the sign is positive or negative. Zero difference scores between pairs ($d = 0$) are dropped from the analysis. Therefore, the total number of signed ranks (*n*) in determining the criterion for rejecting H_o is 9. Finally, in the last column of the table, sum the absolute value of the ranked difference scores having the *least* frequent sign. This last operation yields *T*: the smaller sum of the least frequent rank.

Step 5. Draw conclusions of the basis of critical value(s). Critical values for one-tailed and two-tailed tests have been developed for T, which has its own sampling distribution developed by Wilcoxon. Recall that in the case of the parametric t, values of t *larger* than the critical values listed in the probability table under the chosen significance level serve as a basis for rejecting the null hypothesis in favor of a significant finding. However, in the case of the Wilcoxon T, values *smaller* than the listed table values under a particular for the *total number of signed ranks* (n) is the basis for rejecting the null hypothesis. Turning to Appendix Q, we find that the critical value for an n of 9 is 8.

Because our observed T-value is less than the critical value of 8, we would reject H_o in favor of H_1. More specifically, we can conclude that the complexity of imitated sentences seems to have a direct bearing on phonological productions. Thus, the outcome of our hypothetical study is consistent with the results of previous investigations that have found more phonological errors in children occurring during imitation of complex sentences than of simple sentences.

The **Mann-Whitney *U*-test** is a highly useful test for determining the probability that two independent samples came from the same population. It is variously called the Mann-Whitney U or Wilcoxon-rank sum test. In contrast with its parametric equivalent, the unpaired t-test for independent samples, the Mann-Whitney U-test is concerned with the equality of medians rather than means.

Suppose we are interested in knowing whether the physical status of newborns is related to their subsequent development of receptive language. For this purpose, we conduct a prospective study in which Apgar scores are collected on a random sample. Such scores are used to denote the general condition of an infant shortly after birth based on five physical indices including skin color, heart rate, respiratory effort, muscle tone, and reflex irritability. The maximum score of 10 is indicative of excellent physical condition. Using these numerical values as our independent variable, we divide our sample into two groups: (1) 10 children with high Apgar scores (greater than 6) and (2) 8 children with low Apgar scores (less than 4). Composite receptive language scores, obtained for these same children at ages 3 to 3.5 years on the appropriate subtests of the Clinical Evaluation of Language Functions-Preschool (CELF-P) (Wig et al., 1992), serve as the dependent variable. The results were summarized in Table 13–13.

We now use some fictitious data in order to illustrate an application of the Mann-Whitney U-test. The steps for calculating the Mann-Whitney U statistic are shown below:

Step 1. Form the hypothesis in statistical terms.

H_o: There is no difference in the receptive language ability of children who scored high on the Apgar scale versus those who scored low.

H_1: There is a difference in the receptive language ability of children who scored high on the Apgar scale versus those who scored low.

Step 2. Select an appropriate statistical test.
As an alternative to the unpaired t-test, the Mann-Whitney U is chosen because it is an appropriate test for detecting differences between two independent groups. It is commonly used when the parametric t-test's assumptions of normality and homogeneity of variance are violated.

Table 13–13. Receptive Language Scores for Children with High and Low Apgars: Fabricated Data

Language Score (High Apgar Group)	Rank	Language Score (Low Apgar Group)	Rank
37	14.5	22	1
32	11.5	23	2
34	13	30	9.5
28	6.5	37	14.5
32	11.5	24	3
47	18	27	5
29	8	30	9.5
45	17	28	6.5
39	16		Sum = 51
26	4		
	Sum = 120		

T_L = Larger sum of the ranks = 120.
N_L = number of subjects in the group with the larger sum of ranks = 10.
N_S = number of subjects in the other group = 8.

Source: From *Research and Statistical Methods in Communication Sciences and Disorders* (p. 343), by D. L. Maxwell and E. Satake, 2006, Clifton Park, NY: Thomson Delmar Learning.

Step 3. Choose the significance level. The significance level (a) is set at 0.05 in a two-tailed test. In the case of our problem, a two-tailed test is appropriate because we are assuming that no prior knowledge is available that can be used as a basis for predicting the outcome of our study.

Step 4. Organize a table to include test scores, their ranks, and the sum of their ranks, and calculate the test statistic (see Table 12–6). Table 12–6 shows the results for our hypothetical study including CELF-P scores for the two groups, their corresponding ranks, and the sum of their ranks. The Mann-Whitney U is calculated as the smaller of U_1 and U_2, where

$$U_1 = (n_L)(n_s) + \frac{n_L(n_L + 1)}{2} - T_L$$
$$U_2 = (n_L)(n_s) - U_1$$

n_L = the number of subjects in the group with the larger sum of ranks (denoted by n_1), and

n_S = the number of subjects in the other group (denoted by n_2).

See Appendix R. Given our hypothetical data, U_1 and U_2 are found to be 15 and 65, respectively. Thus, the value of the Mann-Whitney U is 15.

Step 5. Draw conclusions on the basis of the critical value(s). By consulting a special table for Mann-Whitney critical values like that found in Appendix R, we can observe that the obtained U of 15 is less than the table value of 17 ($n_L = 10$, $n_s = 8$ for a two-tailed test at $\alpha = 0.05$). In Appendix R, n_L is labeled as n_1 and n_s is labeled as n_2. The criterion rule for rejecting the null hypothesis (H_o) indicates that we reject H_o when the observed value of U *is less than or equal to* the critical value of U. Therefore, because the observed value of U is less than the critical value, we conclude that the receptive language abilities of the two groups as distinguished on the basis of their Apgar scores are significantly different.

Multigroup Designs: Testing Hypotheses for Three or More Groups

In previous sections of this chapter we discussed a variety of parametric and non-parametric tests for analyzing data from two different experimental conditions or from two different groups of subjects in order to test hypotheses. However, researchers often wish to set up experiments in which a single independent variable (factor) may be represented by more than two treatments (levels) and/or two or more factors may be manipulated consecutively.

Analysis of Variance (ANOVA)

More complex designs than the *t*-test are often necessary for answering questions that go beyond the two-sample case—such as, "Is treatment *A* more effective than treatment *B*?" In some cases, we might want to compare the treatment effectiveness of approaches (*A, B, C,* etc.) or the performance of several groups on a par-

ticular dependent variable. It is also possible to study combined treatment effects that might result from the interactions of treatment ($A \times B$, $A \times C$, $B \times C$, etc.).

One could ask, "Why not perform a single *t*-test for each statistical comparison of mean scores that might need to be made?" There are two main answers to this question. First, if no significant differences exist among any of the comparisons, then conducting numerous *t*-tests in order to make this "dry gulch" determination is a needless waste of time. If this could be achieved by a single omnibus test, the goal of research efficiency is better served. Such a test, called the *analysis of variance (ANOVA),* invented by the British statistician Sir Ronald Fisher, accomplishes this very goal. Although the ANOVA can be used for the analysis of two means, its greater utility lies in testing variation among three or more means.

A second problem relating to the use of multiple *t*-tests is the probability of one or more of them reaching significance merely by chance. Because multiple *t*-tests typically are not independent of one another, the probability of a type I error becomes greater with the number of tests performed. For example, assuming that three *t*-tests are performed where $\alpha = 0.05$, the actual probability of obtaining a significant result by chance from any of the three tests (there are three different *t*-tests that can be performed when we compare three group means simultaneously, such as A versus B, A versus C, and B versus C) is not 0.05. Rather, the true probability is given by:

$$p \text{ (type I error)} = 1 - (1 - \alpha)^n$$

where n represents the number of tests performed. Thus, the true probability is $1 - (1 - 0.05)^3 = 0.14$, not 0.05.

Logic of ANOVA

The use of ANOVA for hypothesis testing is somewhat analogous to a familiar problem encountered in studies involving the electronic transmission of signals called the "signal to noise ratio." For example, a "good" tape recorder is one that allows for the input of signals at high sound pressure levels with as little as possible distortion owing to extraneous noise. No doubt, we have all experienced the unpleasant "hum" that occurs on playback when the capacity of the recording unit has been exceeded. Thus, a good recording device is one in which the ratio of the signal to the noise is large—that is, one that is able to maximize the transmission of salient information (the signal) while minimizing the transmission of artifacts (noise). In designing instrumentation, an oscilloscope can be helpful to electronic engineers in the computation of the signal-to-noise ratio. Similarly, the main goal in using the ANOVA is to "scope the data" in an effort to isolate systematic treatment effects intended by the experimenter (the signal) from sources of error (noise).

In the early part of Chapter 13, we discussed the conceptual basis of systematic variance versus error variance in accounting for the results of an experiment. The main goal of ANOVA is to compute the ratio of systematic variance (the amount of variation owing to a treatment effect) to the degree of error variance that may involve both sampling errors and measurement errors. Recall that a statistical term for systematic variance is *between-group variance*, whereas the statistical moniker for error variance is *within-group variance*. As we also noted, the difference between these types of variance can be expressed symbolically as an *F*-ratio, or $F = \frac{V_n}{V_e}$ where the denominator in the equa-

tion is error variance and the numerator is systematic variance.

In reality, the degree of systematic variance in any experiment is the consequence of not only treatment effects but some chance fluctuations as well. Therefore, the *total variability* in data sets can also be expressed as:

S^2 within groups = error variance

S^2 between groups = error variance + treatment effects

ANOVA provides a convenient method of calculating whether the variability between group means is greater than the variability within group means. This is accomplished by dividing up sources of variance into two major components: (1) the variation of the score of each subject from the mean of their group and (2) the variation between each group mean and the grand mean for the sample. If there are large differences between the group means, the variation between them and the grand mean will be large compared with the amount of variation within each group. If this is found to be true on the basis of an **F-test**, then the null hypothesis of equivalence between groups is rejected. On the other hand, if the group means are similar in size, their variation from the grand mean should not differ substantially from the variation among the subjects within each group beyond chance expectations. In such a case, the null hypothesis is retained.

Calculation of ANOVA

In order to illustrate the use of ANOVA in hypothesis testing, let us examine its application in estimating the significance of difference among three independent means. For this purpose, the simplest of the ANOVA designs involving the analysis of a single factor will be used. This method, called a *one-way ANOVA*, may be viewed as an extension of the unpaired *t*-test for two independent means discussed previously in this chapter.

Suppose we are interested in exploring the relationship between auditory processing abilities and phonological disorders. We model our hypothetical study, in part, after the investigation of Thayer and Dodd (1996), who evaluated the auditory perceptual abilities of children whose speech sound errors consisted of either *delayed* phonologic acquisition or *disordered* phonology against a control group.

For purposes of our example, we will fabricate some data for three groups of children: Control group (A), Consistent group (B), and Delayed group (C). The consistent group are children who display consistent phonologic errors that are atypical of normal phonologic development. On the other hand, the delayed group is constituted of those subjects whose speech sound errors are inappropriate for age but typical of earlier stages of phonologic development. Assume that there are 10 children in each of the three groups. As in the study by Thayer and Dodd, the Pediatric Speech Intelligibility (PSI) Test will be used for the assessment of the subjects' auditory processing abilities. This test involves assessment of the ability to process messages in the presence of competing but semantically related sentences presented either contralaterally (one sentence to each ear) or ipsilaterally (both sentences to the same ear). For purposes of simplifying the analysis, we limit our discussion to some hypothetical outcomes for the right ear results under contralateral testing conditions.

Let us now illustrate the steps in testing the hypotheses associated with this problem and the procedures necessary for their evaluation based on a one-way ANOVA.

Step 1. Form the hypothesis in statistical terms.

H_o: There is no difference in the auditory processing ability among the three groups. Symbolically, we can also state that $f.L_A = f.L_B = f.L_C$.

H_1: There is a difference in the auditory processing ability among the three groups. Symbolically, we can also state that at least one f.L is different from other f.L's.

Step 2. Select an appropriate statistical test.
The use of a one-way ANOVA is predicated on the following three assumptions: (1) there is independence among the groups; (2) the sampling distribution of the groups follows a normal curve; and (3) the variances of the scores in each group are equal. Symbolically, we can state that the population variances of all groups are equal (homogeneity of variance). The first two assumptions are also necessary for the use of the *t*-test for two independent groups, as previously described. However, the third assumption is an additional component underlying the use of any parametric ANOVA. In cases in which the homogeneity of variance among groups is questionable, the **Bartlett test** should be used for making this determination. When each group is constituted by an equal number of subjects or scores, the assumptions of homogeneity of variance are better met. Thus, the one-way ANOVA design is appropriate for hypothesis testing given our hypothetical research problem.

Step 3. Organize a table to include the necessary numerical values and calculate the test statistic (see Table 12–8). The mathematical formula for the one-way ANOVA F-value is given by:

$$F = \frac{\left[\Sigma n_j(\bar{Y}_j - \bar{Y})^2\right]/(J - 1)}{\left[\Sigma(\bar{Y}_{ij} - \bar{Y}_j)^2\right]/(N - J)}$$

$$= \frac{Between\text{-}group\ variance}{Within\text{-}group\ variance}$$

with df (between) $= J - 1$ and df (within) $= N - J$.

The actual calculation of an observed F-value involves the following substeps:

a. Calculate the between-group variance (numerator).

$$Between - group =$$

$$\frac{10[(2.33)^2 + (0.33)^2 + (-2.67)^2]}{3 - 1} = 63.34$$

b. Calculate the within-group variance (denominator).

$$Within - group =$$

$$\frac{628 + 840 + 888}{30 - 3} = 87.26$$

c. Calculate the observed F-value.

$$F = \frac{63.34}{87.46} = 0.73 \text{ with } df \text{ (numerator)} = 2$$

$$\text{and } df \text{ (denominator)} = 27$$

Step 4. Draw conclusions on the basis of critical value(s). By consulting the appropriate table for F in Appendix N, we can observe that the critical value of the test statistic at alpha $(\alpha) = 0.05$ for df (numerator) $= 2$ and df (denominator) $= 27$ is 3.35.

Because the calculated (observed) F-value does not exceed the critical F-value, we must retain H_o in rejection of H_1. More specifically, as in the case of the actual study by Thayer and Dodd, our hypothetical findings indicate that the consistent and delayed groups did not perform neither differently from one another nor from the control group. Therefore, we can conclude that auditory processing abilities as operationally defined in our investigation do not appear to provide a basis for determining the risk for phonologic disorders. All data values and necessary calculations are summarized in Table 13–14.

Two-Way ANOVA

In cases in which an investigator is interested in the effect of two independent variables on one dependent variable involving two or more groups, a two-way analysis of variance (two-way ANOVA) may be performed. For example, if we are interested in comparing the effect of individual therapy (factor 1) versus group therapy (factor 2) on some specific measure of language performance (dependent variable), this statistical method would be suitable for data analysis. Based on a hypothetical problem of this kind, there are three different ways to measure the relative effect of the individual variables under investigation. These are: (1) the main effect owing to factor 1, (2) the main effect owing to factor 2, and (3) the interaction.

Illustrations of three possible types of interaction pattern. (I) No interaction exists between Factor A and Factor B. It indicates that, regardless of the level of treatment (Factor A), there is a constant difference between the means at each level of the other factor (Factor B). (II) Ordinal interaction exists between Factor A and

Table 13–14. PSI Scores for the Right Ear Under Contralateral Testing Conditions for Three Groups of Children Classified According to Pattern of Phonological Development: Fabricated Data

Control (A)	Consistent (B)	Delayed (C)
73	74	86
98	100	76
100	100	90
99	100	88
99	96	99
100	78	74
100	100	100
98	95	98
100	97	100
93	100	99

$n_A = 10$ $n_B = 10$ $n_C = 10$

$\overline{Y}_A = 96$ $\overline{Y}_B = 94$ $\overline{Y}_C = 91$

$\Sigma(\overline{Y}_{nj} - \overline{Y}_A)^2 = 628$ $\Sigma(\overline{Y}_{nj} - \overline{Y}_B)^2 = 850$ $\Sigma(\overline{Y}_{nj} - \overline{Y}_C)^2 = 888$

$\overline{Y}_A - \overline{Y} = 2.33$ $\overline{Y}_B - \overline{Y} = 0.33$ $\overline{Y}_C - \overline{Y} = 2.67$

Where

Overall mean $= \frac{96 + 94 + 91}{3} = 93.67$

J = Total number of groups = 3

N = Total number of subjects in all groups combined = 30

j = Group of identification where j = A, B, C

nj = Number of subjects in each group where $n_A = 10$, $n_B = 10$, and $n_C = 10$

$\overline{Y}_j$ = Sample mean of each group such as $\overline{Y}_A = 96$, $\overline{Y}_B = 94$, $\overline{Y}_C = 91$

$\overline{Y}_{nj}$ = Sample scores in rows (i) by group (j), for example, $\overline{Y}_{1A}$ is the score of the first row in the control group (A) or 73

$\Sigma(\overline{Y}_{nj} - \overline{Y}_j)^2$ = Sum of the squares of between-group differences

$\overline{Y}_j - \overline{Y}$ = Between group differences

Source: From *Research and Statistical Methods in Communication Sciences and Disorders* (p. 347), by D. L. Maxwell and E. Satake, 2006, Clifton Park, NY: Thomson Delmar Learning.

Factor B. It indicates a greater difference between groups at one level of Factor A and Factor B. It indicates a greater differ-ence—effect owing to Factor 1 and Factor 2 (denoted by Factor 1 × 2). The **main effect** can be defined as the average effect of an independent variable across levels of the dependent variable—for instance, how each *separate* therapy factor will contribute to the outcome measure of language performance. The **interaction effect** can be defined as the *joint* effect of the two independent variables—for instance, how the two therapies combine or interact to influence measured language performance. The latter effect is extremely important in many clinical studies because clinicians often combine treatment modalities instead of using a single treatment approach. Box 13–3 illustrates the three possible types of interaction patterns that can be identified for each pair of lines indicating two factors, 1 and 2, when the two-way ANOVA is performed. The conceptual basis for computing the two-way ANOVA is illustrated below:

Total variability of effects = variability owing to main effect of factor 1

+ variability owing to main effect of factor 2

+ variability owing to interaction effect (1 × 2)

+ variability within groups (error variance)

Multiple Comparison Methods

As noted previously, in cases in which three or more group comparisons are to be made, ANOVA is typically performed as the first step in statistical testing. If the result of the *F*-test indicates that the null hypothesis should be rejected, we conclude that at least one of the group means is different from the other group means. However, we are unable to know on the basis of the *F*-test alone which *specific* group means among the various comparisons are significantly different from others. In order to make this determination, several so-called post hoc multiple comparison tests are available, such as **Scheffe's method** or **Tukey's method.**

In the case of an unequal sample size among the comparison groups, Scheffe's test is highly useful for calculating the significance of the observed *F* and *t*-values for each combination of two group means. For instance, having found a significant *F*-value among three groups (say groups A, B, C) based on calculation of an ANOVA, the null hypothesis for Scheffe's test can be stated as:

$$H_o: \mu_A = \mu_B, \mu_A = \mu_C, \text{ and, } \mu_B = \mu_C$$

In a statistical sense, this procedure is considered to be somewhat conservative; that is, the alpha (α) level is generally set at 0.10 if the alpha (α) level of the ANOVA was previously set at 0.05. Scheffe's method is used to control a type I error, entailing the rejection of the null hypothesis when it is correct.

When the sample sizes among comparison groups are equal, then the Tukey test (sometimes called *HSD—Tukey's honestly significant difference*) may be performed instead of the Scheffe's test. Tukey's method is less conservative than Scheffe's test and is designed to make all possible pairwise comparisons among group means while maintaining the type I error rate at the same as set in the ANOVA. The null hypothesis is identical to that of the Scheffe's test.

Finally, we briefly mention three **planned** (a priori) **comparison** procedures used in cases in which an investigator wishes to accomplish the analysis of a limited number of pairwise comparisons in lieu of performing a more comprehensive

Box 13–3. Types of Interactions

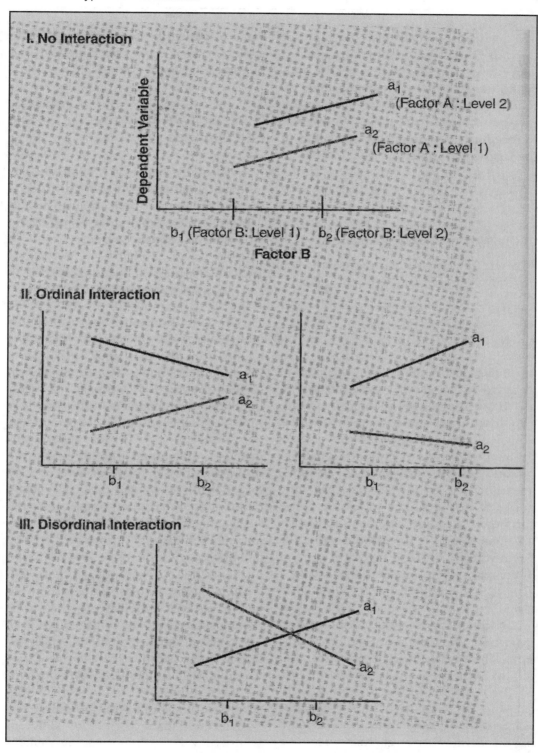

Source: *Research and statistical methods in communication sciences and disorders* (p. 348), by D. L. Maxwell & E. Satake, 2006, Clifton Park, NY: Thomson Delmar Learning.

and time-consuming ANOVA. Such procedures are used when prior theory leads to specific hypotheses about where significant differences between means might be found. For this purpose, we might use a revised version of the t-test. The revised t procedure is accomplished by means of the following formula:

$$t = \frac{(\bar{X}_i - \bar{X}_j)}{\sqrt{2MS_E n}}$$

with $df = N - j$ as defined above

where subscripts i and j represent group identifications and

$$MS_E = \sqrt{\left(\frac{s_i^2}{n_i} + \frac{s_j^2}{n_j}\right)}$$

Thus, rather than using the pooled standard deviation in the denominator, we use MS_E (the error mean square) instead.

Another planned comparison method designed to reduce the probability of making a type I error is to shift the alpha (significance level α) downward. For example, given the probability that approximately one t-test in four will be significant as the consequence of chance alone ($4 \times 0.05 = 0.20$), an option is to shift the alpha (α) downward by dividing it by the number of comparisons to be made. Thus, $0.05/4 = 0.0125$—a more stringent significance level.

Another approach to making a priori pairwise comparisons of group means is called the **Bonferroni t procedure**, also termed *Dunn's multiple-comparison procedure*. This method increases the critical value (table value) of an F needed for reaching statistical significance, depending on the number of comparisons to be made and the sample size. It is used in

cases in which the researcher wishes to avoid a type I error (rejecting the null hypothesis when it is true).

Other ANOVA Designs and Methods

Numerous variations of ANOVA designs and methods are available for special types of research applications. The following sections summarize some of the more widely used techniques.

Randomized-Blocks Analysis of Variance (RBANOVA)

This test is especially appropriate for within-subject designs in which the data comes from repeated measures on the same subject. According to Shavelson (1988), "the RBANOVA is to the t-test for dependent samples what the one-way ANOVA is to the t-test for two independent samples" (p. 487). Its primary purpose is to determine whether or not the differences between two or more groups may be due to chance or to systematic differences among the groups. Although RBANOVA is similar to ANOVA, the former method also takes into account the fact that two or more observations can be made on the same subject, as opposed to a single observation as in the case of the latter. This is accomplished by: (1) partitioning subjects into homogeneous blocks and (2) randomly assigning subjects to different levels within each treatment. For example, this design would be appropriate if we were interested in studying the relative influence of three conditions (A, B, C) as these interact with three different severity levels (1, 2, 3) on some element of measured performance.

In many research studies, a *Latin square* is used in conjunction with a block design when order effects may otherwise confound the influence of two or more treatment conditions. To control for the unwanted influence of confounding factors, a contingency table can be used to form a Latin square in which the confounding factors are assigned to rows and columns and the cells within the Latin Square table are used to denote the observations (treatments) of interest. The objective of this procedure is to arrange the order of treatment conditions so that each condition precedes and follows each treatment condition. The number of ordinal arrangements should equal the number of treatment conditions, and each treatment (letter) should appear only once within a cell of each column and row. For example, in a study of treatment efficacy in aphasia, suppose we wish to control for the possible confounding influences of language severity and time post-onset, as these nuisance variables might interact with three levels of an independent variable, say, the number of therapy sessions per

week. In accordance with the blocking principle of the Latin square, the levels of the confounding factors could be assigned to columns and rows of a square, with the cells of the square then used to identify the levels of treatment. Given this arrangement, there are three blocks of severity, three blocks of time post-onset, and three treatment levels (A, B, C) forming a Latin square consisting of nine cells for analysis. This hypothetical design is illustrated in Table 13–15.

An example of a clinical research study that used a RBANOVA in conjunction with a Latin square design can be found in Appendix B.

Analysis of Covariance (ANCOVA)

The major purpose of the analysis of covariance is to allow for an adjustment in factors that might potentially influence the results of an experiment *before* the experiment begins. More specifically, this test, abbreviated ANCOVA, allows for the statistical adjustment of data values of a dependent variable in accordance with

Table 13–15. Forming a Latin Square Design Consisting of Nine Cells for Analysis Based on Time Post-Onset and Severity of Language Disorders

		Time Post-Onset (in Months)		
		1	*2*	*3*
Severity Based on Percentile Rank	≤35	A	B	C
	36–55	B	C	A
	>55	C	A	B

Source: From *Research and Statistical Methods in Communication Sciences and Disorders* (p. 351), by D. L. Maxwell and E. Satake, 2006, Clifton Park, NY: Thomson Delmar Learning.

known quantities of a variable that the investigator might wish to control (control variable). In effect, this adjustment removes from a dependent variable the degree of variability that otherwise could be attributed to the control variable.

Mathematically, the calculation of such variance is made possible by the use of the linear regression line, discussed previously in Chapter 6, to specify the slope of the relationship between a dependent variable and control variable. By using the regression line, scores on the dependent variable can be predicted based on knowledge of corresponding scores on the control variable. Residual deviation scores are used to specify the degree of variability in the dependent variable that is not associated with the control variable.

Suppose we wish to measure the maintenance of clinical gains in response to some treatment for three groups of subjects following the termination of therapy. Group A will be evaluated 6 months after therapy, Group B after 12 months, and Group C after 18 months. There are several within-group and between-group variables besides the independent variable that might potentially influence the outcome of such a study. For example, the researcher may wish to control for the degree of improvement that occurred during the course of therapy. It is possible that subjects who made more progress in therapy will be the same individuals who best maintain clinical gains through time. Although this is an interesting question in its own right, it is not the purpose of our study, which seeks only to determine the degree of maintenance across different spans of time. Thus, we might wish to control for within- and between-group differences for the *degree* of progress that occurred during therapy by factor-

ing these *gain scores* into the analysis of the dependent variable. The intelligence and the motivation of subjects are examples of other control variables that might need to be considered. Because the mathematical calculation of ANCOVA is highly complex, we refer the reader to Appendix B where the necessary computational steps are outlined in relation to an actual research study along with a discussion of the relative advantages and disadvantages of ANCOVA as compared with ANOVA.

Nonparametric Tests for Multigroup Designs

There are several nonparametric tests that can serve as alternative methods to ANOVA for testing hypotheses for multigroup designs. As an alternative to the two-way ANOVA, one of the most commonly used of these is the **Friedman two-way analysis of variance by ranks**. Remember that nonparametric tests of this kind should be chosen when the assumption of homogeneity of variance is questionable or has been violated.

Just as the Wilcoxon matched-pairs signed ranks test is a useful distribution-free method for detecting a significant difference between two matched or related groups, the Friedman two-way analysis of variance by ranks test is also useful with a randomized block design when a block consists of three or more repeated measures obtained from the same subject. As an example application of the Friedman test, let us consider a question in the aural rehabilitation of profoundly hearing-impaired children related to the effectiveness of various communication methods in facilitating the accuracy of speech reception. More specifically, imagine that we wish to evaluate the use of a training system known as *cued speech* in association with other training modalities. Cued speech involves the use of a set of hand cues to reduce or resolve ambiguities in speech reception (Cornett, 1967). In our hypothetical study, this system will be examined as it might be used in conjunction with three other conditions, namely: (1) audition (AC), (2) lip reading (LC), and (3) audition and lip reading (ALC). For this purpose, a group of 10 profoundly hearing-impaired adolescents will serve as subjects. Assume that a speech recognition task is designed that requires subjects in each of the groups to identify key words embedded in sentences. Subjects' responses to the stimulus items are recorded in terms of the percentage of correct identifications made, and the results were summarized

in Table 13–16. Let us now illustrate the steps in conducting the Friedman test in the context of our example.

Step 1. Form the hypothesis in statistical terms.

H_o: There is no difference in the subjects' speech recognition scores under the three conditions.

H_1: There is a difference in the subjects' speech recognition scores under the three conditions.

Step 2. Select an appropriate statistical test.
As noted above, the Friedman test is an appropriate statistic for data involving repeated measures of subjects tested on three or more conditions when scores

Table 13–16. Hypothetical Results for a Study of Cued Speech Training in Association with Audition, Lip-Reading, and Audition and Lip-Reading

Subjects	AC	LC	ALC	Ranks (R) AC	LC	ALC
1	31	83	63	1	3	2
2	42	77	81	1	2	3
3	44	81	76	1	3	2
4	33	69	65	1	3	2
5	37	69	74	1	2	3
6	32	70	72	1	2	3
7	35	87	82	1	3	2
8	39	88	73	1	3	2
9	46	95	96	1	2	3
10	35	81	79	1	3	2
n = 10				Sum = 10	26	24

Source: From *Research and Statistical Methods in Communication Sciences and Disorders* (p. 353), by D. L. Maxwell and E. Satake, 2006, Clifton Park, NY: Thomson Delmar Learning.

are to be ranked. The specific goal of the test is to determine whether the sums of the ranks for the various conditions differ significantly.

Step 3. Choose the significance level. An alpha level of 0.05 will be used to test the null hypothesis in a one-tailed test. A one-tailed test is always applied in testing the significance of three or more treatment conditions or groups.

Step 4. Organize a table to include test scores, their ranks, and the sum of their ranks, and calculate the test statistic (see Table 13–16). The test scores for the subjects in the three conditions of our hypothetical experiment are cast in a two-way table of n rows (subjects) and k columns (conditions).

It can be seen that:

n = total number of subjects = 10

k = total number of conditions = 3

'SR = a column sum of ranks such as AC-10, LC-26, and ALC-24

The observed value of the Friedman test statistic approximates the chi-square distribution with $df = k - 1$. Therefore, the general formula for the Friedman test statistic is given by:

$$X^2 = \frac{12(\Sigma R^2)}{nk(k + 1)} - 3n(k + 1)$$

with $df = k - 1$

Entering the appropriate values into the formula above,

$$X^2 = \frac{12[10^2 + 26^2 + 24^2]}{10 \cdot 3 \cdot (3 + 1)} - 3 \cdot 10 \cdot (3 + 1)$$

$$= 15.2$$

Step 5. Draw conclusions on the basis of critical value(s). Appendix P lists critical values of the chi-square distribution. For a critical value of 5.991 where $\alpha = 0.05$ and $df = 3 - 1 = 2$, it can be seen that the observed value of x^2 is greater than the critical value of 5.991 listed in Appendix P. Thus, we would reject the null hypothesis and conclude that there was a difference in the speech recognition abilities of subjects among the three conditions. Our hypothetical results are compatible with the findings of an actual experiment concerned with a similar problem (Nicholls & Ling, 1982).

Another nonparametric alternative to the ANOVA is the **Kruskal-Wallis one-way analysis of variance by ranks (KWANOVA).** This test, a nonparametric version of the one- way ANOVA and extension of the Mann-Whitney U-test, is useful for deciding whether the distribution of scores in the populations underlying each group are identical. Instead of using actual test scores, ranks are substituted in order to represent the dependent variable. As in the case of the Friedman, scores are entered into a table and rank ordered from lowest to highest without regard to group membership. After summing the ranks of each group, if their respective sums are similar, then the null hypothesis is retained. Otherwise, H_o is rejected.

The p-Value Approach in Testing Hypotheses

The approach to testing hypotheses we have discussed so far is called the **classical approach** to hypothesis testing. However, current widespread use of computers and statistical software packages make another approach called the **p-value approach** an important method in drawing the final conclusion, because many scholastic journal articles in the field of communication sciences and disorders report the final results in a p-value form. The general definition of a p-value is the probability of obtaining a value of the sample test statistic as favorable or more favorable to the alternative hypothesis (H_1) than the null hypothesis (H_o); if H_o were true, a p-value measures how credible your alternative hypothesis is (or how confident you are in rejecting the null hypothesis), whereas the classical approach simply reports the conclusion by stating "reject or fail to reject the null hypothesis," and it does not calculate the amount of confidence when you reject the null hypothesis. Conversion from the classical approach to the p-value approach and mathematical derivation of the p-value are as follows:

- *Reject* the null hypothesis if the p-value is less than or equal to the predetermined value of α.
- *Fail to reject* the null hypothesis if the p-value is greater than α.
- In a one-tailed test, the p-value is the area to the right (if H_1 contains >) of an observed value or the area to the left (if H_1 contains <) of an observed value. In a two-tailed test, the p-value is twice the area to the right or left of an observed value.

If the conclusion is reported solely by the p-value, many researchers will use the following guide to determine the significance of their test results based on the sample test statistic.

$p < 0.01$ the result is highly significant—very strong evidence against H_o

$0.01 < p < 0.05$ the result is significant—sufficient evidence against H_o

$p > 0.05$ the result is not significant—insufficient evidence against H_o

Figure 13–4 summarizes the general procedure of hypothesis testing and how to formulate the correct wording of the conclusion by both classical approach and p-value approach. As noted earlier, the p-value approach has become more common and important in research because a vast majority of commonly used statistical software packages, like MINITAB, SPSS, and the like, always display only p-value with output in determining the significance of the final test result.

Meta-Analysis

An increasingly popular methodology for statistically combining the results from two or more independent studies is called **meta-analysis**—a term introduced by Glass (1977) to describe a kind of higher-order level of data synthesis. Meta-analytic techniques should not be confused with traditional reviews of literature in which the findings of separate but related studies are summarized in an effort to "make sense out of the data." However, the underlying concern of meta-analysis is focused on the same problem, namely, the tendency of many research studies, designed to answer the same or a highly similar question, to yield conflicting results.

According to Sachs et al. (1987), meta-analysis has four main objectives:

1. Increasing statistical power by enlarging the size of the sample
2. Resolving the uncertainty associated with conflicting results

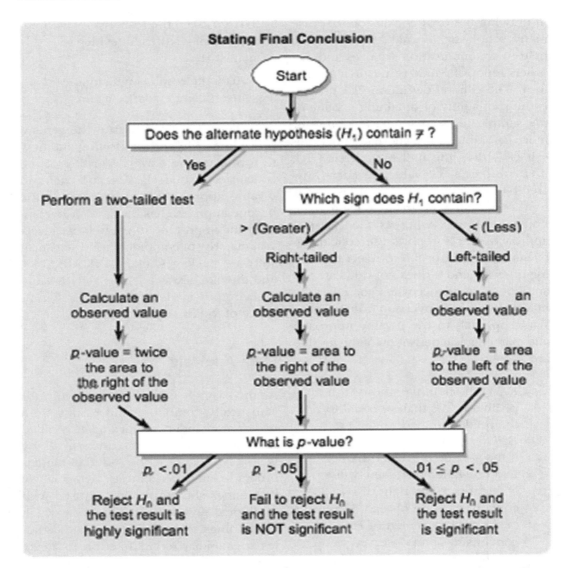

Figure 13–4. A flowchart of classical and *p*-value approaches in testing hypotheses. From *Research and Statistical Methods in Communication Sciences and Disorders* (p. 355), by D. L. Maxwell and E. Satake, 2006, Clifton Park, NY: Thomson Delmar Learning.

3. Improving estimates of effect size
4. Answering questions not posed at the beginning of the study

Among these aims, number 3, relating to effect size, is a key concept underly-

ing the application of many meta-analysis techniques. **Effect size** is an index of the degree to which the phenomenon of interest exists in the population (Cohen, 1977). There are several methods of determining effect size, depending on the unit of analysis. In the case of mean scores, effect size is the difference between the means divided by the averaged standard deviations between the groups.

As noted above, effect size relates to the *power of the test* to yield a significant finding if the research hypothesis is true. The greater the difference between means, and the smaller the population variance, the larger will be the effect size. Criteria for interpreting effect sizes have been established by Cohen (1977). An effect size of 0.2 (interpreted as small) indicates that the means of two groups are separated by 0.2 standard deviations. Effect sizes of 0.5 (moderate) and 0.8 (large) indicate that the means are separated by 0.5 and 0.8 standard deviations, respectively. Meta-analytic technique can be used to combine effect sizes from independent studies into an overall average effect size and probability value based on the pooled results.

As an example of the use of effect size in conjunction with meta-analysis, a study by Nye and Turner (1990) is noteworthy. Using a database of 65 studies to evaluate the effectiveness of articulation therapy, the authors reported a mean effect size (ES) of 0.892, "indicating that articulation treated subjects moved from the 50th to the 81st percentile as a result of intervention." Several variables where sorted out that appeared to have the greatest influence on articulation improvement.

In the field of communication sciences and disorders, some researchers have held that statistical significance testing has been overly emphasized (Attansio, 1994; Maxwell & Satake, 1993) or should be supplemented by additional tests (Attansio, 1994; Maxwell & Satake, 1993; Young, 1993). Although the authors of this text firmly believe that statistical significance testing has value, the calculation of effect size can be of equal importance, particularly in the context of applied research as demonstrated in studies like those of Nye and Turner and others as completed by Andrews et al. (1980) in assessing the effects of stuttering treatment. In discussing the future role of meta-analysis, Attanasio (1994) noted that its importance lies in providing "an estimate of the practical significance of a statistically significant finding" (p. 758). For a more detailed discussion of meta-analysis, see Pillemer and Light (1980); Cooper and Lemke (1991); and Wolf (1986), as well as many advanced statistical textbooks that provide a review of the subject. Also, for the more mathematically inclined reader, the author highly recommends that they should read such a book as *Research and Statistical Methods in Communication Sciences and Disorders* (Maxwell, L. D., & Satake, E., Thomson Delmar Learning, 2006) for further reading to deepen and promote their learning to a much greater extent.

Key Terms and Concepts

Analysis of variance

Independent variable

Dependent variable

Error variance

Within-in group variance

Between-group variance

F-test

Variance estimate

F-Ratio

Experiment-wise error rate

Mean squares

Multiple comparison tests

Tukey test

Scheffe's test

F' critical value

Q distributions

Q_{cv} critical value

Feedback Review of Chapter 13

1. Analysis of variance tests for differences between
   a. individual scores.
   b. group scores.
   c. means.
   d. variances.
   e. standard deviations.

2. Which test of significance is inappropriate for an ANOVA?
   a. t-test
   b. z-test
   c. F-test
   d. a & b
   e. a & c

3. In a one-way analysis of variance, which sum of squares (SS) is not calculated?
   a. SS_b
   b. SS_n
   c. SS_w
   d. SS_t
   e. none of the above (all are calculated)

4. In a one-way ANOVA, the scores of all participants combined are partitioned between and within
   a. two components.
   b. three components.

   c. sums of squares.
   d. mean squares.
   e. b & c

5. To locate the critical value for a one-way ANOVA (F_{cv}), we use the F table referencing
   a. two different degrees of freedom.
   b. three different degrees of freedom.
   c. four different degrees of freedom.
   d. $N - K$ degrees of freedom.
   e. none of the above

6. To calculate the mean squares (MS) in an ANOVA, we divide the sum of squares by
   a. N (total sample size).
   b. n (size of the sample or treatment group).
   c. the number of sub- or treatment groups.
   d. $N - 1$ or $n - 1$.
   e. degrees of freedom.

7. Another name for "mean square" is
   a. sum of squares.
   b. variance.
   c. F.
   d. alpha.
   e. beta.

8. In a one-way ANOVA, the F-ratio is calculated by
   a. MS_w/MS_t.
   b. MS_w/MS_b.
   c. MS_t/MS_b.
   d. MS_b/MS_w.
   e. MS_b/MS_t.

9. In one-way ANOVA, degrees of freedom for within-groups (df_w) is calculated by
   a. $N - 1$.
   b. $F - 1$.

c. n of groups – 1.

c. $df_b - df_t$.

d. $df_t - df_b$.

10. A mean square (MS) is a/an _____ estimate.
    a. sample
    b. population
    c. error
    d. mean
    e. variance

11. In one-way ANOVA, the null hypothesis is rejected when the observed F-ratio
    a. equals the critical value (F_{cv}).
    b. is less than the critical value (F_{cv}).
    c. is greater than the critical value (F_{cv}).
    d. exceeds the degrees of freedom (df).
    e. is less than the degrees of freedom (df).

12. When we reject the null hypothesis in an analysis of variance, we conclude that
    a. not all of the populations are equal.
    b. some of the populations are equal.
    c. all of the populations have unequal means.
    d. all of the populations have unequal variances.
    e. all of the above.

13. Experiment-wise error rate refers to the probability rate of rejecting a
    a. false alternative hypothesis.
    b. true alternative hypothesis.
    c. false true hypothesis.
    d. true null hypothesis.
    e. a or c.

Fill-Ins

14. Which multiple comparison tests is used to determine significant differences among the sample means of unequal size groups? _____

15. Which multiple comparison test is used to determine significant differences among the sample means of equal size groups? _____

16. The between-groups variance estimate is denoted by the symbol _____.

Short Answer

17. Write the null and alternative hypotheses for a one-way ANOVA with three treatment groups.

18. Why is it inappropriate to use multiple t-tests to test the null hypothesis for multiple sample means?

19. Briefly describe the three assumptions that must be met in order to conduct a one-way ANOVA.

Review Problems

1. A clinical scientist conducts a survey to determine if there is a significant difference in attitude among students, clinical practitioners, and clinical researchers on the particular issue of professional ethics. The results are shown in Table 13–17.

   At $\alpha = 0.05$, can the researcher conclude that there is a difference in attitudes toward professional ethics issue among the three groups? If

Table 13–17. Hypothetical Results Concerning Attitude Among Students, Clinical Practitioners, and Clinical Researchers on the Particular Issue of Professional Ethics

Groups		
Students (s)	Practitioners (p)	Researchers (r)
42	40	40
41	38	39
41	37	38
40	37	37
40	36	37
37	36	37
		34
		34

Table 13–18. Hypothetical Results Concerning the Primary Motives for Interpersonal Communication Between Clinicians and Clients Is to Seek Affection

Elderly (e)	Middle Aged (ma)	Young Adults (ya)
22	12	13
16	18	12
23	22	16
28	16	15
27	15	12
26	13	10
16	14	18

so, apply the appropriate multiple comparison test at the same level of significance. Which group(s) should be considered significantly different from the other(s)?

2. Research indicates that one of the primary motives for interpersonal communication between clinicians and clients is to seek affection. A speech-pathologist wants to know if there is a significant difference among the elderly, middle-aged, and young adults in the use of humor to obtain affection. The results of a questionnaire survey are summarized in Table 13–18.

At the 0.01 level of significance, can the researcher conclude that there is a difference in the use of humor in seeking affection among the three age groups? If a significant difference exists, apply the appropriate multiple comparison test at the same significance level (0.01) and indicate which age group(s) is significantly different from the others. Assume the research participants were randomly selected and that the populations from which the samples were drawn are normal with equal variances.

3. Twenty-four (24) graduate students in the communication disorders program are randomly assigned to one of four learning groups, 3 treatment groups and one control group. Students in the treatment groups, designated G_1, G_2, and G_3, learn a task receiving a particular schedule of reinforcement. Students in the control group, designated *Ctrl*, are given no reinforcement. The results of an achievement test following the experiment are summarized in Table 13–19.

Table 13–19. Hypothetical Results of Achievement Test Scores Concerning the Effectiveness of Four Different Treatments

G_1	G_2	G_3	Ctrl
49	52	51	48
54	57	55	54
50	56	49	51
57	54	54	50
48	55	50	52
52	62	48	47

At the 0.05 level of significance, should the researcher reject the null hypothesis of no difference in achievement between the four learning groups? If "yes," apply the appropriate multiple comparison test at the same significance level (0.05). Assume the research participants were randomly selected and that the populations from which the samples were drawn are normal with equal variances. Which reinforcement schedule(s) should be considered more effective than the others?

Calculation Guides

Preliminary Data Analysis for a One-Way ANOVA

Step 1: Construct a distribution table summarizing the sample size (n), mean ($\overline{X}$), sum of scores ($\sum X_1$), and sum of squared scores ($\sum X_1^2$) for each group and all groups combined.

Step 2: Compute the sum of squares for the total group (SS_t), the between-group (SS_b), and the within-group (SS_w) using Method One (Formula 13–1 through Formula 13–3) or Method Two (Formula 13–5 through Formula 13–8).

Step 3: Calculate the degrees of freedom for the total group (df_t), the between-group (df_b), and the within-group (df_w) using Formula 13–9 through Formula 13–11.

Step 4: Calculate the mean squares (variance estimates).

Between-group

$$MS_b = \frac{SS_b}{df_b} \quad \text{Formula 13–12}$$

Within-group

$$MS_w = \frac{SS_w}{df_w} \quad \text{Formula 13–13}$$

Conducting *F*-test for One-Way ANOVA

Step 1: State the Hypotheses

H_o: $\mu_{bm} = \mu_{cr} = \mu_{sd}$

H_1: *At least one mean is different from the others.*

Step 2: Find the Critical Value for Rejecting H_o:

$\alpha = $ _____ $F_{cv} = $ _____ (Tables N–1, N–2, and N–3 in Appendix N)*

Step 3: Compute the Test Statistic

$$F = \frac{MS_b}{MS_w}$$

Step 4: Apply the Decision Rule

If F is greater than F_{cv}, reject H_o:

If F is less than F_{cv}, do not reject H_o:

*Where df_b is the numerator and df_w is the denominator

14

Categorical Analysis: Chi-Square Tests

Overview

The tests of significance (z, t, and F) introduced in previous chapters are based on certain assumptions about the parameters in the populations from which the samples are selected. One such assumption requires that the variable or variables in the population under study be normally distributed. Statistical tests, such as z-, t-, and F-tests, are generally known as **parametric tests**, because they are based on population parameters. However, very often the data obtained in social and behavioral research, as well as in other disciplines, do not satisfy parametric assumptions. This is particularly true when there is little or no information about the population parameters of interest or when the sample data clearly indicate that parametric assumptions cannot be met. In such cases, researchers utilize statistical techniques that make less restrictive assumptions about the data and populations from which the samples were drawn. These techniques are generally known as **nonparametric tests**, which are appropriate when data are obtained on nominal or ordinal measures. In this chapter, we

focus on one of the most commonly used nonparametric techniques.

Parametric tests, such as z-, t-, and F-tests, are based on population parameters and are used to test hypotheses and estimate parameters, provided that certain assumptions regarding the nature and shape of distributions are satisfied. *Nonparametric tests* are used when little or no information about population parameters is known and/or when parametric assumptions cannot be met.

In Chapter 1, we noted that *nominal variables* are qualitative in nature and do not have the implicit quantity or magnitude of interval and ratio variables such as intelligence, height, weight, or time. Nominal variables are expressed broadly as names, such as "gender," "political affiliation," "religious preference," and broken down into mutually exclusive categories such as "male" and "female," "Democrat," "Republican," and "Independent," or "Catholic," "Protestant," "Jew," and "Buddhist." For this reason, nominal variables often are referred to as **categorical variables**.

Nominal data values usually are obtained from surveys and public opinion polls where responses are assigned to discrete categories, such as "yes" or "no," "in favor of," "against," or "neutral," and so on. In this chapter we introduce a nonparametric statistic known as *chi square,* which is commonly used when the data are obtained from nominal variables.

> Nominal variables, which are expressed broadly as names, also are referred to as *categorical variables.*

The Nature of Chi-Square Tests

There are several nonparametric methods that can be applied to nominal data expressed as frequencies or proportions. The method most commonly used is known as **chi-square tests**. The technique is quite versatile. It can be used with any number of variables that can be divided into specified categories, and it can be applied to a variety of research problems that do not meet the conditions of parametric tests. In fact, the assigned frequency values may be from any of the four types of measurement scales. For example, the nominal variable "income level" may be divided into ordinal categories, such as "low," "middle," and "high." The only condition imposed is that the categories be mutually exclusive and exhaustive and that frequencies are used in the test of significance.

The chi-square test statistic is denoted by the symbol, χ^2. The symbol, χ, is the Greek letter chi, pronounced *"ki,"* which rhymes with "eye." The statistical question posed in chi-square tests asks: Does the distribution of *observed frequencies* across a set of mutually exclusive categories differ significantly from the theoretical distribution of *expected frequencies* for these categories? The probability distribution used to test the significance of differences is the *chi-square sampling distribution,* which we soon discuss.

Observed frequencies in a chi-square problem are those obtained from research measures, such as questionnaires, surveys, and scales. While many applications of the chi-square test are used to analyze discrete data, the technique also is applicable when continuous data is reduced to categories. The **expected frequencies** are based on a research hypothesis. For example, in an experiment of 100 flips of an unbiased coin, we would hypothesize or *expect* 50 heads and 50 tails. Suppose in the course of 100 flips, we *observe* 45 heads and 55 tails. Would we reject the hypothesis that the coin is fair, or would we attribute the difference between what we observed and what we expected to chance or random fluctuation (error)? This is the basic question that frames chi-square tests.

> *Observed frequencies* are those obtained from research measures, such as questionnaires, surveys, and scales. *Expected frequencies* are those based on a research hypothesis.

Chi-square tests are always tests of nondirectional hypotheses that claim no difference between and/or among the distributions of the categories under study. They determine whether there is a significant difference between the observed and expected frequencies, not whether one category has a larger frequency than another. If the test statistic equals or exceeds the hypothesized probability level (critical value), the null hypothesis is rejected.

The equation for comparing observed and expected frequencies in chi-square tests is given in Formula 14–1.

Formula 14–1

$$\chi^2 = \Sigma^k_{i=1} = \frac{(O_i - E_i)^2}{E_i}$$

Where

k = number of possible outcomes, categories, levels, and so on

O = observed frequencies

E = expected frequencies

Note that the subscript $i = 1$ means that the function following the summation sign is conducted for each value of k or number of categories tested. When the observed frequencies and the expected frequencies are close together, the test statistic (χ^2) will be small, and the null hypothesis of no difference cannot be rejected. Conversely, when the observed and expected frequencies are far apart, χ^2 will be larger and the likelihood of rejecting the null hypothesis will be greater.

Assumptions and Conditions

Some chi-square tests have particular assumptions or conditions that must be satisfied in order to use the technique. However, in general, all chi-square tests are based on four assumptions: (1) the samples are independent; (2) the participants in each subgroup or sample have been randomly and independently selected; (3) the classification categories in the distribution are mutually exclusive and exhaustive; and (4) the sample size is reasonably large so that the expected

frequency in each category or cell within a table is 5 or more. Sometimes a researcher will combine the frequencies in two categories to increase the size of cells. This may be appropriate as long as the cell categories are germane or meaningful to each other. For example, a researcher may combine the frequencies in the "agree" and "strongly agree" cells into a single "agree" cell. It should be noted that when samples are small, the expected frequencies also are small, which may result in an exaggerated χ^2 statistic and the possible rejection of a true null hypothesis (Type I error).

The χ^2 Distribution

The chi-square sampling distribution, like the z, t, and F distributions, is actually a family of distributions based on degrees of freedom associated with the number of categories in the sample. As with t and F distributions, there is a distinct χ^2 distribution for every possible value of degrees of freedom. For the most basic chi-square test, the degrees of freedom are determined by the number of categories under study minus 1, as given in $df = k - 1$, where k is the number of categories. However, the degrees of freedom of a particular χ^2 test (α) are based on the number of categories in the distribution and *not* the number of subjects in the sample as in the case of t and F distributions. Rather, degrees of freedom represent the number of cells in which observed frequencies are free to vary.

Chi-square distributions are nonsymmetrical and skewed to the right; their values range from zero to positive infinity. Figure 14–1 reflects the shapes of varying sampling distributions of chi-square for 1, 5, and 15 degrees of freedom. Note that

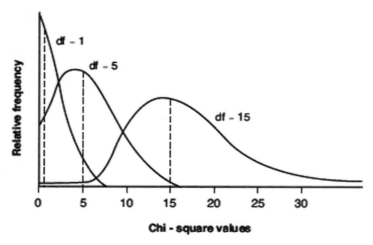

Figure 14–1. Shapes of varying samples of distributions of chi-squares for 1, 5, and 15 degrees of freedom.

for every possible value of degrees of freedom, there is a distinct distribution with its own curve.

Figure 14–1 also reveals some important characteristics of chi-square distributions. For example, notice that all of the values along the horizontal x-axis are positive, with $\chi^2 = 0$ as the left-hand limit of the distribution. Since the lowest possible value of the test statistic is zero, indicating no difference between the observed and expected frequencies, chi-square tests are essentially one-tailed tests of significance, even though the claim of the hypothesis is nondirectional. In short, only the right-hand side of the χ^2 sampling distribution is used for rejection of the null hypothesis.

Another characteristic of chi-square distributions is they are unimodal. Also, while the initial chi-square distribution is positively skewed, as the degrees of freedom increase, the shape of the distributions approach the normal curve. Finally, as the number of degrees of freedom ($k - 1$) increases, the value the χ^2 observed is

expected to increase. Therefore, if the null hypothesis is assumed to be true, we can expect the value of χ^2 to equal the df associated with it. For example, for chi-square with $df = 15$, we would expect to obtain $\chi^2 = 15$ if the null hypothesis is true.

The critical values for chi-square tests, symbolized as χ^2_{cv}, are obtained from Table P–1 in Appendix P. The critical values are determined by two values: degrees of freedom (df) and the probability level. To find a particular χ^2_{cv} in Table P–1, locate the level of significance (α) across the top of the table (column headings) and the degrees of freedom (df) along the left margin (row headings). The critical value lies at the intersection of these two points. For example, given a 0.01 level of significance with 3 degrees of freedom, $\chi^2_{cv} = 11.34$, as shown in Figure 14–2.

While the chi-square distribution can be used for many purposes, its most common use is in the analysis of nominal data. In this chapter, we examine three com-

df	.10	.05	Levels of Significance - α .02	**.01**	.001
1				6.64	
3			---->	**11.34**	
30				50.89	

Figure 14–2. Critical value.

monly used chi-square techniques, the "goodness-of-fit test," the "test for independence," and the "test for homogeneity of proportions." The **goodness-of-fit test** is used to determine whether an observed frequency distribution of a single variable *fits* a specific pattern of what can theoretically be expected. The **test of independence** is used to determine whether two variables are independent. The **test for homogeneity of proportions** is used to determine the equality of proportions. All three tests are used when the variables under study do not come from normally distributed populations. All three use Formula 14–1 to compute the test statistic χ^2 and the chi-square sampling distribution to determine the probability of significance. They differ, however, in the research problems addressed and hypotheses tested.

The Chi-Square Goodness-of-Fit Test

The nonparametric technique known as the **chi-square goodness-of-fit test** is often used to determine if the frequencies observed in a distribution fit an expected pattern for a single variable. In the 100 coin flips experiment described above, how well does the observed outcome fit the theoretical or hypothesized expectation? Is the difference between the 45 heads, 55 tails observed outcome significantly different from the 50 heads, 50 tails split we theoretically would expect? Is the observed outcome within the realm of chance, or is the coin biased in favor of tails? We could attempt to answer this question by subjecting the results to a goodness-of-fit test to see how "good" the *observed* frequencies "fit" the theoretical *expected* frequencies.

The number of categories for a specified variable in the goodness-of-fit test can range from the simplest form of two to any number of categories. For example, if a random sample of individuals is presented with four options, will each option be selected with the same frequency? Consider the following. It was assumed that the Digital Millennium Copyright Act (DMCA) passed in 2003 would dramatically curb the illegal downloading of music over the Internet. However, an article in *The Chronicle of Higher Education* the following January (2004), indicated that efforts to enforce the law were not very effective. Suppose a researcher today, interested in determining the impact of the DMCA among students at a particular college, surveys a random sample of 100 students and asks, "How often, if ever, have you downloaded or shared copyrighted music files *without* using a legal version of a music service such as Napster?" He observes the following results: 40 students responded "frequently," 36 "sometimes," 14 "seldom," and 10 "never."

In the absence of prior information regarding how students might respond to the question, the researcher theoretically could expect that the frequency of each response would be 25 for each response, as shown in Table 14–1. Note that the data collected are in the form of frequencies that fall into mutually exclusive categories or cells (we will use the terms interchangeably). Obviously, there is quite a difference between the distribution of *observed frequencies* (40, 36, 14, 10) and the theoretically or hypothesized *expected frequency* of 25 for each category. Is the difference due to chance or sampling error, or is there a "goodness of fit" between the observed and expected? Let's assume that the researcher decides

to conduct a chi-square goodness-of-fit hypothesis test as follows.

Step 1: State the Hypotheses

The null hypothesis in this goodness-of-fit test claims that there is no difference in the frequency with which students illegally download or share music files over the Internet. The alternative hypothesis claims that there is a difference. Symbolically, the hypotheses may be expressed as:

$$H_o: f_o = f_e \qquad H_1: f_o \neq f_e$$

Where f_o and f_e represent the observed and expected frequencies.

Step 2: Set the Criterion for Rejecting H_o

Assume that the researcher selects an $\alpha = 0.05$ level of significance. The degrees of

Table 14–1. Summary Data for Digital Music Download Survey

SUMMARY DATA FOR COMPUTING GOODNESS-OF-FIT		
Response	*Observed Frequencies (O)*	*Expected Frequencies (E)*
Frequently	40	25
Sometimes	36	25
Seldom	14	25
Never	10	25
Total	100	100

freedom for the goodness-of-fit test are defined as $k - 1$, where k is the number of categories or cells. For this example, $df = 4 - 1 = 3$. Referring to Table P–1, the critical value, χ^2_{cv} for a two-tailed, $\alpha = 0.05$, chi-square test, is 7.82. Thus, the criterion for rejecting the null hypothesis may be stated as follows:

$\alpha = 0.05$ two-tailed test $\chi^2_{cv} = 7.82$

$$\chi^2 = \Sigma^k_{i=1} = \frac{(O_i - E_i)^2}{E_i}$$

$$= \frac{(40 - 25)^2}{25} + \frac{(36 - 25)^2}{25} +$$

$$\frac{(40 - 25)^2}{25} + \frac{(10 - 25)^2}{25}$$

$$= 27.68$$

Step 3: Compute the Test Statistic

The statistical question posed is whether the distribution of observed frequencies for student responses differs substantially from the theoretical expected frequencies to justify rejection of the null hypothesis. The test statistic, χ^2, is computed using Formula 14–1, where the results of subtracting the expected frequency from the observed frequency, squaring the result, and dividing by the expected frequency for each category are summed.

For this illustration, χ^2 is computed as follows, and the data is summarized in Table 14–2.

Step 4: Apply the Decision Rule

Since the test statistic $\chi^2 = 27.68$ is greater than the critical value $\chi^2 = 7.82$, the null hypothesis is rejected, $p < 0.05$. Thus, the researcher can conclude that the probability is less than 5% that there is no difference among the responses of the students. Moreover, a review of the observed frequency distribution indicates that the frequency with which music files are illegally downloaded or shared over the Internet is skewed in the direction of "frequently" and "sometimes." The four steps followed for this example are summarized in Box 14–1.

Table 14–2. Summarized Results of Goodness-of-Fit Test

SUMMARIZED RESULTS FOR GOODNESS-OF-FIT TEST					
Response	*O*	*E*	*O – E*	*(O – E)²*	*(O – E)²/E*
Frequently	40	25	15	225	9.00
Sometimes	36	25	11	121	4.84
Seldom	14	25	−11	121	4.84
Never	10	25	15	225	9.00
Total (Σ)	100	100			27.68

Box 14–1. A Summary of Four Basic Steps of Table 14–1 Example

---

Stem 1: State the Hypotheses

$$H_0: \quad f_o = f_e \qquad H_1: \quad f_o \neq f_e$$

Step 2: Find the Critical Value for Rejecting Ho

$$\alpha = .05 \quad 1 \text{ tailed test} \quad df = 4\text{-}1\text{=}3 \quad \chi^2_{cv} = 7.815$$

Step 3: Compute the Test Statistic

$$\chi^2 = \sum_{i=1}^{k} \frac{(O - E)^2}{E}$$

$$= \frac{(40 - 25)^2}{25} + \frac{(36 - 25)^2}{25} + \frac{(14 - 25)^2}{25} + \frac{(10 - 25)^2}{25} = 27.68$$

Step 4: Apply the Decision Rule

<u>Decision Statement:</u> Since $\chi^2 = 27.68 > \chi^2_{cv} = 7.815$, H_0 is rejected; $p < .05$

The Chi-Square Test of Independence

The chi-square technique also can be used to test the independence of two variables. For example, are the opinions in support of national identity cards independent of political philosophy? Does a relationship exist between gender and level of willingness to self-disclose in interpersonal transactions? Are attitudes toward career paths dependent on family income level? When the data of studies considering these questions are reported in terms of frequency of responses, the **chi-square test for inde-pendence** can be used to test the null hypothesis asserting the independence of the two variables of interest. In general terms, the question asked is whether the population frequency distribution of the categories of one variable is independent of the population frequency distribution of another variable. The hypotheses of the test of significance, in general terms, are stated as follows:

H_o: The two variables *are* independent.

H_1: The two variables *are not* independent.

The *chi-square test for independence* is used to determine the independence of two variables.

In the chi-square test for independence, the data are tabulated and arranged in a **contingency** or **cross-tabulation table**, showing the frequency distributions of two categorical variables. The table is made up of rows and columns in matrix form, with the number of rows times the number of columns ($R \times C$) defining the number of cells. For example, a table with 2 rows and 3 columns contains 6 cells and is known as a 2×3 contingency or cross-tabulation table; a table with 3 rows and 3 columns is known as a 3×3 table, and so on. The cells are labeled 1 to *n*, in a clockwise fashion, as shown in Figure 14–3.

The equation for computing the expected frequency (E) for each cell is given in Formula 14–2.

Formula 14–2

$$E = \frac{R_t \times C_t}{N_t}$$

Where

R_t = row total

C_t = column total

N_t = grand total ($R_t + C_t$)

Row and column totals are frequently called **marginal totals** and obtained by adding the observed frequency of each cell in a row (R_t) and in each column (C_t). The **grand total** is the sum of the row and column totals ($R_t + C_t$).

The data in the chi-square test for independence are tabulated and arranged in a *contingency* or *cross-tabulation table*, showing the frequency distributions of two categorical variables.

Row and column totals in contingency or cross-tabulation tables are frequently called *marginal totals*, and are obtained by adding the frequency of each cell in a row (R_t) and in each column (C_t). The sum of the row and column totals ($R_t + C_t$) are referred to as the *grand total*.

Scenario 1. A researcher wants to know if the preference for strong gun control among Democrats is related to their level of education. The two variables in this case

	Col.$_1$	Col.$_2$	Col.$_3$	Row Totals
Row$_1$	1	2	3	
Row$_2$	4	5	6	
Column Totals				

Figure 14–3. Contingency or cross-tabulation table.

are preference-for-strong-gun-control and education-level. The researcher randomly selects and surveys a sample of 255 Democrats on the question of whether they are in favor of or against strict gun control. Of the 255 participants, 120 completed high school and 135 completed college. Table 14–3 presents the results in a 2 × 2 contingency table. The underlying research question is: Is the frequency distribution of education level responses independent of the frequency distribution of preference for strong gun control responses, or is a preference for strong gun control contingent on one's education level. For this reason, the data are sometimes referred to as *contingency* or *cross-tabulation data*. Let us assume that the researcher decides on a 0.05 level of significance in testing the null hypothesis that the preference for gun control is "independent" of educational level. The chi-square solution to this research problem is illustrated using a four-step hypothesis test.

Step 1: State the Hypotheses

H_o: Preference for gun control is *independent* of education level

H_1: Preference for gun control is *contingent* on education level

Step 2: Set the Criterion for Rejecting H_o

The degrees of freedom for chi-square tests of independence are determined by subtracting the number of rows in a data table by 1, multiplied by the number of columns minus 1, as given in Formula 14–3.

Formula 14–3

$$df = (r - 1)(c - 1)$$

Where

r = number of cell rows

c = number of cell columns

Thus, the degrees of freedom for this scenario are as follows: $df = (2 - 1)(2 - 1) = 1$. Given that the level of significance selected for this problem is $\alpha = 0.01$, the critical value, using Table P–1, is $\chi^2_{cv} = 6.64$, and the criterion is stated as follows:

$$\alpha = 0.01 \quad \text{one-tailed test} \quad \chi^2_{cv} = 6.64$$

Table 14–3. Contingency Table of Preference for Strong Gun Control and Education Level

SUMMARY DATA FOR CHI-SQUARE TEST FOR INDEPENDENCE			
Preference	*Education High School*	*Level*	*Total*
Favor	75	105	180
Against	45	30	75
Total	120	135	255

Step 3: Compute the Test Statistic

In order to derive the test statistic, the expected frequencies for each cell in the contingency table must first be determined. The reasoning for the expected frequencies is as follows. The total number of responses by all voters was 255. The proportion of the total saying that they favor strong gun control measures is as follows:

$$\frac{180}{255} = 0.7059$$

If there is no difference in response for voters with a high school education and those who graduated college, we would expect approximately 70.59% in each group to favor the measure. Thus, expected frequencies for Cell 1 and Cell 2 of Table 14–3 are computed as follows:

Expected number of high school voters in favor = 0.7059(120) = 84.71

Expected number of college voters in favor = 0.7059(135) = 95.30

The same reasoning can be applied in determining expected frequencies for Cell 3 and Cell 4 responses "against" strong gun control measures. However, it probably is more convenient to use Formula 14–2 ($E = \frac{R_t \times C_t}{N_t}$) in determining expected frequencies (E) for a contingency table. For example, applying Formula 14–2 to the data in this study, we find that the theoretical expected frequency for the 75 participants with a high school education who favor strong gun control measures (Cell 1) is 84.71 ($E = \frac{180 \times 120}{255}$). Similarly, the expected frequency for the 105 participants with a college education in Cell 2 who favor strong gun control measures is 95.29, ($E = \frac{135 \times 180}{255}$). The observed ($O$) and expected ($E$) frequencies for all cells are summarized in Table 14–4. Note that the data in Table 14–4 illustrates the principle that the observed and expected frequencies should be equal to the sum of the observed frequencies for each row and column in the contingency table.

The test statistic χ^2 for the test of independence is computed using the same equation as that for the goodness-of-fit test (Formula 14–1). For this example, χ^2 is computed as follows:

Table 14–4. Summary of Observed and Expected Frequencies for All Cells

SUMMARIZED O AND E FREQUENCY DATA FOR X² TEST OF INDEPENDENCE

| | Education Level | | | | Total | |
| | High School | | College | | | |
Preference	Observed	Expected	Observed	Expected	Observed	Expected
Favor	75	84.71	105	95.30	180	180*
Against	45	35.29	30	39.70	75	75*
Total	120	120.00*	135	135.00*	255	255*

*Statistically significant.

$$\chi^2 = \Sigma_{i-1}^k \frac{(O-E)^2}{E}$$

$$= \frac{(75-84.71)^2}{84.71} + \frac{(45-35.29)^2}{35.29} +$$

$$\frac{(105-95.30)^2}{95.30} + \frac{(30-39.70)^2}{39.70}$$

$$= 7.142$$

Step 4: Apply the Decision Rule

Since the test statistic $\chi^2 = 7.142$ is greater than the critical value $\chi^2_{cv} = 6.64$, the null hypothesis is rejected, $p < 0.01$. In other words, the probability is *less* than 1% that the two variables are independent. Therefore, the researcher can conclude that the preference for strong gun control measures among Democrats is contingent or dependent on education level. The four steps followed in the hypothesis test are summarized below.

The Chi-Square Test for Homogeneity of Proportions

While the chi-square test for independence is useful in determining the association between two categorical variables in a single population, researchers often are interested in testing hypotheses where the frequency data are obtained from two or more samples with multiple categories of a variable. In these situations, the researcher is interested in determining whether the proportions in each category of a variable(s) are the same for the different populations sampled.

Recall that in Chapter 11, we used a z-test to determine the significance between two proportions when parametric assumptions are satisfied. However, as noted at the outset of this chapter, when little is known about the population or when the sample data clearly indicate that parametric assumptions cannot be met, a

---

Step 1: State the Hypotheses

H_o: Preference for gun control is *independent* of education level

H_1: Preference for gun control is *contingent* on education level

Step 2: Find the Critical Value for Rejecting H_o

$\alpha = 0.01$ one-tailed test

$df = (2-1)(2-1) = 1$

$\chi^2_{cv} = 6.64$

Step 3: Compute the Test Statistic

$$\chi^2 = \Sigma_{i-1}^k \frac{(O-E)^2}{E}$$

$$= \frac{(75-84.71)^2}{84.71} + \frac{(45-35.29)^2}{35.29} +$$

$$\frac{(105-95.30)^2}{95.30} + \frac{(30-39.70)^2}{39.70}$$

$$= 7.142$$

Step 4: Apply the Decision Rule

Decision Statement: Since $\chi^2 = 7.142 > \chi^2_{cv} = 6.64$, H_o is rejected; $p < 0.01$

nonparametric test of significance is more appropriate. Therefore, in cases where a researcher is interested in determining whether the proportions in each category of a variable(s) are the same for the different populations sampled, the **chi-square test for homogeneity of proportions** is an appropriate measure.

The statistical question in the chi-square test for homogeneity of proportions is not whether the proportions for each category are exactly the same, but whether the observed differences are statistically significant. If the null hypothesis is *not* rejected, the researcher will assume that the obtained differences are due to chance or random fluctuation from sampling. When the null hypothesis *is* rejected, the assumption is that differences are due to some relationship between the variables. The computational procedures for the test are the same as that for the test chi-square for independence. Both use contingency tables in analyzing data, as well as Formula 14–1, to compute the test statistic χ^2. However, in this case, the researcher is interested in determining whether the proportions of scores are the same for each population from which the samples were drawn.

> *The chi-square test for homogeneity of proportions* is used to determine if the proportions in each category of a variable(s) are the same for the different populations sampled.

Scenario 2. A researcher wants to determine if the responses to a survey item concerning the attractiveness of body jewelry are significantly different among 187 randomly selected students attending urban, suburban, and rural high schools. The responses to item categories by geographic areas are arranged in a twelve-cell, 4 × 3 contingency table, shown in Table 14–5. In this example, the research question is whether the proportion of responses are the same for students attending high school in urban, suburban, and rural areas. We illustrate the solution to the problem using the four steps in hypothesis testing.

Table 14–5. Contingency Table of Attractiveness of Body Jewelry in Urban, Suburban, and Rural High Schools

SUMMARIZED DATA FOR TEST OF HOMOGENEITY OF PROPORTIONS				
	Geographic Region			
Response Category	*Urban*	*Suburban*	*Rural*	*Row Total*
Very attractive	22	19	10	51
Somewhat attractive	19	21	8	48
Unattractive	12	14	21	47
Somewhat unattractive	9	11	21	41
Column total	62	65	60	187

Step 1: State the Hypotheses

The null hypothesis in this study claims that the proportion of students selecting each category of the variable (attractiveness-of-body-jewelry) is the same for each population from which the samples were drawn. For example, the proportion of students selecting "very attractive" will be the same for students attending high school in urban, suburban, and rural areas. The same claim is made about students selecting "attractive," "unattractive," and "very unattractive." Therefore, the null and alternative hypotheses may be stated in symbolic terms as follows:

$$H_o: P_{urban} = P_{suburban} = P_{rural}$$

H_1: At least one proportion is different from the others

Step 2: Set the Criterion for Rejecting H_o

The degrees of freedom (df) for the chi-square test for independence is determined using Formula 14–3. For this illustration, $df = (r - 1)(c - 1) = (4 - 1)(3 - 1) = 6$. The level of significance selected for this problem is $\alpha = 0.01$. Referring to Table P–1, we find the critical value to be $\chi^2_{cv} = 12.59$. Therefore, the criterion for rejecting the null hypothesis is set as follows:

$\alpha = 0.05$ one-tailed test $\chi^2_{cv} = 12.59$

Step 3: Compute the Test Statistic

The test statistic χ^2 for the test for proportions is computed using the same equa-tion used in the goodness-of-fit test and the test of independence (Formula 14–1). Although the null hypotheses in tests for homogeneity of proportions claims equal-ity of proportions, the calculations in deriving the test statistic, χ^2, are based on the frequencies given in the contingency table. Therefore, we must first determine the expected frequencies (E) of the cells in the contingency table. As in the case of the test of independence, the expected frequency for each cell is computed using Formula 14–2, $E = \frac{R_t \times C_t}{N_t}$. For example, the expected frequency for Cell 1 of Table 14–5, containing the frequency of 22 urban high school students is 16.91, ($E = \frac{62 \times 51}{187}$). In this case, we would expect 16.91 students from urban high schools to find body jew-elry attractive. The expected frequencies for the other eleven cells are computed the same way and are presented within parentheses in Table 14–6.

Applying Formula 14–1, we deter-mine test statistic χ^2 to be:

$$\chi^2 = \Sigma^k_{i=1} = \frac{(O_i - E_i)^2}{E_i}$$

$$= \frac{(22 - 16.91)^2}{16.91} + \frac{(19 - 17.73)^2}{17.73} + \frac{(10 - 16.36)^2}{16.36} +$$

$$\frac{(19 - 15.91)^2}{15.91} + \frac{(21 - 16.68)^2}{16.68} + \frac{(8 - 15.40)^2}{15.40} +$$

$$\frac{(12 - 15.58)^2}{15.58} + \frac{(14 - 16.34)^2}{16.34} + \frac{(21 - 15.08)^2}{15.08} +$$

$$\frac{(9 - 13.59)^2}{13.59} + \frac{(11 - 14.25)^2}{14.25} + \frac{(21 - 13.16)^2}{13.16}$$

$$= 9.81$$

Step 4: Apply the Decision Rule

Since the test statistic $\chi^2 = 19.81$ is greater than the critical value $\chi^2_{cv} = 12.59$, the null hypothesis is rejected, $p < 0.05$. The probability is less than 5% that there is

Table 14–6. Expected Frequencies for Data in Table 14–5

Response Category	Geographic Region			Row Total
	Urban	Suburban	Rural	
Very attractive	22 (16.91)	19 (17.73)	10 (16.36)	51 (51)
Somewhat attractive	19 (15.91)	21 (16.68)	8 (15.40)	48 (48)*
Unattractive	12 (15.58)	14 (16.34)	21(15.08)	47 (47)
Somewhat unattractive	9 (13.59)	11 (14.25)	21 (13.15)	41 (41)
Column total	62 (62.00)*	65 (65.00)	60 (60.00)	187 (187)

*Statistically significant.

no difference in the responses among students from urban, suburban, and rural high schools. Put another way, the results of the chi-square test for proportions suggest that the perceived attractiveness of body jewelry among high school students is contingent on the geographical location of the high school they attend. The four-step hypothesis test for this example is summarized below.

Step 1: State the Hypotheses

H_o: $P_{urban} = P_{suburban} = P_{rural}$

H_1: At least one proportion is different from the others

Step 2: Find the Critical Value for Rejecting H_o

5   one-tailed test

$df = (4 - 1)(3 - 1) = 6$

$\chi^2_{cv} = 12.59$

Step 3: Compute the Test Statistic

$$\chi^2 = \Sigma^k_{i=1} \frac{(O-E)^2}{E}$$

$$= \frac{(22 - 16.91)^2}{16.91} + \frac{(19 - 17.73)^2}{17.73} + \frac{(10 - 16.36)^2}{16.36} +$$

$$\frac{(19 - 15.91)^2}{15.91} + \frac{(21 - 16.68)^2}{16.68} + \frac{(8 - 15.40)^2}{15.40} +$$

$$\frac{(12 - 15.58)^2}{15.58} + \frac{(14 - 16.34)^2}{16.34} + \frac{(21 - 15.08)^2}{15.08} +$$

$$\frac{(9 - 13.59)^2}{13.59} + \frac{(11 - 14.25)^2}{14.25} + \frac{(21 - 13.16)^2}{13.16}$$

$$= 9.81$$

Step 4: Apply the Decision Rule

Decision Statement: Since $\chi^2 = 19.81$ > $\chi^2_{cv} = 12.59$, H_o is rejected; $p < 0.05$.

Clinical Applications of Chi-Square Tests: Goodness-of-Fit, Independence, and Homogeneity

As discussed in this chapter, in essence, the chi-square test provides a means of determining the ability of fit, independence, and homogeneity between the variable(s) of an investigator's interest by calculating the discrepancy between the observed frequencies (actual counts) for a set of categories and the expected frequencies for the same categories (probability estimates). Suppose we wish to determine whether graduate students preparing for their clinical careers in either speech-language pathologist (SLP) or audiology (Aud) have different preferences of the type of setting in which they might choose to work, say, four different categories of their workplace preferences, namely hospital, rehab center, school, or private practice. Imagine further that our case sample is based on the job preferences expressed by 200 SLP and 200 Aud. Let us now illustrate the procedure of the *test of independence* to see whether the variables of interest are independent or in some way associated. The frequencies of the observed counts are summarized in Table 14–7 shown below.

As we discussed before, we first state two hypotheses for independency:

H_o: Specialization and workplace preference are independent.

H_a: They are NOT independent.

Using either the formula (as presented earlier) or statistical software packages, we obtained the following results: observed chi-square value = 57.682, $df = 3$, and its corresponding p-value = 0.000 ($p < 0.01$). So, the amount of evidence against H_o is large enough to conclude that the result is "statistically significant" or "reject H_o" at the 5% level of significance under the frequentists methods.

Next, we illustrate the test of homogeneity, followed by the conceptual difference between two different tests (independence versus homogeneity). Suppose a total of 300 people are attending the annual ASHA convention (100 graduate students, 100 clinical practitioners, and 100 clinical researchers). We are interested in investigating the relationship of homogeneity (similarity) of the three different populations with respect to the choice

Table 14–7. Hypothetical Survey of Work Preferences Among SLP and Audiology Students

Specialization	Workplace Preference				Row Total
	Hospital	Rehab Center	School	Private Practice	
SLP	90	70	30	10	200
Aud	70	40	20	70	200
Column Total	160	110	50	80	400

of educational sessions (short courses, research seminar, and poster session). As the readers are already aware, the mathematical derivations of the observed chi-square values for both tests of independence and homogeneity are identical. For the test of independence, we were interested in whether two characteristics are related for individuals of the *same* population, that is, we treat area of specialization (SLP and Aud) as a whole population as one unit, and workplace preferences are also treated as one population. A test of homogeneity provides another perspective to the problem. Such a test considers one characteristic for *different* populations: those who are SLP and those who are Aud. The main issue here is similarity of their choices of workplace preference, that is, we now examine whether these two different populations are homogeneous (similar) with respect to the characteristic of workplace preference, that is to say, two populations show similar trend (or tendency) when they choose their workplace. Therefore, in conducting the test of homogeneity, we need to change our focus to similarity of two different populations based on the characteristics of interest. This change of the focus reflects the hypotheses. Now, we state H_o and H_a based on homogeneity of two different populations. Namely:

H_o: SLP and Aud are homogeneous with respect to their workplace preferences.

H_a: SLP and Aud are NOT homogeneous with respect to their workplace preferences.

The result revealed that we will still reject H_o at $\alpha = 5\%$ or the difference between two populations is statistically significant ($p < 0.01$) under the frequentists methods.

Let us go back to the question concerning the choice of educational sessions offered at the ASHA convention. In this example, we state H_o and H_a as follows:

H_o: All groups are homogeneous with respect to their choices of educational sessions.

H_a: All groups are NOT homogeneous with respect to their choices of educational sessions.

Hypothetical counts are summarized in Table 14–8. Under the hypothesis tests at 5% level of significance, we reject H_o, and the p-value suggests that the amount of evidence against H_o is large enough to conclude statistically significant.

Third, suppose a random sample of 216 clients having the particular speech fluency disorders were investigated. They were classified into the four age categories (I, II, III, and IV) and their diagnoses based on a screening test were also categorized as normal, mildly severe, and severe. The summary of all actual frequencies are summarized in Table 14–9.

If we wish to test the independency, H_o and H_a can be written as follows:

H_o: Age and level of severity are independent

H_a: Age and level of severity are NOT independent

On the other hand, if we wish to test the homogeneity of the variables of interest, we can state H_o and H_a as follows:

Table 14–8. Hypothetical Survey of Participant's Choices of Educational Sessions Among Graduate Students, Clinical Practitioners, and Clinical Researchers

Type of Educational Sessions	PARTICIPANT'S STATUS			Row Totals
	Graduate Students	Clinical Practitioners	Clinical Researchers	
Short Courses	15	25	35	75
Research Seminar	35	40	60	135
Poster Sessions	50	35	5	90
Column Totals	100	100	100	Grand Total of 300

Observed chi-square value = 50.778, $df = 4$, and p-value of 0.000 ($p < 0.01$).

Table 14–9. The Results of the Hypothetical Study Concerning the Severity of the Particular Speech Fluency Disorders by the Clients' Age Categories and Their Diagnoses

Diagnosis	I	II	III	IV	Row Total
Normal	15	32	18	5	70
Mildly Severe	8	29	23	18	78
Severe	1	24	24	19	68
Column Total	24	85	65	42	216

H_o: All age groups are homogeneous with respect to the level of severity

H_a: All age groups are NOT homogeneous with respect to the level of severity

Using the formulas or statistical software packages, we can obtain such the p-value as 0.0001 ($p < 0.01$). Under the frequentists methods, we reject H_o and the amount of evidence against H_o showed that the result is statistically significant. You may use the Minimum Bayes Factor (MBF) to measure the strength of the exact evidence in a most precise and accurate manner, as explained in Appendix S.

Goodness of-fit is often used to identify the most appropriate probability distribution where a given set of actual data values form. In a clinical setting in which an investigator has count data, for example, a clinician is interested in determining if a particular probability model (e.g., Normal, t, F, Binomial, Poisson, Geometric, and many others) adequately fits the data collected. Does a binomial or Poisson probability model provide a reasonable model for the observed data values? The measure of how well the actual observed data fits the particular probability model is the most widely used application of chi-square goodness-of-fit statistical method. For instance, suppose the clinician wants to investigate whether or not all observed data will form a Poisson distribution. She may state the following hypotheses:

H_o: Data come from a Poisson distribution. (Poisson probability model is well-fit.)

H_a: Data do NOT come from a Poisson distribution. (The model is NOT well-fit.)

Using the formula or statistical software package, we can obtain the observed chi-square values and its p-value to determine whether or not a Poisson distribution is adequate. In this case, the p-value assesses how well a Poisson probability model fits the observed data. Guidelines for assessing the quality of the fits are given as follows:

If $p \geq 0.25$, it is "excellent" fit

If $0.15 \leq p < 0.25$, it is "good" fit

If $0.05 \leq p < 0.15$, it is "moderately good" fit

If $0.01 \leq p < 0.05$, it is "poor" fit

If $p < 0.01$, it is "unacceptable" fit

The main disadvantage of the clinical use of chi-square goodness-of-fit is the potential for committing a higher incidence rate of a Type 2 error when an investigator retain H_o, because the investigator wants to show that sample data conform to or fit her theory without having the substantial amount of external evidence. Also, the calculation of a Type 2 error (β) is complex, and even we set $\beta \leq 20\%$ or 10% (a typical choice for communication disorders), it is still difficult for testing the composite hypothesis such as "the treatment is beneficial or effec-

tive." It is also very time-consuming work to choose the alternative hypothesized value against H_o. So, do not automatically give the full acceptance to the null hypothesis (all data values adequately fit a given probability model), just because H_o was not rejected. In replacement or as an alternative to goodness-of-fit test, the Bayesian probability model will successfully accomplish the task. For further details, especially when calculating MBF for chi-square values, the readers should visit the following site: Sources for Calculation of MBF: Perception and Cognitive Lab, Department of Psychological Sciences, University of Missouri (http://www.pcl.missouri.edu/bayesfactor).

Key Terms and Concepts

Parametric tests

Nonparametric tests

Nominal variables

Categorical variables

Mutually exclusive categories

Expected frequencies

Contingency table

Marginal totals

Grand total

Cross-tabulation table

Observed frequencies

χ^2 sampling distribution

Test of homogeneity of proportions

Goodness-of-fit test

Test of independence

Feedback Review of Chapter 14

1. Compared with the normal distribution, distributions are
   a. symmetrical.
   b. positively skewed.
   c. negatively skewed.
   d. all of the above.
   e. none of the above.

2. If the computed chi square for a test of significance equals 2.97, and the critical value equals 1.96, the decision of the researcher should be to
   a. gather more data.
   b. accept the null hypothesis.
   c. reject the null hypothesis.
   d. fail to reject the null hypothesis.
   e. accept the alternative hypothesis.

3. A psychologist wants to determine whether a person's confidence is heightened by a particular confidence building strategy. During an experiment, she counts the number of times each response is made in reference to a self-confidence expression. In this study, the variable self-confidence is *best* described as a/an _____ variable.
   a. nominal
   b. ordinal
   c. interval
   d. ratio
   e. confounding

4. All of the following are steps in computing the chi-square statistic for the goodness-of-fit technique, EXCEPT
   a. determine the expected frequencies in each category or cell.
   b. determine the actual, observed frequencies in each category or cell.
   c. determine the difference between the observed and expected frequencies in each category or cell.
   d. divide the squared expected frequencies by the observed frequencies for each category or cell.
   e. divide each squared difference of the observed minus expected frequencies by the expected frequency for each category or cell.

5. The degrees of freedom for the chi-square test of independence is
   a. the number of categories minus one.
   b. the number of categories times the number of columns.
   c. the number of columns-minus-one times the number of columns.
   d. the number of rows-minus-one times the number of categories.
   e. the number of rows-minus-one times the number of columns-minus-one.

6. Rejecting the null hypothesis in the chi-square tests of independence and homogeneity, means that:
   a. there is a relationship between the variables under study.
   b. there is no relationship between the variables under study.
   c. the observed frequencies are smaller than the expected frequencies.
   d. the observed frequencies are larger than the expected frequencies.
   e. a & d.

7. The chi-square technique can be used for testing
   a. goodness-of-fit.
   b. the independence of two variables.
   c. the homogeneity of proportions.
   d. all of the above.
   e. none of the above.

8. The goodness-of-fit test is used to test the null hypothesis.
   a. H_o: $\mu_1 = \mu_2$
   b. H_o: $\mu_o = \mu_e$
   c. H_o: $f_0 = f_e$

9. A table representing a two-way classification of variables is known as a
   a. class interval.
   b. classification table.
   c. chi-square table.
   d. divergent table.
   e. contingency table.

10. Chi-square tests are used when data are expressed in
    a. frequencies.
    b. proportions that can be reduced to frequencies.
    c. percentages that can be reduced to frequencies.
    d. all of the above.
    e. none of the above.

11. Which chi-square technique is most appropriate when the frequency data are obtained for two or more samples with multiple categories of a variable?
    a. Chi-square test for homogeneity of proportions
    b. Chi-square goodness-of-fit test
    c. Chi-square test of independence
    d. a and c
    e. none of the above

12. When $\chi^2 > \chi^2_{cv}$, the decision rule is
    a. reject H_o.
    b. fail to reject H_o.
    c. assume that the population frequencies are the same.
    d. e & c.
    e. b & c.

13. As the number of degrees of freedom increases, the curve of the distribution becomes
    a. increasingly positively skewed.
    b. increasingly negatively skewed.
    c. increasingly more symmetrical.
    d. bimodal.
    e. multimodal.

14. In a test of independence using a 2×3 contingency table, the degrees of freedom are determined mainly by the
    a. frequency of each cell.
    b. number of rows and columns.
    c. size of the sample.
    d. size of the sample and number of rows.
    e. size of the sample and number of columns.

Review Problems

1. A speech-language pathologist (SLP) wants to determine if office workers differ in preference for two types of management leadership styles at a certain speech clinic. She selects a random sample of 84 precertified SLP and asks whether they prefer a supervisor whose management style in interpersonal interactions with subordinates is usually formal (labeled "Formal Leadership Style") or a supervisor whose interpersonal communication is more informal (labeled "Informal

Leadership Style"). She obtains the results in Table 14–10. Using a 0.01 level of significance and following the four steps in hypothesis testing, what will she conclude?

2. A researcher wants to determine if newly licensed speech therapists differ in their preference for three types of therapy, labeled: Type A, Type B, and Type C. She selects a random sample of 81 therapists from the target population and obtains the results in Table 14–11. Using $\alpha = 0.01$ as her level of significance and following the four steps in hypothesis testing, what will she conclude?

3. A behavioral scientist is interested in determining whether male and female high school speech teachers differ in their attitudes toward compliance gaining strategies (tactics used to get others to do what you want them to do). He selects separate samples of 120 female teachers and 105 male teachers and asks them to respond to the following statement: "Teenagers are more likely to comply with teachers who use humor to correct antisocial behavior in the classroom." A Likert-type response scale was used for recording responses; the scale consisted of the following choices: "Strongly Agree," "Agree," "Neutral,"

"Disagree," "Strongly Disagree." Table 14–12 shows the results.

4. The statistical question confronting the researcher is whether the proportions in the different response categories are the same for male and female populations. Using $\alpha = 0.01$ as her level of significance and following the four steps in hypothesis testing, what will she conclude?

Table 14–10. The Results of the Hypothetical Study Concerning Preference for Two Types of Management Leadership Styles

Type of Leadership	f
Formal leadership style	50
Informal leadership style	34
	Total 84

Table 14–11. The Results of the Hypothetical Study Concerning Newly Licensed Counseling Therapists' Preference for Three Different Types of Therapy

Type of Therapy	f
Type A	22
Type B	47
Type C	12
	Total 81

Table 14–12. The Results of the Hypothetical Study Concerning the Gender Difference in Their Attitudes Toward Compliance Gaining Strategies

| Gender | Responses | | | | |
	Strongly Agree	Agree	Neutral	Disagree	Strongly Disagree
Female	9	11	13	50	37
Male	33	45	10	9	8

15

Not the Most Widely Used Methods but Important to Know for Determining "Practical and Personal Significance"

Factor Analysis

A major goal of scientific research is to organize data in such a way that existing relationships among variables can be more readily comprehended. An important statistical method for accomplishing this goal is termed *factor analysis*. Some of the earliest work on factor analysis was carried out by Thurstone (1947), who believed it to be a powerful tool for exploring "vectors of the mind." Its primary aim is to reduce or condense a large number of observations (e.g., test items in a questionnaire) into a small number of key indicators (commonality) of underlying constructs (factors). Over the years, factor analysis has found many theoretical and practical applications. It is especially useful in the development of clinical tests and rating scales for determining especially personal significance by summarizing the relationships among variables in a concise way.

Suppose we are interested in uncovering some of the principal dimensions of intelligence in children. Assume further that we do not know what these dimensions are and therefore decide to collect several types of measures on a large number of subjects. We select our measures given the presumption that some of them ought to be related to intelligence, but we are uncertain how or to what extent this is true. After administering, a large array of tests is shown in Table 15–1.

The second step is to determine the appropriateness of the sample size for factor analysis. Two of the most common tests are Bartlett's test of sphericity and the Kaiser-Meyer-Olkin measure of sampling adequacy (KMO). These methods can be found from several widely used statistical software packages like MINITAB, SPSS, SAS, and so on. Without

Table 15–1. Factor Analysis Study of Intelligence Based on Thirteen Items

1. Arithmetic	**6. Information**	**11. Similarities**
2. Block Design	**7. Mazes**	**12. Symbol Search**
3. Coding	**8. Object Assembly**	**13. Vocabulary**
4. Comprehension	**9. Picture Arrangement**	
5. Digit Span	**10. Picture Completion**	

Source: From *Research and Statistical Methods in Communication Sciences and Disorders* (p. 358), by D. L. Maxwell and E. Satake, 2006, Clifton Park, NY: Thomson Delmar Learning.

going into the details of how each method is calculated to derive sampling adequacy (mathematical derivations of these methods are extremely complex), some general rules can be used. The closer the KMO measure is to 1, the better. The KMO is based on squared partial correlations. Therefore, a KMO of 1 would represent perfect correlation, whereas a KMO of 0 would indicate no correlation. Some users look for values greater than 0.50 for each variable, as well as for the set of variables, but Kaiser suggests a more conservative criterion, that the KMO should be at least 0.60 if one is to continue to the next step of extracting dimensions. Bartlett's test of sphericity generates a chi-square statistic and tests the null hypothesis that the correlation matrix is made up of diagonal elements equal to 1 and off-diagonal elements equal to 0. The clinical investigator wishes to reject this null hypothesis in hopes of being able to proceed to the next step, extracting dimensions. If the chi-square is high and its p-value is low (e.g., $p < 0.05$), it is likely safe to proceed to the next step. In other words, low scores from a KMO test or a nonsignificant Bartlett's F statistics (test of sphericity is measured by an F-test statistic) indicate that the variables probably are independent of one another, or at least not dependent enough

to be interesting from the point of views of factor analysis (Hodgetts, Hagler, & Thompson 2006).

Hypothetical outputs from the statistical software package are shown in Table 15–2.

Sample Output from Bartlett's Test of Sphericity and KMO

Next, we calculate correlations (or more specifically, intercorrelation matrix) among each and every one of the test items. The results of our hypothetical study are shown later.

Third, we need to identify the dimensions by looking for the strength of intercorrelation relationships among variables, and rank ordering dimensions that account for the greatest variance (R^2). The clinical investigator must decide which dimensions to retain (or which dimensions to drop) to successfully condense a large number of items into a smaller one. This step is very crucial in the process and very controversial because of many different views. Generally speaking, the key index number to identify the dominant factor is termed as *eigenvalue* (it measures the strength of intercorrelations among the variables). Also, the eigenvalues that are normally calculated for each dimension (component) are an index of the variances in the data set, specifically the amount of variance explained by that particular dimension. We normally use the criteria *eigenvalue >1* to retain the factor. In other words, we need to find out how the measure tends to cluster based on their intercorrelations. This can be done by constructing a matrix that displays the correlation between each possible variable, or, more conveniently, by a use of a software package. Some measures will be strongly correlated with each other but not with other measures. Measures that are found to be correlated are called *factors*. The fourth step is to determine the factor loadings for the various measures. Generally, this is done by determining the degree to which the measure correlates with a certain factor. As a general and most widely used method, we use the criteria *the absolute value of r >0.6 for clustering* (Table 15–3).

As it can be seen in Table 15–3, we retained four factors whose eigenvalue is greater than a 1 and drop the rest of

Table 15–2. Sample Output from Bartlett's Test of Sphericity and KMO

KMO		0.783
Bartlett's Test of Sphericity	Chi-Square *p*-value	$p < 0.01$

Table 15–3. Hypothetical Outputs from Bartlett's Test of Sphericity and KMO

Component (test items)	Eigenvalue	% of Variance	Cumulative % of Variances
1. Arithmetic	7.25	41.56	41.56
2. Block Design	2.33	16.44	58.00
3. Coding	2.05	13.50	71.50
4. Comprehension	1.55	10.50	82.00
5. Digit Span	0.89		
6. Information	0.77		
7. Mazes	0.58		
8. Object Assembly	0.52		
9. Picture Arrangement	0.44		
10. Picture Completion	0.33		
11. Similarities	0.22		
12. Symbol Search	0.17		
13. Vocabulary	0.09		

the factors that failed to meet the criteria. This illustration was intended to make this hypothetical example as least complex as possible, of course. If we look back at our 13 components measure, we see that dimension (component) 1 accounts for approximately 41.56% of the total variances, dimension 2 accounts for 16.44%, followed by dimensions 3 and 4 accounts for 13.50% and 10.50%, respectively. So, 82% of the total variances of the test were accounted for by knowing such four factors shown in Table 15–4.

The fifth step in factor analysis is to label the factors based on the theoretical understanding of their nature, as shown in Table 15–4.

The results of the factor analysis shows that there are four factors labeled as (1) Verbal comprehension (see all related test items that can be found in Table 15–4), (2) Perceptual Organization, (3) Freedom from Distractibility, and (4) Processing Speed. Of course, the knowledgeable readers will recognize that the factors named and their associated test measures constitute a well-known intelligence test called the Wechsler Intelligence Scale for Children-Third Edition (WISC-III; Wechsler, 1991).

Although the author has illustrated the use of factor analysis based on 13 components of the test instrument, it is more common for dozens or even hundreds of measures to be included at the

Table 15–4. Four Named Factors of an Intelligence Test and the Subtests of Each Factor

Factor 1	Verbal Comprehension	*Comprehension*
		Information
		Similarities
		Vocabulary
Factor 2	Perceptual Organization	*Block Design*
		Mazes
		Object Assembly
		Picture Arrangement
		Picture Completion
Factor 3	Freedom from Distractibility	*Arithmetic*
		Digit Span
Factor 4	Processing Speed	*Coding*
		Symbol Search

Adapted from Wechsler Intelligence Scale for Children by D. Wechsler, 1991, 3rd ed. (p. 39), San Antonio, TX: Harcourt, Brace, Jovanovich.

Source: From *Research and Statistical Methods in Communication Sciences and Disorders* (p. 359), by D. L. Maxwell and E. Satake, 2006, Clifton Park, NY: Thomson Delmar Learning.

outset of factor analysis studies. Over the years, factor analysis has led to the refinement of the theoretical foundations of the WISC as it has gone through several revisions. A major strength of factor analysis is that it advances conceptualization of the quality being studies. That leads to measuring clinical, practical, and personal significance in a more accurate way, as well as statistical significance. At this time of my writing, factor analysis may be used or considered as one of the alternative methods, the author can see the great potential of the practical use of the method in communication disorders, especially for improvement and/or development of a new screening test and diagnoses for a particular disorder; most importantly, the outcomes derived from factor analysis can answer the question pertaining to practical significance, such as, "What outcome measures should we use to show that my intervention was successful?," "Is there a more effective intervention for this particular client?," or "Can you prove that your intervention has made a difference in that client's speech?"

Discriminant Analysis

A statistical procedure whose purpose is somewhat similar to MANOVA is called discriminant analysis. The name of the test is appropriate because it is often employed to identify which dependent variables in a set of such variables are most responsible for discriminating among groups. Thus, whereas both MANOVA and discriminant analysis are concerned with identifying which variables contribute to group separation, only the latter evaluates the magnitude of the contribution of each variable toward this end. Discriminant analysis can be useful in identifying factors that distinguish among subtypes of communication disorders such as stuttering—for instance, Van Riper's (1982) four developmental tracks that he distinguished on the basis of different communications of factors including age of stuttering onset, manner of onset, symptoms, and general speech skills. Whereas Van Riper's approach to subtyping developmental stuttering was largely based on the methods of clinical observation and description, discriminant analysis has obvious applications to a problem of this kind. Additionally, the clinical application of the method goes beyond identification of most influential factors. Recently, Kramer, Mallet, Schneider, and Hayward (2009) used the discriminant analysis for determining the diagnostic accuracy to calculate specificity and sensitivity of a screening test between two groups. For further details, readers should read the article, entitled "Dynamic Assessment of Narratives with Grade 3 Children in a First Nations Community" (*Canadian Journal of Speech-Language Pathology and Audiology, 33*(3), Fall 2008).

Although mathematically complex, the method essentially involves identifying which variables or combination of the variables are most powerful in discriminating among groups. In addition to its primary use in studies concerned with describing or identifying factors that discriminate groups, the method also has utility in predicting group membership (like logistic regression) of an individual. For example, based on a prior knowledge of certain factors in a client's history, we might calculate the probability that the client belongs to a particular category or subtype of disorder within the population of subjects who stutter. The accuracy of discriminant analysis is based on the percentage of cases that are classified correctly. Some of the basic assumptions of the discriminant analysis are that: (1) there are two or more groups; (2) there are at least two cases per group; and (3) discriminating variables have nominal characteristics for dependent variables and continuous characteristics for independent variables. A clinical researcher with moderately strong background in statistics and mathematics, she or he can make considerable use of the discriminant analysis routines in the standard computer programs (e.g., SPSS, SAT, BMD, etc.) for a more complex data set. The reader who wishes to learn more about any of the features of discriminant analysis can pursue them in texts such as *Discriminant Analysis* by W. R. Klecka (a Sage University Paper, No. 19, 1980).

Cluster Analysis: A Conceptual Basis

To this point, we have been primarily concerned with the statistical relationships that exist among variables. The objects upon which the variables were measured were assumed to be homogeneous by nature, which means, there was no reason to believe, or interest in the possibility, that a given set of objects could be divided into subsets, which displayed reliable nonrandom differences. There are indeed many situations, however, in which our main interest is in dividing a set of objects into subgroups, which differ in meaningful ways.

Cluster analysis, also known by the names of segmentation analysis and taxonomy analysis, is a set of techniques for accomplishing the task of partitioning a set of objects into relatively homogeneous subsets based on the interobject similarities. We can also view cluster analysis as encompassing the clustering of variables, as in the case of factor analysis, although it is usually thought of as being concerned with the clustering of objects.

The clinical applications of cluster analysis are many. For instance, a clinical investigator might be interested in clustering subjects based on their similarities with respect to the severity level of a particular fluency disorder, self-images, or attitudes.

The overall cluster analysis procedure is as follows. We typically begin by measuring each of a set of n objects on each of k variables. Next, a measure of the *similarity*—or the distance or difference —between each pair of objects must be obtained. Then some mathematical algorithm or set of rules must be employed to cluster the objects into subgroups based on the interobject similarities. The main goal is to arrive at clusters of objects that display small within-cluster variation, but large between-cluster variation. The difference between the resultant clusters can then be understood by comparing them with respect to their mean values on the input variables or other characteristics of interest.

The ultimate benefit of forming and describing the clusters will be contingent upon the purpose of the particular analysis. For example, patients clustered on the basis of their complaints can provide insights into the causes of the symptoms as well as for alternative therapies. At the very least, a cluster analysis will serve the heuristic function of generating hypotheses for further research. In a way, cluster analysis is an inductive-natured statistical method.

While superficially similar, it is important to understand the distinction between cluster analysis and discriminant analysis. Whereas in discriminant analysis, we begin with a priori well-defined groups in an attempt to identify the variables that distinguish the groups, in cluster analysis we begin with an undifferentiated group and attempt to form subgroups, which differ on selected variables. That means, in discriminant analysis, we essentially ask how the given groups differ. In cluster analysis, we ask whether a given group can be partitioned into subgroups, which differ.

Given the overall cluster analysis procedure, it will be recognized that the two key problems involve: (1) obtaining a measure of interobject similarity, and (2) specifying a procedure for forming the clusters based on the similarity measures. Understanding the rationale behind the mathematical formulas for cluster analysis requires a good working knowledge of some advanced mathematics and statistics; therefore, the readers should consult with the computer software packages such as SPSS, SAS, BMDP, and the like for data analysis.

Key Terms and Concepts

Factor analysis

Descriminant analysis

Cluster analysis

Review Problems of Chapter 15

1. What are the main purposes and clinical applications of factor analysis, discriminant analysis, and cluster analysis?

2. Find several articles from any one of the ASHA journals that used factor analysis, discriminant analysis, or cluster analysis for data analyses and discuss how such methods were used in answering research questions.

16

Useful Research Designs for Clinical Studies: Fundamental Concepts, Foundations, and Procedures

Introduction to the Types of Research

In a concise review of the history of the profession, Duchan (2002) noted that while some of the early treatments of communication disorders might be viewed as quackery by current standards, "the pioneers, several of whom were the founding group of ASHA, set out to design diagnostic tools, concepts, and normative data for creating a more scientific base for research and practice in the field" (p. 29). An extensive list of references pertaining to the history of speech-language pathology and audiology is available on ASHA's website (http://www.asha.org). This literature makes clear that the knowledge base that underlies the daily work of clinicians has accumulated through systematic investigations, that is, the research process. Such work has entailed the con-

tributions of professionals from diverse disciplines including medicine, psychology, education, and the social sciences, among others.

Regardless of the field of scientific inquiry, the purpose of research is to discover new knowledge by asking questions that can be answered through valid and reliable research methods. In the discussion to follow, you will be introduced to some of the terminology used by researchers to identify several of these methods along with the conceptual basis for their use. From the outset, it is important to recognize that scientific research is not a unitary approach to problem solving but includes a broad range of activities and methods that contribute toward the development or refinement of knowledge. In the field of communication sciences and disorders, perhaps the most common type of research involves the testing of relations presumed to exist among variables underlying the processes of speech, language, and hearing. Two major paradigms that guide scientific inquiry are quantitative research and qualitative research.

Quantitative Research

The traditional quantitative research paradigm used in communication sciences and disorders involves a systematic and highly disciplined approach to problem solving. *Deductive reasoning* is used initially to generate hypotheses that are then tested under tightly controlled conditions designed by the researcher to minimize bias and maximize the reliability and validity of information. In **quantitative research**, formalized tests and measuring instruments are applied to precisely and objectively specify the characteristics of data in numerical terms. Typically, such data are used to compare a group of individuals having a particular communication disorder (experimental group) with a normal group of individuals (control group). As we have seen in Chapters 9, 10, 11, 12, and 13, comparative measures of averages and variances between such groups are considered by many to be the hallmark of valid research. Such an approach can be described as an extensive research model because it involves the aggregation and subsequent analysis of numerous individual scores as unitary indices of performance such as group mean averages. Statistical tests are then used to draw *inductive inferences* as to the probability for finding similar between-group differences in a comparable population of people tested or evaluated under similar conditions or circumstances.

The ultimate goal of most quantitative research is to prove that the hypothesis under evaluation is either true or false. Suppose that the hypothesis being tested is that children who are delayed in some aspect of language development (experimental group) will perform less well on a verbal memory task than children whose language development is normal (control group). The participants (subjects) employed in this study will be selected so as to be equivalent or closely so in all respects except for their differences in language development—that is, the sample of subjects forming the two groups will come from the same socioeconomic sector of the population, be equally represented with respect to age, gender, health status, and so on. Suppose further that we compute the scores on the verbal memory test and find that the control group achieved a relatively high verbal memory score (say, 95%) whereas the experimental group achieved a lower verbal memory score (say, 87%). Is this a difference that makes a difference in statistical terms? To answer the question as to whether or not our hypothesis is true or false, we must ask whether or not this "sample fact," derived from a small number of observations, approximates a "true fact"—the fact that would be obtained should we repeat this study again and again.

By applying various techniques of statistical inference, we are able to determine in quantitative terms just how confident we can be in generalizing our finding to large groups or populations based on our sample results for individuals believed to represent these populations. Referring to our study of verbal memory, if our results were determined to be statistically reliable, we could expect the experimental group to have a lower mean verbal memory score than the control group almost every time the study is repeated. In the jargon of statistics, a statically reliable result is called a **significant result**. On the other hand, should the results of statistical testing suggest that the findings could have resulted from chance (accidental) factors unknown to the researcher, the results from the study would be judged as unreliable or **nonsignificant**. In passing such statistical judgments, researchers evaluate the odds for making certain types of errors (drawing wrong conclusions).

Although the majority of research studies in communication sciences and disorders and related behavioral sciences have been based on what is sometimes called the extensive research approach of quantitative research, there has been a shift in recent years toward increased use of intensive approaches (single-subject research). Such methods are particularly adaptable to studying changes in one or a few individuals over an extended period of time. Such methods should not be confused with the so-called one-shot case studies. Although the latter studies often serve as a basis for a particular clinical focus, because they lack any control over extraneous variables, they have no value in establishing cause-effect relationships.

Several researchers favor the use of intensive single-subject or small-*N* designs over extensive large-*N* studies for some types of problems. Single-subject studies, sometimes called **applied behavior analysis**, are aimed at the precise analysis, control, or modification of behavior. Often, data description procedures are based on the mere visual inspection of results recorded in graphic form. Furthermore, as opposed to most group designs, single-subject research emphasizes numerous *repeated measurements* of single subjects under controlled conditions.

Although there are many types of single-subject designs, the classic paradigm involves: (1) establishing during a

baseline period of recording an operant level of stable responding for a dependent variable prior to treatment; (2) introducing during a treatment period a single independent variable while recording any response changes in the dependent variable; and (3) removing the independent variable during a withdrawal period while recording any response changes in the dependent variable, as shown in Figure 16–1. Although it is impossible to generalize results to a population based on one subject, single-subject designs may attempt to bolster the external validity of experimental findings by: (1) describing the results from a number of individual subjects with similar characteristics (e.g., age, gender, IQ); (2) controlling sources of variability for each subject; and (3) demonstrating replicated findings with different subjects within the same experiment (Sidman, 1960).

The essential criterion for any study is the reliability of findings as judged by their replication in subsequent experiments. As discussed more fully in Appendix J, single-subject designs typically take the form of a series of baseline–treatment trials on the same subject.

Differences between the baseline and treatment conditions are evaluated *within* each individual subject separately. Intensive designs are particularly applicable to many clinical studies in which generalizations about individual subjects rather than groups of subjects are sought. The "clinical situation" can provide a highly fertile source of research because human problems can be seen and intensively evaluated under controlled conditions apart from the ordinary circumstances and confounding influences of everyday life. For further details, the author recommends that readers read Appendix J.

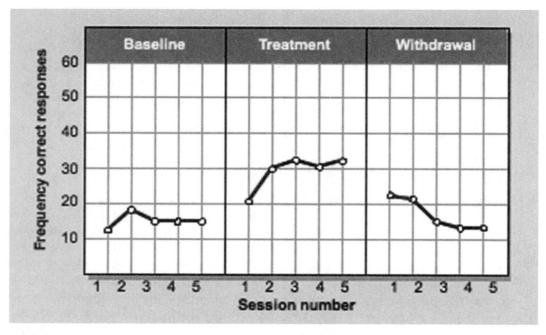

Figure 16–1. Basic paradigm for small-*N* designs. From *Research and Statistical Methods in Communication Sciences and Disorders* (p. 37), by D. L. Maxwell and E. Satake, 2006, Clifton Park, NY: Thomson Delmar Learning.

Qualitative Research

Some researchers hold that qualitative rather than quantitative methods are more appropriate for the study of many social and cultural aspects of human behavior. Such behavior is believed to involve a subject matter that is far more complex, dynamic, and less amenable to quantification than are the phenomena studied by biological and physical scientists. The study of patterns of family interaction in caring for a member with a terminal disease such as amyotrophic lateral sclerosis (ALS), or of the grief and coping mechanisms of parents upon learning that their child was born deaf, or of the attitudes of potential employers toward persons who

stutter—these and problems of a similar kind are not easily reducible to a set of numbers or measures that have meaning.

Qualitative studies involves several types of approaches that emphasize data collection in the "natural setting" such as the home, school, community, and the like. A classic example of naturalistic research is embodied in the early work of Piaget (1932), whose approach to the study of language development consisted primarily of observing and recording children's questions, reflections, and conversations. From such qualitative methods, Piaget published a number of scientific papers concerning various stages of what he termed "egocentric" and "sociocentric" speech development that in turn stimulated much additional research of a similar kind.

Unlike quantitative researchers who define as clearly as possible the concepts, variables, and hypotheses before a study begins, qualitative researchers use a variety of descriptive and interpretative methods that remain more flexible in application and that allow for the discovery of new leads to knowledge as the data emerge. As noted previously, quantitative researchers tend to emphasize relatively rigid research designs to control or eliminate bias and extraneous factors. On the other hand, qualitative researchers are likely to interact more freely with participants while trying to understand and interpret how they construct meaning from the standpoint of their own experiences.

Although the methods employed may differ, all qualitative studies are designed to allow the investigator to "get close to the data." In his seminal research of street corner culture, Liebow (1967) emphasized the importance of the investigator actually entering the experience of the individuals under study in order to adopt their perspective from the "inside." Similarly, Glesne and Peshkin (1992) stated that the main goal of qualitative research is to "understand and interpret how the various participants in a social setting construct the world around them" (p. 6). In this same vein, Kirk and Miller (1986) defined qualitative research as a process of "watching people in their own territory and interacting with them on their own terms" (p. 547).

Depoy and Gitlin (1994) have identified four basic principles of naturalistic inquiry that characterize much of qualitative research: investigator involvement, the interactive process of gathering information and analysis, prolonged engagement in the field, and use of multiple data collection strategies.

- *Investigator involvement* is an integral part of most approaches to qualitative research since the investigator is the major data-gathering tool. Instead of striving to adopt an entirely objective attitude toward the subject under investigation, as do most quantitative researchers, the central premise guiding qualitative research is that the best means of understanding the "lived experiences" of people is to become involved in their life situations or circumstances. To accomplish this goal, the investigator engages in fieldwork —that is, enters the "life field" of the people under study.

- *Gathering and analyzing information* on an ongoing basis is still another principle shared by qualitative researchers. Whereas in quantitative research data collection and analysis occurs during a defined time, qualitative researchers generally collect and evaluate information throughout the entire length of the investigation. Based on an investigator's perceptions, thoughts, and feelings about how one piece of information might link to another, the focus and methods of data gathering, shifting in accordance with "who, what, when, and where," might require further study. Through a dynamic process in which data collection and analysis becomes increasingly refined as new knowledge emerges—becomes "richer," "thicker," "more in-depth," and so forth—so too does the researcher's understanding and interpretation of reality.

- *Prolonged engagement in the field* is required in most qualitative studies. This is necessary to allow the researcher to become sufficiently immersed in the problem under investigation to obtain an in-depth understanding. However, unlike quantitative studies wherein data is typically collected on each participant during a prescribed time period, the length of the data collection period is not predetermined in qualitative studies but can vary widely depending on the researcher's judgment as to whether or not sufficient information has been obtained.

- *Multiple data collection approaches* are employed in qualitative research including observing, listening, and interacting with people in the natural contexts of their lived experiences; asking questions through the use of various interview techniques not only to obtain information from the informants but also to clarify and verify the accuracy of the information; and examining written materials such as records, diaries, charts, and progress notes in a search for reoccurring themes and patterns related to the phenomenon under study. Qualitative data are recorded in a variety of formats including field notes, diaries, photographs,

audiotapes, videotapes, and so on. To facilitate the accuracy and trustworthiness of recording and reporting data, two or more data-gatherers may be used who have been trained for this purpose and who record their observations independently of one another. In addition, to assure the accuracy of information, qualitative researchers sometimes employ the method of triangulation, in which the results of several data collection strategies bearing on the same phenomenon are compared.

Qualitative research is guided by several types of research perspectives or traditions including:

- **Ethnography**—studies that seek to document the customs, social patterns, and rule- governed behavior of a culture or group of individuals. Ethnography grew out of anthropology—the science concerned with the manner in which culture influences and is influenced by how people behave, how they talk to one another, and the things they make.

- **Grounded theory**—studies that focus on the symbolic interactions among people and how they use symbols, such as language, to interpret or "make sense" of their experiences over time. Grounded theory is rooted primarily in the discipline of sociology—the science concerned with generating theories to explain social experiences. Grounded theorists do not begin a study with perceived theories or focused research questions. Instead, concepts and explanations are derived from research findings that emerge gradually in the process of collecting, coding, and analyzing data—the theory that eventually evolves is "grounded" in such data.

- **Phenomenology**—studies that aim to understand how people attribute meaning to events and interactions with others during the course of daily living. As an approach to understanding the experiences of people from their own subjective viewpoint, phenomenology has a long tradition of use in the disciplines of philosophy and psychology. When adopting a phenomenological perspective, the researcher attempts to enter the world of the participants to the greatest extent possible in order to understand their thoughts, attitudes, feelings, and beliefs about various aspects of existence. The researcher gains insight through observations, in-depth interviews, and by participating in and reflecting on the lived experiences of others.

- **Discourse analysis**—studies that are concerned with the analysis of spoken and written text messages used to convey meaning or to perform particular social functions such as asking or answering questions, accusing or complimenting

others, justifying actions, and the like. This approach evolved primarily from the discipline of sociolinguistics. As stated by Coyle (1995), "Discourse analysis sees language not as simply reflecting psychological and social life but as constructing it" (p. 244).

Regardless of their approach, practitioners of qualitative research are likely to eschew the use of preconceived measurements or data analysis techniques that could potentially influence or conceal the natural interaction of research subjects with their environment. When numbers are used, their primary purpose most often is to describe or represent the mere presence or absence of the quality under study rather than quantifying a specific attribute. Categories of behavior are compared, contrasted, and sorted in the search for meaningful patterns and relationships (Shaffir & Stebbins, 1991).

Although an advantage of qualitative methods may be found in their flexibility in studying a wide variety of human problems, the use of nonstandardized procedures can present many difficulties in collecting reliable and valid data. Unless attention is focused carefully on central issues, it is possible that efforts to collect, organize, and interpret data will be rendered meaningless. Another danger of qualitative research is that the interior world of the individuals or groups under study may be distorted by the mere presence of an outside observer or by whatever biases the researcher may impose based on his or her subjective views.

Despite such potential limitations, qualitative approaches of the type described above are frequently used to understand the problems of people and how they perceive these within the context of their own lived experiences. For relevant examples of such applications in the field of communication sciences and disorders, see Chapter 10.

True Experimental Research

A large number of experimental methods are available for use in scientific research that seeks to establish lawful relationships among variables. The use of all such methods goes beyond efforts to observe and describe problems to their prediction and control.

True experimental designs can be distinguished from all others on the basis of three main factors. The first of these involves the random assignment of subjects to at least two or more groups. The second requirement is for some type of active manipulation to be performed. Third, one group of subjects is treated (experimental group), and then compared with another nontreated group (control group). When compared with other research methods, true experimental designs are the most effective in controlling for sources of variance extraneous to the causal relationships under study.

For many practical and ethical reasons, it is sometimes impossible for an investigator to assign subjects randomly to treatment groups or to indiscriminately apply a particular treatment to one group while withholding it from another. This is often the case in clinical studies in which an insufficient number of appropriate subjects may preclude the use of randomization procedures. In addition, it could be argued that withholding a treatment from a target population or admin-istering an alternative treatment with unknown effects rather than one with established benefits is an unethical if not illegal practice.

Quasiexperimental Research

Quasiexperimental research designs are generally selected when true experimentation is impractical or impossible to perform. Typically, subjects are assigned to groups on the basis of preexisting conditions or circumstances. Suppose you work in a hospital clinic where you treat many adult patients for hoarseness accompanied by vocal nodules. Following diagnosis, the availability of therapy is on a "first-come, first-served" basis, so many patients are on a waiting list for three months or more. Although the use of randomization procedures may not be possible, you still wish to draw some conclusions about the efficacy of your treatment program.

An alternative way to estimate your program's effectiveness would be to use a **constructed control group** suitable for comparison with a treated group of patients. The two groups would be matched on a number of variables prior to treatment; these variables would possibly include such factors as degree of hoarseness, size of nodules, duration of illness, occupation, age, gender, or alcohol/tobacco consumption. Such matching would be done to rule out as many extraneous variables as possible, so that any subsequent positive between-group differences could be confidently attributed to your program.

As a means of coping with extraneous variables that might invalidate an experiment, quasiexperimental methods often necessitate the use of more control procedures than do true experiments.

Consequently, they are considered to be less powerful, as stated previously, and are generally recommended only when true experimentation is not possible. Yet, some investigators believe that quasiexperiments can be as effective as true experiments.

Both true experimental and quasiexperimental designs incorporate protocols that are aimed at establishing causal relations among variables. Although it is sometimes impossible in any research study to determine that an experimental manipulation has clearly produced an intended effect, designs of this type offer the greatest promise of producing unambiguous results.

Nonexperimental Research

One type of investigation in which causal relations definitely cannot be established is **nonexperimental research.** In such research, there is no attempt to achieve randomization, nor is any purposeful effort made to manipulate the variables under study. In such studies, many of which involve qualitative approaches of the type described previously, only correlational, as opposed to causal, relations can be evaluated.

Attempting to infer causal relations on the basis of the mere association between factors X, Y, or Z is risky. To illustrate why correlational designs are subject to ambiguity, consider the associative relations often found to exist between attention deficits, low IQ levels, and developmental language delays (Rutter, 1989). It might be argued that any one of these factors could give rise to the others. Alternatively, all three factors could be the common result of still another more generalized delay or abnormality in development.

Efforts to derive causative relations from correlational findings alone can lead to the kind of fallacious reasoning that is represented metaphorically as "putting the cart before the horse." Such reasoning, sometimes described as "vicious circularity," occurs when an answer is based on a question and a question on the answer. For example, one might ask: "Why do slow learners experience academic failure?" Answer: "Because of language-learning disabilities." Question: "But how do we know they are language-learning disabled?" Answer: "Because they exhibit academic failure."

Correlational studies are generally lacking in purposeful experimental manipulations that are external to or independent of the variables under study. For this reason, they are often called ex post facto studies because they search for past causes of a phenomenon that has already occurred. Efforts to derive causal relations in this manner can become hopelessly engulfed in the type of circular reasoning processes described above. As Dember and Jenkins (1970) succinctly noted, "correlational designs are subject to an ambiguity of interpretation considerably greater than the normal uncertainty inherent in any research attempt" (p. 47).

Clinical Research

In evaluating and selecting a particular research design, it is important to bear in mind the purpose of the study. Particularly in the context of the clinical setting, problems are initially encountered in a qualitative form. It is often the case that numerical data are unavailable. Information must be collected from a variety of sources, including written questionnaires, client and family interviews, pre-existing records, formal and informal test procedures, and the like. Ultimately, the clinician must work with whatever historical and current information about individual clients that is available. By examining the possible relations among historical factors and current conditions, an effort is made to form both a tentative hypothesis about the cause(s) of the problem and an appropriate treatment plan.

The research-oriented clinician may collect data on a number of clients with similar problems under controlled conditions of testing or treatment. It is generally the case that such a preliminary or exploratory investigation begins because of the apparent association between two or more variables. For example, the clinician might have noted during his or her work with children that weaknesses in phonological encoding and word retrieval seem to go hand in hand. Subsequently, a formal research study may be performed wherein a strong positive relationship between the two variables is demonstrated based on the strength of their statistical correlation (read Chapters 5 and 6 for further details). The next step may be to sharpen the investigative focus through the use of a true experimental or quasiexperimental design in an effort to determine whether or not the observed relationship is associative or causal in nature. To accomplish this objective, special conditions must be established to determine the extent to which an active manipulation of one factor might cause a significant change in another. Given the hypothesis that phonological encoding skills underlie word retrieval abilities, the clinician might set up a program designed to improve phonological awareness in a randomly assigned experimental group and then evaluate the effects of such training against a ran-

domly assigned control group (true experiment). Alternatively, a comparison group matched on relevant variables might be used instead (quasiexperiment).

In choosing a particular research design, the investigator must weigh the design's relative advantages and disadvantages in view of the questions asked and the answers sought. Some designs are more appropriate at one stage of an investigation than another. Furthermore, the physical limitations imposed by certain experimental settings, the unavailability of suitable subjects and instrumentation or test materials, excessive costs, and the potential for ethical or legal violations are but some of the constraints that may influence the final selection of a specific research plan.

Applied Versus Basic Research

Because the main orientation of the profession of communication sciences and disorders is to help clients solve practical problems, most scientific research focuses on solutions to problems that have immediate application. Such **applied research** is sometimes distinguished from **basic research** (pure research) that might have no presently identifiable application but is done simply to advance knowledge for its own sake. This is not to say that one type of research emphasis, applied versus basic, is better than the other. Indeed, much of the foundation of our clinical knowledge is enlightened and directed by advances in the study of "pure" or "normal" processes of speech, language, and hearing. For example, from the study of normal physiology of the inner ear, invaluable information has been gained leading to applications involving cochlea implantation. Through efforts to understand the molecular genetics of normal hearing, genetically transmitted hearing loss may be preventable in the future. Conversely, an understanding of the genetics of normal hearing may be gained by studying individuals with heritable hearing loss.

In the opinion of the present authors, the applied versus basic research distinction is somewhat irrelevant to the actual work of scientists who, regardless of the problem, engage certain thinking and action processes designed to provide better and more representative solutions to problems. Such work proceeds by what is commonly called the scientific method.

The Scientific Method as a Research Process

As noted in the Introduction Chapter, science involves a systematic way of thinking and behaving to solve problems. Although the term "scientific method" is often used to describe an interconnected series of steps or organized activities that are uniformly followed by scientists in achieving their research goals, such a view can be erroneous or misleading. In reality, the so-called scientific method is better conceived as a **research process** that evolves through several cyclical stages. The process is sometimes depicted in the form of a loop. As shown in Figure 16–2, the major components of this process include:

- Identifying a problem that leads to an idea for a research question or hypothesis
- Developing a research design appropriate for investigating the question or hypothesis
- Collecting data and analyzing results pertinent to the question or hypothesis
- Interpreting the results in a manner that refines understanding and leads to new questions.

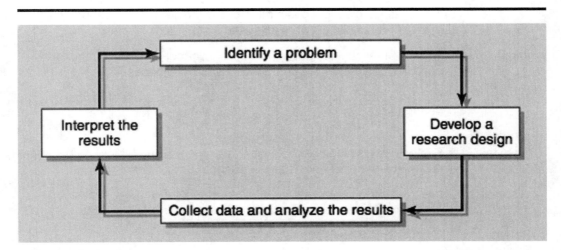

Figure 16–2. Research as a cyclical process. From *Research and Statistical Methods in Communication Sciences and Disorders* (p. 37), by D. L. Maxwell and E. Satake, 2006, Clifton Park, NY: Thomson Delmar Learning.

As we are about to discuss, these components of scientific work are well reflected in the various sections of a scientific article.

Structure and Content of a Research Article

Writing up the results of a research study for publication in a professional journal within one's field is an integral part of scientific work. Why the study was done, how and to whom it was done, as well as the results and implications of the study, must all be made clear. Familiarity with the structure of a research article and the kind of information contained within each section will help the reader assess the degree to which these goals have been achieved. As you gain the ability of scientific literacy and deepen critical thinking about the nature and fundamentals of research in general, you will be able to further sharpen the concepts and skills needed for the critical reading of a research article. Specific criteria for evaluating each component of a research article are covered more thoroughly previously. Meanwhile, we provide a brief overview of the prototypic structure and content of a research article as outlined in Table 16–1.

Abstract

Most research articles begin with an abstract or concise summary of the problem investigated, the methods used, highlights of the results and their statistical significance, and a concluding statement of implications. Key words are sometimes listed at the bottom of the abstract as cues to the specific topics covered. In essence, a good abstract provides a convenient yet accurate means of scanning the substance of

Table 16–1. Structure and Content of a Research Article

Section	Includes
Abstract	Concise summary of the research (approximately 100 to 150 words) that includes a description of the problem, the experimental procedures, highlights of results, and a statement of implications
Introduction	Review of relevant literature, theoretical, foundational, and rationale, purpose statement/research questions or hypotheses
Method	Design of study, subjects, and sampling techniques, controls used, apparatus of test materials, experimental procedures, logical basis for choice of statistics
Results	Systematic discussion of relevant data, figures, and tables, evaluation of data to point out significant/nonsignificant findings
Discussion	Interpretation of the meaning and importance of findings, evaluation of hypotheses and their generality, implications for future studies
References/ Bibliography	Complete citations of the work of others

Source: From *Research and Statistical Methods in Communication Sciences and Disorders* (p. 38), by D. L. Maxwell and E. Satake, 2006, Clifton Park, NY: Thomson Delmar Learning.

the article as a whole. Its main purpose is to provide readers with just enough information to help them decide if they should read the entire article.

Introduction

The introduction section of an article, although usually not labeled as such, includes a historical overview of the theoretical foundations of the problem to be investigated based on the results of previous research. A review of relevant literature is akin to the process of scientific observation that, as noted previously, involves collecting, organizing, and interpreting available background information (data) related to the current problem. Such information is assembled so as to provide the basis for a logical argument or research rationale used to justify the need for additional investigation. Based on a review of pre-existing knowledge and the theoretical propositions of other researchers, the introduction should lead naturally to a statement of the current problem. The researcher might state the problem by denoting the purpose of the research or posing a research question. For example:

> The purpose of this study was to examine the relative frequency of different types of phonological errors (omissions, substitutions, distortions) in the speech of children with verbal apraxia.

or

> What is the relative frequency of different types of phonological errors (omissions, substitutions, distortions) in the speech of children with verbal apraxia?

A third type of problem statement based on theoretical reasoning, prior data, or both is called a research hypothesis. As a means of defining a research problem, the use of a formal hypothesis is typically reserved for predicting associative or causal relations among the variables under study. For example:

> Verbal apraxia in children is associated with (or causative of) a significantly higher frequency of substitutions than other types of phonological errors involving omissions or distortions.

The manner in which the problem is stated in the introduction often provides some hint about the general type of statistical methods used in analyzing the data. Of the problem statements illustrated here, all three imply that measurements will be carried out to quantify the frequency of certain types of phonologic errors. In the case of the first two statements, the frequency measures will at least be totaled, averaged, converted into percentages, or statistically described in other ways. However, it is clear only in the case of the third statement, involving the research hypothesis, that sampling statistics also will be used to infer the *significance of difference* in the frequency of types.

Method

Unfortunately, the method section of a research article is frequently given the least attention by the reader because, as the *structural blueprint* for the investigation, this section often contains many tedious details. Yet, the framework of the entire investigation either stands or falls based on the strength of its methodological foundation.

Most research studies will include important information about how a study was conducted. Such information will pertain to the: (1) design of the study; (2) subjects used and how they were selected; (3) apparatus or test materials employed; (4) procedures for collecting data; and (5) statistical analysis techniques. The researcher must carefully address each of these topics *prior to* conducting a study if it is to be successful. It will be too late to correct methodological errors after the study has been done. Each of these topics is discussed in greater detail below.

Design. It is important for a researcher to provide clear and complete information about how a study was designed. From such information, the reader should learn whether the design used was primarily intended to describe the characteristics and/or associative relations among variables or was the goal to arrive at causal explanations through the use of experimental strategies. Typically, descriptive methods are chosen if an investigator wishes to observe, record, or perhaps measure certain events but has no desire to manipulate the variables of interest. The basic tool of description is systematic observation of the phenomena under investigation. *Observations* of individuals or groups in the clinical or natural setting, *surveys* of attitudes and opinions, *cohort and case-control studies,* and *prevalence and incidence studies* are examples of problems that call for nonexperimental research designs. As we noted previously, descriptive methods are often important in categorizing or classifying variables according to their physical or psychological attributes; this is a preliminary step that leads toward more definitive studies of their causal relations.

When the researcher is primarily interested in explaining the effect of one variable, the independent variable, upon another, the dependent variable, he or she selects either experimental or quasiexperi-

mental techniques. In the field of communication sciences and disorders, such explanatory methods are frequently used to test a hypothesis about a causal relationship. Such methods are commonly employed in the search for explanations for the causes of specific disorders or to evaluate the efficacy of new diagnostic techniques or therapy procedures.

Recall that the defining feature of a true experiment versus a quasiexperiment is that the former requires random assignment of subjects to different treatment conditions, whereas the latter simply involves classifying subjects on the basis of a particular characteristic (e.g., normal hearing versus hearing impairment). Following treatment, the groups are compared on some dependent variable or performance measure. Quasiexperimental designs are weaker than true experiments because of the potential for preexisting subject differences and other extraneous variables to contaminate the results.

Subjects. There are several types of information pertaining to how subjects were chosen that an author should provide. This information should relate to three major factors that must be considered in selecting subjects. First, the subjects should be appropriate given the goals of the study. If an investigator's intention is to study syntactical errors in Broca's aphasics, the inclusion of Wernicke's aphasics, or of other types of aphasic disorders must be avoided. Ultimately, the goal of any research study is to assure the internal validity of the results, or the degree to which they can be directly attributed to the effect of a chosen independent variable as opposed to some unwanted extraneous variable. A confounding effect owing to selection can result if subject characteristics in one group differ from those in a comparison group. The old adage that "apples and oranges can't be compared" summarizes well this particular problem. In the subject section of the methods portion of the research article, the characteristics of all participants, including age, gender, intelligence, type of disorder if present, and any other relevant identifying information should be listed.

A second issue is the degree to which subjects in a study are representative of the population from which they were selected. This concern relates importantly to the establishment of external validity or the degree to which the results can be transferred to the population from which the sample was originally drawn. If a sample of subjects is not highly similar to the parent population from which it was selected, then the results will be of little or no value as they might apply to other cases under comparable conditions or circumstances. Although random selection of a sample of subjects does not assure that the sample will be representative of the population from which it was drawn, it is the best means available for accomplishing this goal (see Appendix G).

A third issue in subject selection pertains to the number of subjects to be used. Decisions as to the number of subjects (denoted as N for the population and n for the sample) to be used in an investigation are complex. From a pragmatic perspective, the investigator will include whatever number of subjects is appropriate and available, given the particular aims of the experiment, keeping in mind that the problem of generality cannot be disposed of simply by employing large numbers of subjects. Nevertheless, it is also the case that, for purposes of detecting significant between-group differences, large samples generally lend greater power to a statistical test than do small samples.

If the sample size is too small, there is a risk of failing to detect the true effect of an independent variable on a dependent variable—the main purpose of the experiment.

Apparatus and Materials. The apparatus used in presenting stimuli and recording responses, test materials, questionnaires, and related measurement tools must also be described. All identifying information including names of manufacturers, model numbers, publishers, calibration procedures for electrical or mechanical equipment, and evidence of the reliability and validity of such instruments should likewise be included.

Procedures. It is necessary that the procedures used in conducting an experiment be precisely delineated. This is important for at least two reasons. First, research procedures reflect the plan for the actual steps to be followed in carrying out the investigation. As far as possible, the following issues should be clarified by describing:

1. The manner in which the independent variable was administered.
2. The way the dependent variable was recorded.
3. The instructions given to subjects.
4. The nature of the test environment.

A second and equally important reason for carefully documenting research procedures is to allow for replication by other investigators. For this to occur, the essential conditions of the original experiment must be reproducible. Unfortunately, in communication disorders and other behavioral fields, replication is not yet given sufficient emphasis as a part of the scientific method as it is in many of the physical sciences. Although replication experiments in several fields, including our own, do not appear to be highly esteemed, the ability to substantiate research findings through experimental replication ought to be an integral goal of all scientific studies irrespective of the nature of the problem. Perhaps greater value will be placed on such research by future investigators and the editors of professional journals as we are increasingly required to justify, through empirical means, the efficacy of our clinical programs.

Statistical Analysis. Often, the types of statistical analyses used and their manner of application are described toward the end of the method section. The type of statistical methods selected will vary according to the purposes they are intended to serve but will essentially consist of one or more types of three major techniques. If the aim of the statistic is only to describe the features of a set of measurable observations, descriptive statistics will be used to *summarize*, *condense*, and *organize* such observations into a more convenient and interpretable form of data. Tables and graphic figures may be used to display the data in a "pictorial" manner. Such descriptive statistics are also used to derive what are called **measures of central tendency** (averages), and the way in which individual scores are dispersed around such averages (**measures of variability**).

A second major type of statistic is based on investigative efforts to describe an apparent association between two or more sets of data. For example, one might wish to know the degree to which academic performance measures in children are related to various aspects of language expression and/or comprehension. Statistical tests of **correlation** may be used to describe the degree of relatedness between these or other sets of data. However, it is impossible to derive causal relationships on the basis of such comparisons alone.

A third type of statistical techniques goes beyond the mere description of variables or their association, to making **statistical inferences** about the degree to which a particular sample of subjects is representative of the population from which it was drawn. In clinical science fields, such as communication sciences and disorders, sampling or inferential statistics are commonly used to study specific disorders or diseases in a specified number of individuals. Subsequently, by means of inductive reasoning, inferences about the general nature of such conditions in the population at large may be drawn. Typically, we do not investigate specific groups of aphasic patients, people who stutter, dysarthric or hearing impaired individuals, or persons with voice disorders for their own sake but to learn more generally about how to explain or modify such problems as found in similar persons from the same population.

Essentially, we want to know the extent to which a "sample fact," derived from a small number of observations, approximates a "true fact"—the fact that would have been obtained had we examined the entire population. By applying the techniques of statistical inference, we are able to determine how confident we can be in generalizing our findings to large groups or populations based on sample results for individuals believed to represent these populations. Such confidence is based on the tolerance for making certain kinds of sampling errors owing to chance factors beyond the investigator's control.

In addition to the need for determining, prior to initiating a study, what type of statistical procedures can best be used, the **risk tolerance** for sampling errors should likewise be decided beforehand if the results are to be fairly evaluated. Such risk is conventionally preset at either a 1% (0.01) or 5% (0.05) chance of error (see Chapter 12). In the first case, the researcher can be at least 99% confident that no error has been made in interpreting the results. In the second case, the researcher can be at least 95% confident in his or her conclusions. Unfortunately, too many researchers are negligent in deciding such matters in advance of conducting a study. In our opinion, this practice is like waiting for the last bounce of the ball at the roulette wheel before finally placing your bets.

Perhaps the best way to conceive of statistics is as an implicit logical reasoning system made explicit in quantitative terms. Statistical probabilities are not to be confused with *certainties* in the sense that a consequent event will always follow a given antecedent cause or condition. More accurately, the "laws of statistics" can be better conceived in terms of the "likelihood" of a particular event occurring a certain percentage of time under highly defined conditions and within specified **confidence limits** (see Chapter 12). Furthermore, although a clinician may be able to predict with 95% confidence that some hypothetical number of cases similar to one's own will improve in response to treatment X under certain conditions, which particular cases might do so cannot be determined. Because statistical methods do not lead to invariant answers, they are best viewed as general guides rather than precise maps in the search for new knowledge and understanding.

Results

The main goal of the results section of a research article is to provide a straightforward presentation of the relevant data. Some research publications include not only a detailed explanation of the empirical data within this section but also a discussion of their theoretical implications. However, it is common practice within the results section to present and explain the data only in relation to the research hypotheses. *Interpretation* of findings should be avoided. The latter task is reserved for the discussion section of the research article.

Within the results section, a systemic presentation of the data should be included beginning with a precise summary of the evidence and then proceeding to a point-by-point report of each statistical analysis. Figures or graphs may be used to illustrate relevant research findings in pictorial form. Tables provide a convenient format for condensing data according to such average measures as the mean and measures of variability (the dispersion of scores around the mean) such as the standard deviation. Based on the comparison of such composite measures, which reflects differences in sets of scores *between* or *within* groups of subjects, statistical formulae can be used to calculate the significance of the results expressed as a probability value or p (see Chapter 12). For example, the notation $p < 0.05$ would be interpreted to mean that one could expect his or her hypothesis to be true at least 95% of the time with less than a 5% chance of error (i.e., one chance in 20 of drawing an incorrect conclusion).

As noted previously, a combination of descriptive and inferential methods, rather than a single statistical technique, is usually employed in the area of communication sciences and disorders. Although descriptive statistics permits observed variables to be specified in mathematical terms, it is only through the use of inferential statistics that generalizations are made from a selected sample of subjects to a larger population.

Discussion

After objectively presenting and explaining the results of a study in relation to the hypotheses under test, the next step is to interpret this factual information in terms of the overall issues that served as the original impetus for the investigation. In essence, the task requires looking for meaningful patterns in the data to see how they might fit within the larger framework of knowledge (i.e., pre-existing theories, conceptual models, and other research findings as reviewed in the introduction).

Whereas the form of scientific reasoning leading up to the results of an experiment was largely deductive in nature, the researcher is now required to inductively draw inferences *back* to the real world based on the specific data obtained. In more specific statistical terms, the degree to which the sample data can be generalized to the population from which it was drawn is carefully evaluated. This requires a rigorous analysis of the strengths and weaknesses of the current research design with respect to such matters as the effectiveness of the sampling procedures and the adequacy of experimental controls in dealing with the unwanted effects of extraneous variables.

In a figurative sense, the discussion section of a research article requires using data not only to look backward at "things as they have been" in the past but also forward as to how "things might be" in the future. Practical recommendations for improving various aspects of the methodology may be offered. Even new hypotheses may be advanced along with suggestions about the types of experiments needed for their testing. Thus, the discussion section of a study provides a mechanism for engaging scientific reasoning processes in ways that foster continuity of knowledge and new understanding.

References

All citations of previous studies must be listed in a reference list at the end of the research article. The references used need not be exhaustive but should reflect the work of previous investigations that are clearly related to the problem under investigation. The specific manner in which references should be cited within text and in the reference list must be carefully and thoroughly evaluated.

Ethics of Research

We end this chapter by briefly mentioning the importance of ethical practice in research (see Chapter 3 for a fuller discussion of ethical guidelines for protecting human subjects). In the field of communication science and disorders, researchers and clinicians might believe that questions pertaining to the ethics of research hold less importance than for professionals in other fields, such as medicine, where violating the rights of human subjects has been vividly documented. Consider, for example, the atrocious practices of Nazi Germany that used Jews, gypsies, the mentally ill, and other segregated minorities as laboratory specimens to study endurance and reaction to various diseases and untested drugs (Polit et al., 2001). More recently, in the United States, we are aware of similar violations that are equally horrifying. Beginning in the early 1930s and continuing until 1972, a study sanctioned by the U.S. Public Health Service examined the influence of syphilis on men from a black community that comprised a control group (treatment was intentionally withheld).

Although the vast majority of studies undertaken in the communication sciences and disorders do not place participants at physical risk, researchers nonetheless are often confronted with important ethical questions such as:

- When a treatment is suspected but not yet proven to have value, is it ethical to assign participants to a control group, thereby denying them a potentially beneficial exposure?
- What are the ethical implications of withholding treatment information from participants (keeping them unaware as to what group they have been assigned, i.e., experimental group, placebo group, or control group)?
- Is it appropriate to publish information obtained from participants when aspects of their physical or mental state have been compromised by a disorder or disease despite having obtained permission from them or their families to do so?
- Are personal questions designed to uncover people's fears, failures, weaknesses, and so on, scientifically justifiable when it is not possible to provide therapeutic assistance?

These are but a few of the ethical dilemmas that researchers frequently encounter. To the greatest extent possible, participants in research should be protected from harm. Generally, codes of ethics have been adopted and public laws enacted to provide such protection.

Key Terms and Concepts

Quantitative research

True experimental research designs

Significant results

Quasiexperimental research designs

Nonsignificant results

Constructed control group

Applied behavior analysis

Nonexperimental research

Baseline period

Applied research

Qualitative research

Basic research

Ethnography research process

Grounded theory

Risk tolerance

Phenomenology

Discourse analysis

Review Problems of Chapter 16

1. Why is quantitative group research called the extensive research model?

2. What is ethnographic research? Give two clinically relevant examples.

3. What kind of data-recording techniques are used in qualitative research?

4. When are quasiexperimental designs selected as alternatives to true experiments?

5. Provide an example of a clinical research question and identify the antecedent treatment conditions and consequent effects to be assessed.

6. Distinguish between applied and basic research. Is one type of research of greater value than the other? Justify your answer.

7. Describe the scientific method and evaluate its clinical utility.

8. Why is the method section of a research article best viewed as the "structural blue print" for the investigation? Identify and briefly describe the four major factors to consider within the method section.

9. Distinguish between the concepts of internal validity and external validity. What is meant by a "confounding effect"?

10. Describe the importance of experimental replication. What is the essential requirement for this to occur?

11. Distinguish between descriptive statistics and inferential statistics.

12. If you were to conduct a clinical research pertaining to a clinical diagnosis based on the results derived from a screening test, what do you think the most important (or essential) components in drawing a more accurate result?

13. In your own words, distinguish "Statistical Significance" and "Clinical Significance" by providing two clinically relevant examples.

14. What kind of research designs do you think best fit to EBP?

APPENDIX A

Review of Basic Mathematics

Although the study of statistics can involve the use of advanced mathematical concepts and procedures, this text requires only the most basic of mathematical skills. In this appendix, we review some of the arithmetic operations and elementary algebra concepts and procedures that you undoubtedly were introduced to in the past but may have forgotten.

Basic Arithmetic Terms

Before considering the basic operations in arithmetic and the order in which they are performed, let us review some basic mathematical terms and concepts that are used in the study of statistics.

1. **Real Numbers.** All positive and negative numbers from negative to positive infinity $(-\infty, +\infty)$, including decimals and fractions are known as *real numbers*.

2. **Signed numbers.** The sign before a number indicates its direction from zero (0) along the number line, which extends to infinity in either direction. We refer to these numbers as *signed numbers*. Any number written without a sign is always considered positive. A negative number must be preceded by a negative sign.

3. **Absolute values.** The value of a real number, without regard to its algebraic sign, is known as its *absolute value* and expressed symbolically with vertical lines. For example, the absolute value of 6 or −8 are given as $|6|$ and $|8|$.

4. **Numerical variables.** Letters of the alphabet, such as X and Y, often are used to represent *numerical variables*. For example, the letter X may be used to represent the value 342 or the set of values 5, 7, 4, and 6. The numeric data or values for these variables may be scores derived from various measures, such as questionnaires, tests, surveys, and scales.

5. **Exponents.** A number above a value represents the number of repeated multiplications performed on that number. The operation is also referred to as "raising" a number to a particular "power." For example, the expression, 2^3, means $2 \times 2 \times 2 = 8$ and may be referred to as "raising two to the third power." The superscript "3" in the

expression is called the *exponent* and the value "2" is known as the *base*. When an exponent is outside parentheses, perform the operations within the parentheses first, then remove the parentheses and complete the operation, as in $(2 \times 3)^2 = 6^2 = 36$.

6. **Evaluate.** To evaluate an expression means to find the value of an expression by replacing the letters with numbers and simplifying. For example, given the following expression: $a + 5b$, where $a = 4$ and $b = -3$, we evaluate as follows:

   a. $a + 5b$
   b. $= 4 + 5(-3)$
   c. $= 4 + (-15)$
   d. $= -11$

Similarly, for the expression: $\overline{X} = \frac{X}{n}$, where $X = 12$ and $n = 4$, we evaluate as follows:

$$\overline{X} = \frac{X}{n}$$
$$= \frac{12}{4}$$
$$= 3$$

7. **Terms.** The parts in an algebraic expression that are added or subtracted are called *terms*. For example, in the expression $5x - 2y - 4$, $5x$, $-2y$, and -4 are *terms*. The plus (+) and minus (−) signs that delineate the terms are a part of the term. (When listing the terms of expression, it is not necessary to include the plus, +, sign before a positive term.)

8. **Coefficient.** The numerical part of a term is called its *coefficient*.

9. **Equation.** An *equation* is a statement expressing the equality of two mathematical expressions, which can be either a numerical expression, as in $6 + 8 = 14$, or a variable expression, as in $5x + 6 = x - 8$, or a symbolic expression, as in $\overline{X} = \frac{\Sigma X}{n}$.

10. **Ratio.** A *ratio* is a comparison between two numbers. It shows a relationship between the two numbers through division and may be expressed in one of two ways: fractionally, as in $\frac{2}{3}$, or with a colon, as in 2:3. Both are read "2 to 3."

Basic Arithmetic Operations

The four basic arithmetic operations are addition, subtraction, multiplication, and division, denoted by the algebraic signs $+$, $-$, $*$, and $/$. Each of the four operations may be performed with numbers and/or letters representing numerical variables. The algebraic sign before a number or letter affects the result of the arithmetic operations.

Addition

The addition of two or more numbers is written with the plus sign (+) separating each numeric value, as in $3 + 5 + 4 + 2 = 14$, or between two or more letters representing numerical values. For example, if $X = 10$ and $Y = 7$, then $X + Y = 17$. The result of an addition operation is known as the **sum**. There are two rules for the addition of signed numbers.

a. One of the addition rules states that the sum of two positive numbers will always be positive, and the sum of two negative numbers will always be negative. When adding two or more numbers with the same sign (positive or negative), add their absolute values and retain their common sign in the sum.

Example: $24 + 15 = (24 + 15) = 39$

Example: $-18 + (-8) =$
$-(18 + 8)| = -26$

b. On the other hand, the sum of two signed numbers with different or opposite signs may be either positive or negative. The sign of the sum will be the same as the sign of the number with the larger value. When adding two numbers of unlike or opposite signs, the addition rule requires that we subtract the value of the smaller number from the value of the larger number and attach the sign of the number with the larger absolute value to the sum.

Example: $9 + (-4) = (9 - 4) = 5$

Example: $6 + (-10) =$
$-(10 - 6) = -4$

Subtraction

Subtraction is the opposite of addition. It is the process of withdrawing or taking away. The subtraction of two or more numbers is written with the minus sign (−) separating each numeric value, as in $5 - 2 = 3$ or $10 - 4 - 2 = 4$ or between one or more letters representing numerical values, as in $7 - X = 4$ or $X - Y = 18$ given $X = 28$ and $Y = 10$. The result of a subtraction operation is known as the *remainder* or *difference*.

There is only one rule for subtracting signed numbers. The rule is as follows: when subtracting signed numbers, first change the sign of the second number (or bottom number) and then apply the rules for addition.

Example: $12 - 4 = 12 + (-4) = 8$

Example: $8 - 19 = 8 + (-19) = -11$

Example: $16 - (-9) = 16 + 9 = 25$

Example: $-12 - (-5) = -12 + 5 = -7$

Multiplication

The operation of multiplication is basically the repeated addition of the same number. The numbers that are multiplied are called *factors*, and the result is called the *product*. Multiplication in an equation may be expressed in one of four ways: (1) with a raised dot between two or more numbers, as in $6 \cdot 5 = 30$, or between two letters, $\chi \cdot y = n$; (2) by enclosed numbers or letters within parentheses, as in $(7)(7) = 49$, or $6(8) = 48$, or $(9)(x) = 36$; (3) by a number and a letter or two or more letters, without the use of a multiplication sign, as in $3x$ or ab; and (4) by the symbol ×, as in $3 \times 4 = 12$.

There are two rules for multiplication of signed numbers.

a. The first rules states that the product of two numbers with like signs (positive × positive or negative × negative) is a positive number.

Example: $3 \times 4 = 12$

Example: $-8 \times (-4) = 32$

b. The second rule states that the product of two numbers with unlike signs is a negative number.

Example: $6 \times (-11) = -66$

Example: $-7 \times 5 = -35$

Division

Division is the inverse of multiplication. Its purpose is to separate objects or values into two equal groups. The process involves finding out how many times one number is contained in another number. The result of division is called the *quotient*. The division of two numbers can be expressed in four different ways: $\frac{15}{5}$ (where 15 is called the *numerator* and 5 the *denominator*); 15/5 (where 15 is called the *numerator* and 5 the *denominator*); $4\overline{)28}^{\,7}$ (where 28 is known as the *dividend* and 4 as the *divisor*); or as $6 \div 2$.

The rules for division of signed numbers are the same general rules used for multiplication.

a. The first rule states that the quotient of two numbers with like signs (positive positive or negative negative) is a positive number.

Example: $30 \div 5 = 6$

Example: $-20 \div (-4) = 5$

b. The second rule states that the quotient of two numbers with unlike signs (positive negative or negative positive) is a negative number.

Example: $-48 \div (+6) = -8$

Example: $27 \div (-9) = -3$.

Summary of Basic Operations

1. The sum of two positive numbers will be a positive number.
2. The sum of two negative numbers will be a negative number.
3. The sum of a positive number and a negative number will be either a positive or negative number, depending on the sign of the larger value.
4. The product (or quotient) of two positive numbers will be a positive number.
5. The product (or quotient) of two negative numbers will be a positive number.
6. The product (or quotient) of a positive number and a negative number will be a negative number.

Order of Operations

The order in which arithmetic operations are performed may affect the answer of a numerical expression. Therefore, it is important the correct order be followed. The four steps and the order in which they are to be performed are as follows:

Step 1. Perform all operations within parentheses. If the parentheses are within brackets, [ ], perform the operations from inside out.

Step 2. Simplify any numeric expressions containing exponents, that is, squaring or raising numbers to the *nth* power or finding the square root of a value.

Step 3. Perform all multiplications and divisions, from left to right.

Step 4. Perform all additions and subtractions, from left to right.

For example, the expression $4 \cdot (5 + 7) - 3^2 + 4 \div \sqrt{4}|$ is evaluated as follows:

Step 1. Operation within parentheses

$= 4 \cdot 12 - 3^2 + 4 \div \sqrt{4}\,|$

Step 2. Exponential operations

$= 4 \cdot 12 - 9 + 4 \div 2\,|$

Step 3. Multiplication and division

$= 48 - 9 + 2\,|$

Step 4. Addition and multiplication

$= 39 + 2\,|$

$= 41$

Many students use the sentence, "**P**lease **E**xcuse **M**y **D**ear **A**unt **S**ally," to recall the order of operations: **P**arentheses, **E**xponents, **M**ultiplication, **D**ivision, **A**ddition, **S**ubtraction.

Rounding Numbers

The process of giving an approximation of a value for an exact number is referred to as *rounding*, and the process is the same both for whole numbers and decimal values. However, before we examine the operations for rounding both types of expressions, let us review some basic concepts and terms we use when discussing the rounding of numbers. For example, in rounding, we often refer to numbers in an expression as *digits*. For example, we say that the number 87.359 contains five digits. We also say that a number is rounded to a given *place* value, and we speak of rounding a number *n* "places after the decimal." Also, we often make reference to the names of the positions of these "places" before and after the decimal, as in "tenths," "hundredths," "thousandths," "ten thousandths," and so on. Finally, the symbol, ≈, often is used as shorthand for

the phrase, "approximately equal to," as in $243.11 \approx 243$.

a. **Rounding Whole Numbers.** A whole number is rounded to a given place value by locating the first digit to the right of the given place value and applying one of two rules.

   i. Rule 1: If the digit to the right of a given place value (referred to as the deciding number) is equal to or greater than 5, the digit in the given place value is increased by 1 and the deciding number becomes zero. For example, the whole number 67 (six tens and seven ones) rounded to the nearest <u>tenth</u> is written as 70; the number 106 rounded to the nearest <u>hundredth</u> is written as 110; and so on.

   ii. Rule 2: If the digit to the right of a given place value is less than 5, that digit and all other digits to the right are deleted. For example, the whole number 560 rounded to the nearest <u>tenth</u> is written as 56; the number 1934 rounded to the nearest <u>thousandth</u> is written as 1900; and so on.

b. **Rounding Decimal Values.** In dividing two numbers, such as 1/6, the decimal values in the quotient 1.6666 can be extended to infinity. The nonzero values to the right of the decimal point are referred to as *significant digits*. To determine when to end the values after a decimal, we follow the same general rules for rounding whole numbers.

   i. Rule 1: If the digit to the right of a given place value after the decimal is equal to or greater than 5, the digit in the given place of interest is increased by 1, and all of the numbers to its right are deleted. For example, in rounding the number 0.8734 to the <u>tenths</u> place, we note that the number in the hundredths position, 7, is greater than 5. Therefore, we increase the tenths digit 8 by 1 to 9 and drop the 734 in the expression. Thus, 0.8634 is written as 0.9. Similarly, 68.384 is written as 68.4.

ii. The number 0.1692 rounded to the nearest <u>hundredth</u> is written as 0.17, since the digit in the <u>thousandths</u> position, 9, is greater than 5.

iii. Rule 2: If the digit to the right of a given place value after the decimal is less than 5, that digit and all other digits to the right are deleted.

For example, the number 0.52436 rounded to the nearest <u>thousandth</u> is written as 0.524, since the <u>ten thousandth</u> digit to the right, 3, is less than 5. Similarly, the number 213.0547 is written as 213.055.

Most of the answers or solutions to problems in this text are rounded to the nearest thousandth. Thus, the answer 325.421786 is rounded to 325.422.

c. **Rounding Decimal Values with Zeros.** Sometimes the calculation of a numerical expression results in a decimal value with two or more zeros immediately to the right of the decimal point, as in .002436 or 273.0000968. In such cases, the suggested rule of thumb is to round to two significant digits (nonzero values) after the decimal. Thus, 0.002436 and 273.0000968 would be written as 0.0024 or 273.000097.

Scientific Notation

When a numerical expression exceeds a particular number of digits, some calculators display the result of a calculation as a positive or negative scientific notation. When the notation is positive, as in 4.5E 4, shift the decimal to the right the number of places following the letter "E" and add the appropriate number of zeros. In this case, 4.5E 4 is written as 45000.0. When the notation is negative, as in 4.5E −4, shift the decimal to the left the number of places following the letter "E" and add the appropriate number of zeros. Thus, 4.5E −4 is written as .00045.

APPENDIX B

Some Statistical Applications and Questions (Adapted from the Literature): Several Case Studies

Appendix Outline

In this appendix, I use selected data values from the published articles of well-respected journals such as the *Journal of Speech and Hearing Disorders*, the *Journal of Speech and Hearing Research*, and the other journals in the field of communication sciences and disorders to illustrate the nature of the study including purposes, methods, and results with several statistical methods as discussed in the main body of the text. By doing so,

I hope that readers will become familiar with some statistical techniques commonly used in the field. The exercises are intended to demonstrate the application and relevance of statistics to "real" problems encountered in the clinic or laboratory. Also, I emphasize the importance of EBP statistical methods and interpretations of the test results, as they can be seen in exercises.

Preliminary Case Study (a)

Epidemiology of Speech and Language Impairment in a Nationally Representative Sample of 4- to 5-Year-Old Children

Source: McLead, S., & Harrison, L. J. (2009, October). Epidemiology of speech and language impairment in a nationally representative sample of 4- to 5-year-old children. *Journal of Speech, Language and Hearing Research, 52*(5), 1213–1229.

Purpose

The purpose of this study was to determine the prevalence of speech and language impairments in 4- and 5-year-old children in Australia. This study drew upon multiple sources to ensure that the population was represented accurately.

Method

Data from 4,983 children between the ages of 4 and 5 years were collected through parent interviews, parent questionnaires, teacher questionnaires, and direct assessments from Growing Up in Australia: The Longitudinal Study of Australian Children

(Australian Institute of Family Studies, 2007). This population was weighted to accurately represent the target age group in Australia.

Results

The results compared the information collected from parents and teachers with the findings on the Adopted Peabody Picture Vocabulary Test-III. This information can be used to determine the need for speech-language pathologists among this population. The results are shown in Figure B–1.

Question

What is a target population of this study? Be specific in your answer.

Preliminary Case Study (b)

Random Sampling

Source: Craig, A., Hancock, K., Tran, Y., & Craig, M., (2003). Anxiety levels of people who stutter: A randomized population study. *Journal of Speech Language & Hearing Research, 46,* 1197–1206.

Purpose

This study investigates the question of whether people who stutter are generally more anxious than people who do not stutter. Previous studies investigating anxiety levels and stuttering have mostly assessed people referred to therapy clinics. The authors of this study note that this is arguably a biased sample. In this study, the authors measure the anxiety levels of people who stutter in the community by using random selection procedures.

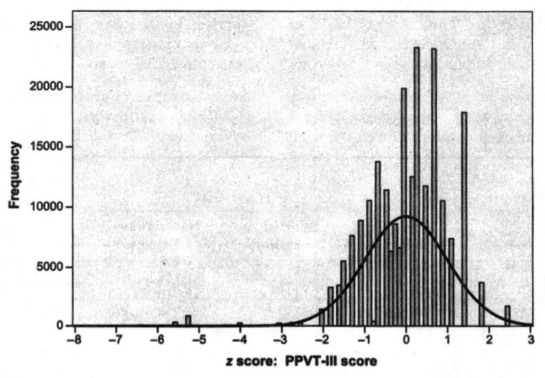

Figure B–1. Weighted population scores for the Adopted Peabody Picture Vocabulary Test-III (PPVT-III). *Source:* McLead, S., and Harrison, L. J. (2009). Epidemiology of speech and language impairment in a nationally representative sample of 4- to 5-year-old children. *Journal of Speech, Language and Hearing Research, 52*(5), 1213–1229.

Method

To recruit participants, this study used a random and stratified selection of households in New South Wales (NSW), Australia. Telephone interviews were conducted with individuals in 4,689 households. Telephone numbers were randomly selected from the New South Wales telephone book in a manner than ensured that the majority of names in each directory had the potential of being selected. During each telephone interview, individuals were asked if they believed that anyone in their household had a stutter. If they answered in the affirmative, the definition of stuttering was presented and a number of corroborative questions were then asked of the person believed to stutter (or to parents if a young child stuttered), such as, "Has the stuttering persisted for the last three months?" or, "Has the stuttering caused fear and avoidance of situations?" In cases where any of the corroborative questions were answered in an affirmative, and someone in the family was believed to stutter, the interviewer inquired about speaking to that person to assess his or her anxiety and tape his or her speech over the telephone. Using this sampling method, 87 individuals were identified as definite cases of stuttering and 63 participants (who were 15 years or older) completed a trait anxiety questionnaire over the telephone.

Results

To test differences in trait anxiety between individuals who stutter and the nonstuttering controls, a one-sample t-test was performed. Independent t-tests were performed to test whether those participants who had received treatment at some time had higher %SS and trait anxiety than those who had never received treatment. Additionally, Pearson correlations were also computed to determine whether associations existed between demographic factors, trait anxiety, and speech measures. No significant difference in anxiety was found between those who had and had not received therapy (mean anxiety of 37.3, SD = 9.9, for the 33 with no therapy; mean anxiety of 40.1, SD = 9.4, for 18 who received therapy). No significant difference in trait anxiety was found ($p = 0.3$) when the 33 who had never received therapy were compared with controls. However, those who had received therapy were significantly more anxious than the controls ($p = 0.02$). The results are summarized in Table B–1.

Question

Explain the type of sampling technique used for the study. Be specific.

Table B–1. The Mean Values for Trait Anxiety, %SS, and SPM for the Stuttering Samples, as well as the Mean Trait Anxiety Values for the Nonstuttering Controls

Group	Trait Anxiety			%SS			SPM		
	M	SD	SE	M	SD	SE	M	SD	SE
Stuttering population sample ($N = 63$)	38.5	9.6	1.2	5.4	4.0	0.51	175	23	2.9
Those who received:									
therapy in their lifetime ($n = 18$)	40.1	9.4	2.2	7.7	5.1	1.20	160	27	6.3
no therapy ($n = 33$)	37.3	9.9	1.7	4.4	3.4	0.60	183	18	3.3
Craig (1990) pretreatment anxiety levels, all of whom received therapy; ($N = 102$)	43.1	11.0	1.1	14.6	7.5	—	138	60	—
Craig (1990) nonstuttering controls ($N = 102$)	35.8	7.0	0.7	—	—	—	—	—	—

Note. 12 of the 63 were unsure that they had ever had south therapy. Dashes indicate no data were taken.

Source: Craig, A., Hancock, K., Tran, Y., & Craig, M. (2003). Anxiety levels of people who stutter: A randomized population study. *Journal of Speech Language & Hearing Research, 46,* 1197–1206.

Case Study 1

Responsiveness to Intervention: Teaching Before Testing Helps Avoid Labeling

Source: Montgomery, J. K., Bielinski, J., & Subin, J. (2005). Responsiveness to intervention: Teaching before testing helps avoid labeling. *Topics in Language Disorders*, *25*(2), 148–167.

Purpose

This study investigates the effectiveness of the responsiveness to intervention (RTI) approach (specifically the Tier 3 level) for improving students' literacy skills. The study set out to answer three questions: (1) Can RTI services prevent students from requiring special education services?, (2) Is the explicit, systematic instruction provided in RTI equally beneficial to English language learners (ELL) and English-only (EO) students?, and (3) Can this program be sustained over time?

Methods

A total of 123 students in the fourth and fifth grades in a public school district in southern California participated in this study. In order to qualify for the intervention, students needed to be at least two grade levels below their peers in reading. The schools' speech-language pathologist or the resource support teacher delivered the intervention. Each program lasted one hour a day, five days a week for nine weeks. Progress was determined by measuring the difference between pretests and post-tests in multiple assessments. Data were collected before, during, and after intervention. Figure B–2 illustrates the results of the study.

Results

The Group Reading Assessment and Diagnostic Evaluation (GRADE; Growth Scale Value [GSV]) was used to measure group change based on scores from pretests and post-tests. The mean score on the pretests was 396.8 with a SD of 29.0. The mean score on the post-tests was 409.3 with a SD of 32.6 ($t = -6.3, p = < 0.01$). The effect size was 0.41. Effect sizes between 0.40–0.60 usually represent a moderate change.

Questions

1. Interpret the results of the study in words, using Fisher's *p*-value.
2. Find MBF (Minimum Bayes Factor) of each of the results and reinterpret the results when $p(H_o) = 0.1, 0.2, 0.3, 0.4, 0.5, 0.6, 0.7, 0.8$, and 0.9.
3. In order to obtain the final posterior probability of H_o to be 0.05, that is, $p(H_o | Data) = 0.05$, what must the prior probability of H_o be?

Case Study 2

Epidemiology of Speech and Language Impairment in a Nationally Representative Sample of 4- to 5-Year-Old Children

Source: McLead, S., & Harrison, L. J. (2009, October). Epidemiology of speech and language impairment in a nationally representative sample of 4- to 5-year-old children. *Journal of Speech, Language and Hearing Research, 52*(5), 1213–1229.

	N	M	SD	ES	t	p
Year 1						
Cycle 1						
Pretest	34	392.2	28.0	0.62	−6.5	<.01
Posttest	34	408.8	25.3			
Cycle 2						
Pretest	29	394.9	25.2	0.61	−4.1	<.01
Posttest	29	412.5	32.8			
Year 2						
Cycle 1						
Pretest	32	392.8	32.7	0.36	−3.8	<.01
Posttest	32	404.6	33.7			
Cycle 4						
Pretest	28	411.4	25.1	0.38	−2.4	.02
Posttest	28	421.2	26.4			
Combined						
Pretest	123	396.8	29.0	0.41	−6.3	<.01
Posttest	123	409.3	32.6			

Figure B–2. GSV average reading scores on paired *t*-tests. *Source:* Montgomery, J. K., Bielinski, J., and Subin, J. (2005). Responsiveness to intervention: Teaching before testing helps avoid labeling. *Topics in Language Disorders, 25*(2), 148–167.

Purpose

The purpose of this study was to determine the prevalence of speech and language impairments in 4- and 5-year-old children in Australia. This study drew upon multiple sources to ensure that the population was represented accurately.

Method

Data from 4,983 children between the ages of 4 and 5 years were collected through parent interviews, parent questionnaires, teacher questionnaires, and direct assessments from Growing Up in Australia: The Longitudinal Study of Australian Children (Australian Institute of Family Studies, 2007). This population was weighted to accurately represent the target age group in Australia. Let us go back to Figure B–1 on page 395 to further investigate the results of the study.

Results

The results compared the information collected from parents and teachers with the findings on the Adopted Peabody Picture Vocabulary Test-III. This information can be used to determine the need for speech-language pathologists among this population.

Questions

1. Define a target population of the study. Write clearly and precisely.
2. Find N.
3. What are independent and dependent variables of the study?
4. What is (or are) the author's research question(s)?
5. Comment on the EBP aspect of the study. Does the study, in general, fulfill the mission of EBP?

Case Study 3

Anxiety Levels of People Who Stutter: A Randomized Population Study

Source: Craig, A., Hancock, K., Tran, Y., & Craig, M., (2003). Anxiety levels of people who stutter: A randomized population study. *Journal of Speech Language & Hearing Research*, 46, 1197–1206.

Purpose

This study investigates the question of whether people who stutter are generally more anxious than people who do not stutter. Previous studies investigating anxiety levels and stuttering have mostly assessed people referred to therapy clinics. The authors of this study note that this is arguably a biased sample. In this study, the authors measure the anxiety levels of people who stutter in the community by using random selection procedures.

Method

To recruit participants, this study used a random and stratified selection of households in New South Wales (NSW), Australia. Telephone interviews were conducted with individuals in 4,689 households. Telephone numbers were randomly selected from the New South Wales telephone book in a manner than ensured that the majority of names in each directory had the potential of being selected. During each telephone interview, individuals were asked if they believed that anyone in their household had a stutter. If they answered in the affirmative, the definition of stuttering was presented and a number of corroborative questions were then asked of the person believed to stutter (or to parents if a young child stuttered), such as, "Has the stuttering persisted for the last three months?" or, "Has the stuttering caused fear and avoidance of situations?" In cases where any of the corroborative questions were answered in an affirmative, and someone in the family was believed to stutter, the interviewer inquired about speaking to that person to assess his or her anxiety and tape his or her speech over the telephone. Using this sampling method, 87 individuals were identified as definite cases of stuttering and 63 participants (who were 15 years or older) completed a trait anxiety questionnaire over the telephone.

Results

To test differences in trait anxiety between individuals who stutter and the nonstuttering controls, a one-sample t-test was performed. Independent t-tests were performed to test whether those participants who had received treatment at some time had higher %SS and trait anxiety than those who had never received treatment. Additionally, Pearson correlations were also computed to determine whether associations existed between demographic factors, trait anxiety, and speech measures. No significant difference in anxiety was found between those who had and had not received therapy (mean anxiety of 37.3, SD = 9.9, for the 33 with no therapy; mean anxiety of 40.1, SD = 9.4, for 18 who received therapy). No significant difference in trait anxiety was found ($p = 0.3$) when the 33 who had never received therapy were compared with controls. However, those who had received therapy were significantly more anxious than the controls ($p = 0.02$). Let us go back to Table B–1 on page 396 to further investigate the results of the study.

Question(s)

1. What is a target population of the study?
2. Is the sampling technique used in the study appropriate for answering research questions accurately?
3. Does this study meet the mission of EBP, as AHSH defined?

Case Study 4

Children with Speech and Language Disability: Caseload Characteristics

Source: Broomfield, J., & Dodd, B. (2004). Children with speech and language disability: Caseload characteristics. *International Journal of Language and Communication Disorders, 39*(3), 303–324.

Purpose

This study aimed to create a profile of the characteristics of children who were referred to speech and language therapy services in the UK over the course of the year in order to help plan for service provision. Researchers aimed to collect meaningful data on the prevalence of specific communication disorders regarding the nature and severity of impairments as well as how they relate to background information such as age, culture, and socioeconomic profiles. Moreover, they wanted to discover the incidence of primary diagnostic categories and the extent of comorbidity, as well as the severity distribution of children with communication disorders.

Methods

Participants included 1,100 children between birth and 16 years who were referred to speech and language therapy services at a certain location (Middlesborough PCT in the UK). Each client referred had an appointment in which a detailed assessment and full case history were taken. Based on their assessment, children were placed in broad diagnostic categories and their severity level based on a range of aspects of speech and language functioning was also determined.

Results

In conclusion, researchers estimated that for Middlesborough, UK, the national incidence of children having speech and language disabilities is about 14.6%. Moreover, data collected provide useful information for how pediatric speech and language therapy services might plan for future caseloads and services. Given various distributions classifying the characteristics of referred clients, service providers can use the data to determine and estimate probability of the potential severity levels and disability categories of future referrals.

Questions

1. What is a target population of the study?
2. State the author's research question(s) clearly.
3. Discuss the EBP appropriateness of the study.

Case Study 5

Effects of Personalized Cue Form on the Learning of Subordinate Category Names by Aphasic and Non-Brain-Damaged Subjects

Source: Marshall, R. C., Karow, C. M., Freed, D. B., & Babcock, P. (2002). Effects of personalized cue form on the learning of subordinate category names by aphasic and non-brain-damaged subjects. *Aphasiology,* *16*(7), 763–771.

Purpose

Personalized cuing is a method designed to help facilitate naming of visual stimuli. It has proven to increase the long-term accuracy in naming. The purpose of this study is to determine if the type of information used to create the personalized cue affects the relative ease in which an individual can label the visual stimulus.

Methods

A total of 600 personalized cues were developed by 30 participants (15 non-brain-damaged and 15 aphasic) to learn the names of dog breeds. Three judges classified these cue forms into 5 different groups on two separate occasions. For 251 cues (127 aphasic and 124 NBD), the judges agreed unanimously on the cue form classification. These cues were used for analysis to determine the effectiveness in increasing long-term accuracy.

Results

An KWANOVA test was used to determine the effectiveness of using cue forms to learn the subordinate category names. The results found that cue forms were effective for aphasiac participants, but not for non-brain-damaged participants. Cues containing semantic information were found to be the most effective. Table B–2 summarizes the results of the study.

Question(s)

1. Statistically, why was KWANOVA used in replace of ANOVA?
2. Does the study meet ASHA's EBP mission? Discuss it and/or comment on it.

Case Study 6

Phonological Abilities of Hearing-Impaired Cantonese-Speaking Children with Cochlear Implants of Hearing Aids

Source: Law, Z. W. Y., & So, L. K. H. (2006). Phonological abilities of hearing-impaired

Table B–2. Mean Ranks for Cue Forms for NBD and Aphasic (APH) Individuals

			Cue Form		
	Feature	*Visual/Literal*	*Experiential*	*Rhyme*	*Comb*
NBD	62.65	59.58	69.57	53.00	72.24
APH	67.91	79.73	76.28	38.24	41.50

Kruskal-Wallis x_2 = 3.040; df = 4; $p > 0.05$ for NBD cues.
Kruskal-Wallis x_2 = 28.80; df = 4; $p < 0.001$ for APH cues.

Pairwise comparisons using Mann-Whitney U analysis for aphasic cues

Comparison	*Significance*
Feature vs. Rhyme	$p < 0.001$
Visual/Literal vs. Rhyme	$p < 0.001$
Experiential vs. Rhyme	$p < 0.001$
Visual/Literal vs. Combination	$p < 0.01$
Experiential vs. Combination	$p < 0.01$
Feature vs. Combination	$p < 0.05$

Source: Marshall, R. C., Karow, C. M., Freed, D. B., & Babcock, P. (2002). Effects of personalized cue form on the learning of subordinate category names by aphasic and non-brain-damaged subjects. *Aphasiology 16*(7), 763–771.

Cantonese-speaking children with cochlear implants or hearing aids. *Journal of Speech, Language, and Hearing Research*, *49*(6), 1342–1353.

Purpose

This study compared the phonological abilities of children fitted with hearing aids, to children with cochlear implants. All participants in the study were Cantonese-speaking children with profound bilateral hearing loss present since the prelingual stage of language development.

Methods

Each of the two groups consisted of 7 children ranging from 5:1 to 6:4 years of age.

The participants were given the task of naming 57 pictures and retelling 2 stories. The phonological units and phonological processes used by each participant were measured.

A part of the research was to compare the receptive phonology between the two groups. A Pearson correlation coefficient found that children with good perception abilities also had good speech abilities in consonant ($r = 0.711$, $n = 14$, $p = 0.04$) and vowel ($r = 0.559$, $n = 14$, $p = 0.038$) production performance.

Conclusion

The findings show that among Cantonese children with similar degrees of hearing loss, those wearing cochlear implants had better phonological skills than those wearing hearing aids.

Questions

1. What do $p = 0.04$ and $p = 0.038$ mean in reference to this study? State two hypotheses H_o and H_a to determine the effectiveness of the treatment.
2. Calculate the Minimum Bayes Factor (set at prior probabilities such as $p(H_o) = \{0.1, 0.2, 0.3, 0.4, 0.5, 0.6, 0.7, 0.8, 0.9, 0.95,$ and $0.99\}$, posterior probabilities for H_o and H_a, and interpret the results.
3. Discuss the changes of ***statistical significance*** and ***clinical significance***.

Case Study 7

Responsiveness to Intervention: Teaching Before Testing Helps Avoid Labeling

Source: Moore-Brown, B. J., Montgomery, J. K., Bielinski, J., & Subin, J. (2005). Responsiveness to intervention: Teaching before testing helps avoid labeling. *Topics in Language Disorders, 25*(2), 148–167.

Purpose

This study investigates the effectiveness of the responsiveness to intervention (RTI) approach (specifically the Tier 3 level) for improving students' literacy skills. The study set out to answer three questions: (1) Can RTI services prevent students from requiring special education services? (2) Is the explicit, systematic instruction provided in RTI equally beneficial to English language learners (ELL) and English-only

(EO) students?, and (3) Can this program be sustained over time?

Methods

A total of 123 students in the fourth and fifth grades in a public school district in southern California participated in this study. In order to qualify for the intervention, students needed to be at least two grade levels below their peers in reading. The schools' speech-language pathologist or the resource support teacher delivered the intervention. Each program lasted one hour a day, five days a week for nine weeks. Progress was determined by measuring the difference between pretests and post-tests in multiple assessments. Data were collected before, during, and after intervention. Let us again go back to Figure B–2 on page 398 to further investigate the results of the study.

Results

The Group Reading Assessment and Diagnostic Evaluation (GRADE; Growth Scale Value [GSV]) was used to measure group change based on scores from pretests and post-tests. The mean score on the pretests was 396.8 with a SD of 29.0. The mean score on the post-tests was 409.3 with a SD of 32.6 ($t = -6.3$, $p = <0.01$). The effect size was 0.41. Effect sizes between 0.40 to 0.60 usually represent a moderate change.

Question(s)

1. Calculate Minimum Bayes Factor of Cycle 4 (set prior probability for H_o at 0.1, 0.25, 0.5, 0.75, and 0.9), and calculate posterior odds of H_o and H_a.
2. Interpret the results in (1).
3. Interpret the results of ES

Case Study 8

Risk Markers for SLI: A Study of Young Language-Learning Children

Source: Conti-Ramsden, G., & Hesketh, A. (2003). Risk markers for SLI: A study of young language-learning children. *International Journal of Language & Communication Disorders, 38* (3), 251–263.

Purpose

This study assessed risk factors that potentially could distinguish whether or not children under 5 with slow language development have symptoms suggesting specific language impairment (SLI). Researchers examined what constitutes a normal variation versus the presence of an abnormality by comparing distributions of scores from risk marker language tasks. The data are informative for clinicians to identify potential key language difficulties young children might have that suggest a risk for SLI and set them apart from what might be considered normal variation.

Methods

Participants included 32 children with SLI (mean age 5 years) and 32 younger, typical language-learning children (mean age 3 years). All children were assessed individually, and data were collected on their skills in four risk marker tasks including a past tense task, noun plural task, nonword repetition, and digit recall.

Results

Researchers discovered that processing tasks in particular such as nonword rep-

etition, involving short-term memory, could potentially suggest a risk of SLI in younger children who are already present with slow language development. Moreover, children whose performance level in nonword repetition falls below the 25th percentile in a normal distribution appear to have a potential risk of SLI. The results of the study are summarized in Table B–3.

Question(s)

1. Define a target population of the study, and find *N*.
2. What does "falls below the 25 percentile in a normal distributions" mean? Explain it in a precise manner.

Case Study 9

Hearing Aid Outcomes: Effects of Gender and Experience on Patient's Use and Satisfaction

Source: Williams, V. A., Johnson, C. E., & Danhauer, J. L. (2009). Hearing aid outcomes: Effects of gender and experience on patient's use and satisfaction. *Journal of the American Academy of Audiology,* 422–431.

Purpose

The purpose of this experiment was to determine how content participants were with their hearing aids across various domains (daily use, benefit, residual activity limitations, satisfaction, residual participation restrictions, impact on others, and quality of life).

Methods

Information was collected using the International Outcome Inventory for Hearing

Table B–3. Means and Standard Deviations for the Four Risk Markers for Children with SLI and Younger NL Controls

Task	SLI	NL
Digital recall (centiles)	mean 28.81	63.10
	SD 21.86	23.42
CNRep (centiles)	mean 27.59	63.89
	SD 29.70	28.89
Past tense (% correct)	mean 20.52	14.50
	SD 20.04	16.26
Plural (% correct)	mean 42.38	43.50
	SD 20.33	23.12

Source: Conti-Ramsden, G., & Hesketh, A. (2003). Risk markers for SLI: A study of young language-learning children. *International Journal of Language & Communication Disorders, 38*(3), 251–263.

Aides (IOI-HA) questionnaire. Participants rated their hearing aids on a scale of 1 to 5 (1 meaning not content, 5 meaning most content).

Results

Participants were categorized into four groups based on their gender and experience using hearing aids (male new user, male previous user, female new user, female previous user). Out of a possible score of 35, the mean score and standard deviation were collected for each group. Table B–4 and Figure B–3, respectively, display the results.

Questions

1. Discuss the characteristics of 4 groups (overall, F1, and F2) in terms of measures of central tendency (mean) and measures of dispersion (SD).

2. Discuss why new users have lower SD as compared with previous users for both male and female.

Case Study 10

The Growth of Tense Productivity

Source: Holt, J. K., Rispoli, M., & Hadley, P. (2009). The growth of tense productivity. *Journal of Speech, Language, and Hearing Research, 52*(4), 930–944.

Purpose

Grammatical development rapidly grows in children between the ages of 21 to 48 months. This study tests the predictions made by maturational models on the increase of tense development by using a type-based productivity measure.

Table B–4. Means and Standard Deviations for Patients' (*N* = 64) IOI-HA Responses

	Overall		F1		F2	
	Mean	*SD*	*Mean*	*SD*	*Mean*	*SD*
Male New User	26.43	3.65	15.57	2.34	10.86	2.18
Male Previous User	27.35	4.99	15.90	3.42	11.45	2.39
Female New User	27.44	4.35	16.31	2.85	11.13	3.20
Plural (% correct)	28.79	5.12	17.21	3.26	11.57	2.41

Note: Overall = scores for all seven questions; F1 = includes questions 1, 2, 4, and 7; F2 = includes questions 3, 5, and 6.

Source: Williams, V. A., Johnson, C. E., & Danhauer, J. L. (2009). Hearing aid outcomes: Effects of gender and experience on patient's use and satisfaction. *Journal of the American Academy of Audiology*, 422–431.

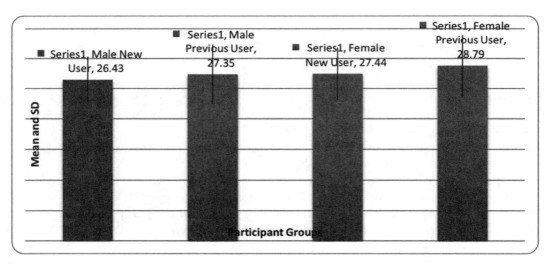

Figure B–3. Histogram for means and standard deviations of all participants' IOI-HA responses by gender and their user status (new or previous user). *Source:* Williams, V. A., Johnson, C. E., and Danhauer, J. L. (2009). Hearing aid outcomes: Effects of gender and experience on patient's use and satisfaction. *Journal of the American Academy of Audiology*, 422–431.

Methods

Samples were taken from 20 typically developing children between the ages of 21 and 33 months of age. These samples were collected every 3 months and measured the subject's growth of productivity of tense morphemes. The children's accuracy of tense marking at 33 months was predicted using empirical Bayes residuals from 21- to 30-month productivity growth trajectories.

Results

To best depict the growth tense markings between 21 and 30 months, a random effects quadratic growth model with no intercept was used. Significant variation was present, but the average development was illustrated by slow instantaneous linear growth (less than 1 morpheme per month at 21 months) and a general trend of acceleration. Linear and quadratic empirical Bayes residuals predicted 33-month accuracy scores ($r = 0.672$, $p = 0.008$). Table B–5 and Figure B–4 summarize the test results.

Question(s)

1. Do research on empirical Bayes residuals and define in a clinical way in reference to this research.
2. Interpret the results of the study in words, using Fisher's p-value.
3. Find MBF (Minimum Bayes Factor) of each of the results and reinterpret the results when $p(H_o) = 0.1, 0.2, 0.3, 0.4, 0.5, 0.6, 0.7, 0.8$, and 0.9.
4. In order to obtain the final posterior probability of H_o to be 0.05, that is, $p(H_o|\text{Data}) = 0.05$, what must the prior probability of H_o be?

Table B–5. Using Empirical Bayes Factor for Prediction Under Linear and Multiple Regression Models and Their Accuracy Index (0 = least, 1 = most)

ID	Linear EB	Quadratic EB	Accuracy
F01	−0.07	0.10	0.93
F04	0.51	0.01	0.88
F05	−0.77	0.05	0.05
F08	−0.01	0.05	0.92
F13	−0.25	0.06	0.82
F14	−0.76	0.01	0.89
F15	1.06	−0.04	0.85
F16	−0.080	0.00	0.48
F17	−0.062	0.03	0.77
F18	−0.78	0.03	0.60
F19	−0.10	−0.01	0.68
M01	−0.57	−0.02	0.54
M04	1.22	−0.05	—
M06	−0.67	−0.02	0.49
M08	1.27	−0.06	0.70
M11	−0.13	−0.01	0.69
M13	1.09	−0.05	0.79
M14	0.88	−0.03	0.93
M16	0.06	−0.08	0.79
M17	−0.057	0.02	0.82

Note. Dash indicates that data were not available for this participant at 33 months.

Source: Holt, J. K., Rispoli, M., & Hadley, P. (2009). The growth of tense productivity. *Journal of Speech, Language, and Hearing Research*, *52*(4), 930–944.

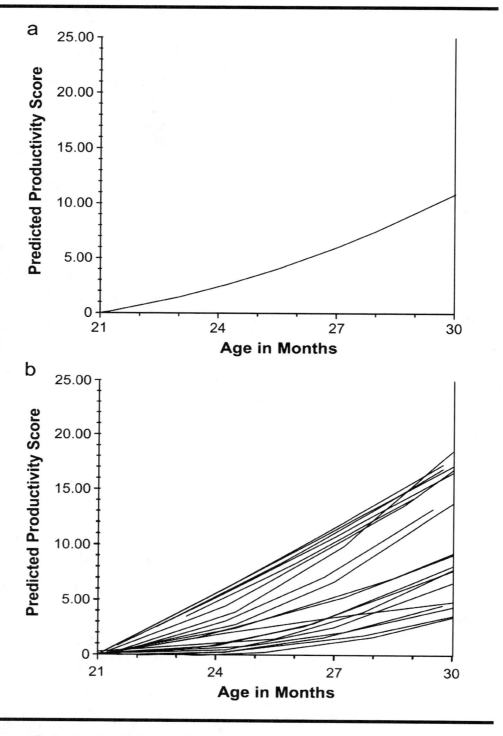

Figure B–4. A. Quadratice productivity growth model for the population average. **B.** Model based empirical Bayes estimates of the individual grown trajectories. *Source:* Holt, J. K., Rispoli, M., and Hadley, P. (2009). The growth of tense productivity. *Journal of Speech, Language, and Hearing Research, 52*(4), 930–944.

APPENDIX C

Calculation of the Power of a Statistical Test

Ideally, one wants to avoid (or at least minimize) making both Type I and Type II errors at the same time. Unfortunately, the two errors always work against one another. That is to say, if one tries to decrease a Type I error (denoted by α), one is likely to increase β (Type II error), and vice versa. In most cases, researchers pay more attention to a Type II error, because it is a β that determines the power of a statistical test, denoted by $1 - \beta$.

The power represents the probability of rejecting a false null hypothesis correctly; that is, it is the ability of a statistical test to detect a difference between the mean under

H_o and the mean under H_1 when it exists. For example, researchers might suspect that the mean IQ score of a certain group of children is 105. Knowing the population mean score (μ) under the null hypothesis is 100, and the standard deviation (a) is 15, the alternative mean is 105 for $n = 36$.

How do we calculate the power of this test? The following steps are necessary:

Step 1: State H_o and H_1

$$H_o: \mu_0 = 100 \qquad H_1: \mu_1 = 105$$

Step 2: Draw a diagram of two sampling distributions (Figure C–1).

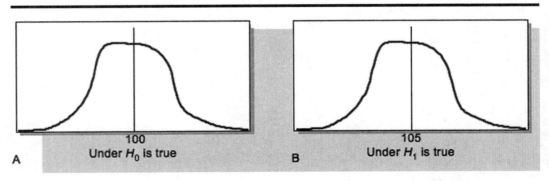

Figure C–1. A. A sampling distribution when H_o is true. **B.** A sampling distribution when H_1 is true.

Step 3: Set up (say, 0.05) and drop a line down through $Z_{critical}$ to meet part B in Figure C–1. The point at which this line meets the abscissa in part B in Figure C–1 is referred to as μ_M. Identify the "rejection areas" for both diagrams by drawing a dashed line.

Step 4: Calculate β and power $(1 - \beta)$.

Under H_1 distribution, Z is calculated as follows:

$Z = (104.125 - 105) / 2.5 = -0.35$

104.125 is mathematically derived from the formula in Chapter 9, that is $100 + (1.65) \times (15/6) = 104.125$, since the critical value is 1.65 and the standard error of the mean can be derived from the ratio of a population standard deviation (15) to the square root of n (36).

Using the Z table (or statistical software program), the probability of β is calculated as: $50\% - 13.68\% = 36.32\%$. (13.68% was derived from the area under the curve between $Z = 0$ and $Z = -0.35$), that is, Type 2 error rate (β).

Hence, the power of the test is given by: $100\% - 36.32\% = 63.68\%$.

This means that given a specific alternative hypothesis, researchers will correctly reject a false null hypothesis about 63.68% of the time.

It is extremely important to do what you can to increase the power of a test at least 80%. The following are some factors that influence power.

1. Sample Size (n): The power of a statistical test increases as n increases, because increasing n decreases the variability in the sampling distribution, which eventually increases power.
2. Significance level (α): As α increases, the power of a test also increases, because the ability to detect a difference when it exists becomes better if you use a less credible level of significance.
3. Standard deviation (s or σ): The power of a statistical test increases if the standard deviation decreases.

APPENDIX D

Evidence-Based Medicine: Calculations of Various Probabilities with Nomogram

Evidence-based medicine (EBM) is the conscientious, explicit, and judicious use of current best evidence in making clinical decisions about the care of individual clients. The practice of EBM integrates individual clinical expertise with the best available external clinical evidence from systematic research. One of the clinical techniques, developed by the Oxford Centre for Evidence-Based Medicine, is the likelihood ratio nomogram. It calculates the post-test probability (posterior probability) for both positive and negative test results, by means of graphing that is based on pretest probability (prior probability), sensitivity, and specificity. Let us now illustrate the necessary steps in calculating the post-test probability in the context of our example. For the purpose of calculations of the various types of the probabilities, readers should refer to Table D–1.

Exercises

Calculate the following probabilities.

1. Prevalence for a positive and negative test, that is, P (D$^+$) and P (D$^-$).
2. Find sensitivity, specificity, LR$^+$, LR$^-$, predictive values positive and negative, and posterior probability (+ and –).
3. Calculate absolute risk reduction (ARR) and number needed to treat (NNT; Notes).
   - Recall that posterior odds (+) = prior odds (+) × LR$^+$ and posterior odds (–) = prior odds (–) × LR$^-$
   - Alternatively, instead of doing all of the above calculations, we could simply graph the posterior probability in relation to the pretest probability. Such

Table D–1. The Sample Data, Projected to a Hypothetical Population with 13% Prevalence of Language Delay (N = 1000), with Positive and Negative Predicative Values Expected

	N = 1000		
	Clinical Outcome		
Screening	*D (D⁺)*	*LN (D⁻)*	*Row Total*
Positive (T⁺)	118	113	231
Negative (T⁻)	12	757	769
Column Totals	130	870	1000

Note: LD represents "Language Delayed"; LN represents "Language Normal."

Source: From Improving the positive predicative value of screening for developmental language disorder by T. Klee, K. Pearce, and D. K. Carson (2000). *Journal of Speech, Language, and Hearing Research, 43,* 823. ©American Speech-Language-Hearing Association. Reprinted by permission.

a graphical method is called a nomogram. For further details, readers should visit the website: http://www.jamaevidence.com/calculators

APPENDIX E

Measures of Disorder/ Disease Occurrence

Descriptive Studies

According to our view, studies can be best classified based on the degree to which they explain the causal relations among variables. In achieving this goal, the weakest of the lot are *descriptive studies*, or those intended to observe, illustrate, record, classify, or by other means attempt to clarify the distinctive features of research variables. The methods of description include surveys, case histories, clinical reports, prevalence/incidence studies, and field studies. Such studies often result in a better understanding of phenomena as they exist *in the here and now*, thereby establishing the conditions for later scientific work when questions as to the relationship among variables might arise.

Prevalence/Incidence

Measures of disorder occurrence describe either the pool of actual existing cases, or the occurrence of new cases. *Prevalence* is defined as the proportion of the target population who carry a particular disorder (under discussion) at one specific point in time, whereas *incidence* is defined as the frequency of disorder occurrence of new cases during a time period. Each subject is categorized into two states, namely disorder (D^+) or normal (D^-). The prevalence, in this framework, is the proportion of the given population that is in D^+ at a specific time. The incidence describes the rate of flow from D^- to D^+. The magnitude of prevalence always depends on incidence, because a greater rate of occurrence of new cases will be likely to increase the number of actual existing cases. We now present the formulas for two specific measures of disorder occurrence. The first one is a prevalence measure, and the second is an incidence measure.

Prevalence, denoted by P, is calculated as follows:

$$P = \frac{\textit{Number of subjects carrying the disorder at a specific time}}{\textit{Size of a target population at that point in time}}$$

or symbolically,

$$P = \frac{D^+}{N}$$

A $(1 - \alpha)$ confidence interval for P is given as

$$P \pm |Z_{\alpha/2}| \times \text{SQR} [P \times (1 - P)/N]$$

The Relationship Between Prevalence (*P*) and Incidence Rate (*I*)

As noted earlier, prevalence is dependent on the incidence rate and the duration of a particular disorder. This association can be expressed as follows:

$$\frac{P}{(1 - P)} = I \times B$$

where B denotes average duration of the disorders.

The denominator of the fraction that appears on the left-hand side of the equation above represents the part of the population that is free from the disorder. It is included in the formula because only those who are free from the disorder are at risk of getting it. Therefore, in case of rare disorders, $(1 - P)$ will get closer to 1; that is, P is very small. Then the formula will be revised as simply $P = I \times B$.

APPENDIX F

Flowchart for Classical Statistics Versus Bayesian Statistical Approach in Hypothesis Testing

Illustrated Example: Calculations of Fisher's *p*-Value and MBF

In this section, the following issues are discussed: (1) how are Fisher's and MBF calculated under H_o distribution?; (2) why the MBF approach produces a more accurate and reliable result than the Fisher's *p*-value approach when we measure the strength of evidence against H_o?; and (3) why is it important to teach MBF, in addition to Fisher's traditional *p*-value approach, in a statistics classroom?

For the illustration purpose, the author provides a relevant working example that is typically taught in an introductory statistics course.

Working Example

Adapted from the book *General statistics* (4th ed.), by W. Chase & F. Bown.

To confirm her belief that abused children will show elevated levels of depression, a psychologist gave a test called the Profile of Mood States (POMS) to a sample of 49 abused children. The results showed a mean depression score of 16.6 and a standard deviation of 5.6. Can she conclude that abused children in general have a mean depression level that is different from the national norm of 15?

Solution

Calculating an observed value based on a sample, assuming that a two-sided test is conducted.

Step 1: State H_o and H_a.

$$H_o: \mu = 15 \qquad H_a: \mu \neq 15$$

Step 2: Calculate an observed value $\hat{\theta}$.

$$\hat{\theta} = \frac{16.6 - 15}{5.6/\sqrt{49}} = \frac{1.6}{0.8} = 2$$

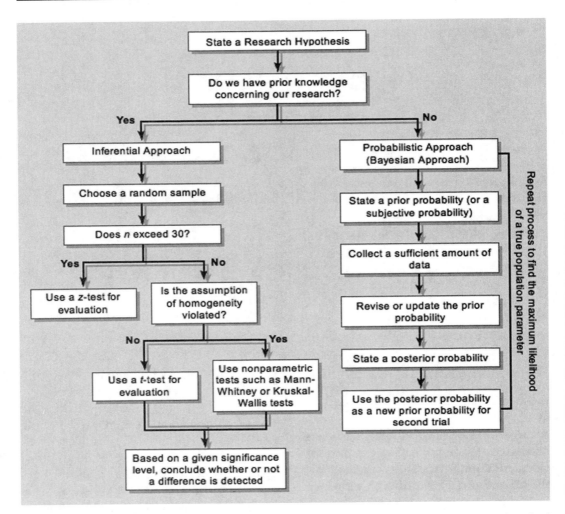

Figure F–1. Flowchart for hypothesis testing process: Comparison between classical approach and Bayesian approach. Reprinted with permission from Thomson Delmar Learning (Maxwell and Satake).

Step 3: Calculate Fisher's p-value and MBF.

Fisher's p-value = $0.0228 \times 2 = 0.0456$ (since it is a two-sided test)

Symbolically, it is written as

$$\text{Fisher's } p\text{-value} = p[(\hat{\theta} \geq 2), \text{ given that } (H_o \text{ is true})] = 0.0456$$

Symbolically,

$$MBF = p[(\hat{\theta} = 2) \text{ given } (H_o \text{ is true})]$$
$$= e^{-\frac{(z)^2}{2}} = e^{-2} = 0.1353, \text{ where}$$

0.0456 corresponds to z-value of 2, shown in Appendix K. Note that θ is exactly the same as the corresponding z-value of 0.0456, that is, $\theta = z = 2$ in our case.

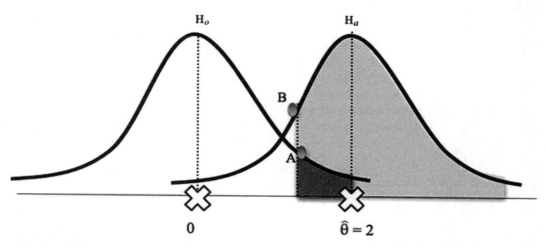

Figure F–2. Graphical illustration of Fisher's *p*-value and Minimum Bayesian Factor (MBF) when measuring the strength of evidence.

As it can be seen from the results in Figure F–2, Fisher's *p*-value greatly overstates the amount of evidence against H_o 2.97 times $\left(\frac{A}{\text{Fisher's } p\text{-value}} = \frac{0.135}{0.0456} \right) = 2.97$ as much as MBF. This means that Fisher's *p*-value exaggerates *statistical significance* almost 3 times as much as MBF; therefore, the conclusion derived from Fisher's *p*-value is seemingly less credible as a measure of the strength of evidence against H_o. For mathematically-inclined readers, all calculations necessary for deriving clinical significance (aka Prior Odds), statistical significance (aka Bayes factor), and a combination of both (aka Posterior odds) are presented in Appendix S.

APPENDIX G
Sampling Techniques

As with randomness, the concept and methodologies of sampling are central to the rationale underlying inferential statistics. There are two reasons for sampling's importance. First, in probability theory, how we sample affects the probability of an outcome. The probability observed in a situation where the object selected is returned to the population from which it was drawn (*sampling with replacement*) is significantly different from the probability derived when the object is not returned (*sampling without replacement*). Second, in the design of experiments and research studies in general, the method of sampling is central to inferences that are to be drawn from results of the research. If the sampling method is inappropriate or biased, the inferences and conclusions of a study will be flawed and meaningless. (Recall the dictum, "garbage in, garbage out.") As we shall see, the consequence of inappropriate, and, particularly, biased sampling is not as easily discernable as it would appear.

The methods used in drawing inferences from observations made in scientific research differ significantly from the intuitive procedures we use in everyday life, in that they are more structured, less subjective, and statistically based. The term **statistical inference** refers to gener-

alizations about descriptive measures of a population's characteristics (*parameters*) based on corresponding characteristics (*statistics*) of samples. For example, the mean of a sample is used, as an estimate, to describe the mean of the population from which it was drawn. However, the efficacy of the inference or generalization, as we have said, is valid only if the sampling method or process is appropriate and/or free of bias.

Basically, there are two types of samples, *probability samples* and *nonprobability samples*. In probability sampling, each unit or member of a population has an equal chance of being selected for inclusion in the sample. Nonprobability sampling methods do not or cannot provide for equal representation of membership in a sample. We briefly examine some of the more common techniques to derive each of these types of samples.

Probability Sampling

Statistical inferences drawn from probability sampling differ significantly from those derived by nonprobability sampling in that they involve random samples and particular statistical techniques or methods.

As we noted earlier, a random sample is one in which every individual in the population has an equal chance (probability) of being selected as one of its members. (We could use objects or animals or pizzas, but for the most part, we refer to people in our illustrations.) The theoretical assumption underlying random samples is that they will contain a representative cross-section of all members of the population. This may not always be the case because any representation of a population is one of degree and subject to some margin of error, referred to as *sampling error*. **Sampling error** is a value that expresses the degree to which the characteristic observed in a sample differs from the corresponding characteristic in the population from which the sample is drawn. Nevertheless, most researchers would agree that random sampling methods provide the most consistent way of ensuring that the selected samples are sufficiently representative of the populations from which they are drawn. Generally, researchers used one of four common probability sampling techniques: *simple random sampling*, *systematic sampling*, *stratified random sampling*, and *cluster sampling*, each of which attempts to increase the likelihood that a sample is representative of the population of interest.

Simple Random Sampling

In a **simple random sample**, every person has an equal chance of being selected to participate in a study or experiment. There are several ways of generating simple random samples. For very small populations, we can use the same basic *sampling-without-replacement* procedures intro-

duced in Chapter 7 for nonindependent events. For example, suppose you are interested in determining how students in your class feel about a particular issue, and suppose you decide to conduct a survey using a simple, random sample. At a very basic but perfectly valid level, you could derive a simple random sample as follows:

Step 1: Decide on the size of the sample you wish to use.

Step 2: Write the name of each student in the class (*population* or *sample frame*) on same-sized slips of paper.

Step 3: Place the slips in a container, and shake it well so that each student has an equal chance of being selected.

Step 4: Draw a name and put the slip aside. (Do not return it to the container.)

Step 5: Shake the container again and draw another slip, continuing the process until you have the desired sample size.

In cases of larger populations, we could assign a number for each member of the population or sample frame, starting with the number 1, and select the desired size sample using a list of random numbers, a computer or hand-calculator program, or a random number table. Random number lists/tables consist of numbers in a nonpurposive arrangement, where there is no predetermined order or relationship for and among the numbers and where each number had an equal chance of being included. The steps in using a random number list or table are as follows:

Step 1: Take a pencil, close your eyes, and put the pencil down on the list or table of random numbers.

Step 2: If the desired sample size is less than 100, take the number closest to where the pencil lands and link it to the next number; if the sample size is to consist of less than 1000 objects or individuals, take the next two numbers; and so on. The numbers could be to the right, left, above, or below, just so long as you follow the same process throughout the procedure.

Step 3: Continue the selection process until you have the desired number for your sample.

Simple random sampling is the simplest and easiest method of selecting a random probability sample. However, it is not appropriate for all situations, particularly if it is impossible to obtain or identify a complete list of members in the population, such as the complete list of residents in a large city. It also should not be used when it's important that subgroups of a population be represented in the sample.

Systematic Sampling

A second type of random sampling is known as *systematic sampling*, which is sometimes referred to as *ordinal sampling*. In a **systematic sample,** every *n*th person from a population list or table, starting at some random point, is selected as a member. To select a systematic sample, you follow the following three steps:

Step 1: Determine the number of individuals or objects in the population (sample frame) and assign a number to each one beginning with the number 1, as in Table D–1.

Step 2: Determine the *sampling rate*, that is, the interval used to choose every *n*th person.

Step 3: Take a pencil, close your eyes, and put the pencil down on the list of names. The number closest to where the pencil lands is the starting point from which to select every *n*th person.

Systematic samples tend to be easier to generate from large populations than simple random samples. In most cases, the two methods produce near identical results, *except* in cases where the order of names or objects in a population is such that it results in a nonrepresentative (biased) sample. The problem is known as **periodicity.** For example, if the subjects in the list are arranged in a cyclical manner or particular pattern, it might bias the outcome. Given the example above, such bias would occur if every 10th name on the ASHA list happened to be male, or Hispanic, or a new member, or whatever may potentially create bias.

Stratified Sampling

When it is important that subgroups of a population be represented in a sample, the stratified sampling technique should be used. A **stratified sample** consists of randomly selected members from each of the subgroups or categories of the population of interest. In stratified sampling, a population is divided into mutually exclusive subgroups or categories, meaning a person or element cannot be a member of more than one subgroup or category. The goal is to ensure that each subgroup of the population is represented in the sample. In general, college students may be stratified by year, families may be stratified by income level, and voters may be stratified by party affiliation, and so on.

If a sample of participants for a research study is selected in proportion to the participants' representation in a population, the sample is known as a **proportional stratified sample**. To illustrate, suppose that in surveying ASHA membership attitudes regarding some issue, we wanted to assure adequate representation according to the factor of gender. For purposes of illustration, let us further assume that we learn that the professional membership is approximately 80% female and 20% male. Given this knowledge, we decide that we want our sample to represent this same gender population. One way to accomplish such a sampling distribution is to divide the population into two groups and then randomly select four females for every male using a random numbers table. This particular strategy is designed to proportionally represent elements of a population as these elements are found in the world or to create what has been called "miniature of the population." The same stratified random sampling procedure could be used to assure adequate representation of age, ethnicity, employment setting, and specialty area of interest, among other factors. When the number of such stratified variables is large, it is often necessary to increase the size of the sample substantially to satisfy the minimum number of subjects that an investigator might wish to have in each category.

Cluster Sampling

Each of the three types of sampling methods described so far requires the complete list of a population or elements in the sample frame. This is not always possible or practical, particularly when a population is spread out over a wide, geographical area. In such cases, researchers use a technique known as *cluster sampling*. A **cluster sample** consists of randomly selected units or clusters of a population. The sampling process consists of two or more stages. In a two-stage process, for example, clusters are first randomly selected from among those in the population; in the second stage, individuals are randomly selected from each cluster. Referring once again to our hypothetical example of ASHA membership, we might decide to conduct an area sampling survey in clusters of people based on gender and geographical location (hypothetically, we are interested in the state of California and Idaho); that is, if we were interested in developing a two-stage cluster sample to measure the proportion of gender in an ASHA directory first, and then the proportion of the states (California and Idaho). Third, we combine these two proportions to determine how many subjects (gender by state) must be chosen for each sample to optimize representativeness in sampling to minimize the selection bias as much as we could. To do so, the researcher must strive to form clusters that are as heterogeneous as possible.

Nonprobability Sampling

Sometimes it is not possible or even appropriate to use random sampling methods.

This is particularly true in cases where no population list for the characteristic(s) of interest to the researcher exists. Suppose you are interested in levels of aggressiveness among disfluency children with a particular disorder in rural areas. It is unlikely that a list of subjects is always available. Nor is it likely that you could easily find or create a list of subjects who fit the description perfectly. In such cases, researchers employ *nonprobability samples*, also referred to as *nonrandom samples*.

The major limitation of nonprobability sampling is that it is difficult to draw accurate statistical inferences from the results of studies with samples selected on a nonrandom basis. When the selection process is nonrandom, there is no way of knowing the extent to which a sample is representative of the population of interest; nor is it possible to estimate sampling error. Therefore, researchers must be very careful in the inferences they draw from nonprobability sample data. Here, we briefly discuss three common types of nonprobability samples and their selection techniques: *convenience sampling*, *purposive sampling*, and *quota sampling*.

Convenience Sampling

In human subject research, a **convenience sample** consists of individuals selected on the basis of availability. It is the method frequently used by researchers who teach at colleges and universities and who ask or require students in introductory courses to participate in a survey or quasiexperiment study. It is also called "on-the-sheet" or opportunistic sampling. The technique is commonly used by the media to poll attitudes or opinions about current events.

Often, the general public may be invited to write or telephone or electronic survey to express their opinion about a particular issue such as new innovative treatment, ASHA's future direction, implementation of EBP to the graduate course curriculum, and so forth. Obviously, such survey data are potentially fraught with bias because of the restricted pool of respondents who may just happen to be available at a given time. For a more generic example, shoppers at malls represent another population from which convenience samples are selected, especially by marketing researchers. Radio and television newscasts that ask listeners and viewers to respond to a particular question or issue related to a news story are more recent examples of how convenience sampling is used. Such surveys or polls are virtually worthless, but are nevertheless often viewed by many in the lay public as indicative of beliefs and attitudes.

Purposive Sampling

A **purposive sample** consists of individuals with a particular characteristic of interest to the researcher. The technique is similar to stratified sampling, except the members or elements within the categories of the stratification are not selected at random. Purposive samples also are known as *judgment samples* because they depend on the informed judgment of the researcher. However, to be effective in the selection process, the researcher must be knowledgeable in the variable of interest and of the population from which the sample is to be drawn. Thus, a researcher interested in how emergency medical technicians (EMTs) deal with on-the-job stress should be well-informed both in the area of stress and in the daily activities and functions of EMTs.

Quota Sampling

A **quota sample** consists of individuals or elements selected nonrandomly on the basis of their known proportion in a population. The technique used in quota sampling is similar to that used in proportional stratified sampling, except that the proportional selection of members of each subgroup is not done on a random basis. Suppose the workplace preferences of CD majors at a particular college are known to be as follows: 45% medical center, 25% school system, 25% private practice, and 5% other. A researcher using the quota sampling technique would ensure that the selected sample would reflect these percentages. However, the students in each subgroup would not be selected at random. This is contrary with proportional stratified sampling in which the selection process would ensure that all students in each subgroup would have an equal chance of being selected.

APPENDIX H

Writing a Proposal of ASHA Convention Paper

Whether writing a research proposal, thesis, or PhD dissertation, or an article for publication, it is important to attend closely not only to the content but also to the mechanics of the written result. This leads to a successful research or clinical career and development of scientific literacy as noted earlier. The following is the sample of ASHA's Short Course Proposal.

ASHA Short Course Proposal

Title: Beyond p-value: Measuring Clinical Significance by Bayesian Methods

Abstract: Although Bayesian methods have recently been the center of attention in EBP sciences, they are rarely used in communication disorders research. The purpose of this course is to discuss the potential application of Bayesian methods as an alternative to the frequentist methods most often used by communication disorders researchers.

Main Body of the Short Course

The growing interest among medical and clinical science communities in Bayesian statistical methods and its potential application in decision-making research has not as yet extended to the field of communication disorders. A major obstacle to its acceptance is the nearly singular use of frequentist statistical methods. This is unfortunate for several reasons, particularly the lack of understanding of the nature of p-values as measures of so-called statistical significance.

Frequentist Statistics

The frequentist or classical statistics approach to research questions is commonly referred to as hypothesis testing or null hypothesis significance testing (NHST). The procedures used involve a null hypothesis (H_o) that states that there

425

is no effect or relationship; an alternative hypothesis (H_a) that essentially says H_o is not true at alpha or pretrial significance level (typically 0.05) and a calculated p-value to determine statistical significance. If the p-value is less than 0.05, the result is considered significant. Other factors that come into play in frequentist statistics include Type I and Type II errors and power of tests.

Frequentist statistical methods have been criticized for a number of reasons. For example, the null hypothesis (H_o) is often known to be false prior to a study. But perhaps the most serious criticism centers on the misinterpretation of p-values.

1. **The nature of p-values and common misunderstanding.** According to Sir Ronald Fisher, the founder of frequentist statistics, "The p-value is the probability of occurrence (or rarity) of the actual observed outcome (or evidence) plus 'more extreme' than the actual observed outcome, given that the null hypothesis, H_o, is true." Since the calculation of a p-value is based on the assumption that H_o is true, it cannot be a direct measure of the credibility of H_o, that is, it does not answer the question most researchers want to know, specifically, "How credible is the hypothesis based on actual data?" or "How effective is a treatment based on actual data?" p-values invite users to commit an interpretation error called "*transposition of conditioning fallacy*" in which:

   Probability of evidence, given H_o is true, is mistaken for probability H_o is true, given evidence.

   Unfortunately, many clinical professionals and researchers in communication disorders incorrectly interpret p-values as the probability that H_o (presence of a null treatment effect) is true based on what was actually observed in a sample. But this is not the case. A p-value is not the probability of truth of the hypothesis of one's interest.

2. **Misdirection of p-values.** In addition to not telling us what we want to know, there is a tendency of p-values to mislead clinicians and researchers. For instance, a small p-value (one assumed to be significant) often reflects sample size rather than a meaningful difference between the null and alternative hypotheses. Simply put, p-values are notorious exaggerators. Consequently, the conclusion becomes less accurate and less credible thereby threatening statistical conclusion validity. To prove this point, using clinically relevant examples, the authors will show that the weight of evidence against H_o is not nearly as strong in magnitude as frequentist p-values often suggest.

3. **Frequentist approach does not meet EBP criteria.** According to Sackett (1996), evidence-based practice (EBP) is defined as "The conscientious, explicit and judicious use of current best evidence in making decisions about the care of individual patients. It means integrating individual clinical expertise with the best available external clinical evidence from systematic research."

   a. In research and practice in the field of communication disorders, one of the main concerns involves accurately interpreting the results of a treatment(s). Clinically, placing excessive importance on *p*-values resulting from NHST may impede instead of enhance the goals of EBP. What is needed is an alternative approach to clinical decision making based on actual data rather than *p*-values.

Bayesian Statistics

As an alternative to the *p*-value approach, Bayesian statistics are well suited to the needs of clinical practitioners and the objectives of evidence-based research. Bayesian methods provide a means for determining how a clinician's initial belief about a disorder of interest can be modified and updated by actual data. Perhaps the main reason why Bayesian methods have not caught on in communication sciences and disorders is because they are believed by many professionals to entail a subjective approach to data analysis. Contrary with this belief, Bayesian methods have a data-based core that can be used mathematically as a calculus of evidence. This statistical core is the Bayes factor, that is, the Bayesian counterpart of the *p*-value. The Bayes factor measures the strength of evidence more accurately than the frequentist *p*-value because it calculates the rarity of exact evidence, rather than including "more extreme" evidence, given that H_o is true.

The Bayesian factor has a sound scientific foundation upon which to interpret the meaning of "clinical significance" versus "statistical significance." More importantly, Bayesian methods have an ability to combine external evidence (clinical significance) with experimental evidence (statistical significance) to generate a new probability of truth of the hypothesis of interest, that is, the probability of the effectiveness of a treatment, given the exact evidence observed. In short, Bayesian methods are better suited for clinical decision making in communication disorders because they provide more direct and accurate answers to questions that both clinicians and researchers seek to find.

Learning Outcomes

Participants will learn:

1. Why frequentist statistical methods currently in use are not well designed for EBP and how frequentist *p*-values can actually hinder the development of new knowledge;
2. About several shortcomings in the current publication guidelines of ASHA journals including editorial policies that allow for, if not promote, the frequentist *p*-value approach in the absence of or alongside other forms of evidence;
3. Why Bayesian methods are more clinically relevant to the goals of EBP than frequentist methods in evaluating the strength of evidence; and
4. About the conceptual and practical differences between *statistical significance* and *clinical significance* through several clinically relevant examples, while becoming aware that the differences between these concepts are not often made clear in journal articles and textbooks.

Structure of the Course

The proposed three-hour short course will incorporate both didactic and interactive methods to: (1) create an intellectually stimulating learning environment, and

(2) promote audience's active participation to facilitate learning goals. Copies of Powerpoint slides and a comprehensive outline of the topics to be discussed will be distributed.

- 10 minutes—Overview of the course.
- 20 minutes—Tutorial and discussion: foundation of frequentist p-value.
- 20 minutes—Tutorial and discussion: logical fallacies of frequentist statistical methods such as p-values, hypothesis tests, confidence intervals, and effect size.

- 20 minutes—Tutorial and discussion: evidence based statistics in communication sciences and disorders.
- 40 minutes—Tutorial and discussion: statistical significance and clinical significance.
- 40 minutes—Tutorial and discussion: what are Bayesian statistical methods? How do we measure the strength of evidence and interpret the results in Bayesian research.
- 10 minutes—Summary.
- 20 minutes—Questions and answers.

APPENDIX I

The Fisher's *p*-Value Method for Hypothesis Testing (aka Combined Method)

Overview

As we noted in Chapter 9, there are two approaches to testing hypotheses, the traditional method used in this text, and the *p*-value method, presented here. Understanding the concept and methods of calculating *p*-values becomes increasingly important as one includes the use of computers in hypothesis testing and data analysis. Many computer statistical packages report both alpha (α) values, such as 0.05 and 0.01, and *p*-values in their output of statistical tests.

A *p*-value is a probability value. It may be defined as the probability of obtaining a test statistic, such as a z or t, favoring the direction of the alternative or research hypothesis (H_1), when the null hypothesis (H_o) is true. In the traditional method of testing hypotheses, we compare the test statistic to the critical value set as the criterion for rejecting H_o. For example, if the computed value of the test statistic (z or

t) is equal to or greater than the selected critical value, H_o is rejected. In such cases, we concluded that the probability of the null hypothesis being true is less than the α level (such as 0.05, or 0.01) set in advance of the data analysis.

The Fisher's *p*-Value Method

In the *p*-value method, we do not set a critical value for rejecting H_o, rather we compare the computed test statistic to the computed *p*-value generated by a computer statistical package or calculator, or the value we calculate by hand. The observed *p*-value represents the probability of the observed test statistic.

For example, suppose the null and alternative hypotheses for a one-tailed hypothesis test are stated as: H_o: $\mu = 60$ and H_1: $\mu > 60$, respectively. Suppose further that the observed sample mean ($\overline{X}$) is 66. If the computed *p*-value for the test statistic is 0.0325, then we conclude that the probability of obtaining a sample mean equal to or greater than 60 is 0.0325. Put another way, the chances of obtaining a sample mean of 66, given that the population mean is truly 60, is approximately 3%. Such a low probability would appear to not support the claim of the alternative hypothesis (H_1).

Whether or not a *p*-value of 0.325 is sufficiently low enough to reject the null hypothesis is conditioned by several factors, including the size and variance of the sample and our desire to avoid Type I error. The relationship between a *p*-value and an *alpha* (α) value may be illustrated as follows. We would reject the null hypothesis with a *p*-value of 0.0325 at $\alpha = 0.10$ or 0.05, but not $\alpha = 0.01$ or 0.001 levels.

The Hypothesis Test Model

The hypothesis testing model used in the *p*-value method consists of five steps:

Step 1: State the hypotheses.

Step 2: Compute the test statistic.

Step 3: Find the *p*-value.

Step 4: Apply the decision rule.

Step 5: State the conclusion.

The model is nearly identical to the traditional model for testing hypotheses introduced in Chapter 9 and used throughout the text. One major difference between the two methods, as mentioned earlier, is the focus on the claim of the researcher whether implied or stated in the alternative (H_1) or null hypothesis (H_o). Another distinction is in the use of *p*-values rather than critical values (traditional model)

in the decision-making process. Specifically, in the traditional approach, the value is selected by the researcher *before* the test statistic is computed, whereas the *p*-value is derived *after* the test statistic is computed. We illustrate how the *p*-value model functions in hypothesis tests for large and small sample cases for the mean.

Fisher's *p*-Value Method for Large Samples

Recall that when the size of a sample is greater than 30 ($n > 30$), the sampling distribution for the mean is the standard normal *z* distribution and the test of significance is the *z*-test. Since the focus here is to illustrate the *p*-value calculation, the author decided to provide more general themes of the questions, rather than the ones that are more clinically relevant. The readers are encouraged to apply the calculation method to the field of the clinical sciences. First, consider the following problem.

Scenario One

A national survey company reports that the average college student spends more than the 4,195 minutes per month on cell phones. A researcher believes that college students in New England spend more time on cell phones than their national counterparts and decides to test her claim. She selects a random sample of 40 students from New England colleges, and finds that the students in her sample spend an average ($\overline{X}$) of 4,485 minutes per month on their cell phones, with a standard deviation (*s*) of 680 minutes. Is there evidence to support the researcher's alternative hypothesis claim at the $\alpha = 0.05$ level of significance?

Relevant Data: $\mu = 4195$, $N = 40$, $\bar{X} = 4485$, $s = 680$, $\alpha = 0.05$, One-tailed test

Step 1: State the Hypotheses

H_o: $\mu = 4195$ H_1: $\mu > 4195$

Step 2: Compute the Test Statistic

$$z = \frac{\bar{X} - \mu}{s_{\bar{X}}} = \frac{4485 - 4195}{107.501}$$

$$= \frac{290}{107.51} = 2.697 \approx 2.70$$

Where $s_{\bar{X}} = \frac{s}{\sqrt{n}} = \frac{680}{\sqrt{40}} = \frac{680}{6.325} = 107.501$

Step 3: Find the *p*-Value. The *p*-values for one- and two-tailed *z*-tests are derived using Tables K–1, K–2, and K–3 in Appendix K. There are two ways to find a particular *p*-value. One way is to locate the corresponding area for the computed test statistic *z* in the "Area between *X* and *z*" column in Tables K–1, K–2, and K–3 and subtract the value from 0.5000.

The *remainder* is the *p*-value. The second, and perhaps more efficient way, is simply to locate the "Area beyond *z*" value corresponding to the computed test statistic *z* in Tables K–1, K–2, and K–3. In the scenario illustrated here, the corresponding "Area between *X* and *z*" for $z = 2.70$ in Tables K–1, K–2, and K–3 is 0.4965, which is subtracted from 0.5000 to find the area in the right tail of the normal curve, as given in:

$$0.5000 - 0.4965 = 0.0335$$

Hence, the *p*-value or probability value for this scenario is 0.0335. This value is exactly the same as the one listed in the "Area beyond *z*" column for $z = 2.70$ in Table K–3. This segment of Table K–3 is shown in Figure I–1.

Step 4: Apply the Decision Rule. Since the *p*-value of 0.0335 is less than $\alpha = 0.05$, the decision is to reject the null hypothesis (H_o). See Figure I–2.

z	Area between X and z	Area beyond z	z	Area between X and z	Area beyond z	z	Area between X and z	Area beyond z
1.38	0.4162	0.0838	1.76	0.4608	0.0392	2.14	0.4838	0.0162
1.39	0.4177	0.0823	**1.77**	**0.4616**	**0.0384**	2.15	0.4842	0.0158
1.40	0.4192	0.0808	1.78	0.4625	0.0375	2.16	0.4846	0.0154
2.31	0.4896	0.0104	2.69	0.4964	0.0036	3.07	0.4989	0.0011
2.32	0.4898	0.0102	**2.70**	**0.4965**	**0.0035**	3.08	0.4990	0.0010
2.33	0.4901	0.0099	2.71	0.4966	0.0034	3.09	0.4990	0.0100

Figure I–1. Selected values under the standard normal distribution for values of *z*. Courtesy of Karen Weasen.

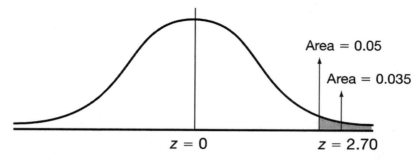

Figure I–2. Test statistic and corresponding area of region of rejection for one-tailed test at $\alpha = 0.05$: Scenario One. Courtesy of Karen Weasen.

Step 5: State the Conclusion. There is sufficient evidence to support the claim of the alternative hypothesis, H_o, that college students in New England spend more time on cell phones than their national counterparts.

Scenario Two

A researcher is interested in testing his belief (claim) that college undergraduates believe consuming 4.1 drinks in an hour constitutes binge drinking. He surveys a random sample of 50 college undergraduates, and finds that the average belief of what constitutes binge drinking among the sample members is 4.3 drinks, with a standard deviation of 0.8. At $\alpha = 0.05$ is there sufficient evidence to reject the claim?

Relevant Data: $\mu = 4.1$, $n = 50$,
$\overline{X} = 4.3$, $s = 0.8$, $\alpha = 0.05$,
Two-tailed test

Step 1: State the Hypotheses

$$H_o: \mu = 4.1 \qquad H_1: \mu \neq 4.1$$

Step 2: Compute the Test Statistic

$$z = \frac{\overline{X} - \mu}{s_{\overline{X}}} = \frac{4.3 - 4.1}{0.113} = \frac{0.2}{0.113} = 1.77$$

Where $s_{\overline{X}} = \frac{s}{\sqrt{n}} = \frac{0.8}{\sqrt{50}} = \frac{0.8}{7.071} = 0.113$

Step 3: Find the p-Value. When the test of significance is a two-tailed test, the area in one tail must be doubled in deriving the p-value. For example, if the hypothesis test in Scenario One was two-tailed at $\alpha = 0.05$, the 0.0384 area in the one-tailed would be doubled, and the p-value would be 2(0.0384) or 0.0768. In such a case, the null hypothesis (H_o) would not have been rejected, since 0.0768 is greater than 0.05 and would fall outside the region of rejection.

In Scenario Two illustrated here, the corresponding "Area between X and z" for $z = 1.77$ in Table K–2 is 0.4616, which, subtracted from 0.5000 equals to 0.0384 (see Figure I–1).

$$0.5000 - 0.4616 = 0.0384$$

Since this is a two-tailed test, the area 0.0384 must be doubled to obtain the p-value.

$$2(0.0384) = 0.0768$$

Hence, the p-value or probability value for Scenario Two is 0.0768.

Step 4: Apply the Decision Rule. Since the *p*-value of 0.0768 is greater than the $\alpha = 0.05$ level of significance, the decision is *not* to reject the null hypothesis (H_o). See Figure I–3.

Step 5: State the Conclusion. There is insufficient evidence to support the claim of the null hypothesis, H_o, that college undergraduates believe consuming 4.1 drinks in an hour constitutes binge drinking.

Fisher's *p*-Value Method for Small Samples

As we illustrated in Chapter 9, when the standard deviation of the population is unknown and the size of the sample is less than 30, the *t*-test is more appropriate for testing hypotheses involving population means. The *p*-values for *t*-test are derived via a four-step process, using the test statistic, *t*, the degrees of freedom ($n - 1$), and Table M–1 in Appendix M.

For example, assume the following data: $n = 15$, $df = 15 - 1 = 14$, $t - 1.987$ and proceed as follows:

1. Compute *t* using Formula 9–4 $\left[\frac{\bar{X} - \mu}{s_{\bar{x}}}\right]$ introduced in Chapter 9 $\left(\text{where } s_{\bar{x}} = \frac{s}{\sqrt{n}}\right)$. In this case, $t = 1.987$.

2. Locate the appropriate row of values corresponding to the number of degrees of freedom for the sample in Table M–1 in Appendix M. In this case, since $df = 14$, we would look at row 14.

3. Table B3 does not lend itself to finding exact *p*-values. However, by looking across the row of values in which the *t*-values for $n - 1$ degrees of freedom falls, we can identify the upper and lower limits of an exact *p*-value. This approach is known as the *interval estimate method*. In this case, looking across row 14, where $t = 1.987$ falls, we find the lower and upper limits of the exact *p*-value interval to be 1.761 and 2.145, respectively, as shown in Figure I–4.

These values correspond to the $\alpha = 0.05$ and $\alpha = 0.025$ levels of significance for a one-tailed test, and $\alpha = 0.10$ and $\alpha = 0.05$ for a two-tailed test.

4. Reject or do not reject the null hypothesis depending on the alpha level chosen for the hypothesis test. In this case, for example, the null would be rejected for both a one- and two-tailed test if $\alpha = 0.05$ was chosen as the significance level but not rejected if the significance level was set at $\alpha = 0.01$.

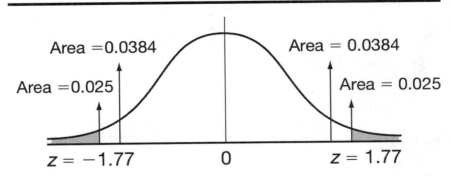

Figure I–3. Test statistic and corresponding area of regions of rejection for two-tailed test at $\alpha = 0.05$: Scenario Two. Courtesy of Karen Weasen.

	Level of significance for one-tailed tests					
	.10	.05	.025	.01	.005	.0005
	Level of significance for two-tailed tests					
df	.20	.10	.05	.02	.01	.001
1	3.078	6.314	12.706	31.821	63.657	636.619
2	1.886`	2.920	4.303	6.965	9.925	31.598
14	1.345	**1.761**	**2.145**	2.624	2.977	4.140
15	1.341	1.753	2.131	2.602	2.947	4.073
16	1.337	1.746	**2.120**	**2.583**	2.921	4.015
120	1.289	1.658	1.980	2.358	2.617	3.373
∞	1.282	1.645	1.960	2.326	2.576	3.291

Figure I–4. Selected critical values and levels of the t distribution. Courtesy of Karen Weasen.

Scenario Three

A sociologist claims that the mean age of listeners of conservative talk shows is over 40. He selects and surveys a random sample of 17 and finds the mean age of the sample to be 43, with a standard deviation of 5 years. At $\alpha = 0.05$, is there sufficient evidence to reject the claim?

Relevant Data: $\mu = 40$, $n = 17$,
$\overline{X} = 4.3$, $s = 5$, $\alpha = 0.05$,
$df = 17 - 1 = 16$, one-tailed test

Step 1: State the Hypotheses

$$H_o: \mu = 40 \qquad H_1: \mu > 40$$

Step 2: Compute the Test Statistic

$$t = \frac{\overline{X} - \mu}{s_{\overline{X}}} = \frac{43 - 40}{1.213} = \frac{3}{1.213} = 2.473$$

Where $s_{\overline{X}} = \frac{s}{\sqrt{n}} = \frac{5}{\sqrt{17}} = \frac{5}{4.123} = 1.213$

Step 3: Find the p-Value. Looking across row 16 (df) in the abbreviated version of Table M–1, we see that $t = 2.473$ falls between 2.120 and 2.583, which correspond to $\alpha = 0.025$ and $\alpha = 0.01$. Therefore the p-value falls between the 0.01 and 0.25 levels of significance.

Step 4: Apply the Decision Rule. Since the level of significance of interest to the researcher is $\alpha = 0.05$, and the p-value of $t = 2.473$ falls between the $\alpha = 0.025$ and $\alpha = 0.01$ levels, the null hypothesis (H_o) is rejected (i.e., p-value < α). See Figure I–5.

Step 5: State the Conclusion. There is sufficient evidence to support the sociologist's claim (H_1) that the average age of listeners of conservative talk shows is over 40.

Summary Notes

The calculation of p-values for hypothesis tests for the mean involve: (1) the type or direction of the test (right-tailed, left-tailed, or two-tailed); and (2) an observed test statistic, z or t-value (including the number of degrees of freedom). A summary of the location of p-values are presented in Figure I–6.

There are two approaches to using the p-value method. Some researchers decide on the alpha (α) level value in advance of the hypothesis test and then use the p-value to make a decision regarding the null hypothesis. This is the approach we have taken here.

On the other hand, some researchers chose not to set an α level, but simply report the p-value and leave it to the reader to decide whether the null hypothesis should be rejected or retained.

In cases where only a p-value is reported, many researchers will use guidelines, such as the one offered below, in deciding whether to reject or retain the null hypothesis.

If p-value < 0.01, the result is highly significant. Reject H_o.

If p-value ≥ 0.01 but < 0.05, the result is significant. Reject H_o.

If p-value ≥ 0.05, the result is not significant. Do not reject H_o.

Some statisticians use an even simpler set of guides of the combined method (although theoretically and logically incorrect, as noted earlier), such as:

If p-value $\leq \alpha$, reject H_o.

If p-value $> \alpha$, do not reject H_o.

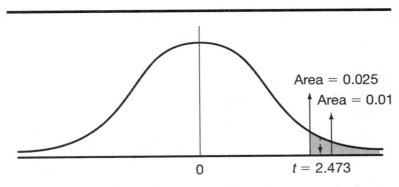

Figure I–5. Test statistic and corresponding area of region for rejection for one-tailed test at $\alpha = 0.05$: Scenario Three. Courtesy of Karen Weasen.

If H_1 contains	> (more than)	< (less than)	≠ (not equal to)
Location of the p-value	The area to the right of an observed value	The area to the left of an observed value	Twice the area to the right or left of an observed value*

Figure I–6. Location of p-values for directional and nondirectional tests. Courtesy of Karen Weasen.

APPENDIX J

Single-Subject Designs

Theoretical Foundations and Statistical Methods of Single-Subject Research: Most Frequently Asked Questions

Historical and Theoretical Foundations of Single-Subject Research

Most Frequently Asked Questions and Their Answers

Question 1. What Is Single-Subject Research?

■ It refers to the study of a single subject over a period of time (or phases) to determine whether or not a given treatment (intervention) is effective in changing one's behavior or score. Typically, the most widely used single-subject research designs are illustrated as follows:

1. The investigator obtains pretreatment measures (baseline, denoted by A) before intervention (treatment, denoted by B).
2. Then, the investigator introduces an intervention to a certain subject.
3. The investigator continues to measure the subject's scores after an intervention is introduced.

4. Then, the investigator determines whether or not any evident change in the dependent variable from the baseline has occurred. (This design is called the A-B design.)
5. The investigator, who wants to go further, may remove the intervention to determine if the subject's score returns to the baseline phase. (This design is called the A-B-A design.)

Question 2. What Are the Other Names for Single-Subject Designs?

■ Single-subject designs are variously called (a) small-N designs, (b) $N = 1$ designs, (c) intensive designs, (d) idiographic designs, and so on.

Question 3. What Are Philosophical and Historical Foundations of Single-Subject Designs?

■ It is rooted in the work of B. F. Skinner and many other advocates of "operant conditioning" or "applied behavioral analysis."
■ Skinner stated: "Establish the behavior in which you are interested, submit the organism to a particular treatment, and look again at the behavior."
■ Advocates argue that such methods may prove more useful than therapies

based on group research concerned with the classical hypothesis testing.

- The movement toward the adoption of such forms of evidence and experimentation will lead to greater acceptance by:
  a. "the public,
  b. those influential in the creation of public policy" (Robey et al., 1999).

Question 4. What Are the Advantages of Single-Subject Designs?

- They are advantageous when the number of subjects appropriate for study is limited.
- They allow for better intrasubject control than group studies.
- They are well adapted for meeting quality-assurance standards demanded by public and private health care agencies and organizations.
- They are applicable to psychological counseling and related areas. They are described as "the best kept secret in counseling" (Lundervold & Belwood, 2000).
- The design identifies functional relationships between an independent variable and a dependent variable, something a typical case study does not allow.
- Another merit of the use of the single-subject designs is the capability for examinations of both intersubject and intrasubject variability.
- The design allows an investigator to be able to correctly identify a confounding (extraneous) variable easier than a group design.

Question 5. What Are the Major Goals of Single-Subject Research?

- They must
  a. Gain precise control over the experimental conditions by eliminating extraneous variables.
  b. Establish a stable level of responding (baseline) before administering an intervention.
  c. Record the treated behavior within a given time period.
  d. Perform a visual and/or statistical/probabilistic analysis of the data to determine the treatment outcome.

Question 6. What Are the Limitations of Single-Subject Designs?

- A major concern about the single-subject design is external validity, that is, the result of one observation that can accurately generalize others or a target population. Some could easily argue that such a lack of external validity may be corrected in replication.
- Assessing change with single-subject data is difficult because current statistical and nonstatistical (visual approach) methods are unreliable and cannot control Type 1 and Type 2 errors effectively.

Question 7. What Are the Commonly Used Single-Subject Designs?

1. A-B Design. The most basic of the small-N (time series) designs in which observations are made over a period of time to establish a baseline (A, prior to a treatment) for the subsequent comparison of retest data. Next, a treatment (or an intervention) is introduced (B) and an investigator observes changes in the dependent variable to determine the effectiveness of the treatment.

2. A-B-A Design. A type of small-N time series design in which a baseline (A) condition is first established, followed by a treatment (intervention) condition, denoted by B, and then finally by the withdrawal of the treatment

condition, that is, return to baseline (A). It is also called a reversal design. The logic of the A-B-A design is as follows: If the treatment is effective, there exist some changes (most likely a positive change) in the dependent variable after treatment is introduced, and there will be a return to the baseline condition when the treatment is withdrawn.

3. A-B-A-B Design. The most commonly used of the small-N time series designs. First, a baseline (A) phase is established. Second, treatment (B) is introduced. Third, treatment is withdrawn, that is, return to the baseline (A). Fourth, treatment (B) is introduced again to assess its reliability. A variation of this design involves substituting an independent variable in the final B condition that is different than the first B condition. In effect, the A-B-A-B sequence involves the study of the treatment effect as it both precedes and follows a baseline phase. Clinically, the fourth phase of such a design is highly desirable since it avoids the negative consequences of the A-B-A experiment that leaves the subject at the end of the study as they were in the beginning—namely, in a state comparable with their original baseline level of responding. It is also called replication designs.

4. Alternating Treatment Design. Two treatments, A and B, are alternated randomly as they are applied to a single subject. The results are examined to determine whether one of the two treatments is more effective than the other. It is also called a "between-series design."

5. Reversal Design. Baseline measures are first recorded prior to a treatment. An intervention is then introduced that is followed in the next phase by a therapeutic reversal in intervention.

6. Multiple-Baseline Design. Small-N designs that involve the application of a treatment to different baselines at different times. The main steps in the use of any multiple-baseline designs are as follows:

a. Establish reliable and stable baselines on all behaviors selected for modification.

b. Randomly select a behavior (or a subject or setting) for treatment while simultaneously observing an untreated behavior (or subject or setting).

c. Randomly select another untreated baseline and introduce the experimental treatment.

d. Continue until all baselines have been treated.

e. Demonstrate treatment effectiveness by showing systematic modifications in performance across more than one baseline.

7. Changing Criterion Design. A variation of the small-N designs. First, a series of behavioral criteria are established. A treatment plan is then introduced, and its effectiveness is judged based on the extent to which the response level of the target behavior matches the present criteria.

Question 8. What Are the Advantages/Disadvantages of Each Design?

See Table J–1.

Question 9. How Do We Evaluate Treatment Efficacy in Single-Subject Research?

See Table J–2.

Table J–1. Advantages and Limitations of the Most Widely Used Single Subject Designs

Name of Design	Advantages	Limitations
A-B	• Least complicated design and easy to construct.	• The lack of control of extraneous variables for determining a treatment efficacy, that is, internal validity issue should be noted. Replication may correct the problem.
A-B-A	• It affords greater experimental control by adding a second A.	• Difficult to interpret the follow-up data (a second A), after the treatment (B) is terminated. • A possible ethical concern for some investigators relates to withholding treatment when a second baseline is used.
A-B-A-B	• It allows for demonstrating the influence of the independent variable on two occasions. • Clinically, the fourth phase B is highly desirable since it avoids the negative consequences of the A-B-A design that leaves the subject at the end of the study as they were in the beginning—namely, in a state comparable with their original baseline level of responding.	• A same ethical concern, as stated in A-B-A, should be noted. The possible answer to that is to gain more confidence in its potential efficacy by demonstrating its positive influence during a second treatment period.
Alternating Treatments	• Some type of treatment is always being used. • Comparing differences between alternative treatments can assess their relative effectiveness.	• Can be associated with multiple-treatment interference effects, that is, the tendency of preceding treatments to make later treatments more or less effective. • Can result from the order in which treatments are given or from the effects of one treatment carrying over to another.
Multiple-Baseline	• Do not necessitate withdrawal of treatment to demonstrate treatment efficacy. • Well suited for a variety of clinical applications, especially when an investigator wishes to monitor several treatments concurrently.	• Effects arising from treating the first behavior in a series might spread across to other behaviors under treatment. • Problems resulting from failure to achieve stable baselines prior to intervention. • Large amount of time needed to collect data.

Name of Design	Advantages	Limitations
Reversal	• Gains power in illustrating the efficacy of a clinical intervention.	• Possibility of being unable to reverse some negative consequence associated with the effort to demonstrate experimental control over the targeted behavior. Thus, for practical and ethical reasons, caution should be exercised in the use of this design.
Changing Criterion	• It has many useful applications to clinical or applied settings in which random assignment of individuals to treatment conditions is impractical or impossible to achieve.	• Falls short of meeting the randomization requirement of true experiments.

Table J–2. The Strengths and Limitations of the Most Widely Used Approaches for Evaluating Treatment Efficacy in Single Subject Research

Approach	Method	Strengths/Limitations
Visual/ Graphical	1. Split-Middle 2. Celeration Line 3. Two Standard Deviation Rule 4. Frequency Histogram 5. Bar Graph	**Strengths** • All data values are presented in a single source, so that it is less time-consuming and less complex when we analyze and interpret the results. • It uses a more direct descriptive approach to describe the population parameter (a single subject) in which one has all information, whereas inferential statistics are used to make predictions about an entire population based on representative samples of behavior. **Limitations** • It tends to produce a low level of agreement among raters concerning the research result. • There is a lack of universally accepted decision criteria in detecting a change. • Excessive risk of a Type 1 error (no actual change but rated as showing a treatment effect) especially when a number of sample data points is small. • Less statistical power, that is, more Type II error (actual change but rated as showing no treatment effect) may be committed when a number of sample data points is small.

continues

Table J–2. *continued*

Approach	Method	Strengths/Limitations
Statistical	**Inferential** 1. t-Test 2. ANOVA 3. Mann-Whitney U-test 4. Regression **Time Series** 1. Moving Average 2. Interrupted Time-Series Analysis (ITSA) 3. A New Interrupted Time-Series Analysis (ITSACORR) 4. The C Statistic **Probabilistic** 1. Binomial Tests 2. Bayesian Analysis with C Statistic (Jones, 2003) 3. Bayesian Analysis with Beta Probability (Satake & Maxwell, 2005) **Nonparametric** 1. Chi-Square Test	**Strengths** • It is reliable when its assumptions (normality, independence, and homogeneity or variances) are met; it maintains Type 1 error at the satisfactory level. • It can detect small but consistent treatment effects. • In contrast with the visual approach, it produces consistent and more scientific results across data analysis. **Limitations** • The results of a hypothesis test depend on both effect size and sample size in the study. Small effects that may be statistically significant may have very little practical or clinical significance. • An inappropriate conclusion is often associated with rejecting a null hypothesis. • Parametric assumptions must be satisfied in order to obtain an accurate result. • When data values are positively autocorrelated (each value is more similar to its preceding value than to the mean), observations are more similar to each other. This leads to artificial deflation of error variances and inflation of a t(F) value. Hence, it increases the probability of making a Type 1 error. • Negatively autocorrelated data values (each value is less similar to its preceding value than to the mean) are more dissimilar to each other than would occur by chance. This leads to artificial inflation of error variance and deflation of a t(F) value. Hence, it increases the probability of making a Type II error. • When we use regression analysis, many actual data points that are further away from the central zone will be dropped and removed from the final analysis. It may produce an inaccurate result especially when a number of sample data points are small. • When we use moving average time-series analysis, moving average values can be extremely inconsistent and discrepant with the actual trend of existing data set, that is, the mean (or median) value neglects the true value of measure of dispersion. It must be calculated on the actual data values, not the average values, to increase the accuracy of the results.

Question 10. What Is the Significance of the Use of Statistical Analysis in Single-Subject Research?

■ Investigators need to know the likelihood of the change due to either pure random chance or a true treatment effect in many cases, that is, "what is the probability that the successful outcome derived from a particular study was the result of chance or a true treatment effect?"

Question 11. Statistically, How Do We Control Error Variance (due to Chance)?

■ With group-designs, error variance (V_e) is controlled experimentally (by means of randomization).
■ With single-subject designs, error variance (V_e) is controlled using replication and as much as possible experimentally.

Question 12. What Do We Mean by "Experimentally"?

■ Investigators must identify the factor(s) that is affecting one's behavior and the confounding factor(s), other than treatment through therapy, counseling, and so on.
■ Using individuals as their own controls, comparing no intervention and intervention time periods.
■ Replication across subjects is also used in single-subject research to enhance control.

Question 13. What Are the General Procedures of the Classical Statistical Methods in Single-Subject Research?

■ If autocorrelation r (Pearson correlation coefficient involving serial dependency in a temporally order sequence of data points) are not statistically significant (or it is believed to be nonsignificant visually), you may proceed with a t-test, ANOVA, or the nonparametric Mann-Whitney U-test.

Question 14. What Is a Time Series? How Do We Evaluate Data Values?

■ Time series analysis is about whether there is an evident "trend" in the sequential measurements.
■ Trend is evaluated by two components: slope (evaluated visually by the time series graph) and magnitude (y intercept: it is evaluated using the C statistics).
■ The most commonly used methods are moving average (a series of the mean of successive data point values), interrupted time-series analysis (autocorrelational time series), and a revised interrupted time-series analysis (improved version of interrupted time-series analysis).

Question 15. What Are the Limitations of Time Series Analysis?

■ Moving average values can be extremely inconsistent (a greater degree of fluctuation) with the actual trend of real existing data set, that is, the mean (or median) value of lag 1 (or 2, 3, etc.) neglects the true value of measure of dispersion. It must be calculated on the actual data values, not the average values, to increase the accuracy of observation.

Question 16. What Is the Limitation of the Regressional/ Correlational Method?

■ To find a line of best fit, many actual data points (that are further away from the central zone) will be dropped and removed from the final analysis.

Question 17. How Do We Maintain the Power of a Statistical Test in Single-Subject Research?

■ In many cases, the quality and form of the data would suggest that you choose a more conservative approach (if one of the parametric assumptions is violated, i.e., normality, independence, and homogeneity of variances) with the nonparametric test for data analysis.

■ The disadvantage of the use of the nonparametric test is "Less Power" (or "increment of Type II error") in detecting a significant change between the phases, that is, you may risk failing to reject a null hypothesis when differences between phases (variables) are in fact unlikely to have occurred by chance alone.

■ You can still choose to perform the parametric methods, regardless of the violation of assumptions. With that decision, the risk is that you will reject the null hypothesis when the differences were actually the result of peculiarities in the data rather than differences in the treatment.

■ The best approach is to use both visual and statistical (including probabilistical) methods when we analyze single-subject data values. Also, you must remember that statistical analysis is exclusively designed for determining whether or not a change is "statistically significant" and does not address whether or not the change is "clinically or theoretically significant."

Question 18. What Is the C Statistic?

■ One of the simplest ways to calculate the change of "slope of the baseline" and "slope of the intervention period."

■ A primary advantage of the C statistic for single-subject data series is the significant reduction in the number of data points required—as few as eight data points per phase to have little loss in power to detect a change of slope and trend (Jones, 2003).

Question 19. How Do We Calculate C?

■ The value of C is given by:

$$C = 1 - \frac{\sum_{i-1}^{n-1}(x_i - x_{i+1})^2}{2 \cdot \sum_{i-1}^{n}(x_i - \bar{x})^2}$$

where x_i = the ith data point in the combined stream of n data points in phases A and B and $\bar{x}$ = overall mean

■ The ratio of C to its standard deviation (SD) gives a z-value, which provides the probability value of assessing the tenability of the null hypothesis.

■ $Z = \dfrac{C}{SD}$ where $SD = \sqrt{\dfrac{n-2}{(n-1)(n+1)}}$

Question 20. What Is the Rationale Behind the C Statistic in Actual Practice?

■ The logic of the C statistic for application with actual practice is: (1) continue baseline measures until there is no evident random variation (almost stable horizontally) and (2) after a treatment is given, you observe whether or not data points in treatment phase become statistically significantly different from data points in baseline phase based on a p-value.

Question 21. What Is the Difference, in Terms of Usage, between Time-Series with the C Statistic and Time-Series with Autocorrelation?

■ In essence, autocorrelation is a form of Pearson's product moment correlation coefficient (r). The most widely used autocorrelation in single-subject research is called "Lag 1," that is a correlation of each data point with the immediately following observed point in the series. It calculates only within each of the phase.

■ In the C statistic, you conduct an analysis of each phase separately and then the analysis of the outcome of two phases combined, for example, baseline analysis, treatment analysis, and both baseline + treatment analysis.

Question 22. How Do We Conduct a Chi-Square Test in Single-Subject Design?

■ Categorize "desired" (falls at or above the celeration/split-middle line) and "undesired" (falls below the celeration/split-middle line) outcomes using either a celeration or split-middle line for a 2 × 2 contingency table analysis. It is shown in Table J–3 in A-B design.

■ The basic steps for the method are summarized as follows:

1. Identify whether or not there is evident change (increase or decrease) in the baseline phase.
2. Extend the celeration (or split-middle) line through the treatment phase.
3. The two columns in the first row for the analysis are the number of points in the baseline data that are at or above the celeration line (or split-middle line), called "Desired," and the number of data points that are below the line, called "Undesired."
4. Comparable data for the treatment phase provides the second row for the analysis.
5. Calculate an observed χ^2 value and conclude it.

H_o: No change

H_a: Evident Change

$$\text{Observed } \chi^2 \text{ value} = \sum \frac{(0 - E)}{E}$$

with degrees of freedom = $(Row - 1) \times (Column - 1)$

O = number of data points

E = expected number of data points = $\frac{(Row\ Subtotal) \times (Column\ Subtotal)}{Grand\ Total}$ for an appropriate category

Question 23. What Is a Binomial Expansion Test and How Is It Performed?

■ A binomial test is focused on the consistency of whatever differences may occur whereas a *t*-test, ANOVA, and

Table J–3. A Two-by-Two Chi-Square Table

Outcomes Phase	Desired	Undesired	Subtotal
Baseline (A)			
Treatment (B)			
Subtotal			Grand Total

Mann-Whitney *U*-test focus on "how much" difference exists between the phases. The outcome of the binomial analysis is a direct probability of occurrence of a particular event of interest.

■ To calculate the binomial probability, we need (a) number of trials, and number of "successful" outcomes (it means "how many" data points meet your criteria). Then, we calculate it as follows:

p (k successes in n trials)
$= {}_nC_k \cdot p^k \cdot (1 - p)^{n-k}$

where ${}_nC_k$ = number of different arrangements can be made in selecting k successes from a total of n trials,

$${}_nC_k = \frac{n!}{k! \cdot (n-k)!}$$

$n!$ represents (n factorial) the product of n consecutive integers from n to 1.

p = probability of a success

Question 24. In a Binomial Analysis, How Do We State Hypotheses?

■ The null hypothesis (H$_o$) states that a population proportion in the baseline phase (A), denoted by π_b, is equal to the population proportion in the intervention phase (B), denoted by π_i, that is, symbolically it is written as follows:

H$_o$: $\pi_b = \pi_i$ (No evident change)
H$_a$: $\pi_b \neq \pi_i$ (Evident change)

■ Count the number of data points that fall below the celeration (or split-middle) line, and we write:

$$\hat{\pi}_b = \frac{number\ of\ data\ points\ falling\ below\ the\ line}{total\ number\ of\ data\ points}$$

(baseline)

$$\hat{\pi}_i = \frac{number\ of\ data\ points\ falling\ below\ the\ line}{total\ number\ of\ data\ points}$$

(intervention)

where $\hat{\pi}_b$ and $\hat{\pi}_i$ are called "a point estimate" for $\hat{\pi}_b$ and $\hat{\pi}_b$, respectively.

■ Cohen (1988) recommends that the test of H$_o$ should be rewritten as:

H$_o$: $\varnothing_b = \varnothing_i$
where $\hat{\varnothing}_b = 2 \arcsin \sqrt{\hat{\pi}_b}$

Using the critical value given by Cohen (1988), we may draw a conclusion whether or not evident change occurred.

Question 25. Are There Any New Developments on Statistical Methods for Single-Subject Designs?

■ We have successfully implemented the so-called Bayesian probabilistic approach with C-statistics (Jones, 2003) and/or beta distribution (Satake & Maxwell, 2005) into the single-subject designs. Using this approach, we do not have to be concerned about the usual parametric assumptions, such as "Normality," "Independence," and "Homogeneity of Variances."

Question 26. What Is the Bayesian Analysis?

■ A mathematical basis for determining the degree to which a prior belief corresponds with the actual facts of subsequent observations. Statistically, a formula of calculating the inverse conditional probability of an event, p (A given B), from the conditional probability of another event, p (B given A), and the unconditional probability of the event p (A).

■ First described by an English clergyman by the name of Thomas Bayes in

1763, the Bayesian method provides a mathematical basis for expressing one's beliefs in the language of probability prior to collecting data. Such a statement, called the prior probability, is akin to the research hypothesis (or alternate hypothesis) with the additional requirement of including a numerical or quantitative estimate or "bet" reflecting the degree of belief about a predicted result. The next step is to derive a data probability based on the sample of data actually collected. The data probability can be regarded as the conditional credibility of a particular view pending the calculation of a posterior probability. The latter probability, reflecting the updated credibility of an original opinion or viewpoint, is derived from a mathematical combination of the prior and data probabilities.

Question 27. How Does Bayesian Analysis Work?

■ Prior Probability (one's subjective belief) → New Data → Combined New Data with Prior Probability → Update Prior Probability → Posterior Probability (or a new prior probability) → New Data → Combined New Data with New Prior Probability → Update New Prior Probability → New Posterior Probability (or a new prior probability)

Keep repeating this cycle process to derive the maximum likelihood of a particular event of your interest. This cumulative process provides a guide for changing and existing one's belief as new evidence emerges.

Question 28. What Is the Rationale behind Bayesian Analysis?

■ For instance, in a clinical setting, an investigator needs to know the appropriate time/situation of providing a necessary treatment to his or her clients to prevent them from further damages. In order to accomplish this task, what they need is the study design that is continuous (from day to day) and cumulative [(In Bayesian view, the likelihood of the occurrence of the 2nd data value is contingent on the occurrence of the 1st data value, symbolically we write p(2nd) data given that 1st data have already been observed)], and the statistical analysis that can operate in a cumulative way, rather than a terminal way.

■ Early detection is extremely crucial, so the investigator must be sensitive enough to know and detect their client's changes (evident or not) on a daily basis, rather than the overall mean or median changes over a long period of time.

■ The ideal statistical model is a mixture of time series analysis and cumulative probabilistic model. Bayesian analysis rests on a premise that the probability of a particular outcome on a particular day is contingent on the fact that all other outcomes in the preceding stages have already observed/occurred.

Question 29(a). How Do We Determine "Changes in Level" and "Changes in Trend" Graphically?

See Figure J–1.

Question 29(b). In General, How Do We Analyze Single-Subject Data Visually, that is, How Do We Detect a Change of One's Response by Using the Visual/Graphical Approach?

■ To determine the cause of one's change, a horizontal stable baseline is a desired characteristic in single-subject research.

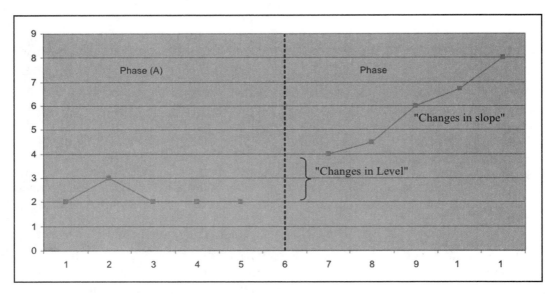

Figure J–1. Illustration of "changes in slope" and "changes in level" in A-B design.

■ **Phase Length.** A minimum of at least three consecutive observations should be used for purposes of plotting data points during each phase of the experiment. So far as possible, the baseline phase should continue until stability in the targeted behavior has been established.

■ **Change one variable at a time.** When moving from one phase to another, only one independent variable should be altered so that its influence can be observed and recorded independent of any other influence.

■ **Level.** Refers to the magnitude of the data points on a graph. Typically, the change of the y intercept indicates the level change between baseline phase (A) and intervention phase (B). Two aspects to examine include the level stability and level change of data.

   a. **Level Stability.** The range of the data point value determines level stability within a particular phase of the experiment regardless of whether it is a baseline phase or treatment phase. As a general guide, if 80% to 90% of the data points of a condition fall within a 15% range of the mean level of all data point values of a condition, they are considered to be level stable (Tawney & Gast, 1984).

   b. **Level Change.** To determine the change in the level of the dependent variable between the baseline and treatment phases of an experiment, compare the last data point of the baseline phase with the first data point of the treatment phase. Only adjacent phases can serve as valid comparisons of data points. Generally, the sooner a change in response level is observed following the introduction of treatment and the greater its magnitude in relation to baseline, the more confidence we can have in the treatment effect. It is also possible to identify the degree of level change within a particular phase. A simple way to accomplish this is to: (a) identify the first and last data points of a phase, (b) subtract the smaller of the values from the larger, and (c) observe whether the change in level is in a positive or negative direction based on the treatment objectives.

■ **Trend.** In general, it refers to the slope (rate of change) of the data points on a graph. The data points can be said to be accelerating (increasing with respect to their ordinate values), decelerating (decreasing with respect to their ordinate values), or may show zero slope (data points are level with abscissa). Figure J–2 illustrates these three trend characteristics found in single-subject data.

■ However, should the slopes of the data points in adjacent phases move in the same direction, it is difficult to detect a treatment effect under such circumstances. This is because such a change simply may be due to extraneous variables such as maturation, history, and the like.

■ Furthermore, should the data points illustrate a large degree of fluctuation during the baseline phase, the number of trials during this phase should be increased until either: (1) a stable response rate is demonstrated, that is, response rate $= \frac{response\ frequency}{time}$, or (2) the trend of the direction of behavior of interest is opposite to that of the intended treatment effect.

Question 30. What Is a Celeration Line?

■ To estimate the slope of the trend, the most commonly used visual approach is to draw a straight line that most closely approximates the majority of the data

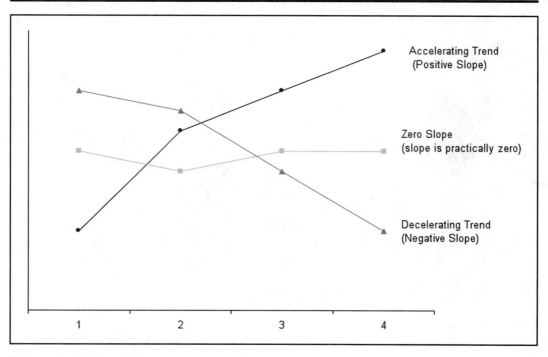

Figure J–2. Three different trend characteristics.

points in a series. Such a line is called a celeration line. The procedures for obtaining a celeration line are identical to those for obtaining a split-middle line except that means are used instead of medians. The instructions of drawing such a line for a hypothetical series of data points are shown in Figure J–3 and described below.

Instructions for Drawing a Celeration Line (refer to Figure J–3).

X represents the intersection point between the median data point and the dashed vertical line.

1. Step 1: Count the total number of data points in the baseline phase (pretest 1 to pretest 10) and divide this number so that half fall on one side of a solid vertical line and the remaining

half fall on the other side. As can be seen, the solid line falls directly in the center of the graph. Next, draw a second dashed vertical line on each side of the solid vertical line that again divides the data points in half.

2. Step 2: Identify the median score for the data distribution on each side of the solid vertical line. The median is the middle value of the data points with respect to their magnitude.

3. Step 3: Draw a dashed horizontal line through the median data point on each side of the solid vertical line, so it intersects the dashed vertical lines.

4. Step 4: Draw a straight solid line by connecting the two points of intersection (denoted by X) passing through the solid vertical line. This final step completes the construction of the celeration line. In this case, we can visually determine that the trend of

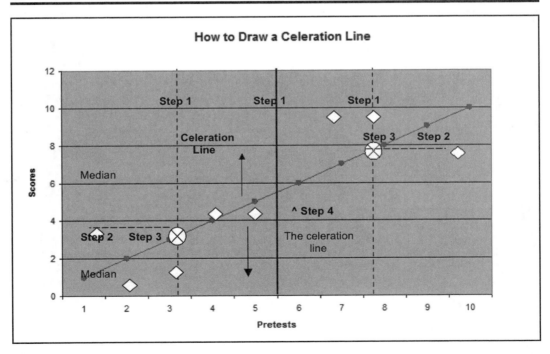

Figure J–3. Illustration of a celeration line.

the data points is accelerating. However, based on such a visual analysis alone, we cannot determine the *rate of change*—how fast the dependent variable changes over time. This determination can only be made by the use of statistical methods that are beyond the scope of this appendix.

Question 31. What Are the Differences between the Classical Statistical Approach and the Bayesian Probabilistic Approach?

■ A table for classical statistical approach versus Bayesian approach in hypothesis testing is illustrated in Table J–4.

Table J–4. Classical Versus Bayesian Statistics

Sources	Classical Statistics	Bayesian Statistics
Number of hypotheses	Only two (null and alternative) hypotheses can be stated each time	Allowed to have two or more hypotheses at one time
Hypothesized values in initial hypotheses	More objective, views, or well-defined previous knowledge	Researcher is free to express subjective views from previous experience
Data analysis	Normal z, t, or F distributions	Beta distribution with Gamma function
Assumptions of data analysis	1. Independence 2. Homogeneity of variances	None
Type of conclusion derived	Rejection or nonrejection of null hypothesis. The hypothesis rejected is totally disregarded. No specific value of a true population parameter is derived.	None of the hypotheses disregarded. Researcher estimates the credibility of each hypothesized value and derives the maximum likelihood of a true population parameter.
ANOVA	Researcher determines whether or not there are treatment effects on dependent variable(s). Significant or not	Researcher considers how much parameter (treatment effect) affects dependent variable(s); measures the strength of each treatment. Specific values that represent the degree of strength are derived.
ANOVA model selection	Trial and error	The most powerful and suitable model can be found. How accurately does each model predict a future value?
MANOVA and ANOVA	Trial and error	Same as above

- Table J–4 also summarizes the main differences between two approaches.

Question 32. What Is Bayesian Analysis with C Statistic?

- Jones (2003) invented a method to test the hypothesis of randomness (evident change or not) of baseline + treatment phases by means of Bayesian analysis. Tables J–5, J–6, and J–7 illustrate step-by-step the procedure for this method of hypothesis testing.

1. Step 1: Calculate a p-value from baseline + treatment phase.
2. Step 2: First replication: Calculate a new likelihood, a p-value of $z = \frac{C}{SD}$ again using a set of new data values (baseline + treatment).
3. Step 3: Second replication: Calculate a new likelihood, a p-value of $z = \frac{C}{SD}$ once again using a set of new data values (baseline + treatment), and so on. Keep repeating the procedure and

we would eventually obtain the maximum likelihood posterior probability of H_o and H_a. Murphy (2000) stated that the essence of the Bayesian approach is a mathematical rule to guide the change of existing belief when there is new evidence, rather than any one study serving a "stand-alone" role, each new set of observations or study is conceptualized instead as just a tool for modifying the prior belief.

Question 33. What Is the Bayesian Analysis with Beta Probabilities?

- Satake and Maxwell (2005) formulated and applied an alternative method using a probability distribution called "Beta Distribution" for updating one's prior belief to eventually allow one to be able to derive the maximum likelihood of p-value of the belief by means of replications, that is, testing. (For further details, see Satake's book, entitled *Handbook of Statistical Methods in*

Table J–5. Initial Calculation Procedures of the Bayesian Analysis with a *C* Statistic

Hypotheses	Prior Probability	Likelihood	Data Probability Prior Likelihood	Posterior Probability
H_o: No evident change (Random)	0.5	p	$0.5p$	$\frac{0.5p}{\Sigma(sum)} = a$
H_a: Evident change (Not Random)	0.5 Not having any substantial knowledge about the matter, it is recommended that the series start with equal prior probabilities, that is, 50%–50%	$1 - p$ p is derived from a normal obtained z score, that is, $z = \dfrac{C}{SD}$	$0.5(1 - p)$ $\Sigma(sum) =$ $0.5p + 0.5(1 - p)$	$\dfrac{0.5(1 - p)}{\Sigma(sum)}$ $= 1 - a$ $\dfrac{Posterior\ Data}{\Sigma(sum)}$

Single Subject Design, Plural Publishing, 2008).

H_o: No evident change, H_a: Evident change, without using the classical parametric statistics assumptions.

Let us define:

- π = a point estimate (subjective or objective) of the binomial experiment
- n = sample size

Table J–6. Calculation Procedure in the First Replication Stage

Hypothesis	Prior	Likelihood	Data: Prior × Likelihood	Posterior
H_o: No evident change (Random)	a	p'	ap'	$\dfrac{ap'}{\Sigma(sum)} = b$
H_a: Evident change (Not Random)	$1 - a$	$1 - p'$	$(1 - a) \cdot (1 - p')$	$\dfrac{(1 - a)(1 - p')}{\Sigma(sum)}$ $= 1 - b$
	Note that prior of the 1st replication is equal to posterior of the preceding series.	p' = a p-value of the 1st replication, using $z = \dfrac{C}{SD}$	$\Sigma(sum) = ap' + (1 - a)(1 - p')$	$\dfrac{Data}{\Sigma(sum)}$

Table J–7. Calculation Procedure in the Second Replication

Hypothesis	Prior	Likelihood	Data: Prior × Likelihood	Posterior
H_o: No evident change (Random)	b	p''	bp''	$\dfrac{bp''}{\Sigma(sum)} = C$
H_a: Evident change (Not Random)	$1 - b$	$1 - p''$	$(1 - b) \cdot (1 - p'')$	$\dfrac{(1 - b)(1 - p'')}{\Sigma(sum)}$ $= 1 - C$
	Again, note that the prior probability of the 2nd replication is equal to the posterior probability of the 1st replication.	p'' = a p-value of the 2nd replication, using $z = \dfrac{C}{SD}$	$\Sigma(sum) = bp'' + (1 - b)(1 - p'')$	$\dfrac{Data}{\Sigma(sum)}$

■ x = number of observations having a particular characteristic we are investigating

Then, the prior distribution of "Beta" may be written as follows:

$$f(\pi) = \frac{(a + b - 1)!}{(a - 1)!(b - 1)!} \cdot \pi^{a-1} \cdot (1 - \pi)^{b-1}$$

where μ' (1st prior mean) and σ'^2 (1st prior variance) are calculated as:

$$\mu' = \frac{a}{a + b}, \quad \sigma'^2 = \frac{\mu'(1 - \mu')}{a + b + 1}$$

Note that a and b are two nonnegative integer parameters for π, and the purpose of such constants is to simply adjust the beta curve in such a way that the area under the curve equals 100%, thereby making the function a probability distribution. The shape of the curve is adjusted by the exponents for π and $1 - \pi$. Using a great deal of algebra, we can compute a and b as follows:

$$a = \mu' \left[\frac{\mu'(1 - \mu')}{\sigma'^2} - 1 \right]$$

$$b = (1 - \mu') \left[\frac{\mu'(1 - \mu')}{\sigma'^2} - 1 \right]$$

The data values are assumed to satisfy the binomial distribution, such that for the true value of π the probability of the data can be found.

Data Probability =

$$f(x|\pi) = \frac{n!}{x!(n - x)!} \cdot \pi^x \cdot (1 - \pi)^{n-x}$$

$$f\langle x|\pi\rangle = \frac{n!}{x!(n - x)!} \cdot \pi^x \cdot (1 - \pi)^{n-x}$$

$f\langle x|\pi\rangle$ means f(x given π)

Next, we combine the prior probability and data probability together by Bayes's rule, and it gives the posterior probability:

$$f\langle \pi|x\rangle = \frac{(n + a + b - 1)!}{(x + a - 1)!(n - x + b - 1)!} \cdot \pi^{x + a - 1} \cdot (1 - \pi)^{n - x + b - 1}$$

which is a beta distribution with parameters $x + a$ and $n - x + b$. The posterior mean μ'' and variance σ''^2 can be computed as:

$$\mu'' \frac{x + a}{n + a + b} \quad \sigma''^2 = \frac{\mu''(1 - \mu'')}{n + a + b + 1}$$

Keep repeating this process (complexity of beta probability calculations can easily be done by using the statistical software packages like MINITAB, SPSS, etc.). We would again be able to derive the maximum likelihood p-value of a particular event of interest. One of the major advantages of this approach over others is that, for reasonably large exponents, the beta distribution can be approximated by the normal distribution and Bayesian probability intervals for π, regardless of n, can be easily found from $\mu \pm z_{\frac{a}{2}} \cdot \sigma$. Even when the beta curve is not entirely symmetric, the normal approximation is still quite good. Finally, Iversen (1984) stated "the reason Bayesian inference is so much more natural is that it is more closely geared to the research process itself than is classical inference. The research problem starts with an initial uncertainty about one or more parameters, data are collected in order to increase our information about the parameters, and in light of the new information, the initial uncertainty has been reduced."

Clinically Relevant Example: A Hypothetical Case

Analysis of Single-Subject Data Using the Beta Probability Distribution (for Mathematically Inclined Readers)

Bayesian Approach with Beta Distribution: A Hypothetical Example in AB Design

Given the following set of hypothetical data values in AB design, we derive the maximum likelihood (aka Bayesian p-value) of a subject's score change in day-to-day to determine the strength of evidence.

A_1: 5, 4, 4, 2, 3, 4, 4, 6 (out of 10)

B_1: 7, 5, 4, 6, 6, 7, 5, 4, 7, 7 (out of 10)

It is mathematically convenient for us to convert each score into its decimal equivalent, so that we now have:

A_1: 0.5, 0.4, 0.4, 0.2, 0.3, 0.4, 0.4, 0.6

B_1: 0.7, 0.5, 0.4, 0.6, 0.6, 0.7, 0.5, 0.4, 0.7, 0.7

Using the formulas for two constant values (a, b) for the beta probabilities, shown on p. 454, we calculate them as follows:

A_1: $\mu (A_1) = 0.4$, $\sigma^2(A_1) = 0.125$,

$$a = \mu \left[\left(\frac{\mu \times (1 - \mu)}{\sigma^2} \right) - 1 \right] = 0.368,$$

$$b = (1 - \mu) \left[\left(\frac{\mu \times (1 - \mu)}{\sigma^2} \right) - 1 \right] = 0.552,$$

$$\mu = \frac{(a + x)}{(a = b = n)}, \ \sigma^2 = \left[\mu \times \frac{(1 - \mu)}{(a + b + n + 1)} \right]$$

B_1: 1st value = 0.7, so that the cumulative density function $F(X)$ can be calculated $P(X = 0.7$, given that B (0.368, 0.552) is provided) as follows:

$$F(0 < X < 0.7) =$$

$$\int^{0.7} \frac{\left[t^{0.368 - 1} \times (1 - t)^{0.552 - 1} \right]}{B} (0.368, 0.552)$$

$$= 0.72774$$

The Bayesian p-value is given as $1 - F(X)$ $= 1 - 0.72774 = 0.27226$; therefore, after the 1st day of intervention period, we did not detect a significant treatment effect $(p > 0.05)$. The software packages such as MINITAB 14 or SPSS can easily derive the calculation shown above.

By the same token, we have a 2nd value 0.5, so that we calculate a and b for the new beta density function $B(a, b)$ such that $\mu = (0.368 + 0.7)/ (0.368 + 0.552 + 1) = 0.55625$,

$$\sigma = SQR \left[\frac{(0.55625) \times (1 - 0.55625)}{(0.368 + 0.552 + 1 + 1)} \right]$$

$= 0.17$, where $n = 1$ and $x = 0.7$,
$a = 1.06805$, $b = 0.85204$, and
$F (0 < X < 0.5) = F (0.5) = 0.42330$

Therefore, the Bayesian p-value after Day 2 is 0.57670 $(1 - 0.42330)$. Again, we did not detect a significant treatment effect. The p-value after Day 2 is actually larger than the one after Day 1, so the strength of evidence of the treatment got weaker by almost 30%.

By repeating this process to update the maximum likelihood of each of the intervention data values, we can obtain the results shown in Table J–8.

Figure J–4 shows the beta distribution curve of each trial graphically. The interval for probability density distribution gets

Table J–8. Summary of Beta Distribution, Beta (a,b), in Each of 10 Days' Actual Observations: A Hypothetical Study

Intervention (B₁)	Data Values	μ	σ	Beta (a,b)	F(X)	p-Value 1 – F(X)	Change (+ or –)
Day 1	0.7	0.5563	0.17	(0.37, 0.55)	0.7277	0.2723	
Day 2	0.5	0.5370	0.2518	(1.07, 0.85)	0.4233	0.5767	−0.304
Day 3	0.4	0.5021	0.2254	(1.57, 1.35)	0.3214	0.6786	−0.1020
Day 4	0.6	0.5220	0.2053	(1.97, 1.95)	0.6430	0.3570	+0.322
Day 5	0.6	0.5352	0.1896	(2.57, 2.35)	0.6253	0.3747	−0.0177
Day 6	0.7	0.5590	0.1764	(3.17, 2.75)	0.7846	0.2154	+0.159
Day 7	0.5	0.5515	0.1665	(3.87, 3.05)	0.3706	0.6294	−0.414
Day 8	0.4	0.5345	0.1584	(4.37, 3.55)	0.1956	0.8044	−0.175
Day 9	0.7	0.5512	0.1505	(4.77, 4.15)	0.8398	0.1602	+0.644
Day 10	0.7	—	—	(5.47, 4.45)	0.8264	0.1736	−0.0134
Day 11	x	—	—				

narrower, and for larger values of a and b, the distribution are seen to have less spread or variance and relatively more peaked. Prior specification of beta distribution with larger a and b corresponds to having more information (messages), or a more precise view initially, about the true population parameter of interest than the case that a and b are smaller. It means that the maximum likelihood of μ (the central value of the probability density distribution) converges to a true population mean μ. Technically, the beta distribution shown below is a continuous distribution, for which the total area under the beta curve is 100%. The height of the beta curve is described as the probability density for the parameter values and the distribution function represents the cumulative probabilities of the random variable.

The Bayesian capacity to accommo-date continuous revision of a probability from one behavioral act to the next makes it quite suitable for detecting and determining a subject's behavioral change from a variety of perspectives in which prediction is an important factor. The cumulative treatment of the data from behavioral shift to behavioral shift adjusts the margin of error and increases the predictability of the final results. Theoretically, through beta distribution, the predictability of the parameter of your interest will increase as more new empirical data emerge.

Both the Bayesian and classical methods to statistical inference and a typical hypothesis testing, each method should be viewed as mere tools in a toolkit. More specifically, a clinical practitioner should retain the freedom to choose and apply whichever the method that is most suitable in answering the research questions.

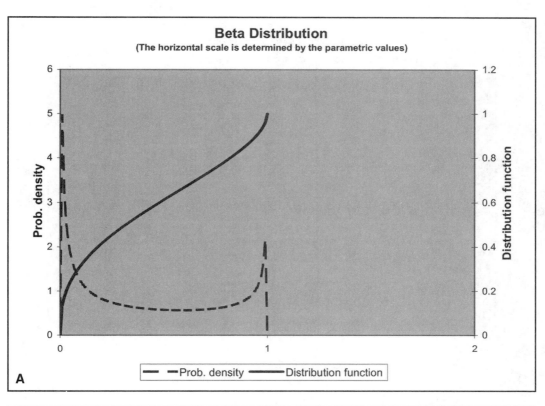

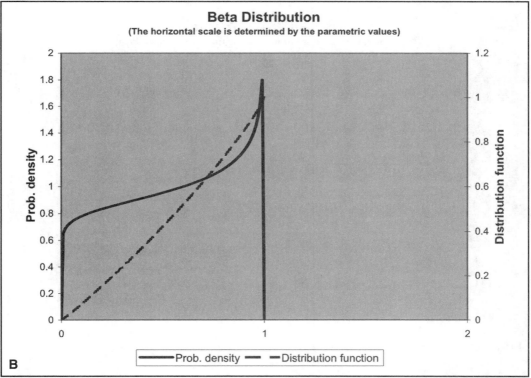

Figure J–4. A. Beta graph of Day 1. **B.** Beta graph of Day 2. *continues*

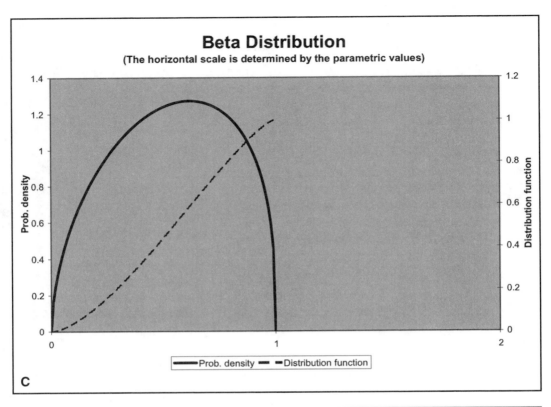

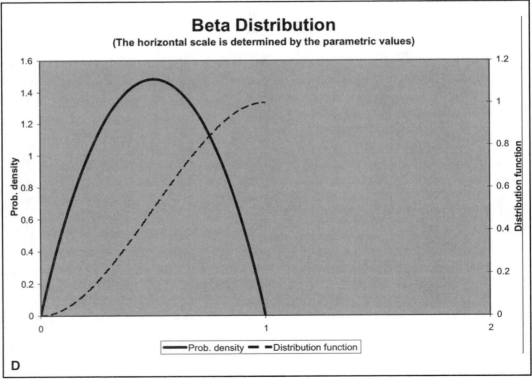

Figure J–4. *continued* **C.** Beta graph of Day 3. **D.** Beta graph of Day 4. *continues*

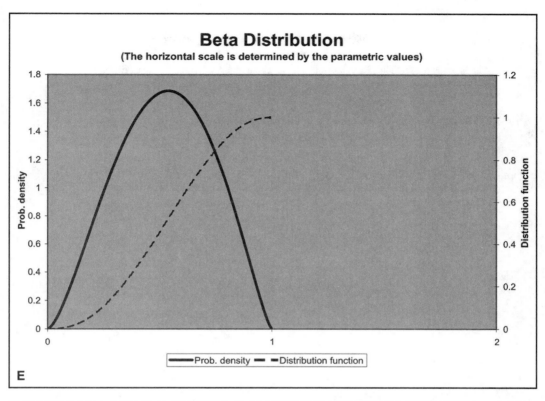

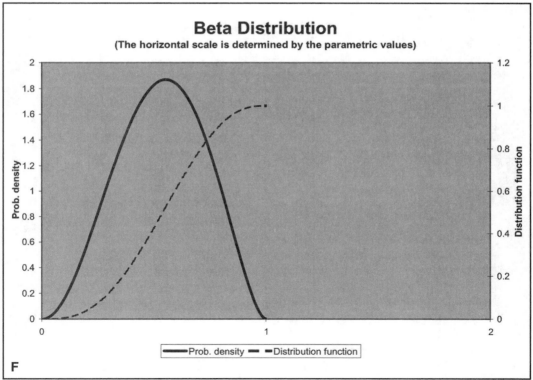

Figure J–4. *continued* **E.** Beta graph of Day 5. **F.** Beta graph of Day 6. *continues*

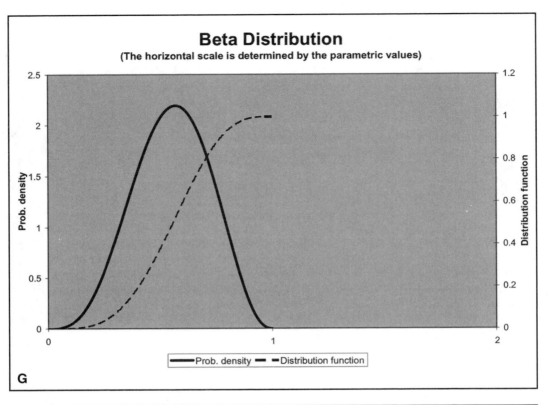

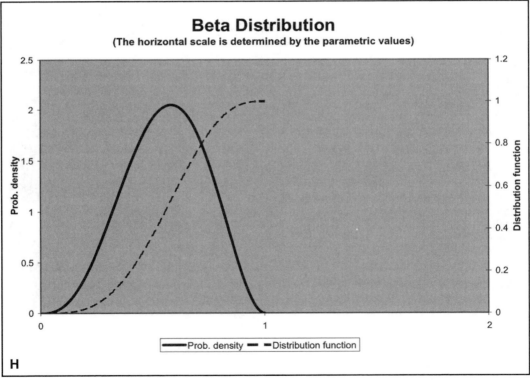

Figure J–4. *continued* **G.** Beta graph of Day 7. **H.** Beta graph of Day 8. *continues*

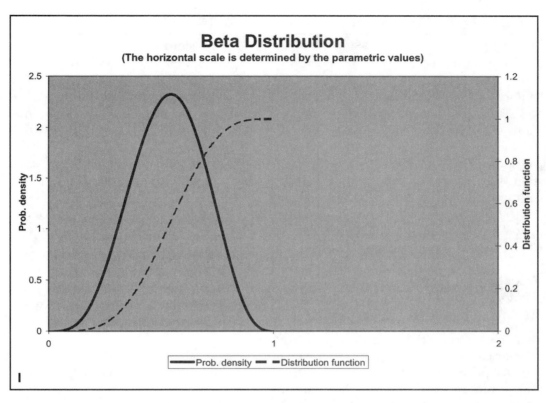

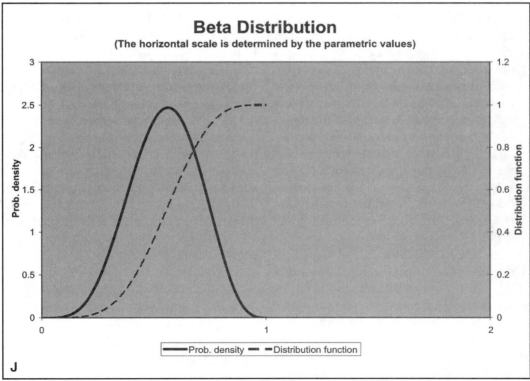

Figure J–4. *continued* **I.** Beta graph of Day 9. **J.** Beta graph of Day 10.

Predicting the future is always risky business, and a Bayesian analysis does not reduce or remove the risk. As with classical statistics, the analyses and interpretations of beta probabilities are complicated by the factors that go into any measure of human behavior. Nevertheless, prediction is dependent on the statistical nature of human behavior, and as noted earlier, Bayesian statistical methodologies are more suitable with process-oriented phenomena than classical statistical methodologies.

Question 34. What Is the Bayes Factor and How Do We Interpret the Test Results with the Bayes Factor?

■ In recent years, there has been growing interest and awareness of the Bayesian approach as an alternative to the p-value approach within the clinical and behavioral research fields, and increasing discussions of its potential applications to the various research questions. The p-value approach has been criticized by many researchers over a long period of time, largely due to such deficiencies as: (a) misinterpretation of a conclusion, (b) arbitrariness of the widely used $p = 0.05$ or 0.01 criteria for statistical significance to reject the null hypothesis (H_o), and (c) the p-value method is not an "evidence-based" method. Most importantly, on the contrary to what most clinical practitioners believe, the p-values are conditional probabilities and calculated on the assumption that the null hypothesis (H_o) is true. Symbolically, the p-values are expressed as p (Data$|H_o$ is true). That is to say, a typical p-value user tends to commit a crucial error, called "transposition of conditional fallacy," in which p (Data$|H_o$ is true) is mistaken for p (H_o is true$|$Data). Basically, what clinical practitioners want to derive

is the latter conditional probability (the inverse of the p-value, i.e., p (H_o is true$|$Data)), indicating the evidential strength or credibility for the null hypothesis (H_o) versus the research hypothesis (H_A) after actual data is observed and studied. Mathematically, we can write this as follows:

$[p$ (H_o is true$|$Data)$/p$ (H_A is true$|$Data)$]$
$= [p$ (H_o is true)$/p$ (H_A is true)$] \times \lambda$

where λ = Bayes Factor = $[p$ (Data$|H_o$ is true)$/p$ (Data$|(H_A$ is true)$]$

Simply, from the left to the right, we can also express it as follows:

Posterior odds =
Prior odds × Bayes factor.

Hence, the Bayes factor, sometimes called the weight of evidence of two hypotheses, is a comparison ratio of how well two hypotheses predict the actual empirical data. Furthermore, we can interpret the Bayes factor as the ratio of credibility of two hypotheses, not a probability itself. Unlike the p-value, the Bayes factor requires two hypotheses and is contingent on the probability of the observed data alone, not including unobserved "long run" results that are part of the calculation of the p-value. The formula of the Bayes factor allows us to establish the relationship between the Minimum Bayes Factor required and p-values.

Comparison Between p-Values and the Bayesian Factor and the Evidential Effects on the Null Hypothesis (Goodman, 1999) (Table J–9)

For instance, when an observed value of a sample results in $z = 1.96$ (p-value = 0.05),

Table J–9. Comparison Between p-Values and the Bayesian Factor and the Evidential Effects on the Null Hypothesis (Goodman, 1999)

Two-Tailed p-Value	Minimum Bayes Factor	Strength of Evidence (Bayesian Conclusion)
0.10 ($z = 1.645$)	$0.26\left(\frac{1}{3.8}\right)$	Weak
0.05 ($z = 1.96$)	$0.15\left(\frac{1}{6.8}\right)$	Weak to Moderate
0.03 ($z = 2.17$)	$0.095\left(\frac{1}{11}\right)$	Moderate
0.01 ($z = 2.58$)	$0.036\left(\frac{1}{28}\right)$	Moderate to Strong
0.001 ($z = 3.28$)	$0.005\left(\frac{1}{216}\right)$	Strong to Very Strong
Less than 0.001	Less than 0.005	Very Strong

the Minimum Bayes Factor is 0.15, that is, three times as large as 0.05. It means that the credibility of the null hypothesis is 15% whereas the research hypothesis gets credibility of 85%. This indicates that the strength of evidence against the null hypothesis is not quite as significant as "$p = 0.05$" actually suggests. Rather, much weaker evidence is derived. The main goal of statistical inference is to quantify uncertainty about unknown facts. Unlike the p-value approach, the Bayes factor provides both a framework for quantifying uncertainty of two hypotheses and a method for revising such uncertainty measures in the light of acquired empirical evidence.

Additional Comments

1. There are several important issues in relation to the selection of an experimental approach for determining the existence of the treatment effect(s). Namely, they are: (a) inter- and intra-subject variability and averaging of the data values (in both baselines and treatment periods), (b) the external validity, (c) generalization of treatment effects across responses and stimulus conditions, (d) ethical issues, and (e) other practical issues, that is, clinical significance rather than statistical and/or theoretical significance of the test results. All clinicians and investigators must carefully review all these issues to increase the accuracy of their diagnoses.

2. Again, the basic requirements of single-subject research designs for investigating the treatment efficacy is very similar to those for group designs. These are: (a) demonstration of experimental control/internal validity, (b) defining both independent variable (treatment) and dependent variable (outcome) clearly, (c) repeated measurements, (d) reliability of measurement, and (e) description of participants.

3. While single-subject designs are often used in clinical and psychological research, there remain a fair number of case studies that lack the experimental control that allows an investigator to draw valid conclusions about the functional relationship between treatment and their outcomes. Furthermore, some investigators continue to use only one participant in their studies and even when more participants are observed, the total number is inadequate for proper, within and across, subject replication.

4. Not all studies mention reliability on the independent and dependent measures. This leads to many unanswered questions concerning treatment effects, questions such as: (a) when is the treatment most effective, (b) how often should treatment be given, and (c) what treatment(s) are the most effective with whom. Unless we investigate the reliability of both independent and dependent measures, we will be unable to answer these crucial questions.

APPENDIX K

Area Under the Standard Normal Curve for Values of z

See Tables K–1, K–2, and K–3 on the following pages.

Table K-1. Areas Under the Standard Normal Distributions for Values of z Between 0.00 and 1.19

z	Area between $\bar{X}$ and z	Area beyond z	Ordinate	z	Area between $\bar{X}$ and z	Area beyond z	Ordinate	z	Area between $\bar{X}$ and z	Area beyond z	Ordinate
0.00	.0000	.5000	.3989	0.40	.1554	.3446	.3683	0.80	.2881	.2119	.2897
0.01	.0040	.4960	.3989	0.41	.1591	.3409	.3668	0.81	.2910	.2090	.2874
0.02	.0080	.4920	.3989	0.42	.1628	.3372	.3653	0.82	.2939	.2061	.2850
0.03	.0120	.4880	.3988	0.43	.1664	.3336	.3637	0.83	.2967	.2033	.2827
0.04	.0160	.4840	.3986	0.44	.1700	.3300	.3621	0.84	.2995	.2005	.2803
0.05	.0199	.4801	.3984	0.45	.1736	.3264	.3605	0.85	.3023	.1977	.2780
0.06	.0239	.4761	.3982	0.46	.1772	.3228	.3589	0.86	.3051	.1949	.2756
0.07	.0279	.4761	.3980	0.47	.1808	.3192	.3572	0.87	.3078	.1922	.2732
0.08	.0319	.4721	.3977	0.48	.1844	.3156	.3555	0.88	.3106	.1894	.2709
0.09	.0359	.4681	.3973	0.49	.1879	.3121	.3538	0.89	.3133	.1867	.2685
0.10	.0398	.4602	.3970	0.50	.1915	.3085	.3521	0.90	.3159	.1841	.2661
0.11	.0438	.4562	.3965	0.51	.1950	.3050	.3503	0.91	.3186	.1814	.2637
0.12	.0478	.4522	.3961	0.52	.1985	.3015	.3485	0.92	.3212	.1788	.2613
0.13	.0517	.4483	.3956	0.53	.2019	.2981	.3467	0.93	.3238	.1762	.2589
0.14	.0557	.4443	.3951	0.54	.2054	.2946	.3448	0.94	.3264	.1736	.2565
0.15	.0596	.4404	.3945	0.55	.2088	.2912	.3429	0.95	.3289	.1711	.2541
0.16	.0636	.4364	.3939	0.56	.2123	.2877	.3410	0.96	.3315	.1685	.2516
0.17	.0675	.4325	.3932	0.57	.2157	.2843	.3391	0.97	.3340	.1660	.2492
0.18	.0714	.4286	.3925	0.58	.2190	.2810	.3372	0.98	.3365	.1635	.2468

0.19	.0753	.4247	.3918	0.59	.2224	.2776	.3352	0.99	.3389	.1611	.2444
0.20	.0793	.4207	.3910	0.60	.2257	.2743	.3332	1.00	.3413	.1587	.2420
0.21	.0832	.4168	.3902	0.61	.2291	.2709	.3312	1.01	.3438	.1562	.2396
0.22	.0871	.4129	.3894	0.62	.2324	.2676	.3292	1.02	.3461	.1539	.2371
0.23	.0910	.4090	.3885	0.63	.2357	.2643	.3271	1.03	.3485	.1515	.2347
0.24	.0948	.4052	.3876	0.64	.2389	.2611	.3251	1.04	.3508	.1492	.2323
0.25	.0987	.4013	.3867	0.65	.2422	.2578	.3230	1.05	.3531	.1469	.2299
0.26	.1026	.3974	.3857	0.66	.2454	.2546	.3209	1.06	.3554	.1446	.2275
0.27	.1064	.3936	.3847	0.67	.2486	.2514	.3187	1.07	.3577	.1423	.2251
0.28	.1103	.3897	.3836	0.68	.2517	.2483	.3166	1.08	.3599	.1401	.2227
0.29	.1141	.3859	.3825	0.69	.2549	.2451	.3144	1.09	.3627	.1379	.2203
0.30	.1179	.3821	.3814	0.70	.2580	.2420	.3123	1.10	.3643	.1357	.2179
0.31	.1217	.3783	.3802	0.71	.2611	.2389	.3101	1.11	.3665	.1335	.2155
0.32	.1255	.3745	.3790	0.72	.2642	.2358	.3079	1.12	.3686	.1314	.2131
0.33	.1293	.3707	.3778	0.73	.2673	.2327	.3056	1.13	.3708	.1292	.2107
0.34	.1331	.3669	.3765	0.74	.2704	.2296	.3034	1.14	.3729	.1271	.2083
0.35	.1368	.3632	.3752	0.75	.2734	.2266	.3011	1.15	.3749	.1251	.2059
0.36	.1406	.3594	.3739	0.76	.2764	.2236	.2989	1.16	.3770	.1230	.2036
0.37	.1443	.3557	.3725	0.77	.2794	.2206	.2966	1.17	.3790	.1210	.2012
0.38	.1480	.3520	.3712	0.78	.2823	.2177	.2943	1.18	.3810	.1190	.1989
0.39	.1517	.3483	.3697	0.79	.2852	.2148	.2920	1.19	.3830	.1170	.1965

*For values of z greater than 3.09, the height of the curve is negligible and the value of the ordinate is close to zero.

Source: From Table III of Fisher, R. A., & Yates, F. (1974). *Statistical tables for biological, agricultural, and medical research* (6th ed.). London: Longman Group.

Table K–2. Areas Under the Standard Normal Distribution for Values of z Between 1.20 and 4.00

z	Area between $\bar{X}$ and z	Area beyond z	Ordinate	z	Area between $\bar{X}$ and z	Area beyond z	Ordinate	z	Area between $\bar{X}$ and z	Area beyond z	Ordinate
1.20	.3849	.1151	.1942	1.60	.4452	.0548	.1109	2.00	.4772	.0228	.0540
1.21	.3869	.1131	.1919	1.61	.4463	.0537	.1092	2.01	.4778	.0222	.0529
1.22	.3888	.1112	.1895	1.62	.4474	.0526	.1074	2.02	.4783	.0217	.0519
1.23	.3907	.1093	.1872	1.63	.4484	.0516	.1057	2.03	.4788	.0212	.0508
1.24	.3925	.1075	.1849	1.64	.4495	.0505	.1040	2.04	.4793	.0207	.0498
1.25	.3944	.1056	.1826	1.65	.4505	.0495	.1023	2.05	.4798	.0202	.0488
1.26	.3962	.1038	.1804	1.66	.4515	.0485	.1006	2.06	.4803	.0197	.0478
1.27	.3980	.1020	.1781	1.67	.4525	.0475	.0989	2.07	.4808	.0192	.0468
1.28	.3997	.1003	.1758	1.68	.4535	.0465	.0973	2.08	.4812	.0188	.0459
1.29	.4015	.0985	.1736	1.69	.4545	.0455	.0957	2.09	.4817	.0183	.0449
1.30	.4032	.0968	.1714	1.70	.4554	.0446	.0940	2.10	.4821	.0179	.0440
1.31	.4049	.0951	.1691	1.71	.4564	.0436	.0925	2.11	.4826	.0174	.0431
1.32	.4066	.0934	.1669	1.72	.4573	.0427	.0909	2.12	.4830	.0170	.0422
1.33	.4082	.0918	.1647	1.73	.4582	.0418	.0893	2.13	.4834	.0166	.0412
1.34	.4099	.0901	.1626	1.74	.4591	.0409	.0878	2.14	.4838	.0162	.0404
1.35	.4115	.0885	.1604	1.75	.4599	.0401	.0863	2.15	.4842	.0158	.0395
1.36	.4131	.0869	.1582	1.76	.4608	.0392	.0848	2.16	.4846	.0154	.0387
1.37	.4147	.0853	.1561	1.77	.4616	.0384	.0833	2.17	.4850	.0150	.0379
1.38	.4162	.0838	.1539	1.78	.4625	.0375	.0818	2.18	.4854	.0146	.0371

1.39	.4177	.0823	.1518	1.79	.4633	.0367	.0804	2.19	.4857	.0143	.0363
1.40	.4192	.0808	.1497	1.80	.4641	.0359	.0790	2.20	.4861	.0139	.0355
1.41	.4207	.0793	.1476	1.81	.4649	.0351	.0775	2.21	.4864	.0136	.0347
1.42	.4222	.0778	.1456	1.82	.4656	.0344	.0761	2.22	.4868	.0132	.0339
1.43	.4236	.0764	.1435	1.83	.4664	.0336	.0748	2.23	.4871	.0129	.0332
1.44	.4251	.0749	.1415	1.84	.4671	.0329	.0734	2.24	.4875	.0125	.0325
1.45	.4265	.0735	.1394	1.85	.4678	.0322	.0721	2.25	.4878	.0122	.0317
1.46	.4279	.0721	.1374	1.86	.4686	.0314	.0707	2.26	.4881	.0119	.0310
1.47	.4292	.0708	.1354	1.87	.4693	.0307	.0694	2.27	.4884	.0116	.0303
1.48	.4306	.0694	.1334	1.88	.4699	.0301	.0681	2.28	.4887	.0113	.0297
1.49	.4319	.0681	.1315	1.89	.4706	.0294	.0669	2.29	.4890	.0110	.0290
1.50	.4332	.0668	.1295	1.90	.4713	.0287	.0656	2.30	.4893	.0107	.0283
1.51	.4345	.0655	.1276	1.91	.4719	.0281	.0644	2.31	.4896	.0104	.0277
1.52	.4357	.0643	.1257	1.92	.4726	.0274	.0632	2.32	.4898	.0102	.0270
1.53	.4370	.0630	.1238	1.93	.4732	.2068	.0620	2.33	.4901	.0099	.0264
1.54	.4382	.0618	.1219	1.94	.4738	.0262	.0608	2.34	.4904	.0096	.0258
1.55	.4394	.0606	.1200	1.95	.4744	.0256	.0596	2.35	.4906	.0094	.0252
1.56	.4406	.0594	.1182	1.96	.4750	.0250	.0584	2.36	.4909	.0091	.0246
1.57	.4418	.0582	.1163	1.97	.4756	.0244	.0573	2.37	.4911	.0089	.0241
1.58	.4429	.0571	.1145	1.98	.4761	.0239	.0562	2.38	.4913	.0087	.0235
1.59	.4441	.0559	.1127	1.99	.4767	.0233	.0551	2.39	.4916	.0084	.0229

continues

Table K-2. *continued*

z	Area between $\bar{X}$ and z	Area beyond z	Ordinate
2.40	.4918	.0082	.0224
2.41	.4920	.0080	.0219
2.42	.4922	.0078	.0213
2.43	.4925	.0075	.0208
2.44	.4927	.0073	.0203
2.45	.4929	.0071	.0198
2.46	.4931	.0069	.0194
2.47	.4932	.0068	.0189
2.48	.4934	.0066	.0184
2.49	.4936	.0064	.0180
2.50	.4938	.0062	.0175
2.51	.4940	.0060	.0171
2.52	.4941	.0059	.0167
2.53	.4943	.0057	.0163
2.54	.4945	.0055	.0158
2.55	.4946	.0054	.0154
2.56	.4948	.0052	.0151
2.57	.4949	.0051	.0147
2.58	.4951	.0049	.0143

z	Area between $\bar{X}$ and z	Area beyond z	Ordinate
2.80	.4974	.0026	.0079
2.81	.4975	.0025	.0077
2.82	.4976	.0024	.0075
2.83	.4977	.0023	.0073
2.84	.4977	.0023	.0071
2.85	.4978	.0022	.0069
2.86	.4979	.0021	.0067
2.87	.4979	.0021	.0065
2.88	.4980	.0020	.0063
2.89	.4981	.0019	.0061
2.90	.4981	.0019	.0060
2.91	.4982	.0018	.0058
2.92	.4982	.0018	.0056
2.93	.4983	.0017	.0055
2.94	.4984	.0016	.0053
2.95	.4983	.0016	.0051
2.96	.4985	.0015	.0050
2.97	.4985	.0015	.0048
2.98	.4986	.0014	.0047

z	Area between $\bar{X}$ and z	Area beyond z	Ordinate
3.20	.4993	.0007	
3.21	.4993	.0007	
3.22	.4994	.0006	
3.23	.4994	.0006	
3.24	.4994	.0006	
3.25	.4994	.0006	
3.30	.4995	.0005	
3.35	.4996	.0004	
3.40	.4997	.0003	
3.45	.4997	.0003	
3.50	.4998	.0002	
3.60	.4998	.0002	
3.70	.4999	.0001	
3.80	.4999	.0001	
3.90	.49995	.00005	
4.00	.49997	.00003	

z				z			
2.59	.4952	.0048	.0139	2.99	.4986	.0014	.0046
2.60	.4953	.0047	.0136	3.00	.4987	.0013	.0044
2.61	.4955	.0045	.0132	3.01	.4987	.0013	.0033
2.62	.4956	.0044	.0129	3.02	.4987	.0013	.0024
2.63	.4957	.0043	.0126	3.03	.4988	.0012	.0017
2.64	.4959	.0041	.0122	3.04	.4988	.0012	.0012
2.65	.4960	.0040	.0119	3.05	.4989	.0011	.0009
2.66	.4961	.0039	.0116	3.06	.4989	.0011	.0006
2.67	.4962	.0038	.0113	3.07	.4989	.0011	.0004
2.68	.4963	.0037	.0110	3.08	.4990	.0010	.0003
2.69	.4964	.0036	.0107	3.09	.4990	.0010	.0002*
2.70	.4965	.0035	.0104	3.10	.4990	.0010	
2.71	.4966	.0034	.0101	3.11	.4991	.0009	
2.72	.4967	.0033	.0099	3.12	.4991	.0009	
2.73	.4968	.0032	.0096	3.13	.4991	.0009	
2.74	.4969	.0031	.0093	3.14	.4992	.0008	
2.75	.4970	.0030	.0091	3.15	.4992	.0008	
2.76	.4971	.0029	.0088	3.16	.4992	.0008	
2.77	.4972	.0028	.0086	3.17	.4992	.0008	
2.78	.4973	.0027	.0084	3.18	.4993	.0007	
2.79	.4974	.0026	.0081	3.19	.4993	.0007	

*For values of z greater than 3.09, the height of the curve is negligible and the value of the ordinate is close to zero.

Source: From Table III of Fisher, R. A., & Yates, F. (1974). *Statistical tables for biological, agricultural, and medical research* (6th ed.). London: Longman Group.

Table K–3. Areas Under the Standard Normal Distribution for Values of z Between 2.40 and 4.00

z	Area between $\bar{X}$ and z	Area beyond z	Ordinate	z	Area between $\bar{X}$ and z	Area beyond z	Ordinate	z	Area between $\bar{X}$ and z	Area beyond z	Ordinate
2.40	.4918	.0082	.0224	2.59	.4952	.0048	.0139	2.78	.4973	.0027	.0084
2.41	.4920	.0080	.0219	2.60	.4953	.0047	.0136	2.79	.4974	.0026	.0081
2.42	.4922	.0078	.0213	2.61	.4955	.0045	.0132	2.80	.4974	.0026	.0079
2.43	.4925	.0075	.0208	2.62	.4956	.0044	.0129	2.81	.4975	.0025	.0077
2.44	.4927	.0073	.0203	2.63	.4957	.0043	.0126	2.82	.4976	.0024	.0075
2.45	.4929	.0071	.0198	2.64	.4959	.0041	.0122	2.83	.4977	.0023	.0073
2.46	.4931	.0069	.0194	2.65	.4960	.0040	.0119	2.84	.4977	.0023	.0071
2.47	.4932	.0068	.0189	2.66	.4961	.0039	.0116	2.85	.4978	.0022	.0069
2.48	.4934	.0066	.0184	2.67	.4962	.0038	.0113	2.86	.4979	.0021	.0067
2.49	.4936	.0064	.0180	2.68	.4963	.0037	.0110	2.87	.4979	.0021	.0065
2.50	.4938	.0062	.0175	2.69	.4964	.0036	.0107	2.88	.4980	.0020	.0063
2.51	.4940	.0060	.0171	2.70	.4965	.0035	.0104	2.89	.4981	.0019	.0061
2.52	.4941	.0059	.0167	2.71	.4966	.0034	.0101	2.90	.4981	.0019	.0060
2.53	.4943	.0057	.0163	2.72	.4967	.0033	.0099	2.91	.4982	.0018	.0058
2.54	.4945	.0055	.0158	2.73	.4968	.0032	.0096	2.92	.4982	.0018	.0056
2.55	.4946	.0054	.0154	2.74	.4969	.0031	.0093	2.93	.4983	.0017	.0055
2.56	.4948	.0052	.0151	2.75	.4970	.0030	.0091	2.94	.4984	.0016	.0053
2.57	.4949	.0051	.0147	2.76	.4971	.0029	.0088	2.95	.4983	.0016	.0051
2.58	.4951	.0049	.0143	2.77	.4972	.0028	.0086	2.96	.4985	.0015	.0050

z				z		
2.97	.4985	.0015	.0048	3.18	.4993	.0007
2.98	.4986	.0014	.0047	3.19	.4993	.0007
2.99	.4986	.0014	.0046	3.20	.4993	.0007
3.00	.4987	.0013	.0044	3.21	.4993	.0007
3.01	.4987	.0013	.0033	3.22	.4994	.0006
3.02	.4987	.0013	.0024	3.23	.4994	.0006
3.03	.4988	.0012	.0017	3.24	.4994	.0006
3.04	.4988	.0012	.0012	3.25	.4994	.0006
3.05	.4989	.0011	.0009	3.30	.4995	.0005
3.06	.4989	.0011	.0006	3.35	.4996	.0004
3.07	.4989	.0011	.0004	3.40	.4997	.0003
3.08	.4990	.0010	.0003	3.45	.4997	.0003
3.09	.4990	.0010	.0002*	3.50	.4998	.0002
3.10	.4990	.0010		3.60	.4998	.0002
3.11	.4991	.0009		3.70	.4999	.0001
3.12	.4991	.0009		3.80	.4999	.0001
3.13	.4991	.0009		3.90	.49995	.00005
3.14	.4992	.0008		4.00	.49997	.00003
3.15	.4992	.0008				
3.16	.4992	.0008				
3.17	.4992	.0008				

*For values of z greater than 3.09, the height of the curve is negligible and the value of the ordinate is close to zero.

Source: From Table III of Fisher, R. A., & Yates, F. (1974). *Statistical tables for biological, agricultural, and medical research* (6th ed.). London: Longman Group.

APPENDIX L

Standard Scores Corresponding to Percentile from 0.5000 to 0.9995

Table L–1. *Z*-Scores Corresponding to Percentiles from 0.500 to 0.9995

A	B	A	B	A	B
Percentile	***Z*-score**	**Percentile**	***Z*-score**	**Percentile**	***Z*-score**
0.500	0.000	0.675	0.4538	0.850	1.0364
0.505	0.0125	0.680	0.4677	0.855	1.0581
0.510	0.0251	0.685	0.4817	0.860	1.0803
0.515	0.0376	0.690	0.4959	0.865	1.1031
0.520	0.0502	0.695	0.5101	0.870	1.1264
0.525	0.0627	0.700	0.5244	0.875	1.1503
0.530	0.0753	0.705	0.5388	0.880	1.1750
0.535	0.0878	0.710	0.5534	0.885	1.2004
0.540	0.1004	0.715	0.5681	0.890	1.2265
0.545	0.1130	0.720	0.5828	0.895	1.2536
0.550	0.1257	0.725	0.5978	0.900	1.2816
0.555	0.1383	0.730	0.6128	0.905	1.3106

continues

Table L–1. *continued*

A Percentile	B Z-score	A Percentile	B Z-score	A Percentile	B Z-score
0.560	0.1510	0.735	0.6280	0.910	1.3408
0.565	0.1637	0.740	0.6433	0.915	1.3722
0.570	0.1764	0.745	0.6588	0.920	1.4051
0.575	0.1891	0.750	0.6745	0.925	1.4395
0.580	0.2019	0.755	0.6903	0.930	1.4757
0.585	0.2147	0.760	0.7063	0.935	1.5141
0.590	0.2275	0.765	0.7225	0.940	1.5548
0.595	0.2404	0.770	0.7388	0.945	1.5982
0.600	0.2533	0.775	0.7554	0.950	1.6449
0.605	0.2663	0.780	0.7722	0.955	1.6954
0.610	0.2793	0.785	0.7892	0.960	1.7507
0.615	0.2924	0.790	0.8064	0.965	1.8119
0.620	0.3055	0.795	0.8239	0.970	1.8808
0.625	0.3186	0.800	0.8416	0.975	1.9600
0.630	0.3319	0.805	0.8696	0.980	2.0537
0.635	0.3451	0.810	0.8779	0.985	2.1701
0.640	0.3585	0.815	0.8965	0.990	2.3263
0.645	0.3719	0.820	0.9154	0.995	2.5758
0.650	0.3853	0.825	0.9346	0.996	2.6521
0.655	0.3989	0.830	0.9542	0.997	2.7478
0.660	0.4125	0.835	0.9741	0.998	2.8782
0.665	0.4261	0.840	0.9945	0.999	3.0902
0.670	0.4399	0.845	1.0152	0.9995	3.2905

APPENDIX M

Critical Values of the *t*-Distribution

Table M–1. Critical Values and Levels of Significance of the Student's *t*-Distribution

	Levels of Significance for One-Tailed Test					
	0.10	0.05	0.025	0.01	0.005	0.0005
	Levels of Significance for Two-Tailed Test					
df	0.20	0.10	0.05	0.02	0.01	0.001
1	3.078	6.314	12.706	31.821	63.657	636.619
2	1.886	2.920	4.303	6.965	9.925	31.598
3	1.638	2.353	3.182	4.541	5.841	12.941
4	1.533	2.132	2.776	3.747	4.604	8.610
5	1.476	2.015	2.571	3.365	4.032	6.859
6	1.440	1.943	2.447	3.143	3.707	5.959
7	1.415	1.895	2.365	2.998	3.499	5.405
8	1.397	1.860	2.306	2.896	3.355	5.041
9	1.383	1.833	2.262	2.821	3.250	4.781
10	1.372	1.812	2.228	2.764	3.169	4.587
11	1.363	1.796	2.201	2.718	3.106	4.437
12	1.356	1.782	2.179	2.681	3.055	4.318
13	1.350	1.771	2.160	2.650	3.012	4.221

continues

Table M–1. *continued*

df	Levels of Significance for One-Tailed Test

	0.10	0.05	0.025	0.01	0.005	0.0005
	Levels of Significance for Two-Tailed Test					
df	0.20	0.10	0.05	0.02	0.01	0.001
14	1.345	1.761	2.145	2.624	2.977	4.140
15	1.341	1.753	2.131	2.602	2.947	4.073
16	1.337	1.746	2.120	2.583	2.921	4.015
17	1.333	1.740	2.110	2.567	2.898	3.965
18	1.330	1.734	2.101	2.552	2.878	3.922
19	1.328	1.729	2.093	2.539	2.861	3.883
20	1.325	1.725	2.086	2.528	2.845	3.850
21	1.323	1.721	2.080	2.518	2.831	3.819
22	1.321	1.717	2.074	2.508	2.819	3.792
23	1.319	1.714	2.069	2.500	2.807	3.767
24	1.318	1.711	2.064	2.492	2.797	3.745
25	1.316	1.708	2.060	2.485	2.787	3.725
26	1.315	1.706	2.056	2.479	2.779	3.707
27	1.314	1.703	2.052	2.473	2.771	3.690
28	1.313	1.701	2.048	2.467	2.763	3.674
29	1.311	1.699	2.045	2.462	2.756	3.659
30	1.310	1.697	2.042	2.457	2.750	3.646
40	1.303	1.684	2.021	2.423	2.704	3.551
60	1.296	1.671	2.000	2.390	2.660	3.460
120	1.989	1.658	1.980	2.358	2.617	3.373
∞	1.282	1.645	1.960	2.326	2.576	3.291

Source: From Table III of Fisher, R. A., & Yates, F. (1974). *Statistical tables for biological, agricultural and medical research* (6th ed.) London, UK: Longman Group.

APPENDIX N

The *F*-Distribution Values of $F_{0.05}$, $F_{0.025}$, and $F_{0.01}$

See Tables N–1, N–2, and N–3 on the following pages.

Table N–1. The *F*-Distribution Values of $F_{0.05}$

		Degrees of Freedom of the Numerator								
	df_1/df_2	1	2	3	4	5	6	7	8	9
Degrees of Freedom of the Denominator	1	161.4	199.5	215.7	224.6	230.2	234.0	236.8	238.9	240.5
	2	18.51	19.00	19.16	19.25	19.30	19.33	19.35	19.37	19.38
	3	10.13	9.55	9.28	9.12	9.01	8.94	8.89	8.85	8.81
	4	7.71	6.94	6.59	6.39	6.26	6.16	6.09	6.04	6.00
	5	6.61	5.79	5.41	5.19	5.05	4.95	4.88	4.82	4.77
	6	5.99	5.14	4.76	4.53	4.39	4.28	4.21	4.15	4.10
	7	5.59	4.74	4.35	4.12	3.97	3.87	3.79	3.72	3.68
	8	5.32	4.46	4.07	3.84	3.69	3.58	3.50	3.44	3.39
	9	5.12	4.26	3.86	3.63	3.48	3.37	3.29	3.23	3.18
	10	4.96	4.10	3.71	3.48	3.33	3.22	3.14	3.07	3.02
	11	4.84	3.98	3.59	3.36	3.20	3.09	3.01	2.95	2.90
	12	4.75	3.89	3.49	3.26	3.11	3.00	2.91	2.85	2.80
	13	4.67	3.81	3.41	3.18	3.03	2.92	2.83	2.77	2.71
	14	4.50	3.74	3.34	3.11	2.96	2.85	2.76	2.70	2.65
	15	4.54	3.68	3.29	3.06	2.90	2.79	2.71	2.64	2.59
	16	4.49	3.63	3.24	3.01	2.85	2.74	2.66	2.59	2.54
	17	4.45	3.59	3.20	2.96	2.81	2.70	2.61	2.55	2.49
	18	4.41	3.55	3.16	2.93	2.77	2.66	2.58	2.51	2.46
	19	4.38	3.52	3.13	2.90	2.74	2.63	2.54	2.48	2.42
	20	4.35	3.49	3.10	2.87	2.71	2.60	2.51	2.45	2.39
	21	4.32	3.47	3.07	2.84	2.68	2.57	2.49	2.42	2.37
	22	4.30	3.44	3.05	2.82	2.66	2.55	2.46	2.40	2.34
	23	4.28	3.42	3.03	2.80	2.64	2.53	2.44	2.37	2.32
	24	4.26	3.40	3.01	2.78	2.62	2.51	2.42	2.36	2.30
	25	4.24	3.39	2.99	2.76	2.60	2.49	2.40	2.34	2.28
	26	4.23	3.37	2.98	2.74	2.59	2.47	2.39	2.32	2.27
	27	4.21	3.35	2.96	2.73	2.57	2.46	2.37	2.31	2.25
	28	4.20	3.34	2.95	2.71	2.56	2.45	2.36	2.29	2.24
	29	4.18	3.33	2.93	2.70	2.55	2.43	2.35	2.28	2.22
	30	4.17	3.32	2.92	2.69	2.54	2.43	2.33	2.27	2.21
	40	4.08	3.23	2.84	2.61	2.45	2.34	2.25	2.18	2.12
	60	4.00	3.15	2.76	2.53	2.37	2.25	2.17	2.10	2.04
	120	3.92	3.07	2.68	2.45	2.29	2.17	2.09	2.02	1.96
	∞	3.84	3.00	2.60	2.37	2.21	2.10	2.01	1.94	1.88

Source: From Pearson, E. S., & Hartley, H. O. (Eds.). (1958). *Biometrika tables for statisticians* (Vol. 1, 2nd ed.), 171–173.

Degrees of Freedom of the Numerator									
10	12	15	20	24	30	40	60	120	∞
241.9	243.9	245.9	248.0	249.1	250.1	251.1	252.2	253.3	254.3
19.40	19.41	19.43	19.45	19.45	19.46	19.47	19.48	19.49	19.50
8.79	8.74	8.70	8.66	8.64	8.62	8.59	8.57	8.55	8.53
5.96	5.91	5.86	5.80	5.77	5.75	5.72	5.69	5.66	5.03
4.74	4.68	4.62	4.56	4.53	4.50	4.46	4.43	4.40	4.36
4.06	4.00	3.94	3.87	3.84	3.81	3.77	3.74	3.70	3.87
3.64	3.57	3.51	3.44	3.41	3.38	3.34	3.30	3.27	3.23
3.35	3.28	3.22	3.15	3.12	3.08	3.04	3.01	2.97	2.93
3.14	3.07	3.01	2.94	2.90	2.88	2.83	2.79	2.75	2.71
2.98	2.91	2.85	2.77	2.74	2.70	2.66	2.62	2.58	2.54
2.85	2.79	2.72	2.65	2.61	2.57	2.53	2.49	2.45	2.40
2.75	2.69	2.62	2.54	2.51	2.47	2.43	2.38	2.34	2.30
2.67	2.60	2.53	2.46	2.42	2.38	2.34	2.30	2.25	2.21
2.60	2.53	2.46	2.39	2.35	2.31	2.27	2.22	2.18	2.13
2.54	2.48	2.40	2.33	2.29	2.25	2.20	2.16	2.11	2.07
2.49	2.42	2.35	2.28	2.24	2.19	2.15	2.11	2.06	2.01
2.45	2.38	2.31	2.23	2.19	2.15	2.10	2.06	2.01	1.96
2.41	2.34	2.27	2.19	2.15	2.11	2.06	2.02	1.97	1.92
2.38	2.31	2.23	2.16	2.11	2.07	2.03	1.98	1.93	1.88
2.35	2.28	2.20	2.12	2.08	2.04	1.99	1.95	1.90	1.84
2.32	2.25	2.18	2.10	2.05	2.01	1.96	1.92	1.87	1.81
2.30	2.23	2.15	2.07	2.03	1.98	1.94	1.89	1.84	1.78
2.37	2.20	2.13	2.05	2.01	1.96	1.91	1.86	1.81	1.76
2.35	2.18	2.11	2.03	1.98	1.94	1.89	1.84	1.79	1.73
2.34	2.16	2.09	2.01	1.96	1.92	1.87	1.82	1.77	1.71
2.33	2.15	2.07	1.99	1.95	1.90	1.85	1.80	1.75	1.69
2.30	2.13	2.06	1.97	1.93	1.88	1.84	1.79	1.73	1.67
2.19	21.2	2.04	1.96	1.91	1.87	1.82	1.77	1.71	1.65
2.18	2.10	2.03	1.94	1.90	1.85	1.81	1.75	1.70	1.64
2.16	2.09	2.01	1.93	1.89	1.84	1.79	1.74	1.68	1.62
2.08	2.00	1.92	1.84	1.79	1.74	1.69	1.64	1.58	1.51
1.99	1.92	1.84	1.75	1.70	1.65	1.59	1.53	1.47	1.39
1.91	1.83	1.75	1.66	1.61	1.55	1.50	1.43	1.35	1.25
1.83	1.75	1.67	1.57	1.52	1.46	1.39	1.32	1.22	1.00

Table N–2. The *F*-Distribution: Values of $F_{0 \cdot 025}$

		Degrees of Freedom of the Numerator								
	df_1/df_2	1	2	3	4	5	6	7	8	9
Degrees of Freedom of the Denominator	1	647.8	799.5	864.2	899.6	921.8	937.1	948.2	956.7	963.3
	2	38.51	39.00	39.17	39.25	39.30	39.33	39.36	30.37	39.39
	3	17.44	16.04	15.44	15.10	14.88	14.73	14.62	14.54	14.47
	4	12.22	10.65	9.98	9.60	9.36	9.20	9.07	8.98	8.90
	5	10.01	8.43	7.76	7.39	7.15	6.98	6.85	6.76	6.68
	6	8.81	7.26	6.60	6.23	5.99	5.82	5.70	5.60	5.52
	7	8.07	6.54	5.89	5.52	5.29	5.12	4.99	4.90	4.82
	8	7.57	6.06	5.42	5.05	4.82	4.65	4.53	4.43	4.36
	9	7.21	5.71	5.08	4.72	4.48	4.32	4.20	4.10	4.03
	10	6.94	5.46	4.83	4.47	4.24	4.07	3.95	3.85	3.78
	11	6.72	5.26	4.63	4.28	4.04	3.88	3.76	3.66	3.59
	12	6.55	5.10	4.47	4.12	3.89	3.73	3.61	3.51	3.44
	13	6.41	4.97	4.35	4.00	3.77	3.60	3.48	3.39	3.31
	14	6.30	4.86	4.24	3.89	3.66	3.50	3.38	3.29	3.21
	15	6.20	4.77	4.15	3.80	3.58	3.41	3.29	3.20	3.12
	16	6.12	4.69	4.08	373	3.50	3.34	3.22	3.12	3.05
	17	6.04	4.62	4.01	3.66	3.44	3.28	3.16	3.06	2.98
	18	5.98	4.56	3.95	3.61	3.38	3.22	3.10	3.01	2.93
	19	5.92	4.51	3.90	3.56	3.33	3.17	3.05	2.96	2.88
	20	5.87	4.46	3.86	3.51	3.29	3.13	3.01	2.91	2.84
	21	5.83	4.42	3.82	3.48	3.25	3.09	2.97	2.87	2.80
	22	5.79	4.38	3.78	3.44	3.22	3.05	2.93	2.84	2.76
	23	5.75	4.35	3.75	3.41	3.18	3.02	2.90	2.81	2.73
	24	5.72	4.32	3.72	3.38	3.15	2.99	2.87	2.78	2.70
	25	5.69	4.29	3.69	3.35	3.13	2.97	2.85	2.75	2.68
	26	5.66	4.27	3.67	3.33	3.10	2.94	2.82	2.73	2.65
	27	5.63	4.24	3.65	3.31	3.08	2.92	2.80	2.71	2.63
	28	5.61	4.22	3.63	3.29	3.06	2.90	2.78	2.69	2.61
	29	5.59	4.20	3.61	3.27	3.04	2.88	2.76	2.67	2.59
	30	5.57	4.18	3.59	3.25	3.03	2.87	2.75	2.65	2.57
	40	5.42	4.05	3.46	3.13	2.90	2.74	2.62	2.53	2.45
	60	5.29	3.93	3.34	3.01	2.79	2.63	2.51	2.41	2.33
	120	5.15	3.80	3.23	2.89	2.67	2.52	2.39	2.30	2.22
	∞	5.02	3.69	3.12	2.79	2.57	2.41	2.29	2.19	2.11

Source: From Pearson, E. S., & Hartley, H. O. (Eds.). (1958). *Biometrika tables for statisticians* (Vol. 1, 2nd ed.), 171–173.

Degrees of Freedom of the Numerator									
10	12	15	20	24	30	40	60	120	∞
986.6	976.7	984.9	993.1	997.2	1001	1006	1010	1014	1018
39.40	39.41	39.43	39.45	39.46	39.46	39.48	39.48	39.49	39.50
14.42	14.34	14.25	14.17	14.12	14.08	14.04	13.99	13.95	13.90
8.84	8.75	8.66	8.56	8.51	8.46	8.41	8.36	8.31	8.26
6.62	6.52	6.43	6.33	6.28	6.23	6.18	6.12	6.07	6.02
5.46	5.37	5.27	5.17	5.12	5.07	5.01	4.96	4.90	4.85
4.76	4.67	4.57	4.47	4.42	4.36	4.31	4.25	4.20	4.14
4.30	4.20	4.10	4.00	3.95	3.89	3.84	3.78	3.73	3.67
3.96	3.87	3.77	3.67	3.61	3.56	3.51	3.45	3.39	3.33
3.72	3.62	3.52	3.42	3.37	3.31	3.26	3.20	3.14	3.08
3.53	3.43	3.33	3.23	3.17	3.12	3.06	3.00	2.94	2.88
3.37	3.28	3.18	3.07	3.02	2.96	2.91	2.85	2.79	2.72
3.25	3.15	3.05	2.95	2.89	2.84	2.78	2.72	2.66	2.60
3.15	3.05	2.95	2.84	2.79	2.73	2.67	2.61	2.55	2.49
3.06	2.96	2.86	2.76	2.70	2.64	2.59	2.52	2.46	2.40
2.99	2.89	2.79	2.68	2.63	2.57	2.51	2.45	2.38	2.32
2.92	2.82	2.72	2.62	2.56	2.50	2.44	2.38	2.32	2.25
2.87	2.77	2.67	2.56	2.50	2.44	2.38	2.32	2.26	2.19
2.82	2.72	2.62	2.51	2.45	2.39	2.33	2.27	2.20	2.13
2.77	2.68	2.57	2.46	2.41	2.35	2.29	2.22	2.16	2.09
2.73	2.64	2.53	2.42	2.37	2.31	2.25	2.18	2.11	2.04
2.70	2.60	2.50	2.39	2.33	2.27	2.21	2.14	2.08	2.00
2.67	2.57	2.47	2.36	2.30	2.24	2.18	2.11	2.04	1.97
2.64	2.54	2.44	2.33	2.27	2.21	2.15	2.08	2.01	1.94
2.61	2.51	2.41	2.30	2.24	2.18	2.12	2.05	1.98	1.91
2.59	2.49	2.39	2.28	2.22	2.16	2.09	2.03	1.95	1.88
2.57	2.47	2.36	2.25	2.19	2.13	2.07	2.00	1.93	1.85
2.55	2.45	2.34	2.23	2.17	2.11	2.05	1.98	1.91	1.83
2.53	2.43	2.32	2.21	2.15	2.09	2.03	1.96	1.89	1.81
2.51	2.41	2.31	2.20	2.14	2.07	2.01	1.94	1.87	1.79
2.39	2.29	2.18	2.07	2.01	1.94	1.88	1.80	1.72	1.64
2.27	2.17	2.06	1.94	1.88	1.82	1.74	1.67	1.58	1.48
2.16	2.05	1.94	1.82	1.76	1.69	1.61	1.53	1.43	1.31
2.05	1.94	1.83	1.71	1.64	1.57	1.48	1.39	1.27	1.00

Table N–3. The F-Distribution: Values of $F_{0.01}$

df₁/df₂	Degrees of Freedom of the Numerator								
	1	2	3	4	5	6	7	8	9
1	4054	4999.5	5403	5625	5764	5859	5928	5981	6022
2	98.50	99.00	99.17	99.25	99.30	99.33	99.36	99.37	99.39
3	34.12	30.82	29.46	28.71	28.24	27.91	27.67	27.49	27.35
4	21.20	18.00	16.69	15.98	15.52	15.21	14.98	14.80	14.66
5	16.26	13.27	12.06	11.39	10.97	10.67	10.46	10.29	10.16
6	13.75	10.92	9.78	9.15	8.75	8.47	8.26	8.10	7.98
7	12.25	9.55	8.45	7.85	7.46	7.19	6.99	6.84	6.72
8	11.26	8.65	7.59	7.01	6.63	6.37	6.18	6.03	5.91
9	10.56	8.02	6.99	6.42	6.06	5.80	5.61	5.47	5.35
10	10.04	7.56	6.55	5.99	5.64	5.39	5.20	5.06	4.94
11	9.65	7.21	6.22	5.67	5.32	5.07	4.89	4.74	4.63
12	9.33	6.93	5.95	5.41	5.06	4.82	4.64	4.50	4.39
13	9.07	6.70	5.74	5.21	4.86	4.62	4.44	4.30	4.19
14	8.86	6.51	5.56	5.04	4.69	4.46	4.28	4.14	4.03
15	8.58	6.36	5.42	4.89	4.56	4.32	4.14	4.00	3.89
16	8.53	6.23	5.29	4.77	4.44	4.20	4.03	3.89	3.78
17	8.40	6.11	5.18	4.67	4.34	4.10	3.93	3.79	3.68
18	8.29	6.01	5.09	4.58	4.25	4.01	3.84	3.71	3.60
19	8.18	5.93	5.01	4.50	4.17	3.94	3.77	3.63	3.52
20	8.10	5.85	4.94	4.43	4.10	3.87	3.70	3.56	3.46
21	8.02	5.78	4.87	4.37	4.04	3.81	3.64	3.51	3.40
22	7.95	5.72	4.82	4.31	3.99	3.76	3.59	3.45	3.35
23	7.88	5.66	4.76	4.26	3.94	3.71	3.54	3.41	3.30
24	7.82	5.61	4.72	4.22	3.90	3.67	3.50	3.36	3.26
25	7.77	5.57	4.68	4.18	3.85	3.63	3.46	3.32	3.22
26	7.72	5.53	4.64	4.14	3.82	3.59	3.42	3.29	3.18
27	7.68	5.49	4.60	4.11	3.78	3.56	3.39	3.26	3.15
28	7.64	5.45	4.57	4.07	3.75	3.53	3.36	3.23	3.12
29	7.60	5.42	4.54	4.04	3.73	3.50	3.33	3.20	3.09
30	7.56	5.39	4.51	4.02	3.70	3.47	3.30	3.17	3.07
40	7.31	5.18	4.31	3.83	3.51	3.29	3.12	2.99	2.89
60	7.08	4.98	4.13	3.65	3.34	3.12	2.95	2.82	2.72
120	6.85	4.79	3.95	3.48	3.17	2.96	2.79	2.66	2.56
∞	6.63	4.61	3.78	3.32	3.02	2.80	2.64	2.51	2.41

Source: From Pearson, E. S., & Hartley, H. O. (Eds.). (1958). *Biometrika tables for statisticians* (Vol. 1, 2nd ed.), 171–173.

Degrees of Freedom of the Numerator									
10	**12**	**15**	**20**	**24**	**30**	**40**	**60**	**120**	**∞**
6056	6016	6157	6209	6235	6261	6287	6313	6339	6366
99.40	99.42	99.43	99.45	99.46	99.47	99.47	99.48	99.49	99.50
27.23	27.05	26.87	26.69	26.60	26.50	26.41	26.32	26.22	26.13
14.55	14.37	14.20	14.02	13.93	13.84	13.75	13.65	13.56	13.46
10.05	9.89	9.72	9.55	9.47	9.38	9.29	9.20	9.11	9.02
7.87	7.72	7.56	7.40	7.31	7.23	7.14	7.06	6.97	6.88
6.62	6.47	6.31	6.16	6.07	5.99	5.91	5.82	5.74	5.65
5.81	5.67	5.52	5.36	5.28	5.20	5.12	5.03	4.95	4.86
5.26	5.11	4.96	4.81	4.73	4.65	4.57	4.48	4.40	4.31
4.85	4.71	4.56	4.41	4.33	4.25	4.17	4.08	4.00	3.91
4.54	4.40	4.25	4.10	4.02	3.94	3.86	3.78	3.69	3.60
4.30	4.16	4.01	3.86	3.78	3.70	3.62	3.54	3.45	3.36
4.10	3.96	3.82	3.66	3.59	3.51	3.42	3.34	3.25	3.17
3.94	3.80	3.66	3.51	3.43	3.35	3.27	3.18	3.09	3.00
3.80	3.67	3.52	3.37	3.29	3.21	3.13	3.05	2.96	2.87
3.69	3.55	3.41	3.26	3.18	3.10	3.02	2.93	2.84	2.75
3.59	3.46	3.31	3.16	3.08	3.00	2.92	2.83	2.75	2.65
3.51	3.37	3.23	3.08	3.00	2.92	2.84	2.75	2.66	2.57
3.43	3.30	3.15	3.00	2.92	2.84	2.76	2.67	2.58	2.49
3.37	3.23	3.09	2.94	2.86	2.78	2.69	2.61	2.52	2.42
3.31	3.17	3.03	2.88	2.80	2.72	2.64	2.55	2.46	2.36
3.26	3.12	2.98	2.83	2.75	2.67	2.58	2.50	2.40	2.31
3.21	3.07	2.93	2.78	2.70	2.62	2.54	2.45	2.35	2.26
3.17	3.03	2.89	2.74	2.66	2.58	2.49	2.40	2.31	2.21
3.13	2.99	2.85	2.70	2.62	2.54	2.45	2.36	2.27	2.17
3.09	2.96	2.81	2.66	2.58	2.50	2.42	2.33	2.23	2.13
3.06	2.93	2.78	2.63	2.55	2.47	2.38	2.29	2.20	2.10
3.03	2.90	2.75	2.60	2.52	2.44	2.35	2.26	2.17	2.06
3.00	2.87	2.73	2.57	2.49	2.41	2.33	2.23	2.14	2.03
2.98	2.84	2.70	2.55	2.47	2.39	2.30	2.21	2.11	2.01
2.80	2.66	2.52	2.37	2.29	2.20	2.11	2.02	1.92	1.80
2.63	2.50	2.35	2.20	2.12	2.03	1.94	1.84	1.73	1.60
2.47	2.34	2.19	2.03	1.95	1.86	1.76	1.66	1.53	1.38
2.32	2.18	2.04	1.88	1.79	1.70	1.59	1.47	1.32	1.00

APPENDIX O

Critical Values of Q

Table O–1. Critical Values of Q

df_w	α	2	3	4	5	6	7	8	9	10
2	0.05	6.08	8.33	9.8	10.88	11.74	12.44	13.03	13.54	13.99
	0.01	**14.04**	**19.02**	**22.29**	**24.72**	**26.63**	**28.20**	**29.53**	**30.68**	**31.69**
3	0.05	4.50	5.91	6.82	7.50	8.04	8.48	8.85	9.18	9.46
	0.01	**8.26**	**10.62**	**12.17**	**13.33**	**14.24**	**15.00**	**15.64**	**16.20**	**16.69**
4	0.05	3.93	5.04	5.76	6.29	6.71	7.05	7.35	7.60	7.83
	0.01	**6.51**	**8.12**	**9.17**	**9.96**	**10.58**	**11.10**	**11.55**	**11.93**	**12.27**
5	0.05	3.64	4.60	5.22	5.67	6.03	6.33	6.58	6.86	6.99
	0.01	**5.70**	**6.98**	**7.80**	**8.42**	**8.91**	**9.32**	**9.67**	**9.97**	**10.24**
6	0.05	3.46	4.34	4.90	5.30	5.63	5.90	6.12	6.32	6.49
	0.01	**5.24**	**6.33**	**7.03**	**7.56**	**7.97**	**8.32**	**8.61**	**8.87**	**9.10**
7	0.05	3.34	4.16	4.68	5.06	5.36	5.61	8.82	6.00	6.16
	0.01	**3.95**	**5.92**	**6.54**	**7.01**	**7.37**	**7.68**	**7.94**	**8.17**	**8.37**
8	0.05	3.26	4.04	4.53	4.89	5.17	5.40	5.60	5.77	5.92
	0.01	**4.75**	**5.64**	**6.20**	**6.62**	**6.96**	**7.24**	**7.47**	**7.68**	**7.86**
9	0.05	3.20	3.95	4.41	4.76	5.02	5.24	5.43	5.59	5.74
	0.01	**4.60**	**5.43**	**5.96**	**6.35**	**6.66**	**6.91**	**7.13**	**7.33**	**7.49**
10	0.05	3.15	3.88	4.65	4.65	4.91	5.12	5.30	5.46	5.60
	0.01	**4.48**	**5.27**	**6.14**	**6.14**	**6.43**	**6.67**	**6.87**	**7.05**	**7.21**
11	0.05	3.11	3.82	5.57	5.57	4.82	5.03	5.20	5.35	5.49
	0.01	**4.39**	**5.15**	**5.97**	**5.97**	**6.25**	**6.48**	**6.67**	**6.84**	**6.99**

continues

Table O–1. *continued*

df_w	α	2	3	4	5	6	7	8	9	10
12	0.05	3.08	3.77	4.51	4.51	4.75	4.95	5.12	5.27	5.39
	0.01	**4.32**	**5.05**	**5.84**	**5.84**	**6.10**	**6.32**	**6.51**	**6.67**	**6.81**
13	0.05	3.06	3.73	4.45	4.45	4.69	4.88	5.05	5.19	5.32
	0.01	**4.26**	**4.96**	**5.73**	**5.73**	**5.98**	**6.19**	**6.37**	**6.53**	**6.67**
14	0.05	3.03	3.70	4.41	4.41	4.64	4.83	4.99	5.13	5.25
	0.01	**4.21**	**4.89**	**5.63**	**5.63**	**5.88**	**6.08**	**6.26**	**6.41**	**6.54**
15	0.05	3.01	3.67	4.37	4.37	4.59	4.78	4.94	5.08	5.20
	0.01	**4.17**	**4.84**	**5.56**	**5.56**	**5.80**	**5.99**	**6.16**	**6.31**	**6.44**
16	0.05	3.00	3.65	4.05	4.33	4.56	4.74	4.90	5.03	5.15
	0.01	**4,13**	**4.79**	**5.19**	**5.49**	**5.72**	**5.92**	**6.08**	**6.22**	**6.35**
17	0.05	2.98	3.63	4.02	4.30	4.52	4.70	4.86	4.99	5.11
	0.01	**4.10**	**4.74**	**5.14**	**5.43**	**5.66**	**5.85**	**6.01**	**6.15**	**6.27**
18	0.05	2.97	3.61	4.00	4.28	4.49	4.67	4.82	4.96	5.07
	0.01	**4.07**	**4.70**	**5.09**	**5.38**	**5.60**	**5.79**	**5.94**	**6.08**	**6.20**
19	0.05	2.96	3.59	3.98	4.25	4.47	4.65	4.79	4.92	5.04
	0.01	**4.05**	**4.67**	**5.05**	**5.33**	**5.55**	**5.73**	**5.89**	**6.02**	**6.14**
20	0.05	2.95	3.58	3.96	4.23	4.45	4.62	4.77	4.90	5.01
	0.01	**4.02**	**4.64**	**5.02**	**5.29**	**5.51**	**5.69**	**5.84**	**5.97**	**6.09**
24	0.05	2.92	3.53	3.90	4.17	4.37	4.54	4.68	4.81	4.92
	0.01	**3.96**	**4.55**	**4.91**	**5.17**	**5.37**	**5.54**	**5.69**	**5.81**	**5.92**
30	0.05	2.89	3.49	3.85	4.10	4.30	4.46	4.60	4.72	4.82
	0.01	**3.89**	**4.45**	**4.80**	**5.05**	**5.24**	**5.40**	**5.54**	**5.65**	**5.76**
40	0.05	2.86	3.44	3.79	4.04	4.23	4.39	4.52	4.63	4.73
	0.01	**3.82**	**4.37**	**4.70**	**4.93**	**5.11**	**5.26**	**5.39**	**5.50**	**5.60**
60	0.05	2.83	3.40	3.74	3.98	4.16	4.31	4.44	4.55	4.65
	0.01	**3.76**	**4.28**	**4.59**	**4.82**	**4.99**	**5.13**	**5.25**	**5.63**	**5.45**
120	0.05	2.80	3.36	3.68	3.92	4.10	4.24	4.36	4.47	4.56
	0.01	**3.70**	**4.20**	**4.50**	**4.71**	**4.87**	**5.01**	**5.12**	**5.21**	**5.30**
∞	0.05	2.77	3.31	3.63	3.86	4.03	4.17	4.29	4.39	4.47

r = number of means being compared.

Source: Based on Table 29 of Pearson, E. S., & Hartley, H. O. (Eds.). (1966). *Biometrika tables for statisticians.* Cambridge: Cambridge University Press.

APPENDIX P

The Chi-Square Distribution

See Table P–1 on the following page.

Table P–1. Levels of Statistical Significance (α)

df	0.10	0.05	0.02	0.01	0.001
1	2.71	3.84	5.41	6.64	10.38
2	4.60	5.99	7.82	9.21	13.82
3	6.25	7.82	9.84	11.34	16.27
4	7.78	9.49	11.67	13.28	18.46
5	9.24	11.07	13.39	15.09	20.82
6	10.64	12.59	15.03	16.81	22.46
7	12.02	14.07	16.62	18.48	24.32
8	13.36	15.51	18.17	20.09	26.12
9	14.68	16.92	19.68	21.67	27.88
10	15.99	18.31	21.16	23.21	29.59
11	17.28	19.68	22.62	24.72	31.26
12	18.55	21.03	24.05	26.22	32.91
13	19.81	22.36	25.47	27.69	34.53
14	21.06	23.68	26.87	29.14	36.12
15	22.31	25.00	28.26	30.58	37.70
16	23.54	26.30	29.63	32.00	39.25
17	24.77	27.59	31.00	33.41	40.79
18	25.99	28.87	32.35	34.80	42.31
19	27.20	30.41	33.69	36.19	43.82
20	28.41	31.41	35.02	37.57	45.32
21	29.62	32.67	36.34	38.93	46.80
22	31.81	33.92	37.66	40.29	48.27
23	32.01	35.17	38.97	41.64	49.73
24	33.20	36.42	40.27	42.98	51.18
25	34.38	337.65	41.57	44.31	52.62
26	35.56	38.88	42.86	45.64	54.05
27	36.74	30.11	44.14	46.96	55.48
28	37.92	41.34	45.42	48.28	56.89
29	39.08	42.56	46.68	49.59	58.30
30	40.26	43.77	47.96	50.89	59.70

Source: Based on Table A–5, Owen, D. B. (1962). *Handbook of statistical tables.* Reading, MA: Addison-Wesley Longman.

APPENDIX Q

Critical Values for the Wilcoxon Signed-Rank Test for *n* = 5 to 50

See Table Q–1 on the following page.

Table Q–1. Critical Values for the Wilcoxon Signed-Rank Test for n = 5 to 50

One-Sided	Two-Sided	$n=5$	$n=6$	$n=7$	$n=8$	$n=9$	$n=10$	$n=11$	$n=12$	$n=13$	$n=14$	$n=15$	$n=16$
$\alpha = 0.05$	$\alpha = 0.10$	1	2	4	6	8	11	14	17	21	26	30	36
$\alpha = 0.025$	$\alpha = 0.05$		2	2	4	6	8	11	14	17	21	25	30
$\alpha = 0.01$	$\alpha = 0.02$			0	2	3	5	7	10	13	16	20	24
$\alpha = 0.005$	$\alpha = 0.01$				0	2	3	5	7	10	13	16	19

One-Sided	Two-Sided	$n=17$	$n=18$	$n=19$	$n=20$	$n=21$	$n=22$	$n=23$	$n=24$	$n=25$	$n=26$	$n=27$	$n=28$
$\alpha = 0.05$	$\alpha = 0.10$	41	47	54	60	68	75	83	92	101	110	120	130
$\alpha = 0.025$	$\alpha = 0.05$	35	40	46	52	59	66	73	81	90	98	107	107
$\alpha = 0.01$	$\alpha = 0.02$	28	33	38	43	49	56	62	69	77	85	93	102
$\alpha = 0.005$	$\alpha = 0.01$	23	28	32	37	43	49	55	61	68	76	84	98

One-Sided	Two-Sided	$n=29$	$n=30$	$n=31$	$n=32$	$n=33$	$n=34$	$n=35$	$n=36$	$n=37$	$n=38$	$n=39$	
$\alpha = 0.05$	$\alpha = 0.10$	141	152	163	175	188	201	214	228	242	256	271	
$\alpha = 0.025$	$\alpha = 0.05$	127	137	148	159	171	183	195	208	222	235	250	
$\alpha = 0.01$	$\alpha = 0.02$	111	120	130	141	151	162	174	186	198	211	224	
$\alpha = 0.005$	$\alpha = 0.01$	100	109	118	128	138	149	160	171	183	195	208	

One-Sided	Two-Sided	$n=40$	$n=41$	$n=42$	$n=43$	$n=43$	$n=45$	$n=46$	$n=47$	$n=48$	$n=49$	$n=50$	
$\alpha = 0.05$	$\alpha = 0.10$	287	303	319	336	353	371	389	408	427	427	466	
$\alpha = 0.025$	$\alpha = 0.05$	264	279	295	311	327	344	361	379	397	397	434	
$\alpha = 0.01$	$\alpha = 0.02$	238	252	267	281	297	313	329	345	362	362	398	
$\alpha = 0.005$	$\alpha = 0.01$	221	234	248	262	277	292	307	323	339	356	373	

Source: From Wilcoxon, F., & Wilcox, R. A. (1964). *Some rapid approximate statistical procedures.* Pearl River, NY: Lederle Laboratories of the American Cyanamid Company, p. 28.

APPENDIX R

Critical Values for a Mann-Whitney *U*-Test

See Tables R–1 and R–2 on the following pages.

Table R–1. Critical Values for a Mann-Whitney U-Test for a One-Tailed Test at $\alpha = 0.01$ (Roman Type) and $\alpha = 0.005$ (Boldface Type) and for Two-Tailed Test at $\alpha = 0.02$ (Roman Type) and $\alpha = 0.01$ (Boldface Type)

n_1/n_2	1	2	3	4	5	6	7	8	9	10	11	12	13	14	15	16	17	18	19	20
1	None	—	—	—	—	—	—	—	—	—	—	—	—	—	—	—	—	—	—	—
	—	—	—	—	—	—	—	—	—	—	—	—	—	—	—	—	—	—	—	—
2	—	—	—	—	—	—	—	—	—	—	—	—	0	0	0	0	0	0	1	1
	—	—	—	—	—	—	—	—	—	—	—	—	—	—	—	—	—	—	**0**	**0**
3	—	—	—	—	—	—	0	0	1	1	1	2	2	2	3	3	4	4	4	5
	—	—	—	—	—	—	—	—	**0**	**0**	**0**	**1**	**1**	**1**	**2**	**2**	**2**	**2**	**3**	**3**
4	—	—	—	—	0	1	1	2	3	3	4	5	5	6	7	7	8	9	9	10
	—	—	—	—	—	**0**	**0**	**1**	**1**	**2**	**2**	**3**	**3**	**4**	**5**	**5**	**6**	**6**	**7**	**8**
5	—	—	—	0	1	2	3	4	5	6	7	8	9	10	11	12	13	14	15	16
	—	—	—	—	**0**	**1**	**1**	**2**	**3**	**4**	**5**	**6**	**7**	**7**	**8**	**9**	**10**	**11**	**12**	**13**
6	—	—	—	1	2	3	4	6	7	8	9	11	12	13	15	16	18	19	20	22
	—	—	—	**0**	**1**	**2**	**3**	**4**	**5**	**6**	**7**	**9**	**10**	**11**	**12**	**13**	**15**	**16**	**17**	**18**
7	—	—	0	1	3	4	6	7	9	11	12	14	16	17	19	21	23	24	26	28
	—	—	—	**0**	**1**	**3**	**4**	**6**	**7**	**9**	**10**	**12**	**13**	**15**	**16**	**18**	**19**	**21**	**22**	**24**
8	—	—	0	2	4	6	7	9	11	13	15	17	20	22	24	26	28	30	32	34
	—	—	—	**1**	**2**	**4**	**6**	**7**	**9**	**11**	**13**	**15**	**17**	**18**	**20**	**22**	**24**	**26**	**28**	**30**
9	—	—	1	3	5	7	9	11	14	16	18	21	23	26	28	31	33	36	38	40
	—	—	**0**	**1**	**3**	**5**	**7**	**9**	**11**	**13**	**16**	**18**	**20**	**22**	**24**	**27**	**29**	**31**	**33**	**36**
10	—	—	1	3	6	8	11	13	16	19	22	24	27	30	33	36	38	41	44	47
	—	—	**0**	**2**	**4**	**6**	**9**	**11**	**13**	**16**	**18**	**21**	**24**	**26**	**29**	**31**	**34**	**37**	**39**	**42**

n																				
11	53/**48**	50/**45**	47/**42**	44/**39**	41/**36**	37/**33**	34/**30**	31/**27**	28/**24**	25/**21**	22/**18**	18/**16**	15/**13**	12/**10**	9/**7**	7/**5**	4/**2**	1/**0**	–/**–**	–/**–**
12	60/**54**	56/**51**	53/**47**	49/**44**	46/**41**	42/**37**	38/**34**	35/**31**	31/**27**	28/**24**	24/**21**	21/**18**	17/**15**	14/**12**	11/**9**	8/**6**	5/**3**	2/**1**	–/**–**	–/**–**
13	67/**60**	63/**56**	59/**53**	55/**49**	51/**45**	47/**42**	43/**38**	39/**34**	35/**31**	31/**27**	27/**24**	23/**20**	20/**17**	16/**13**	12/**10**	9/**7**	5/**3**	2/**1**	0/**–**	–/**–**
14	73/**67**	69/**63**	65/**58**	60/**54**	56/**50**	51/**46**	47/**42**	43/**38**	38/**34**	34/**30**	30/**26**	26/**22**	22/**18**	17/**15**	13/**11**	10/**7**	6/**4**	2/**1**	0/**–**	–/**–**
15	80/**73**	75/**69**	70/**64**	66/**60**	61/**55**	56/**51**	51/**46**	47/**42**	42/**37**	37/**33**	33/**29**	28/**24**	24/**20**	19/**16**	15/**12**	11/**8**	7/**5**	3/**2**	0/**–**	–/**–**
16	87/**79**	82/**74**	76/**70**	71/**65**	66/**60**	61/**55**	56/**50**	51/**45**	46/**41**	41/**36**	36/**31**	31/**27**	26/**22**	21/**18**	16/**13**	12/**9**	7/**5**	3/**2**	0/**–**	–/**–**
17	93/**86**	88/**81**	82/**75**	77/**70**	71/**65**	66/**60**	60/**54**	55/**49**	49/**44**	44/**39**	38/**34**	33/**29**	28/**24**	23/**19**	18/**15**	13/**10**	8/**6**	4/**2**	0/**–**	–/**–**
18	100/**92**	94/**87**	88/**81**	82/**75**	76/**70**	70/**64**	65/**58**	59/**53**	53/**47**	47/**42**	41/**37**	36/**31**	30/**26**	24/**21**	19/**16**	14/**11**	9/**6**	4/**2**	0/**–**	–/**–**
19	107/**99**	101/**93**	94/**87**	88/**81**	82/**74**	75/**69**	69/**63**	63/**56**	56/**51**	50/**45**	44/**39**	38/**33**	32/**28**	26/**22**	20/**17**	15/**12**	9/**7**	4/**3**	1/**0**	–/**–**
20	114/**105**	107/**99**	100/**92**	93/**86**	87/**79**	80/**73**	73/**67**	67/**60**	60/**54**	53/**48**	47/**42**	40/**36**	34/**30**	28/**24**	22/**18**	16/**13**	10/**8**	5/**3**	1/**0**	0/**–**

Critical values for a one–tailed test at α = 0.01 (lightface type) and α = 0.005 (boldface type) and for two–tailed test α = 0.02 (lightface type) and α = 0.01 (boldface type).

Source: From Kirk, R. (1978). *Introductory statistics.* Monterey, CA: Brooks/Cole Publishing Company, pp. 423–424.

Table R–2. Critical Values for a Mann-Whitney U Test for a One-Tailed Test at α = 0.05 (Roman Type) and α = 0.025 (Boldface Type) and for Two-Tailed Test at α = 0.10 (Roman Type) and α = 0.05 (Boldface Type)

n_1/n_2	1	2	3	4	5	6	7	8	9	10	11	12	13	14	15	16	17	18	19	20
1	None	—	—	—	—	—	—	—	—	—	—	—	—	—	—	—	—	—	0	0
	—	—	—	—	—	—	—	—	—	—	—	—	—	—	—	—	—	—	—	—
2	—	—	—	—	0	0	0	1	1	1	1	2	2	2	3	3	3	4	4	4
	—	—	—	—	—	—	—	**0**	**0**	**0**	**0**	**1**	**1**	**1**	**1**	**1**	**2**	**2**	**2**	**2**
3	—	—	0	0	1	2	2	3	3	4	5	5	6	7	7	8	9	9	10	11
	—	—	—	—	**0**	**1**	**1**	**2**	**2**	**3**	**3**	**4**	**4**	**5**	**5**	**6**	**6**	**7**	**7**	**8**
4	—	—	0	1	2	3	4	5	6	7	8	9	10	11	12	14	15	16	17	18
	—	—	—	**0**	**1**	**2**	**3**	**4**	**4**	**5**	**6**	**7**	**8**	**9**	**10**	**11**	**11**	**12**	**13**	**13**
5	—	0	1	2	4	5	6	8	9	11	12	13	15	16	18	19	20	22	23	25
	—	—	**0**	**1**	**2**	**3**	**5**	**6**	**7**	**8**	**9**	**11**	**12**	**13**	**14**	**15**	**17**	**18**	**19**	**20**
6	—	0	2	3	5	7	8	10	12	14	16	17	19	21	23	25	26	28	30	32
	—	—	**1**	**2**	**3**	**5**	**6**	**8**	**10**	**11**	**13**	**14**	**16**	**17**	**19**	**21**	**22**	**24**	**25**	**27**
7	—	0	2	4	6	8	11	13	15	17	19	21	24	26	28	30	33	35	37	39
	—	—	**1**	**3**	**5**	**6**	**8**	**10**	**12**	**14**	**16**	**18**	**20**	**22**	**24**	**26**	**28**	**30**	**32**	**34**
8	—	1	3	5	8	10	13	15	18	20	23	26	28	31	33	36	39	41	44	47
	—	**0**	**2**	**4**	**6**	**8**	**10**	**13**	**15**	**17**	**19**	**22**	**24**	**26**	**29**	**31**	**34**	**36**	**38**	**41**
9	—	1	3	6	9	12	15	18	21	24	27	30	33	36	39	42	45	48	51	54
	—	**0**	**2**	**4**	**7**	**10**	**12**	**15**	**17**	**20**	**23**	**26**	**28**	**31**	**34**	**37**	**39**	**42**	**45**	**48**
10	—	1	4	7	11	14	17	20	24	27	31	34	37	41	44	48	51	55	58	62
	—	**0**	**3**	**5**	**8**	**11**	**14**	**17**	**20**	**23**	**26**	**29**	**33**	**36**	**39**	**42**	**45**	**48**	**52**	**55**

Critical values of the Mann–Whitney U statistic. Lightface: critical values for a one-tailed test at $\alpha = 0.05$ and for a two-tailed test at $\alpha = 0.10$. **Boldface**: $\alpha = 0.025$ (one-tailed) and $\alpha = 0.05$ (two-tailed).

$n_2 \backslash n_1$	1	2	3	4	5	6	7	8	9	10	11	12	13	14	15	16	17	18	19	20
11	—	1	5	8	12	16	19	23	27	31	34	38	42	46	50	54	57	61	65	69
11	**—**	**0**	**3**	**6**	**9**	**13**	**16**	**19**	**23**	**26**	**30**	**33**	**37**	**40**	**44**	**47**	**51**	**55**	**58**	**62**
12	—	2	5	9	13	17	21	26	30	34	38	42	47	51	55	60	64	68	72	77
12	**—**	**1**	**4**	**7**	**11**	**14**	**18**	**22**	**26**	**29**	**33**	**37**	**41**	**45**	**49**	**53**	**57**	**61**	**65**	**69**
13	—	2	6	10	15	19	24	28	33	37	42	47	51	56	61	65	70	75	80	84
13	**—**	**1**	**4**	**8**	**12**	**16**	**20**	**24**	**28**	**33**	**37**	**41**	**45**	**50**	**54**	**59**	**63**	**67**	**72**	**76**
14	—	2	7	11	16	21	26	31	36	41	46	51	56	61	66	71	77	82	87	92
14	**—**	**1**	**5**	**9**	**13**	**17**	**22**	**26**	**31**	**36**	**40**	**45**	**50**	**55**	**59**	**64**	**67**	**74**	**78**	**83**
15	—	3	7	12	18	23	28	33	39	44	50	55	61	66	72	77	83	88	94	100
15	**—**	**1**	**5**	**10**	**14**	**19**	**24**	**29**	**34**	**39**	**44**	**49**	**54**	**59**	**64**	**70**	**75**	**80**	**85**	**90**
16	—	3	8	14	19	25	30	36	42	48	54	60	65	71	77	83	89	95	101	107
16	**—**	**1**	**6**	**11**	**15**	**21**	**26**	**31**	**37**	**42**	**47**	**53**	**59**	**64**	**70**	**75**	**81**	**86**	**92**	**98**
17	—	3	9	15	20	26	33	39	45	51	57	64	70	77	83	89	96	102	109	115
17	**—**	**2**	**6**	**11**	**17**	**22**	**28**	**34**	**39**	**45**	**51**	**57**	**63**	**67**	**75**	**81**	**87**	**93**	**99**	**105**
18	—	4	9	16	22	28	35	41	48	55	61	68	75	82	88	95	102	109	116	123
18	**—**	**2**	**7**	**12**	**18**	**24**	**30**	**36**	**42**	**48**	**55**	**61**	**67**	**74**	**80**	**86**	**93**	**99**	**106**	**112**
19	0	4	10	17	23	30	37	44	51	58	65	72	80	87	94	101	109	116	123	130
19	**—**	**2**	**7**	**13**	**19**	**25**	**32**	**38**	**45**	**52**	**58**	**65**	**72**	**78**	**85**	**92**	**99**	**106**	**113**	**119**
20	0	4	11	18	25	32	39	47	54	62	69	77	84	92	100	107	115	123	130	138
20	**—**	**2**	**8**	**13**	**20**	**27**	**34**	**41**	**48**	**55**	**62**	**69**	**76**	**83**	**90**	**98**	**105**	**112**	**119**	**127**

Critical values for a one–tailed test at $\alpha = 0.05$ (lightface type) and $\alpha = 0.025$ (boldface type) and for two–tailed test $\alpha = 0.10$ (lightface type) and $\alpha = 0.05$ (boldface type).

Source: From Kirk, R. (1978). *Introductory statistics.* Monterey, CA: Brooks/Cole Publishing Company, pp. 423–424.

APPENDIX S

Statistical Inference: A Bayesian Perspective

Beyond a *p*-Value and Hypothesis Testing: Using the Minimum Bayes Factor to Teach Statistical Inference: Moving Forward to EBP Statistics

Overview and Introduction

In recent years, Bayesian statistics has gone from being a controversial theory on the fringe of mainstream statistics to being widely accepted as a valuable alternative to more common classical approach (aka frequentists methods) such as *p*-value and hypothesis testing approaches. Indeed, Bayesian methods have become more and more common in a range of fields, including marketing, economics, school assessment, nuclear waste disposal, medicine, and the law. They have, for example, permeated all of the major areas of medical research, from clinical trials to survival modeling and decision-making in use of new technologies (Ashby, 2006).

Interest in Bayesian statistics also has been growing in statistical education. Increasingly, although not commonly, elementary statistics texts today are introducing Bayesian approach using Bayes's rule

within a section on conditional probability (see for example, Bluman, 2004; De Veaux, Velleman, & Bock, 2007; Larson & Farber, 2006; Sullivan, 2007; Triola, 2007). This is a significant step forward from what was observed more than a decade ago when the Bayes's rule and Bayesian methods were rarely covered or treated as an optional topic at best (Satake, Gilligan, & Amato, 1995). A few texts, such as Berry (1996), Bluman (2004), and Larson and Farber (2006), discuss the theorem in great detail with examples and exercise problems. Unfortunately, for the most part, our informal survey reveals that the treatment of the topic in textbooks, and the classroom instruction is often sparse and inadequate. Since students in many fields today are likely to enter careers that will include a decision making theory that requires a good working knowledge of Bayesian methods and ideas, the importance and practical necessity of integrating the Bayesian approach within *p*-value and hypothesis testing approaches is becoming increasingly clear (Satake & Amato, 2008). In this appendix, we discuss the followings: (1) several fallacies of frequentists statistical methods, specifically *p*-value and hypothesis tests, (2) the use of the Minimum Bayes Factor (MBF) for statistical inference as an alternative to the frequentists methods, (3) the reason why Bayesian approach provides more accurate, credible, and relevant test results than the frequentists statistical methods when we measure the strength of the evidence, and (4) the reason why the Bayesian methods should be included in an introductory statistics course.

Typically, in an introductory statistics course, the primary procedure of statistical inference presented by the instructors is the *combined method* of Fisher's *p*-value approach and Neyman-Pearson's Hypothesis Tests approach. In fact, the method is the most widely used even beyond undergraduate statistics classes. Furthermore, the combined method is considered to be so-called a *best compromised* method by many researchers and practitioners in the various fields, and it has become the standard method in classroom instruction and scientific journal article writings. Unfortunately, the *p*-value approach and hypothesis tests approach are conceptually different and incompatible with each other (Goodman, 1999a, 2005). Therefore, it is illogical to combine the two methods and use it as a single coherent approach to statistical inference. As a matter of fact, the founders of each method, Fisher and Neyman-Pearson, greatly disagreed with each other's approach to statistical inference and disliked each other at a personal level. (Goodman, 1999a, 2005). Based on both authors' informal survey of the most widely used textbooks (reference, for example), almost none of them covers the history of the debate, and most treat these two incompatible approaches as a single coherent method.

The main objective of statistical inference is to best estimate the characteristics of the parameter of a target population based on what was actually observed in a sample drawn from the population. It goes from a specific outcome (sample) to predict a general outcome (population). This process is called *inductive*. Therefore, what one eventually must answer is, "How credible is one's hypothesis based on what was actually observed?" Contrast this with the question, "how credible is one's sample data based on the assumption the null hypothesis being true?" The latter question process is known as *deductive*. Using *p*-value, hypothesis tests, or the combined method approaches to answer the main question of statistical inference is irrelevant and meaningless in many cases because one is using deductive reasoning to answer an inductive-natured question. In other words, one is not interested in measuring the credibility of the data, but rather measuring the truth of the hypotheses based on the data. The deductive quantitative tools such as *p*-value and hypothesis tests do not serve well to answer the inductive-natured statistical inference questions. One needs an inductive tool to answer the question directly related to statistical inference. That is one of the main reasons why students and even instructors in a statistics course often misinterpret the results of their statistical analyses (Gigerenzer et al., 2004).

Regardless of the type, statistical methods were originally intended to measure the strength of *evidence* for drawing an accurate and reliable conclusion about the population parameters of interest, based on a sample. Unfortunately, in most cases, the term "evidence" is not correctly interpreted by students or even correctly defined by instructors. A statistical definition of evidence, according to Goodman and Royall (1988), is given as "a property of data that makes us alter our beliefs about how the world around us is working." In short, what we mean by "measuring the strength of evidence" must lead to a determination of the truth of one's belief (or hypothesis) in the end, based on what is actually observed. It is a simple fact that neither of frequentists methods can accomplish this task. In the next two sections of this paper, we discuss three frequentists approaches to statistical inference, followed by introducing an alternative inductive-natured statistical method called *Bayesian methods*.

I. Fisher's p-Value

Every experiment may be said to exist only in order to give the facts a chance of disproving the null hypothesis —R. A. Fisher (1935)

This approach consists of two components, namely: (1) a null hypothesis (H_o),

and (2) a test statistic, that is, an observed value derived from a sample under the null hypothesis distribution. Graphically, when a right-sided test (or the right-sided area of a two-sided test), the *p*-value is the area under the null hypothesis distribution (H_o distribution) curve from the test statistic (denoted by θ), and beyond it. (See the area beyond and above θ.)

The bell-shaped curve represents the probability of every possible outcome under the null hypothesis. Both α (the Type I error rate) and the *p*-value are "tail areas" under this curve. The tail area for α is set before the experiment, and a result can fall anywhere within it. The *p*-value tail area is known only after a result is observed, and, by definition, the result will always lie on the border of that.

As can be seen in Figure S–1, the correct interpretation of the *p*-value is the probability of obtaining a test sta-

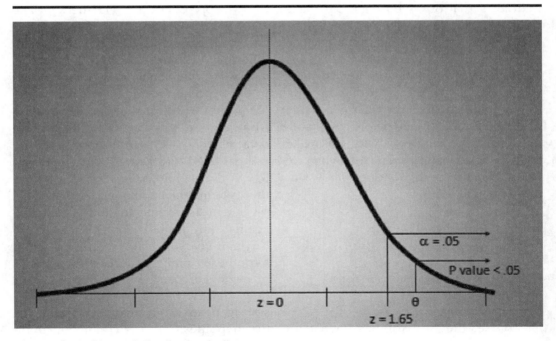

Figure S–1. Normal distribution bell curve.

tistic equal to or *more extreme* than the observed value, assuming that the null hypothesis is true. The basic rule for decision making is that, if any sample data has a corresponding *p*-value less than an ordinary benchmark of 0.05 (a typical choice in the behavioral and social science research, as Fisher stated), the result is interpreted as *statistically significant*.

Although there are many studies on *p*-value fallacies (e.g., Goodman 1999a, 2005; Matthews, 2001; Maxwell & Satake, 2010; Winkler, 2001, etc.), the following two fallacies are the most serious ones in terms of why the *p*-value is not suitable for measuring the strength of evidence and drawing an accurate conclusion about the population of interest. First, the correct definition of the *p*-value is made extremely difficult and complex for interpretation of the results because it is not part of any formal procedure of statistical inference. Especially, the inclusion of the probability of "more extreme" than an actual observed data will make the conclusion imprecise and unreliable. Later, we show how much the *p*-value overstates the amount of evidence against H_o. Second, the *p*-value does not calculate the probability of the truth of a hypothesis of interest based on what is actually observed. As mentioned before, the inability to calculate the probability will make the *p*-value an inappropriate tool when we conduct statistical inference. Symbolically, it is written as follows:

$$(\text{Fisher's}) \ p\text{-value} = p \ [(x \geq \theta) \, | \, (H_o \text{ is true})]$$

where x = the test statistic for a sample

Of course, the probability of what an investigator wishes to find in the end is $p \ [(H_o \text{ is true})] \, | \, (x = \theta)]$. The common error

made by the investigator is to interpret the Fisher's *p*-value as the latter probability, which it is not.

II. Neyman-Pearson's Hypothesis Tests

No test based upon a theory of probability can by itself provide any valuable evidence of the truth or falsehood of a hypothesis.

But we may look at the purpose of tests from another viewpoint. Without hoping to know whether each separate (conflicting) hypothesis is true or false, we may search for rules to govern our behavior with regard to them, in following which we insure that, in the long run of experience, we shall not often be wrong. —J. Neyman & E. Pearson (1933)

The major conceptual differences between the two approaches are: (1) Fisher's *p*-value was originally intended for a flexible inferential measure in a single experiment, whereas Neyman-Pearson's hypothesis tests was a rule of *behavior*, not inference, in the hypothetical long run experiment, (2) *p*-value indicates tail area starting from a point calculated by the sample data, whereas Neyman-Pearson uses the pretrial fixed "error rates," such as α and β, and the region for rejecting H_o before the experiment begins, and (3) Fisher's *p*-value measures the amount of evidence against only a null hypothesis, whereas Neyman-Pearson states two conflicting hypotheses and measures the strength of evidence based on the pretrial error rates and the rejection region. The decision to reject H_o in favor of the alternative hypothesis (H_a) is contingent upon whether or not the test statistic falls into the rejection region.

Philosophically, Neyman and Pearson held a strong position on the use of deductive reasoning (from *general to specific*), whereas Fisher rejected their deductive and mechanistic approaches to statistical inference. Although both p-values and pretrial Type 1 error rates (α) are *tail area* probabilities under the null hypothesis distribution, p-value is a post-experiment probability calculated from the actual sample data, while α is a fixed pre-experiment error rate prior to sample data analysis (see Figure 1 in front matter). Therefore, they are conceptually different probability values. Note that the symbol θ represents a post-sample statistic that generates the p-value that is less than the pretrial error rate $\alpha = 0.05$, as previously shown in Figure S–1.

Importantly, Neyman-Pearson hypothesis test method lacks the ability to accomplish the following tasks:

1. Measure the strength of evidence accurately
2. Assess truth from a single experiment (Goodman, 1999a)

In other words, in Neyman-Pearson's hypothesis testing, the statistical inference doesn't tell one how confident one can be in two different hypotheses before and after an experiment in terms of the numerical probability values. It only gives conventions for dichotomous results such as, "Reject H_o" or "Do not reject H_o" based on preset long-term error rates. One cannot conclude how a particular decision justified is after, or how credible a hypothesis is prior to, an experiment. More importantly, one cannot derive a probability value to how much actual sample data support a given hypothesis, which is the essential meaning of *measuring the strength of evidence*. One is only able to conclude that the final decision was made by a standard

procedure that in the long run controls error frequencies (Dienes, 2011).

Fundamentally, as we noted earlier, Fisher's p-value and Neyman-Pearson's hypothesis tests are two incompatible methods in many respects. But, somehow, the two approaches were blended into a single approach, and the method has mistakenly become a coherent approach to statistical inference (Maxwell & Satake, 2010).

III. The Combined Method

In the previous section, we noted that neither Fisher's p-value nor Neyman-Pearson's hypothesis tests can accurately measure the strength of evidence to calculate the probability of the truth of one's belief. Specifically, Fisher's p-value calculates the rarity of the observed value plus "more extreme" than the value, given that the null hypothesis is true. On the other hand, as discussed earlier, the Neyman-Pearson's hypothesis tests are not perfect, either. The method also prevents one from calculating the probability of the truth, one can only obtain the dichotomous decision, namely, "Reject H_o" or "Do not reject H_o," without any specific numerical probability value indicating how strongly the evidence is against or for H_o. Therefore, both methods need each other to compensate their own limitations to make it better logically and statistically. This means that the researchers needed to create "something" to make statistical inference procedure nearly perfect. Goodman (1999a) stated on this particular issue as follows:

The hypothesis tests approach offered scientists a Faustian bargain—a seemingly automatic way to limit the number of mistaken conclusions in the long run, but only by abandoning the ability to measure evidence and assess truth from a single experiment. It is doubtful that hypothesis tests would have achieved their current degree of acceptance if something had not been added that let scientists mistakenly think they could avoid that trade-off. That something turned out to be Fisher's "*p*-value," much to the dismay of Fisher, Neyman, Pearson, and many experts on statistical inference who followed. (p. 999)

This is how the combined method operates. First, an investigator sets Type 1 error of his choice (usually 5%) and power (usually the value exceeding 80%) before the experiment. Then the investigator calculates a *p*-value from a sample and reject the null hypothesis if the *p*-value is less than the preset Type 1 error rate, that is, reject H_o if $p < \alpha$. This combined method procedure appears, completely deductively, to associate a probability with the null hypothesis, like Fisher's *p*-value method, within the context of a method that controls the chance of errors. On this issue, Goodman (1999a) states, "The key word here is 'probability,' because a probability has an absoluteness that overwhelms caveats that it is not a probability of truth or that it should not be used mechanically" (p. 1000).

As a result, the combined method is currently considered by many scientists, educators, practitioners, and the others as "more scientific and objective" method for measures of the strength of evidence in statistical inference (Satake, 2010). However, the combined method is also far from perfect. On the contrary to what many believe, the combined method still cannot answer the bottom line question, that is, "What is the probability of the truth of one's belief based on what was actually observed?" If the main goal

of statistical inference were to calculate the truth of the hypothesis of interest, the combined method is not the way to go. So, is there any method that can meet the goal to calculate the probability of the truth in one's hypothesis based on the actual sample data? This is the main scope of this appendix, and such a method is called the *Bayesian method*.

Prelude to Bayesian Methods: Several Key Points on Frequentists Methods

Goodman (2008) pointed out that the correct interpretation of *p*-value is made extraordinarily difficult, even among skilled researchers, because it is not part of any formal system of statistical inference. Therefore, the *p*-value's inferential meaning is widely, and often wildly, misunderstood. For instance, Oakes (1986) asked 70 academic psychologists to define $p < 0.01$; only 8 out of 70 participants interpreted it correctly. The results of other surveys of professionals in the social and clinical sciences indicate similar, apparently widespread misunderstanding of *p*-value and hypothesis testing approaches (Dar, Serlin, & Omer, 1994; Mittag & Thompson, 2000; Nelson, Rosenthal, & Rosnow, 1986). Given that many academics and researchers have spent hundreds of hours studying and teaching *p*-value and hypothesis testing in statistics courses at both the undergraduate and graduate levels, the natural question arises: Why are we not successful in teaching these concepts?

Klein (2005) offers two factors as an explanation. The first is that *p*-value and hypothesis testing are not the most transparent of inference systems (Pollard & Richardson, 1987). On the probability of making a Type 1 error, *Psychological*

Bulletin (*102*, 159–163) noted that it is difficult to explain the logic of these methods and dispel confusion about them. The second, and more disturbing, factor is that it is a general human weakness in reasoning with conditional probabilities, especially ones best viewed from a relative frequency perspective (Andersen, 1990).

Furthermore, many people mistakenly believe the incorporation of the *p*-value into the hypothesis test framework is the right way to measure the strength of statistical evidence. These confusions and misconceptions have created several myths and illusions in statistics education. Before we proceed to the main theme of the paper, we itemize several important points regarding the myths of the frequentists methods.

Facts about the *p*-value, hypothesis tests, and combined approaches that are most commonly misunderstood are summarized below (Goodman, 1999a):

1. Fisher's *p*-value is intended to measure the strength of the evidence using a flexible inferential measure and Neyman-Pearson's hypothesis test is a rule of behavior, not inference. Neyman and Pearson held that inductive reasoning was an illusion and that the only meaningful parameters of importance in an experiment were constraints on the number of statistical "errors" we would make, defined before an experiment (α). Fisher rejected mechanistic approaches to inference, believing in a more flexible, inductive approach to science, such as mathematical likelihood.

2. The two methods are philosophically and conceptually different, that is to say, it is incorrect to conclude that "Reject H_o if $p < \alpha$" and "Do not reject H_o if $p \geq \alpha$." Because of *p*-value's

resemblance to the pretrial α error, *p*-value was absorbed into the hypothesis test framework. This created two illusions; that an "error rate" could be measured after an experiment and that this post-trial "error rate" could be regarded as a measure of inductive evidence.

3. α is a prespecified error rate (before studying a sample), while *p*-value is the probability of the actual observed sample data value or "more extreme" than that value, given that H_o is true. Furthermore, α is the probability of a set of future outcomes, represented by the "tail area" of the null distribution. Implicit in the concept is that we don't know which of those outcomes will occur. The tail area represented by the *p*-value is quite different; we know the outcome, and by definition it lies exactly on the border of the tail area. The "error rate" concept requires that a result can be anywhere within the tail area, which is not the case with the *p*-value. An error rate interpretation of the *p*-value implies partial ignorance about the results, but if we had such ignorance, we could not calculate the *p*-value. Another factor that makes the error rate interpretation of *p*-values problematic is that they are always calculated conditionally (given that H_o is true). Fisher felt that aspects of the data irrelevant to the effect under study should not affect the *p*-value.

4. *p*-value is calculated based on a single experiment while α value is set before an experiment designed for the long run.

5. As a practicing scientist, Fisher had an abiding interest in creating an objective, quantitative method to aid the process of inductive inference-drawing

conclusions from observations. He did not believe that the use of the Bayes's formula to convert *prior probabilities* (the probability, before an experiment, that H_o is true) of hypotheses *to posterior probabilities* (the probability, after an experiment, that H_o is true) was justified in scientific research, where prior probabilities are usually uncertain. He ultimately proposed the inferential methods that did not require prior probabilities of hypotheses. *p*-value approach is one of those inferential methods.

6. The statement, "One can never accept H_o, only fail to reject it," was a feature, not of Neyman-Pearson hypothesis tests, but of Fisher's significance (*p*-value) tests, which had no H_a. There was no measure of evidence in the Neyman-Pearson hypothesis tests, although some have attempted to interpret it that way.

7. Neyman and Pearson held that the best we can do with deductive probability theory is a rule for statistically dictated behavior, which they claimed would serve us well in the long run. They also stated that there does not exist reasoning called "Inductive"; if it were to be used properly, the term should be called "inductive behavior."

8. There is no definitive measure tool to calculate the strength of the evidence in the hypothesis test, developed by Neyman-Pearson, although many people used the *p*-value as such a tool. All that can be said is either "Reject H_o under a given Type 1 error" or "Fail to reject H_o under the given Type 1 error." Also, as we have repeatedly noted, the two methods are incompatible with each other. Therefore, the *p*-value cannot be any part of the hypothesis testing process. In fact, both Fisher and Neyman-Pearson were actually aware of this.

9. Even Fisher thought that null hypothesis testing was the most primitive type in a hierarchy of statistical analyses and should be used only for problems about which we have very little knowledge or none at all (Gigerenzer et al., 1989). Fisher also thought that using a 5% level of significance indicated lack of statistical thinking.

Bayesian Perspectives: How to Measure the Strength of the Evidence

Many of the fallacies about the *p*-value and hypothesis testing are the result of researchers, teachers, and students wishing to determine posterior probabilities without using Bayesian techniques. Unfortunately, frequentists' statistical tests only calculate the probability of occurrence of the observed data value and more extreme than the value on the assumption of H_o being true. Additionally, even if the *p*-value were correctly used, frequentists still neglect to include the "more extreme" values when they draw a conclusion. What is desired is to calculate the probability of truth for a hypothesis based on data that were actually observed in a sample, while excluding "more extreme" hypothetical outcomes that could be observed in the long run. Such a probability can only be obtained using Bayesian methods.

In Bayesian methods, there are three main components; namely, *prior odds of the null hypothesis* (a subjective component stated by an investigator before seeing data), *Bayes factor* (an index that measures the strength of actual evidence), and *posterior odds of the null hypothesis* (a more objective component derived through a combination of prior odds and Bayes factor; the result is the probability of truth of the null hypothesis; Maxwell & Satake, 2010).

Bayesian methods provide a proper way to measure and to combine evidence. They are symbolically written as follows:

$$\frac{P(H_o|\text{Data})}{P(H_a|\text{Data})} = \frac{P(H_o)}{P(H_a)} \cdot \frac{P(\text{Data}|H_o)}{P(\text{Data}|H_a)}$$

In words, the left-hand side of the equation above represents the posterior odds ratio, and the right-hand side is the product of the prior odds ratio and Bayes factor (aka the likelihood ratio). Because the likelihood ratio (Bayes factor) is a factor of the posterior odds ratio, from the Bayesian standpoint, the better the hypothesis predicts the data, the stronger the evidential support for that hypothesis.

There are two main differences between Fisher's *p*-value and Bayes factor. First, the calculation of Fisher's *p*-value involves both observed data and "more extreme" hypothetical outcomes, whereas one calculates Bayes factor using only observed data. Second, Fisher's *p*-value is calculated in relation to only the null hypothesis, whereas Bayes factor is calculated in relation to both the null and alternative hypotheses. In other words, Bayes factor is a comparison of how well two competing hypotheses (H_o and H_a) predict the data. The hypothesis that predicts the actual observed data better is the one that is said to have more evidence supporting it (Goodman, 1999b).

Furthermore, Bayes factor can be interpreted as the mathematical ratio of the credibility of evidence under two conflicting conditions (the null hypoth-

esis versus the alternative hypothesis). For instance, if the Bayes factor is 1/3, the result can be interpreted in three ways:

1. Objective probability: the actual observed result is three times as probable under H_a as it is under H_o.
2. Inductive inference: the evidence supports H_a three times as strong as it does H_o.
3. Subjective probability: assuming that we start with $p(H_o) = p(H_a)$, the odds of H_o to H_a after we observed data are one-third what they were before seeing data.

Therefore, the Bayes factor modifies one's initial belief about an event of interest and, after observing how much Bayes factors of certain sizes change various initial beliefs, one is able to determine the strength of evidence. In other words, one can precisely distinguish between "strong evidence" and "weak evidence" with the Bayes factor.

Minimum Bayes Factor (MBF)

In a typical research study, a *composite alternative hypothesis* against a null hypothesis is seen more often than not, for example, "the treatment is beneficial and/ or effective." Katki (2008) noted that the superiority of the Bayes factor over *p*-values for measuring the strength of evidence is a consequence of considering alternative values of the composite hypothesis mentioned above. At the same time, he also stated that the difficulty of using the Bayes factor is related to the selection of a specific alternative value to be compared with the null value. The Bayes factor is sensitive to the choice of alternative values, and it may lead to unreasonable test results if not chosen properly. Therefore, an investigator must choose the alternative value that best represents all possible distinct alternative values. One way to measure the evidence for a composite hypothesis requires averaging all possible distinct alternative values (infinitely many alternative values exist, for instance, when we say "the mean is different from 0"). Choosing just that hypothesis among all components of the composite is like looking across all patient subgroups in clinical decision making. This process can be extremely complex and time consuming. Fortunately, there are simpler ways to select an alternative value. One can select the alternative value with the largest effect against the null hypothesis, and cite this value as the summary of evidence across all subgroups of all possible distinct alternative values contained in a composite hypothesis. This technique was suggested by Goodman (1999b) and Katki (2008), and is called the Minimum Bayes Factor (aka, MBF). It expresses the largest amount of evidence against the null hypothesis.

So, whatever effect is being investigated, the best-supported alternative hypothesis is always that the unknown true effect is equal to the actual observed effect. Symbolically, it is written as $X = \mu$, where X is the observed value and μ is the hypothesized mean value in H_a. Thus, MBF uses the best-supported alternative hypothesis that has the largest amount of evidence against H_o. It is the worst-case scenario for H_o among all possible distinct Bayes factors, because no alternative value has a larger amount of evidence against H_o than MBF does. So, when we compare p-value with the Bayes factor to measure the strength of the evidence against H_o, we must calculate the Bayes

factor for the hypothesis that corresponds to the actual observed difference. This is an excellent benchmark against Fisher's p-value when comparing frequentists' and Bayesian methods.

Furthermore, Goodman (1999b) addressed the objectivity of MBF as follows:

> The Minimum Bayes Factor is a unique function of the data that is at least as objective as the p-value. In fact, it is more objective because it is unaffected by the hypothetical long-run results that can make the p-value uncertain. (p. 1010)

The process for translating between Fisher's p-value and MBF is summarized below:

Step 1: Since the p-value is always calculated based on the observed value, we need to formulate MBF in exactly the same way. Symbolically, we write

P (Evidence | H_o) and P (Evidence | H_a)

Step 2: Knowing the fact that a smaller p-value means less support for H_o, we must formulate Bayes factor in the same manner. This means, when we calculate the Minimum Bayes Factor, we must place P (Evidence | H_o) in the numerator, while P (Evidence | H_o) is placed in the denominator. Therefore:

$$MBF = \frac{P(\text{Evidence} \mid H_o)}{P(\text{Evidence} \mid H_a)}$$

Step 3: Convert MBF into a Gaussian approximation form

(Standard Normal Distribution form) for calculation purpose. Symbolically, the formula is given as:

$$MBF = \frac{P(\text{Evidence} \mid H_o)}{P(\text{Evidence} \mid H_a)} = e^{-\frac{z^2}{2}}$$

Where z = the corresponding z-value from the null effect. For example, if $p = 0.05$ (two-sided test) is given, z can be obtained as ± 1.96. Hence,

$$MBF = e^{-\frac{(\pm 1.96)^2}{2}} = 0.15 \text{ or } \frac{1}{6.8}$$

This means that the observed value supports H_a 6.8 times as strong as it does H_o (Maxwell & Satake, 2010).

MBF shows that the p-value greatly exaggerates the strength of evidence against the null hypothesis. That is one of the main reasons that the observed effects derived from the various clinical studies often do not predict true effects well (Goodman, 1999b). For mathematically inclined students, the derivation of MBF is shown below.

Mathematical Derivation of MBF

Bayes factor (MBF) under a Gaussian distribution (aka z distribution):

MBF = $e^{-z^2/2}$, where z represents the observed standard score from the mean.

More specifically, the probability of a data value X under a Gaussian distribution is expressed as follows:

$$P(X \mid \mu, \sigma) = \frac{1}{\sigma \cdot \sqrt{2\pi}} \cdot e^{-\frac{(X-\mu)^2}{\sigma}/2}$$

To maximize the value, we need the value of exponent to be zero. This occurs when $\mu = X$, that is, the true population mean is exactly equal to the observed value X. So, by definition, MBF (or LR-Precise when H_a value is unspecified) is calculated by:

$$MBF = \frac{\text{Null Hypothesis } (\mu = 0)}{\text{The maximally supported alternative hypothesis } (\mu = X)}$$

$$= \frac{\frac{1}{\sigma \cdot \sqrt{2\pi}} \cdot e^{-\frac{(X-\mu)^2}{\sigma}/2}}{\frac{1}{\sigma \cdot \sqrt{2\pi}} \cdot e^{-\frac{(X-X)^2}{\sigma}/2}}$$

$$e^{-\frac{(X)^2}{\sigma}/2} = \text{Equation (1)}$$

Since the observed value under a Gaussian distribution (denoted by $\hat{\theta}$ here) is calculated as:

$$\hat{\theta} = \frac{X - \mu}{\sigma} \sim N(0,1),$$

Equation (1) becomes $e^{-\frac{\hat{\theta}^2}{2}}$, since $e^{-\frac{(X)^2}{\sigma}/2} = e^{-\frac{z^2}{2}} = e^{-\frac{\hat{\theta}^2}{2}} = \sim N(0,1)$.

Furthermore, a p-value of 0.05 has a maximum evidential strength of a Bayes factor of about 6.8 (shown below), so it falls in the category of, at most, moderate strength against the null hypothesis.

$$\text{Bayes Factor} = e^{-\frac{(\pm 1.96)^2}{2}} = 0.15 \text{ or } \frac{1}{6.8}$$

$$e^{-\frac{z^2}{2}} = e^{-\frac{(\pm 1.96)^2}{2}} = 0.15 = \frac{1}{6.8}$$

That will bring you from a prior probability of even odds on the alternative hypothesis to about 87%, meaning that a 50:50 hypothesis still has at least a 13% chance of the alternative hypothesis being wrong after observing $p = 0.05$.

$$\frac{P(H_o|\text{Data})}{P(H_a|\text{Data})} = \frac{P(H_o)}{P(H_a)} \cdot \frac{P(\text{Data}|H_o)}{P(\text{Data}|H_a)}$$

Substituting $P(H_o) = P(H_o) = 0.5$ and $\frac{P(\text{Data}|H_o)}{P(\text{Data}|H_a)} = \frac{1}{6.8} = $ into the equation above, we will obtain:

$$\frac{P(H_o|\text{Data})}{P(H_a|\text{Data})} = \frac{0.5}{0.5} \cdot \frac{1}{6.8} = \frac{0.5}{3.4} = \frac{5}{34}$$

$$P(H_o|\text{Data}) = \frac{5}{5 + 34} = \frac{5}{39} = 0.13$$

$$P(H_a|\text{Data}) = 1 - 0.13 = 0.87$$

Another significant advantage of the Bayesian approach over the frequentists' methods is that the conclusion is not dichotomous. For instance, under hypothesis tests, "Reject H_o" leads to "a treatment is effective" and "do not reject H_o" leads to "a treatment is not effective" in a clinical setting. Similarly, "$p < 0.05$" leads to "the treatment is found to be statistically significant" whereas "$p \geq 0.05$" indicates "not significant." In Bayesian methods, a specific prior probability value is assigned in advance to both H_o and H_a to calculate the posterior odds after we see the evidence. Also, unlike the p-value, such odds indicate probabilities of truth of H_o and H_a to calculate the posterior odds. Therefore, an investigator can obtain both "statistical significance" and "practical significance" (the practical meaning of the magnitude of a change between two groups or phases) of an event of interest. This feature should be extremely appealing to researchers, especially in the medical and clinical sciences, because the method allows them to calculate the effectiveness of a treatment directly from the data. It also fulfills the mission of so-called evidence-based practice (Maxwell & Satake, 2010; Satake 2010).

Prior, MBF, and Posterior: Hypothetical Case

Let us assume that we obtained the sample statistic $z = 2$. Using the MBF formula shown above, we calculate MBF = 0.1353. How does this figure affect posterior probabilities of the null and alternative hypotheses as we assign the different values to prior probabilities of such hypotheses? Table S–1 illustrates the computation process of posterior odds, posterior probability of the null hypothesis, and posterior probability of the alternative hypothesis.

Table S–1 also shows us how far the Minimum Bayes Factor (MBF) of 0.1353 moves the various prior probabilities to calculate posterior probabilities. For instance, if we are highly convinced that the probability of H_o before an experiment is 0.9, denoted by $P(H_o) = 0.9$, the MBF of 0.1353 will move to posterior probability of 0.54908 after we observed the data, that is, the actual data (or evidence) reduced almost 35% from prior probability to posterior probability. But if we start out 50% prior probability ($P(H_o) = 0.5$), then the same amount of MBF will move to the posterior probability of 0.11918. This means that as the initial probability of the null hypothesis gets smaller (one becomes less confident of null effect), the final probability of the null hypothesis will get closer to reach at a traditional frequentists' bench mark of 0.05. In the frequentists' methods, we rarely see such a computation process because it lacks prior probability components for statistical inference.

Table S–1. Computation Process of Posterior Odds, Posterior Probability of the Null Hypothesis, and Posterior Probability of the Alternative Hypothesis

$P(H_o)$: Prior for H_o	$P(H_a)$: Prior for H_a	MBF	Posterior Odds: $\dfrac{P(H_o\|Data)}{P(H_a\|Data)}$	$P(H_o\|Data)$ Posterior for H_o	$P(H_a\|Data)$ Posterior for H_a
0.1	0.9	0.1353	0.01503	0.01481	0.98519
0.2	0.8	0.1353	0.033825	0.03272	0.96728
0.3	0.7	0.1353	0.058	0.0548	0.9452
0.4	0.6	0.1353	0.0902	0.08274	0.91726
0.5	0.5	0.1353	0.1353	0.11918	0.88082
0.6	0.4	0.1353	0.2030	0.16871	0.83129
0.7	0.3	0.1353	0.3157	0.23995	0.76005
0.8	0.2	0.1353	0.5412	0.35115	0.64885
0.9	0.1	0.1353	1.12177	0.54908	0.45092

Finally, suppose we wish to know how low prior probability of the null hypothesis must be set to obtain the posterior probability of the null hypothesis of 0.05, as typically used as the threshold for frequentists' methods. The calculation is as follows:

$$\frac{P(H_o \mid Data)}{P(H_a \mid Data)} = \frac{P(H_o)}{P(H_a)} \cdot MBF$$

$$= \frac{x}{1-x} \cdot (0.1353)$$

$$X = P(H_o) = 0.28$$

This means that with Fisher's p-value of 0.0456 (MBF = 0.1353) , the prior probability of the null hypothesis must be set at 28% or below to allow one to conclude with 95% confidence that the null hypothesis is false. That is to say, through this calculation, one can see that the amount of evidence against the null hypothesis is not nearly as strong and credible as the magnitude of Fisher's p-value suggests. Also, with Neyman-Pearson's hypothesis tests, MBF reveals that the result at $\alpha = 0.05$ greatly overstates "statistical significance."

Summary of Bayesian Methods: General View with Clinically Relevant Scenario

Boxes S–1 through S–10, along with Table J–4 of Appendix J (reproduced below), illustrate and summarize how Bayesian methods and MBF can be used through a clinically relevant example. As the readers recall in Appendix J, Table J–4 gives a good and concise comparison between classical and Bayesian approaches in testing hypothesis procedure. The author firmly believes that the readers should have a good working knowledge and understanding of fundamental, conceptual, and procedural differences between such two approaches when testing one's research hypothesis. Such knowledge and understanding are absolutely essential and necessary in not only promoting and developing one's knowledge about the subject matter of evidence-based statistics to a much larger extent, but also deepening their appreciation toward evidence-based practice in general.

Box S–1. Oral Interpretation of Baye's Theorum

Advantages of the Bayesian Approach

Generally, Bayesian approach can be both "Deductive" ("what causes this particular disorder?" and "what kind of symptoms are associated with the disorder?") and "Inductive" ("what is the probability that a client carries the disorder, given a set of the symptoms are currently present?").

Box S–2. Summary: Bayesian Interpretation

Summary: Bayesian Interpretation

- "Deductive" = Calculating "Prior Probability" from "Posterior Probability"
- "Inductive" = Calculating "Posterior Probability" from "Prior Probability"
- "Minimum Bayes Factor" = A bridge between "Deductive" and "Inductive" inference process

Box S–3. Basic Bayesian Inference of Data Interpretation in Words

Items	Bayesian Approach	Classical Approach	Clinical Merit
Oral interpretation of a conclusion	Direct	Indirect	Bayesian
The use of clinical evidence	All available information	Specific to a particular experiment and design as prespecified	Bayesian
Flexibility	Cumulative	Noncumulative	Bayesian

Box S–4. A Comparison Between Bayesian and Classical (aka Frequentists) Approaches

Items	Bayesian Approach	Classical Approach	Clinical Merit
Forecasting ability	Calculate predictive probabilities of an event of your interest	Does not calculate predictive probabilities of the event	Bayesian
General decision making	It is tailored to clinical decision making to determine the maximum likelihood of our decision based on all available evidence	Not well suited to making clinical decision making	Bayesian
The method of interpretation	Bayes factor (the ratio of the credibility of the two hypotheses)	p-value of prefixed significance level (α) and the power ($1 - \beta$)	Bayesian

Box S–5. The "Odds" Form the Bayes's Theorem

$$\frac{Pr(H_o|Data)}{Pr(H_a|Data)} = \frac{Pr(H_o)}{Pr(H_a)} \cdot \frac{Pr(Data|H_o)}{Pr(Data|H_a)}$$

(Posterior Odds) =
(Prior Odds)(Likelihood Odds)

Box S–6. Fundamentals of Bayes's Rule in Words

Posterior Odds of H_o =

$$\begin{pmatrix} \text{Prior Odds} \\ \text{of } H_o \end{pmatrix} \times \begin{pmatrix} \text{Bayes's} \\ \text{Factor (BF)} \end{pmatrix}$$

(after seeing data) =
(before seeing data) ×
(likelihood ratio)

Box S–7. Exchange Rate for p-Value and Bayes Factor

- Calculate the Bayes factor for the same hypothesis for which the p-value is being calculated; this is why we must calculate the observed difference of H_o and H_1.

- Because smaller p-value means less support for H_o, we must structure the Bayes factor the same way, so that a smaller Bayes factor also means less support for H_o (or more evidence against it).

Box S-8. Exchange Formula for Bayes Factor

(Minimum) Bayes Factor (BF or MBF) is calculated as follows:

$$MBF = e^{-z^2/2}$$

Where z is the number of standard errors from the null effect (H_o effect). BF is considered to be the Bayesian p-value.

Box S–9. Scenario (Stuttering)

A clinician wants to determine whether the prevalence rate of stuttering is 0.8% (Morley, 1957; Hull, Mielk, Willeford, & Timmons, 1976) or not. She used SSI-3 (Stuttering Severity Instrument-3) to examine the level of severity of stuttering. Based on her observation of 100 subjects, two were diagnosed as "severe" and "very severe" (Total overall score ≥32).

Box S–10. A Hypothetical Scenario for Illustration of Exchange Between Fisher's p-Value and Minimum Bayes Factor

A. p-value calculation for SSI-3 example:

Given $n = 100$, $x = 2$, $p = 0.008$, and $H_o: p = 0.008$, $H_a \neq 0.008$ (two-tailed), we can calculate the p-value as follows:

B. Using the binomial probability distribution (Frequentists approach),

p-value = $P[\text{Data*} | H_o \text{ is true}]$

a. = $P[n \geq 100 \text{ and } x = 2 | p = 0.008]$

    i. $P[n = 100, x = 2 | p = 0.008]$ +

    ii. $P[n = 101, x = 2 | p = 0.008]$ +

    iii. $P[n = 102, x = 2 | p = 0.008 + \ldots = .04673$

(H_o is rejected, i.e., "statistically significant")

The corresponding z-value for $p = 0.04673$ (two-tailed) is 1.989.

C. Using Bayesian, (Minimum) Bayes Factor is calculated as:

   a. Bayes Factor (BF) = $e^{-\frac{z^2}{2}} = e^{-\frac{(1.989)^2}{2}} = 1.383$ or $\frac{1}{7.23}$

   What does this number indicate?

D. What is the exchange rate for $p = 0.4678$ in the language of Bayesian?

   a. $P[\text{Data}|H_o \text{ is true}] = p\text{-value} = 0.4673$

   In Bayesian, we calculate:

   b. $P[H_o \text{ is true}|\text{Data}] = 0.1215^*$ if we start out

   c. $P(H_o) = P(H_a) = 0.5$

E. (Posterior odds) = (Prior odds) × (Likelihood Odds or MBF)

   Given

   $P(H_o) = 0.5, P(H_a) = 1 - P(H_o) = 0.5$

   and

   $MBF = \dfrac{1}{7.23}$

   Symbolically,

   $$\frac{P(H_o \mid Data)}{P(H_a \mid Data)} = \frac{P(H_o)}{P(H_a)} \cdot \frac{P(Data \mid H_o)}{P(Data \mid H_a)}$$

   $$\frac{0.5}{3.615} = \frac{0.5}{0.5} \cdot \frac{1}{7.23}$$

F. Therefore,

   a. $P(H_o|Data) = \dfrac{0.5}{3.615} = \dfrac{0.5}{0.5} \cdot \dfrac{1}{7.23} = 0.1215$

   b. $P(H_a|Data) = 1 - 0.1215 = 0.8785$

G. Comparison between Fisher's p-value and Bayes factor (BF): interpretation of test results of the "stuttering" example.

continues

Fisher's Imprecise p-Value	*Bayes Factor: Precise p-Value*	**Confidence in H$_o$**	**Strength of Evidence**
$p = 0.04673$	0.1383	Frequentist: 4.673%	Frequentist: "significant"
$(z = 1.989)$	$\left(\dfrac{1}{7.23}\right)$	Bayesian: 12.15%	Bayesian: "weak/moderately weak"

H. With a p-value of 4.673% (equivalently, BF = 0.1383), the prior probability of H$_o$ must be *27.61%* or less to allow one to conclude with 95% confidence that H$_o$ is false. In other words, we must start out $P(H_o) = 0.2761$, instead of $P(H_o) = 0.5$, to eventually obtain p-value = 0.04673.

I. Correspondence of two-sided, fixed sample size p-value under Gaussian distribution with the Minimum Bayes Factor, that is, the strongest against the null hypothesis.

p-Value (z-score)	Minimum Bayes Factor	Strength of Evidence	From	Decrease in probability of the null hypothesis, % To no less than
0.10	0.26	Weak	75	44
(1.64)	(1/3.8)		50	21
			17	5
0.05	0.15	Moderate	75	31
(1.96)	(1/6.8)		50	13
			26	5
0.03	0.1	Moderate	75	22
(2.17)	(1/10.5)		50	9
			33	5
0.01	0.04	Moderate to strong	75	10
(2.58)	(1/28)		50	3.5
			60	5
0.001	0.0005	Strong to very strong	75	1
(3.28)	(1/217)		50	0.5
			92	5

Table J–4. Classical Versus Bayesian Statistics

Sources	Classical Statistics	Bayesian Statistics
Number of hypotheses	Only two (null and alternative) hypotheses can be stated each time	Allowed to have two or more hypotheses at one time
Hypothesized values in initial hypotheses	More objective, views, or well-defined previous knowledge	Researcher is free to express subjective views from previous experience
Data analysis	Normal z, t, or F distributions	Beta distribution with Gamma function
Assumptions of data analysis	1. Independence 2. Homogeneity of variances	None
Type of conclusion derived	Rejection or nonrejection of null hypothesis. The hypothesis rejected is totally disregarded. No specific value of a true population parameter is derived.	None of the hypotheses disregarded. Researcher estimates the credibility of each hypothesized value and derives the maximum likelihood of a true population parameter.
ANOVA	Researcher determines whether or not there are treatment effects on dependent variable(s). Significant or not	Researcher considers how much parameter (treatment effect) affects dependent variable(s); measures the strength of each treatment. Specific values that represent the degree of strength are derived.
ANOVA model selection	Trial and error	The most powerful and suitable model can be found. How accurately does each model predict a future value?
MANOVA and ANOVA	Trial and error	Same as above

Correspondence of two-sided, fixed sample side p-value under Gaussian distribution with the Minimum Bayes Factor, that is, the strongest against the null hypothesis. Boxes S–11 through S–13 summarize the author's points why Bayesian approach is more clinically relevant, philosophical standpoint (see Box S–11), statistical standpoint (see Box S–12), and clinical standpoint (see Box S–13).

Box S–11. Bayesian Interpretations of Deductive, Inductive, and Bayes Factor

---

Bayesian Interpretations

I. "Deductive" = Calculating "Prior Probability" from "Posterior Probability"
II. "Inductive" = Calculating "Posterior Probability" from "Prior Probability"
III. "Bayes Factor" = A bridge between "Deductive" and "Inductive"

Box S–12. Correspondence of Two-Side, Fixed Sample Size Fisher's p-Value Under the Standard Normal Distribution with Minimum Bayes Factor

---

Classical "statistical significance" p-value

versus

Bayesian "Clinical significance" p-value

Symbolically,

Classical p-value = P(Actual Data plus "More Extreme" than Actual Data | H_o)

Bayesian p-value = P(H_o) | Actual Data)

Graphical Illustrations of Fisher's p-Value and Minimum Bayes Factor (MBF) Under the Standard Normal (Gaussian) Distribution Curve

Figures S–2 and S–3 illustrate the conceptual difference between Fisher's p-value and MBF graphically with the fundamental logic behind statistical philosophy.

Box S–13. Why Bayesian Methods Are More Clinically Relevant and Useful

---

Key Points

■ Clinical decision making is fundamentally Bayesian because of its cumulative nature and inductive reasoning pattern.
■ Clinicians' experience and (subjective beliefs) must NOT be ignored. They should be cherished and implemented into the decision-making process for a more accurate conclusion.
■ Clinicians apply Bayesian statistical reasoning in framing and revisiting differential diagnoses.
■ A Bayesian approach is essential for evidence-based practice.

As can be seen, Fisher's p-value is the tail area under the curve of an observed value, whereas MBF is the curve height that corresponds to the observed value. This means that Fisher's p-value includes the probability of occurrence of "more extreme" than what was actually observed (aka, imprecise p-value) while MBF excludes such the probability (aka, precise p-value). Graphical illustrations of Fisher's p-value (aka Imprecise p-value) and the Minimum Bayes Factor (aka MBF) are illustrated in Figures S–2 and S–3.

In words, we can distinguish Fisher's p-value from MBF using the following example in a more practical and clearer manner. Box S–14 summarizes the important conceptual differences between Fisher's p-value and MBF. Additionally, Box S–15 explains the philosophical foundation of the Bayesian approach (aka evidence-based statistics approach) in a concise manner.

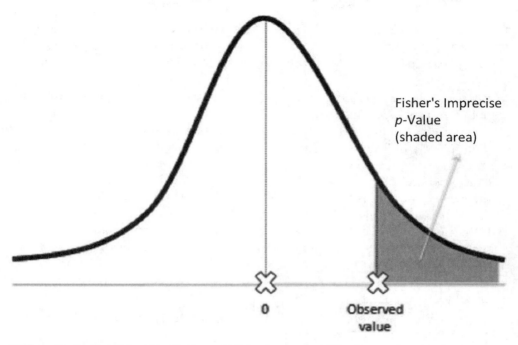

Figure S–2. Graphical illustration of Fisher's *p*-value (aka imprecise *p*-value).

Graphical illusration of MBF (Precise *p*-Value)

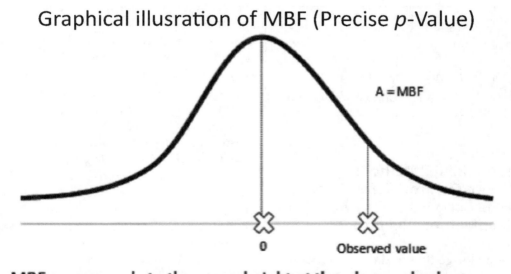

MBF corresponds to the curve height at the observed value, denoted by A.

Figure S–3. Graphical illustration of Minimum Bayes Factor (MBF).

Box S–14. Practical Example

Practical Example

■ If a particular subject ranks 10th out of 100 subjects, that subject is reported as being "within the top 10%." Imprecise p-value (Fisher's) idea; we don't know exactly where (s)he ranks, but the ranked number is between 1st and 10th inclusively.

■ If the same subject is reported as being "exactly the 10th in rank." Precise p-value (MBF) idea; we know exactly where (s)he ranks, and there is no need to include other ranking numbers.

Box S–15. Philosophical Foundation of Bayesian Approach

"If we begin with certainties, we shall end in doubts; but if we begin with doubts, and are patient with them, we shall end with certainties."

—Sir Francis Bacon, 1605

Frequentists' Methods Cannot Control "Error Rates" in the Long Run: Why Are Their Methods Incorrect?

The major goal in traditional frequentists statistical methods, especially Neyman-Pearson's hypothesis tests, is to use decision procedures with known controlled long-term error rates (α and β) for rejecting and retaining the null hypothesis H_o.

As the readers are quite aware by now, you can be in error by rejecting when it is actually true (Type 1 error rate α) or failing to reject H_o (retaining H_o) when it is actually false (Type 2 error rate β). To draw a reliable and credible conclusion, that is to say, accurately measure the strength of evidence against or for H_o, both of the error rates must be controlled to minimize potential damages to the conclusion you desire to derive about a true treatment effect. So first, let me start out explaining how frequentists normally control Type 1 error rate, Type 2 error rate, and finally how the limitations and incorrect procedures are remedied by Bayesian methods.

Controlling Type 1 Error Rate

In the classroom instructions, students are in general taught about controlling Type 1 error rate as follows: Type error rate must be set small enough (usually its threshold is set at 0.05) to determine whether or not an observed value (z, t, chi-square, F, and so on) derived from an actual sample will fall under the critical region of α. Using a combined method (although the method is incorrect, as noted earlier), the result is said to be *statistically significant if $p < 0.05$ (or "reject H_o")*, or otherwise, the result is said to be *statistically nonsignificant (or "failing to reject H_o")*. It is this sentiment that has led to some of the frequent criticism of the traditional methods (e.g., Fisher's p-value, Neyman-Pearson's hypothesis tests, combined method, and so on). To some extent, these criticisms reflect the clinical practice of only trying to control α and not employing the rest of the Neyman-Pearson's logic. As far as an investigator conducts an experiment that involves two or less populations, such as paired t-test, unpaired Z-test, or unpaired *t*-test, it will not be a complicated task to control and maintain the original Type 1 error rate throughout. But when more than two significant pairwise tests (e.g., (M)ANOVA post hoc pairwise test) are conducted, the question will arise as to the long-term error rates of the group (or "family") of tests as a whole. The family-wise error rate is the probability of falsely rejecting *at least one null hypothesis*. Usually, Bonferonni is a generic and most widely used method when we conduct a multiple number of significant family-wise pairwise tests. For instance, suppose your family consists of *K*-tests and wish to set the original α at 0.05. If this is the case, we need to make some adjustment to maintain $\alpha = 0.05$ throughout the whole process. This can be accomplished by setting $\alpha = (0.05)/K$ (or more mathematically, the precise formula is $\alpha^* = 1 - (1 - 0.05)^{1/K}$) as the significance level for each individual pairwise post hoc test. For example, if you were conducting three *t*-tests ($K = 3$), you could reject any individual null hypothesis only if its $p < [(0.05)/3] = 0.17$. With such a decision procedure, you would reject one or more of three null hypotheses no more than 5% of the time in the long run. Bonferonni method controls family-wise error rate to be no more than 5%, but it does so more severely than needed. So, suppose that your *p*-values from post hoc test were given as 0.022, 0.003, 0.15, and 0.023 ($K = 4$, in this hypothetical case example), you would first order them from lowest *p*-value to highest *p*-value. Namely, it is shown in Table S–2.

Next, we construct a threshold value for each *p*-value: $p(1)$'s threshold is $[(0.05)/K]$, $p(2)$'s threshold is $[(0.05)/(K - 1)]$, $p(3)$'s is $[(0.05)/(K - 2)]$, and so forth till the value in the denominator becomes 1. It is illustrated in Table S–2.

Table S–2. *p*-Values from Pairwise Comparison and Threshold for Bonferonni Test

p-Values from Pairwise Comparison	Threshold for Bonferonni Test
$p(1) = 0.03$	$\dfrac{(0.05)}{4} = 0.125$
$p(2) = 0.022$	$\dfrac{(0.05)}{3} = 0.017$
$p(3) = 0.023$	$\dfrac{(0.05)}{2} = 0.025$
$p(4) = 0.15$	$\dfrac{(0.05)}{1} = 0.5$

Next, we start at the bottom of Table S–2 and check if the last value there is less than its threshold. It is not in our case, since $p(4) = 0.15$ exceeds its threshold of 0.05, so that this test is nonsignificant. Move up to the next level and check the value. Here we have $p(3) = 0.023$ is less than the threshold value of 0.025, so it is significant and all *p*-values above it in Table S–2 are automatically significant too whether they exceed their threshold or not. For example, in our case, $p(2)$ is significant even though it is higher than its threshold value of 0.017. Under Bonferonni's rule, $p(2)$ would not have been significant if the other tests below it had not been. This decision rule is guaranteed to control family-wise error rate at 0.05 as a whole if you were to use Bonferonni instead of the usual ANOVA methods for detecting statistical significance. But you can see the major flaw of the process. The method clearly overstates the amount of evidence against or for H_o; therefore, whatever the conclusion we derive from this method, it is more likely that we exaggerate the degree of statistical significance.

Controlling Type 2 Error Rate: How Do We Calculate and Interpret the Power of a Test

As noted earlier, the most common conceptual error in the practical use of inferential statistical methods is that many investigators ignore the sensitivity of a test. Sensitivity can be determined by power of a test (basic calculation of power is illustrated in Appendix C) and confidence intervals. For calculations, most statistical software packages (e.g., SPSS, SAS, BMDP, MINITAB, and the like) will report them.

Power calculation involves determining the minimally interesting effect size (as measured by Cohen's d). Based on Cohen's rule, the following guideline is normally used: $d = 0.2$ (small effect), $d = 0.5$ (medium effect), and $d = 0.8$ (large effect) for the between-subject case. If you were to use Cohen's d to determine effect size and its impact on effectiveness of a treatment in a simpler yet practical manner, you could follow such a procedure: Set up power (almost always 80% to 90%) to detect a medium effect size, and the follow the Cohen's guideline for whatever experiment you run. However, power is something you decide on before running an experiment in order to determine subject number. Many statistical software packages offer automatic power calculations along with significance tests results. These power calculations have very little practical meaning and are indeed worthless. They calculate a power to detect the effect size actually measured, and this is a straightforward function of the p-value.

You will obtain very little information from such automatic power calculations. Power should be calculated for the effect size you are interested in detecting. Under the frequentists methods, the best way to determine the sensitivity of the experiment after collecting data is with confidence intervals. They tell you the set of values you reject as possible population means and the set you still hold under consideration. Furthermore, confidence intervals naturally allow you to assess if the effects allowed by the data are larger than some minimal interesting amount.

Using the Minimum Bayes Factor (MBF) to Control Long-Term Error Rates

The hypothesis with the largest amount of evidence for it has the maximum (mathematical) likelihood against H_o that means that it predicts the observed data best among all possible distinct alternative values. If a clinical investigator observes a 15% difference on the cure rates for stuttering between two different speech therapy treatments, the alternative (testing) hypothesis with the maximum likelihood would be that the true population mean difference would be 15%. In other words, whatever effect size we are measuring, the best-supported hypothesis is always that the unknown true population's mean effect is equal to the observed effect. This fact makes the calculation of power with effect size (aka meta-analysis) straightforward and more clinically relevant and practical under the Bayesian methods. The Bayesian methods are conceptually different than frequentists methods as discussed earlier. The Bayesian methods can allow us to combine the evidence provided by each experiment for each hypothesis and directly test H_o and H_a (the best-supported hypothesis) for measuring the strength of evidence to calculate truth of H_o and H_a. With frequentists methods, an investigator must take a weighted average of the observed effects derived from all possible distinct samples and pool their standard errors. Then we recalculate a new p-value based on the average effect and pooled standard error. But, in reality, this new p-value and standard error have little relation to the p-values for the individual effects, and taking a weighted average of all observed effects obscures the fact that all experiments actually provide the identical evidence for the same hypothesis. So, while the frequentists claim that they are combining evidence from similar studies, they do not have a standard measure of evidence that is directly combined. Furthermore, in securing the assumptions of normality and homogeneity of several variances, the investigator must check all necessary conditions required for meta-analysis. As we discussed previously, the use of MBF definitely has an edge when we measure the strength of evidence against H_o because of the Bayesian statistics' cumulative nature. Although the calculation of MBF is more complex than those of frequentists methods, the readers can visit the following website for computation: http://www.pcl.missouri.edu/bayesfactor

Additionally, in Bayesian methods, the critical prior intervals (CPS) is often used in replacement of confidence intervals. The CPR gears more toward the clinical decision-making process than confidence intervals. It is more useful and suitable, especially when we have a substantial amount of external evidence prior to an experiment and wish to implement it into clinical diagnoses and the decision-making process in general. Those who are mathematically inclined, the author highly recommends that they should read the article, entitled "Why should clinicians care about Bayesian methods?" (Matthews, R. A. J. (2001). *Journal of Statistical Planning and Inference, 94,* 43–58).

Philosophy Behind Evidence-Based Statistics: Why Is a Bayesian Perspective More Clinically Useful?

As we discussed previously, clinical research is inductive, and Bayesian methods is the way to figure out how new data alters the probability of a hypothesis being true (denoted by p (Truth of a Hypothesis | Exact Data observed)). There is no other way or escaping from this truth. People's opinions already figure heavily in modern clinical research and practice, but p-values, confidence intervals, and meta-analysis under the frequentists methods encourage clinical investigators to pretend that it does not. One of the benefits of Bayesian statistics is to force opinion out into the open where it belongs. Prior probability (aka, external evidence), if stated, must be formally estimated and therefore justified. Yet, the existence of prior probability may be taken not too seriously among scientists, at least those who prefer frequentists methods over Bayesian methods, mainly due to the subjective nature of prior probability. But one thing that they must be aware of is that Bayesian methods are the only ones that allow a clinician to state and express her clinical opinion into the evaluation process of clinical trials. The method shows how the clinician's existing view of the truth of a matter can be altered by new experimental data. Prior probability must be estimated from all existing somewhat reliable evidence such as basic science, the test results derived from previous clinical trials, and all other related sources. How conclusions based on such evidence might be altered by new data is the key issue if we were to move forward to EBP statistics.

Goodman (1999b) also noted that it is the subjective nature of prior probabilities (measuring one's belief before an experiment) that explains why clinical trial literature has shifted away from Bayesian statistics, instead of favoring the familiar frequentists statistical methods including Fisher's p-value, Neyman-Pearson's hypothesis tests, confidence intervals, and effect size—tools that are widely assumed to provide objective measure (deductive) of evidence for hypotheses by looking exclusively at data from trials. But, in reality, it is rather illogical and impractical to ignore and diminish external knowledge and evidence that experts may have, no matter how outrageous it may seem at first. Still, they may have some credibility in that theory. Deductive reasoning appears to be logically sound and scientific, but has obvious limitations as an artistic tool for learning about science. It turns out that frequentists methods not only lack a formal way to consider external evidence, but is inappropriate for evaluating clinical outcomes and measuring the strength of clinical evidence for a more fundamental reason; it applies to only deductive inference, as noted earlier. Some may argue that deductive inference is the way to draw a more scientific sound conclusion. But in actual practice, we need

to make a diagnosis or identify the type of fluency disorders (general) based on a set of symptoms observed (specific). This is the main reason why a clinical investigator needs to change her perspective toward scientific reasoning to: (1) learn how to correctly measure the strength of evidence, and (2) look for clinical, practical, and personal significance beyond statistical significance through EBP Statistical Methods such as Bayesian methods.

In other words, in Neyman-Pearson's hypothesis testing, the statistical inference doesn't tell one how confident one can be in two different hypotheses before and after an experiment in terms of the numerical probability values. It only gives conventions for dichotomous results such as "Reject H_o" or "Do not reject H_o" based on preset long-term error rates. One cannot conclude how a particular decision justified is after, or how credible a hypothesis is prior to, an experiment. More importantly, one cannot derive a probability value to how much actual sample data support a given hypothesis, which is the essential meaning of *measuring the strength of evidence*. One is only able to conclude that the final decision was made by a standard procedure that in the long run controls error frequencies (Dienes, 2011).

Last, we would like to summarize the difference between EBP statistics and non-EBP statistics such as Fisher's p-value and Neyman-Pearson hypothesis testing. As we emphasized repeatedly, the author must remind the reader that Fisher's p-value approach and Neyman Pearson's testing hypothesis are conceptually and philosophically different within non-EBP methods. Box S–16 illustrates such conceptual differences between two methods.

Box S–16. Comparisons of Two Non-EBP Statistical Approaches

	p-Value Approach	Hypothesis Tests
Originator	Fisher	Neyman and Pearson
Number of Hypotheses Tested	One (Null Hypothesis H_o)	Two (Null H_o and Alternative H_a)
Is it Inferential?	Yes, it is intended to use as a flexible measure	No, it is a rule of behavior
Assessment Tools	Posttrial Conditional Probability based on an observed value of the truth of H_o	Pretrial error rate called Type 1 error (α), Type 2 error (β), and Power of a Test ($1 - \beta$)

	p-Value Approach	Hypothesis Tests
Decision Rule	Amount of evidence against H_o is small enough to detect a treatment effect	Reject H_o if | observed value | > Critical Value. Otherwise, do not reject H_o
Specific Benchmark for Decision Making	None, although 5% is frequently used in clinical research	α = 1%, 5%, or 10% $\beta \leq$ 10% or 20% Power > 80% or 90%
Basis for Conclusion	Single experiment	Hypothetical long-run frequencies
Support Bayesian Idea?	No (Fisher refused to implement one's subjective view into decision-making process)	No (Neyman and Pearson believed that all reasoning should be deductive)

Application of EBP Statistical Methods to Diagnosis of Aphasia Type Based on Western Aphasia Battery (WAB) Test Scores

The author recently conducted a three-hour short course, entitled "Evidence-Based Statistics for Clinicians: Basic Concepts & ASHA Guidelines," at the annual 2013 ASHA convention held in Chicago, Illinois. The vast majority of our audiences are clinical practitioners, researchers, and instructors who showed a great deal of interest and enthusiasm toward the clinical diagnostic decision making for aphasia type based on WAB scores. Because of such a strong impact on their research interest in this particular topic, the author decided to include the following Power-Point slides of the short course (Box S–17).

Box S–17. Diagnosing Types of Aphasia from WAB Scores Using EBP Statistical Methods

An Example from the Aphasia Literature: Western Aphasia Battery

- WAB and WAB-R
- Kertesz (1982, 2006)
- Commonly used clinical assessment to identify aphasia severity and type
  - Provides and overall Aphasia Quotient (1–100)
  - Offers information about aphasia type
    - Based on fluency, comprehension, repetition, naming
    - Broca's, Wernicke's, global, and others

Diagnosing Types of Aphasia from WAB (Western Aphasia Battery)

A person with Aphasia may be diagnosed as "Global" type or "Wernicke's" type, if his (or her) WAB scores fall into the specific WAB-R Aphasia Classification. In other words, how does a clinician deal with this particular case?

Hypothetical Case

For instance, imagine the following hypothetical case scenario

WAB-R Chart	Global Type (G)	Wernicke's Type (W)	Actual Score (hypothetical)	Diagnosis
Fluency	<5	>4	4.5	G or W
Auditory Verbal Comprehension	0–3.9	0–6.9	2.5	G or W
Repetition	0–4.9	0–7.9	3.5	G or W
Naming and Word Finding	<7	<10	5	G or W

Key Points of Hypothetical Case

- So, a person described here could be diagnosed as "Global" type or "Wernicke's" type, based on the WAB Chart
- Under the normal circumstances, a clinician combines the scores on the WAB with his (or her) own understanding of what *types* of aphasia actually exist and how the client presents
- In other words, the clinician will use his (or her) own subjective or less subjective clinical judgment to diagnose the client with "Borderline" WAB scores, as illustrated in the hypothetical case scenario
- But the clinicians are fully aware of the fact that WAB itself may not be adequate for an accurate diagnosis of this type

How About Using AQ (Aphasia Quotient) as an Alternative?

■ AQ only focuses on the overall sensitivity (a more generic global measure, that is to say, "The worse the WAB scores, the more severe the Aphasia"). Clearly, AQ is not for the purpose of accurately diagnosing the types of Aphasia. In other words, it is not specific enough for a clinician's interest.

■ So, the bottom line question is, " Is there any way that clinicians (especially novices who have fewer years of clinical experience) can distinguish one type of Aphasia from another type." WAB certainly provides some useful guidance, but WAB itself is not enough to represent the whole clinical picture.

Using Evidence-Based Statistics for Diagnosis

■ To validate and determine the accuracy of WAB Chart, we need to formulate the several probabilities that will be used for the calculation of the EBP probability of an investigator's interest, namely:
  ■ (1) Prevalence Rate of Types of Aphasia, such as P (Global), P (Wernicke's), and so on:
    ▪ Among the people with aphasia in the world, how many actually have certain types of aphasia?
  ■ (2) Sensitivity and Specificity of WAB Score Range:
    ▪ Among those diagnosed as having global aphasia, who actually fulfills all requirements as described on the WAB chart?

Measuring the Strength of Evidence

■ Say, E = Evidence such as WAB test scores for Aphasia
■ D = Diagnosis such as "Global"
■ $P(E|D)$ = Probability of obtaining a certain WAB score, given that he is already diagnosed as Global type
■ $P(D|E)$ = Probability of being diagnosed as Global type, given that her (or his) WAB scores
■ Can you tell the difference between $P(E|D)$ and $P(D|E)$?

Pre-existing Condition

■ $P(E|D)$—D is the pre-existing condition, that is, we already know how one was diagnosed. Based on that, we calculate the likelihood of WAB scores. Measuring the strength of Evidence (E) based on Diagnosis (D).
■ $P(D|E)$—E is the pre-existing condition, that is, we already know how one performed on WAB test. Based on that, we calculate the likelihood of Diagnosis (Aphasia type). Measuring the accuracy of Diagnosis (D) based on Evidence.
■ Both are essential for EBP Statistics.

continues

Four Components of a Screening Test

1. Sensitivity = P (the Test is Positive, given that Disorder exists)
2. Specificity = P (the Test is Negative, given that No Disorder exists)
3. Predictive Value Positive = P (Disorder exists, given that the Test is Positive)
4. Predictive Value Negative = P (No Disorder exists, given that the Test is Negative)

EBP Statistics: Probability Values

- (3) Predictive Values (PV+) for "Global" can be expressed as follows:
- $P(\text{Global} \mid \text{WAB}) = P(G \mid W)$
- $P(G \mid W) = [P(G) \cdot P(W \mid G)] \div [P(G) \cdot P(W \mid G) + P(\text{Not } G) \cdot P(W \mid \text{Not } G)]$
- The formula shown above is called Bayes's Theorem or Bayes's Rule. It has gained some recognition and acceptance in the medical literatures over a decade or so. Goodman (1997) stated that the Bayesian method is most suitable for EBP for the following reasons.

Why Bayesian?

- It allows us to view the problem both deductively (from "general" to "specific") and inductively (from "specific" to "general"). More specifically, it goes from "diagnosis (types of Aphasia)" to "symptoms (WAB scores)," and vice versa.
- Using the Bayesian method, a clinician can more effectively and more accurately diagnose his (or her) client's type of Aphasia based on what was actually observed on WAB scores. Also, the method allows the clinician to implement his (or her) subjective clinical belief into the process of diagnosis. This generates both "statistical significance" and "clinical significance," whereas the traditional methods (ANOVA, ANCOVA, Meta-Analysis) don't.

Clinical Implications (1)

One of the main strengths of Bayesian method over traditional inferential method is that it permits the use of information from previous clinical research in the analysis of new results. This feature would invite several clinicians with different views (initially) to state their own opinions as a part of their research prior to actual data collection. After analysis of the new common data, the level of subjectivity about the event of interest (e.g., Prevalence rate of Global type or Wernicke's type) will be reduced because of the common data.

Clinical Implications (2)

It also operates in a cumulative manner, not in a terminal way. One who desires to go further than the first trial, one can use the final probability obtained at the end of the 1st trial (posterior probability) as a new initial probability (prior probability) of the second trial, and proceed with new common data collection to update the clinicians' beliefs. This repetition of the process will certainly minimize discrepancies among the different views among several clinicians and increase the credibility of a desired conclusion about the event of clinical interest, whatever it may be. Hence, the Bayesian method is more clinically relevant to the diagnostic process itself than is traditional inferential method.

Bayes's Formula

- $$P(G \mid W) = \frac{P(G) \cdot P(W \mid G)}{P(G) \cdot P(W \mid G) + P(\text{not } G) \cdot P(W \mid (\text{not } G))}$$
- Where $P(G)$ = Prevalence rate of Global type
- Where $P(\text{not } G)$ = Prevalence of non-Global type
- $P(W \mid G)$ = % of those who completely fulfilled WAB charts for Global type among those who are actually diagnosed as Global type
- $P(W \mid (\text{not } G))$ = % of those who completely fulfilled WAB charts for Global type among those who are actually diagnosed as non-Global type

So What Does This Mean for the WAB?

- Right now, we as clinicians move from the WAB chart to diagnosing type:
  - We use a deductive approach.
- If we consider a Bayesian view, then we may reverse this:
  - That is, we may diagnose the type to validate the ranges as shown on the WAB chart.
  - This is an example of the inductive approach.
- Both approaches are useful.

References

Adam, M. (1984). The differential and direct treatment of stuttering. In J. Costello (Ed.), *Speech Disorders in Children* (pp. 261–290). San Diego, CA: College-Hill Press.

Adams, M. R., Freeman, F. J., & Conture, E. G. (1984). Laryngreal dynamics of stutterers. In R. F. Curlee & W. H. Perkins (Eds.), *Nature and treatment of stuttering: New directions.* San Diego, CA: College-Hill Press.

Altman, D., & Brand, J. (1991). Improving doctor's understanding of statistics. *Journal of the Royal Statistical Society, Series A, 154,* 223–267.

Amato, P. P., & Satake, E. (2007). A Bayesian model of interpersonal transactions in a business setting. *International Academy of Business Discipline Research Year Book, 1.*

Andersen, B. (1990). *Methodological Errors in Medical Research.* Oxford, UK: Blackwell Science.

Apel, K. (1999). Checks and balances: Keeping the science in our profession. *Language, Speech, and Hearing Services in Schools, 30,* 99–108.

Apel, K., & Self, T. (2003). The marriage of research and clinical service, *ASHA Leader, 8*(16), 6–7.

Ashby, D. (2006). Bayesian statistics in medicine: A 25-year review. *Statistics in Medicine, 25,* 3589–3631.

Barlow, D. H., Hayes, S. C., & Nelson, R. O. (1984). *The scientist practitioner: Research and accountability in clinical and educational settings.* Oxford, UK: Pergamon Press.

Barlow, D. H., & Hersen, M. (1984). *Single case experimental designs.* New York, NY: Pergamon Press.

Baron-Cohen, S., Tager-Flusberg, H., & Cohen, D. J. (2000). *Understanding other minds: Perspectives from developmental cognitive neuroscience* (2nd ed.). Oxford, UK: Oxford University Press.

Berger, J., & Sellke, T. (1987). Testing a point null hypothesis: The irreconcilability of *p*-values and evidence. *Journal of American Statistical Association, 82,* 112–139.

Bernabei, P., & Camaioni, L. (2001). Developmental profile and regression in a child with autism: A single case study. *Autism, 5*(3), 287–297.

Berry, D. (1985). Interim analyses in clinical trials: Classical vs. Bayesian approaches. *Statistical Medicine, 4,* 521–526.

Berry, D. (1996). *Statistics: A Bayesian perspective.* Belmont, CA: Wadsworth.

Bluman, A. G. (2004). *Elementary statistics: A step by step approach.* New York, NY: McGraw-Hill.

Browner, W., & Newman, T. (1987). Are all significant *p* values created equal? The analogy between diagnostic tests and clinical research, *JAMA, 257,* 2459–2463.

Callahan, C. D., & Barisa, M. T. (2005). Statistical process control and rehabilitation outcome: The single-subject design reconsidered. *Rehabilitation Psychology, 50*(1), 24–33.

Caplan, D. (2003). Aphasic syndromes. In K. M. Heilman & E. Valenstein (Eds.), *Clinical neuropsychology* (4th ed., pp. 14–34). New York, NY: Oxford University Press.

Case-Smith, J., & Bryan, T. (1999). The effects of occupational therapy with sensory integration emphasis on preschool-age children with autism. *The American Journal of Occupational Therapy, 53*(5), 489–497.

Chambless, D. L., & Hollon, S. D. (1998). Defining empirically supported therapies. *Journal of Consulting Clinical Psychology, 66(1)*, 7–18.

Charman, T., Baron-Cohen, S., Swettenham, J., Baird, G., Drew, A., & Cox, A. (2003). Predicting language outcomes in infants with autism and pervasive developmental disorder. *International Journal of Language & Communication Disorders, 38*(3), 265–285.

Charman, T., Swettenham, J., Baron-Cohen, S., Cox, A., Baird, G., & Drew, A. (1997). Infants with autism: An investigation of empathy, pretend play, joint attention, and imitation. *Developmental Psychology, 33*(5), 781–789.

Clare, L., Wilson, B. A., Carter, G., & Hodges, J. R. (2003). Cognitive rehabilitation as a component of early intervention in Alzheimer's disease: A single case study. *Aging & Mental Health, 7*(1), 15–21.

Cochran, W. G., & Cox, G. M. (1957). *Experimental designs.* New York, NY: Wiley.

Cohen, J. (1988). *Statistical power analysis for the behavioral sciences* (2nd ed.), Hillsdale, NJ: Lawrence Erlbaum Associates.

Cook, T. D., & Campbell, D. T. (1979). *Quasi-experimentation.* Chicago, IL: Rand McNally.

Cooper, H. R., & Craddock, L. C. (2006). *Cochlear implants: A practical guide* (2nd ed.). West Sussex, UK: Whurr.

Coyle, A. (1995). Discourse analysis. In G. M. Blackwell, S. Hammond, & C. Fife-Schaw (Eds.), *Research methods in psychology.* Thousand Oaks, CA: Sage.

Crosbie, J. (1993). Interrupted time-series analysis with brief single-subject data. *Journal of Consulting and Clinical Psychology, 61,* 966–974.

Cullington, H. E. (2003). *Cochlear implants: Objective measures.* Philadelphia, PA: Whurr.

Dar, R., Serlin, R. C., & Omer, H. (1994). Misuse of statistical tests in three decades of psychotherapy research. *Journal of Consulting Clinical Psychology, 62,* 75–82.

Dember, W. N., & Jenkins, J. J. (1970). *General psychology: Modeling behavior and experience.* Englewood Cliffs, NJ. Prentice-Hall.

Depoy, E., & Gitlin, L. N. (1994). *Introduction to research.* St. Louis, MO: Mosby.

De Veaux, R. D., Velleman, P. F., & Bock, D. E. (2007). *Stats data and models* (2nd ed.). Boston, MA: Pearson-Addison Wesley.

Diamond, G. A., & Forrester, J. S. (1983). Clinical trials and statistical verdicts: Probable grounds for appeal. *Annals of Internal Medicine, 98,* 385–394.

Dienes, Z. (2011). Bayesian versus Orthodox statistics: Which side are you on? *Perspectives on Psychological Science, 6*(3), 274–290.

Dollaghan, C. (2004, April 13). Evidence-based practice: Myths and realities. *The ASHA Leader.*

Drew, A., Baird, G., Baron-Cohen, S., Cox, A., Slonims, V., Wheelwright, S., . . . Charman, T. (2002). A pilot randomized control trial of a parent training intervention for preschool children with autism: Preliminary findings and methodological challenges. *European Child & Adolescent Psychiatry, 11,* 266–272.

Duchan, J. (2002). What do you know about the history of speech-language pathology and why is it important? *ASHA Leader, 22*(1), 37–49.

Duffy, J. R. (1995). *Motor speech disorders: Substrates, differential diagnosis, and management.* St. Louis, MO: Mosby.

Edgington, E. S. (1987). Randomized single-subject experiments and statistical tests. *Journal of Counseling Psychology, 34*(4), 437–442.

Edwards, W., Lindman, H., & Savage, L. (1963). Bayesian statistical inference for psychological research. *Psychological Review, 70,* 193–242.

Feinstein, A. R. (1998). *p*-Values and confidence intervals: Two sides of the same unsatisfactory coin. *Journal of Clinical Epidemiology, 51*, 355–360.

Feinstein, A. R., & Horwitz, R. I. (1997). Problems in the "evidence" of "evidence-based medicine." *American Journal of Medicine, 103*, 529–535.

Fey, M., & Johnson, B. (1998). Research to practice (and back again) in speech-language intervention. *Topics in Language Disorders, 18*(2), 23–24.

Fisher, R. (1925). *Statistical methods for research workers*. Edinburgh, UK: Oliver & Boyd.

Fisher, R. A. (1935). *The design of experiment*. Edinburgh, UK: Oliver & Boyd.

Fonagy, P., & Moran, G. S. (1990). Studies on the efficacy of child psychoanalysis. *Journal of Consulting and Clinical Psychology, 58*(6), 684–695.

Freed, D., Celery, K., & Marshall, R. C. (2004). Effectiveness of personalized and phonological cueing on long-term naming performance by aphasic subjects: A clinical investigation. *Aphasiology, 18*(8), 743–757.

Fridriksson, J., Holland, A. L., Beeson, P., & Morrow, L. (2005). Spaced retrieval treatment of anomia. *Aphasiology, 19*(2), 99–109.

Frith, U., & Hill, E. L. (2004). *Autism: Mind and brain*. New York, NY: Oxford University Press.

Fryauf-Bertschy, H., Tyler, R. S., Kelsay, D. M., Gantz, B. J., & Woodworth, G. G. (1997). Cochlear implant use by prelingually deafened children: The influences of age at implant and length of device use. *Journal of Speech, Language, and Hearing Research, 40*(1), 183–199.

Fucetola, R., Tucker, F., Blank, K., & Corbetta, M. (2005). A process for translating evidence-based aphasia treatment into clinical practice. *Aphasiology, 19*(3/4/5), 411–422.

Galassi, J. P., & Gersh, T. L. (1993). Myths, misconceptions, and missed opportunity: Single-case designs and counseling psychology. *Journal of Counseling Psychology, 40*(4), 525–531.

Gantz, B. J., & Turner, C. (2004). Combining acoustic and electrical speech processing: Iowa/Nucleus Hybrid implant. *Acta Otolaryngolica, 124*, 344–347.

Gelfaud, D. M., & Hartmann, D. P. (1984). *Child behavior analysis and therapy*. New York, NY: Pergamon Press.

Gigerenzer, G., Swijtink, Z., Porter, T., Datson, L. J., Beatty, L., & Krueger, L. (1989). *The empire of chance: How probability changed science and everyday life*. Cambridge, UK: Cambridge University Press.

Gigerenzer, G., Krauss, S., & Vitouch, O. (2004). The null ritual: What you always wanted to know about significance testing but were afraid to ask. In D. Kaplan (Ed.), *The Sage handbook of quantitative methodology for the social sciences* (pp. 391–408). Thousand Oaks, CA: Sage.

Glesne, C. & Peshkin, A. (1992). *Becoming qualitative researchers: An introduction*. White Plains, NY: Longman.

Goodman, S. (1993). *p*-Values, hypothesis test, and likelihood: Implications for epidemiology of a neglected historical debate. *American Journal of Epidemiology, 137*, 485–496.

Goodman, S. (1999a). Toward evidence-based medical statistics. 1: The p-Value fallacy. *Annals of Internal Medicine, 130*, 995–1004.

Goodman, S. (1999b). Toward evidence-based medical statistics. 2: The Bayes factor. *Annals of Internal Medicine, 130*, 1005–1015.

Goodman, S. (2005). Introduction to Bayesian methods. 1: Measuring the strength of evidence. *Clinical Trials, 2*, 282–290.

Goodman, S., & Royall, R. (1988). Evidence and scientific research. *American Journal of Public Health, 78*, 1568–1574.

Guyatt, G., Jaeschke, R., Heddle, N., Cook, D., Shannon, H., & Walter, S. (1995a). Basic statistics for clinicians. *Canadian Medical Association Journal, 152*(1).

Guyatt, G., Jaeschke, R., Heddle, N., Cook, D., Shannon, H., & Walter, S. (1995b). Basic statistics for clinicians. *Canadian Medical Association Journal, 152*(2).

Guyatt, G., Jaeschke, R., Heddle, N., Cook, D., Shannon, H., & Walter, S. (1995c). Basic statistics for clinicians. *Canadian Medical Association Journal, 152*(3).

Guyatt, G., Jaeschke, R., Heddle, N., Cook, D., Shannon, H., & Walter, S. (1995d). Basic statistics for clinicians. *Canadian Medical Association Journal, 152*(4).

Guyatt, G. H., Sackett, D. L., & Cook, D. J. (1993). Users' guides to the medical literature. II. How to use an article about therapy or prevention. B. What were the results and will help me in caring for my patients? Evidence-Based Medicine Working Group. *JAMA, 271,* 59–63.

Hacking, I. (1975). *The emergence of probability: A philosophical study of early ideas about probability, induction and statistical inference.* Cambridge, UK: Cambridge University Press.

Havstam, C., Buchholz, M., & Hartelius, L. (2003). Speech recognition and dysarthria: A single-subject study of two individuals with profound impairment of speech and motor control. *Logopedics Phoniatrics Vocology, 28,* 81–90.

Higgins, M. B., McCleary, E. A., & Schulte, L. (1999). Altered phonatory physiology with short-term deactivation of children's cochlear implants. *Ear and Hearing, 20*(5), 426–438.

Hodgetts, W. E., Hagler, P., & Thompson, S. L. (2006). Exploring the use of factor analysis to determine the relevant dimensions of outcome for a given population in rehabilitation science: A tutorial. *Journal of Speech-Language Pathology and Audiology, 30*(12), 132–141.

Howson, C., & Urbach, P. (1993). *Scientific reasoning: The Bayesian approach* (2nd ed.). La Salle, IL: Open Court.

Hull, F. M., Mielke, P. W., Willeford, J. A., & Timmons, R. J. (1976). *National speech and hearing survey* (Final Report for Grant OE-32-15-0050-5010 [607], No.50978). Washington, DC: Office of Education.

Iversen, G. R. (1984). *Bayesian statistical inference.* Newbury Park, CA: Sage.

Iyer, S. N., Rothmann, T. L., Vogler, J. E., & Spaulding, W. D. (2005). Evaluating outcomes of rehabilitation for severe mental illness. *Rehabilitation Psychology, 50*(1), 43–55.

Jones, P. W. (2003). Single-case time series with Bayesian analysis: A practitioner's guide. *Measurement and Evaluation in Counseling and Development, 36,* 28–39.

Justice, L. M., & Fey, M. E. (2004). Evidence-based practice in schools. *ASHA Leader, 9,* 17–32.

Kadane, J. (1995). Prime time for Bayes. *Control Clinical Trials, 16,* 313–318.

Katki, H. A. (2008). Invited commentary: Evidence-based evaluation of *p*-values and Bayes factors. *American Journal of Epidemiology, 168*(4), 384–388.

Kaye, M. S. (2000). *Guide to dysarthria management: A client-clinician approach.* Eau Claire, WI: Thinking Publications.

Kazdin, A. E. (1982). *Single-case research designs: Methods for clinical and applied setting.* New York, NY: Oxford University Press.

Kearns, K. P. (2000). Single-subject experimental designs and treatment research. In L. J. Gonzalez-Rothi, B. Crosson, & S. E. Nadeau (Eds.), *Aphasia and language: Theory to practice* (pp. 421–441). New York, NY: Guilford.

Kertesz, A. (1982). *Western Aphasia Battery.* New York, NY: Grace and Stratton.

Kertesz, A. (2006). *Western Aphasia Battery-Revised.* San Antonio, TX: PsychCorp.

Kiran, S., & Thompson, C. K. (2003). The role of semantic complexity in treatment of naming deficits: Training semantic categories in fluent aphasia by controlling exemplar typicality. *Journal of Speech, Language, and Hearing Research, 46,* 773–787.

Kirk, J., & Miller, M. K. (1986). *Reliability and validity in qualitative research.* Beverly Hills, CA: Sage.

Kline, R. B. (2005). *Beyond significance testing: Reforming data analysis methods in behavioral research.* Washington, DC: American Psychological Association.

Kramer, K, Mallett, P., Schneider, P., & Hayward, D. (2009). Dynamic assessment of narratives with grade 3 children in a first nations. *Canadian Journal of Speech-Language Pathology and Audiology, 33*(3), 119–128.

Kupper, Z., & Tschaher, W. (2002). Symptom trajectories in psychotic episodes. *Comprehensive Psychiatry, 43*(4), 311–318.

Larson, R., & Farber, B. (2006). *Elementary statistics: Picturing the world* (2nd ed.). Upper Saddle River, NJ: Pearson-Prentice Hall.

Leder, S. B., Spitzer, J. B., & Kirchner, J. C. (1987). Immediate effects of cochlear implantation on voice quality. *Archives of Oto-Rhino-Laryngology, 244*(2), 93–95.

Liebow, E. (1967). *Tally's Corner: A study of street corner Negro men.* Boston, MA: Little, Brown.

Linebaugh, C. W., Shisler, R. J., & Lehner, L. (2005). Cueing hierarchies and word retrieval: A therapy program. *Aphasiology, 19*(1), 77–92.

Logemann, J. A. (2000). Dysphasia (difficulty swallowing or difficulty moving food from mouth to stomach). *International Encyclopedia of Rehabilitation.*

Maher, C. A. (1985). Training school psychological services directors in organizational behavior management. *Professional psychology: Research and practice, 16*(2), 209–225.

Matthews, R. A. J. (1995). *Quantification and the quest for medical certainty.* Princeton, NJ: Princeton University Press.

Matthews, R. A. J. (2001). Why should clinicians care about Bayesian methods? *Journal of Statistical Planning and Inference, 94*(1), 43–58.

Maxwell, D. L., & Satake, E. (1993). *Applications of Bayesian statistics to the diagnosis of stuttering.* Annual American Speech-Language Hearing Association Convention [two-hour research seminar], Anaheim, CA.

Maxwell, D. L., & Satake, E. (1997). *Research and statistical methods in communication disorders.* Baltimore, MD: Williams and Wilkins.

Maxwell, D. L., & Satake, E. (2005). *Research and statistical methods in communication sciences and disorders.* Clifton Park, NY: Delmar Thomson Learning.

Maxwell, D. L., & Satake, E. (2006). *Research and statistical methods in communication sciences and disorders.* Clifton Park, NY: Thomson Delmar Learning.

Maxwell, D. L., & Satake, E. (2008). *Evidence-based statistics for clinicians and researchers: Current problems and possible solutions.* Annual ASHA conference [two-hour research seminar], Chicago, IL.

Maxwell, D. L., & Satake, E. (November, 2010). *Scientific literacy and ethical practice: Time for a check-up.* Program presented at the annual American Speech-Language Hearing Association Convention, Philadelphia, PA.

McReynolds, L. V., & Thompson, C. K. (1986). Flexibility of single-subject experimental designs: Pt. I. Review of the basics of single-subject design. *Journal of Speech and Hearing Disorders, 51,* 194–203.

Meline, T., & Paradiso, T. (2003). Evidence-based practice in schools. *Language, Speech, and Hearing Services in Schools, 34,* 273–283.

Mittag, K. C., & Thompson, B. (2000). A national survey of AERA members' perceptions of statistical significance tests and other statistical issues. *Educational Researcher, 29*(4), 14–20.

Miyamoto, R. T., Kirk, K. I., Renshaw, J., & Hussain, D. (1999). Cochlear implantation in auditory neuropathy. *The Laryngoscope, 109,* 181–185.

Miyamoto, R. T., Osberger, M. J., Robbins, A. M., Myres, W. A., Kessler, K., & Pope, M. L. (1991). Comparison of speech perception abilities in deaf children with hearing aids or cochlear implants. *Otolaryngology-Head and Neck Surgery, 104*(1), 42–46.

Morley, M. E. (1957). *In the development and disorder of speech in childhood.* Edinburgh and London, UK: E & S Livingstone Limited.

Morrow, K. L., & Fridriksson, J. (2006). Comparing fixed- and randomized-interval spaced retrieval in anomia treatment. *Journal of Communication Disorders, 39,* 2–11.

Mundy, P., Sigman, M., Ungerer, J., & Sherman, T. (1986). Defining the social deficits of autism: The contribution of non-verbal communication measures. *Journal of Child Psychology and Psychiatry, 27,* 657–669.

Murdoch, B. E., Pitt, G., Theodoros, D. G., & Ward, E. C. (1999). Real-time continuous visual biofeedback in the treatment of speech breathing disorders following childhood traumatic brain injury: Report of one case. *Pediatric Rehabilitation, 3*(1), 5–20.

Nelson, N., Rosenthal, R., & Rosnow, R. L. (1986). Interpretation of significance levels and effect sizes by psychological researchers. *American Psychologist, 41*, 1299–1301.

Neyman, J., & Pearson, E. S. (1933). On the problem of the most efficient tests of statistical hypotheses. *Philosophical Transactions of the Royal Society of London. Series A, Containing Papers of a Mathematical or Physical Character, 231*, 289–337.

Oakes, M. (1986). *Statistical inference: A commentary for the social sciences.* New York, NY: Wiley.

Osberger, M. J., Miyamoto, R. T., Zimmerman-Phillips, S., Kemink, J. L., Stroer, B. S., Firszt, J. B., & Novak, M. A. (1991). Independent evaluation of the speech perception abilities of children with the Nucleus 22-channel cochlear implant system. *Ear and Hearing, 12*(4 Suppl.), 66S–80S.

Osberger, M. J., Todd, S. L., Berry, S. W., Robbins, A. M., & Miyamoto, R. T. (1991). Effect of age at onset of deafness on children's speech perception abilities with a cochlear implant. *The Annals of Otology, Rhinology, and Laryngology, 100*(11), 883–888.

Ottenbacher, K. (1986). *Evaluating clinical change: Strategies for occupational and physical therapists.* Baltimore, MD: Williams & Wilkins.

Ottenbacher, K. J. (1993). Interrater agreement of visual analysis in single-subject, decisions: Quantitative review and analysis. *American Journal of Mental Retardation, 98*, 135–142.

Peach, R. K. (1996). Treatment for aphasic phonological output planning deficits. *Clinical Aphasiology, 24*, 109–120.

Pedhazur, E. J., & Schmelkin, L. P. (1991). *Measurement, design and analysis: An integrated approach.* Hillsdale, NJ: Lawrence Erlbaum Associates.

Pedley, K., Giles, E., & Hogan, A. (2005). *Adult cochlear implant rehabilitation.* Philadelphia, PA: Whurr.

Piaget, J. (1932). *The language and thought of the child.* New York, NY: Harcourt, Brace.

Polit, D. F., Beck, C. T., & Hungler, B. P. (2001). *Essentials of nursing research.* Philadelphia, PA: Lippincott.

Pollard, P., & Richardson, J. T. E. (1987). On the probability of making Type 1 errors. *Psychological Bulletin, 10*, 159–163.

Poole, C. (1987). Beyond the confidence interval. *American Journal of Public Health, 77*, 195–199.

Pratt, S. R., Heintzelman, A. T., & Deming, S. E. (1993). The efficacy of using the IBM speech viewer vowel accuracy module to treat young children with hearing impairment. *Journal of Speech and Hearing Research, 36*, 1063–1074.

Proops, D. W. (2006). The cochlear implant team. In H. R. Cooper & L. C. Craddock (Eds.), *Cochlear implants: A practical guide* (2nd ed., pp. 70–79). West Sussex, UK: Whurr.

Rebmann, M. J., & Hannon, R. (1995). Treatment of unawareness of memory deficits in adults with brain injury: Three case studies. *Rehabilitation Psychology, 40*(4), 279–287.

Robey, R. (2004, April 13). Level of evidence. *The ASHA Leader.*

Robey, R. R., Schultz, M. C., Crawford, A. B., & Sinner, C. A. (1999). Single-subject clinical-outcome research: Designs, data, effect sizes, and analyses. *Aphasiology, 13*, 445–473.

Royall, R. (1997). *Statistical evidence: A likelihood paradigm.* London, UK: Chapman and Hall.

Russell, B. (1948). *Human knowledge.* New York, NY: Simon & Schuster.

Rutter, M. (1989). Attention deficit disorder/ hyperkinetic syndrome: Conceptual and research issues regarding diagnosis and classification. In T. Sagvolden & T. Archer (Eds.), *Attention deficit disorder: Clinical and basic research.* Hillsdale, NJ: Lawrence Erlbaum.

Sackett, D., Haynes, R., & Tugwell, P. (1985). *Clinical epidemiology: A basic science for clinical medicine.* Boston, MA: Little Brown.

Sackett, D. L., Rosenburg, W. M., Gray, J. A., Haynes, R. B., & Richardson, W. S. (1996). Evidence-based medicine: What it is and what it isn't. *Bio-Medical Journal, 312*(7023), 71–72.

Salsburg, D. (2001). *The lady tasting tea: How statistics revolutionized science in the twentieth century*. New York, NY: Holt.

Satake, E. (1994). Bayesian inference in polling technique: 1992 presidential polls. *Communication Research, 21*(3), 396–407.

Satake, E. (2008). *Single subject designs and clinical neuropsychology: Statistical methods for clinical practice*. American Academy of Clinical Neuropsychology annual conference on *"Excellence in Clinical Practice,"* Boston, MA.

Satake, E. (2010, August). Moving forward to evidence-based statistics: What really prevents us? *Plural Community.*

Satake, E., & Amato, P. (2012). *Imprecise p-value vs precise p-value: Teaching the minimum Bayes factor as an alternative way to measure the strength of evidence*. Manchester, NH: Annual New England Mathematics Association for two-year colleges convention [two-hour research seminar].

Satake, E., & Amato, P. P. (2008). An alternative version of conditional probabilities and Bayes' rule: An application of probability logic. *The AMATYC Review, 29,* 44–50.

Satake, E., Gilligan, W., & Amato, P. P. (1995). Using *n* × *m* contingency table to determine Bayesian probabilities: An alternative strategy. *The AMATYC Review, 16,* 34–43.

Satake, E., Jagaroo, V., & Maxwell, D. L. (2008). *Handbook of statistical methods: Single subject design*. San Diego, CA: Plural.

Satake, E., & Maxwell, D. L. (2005). *Using Bayesian time series for analyzing and interpreting single-subject data*. Annual Case Studies in Bayesian Statistics Workshop at the Carnegie Mellon University [one-hour research seminar], Pittsburgh, PA.

Satake, E., & Maxwell, D. L. (2006). *Analyzing and interpreting single subject data: A tutorial*. Annual American Speech-Language Hearing Association convention [two-hour research seminar], Miami Beach, FL.

Satake, E., & Maxwell, D. L. (2010). *Scientific literacy and ethical practice: Time for a checkup?* Annual American Speech-Language Hearing Association convention [three-hour short course research seminar], Philadelphia, PA.

Satake, E., & Maxwell, D. L. (2011a). *Analyzing and interpreting single subject data: A tutorial*. Annual American Speech-Language Hearing Association convention [two-hour research seminar], San Diego, CA.

Satake, E., & Maxwell, D. L. (2011b). *Evidence-based statistics: Measuring the strength of evidence*. Annual American Speech-Language Hearing Association convention [three-hour short course research seminar], San Diego, CA.

Shaffir, W. B., & Stebbins, R. A. (Eds). (1991). *Experiencing fieldwork: An inside view of qualitative research*. Newbury Park, CA: Sage.

Simpson, M. B., Till, J. A., & Goff, A. M. (1988). Long-term treatment of severe dysarthria: A case study. *Journal of Speech and Hearing Disorders, 53,* 433–440.

Spiegelhalter, D. J., Abrams, K. R., & Myles, J. P. (2004). *Bayesian approaches to clinical trials and health-care evaluation*. Chichester, UK: Wiley.

Spodich, H. (1996). "Evidence-based medicine": Terminologic lapse or terminologic arrogance? [Letter]. *American Journal of Cardiology, 78,* 608–609.

Spring, B., & Hitchcock, K. (2009). Evidence-based practice in psychology. In I.B. Weiner & W. E. Craighead (Eds.), *Corsini's Encyclopedia of Psychology* (4th ed.). New York, NY: Wiley.

Sullivan, M., III. (2007). *Statistics: Informed decisions using data* (3rd ed.). Upper Saddle River, NJ: Prentice Hall.

Tawney, J. W., & Gast, D. L. (1984). *Single subject research in special education*. Columbus, OH: Charles Merrill.

Thurstone, L. L. (1947). *Multiple factor analysis*. Chicago, IL: University of Chicago Press.

Todman, J. B., & Dugard, P. (2001). *Single-case and small-n experimental design: A practical guide to randomization tests*. Mahwah, NJ: Erlbaum.

Tomblin, J. B., Spencer, L., Flock, S., Tyler, R., & Gantz, B. (1999). A comparison of language achievement in children with cochlear implants and children using hearing aids. *Journal of Speech, Language, and Hearing Research, 42*(2), 497–509.

Tonelli, R. (1998). The philosophical limits of evidence-based medicine. *Academy of Medicine, 73*, 1234–1240.

Triola, M. F. (2007). *Essentials of statistics* (3rd ed.). Boston, MA: Pearson-Addison Wesley.

Tye-Murray, N., Spencer, L., Bedia, E. G., & Woodworth, G. (1996). Differences in children's sound production when speaking with a cochlear implant turned on and turned off. *Journal of Speech and Hearing Research, 39*(3), 604–610.

Tyler, R. S., Fryauf-Bertschy, H., Kelsay, D. M., Gantz, B. J., Woodworth, G. P., & Parkinson, A. (1997). Speech perception by prelingually deaf children using cochlear implants. *Otolaryngology-Head and Neck Surgery, 117*(3, Pt. 1), 180–187.

Waltzman, S. B., & Cohen, N. L. (2000). *Cochlear implants.* New York, NY: Thieme Medical.

Wambaugh, J., Cameron, R., Kalinyak-Fliszar, M., Nessler, C., & Wright, S. (2004). Retrieval of action names in aphasia: Effects of two cueing treatments. *Aphasiology, 18*(11), 979–1004.

Wambaugh, J. L., & Martinez, A. L. (2000). Effects of rate and rhythm control treatment on consonant production accuracy in apraxia of speech. *Aphasiology, 14*, 851–871.

Watling, R., Deitz, J., Kanny, E. M., & McLaughlin, J. F. (1999). Current practice of occupational therapy for children with autism. *The American Journal of Occupational Therapy, 53*(5), 498–505.

Wechsler, D. (1991). *Wechsler Intelligence Scale for Children* (3rd ed., p. 39). San Antonio, TX: Harcourt, Brace, Jovanovich.

Welch, B. L. (1938). The significance of the difference between two means when the population variances are unequal. *Biometrika, 29*, 350–362.

Wilcox, M. J., Hadley, P. A., & Bacon, C. R. (1998). Linking science and practice in management of childhood language disorder: Models and problem-solving strategies. *Topics in Language Disorders, 18*, 10–22.

Wimpory, D., Chadwick, P., & Nash, S. (1995). Brief report: Musical interaction therapy for children with autism: An evaluative case study with two-year follow-up. *Journal of Autism and Developmental Disorders, 25*(5), 541–552.

Winkler, R. L. (2001). Why Bayesian analysis hasn't caught on in healthcare decision making. *International Journal of Technology Assessment in Health Care, 17*, 56–66.

Wolery, M., & Harris, S. R. (1982). Interpreting results of single-subject research designs. *Physical Therapy, 62*, 445–452.

Yorkston, K. M. (1996). Treatment efficacy: Dysarthria. *Journal of Speech and Hearing Research, 39*(5), S46–S57.

Yorkston, K. M., Beukelman, D. R., & Bell, K. R. (1988). *Clinical management of dysarthric speakers.* Austin, TX: Pro-Ed.

Young, M. C. (2003). Anterior aphasia as a natural category of acquired cognitive-communicative impairment: Implications for cognitive neurolinguistic theory, experimental methods, and clinical practice. *Dissertation Abstracts International, 64*(5–B), 2415.

Index

Note: Page numbers in **bold** reference non-text material.